The Routledge Guide to William Shakespeare

William Shakespeare is one of the most widely studied and culturally significant writers of all time, and his language and thought remain interwoven through popular reference and imaginings of the Western canon.

In this concise, structured guide, Robert Shaughnessy:

- introduces Shakespeare's life and works in context, providing crucial historical background
- introduces each of Shakespeare's plays in turn, considering issues of historical context, contemporary criticism and performance history
- provides a detailed discussion of twentieth century Shakespearean criticism, exploring the theories, debates and discoveries that have shaped our understanding of Shakespeare today
- looks at contemporary performance of Shakespeare on stage and screen
- cross-references between sections of the guide to suggest links between texts, contexts and criticism
- provides further reading by play and detailed chronologies.

Demystifying and contextualising Shakespeare for the twenty-first century, this book offers both an introduction to the subject for beginning students and an invaluable resource for more experienced Shakespeareans.

Robert Shaughnessy is Professor of Theatre at the University of Kent.

The Routledge Guide to William Shakespeare

Robert Shaughnessy

Routledge
Taylor & Francis Group

LONDON AND NEW YORK

First edition published 2011 by Routledge
2 Park Square, Milton Park, Abingdon, OX14 4RN

Simultaneously published in the USA and Canada
by Routledge
270 Madison Avenue, New York, NY 10016

Routledge is an imprint of the Taylor & Francis Group, an informa business

Typeset in Minion and Helvetica by Taylor & Francis Books
Printed and bound in Great Britain by MPG Books Ltd, Bodmin, Conwall

British Library Cataloguing in Publication Data
A catalogue record for this book is available from the British Library

Library of Congress Cataloging in Publication Data
Shaughnessy, Robert.
The Routledge guide to Shakespeare / Robert Shaughnessy. – 1st ed.
p. cm.
Includes bibliographical references and index.
1. Shakespeare, William, 1564-1616–Criticism and interpretation–Handbooks, manuals, etc.
I. Title.
PR2976.S3445 2010
822.3'3–dc22
2010024259

ISBN 13: 978-0-415-27539-2 (hbk)
ISBN 13: 978-0-415-27540-8 (pbk)
ISBN 13: 978-0-203-83523-4 (ebk)

For Nicki

Contents

Acknowledgements

This book has taken a long time to complete, and along the way I have had much cause to be grateful to family, friends and colleagues for support, encouragement and advice. For initiating the project and seeing it through the first stages, my thanks to Liz Thompson and to the series editors of the Routledge Guides to Literature, Richard Bradford and Jan Jedrzejewski. Among the many colleagues whose generosity, shared insights, and sometimes indirect but nonetheless much-valued help have helped to make this book what it is, I thank in particular Pascale Aebischer, John Russell Brown, Mark Burnett, Peter Holland, Barbara Hodgdon, Graham Holderness, Kate McLuskie, Carol Rutter, Bill Worthen and Ramona Wray. Colleagues at Roehampton University and the University of Kent provided sympathetic ears and critical companionship: Chris Baugh, Peter Boenisch, Michael Dobson, Darryll Grantley, Susanne Greenhalgh, Patrice Pavis, Alan Read, and Melissa Trimingham; special thanks to Peter Reynolds (who secured this book's first period of leave) and Paul Allain (who enabled its second). I am grateful to the Arts and Humanities Research Council for the award of a further term of research leave. My thanks to the two anonymous reviewers of my leave application, for showing the difference between a hawk and a handsaw.

At Routledge, it has been a pleasure to work with Polly Dodson and especially with Emma Nugent, who has been both immensely supportive and extraordinarily patient, especially in the final stages. Lisa Williams's sharp-eyed and imaginative copy-editing saved me from my errors and untied knots; Andrew Watts calmly steered the book through to publication.

My family have lived with this book for as long as I have, and it has been both their amused refusal to take matters Shakespearean too seriously, and their ability to see through to what really matters, that has kept in view a world elsewhere. For this, and much else, I thank Caitlin, Nathaniel, Gabriel and Erina. My deepest thanks to Nicki, who has travelled through it with me, and who knows what is truly beyond words. This is all for you.

Preface

This book is for anyone, from undergraduate level upwards, who is interested in the works of William Shakespeare, in the stage and screen versions which these have generated and inspired, and in the critical debates that have been provoked by them, with a particular, though not exclusive, emphasis upon the work of the past three decades. Offered as a comprehensive single-volume resource, it combines a biography of Shakespeare as a professional poet and playwright, seen in the context of his theatre, and of the cultural, social and political worlds in which the works took shape, a concise account of every work in the canon, and a summary and overview of modern criticism, performance and film. During the past quarter-century, the field of Shakespeare studies has been one of rapid change, diversification and often fierce debate; the aim of this guide is to indicate to readers how to engage further with the most provocative, stimulating and illuminating criticism that has been produced during this exciting period of literary history, and also to reflect upon its future, perhaps even to contribute to it. At the same time, whilst recognising the legitimate and desirable predominance of the new, the contemporary and the innovative in today's critical reading lists, the guide also aims to position recent and current movements in the context of what came before them, not only to establish their place in the larger historical landscape but also to remind its users that not everything that was published on Shakespeare prior to the last quarter-century has been superseded or discredited (far from it). There are, of course, some areas in which a broad – and, for the time being, seemingly solid – consensus appears to have been reached. For most readers of this book, performance – and, increasingly, performance on screen and online – is the primary, and seemingly natural, medium in which Shakespeare's words and works are encountered and brought to life; in this respect, there is nothing out of the ordinary in this book's use of theatre and performance, actual and imagined, as a key point of reference for the plays. However, since this book aims not only to record and reinforce consensus but, where necessary, to interrogate it, it also highlights the real and growing differences within the discipline of Shakespeare performance studies, particularly as it has begun to register the implications of the new thinking about theatre and performance that has been taking place beyond the Shakespearean critical industry.

The Routledge Guide to William Shakespeare is structured in four parts, which can be consulted independently, and approached in any order. Part I, 'Life and contexts', presents a chronologically ordered account, based on what is known of the professional and occasionally personal circumstances of its subject, which provides the basis for a succinct cultural history of the late sixteenth and early seventeenth century literary and theatre industries. Preferring to refrain from the speculative habits to which Shakespearean biographical writing is liable, this part traces a career trajectory that sees its protagonist engaged as a working playwright, theatre maker and entrepreneur in early modern London's most successful and politically best-connected, playing companies. Part II, 'Works', which follows the ordering of the Oxford and Norton editions, consists of twenty-five sections, each ascribed to a play or group of plays. In some cases the groupings reflect the sequential nature of the works in question (the *Henry VI* and *Henry IV* plays), in others generic affinities and partnerships (the narrative poems, the early comedies, the late plays); elsewhere works have been placed alongside each other in order to encourage readers to consider what may be less familiar works (*King John*, for example) alongside the more well-known ones. There are as many ways of reading Shakespeare as there are readers of Shakespeare; and, partly in order to reflect the spirit of critical and creative diversity of the material addressed in the third and fourth sections of the book, the works in this section are addressed in different ways. Some are considered in terms of their originating historical contexts and conditions of performance; others with regard to subsequent performance histories; in two instances (*Othello* and *The Tempest*) the plays' centrality to recent critical debates around race, ethnicity and postcoloniality make these concerns the focus of discussion. Each section is, however, anchored in the key factual information that is summarised in the inset text boxes. Elsewhere in this volume these are used to summarise supplementary material or matters that lend themselves to digressive treatment. Here will be found information about authorship (whether sole or collaborative), dating, publication history up to the printing of the 1623 Folio, and a brief list of important sources and influences, both known and conjectured. Also provided are listings of noteworthy stage and screen productions, and the significant personnel involved in them, and of the spin-offs and offshoots that the work has generated. In general, these brief performance histories concentrate on the period post-1950, though important earlier twentieth century productions are included when appropriate. Perhaps inevitably, given the provenance of this book, there is an emphasis upon productions within the British context, though important productions taking place beyond the shores of the small island are also acknowledged.

Part III, 'Criticism', begins with a short overview of the development of Shakespeare studies during the twentieth century before moving to a consideration of modern criticism from three interrelated perspectives. Chapter 1, 'Histories', traces the evolution of practices of reading that may be broadly termed contextual and political, beginning with the historicisms of the 1940s and 1950s, and proceeding via the new historicism and cultural materialism of the 1980s and after to the present. Chapter 2, 'Languages', examines those modes of interpretation that have been primarily concerned with literariness, and with the operations of discourse, how and why the works' words work in the ways that they do; it ranges from the close readings of New Criticism to the equally close (but theoretically and methodologically antithetical) readings of post-structuralism. Chapter 3, 'Subjectivities', addresses both the rise and fall (and recent rise again) of character criticism and, in relation to it, the critical work that has made questions of gender and sexuality its central concern. This compartmental sectioning is, of course, an artificial way of organising the vast output of its field of study: as will be seen, many of the critical practices and practitioners considered inhabit overlapping categories, and effective interpretation can, and usually will, draw upon a range of perspectives, methods and analytical tools. In a sense, it is obvious that all of the criticisms considered here that have operated in the wake of the changes that occurred a quarter-century ago can be said to be 'historicist', in that neither language nor gender nor performance can be sensibly considered without reference to the conditions that produced and continue to reproduce them. Rather than serving to act as a marker of firm subdisciplinary boundaries, then, the tripartite classification of Part III aims to offer a set of complementary angles of approach to a critical field. Following this, Part IV looks at Shakespeare on screen and on stage through the lenses of the histories of film and performance criticism.

All quotations are from the *Norton Shakespeare* (1997), edited by Stephen Greenblatt, Walter Cohen, Jean E. Howard and Katharine Eisaman Maus.

Part I
Life and contexts

1 Introduction

Son of Stratford

Each year, on the Saturday nearest to 23 April, the otherwise unremarkable English Midlands town of Stratford-upon-Avon hosts a birthday celebration in honour of its most renowned former inhabitant. In 2009, this began at 9.45 a.m. with a reception at the Shakespeare Centre adjacent to the property known as Shakespeare's Birthplace, hosted by the President of the Shakespeare Birthday Celebrations, the veteran Shakespearean actor Sir Donald Sinden. At 10.30 a.m., a procession departed from the steps of the Birthplace, led by Sir Donald and featuring amongst its numbers Stratford civic dignitaries, representatives of Birmingham, Warwick, London, Oxford and Cambridge Universities, pupils from local schools, members of the theatre profession and delegations from around the world that included the Secretary-General of the Commonwealth, the High Commissioner for the Bahamas, the Political and Press Secretary for Ireland, and the Ambassadors of Kazakhstan, El Salvador, Serbia and China. It fell to the last of these to carry out the task of addressing the several hundred guests in attendance at the Birthday Luncheon, an event lasting nearly four hours, on the topic of 'Worldwide Appreciation of Shakespeare'.

The parade proceeded along Henley Street and down Bridge Street, where it paused for the ceremony of the unfurling of the flags of the nations, institutions and interest groups represented by the parade. Onwards, with each member of the parade clutching floral tributes that ranged from single stems to lavish wreaths, the procession wound its way past bemused Stratford townspeople, up Sheep Street, along Chapel Street and past the site of the house that Shakespeare bought in 1597, New Place. It passed the King Edward VI Grammar School and Mason Croft, home of the University of Birmingham's postgraduate outpost, the Shakespeare Institute, down Old Tow, alongside Hall's Croft (home of Shakespeare's daughter, Susanna), finally to arrive at the Holy Trinity Church. Here members of the procession were invited to add their flora and assorted greenery to a growing pile at the base of the monument to the figure in whose memory the whole event had been orchestrated. Reminiscent simultaneously of a christening, a wedding and a funeral (for this birthday is also a day of death), the celebration traces commemoration as a collective pedestrian act, for one day a year transforming the sites of shopping and sauntering into what is both a mobile shrine and a cradle of possibilities, and into a biographical narrative which begins and ends with the gift of flowers, an act in Shakespeare associated both with the furthest reaches of madness (Ophelia, Lear) and profoundly redemptive grace (Perdita): 'There's rosemary, that's for remembrance' (*Hamlet*, 4.5.173); 'Here's flowers for you' (*Winter's Tale*, 4.4.103).

Most of us would agree to recognise the procession as an enactment of a secular pil-grimage ritual, undertaking a journey that literally takes its participants in Shakespeare's footsteps from the womb to the tomb. The procession thus traces the arc of a biographical narrative that acknowledges key markers of the life (home, school, funerary monument) as well as acknowledging a global cultural afterlife. What might provoke disagreement, how-ever, is what significance to attach to the extraordinary emotional and cultural investment that the event appears to represent. For the idealist, the gathering is a tribute to a spirit of genius capable of transcending history and geography to speak across and beyond cultural differences; for the cynic, the ceremony is a particularly lavish and sentimental perpetua-tion of the myth of that very transcendence. Complicating the meanings of the event, in 2009, was the fact that in this year, for the first time, the procession organisers expanded what had been for many years a rather solemn, dogged (and rather dull) trudge through the streets of Stratford into an extravaganza that included stunts, spectacle, street entertainers and a wide variety of local community groups on parade.

Although, sadly, the plan to mount a Royal Shakespeare Company actor, wrapped in the flag of St George, astride one of six motorcycles and send him down Bridge Street declaiming lines from *Henry V* had to be called off for safety reasons, there was much else for the crowds that had turned out to witness the event to experience. Attractions included stiltwalkers and skateboarders, extras in Elizabethan fancy dress, displays of salsa and line dancing, belly-dancing and Japanese fan dancing, and 'Gramophone Man', whose act consists of playing 'music from 1902 to 1960 on a wind-up gramophone'. If it was not immediately obvious what some of this had to do with the nominal meaning of the pro-cession, it was undoubtedly lively. Moreover, it formed the centrepiece of a long weekend of Shakespeare-themed activities around Stratford that had begun with the unveiling of what was claimed to be a newly discovered likeness of Shakespeare, the Cobbe portrait, and which included Royal Shakespeare Company (RSC) actors reciting sonnets and offering masterclasses, the Shakespeare Marathon and half-Marathon, performances of *Hamlet: Sword of Vengeance*, an adaptation in Mandarin Chinese presented by the Beijing Performing Arts School at the Civic Hall, and Shakespearean face-painting for the under-fives in the grounds of New Place.

The rich variety of activities on offer is at once a testimony to the persistence and the power of Shakespeare, the man, the works and the myth, in twenty-first-century culture, and a sign of the ingenuity and the effort that need to be expended in order to persuade the consumers of everyday culture of his, its and their continuing vitality: ostensibly the focus and meaning of the Birthday festivities, Shakespeare is as much pretext as text and context, and the beneficiary of an afterlife which, depending upon which angle you consider it from, is either joyously inevitable or embarrassingly prolonged.

Shakespeare's biographies

We do not need the annual Birthday celebration to remind us that writing the life of Shakespeare is so much more than a matter of re-examining the documentary record and a legacy of myth: as the story of a local boy made about as good as it is possible to get, it is perhaps one of the greatest, and certainly one of the most enduring, of literary-biographical fables. Yet the desire that is expressed every April in Stratford to follow Shakespeare's tracks is to a certain extent provoked by his own evident wish to cover them: the anniversary of 23 April is a public affirmation of an early modern life which, as far as we can tell, appears to have been lived as privately as possible. Shakespeare's burial site is marked by the bust that was erected by Stratford residents after his death and a tombstone bearing a warning:

> Good friend for Jesus' sake forbear,
> To dig the dust enclosed here!
> Blessed be the man that spares these stones,
> And cursed be he that moves my bones.

The sentiments are conventional, formulaic even; as S. Schoenbaum, author of the definitive biography of Shakespeare's biographers, notes, the curse is intended to descend on the sexton, 'who sometimes had to dig up an old grave in the parish church in order to make room for the newly deceased' (1991: 3).

Whether or not Shakespeare was the composer of these lines, the epitaph seems to contain a veiled warning for the prospective biographer who would hope to 'dig the dust' of their subject's time on this planet. Posthumously memorialising a will to rest undisturbed, and the legacy of his plays and poems aside, Shakespeare left behind a fair few documentary traces of his own life, but little that can be convincingly mined for clues as to how those works came into being. This has not prevented generations of biographers from trying, of course: the first biography, by Nicholas Rowe, was written in 1709 and there have been hundreds since. At the time of writing, the most recent of these include Park Honan's *Shakespeare: A Life* (1999); Anthony Holden's *William Shakespeare* (1999); Katharine Duncan-Jones's *Ungentle Shakespeare* (2001); Michael Wood's *In Search of Shakespeare* (2003, published as a tie-in with a BBC mini-series); the longest entry, at nearly 40,000 words, in the *Oxford Dictionary of National Biography* (Holland 2004); Stephen Greenblatt's *Will in the World* (2004); Peter Ackroyd's *Shakespeare* (2005); James Shapiro's *1599: A Year in the Life of William Shakespeare* (2005); Stanley Wells's *Shakespeare and Co.* (2006); Bill Bryson's *Shakespeare* (2007); Charles Nicholl's *The Lodger: Shakespeare on Silver Street* (2007); Germaine Greer's *Shakespeare's Wife* (2007); and Jonathan Bate's *Soul of the Age* (2008).

Even among mainstream biographers the Shakespeares that are constructed are too many and varied to even begin to summarise here (and out of courtesy to the reader we shall here just once acknowledge, and pass over, the tradition of biographical fantasy that disputes the plain fact that the glover's son from Stratford was author of the works attributed to him; for the definitive account of this topic, see James Shapiro's *Contested Will: Who Wrote Shakespeare?* [2010]). In Greenblatt's account, he was a man whose 'root perception of existence' was 'his understanding of what could be said and what should remain unspoken, his preference for things untidy, damaged, and unresolved over things neatly arranged, well made, and settled', and who, at the end of his life, 'had never found or could never realize the love of which he wrote and dreamed so powerfully' (2004: 324, 388). For Katharine Duncan-Jones, Shakespeare ended his days 'ill and furiously angry with those around him … perhaps almost mad with anger' (2001: 277). As a biographical subject, perhaps more than any other, Shakespeare focuses the preoccupations of biographers who, knowingly or not, construct him in their own image. Biographical writing about Shakespeare, which ranges from highly specialised scholarship to trade publication, always involves a degree of legitimate speculation, and sometimes blatant fictionalisation. The gaps and silences in Shakespeare's life have also invited the attentions of novelists, playwrights and film-makers, who can be less circumspect about the relations they construct between life and works, and who can be far more adventurously speculative about Shakespeare's professional career, his political allegiances and social affiliations, his personal relationships and, above all, his sexuality.

The seemingly irresistible appeal of Shakespeare as a subject of factual and fictional biography stems not only from the matchless eloquence, lyricism, emotional depth and range of his writings but also from the apparent disparity between them and the terseness of a biographical archive comprised mostly of contemporary allusions by fellow writers, legal documents, records of financial transactions and parish records, which give a rather fuller account of Shakespeare as a mildly litigious businessman than as a creative artist. The aim of this chapter is not to add to the ever-expanding corpus of Shakespearean life writing, and certainly not to contribute a further portfolio of speculations about the author and his works, but, in the space available, simply to provide the outlines of the life as indicated by the documentary records, whilst also, where there are lacunae in the records that seem to invite significant further investigation, to direct readers towards their fuller treatment elsewhere. It also aims to flesh out the sketch by dealing more closely with the contexts, both professional and cultural, in which that life and work took shape.

2   Shakespeare's early years

As we have seen, for the purposes of Stratford-upon-Avon's Birthday Celebration, and according to the general understanding, William Shakespeare was born on 23 April 1564. Given Shakespeare's standing since the eighteenth century as a patriotic icon, this is a fitting assumption, being the feast day of England's patron, St George. It is also a reasonable one: although the precise date of his birth is not recorded, he was baptised, three days later, as was customary, on 26 April. William was the third child of John Shakespeare (c.1530–1601) and Mary Arden (d. 1608), having been preceded by two sisters who died in infancy, Joan (1558–c.1560) and Margaret (1562–63); he was followed by two sisters, Joan (1569–1646) and Anne (1571–79), and three brothers: Gilbert (1566–1612), Richard (1574–1613) and Edmund (1580–1607). The next time William is mentioned in the records is in 1582, in a licence issued on 27 November for his marriage to Anne Hathaway (1555/6–1623), who was pregnant at the time with their first child, Susanna (baptised on 26 May 1583). In the eighteen years between his own baptism and marriage nothing is known of his doings and whereabouts, although these have inevitably attracted a great deal of speculation.

Schooling

It is generally assumed that, as the son of an alderman, William was educated at Stratford's grammar school, the New King's School, from the ages of seven to fifteen. There he would been the beneficiary of a daily regime that began at 6 a.m., studying, primarily, Latin language and literature and acquiring formal training in the skills of rhetoric, composition, memorisation and argument. At grammar school, William would have made acquaintance with the classical canon whose traces are everywhere evident in his writing: the works of Cicero, Erasmus, Virgil, Horace and Ovid (especially his *Metamorphoses*, in the Latin original but also in Arthur Golding's [c.1536–c.1605] widely read English translation of 1567). In school and at Holy Trinity Church he would also have imbibed the language, and the lessons, of the Geneva and Bishops' Bibles, published in 1560 and 1568 respectively, the Book of Common Prayer (1549) and the Book of Homilies (1547).

Shakespeare's attitude towards his schooling can only be guessed at; but a flavour of it can be caught in an apparently gratuitous episode in *The Merry Wives of Windsor* (written around 1597), the only one of Shakespeare's plays to be set in contemporary England, in which a schoolboy named William is tested by the Welsh pedagogue Sir Hugh Evans within earshot of the housekeeper Mistress Quickly:

EVANS What is '*lapis*', William?
WILLIAM A stone.

EVANS And what is 'a stone', William?
WILLIAM A pebble.
EVANS No, it is *'lapis'*. I pray you remember in your prain.
WILLIAM *'Lapis'*.

(*The Merry Wives of Windsor*, 4.1.26–31)

The questions and responses quote virtually verbatim the government-prescribed textbook *Short Introduction of Grammar* (1540), by William Lily (c.1468–1522); in this instance, however, the chaste sobriety of the all-male Tudor grammar school classroom is unravelled when William's responses provoke Mistress Quickly to unleash a series of obscene puns. School may also have provided opportunities for amateur dramatics in the form of readings of Roman comedy (Plautus and Terence) and tragedy (Seneca), which respectively provided the templates for early works such as *The Comedy of Errors* (first performed in 1594) and *Titus Andronicus* (published 1595).

Whether or not William completed his education is not known: the question of whether he did so or not is prompted by evidence of a change in his family circumstances which, most biographers agree, can hardly have failed to have had a significant impact upon him both personally and, perhaps, artistically. For his first decade of married life, William's father, John Shakespeare, was a relatively successful and prosperous local businessman who enjoyed property interests in and around Stratford, including the substantial house on Henley Street which provides the point of departure for the Birthday parade; he was also the holder of a number of increasingly important municipal offices: he was appointed as an alderman in 1565 and as bailiff in 1568, rising to the position of chief alderman and deputy bailiff in 1571. But in 1577, the man who had always been scrupulous in his attendance at council meetings stopped going to them altogether, an action that was only the first stage of a pattern of absenteeism and evasion that would persist long term. John Shakespeare had already been in trouble in 1570 for illegally charging interest on a loan to a business partner; in 1572 he was charged with 'brogging', the illegal selling of wool (one of the by-products of his trade as a glover).

In 1576, the Queen's Privy Council acted to counter the growing and serious problem of wool shortages by ordering a temporary suspension of all wool trading, and then calling in all broggers and requiring them to pledge £100 as security against their continuing their illegal activities. Whether or not John Shakespeare was in financial difficulties by this stage, this was a substantial sum, and biographers have generally marked this moment as 'a turning-point for the Shakespeare family' (Honan 1999: 39). John Shakespeare was relieved of his responsibility of contributing to poor relief and military levies; in 1579 he mortgaged property inherited by his wife and then forfeited it when he was unable to repay the debt a year later. In 1592, he was among those listed as having failed to attend church regularly, as the commissioners speculated, 'for fear of process for debt' (Schoenbaum 1977: 42).

Religion and resistance

John Shakespeare's non-attendance at church has been the subject of much speculation, in that it raises questions about not only his own religious beliefs and allegiances but those of his son also. The Stratford-upon-Avon in which William Shakespeare was born and raised had its share of adherents to the Catholicism that had been imposed during the brief reign of Mary Tudor (1516–58, reigned 1553–58) and which, with the accession of Queen Elizabeth I (1533–1603) in 1558, and the Acts of Uniformity and of Supremacy in 1559, had been supplanted by the reinstatement of Anglican Protestantism as the state religion. In common with his contemporaries, John Shakespeare had lived through a period in which matters of faith and conscience were also ones of life and often violent death. Peter Thomson summarises the historical context:

> The English Reformation, precipitated by Henry VIII's failure to win the Pope's agreement to his divorcing Catherine of Aragon in order to marry Elizabeth I's mother, Anne Boleyn, had established an English Church without a secure practice of its own. The return to Rome, led by Catherine's passionately Catholic daughter Mary I, had ended with Mary's death in 1558, and the new queen had wisely mixed tolerance with firmness in re-establishing a Church of England. But throughout her reign the new Church was under threat from two sides, the still-committed papists and the increasingly vocal group whose opposition to popish practices may be imprecisely defined as 'Puritan'.
>
> (Thomson 1994: 10)

The response of the Elizabethan state to this double sectarian threat was, at least at first, somewhat less draconian than recent history might have led its subjects to expect.

On the one hand, the authorities moved decisively to remove the vestiges of Catholic iconography from places of worship; thus between 1564 and 1566, John Shakespeare himself, in his official capacity as town Chamberlain, authorised the systematic desecration of Stratford's Guild Chapel, which involved dismantling its altar and whitewashing its medieval frescoes, thereby both sanctioning what Greenblatt calls 'calculated acts of symbolic violence against the traditional Catholic observance' and enforcing 'ways of compelling the

Elizabeth I (1533–1603)

Queen of England and Ireland

The sole child of Henry VIII and his second wife Anne Boleyn, Elizabeth succeeded her half-sister Mary I in 1558, thus bringing to an end a period of Catholic rule that saw the martyrdom of hundreds of Protestants as well as her own imprisonment in the Tower of London. Revealing herself to her subjects in a coronation procession and ceremony that, according to a contemporary account, turned London into 'a stage wherein was showed the wonderful spectacle of a noble hearted princess toward her most loving people, the people's exceeding comfort in beholding so worthy a sovereign, and hearing so princelike a voice' (Kastan 1999a: 117), Elizabeth maintained her power throughout her reign by cultivating the arts of performance in the political as well as cultural spheres. Protagonist as well as patron of pageants, progresses and processions, Elizabeth cultivated the troupe, led by the celebrated actor, clown and publican Richard Tarlton and the Master of the Revels, Edmund Tilney, known as the Queen's Men from 1583; from 1594, she favoured the Lord Chamberlain's and Lord Admiral's Men at court. Star player in a cult of personality that enabled her to negotiate the contradictions inherent in being both a ruler and a woman by centring on her fabled status as Virgin Queen, Elizabeth sustained the independence of England as a Protestant country by remaining unmarried, though her refusal to nominate a successor was in her final years a source of discontent and political instability. Enjoying the longest reign of an English monarch since Edward III (1312–77, reigned from 1327), Elizabeth represented continuity, though she also weathered a series of political crises that included the Northern rebellion of 1569, the Spanish Armada in 1588 and the failed Essex coup of 1601.

community to acknowledge the new order and to observe its practices' (2004: 95). The Church of England's doctrinal position was set out in its *Thirty Nine Articles of Religion* of 1563, which, among other things, proscribed such fundamentals of Catholicism as belief in Purgatory, the system of indulgences, the worship of relics and images, and transubstantiation (the transformation of altar bread and wine into the body and blood of Christ), outlawed the highly theatricalised ceremonial of the liturgy and firmly repudiated the authority of the 'Bishop of Rome'. On the other hand, what mattered was the show of public conformity rather than private spiritual conviction; Elizabeth, according to Francis Bacon, had no wish to 'make windows into men's hearts and secret thoughts' (Greenblatt 2004: 92). Initially, as long as her subjects demonstrated their loyalty to the Crown by regular attendance at church services in which they imbibed the vernacular liturgy, they were in theory free to believe, if not to practise, as Catholics or nonconformists.

This began to change in 1570, when Pope Pius V (1504–72) excommunicated Elizabeth and urged English Catholics (also on pain of excommunication) henceforward to refuse to acknowledge her legitimacy as either their spiritual or temporal sovereign. At a stroke, Pius V transformed the observance of English Catholicism into an act of potential treason, in the eyes of both its adherents and their Protestant neighbours. A year earlier, in 1569, a rebellion in the north of England, a notorious regional redoubt of the old religion, and led by the Earl of Northumberland and the Earl of Westmorland, was motivated by pro-Catholic sympathies; and although it was swiftly, and bloodily, suppressed, the decade that followed saw the repression of Papists and, to a lesser extent, Puritan recusants, steadily escalate. On a local day-to-day level this was manifested in practices such as the official monitoring of church attendance; periodically, however, it assumed a more spectacular public form, notably in the discovery of alleged or actual Catholic plots and the subsequent torture and execution of their perpetrators. In 1580, following Pope Gregory XIII's (1502–85) declaration calling for the assassination of the queen, a Jesuit mission led by Edmund Campion (1540–81) landed in England and proceeded over the next year to conduct covert, and highly dangerous, missionary work amongst the Catholic enclaves of stubbornly recusant Lancashire; apprehended in 1581, Campion was tortured, charged with treason and, suffering the grisly public fate of the traitor, hanged, drawn and quartered.

Campion was one of the first of the more than one hundred English Catholics publicly martyred during the remainder of Elizabeth's reign: perceived by the authorities, not without some justification, as adherents of a terrorist sect intent on the overthrow of the Crown and the imposition of the rule of Rome, Catholics experienced sustained and frequently violently extreme persecution. During the 1580s, fines for non-attendance at church increased, the priesthood was outlawed and harbouring a priest was declared a treasonable offence. In 1586, the regime's concerns about the connection between Catholic activism and insurrection were apparently corroborated by the discovery of the Babington Plot, in which Mary Stuart, Queen of Scots (1542–87), who was regarded by many Catholics as the legitimate ruler of England and who had illegally imprisoned by the English since 1567, was falsely incriminated in an alleged conspiracy to assassinate Elizabeth. Under the terms of the Act of Association passed in 1585, Mary Stuart was condemned to execution as the alleged beneficiary of the plot, and put to death in 1587.

Religious sedition appeared from a different source the following year, with the publication of the first of a series of satirical pamphlets issued under the pseudonym 'Martin Marprelate' which ridiculed the Anglican episcopacy and, in particular, the Archbishop of Canterbury, John Whitgift (c.1530–1604), who had assumed control of the Stationers' Company and of the printing houses, and whose Calvinist leanings had led him to seek the suppression of Puritan writings he regarded as heretical and seditious. The alleged authors of the pamphlets, John Penry and John Udall, were arrested: Penry was hanged in 1593 and Udall died in prison. But their treatment was not representative. Throughout the 1590s, English culture was characterised by 'a bizarre combination of the extreme politicization of some of the outward forms of "religion" with a form of *de facto* religious pluralism', whereby 'the profession of certain religious opinions and the performance or non-performance of certain "religious" actions became synonymous certainly with political disloyalty and sometimes formally with treason' whilst 'the range of available, self-consciously adversarial or mutually exclusive religious positions in the land greatly increased' (Lake 1999: 64). Catholics, regarded as traitors by definition, rather than Puritans, were the ones subjected to arrest, torture and execution.

With the accession of King James VI of Scotland (1566–1625) to the English throne in 1603, the climate eased. James's succession was viewed by radical puritans as an opportunity for Church reform, and in particular for the eradication of the lingering vestiges of 'popish' rituals and ceremonial; however, as ruler of Scotland, James had taken a stronger line on puritan nonconformity than he did on Catholicism, which he was prepared to tolerate as long as its adherents were prepared to profess their loyalty. In 1604 James called a conference of churchmen at Hampton Court with the aim of thrashing out a settlement between the reformers and the bishops, and for the first years of his reign recusancy fines were reduced, and for a time not even enforced (although the pressure that this exerted on the exchequer meant that they eventually rose again). James's position was maintained even following the provocation of the Gunpowder Plot of November 1605, which could have provided the pretext for the widespread persecution of English Catholics; he appeared to recognise that the conspiracy was the act of a minority of zealots and not supported by the majority, most of whom were prepared to outwardly accommodate themselves to the demands of the Protestant state.

James's twenty-two-year reign produced twenty-five Catholic martyrs, compared to more than two hundred under his predecessor. James's governance of church and state by self-proclaimed divine right (which he had himself eloquently theorised in his political treatises and *The Trew Law of Free Monarchies* [1598] and *Basilikon Doron* [1599], describing himself in the former work as a 'little God to sitte on his throne, and rule over other men') produced a settlement between radical reformists and church hierarchy, and between Crown and Commons, that would eventually unravel during the reign of his son Charles; but it also yielded a more enduring literary monument in the form of the English translation of the Bible authorised by the king himself at the Hampton Court conference and published in 1611. For the period up to the end of Shakespeare's lifetime, the everyday culture of religious observance was, at least on the surface, a considerably more settled one than it had been during the last decades of the previous century.

Placed in the context of the religious controversies of the time, and of the attendant daily anxieties and compromises to which they gave rise, the bare documentary record of John Shakespeare's apparent recusancy nonetheless remains provokingly ambiguous; and if the sparseness of the evidence renders the cases both for and against him being a closet Catholic resolutely unproven, it yields even fewer clues as to the religious beliefs or allegiances of William himself, whose own documentary traces simply indicate that he and his children were baptised, married and buried within the Anglican communion. Nonetheless, there has been a great deal of speculation as to whether Shakespeare was covertly a Catholic, or at least was closely associated with the Catholic underworld, although the evidence for this can at best be described as circumstantial.

One theory that has seen a resurgence of interest in recent decades (following the publication of E. A. J. Honigmann's *Shakespeare: The 'Lost Years'* in 1985) takes its cue from a remark by the seventeenth-century antiquarian and gossip-hunter John Aubrey (1626–97) that Shakespeare 'understood Latin pretty well, for he had been in his younger years a schoolmaster in the country' (Schoenbaum 1977: 110) and from the reference to a 'William Shakeshafte' in the will of the wealthy Lancashire Catholic Alexander Hoghton in 1581. Taken together, these two items have been seen as the basis for a case to be made for identifying Shakespeare's alleged experience as a country schoolmaster as a spot of private tutoring in Hoghton's household. The case is perhaps strengthened by the presence of the Lancashire-born John Cottom at the New King's School in Stratford between 1579 and 1581: Cottom's brother Thomas was a Catholic priest and one of the conspirators tortured and executed alongside Edmund Campion in 1581. It has also been seen as suggestive that Hoghton's bequest connects Shakeshafte with an inventory of the equipment of what appears to be a company of players, 'instruments belonging to musics, and all manner of play clothes'; his will expresses the hope that if his brother Thomas is unable to accommodate the company, his neighbour Sir Thomas Hesketh will assume the responsibility.

If Shakespeare, or Shakeshafte, did manage to secure the patronage of Hesketh during the early 1580s, this would in turn have put him in the vicinity of one of the North's most powerful politicians and a key supporter of the drama, the fourth Earl of Derby, Henry Stanley (1531–93), whose flamboyant son Ferdinando, Lord Strange (1559–94), acted as patron of his own company from 1563 through to the mid-1590s. The fourth earl's own conduct in his capacity as a court commissioner for ecclesiastical causes is indicative of the kind of delicate balancing of political and personal loyalties that was required in Elizabeth's England. As one biographer puts it, '[a]s Lancashire became religiously divided in the 1570s he prosecuted recusants vigorously, but he continued to assist Catholics who had been family friends, and was slow to prosecute them in the face of new legislation which he was empowered to enforce' (Knafla 2004: 212). Shakespeare may have been one of the troupe that played as Lord Strange's Men throughout the 1580s (and, after Ferdinando's accession to his father's title in 1593, as the Earl of Derby's Men) and whose members included the decade's leading tragedian, Edward Alleyn (1566–1626), as well as the key personnel of Shakespeare's company, the Lord Chamberlain's Men: Will Kempe (d. c.1603), Richard Burbage (1568–1619), George Bryan and Thomas Pope (d. 1604). It was Lord Strange's Men who performed several of Shakespeare's earliest works at the Rose playhouse between 1591 and 1594, including the first part of *Henry VI* and *Titus Andronicus*.

3   A life in writing

Early sightings

If Shakespeare did join Strange's Men, it was a short-term engagement; as noted earlier, on 27 November 1582 he obtained a licence to marry Anne Hathaway, and six months later their first daughter, Susanna, was baptised, on 26 May 1583. Two years later, on 2 February 1585, the twins Hamnet and Judith were baptised. It is seven years before Shakespeare appears in the records again, in the form of a vicious *ad hominem* attack on his character and literary reputation in the pamphlet *Greene's Groats-Worth of Witte*, which has been attributed to the playwright, pamphleteer, poet, writer of prose romances and all-round hack Robert Greene (though its authorship has been questioned), and which was published in September 1592. Greene (1558–92), who had been educated at Cambridge and Oxford, was one of the group known as the University Wits, a circle that included Christopher Marlowe (1564–93), Thomas Nashe (1567–1601), Thomas Lodge (1558–1625), Thomas Kyd (1558–94), John Lyly (c.1554–1606) and George Peele (c.1557–96), whose collective output included popular successes such as the two parts of Marlowe's *Tamburlaine the Great* (written and performed 1587–88) and *The Tragical History of Doctor Faustus* (1592), Kyd's *The Spanish Tragedy* (1587) and Greene's *Friar Bacon and Friar Bungay* (1589). Addressing himself to Marlowe, Nashe and Peele, Greene takes aim at the figure he terms an 'upstart Crow',

> beautified with our feathers, that with his *Tygers hart wrapt in a Players hyde* supposes he is as well able to bombast out a blanke verse as the best of you; and, beeing an absolute *Iohannes fac totum*, is in his owne conceit the onely Shake-scene in a countrie.
> (Chambers 1923, 4: 241–42)

What Shakespeare had done to offend Greene, if anything, is a mystery, but the general thrust of his invective is clear enough. Arrogating to himself literary airs to which he is not entitled, either by birth or by education, Shakespeare is a 'jack of all trades' who has dared to emerge from the ranks of the players (whom Greene derides as 'those burres to cleave: those Puppits (I meane) that spake from our mouths, those Anticks garnisht in our colours' [45]) to try his hand as a playwright. Shakespeare had yet to publish at this stage, but Greene's deliberate misquotation of a line from *Henry VI, Part 3* indicates that his earliest works were beginning to be performed or were circulating in manuscript: 'O tiger's heart wrapped in a woman's hide' (*3 Henry VI*, 1.4.138) is a line given to the Duke of York as he is tortured and taunted by the monstrous Queen Margaret, a woman he describes as 'She-wolf of France' (l. 112) an 'Amazonian trull' (l. 115) and 'stern, obdurate, flinty, rough, remorseless' (l. 143); Greene may be ridiculing Shakespeare's pretensions here but he also indicates that his target's work was already well known enough for his readership to have recognised the allusion.

Greene's diatribe confirms that Shakespeare was beginning to write for the London stage in the early 1590s, and suggests that he had been working as an actor prior to this. Shakespeare's putative involvement in Lord Strange's Men has already been mentioned: whether or not he became involved in this or any of the other Elizabethan companies during the 1580s, he would certainly have had opportunities to witness plays and players in performance from a young age. In 1569, when William was five years old, it was his father, in his capacity as bailiff, who authorised payments to the Queen's Players and the Earl of Worcester's Men; from then until 1582 Stratford was visited by many of the country's leading companies. During the 1560s and early 1570s the profession of playing was still an itinerant one, though increasingly subject to the strictures of governmental and municipal regulation that were putting an end to the system of unlicensed, semi-professional performance, rooted in the popular entertainment traditions of tumbling and mumming, that had obtained since the medieval period.

Unlicensed common players had been prohibited from performing in the city of London since 1550, and a year after her succession in 1558 Queen Elizabeth declared that local authorities' licensing responsibilities included enforcing restrictions on performance 'wherein either matters of religion or of the governaunce of the estate of the common weale shall be handled or treated' (Chambers 1923, 4: 263). But it was the 'Act for the punishment of Vagabonds' of 1572, the year in which Leicester's Men performed in Stratford, that decisively shaped the fortunes of the theatre industry in the latter part of the sixteenth century.

A piece of legislation aimed not only at the players but at what the authorities regarded as the large and potentially dangerous rural population of itinerant tinkers, beggars and 'masterless men', the Act criminalised by classing as 'Roges Vacaboundes and Sturdy Beggers' those it described as 'Bearewardes Common Players in Enterludes & Minstrels, not belonging to any Baron of this Realme or towardes any other honourable Personage of greater Degree; all Juglers, Pedlars, Tynkers and Petye Chapmen'. It also specified severe penalties upon apprehension: all such persons 'taken begging in any parte of this

Robert Greene (1558–92)

Pamphleteer, poet, prose writer and dramatist

Best known to posterity as the man who penned the first allusion in print to Shakespeare as a writer, in *Greene's Groats-Worth of Witte* (1592), Greene established himself on graduating from Cambridge University as a writer of prose romances and chronicler of the London low-life culture in which he flamboyantly participated. His *Pandosto: The Triumph of Time* (1588) provided the narrative source for *The Winter's Tale*. Possibly one of Shakespeare's collaborators on the *Henry VI* plays (which possibly accounts for him accusing Shakespeare of insolence and plagiarism), he also turned his hand to popular drama in the mixed-mode genre of comic history: his successes included *Friar Bacon and Friar Bungay* (c.1589), *The Scottish History of James IV* (1591) and *Orlando Furioso* (1591), which he attempted to sell to the Queen's and Admiral's Men simultaneously. According to Henry Chettle, who published *Groats-Worth* posthumously – presumably in order to settle some scores of his own, though he later retracted the allegations against Shakespeare – Greene died as a result of an overdose of wine and pickled herrings.

Realme, or taken vagrant wandring and misordering themselves' should be 'grevouslye whipped, and burnte through the gristle of the right Eare with a hot Yron'. Caught a second time, the player would be judged 'a Felon; and shall in all Degrees receave have suffer and forfayte as Felon'; the third time, he would be 'adjudged & deemed for a Felon, and suffer paynes of Death and losse of Land and Goodes as a Felon without Allowance or Benefyte of Cleargye or Sanctuary' (Chambers 1923, 4: 269–70). The effect on the nascent theatre industry was that the established and successful troupes ensured that they secured the protection and support of an aristocratic patron; classed as his (or, in the unique case of the Queen's Men, her) liveried servants, they were then exempt from the provisions of the Act. Maintaining a retinue of players was, for Elizabethan noblemen, a sign of cultural accomplishment and an important component within the household hospitality economy; in return, the players used their patron's name as a licence to travel and to work.

The security of patronage also helped to foster an environment in which the players could for the first time in England organise themselves along regular commercial lines, in joint-stock companies consisting of sharers, hired men and apprenticed boy players. During the 1570s, these included Oxford's Men, Sussex's Men, Warwick's Men and Essex's Men; theirs was largely a peripatetic existence divided between tours of the English provinces and more lucrative and secure work in the capital, and initially subject to the practical and commercial determinations of playing in venues such as inn yards, the halls of great houses and arenas built to house other forms of entertainment, such as bull- or bear-baiting or fencing, whose owners and managers inevitably staked their own interests in the companies' activities in return for their use.

The theatrical entrepreneur Philip Henslowe (c.1555–1615) was a key figure in this respect, and the records that he left of his day-to-day financial transactions from 1592 to 1603 (Foakes and Rickert 1961) furnish detailed evidence of the organisation of the theatre economy in the period: having established himself as the owner of extensive property interests in the borough of Southwark, he became a substantial backer of playmaking activities, supplying props and costumes, commissioning scripts and, especially after 1587, when he built the Rose, leasing playhouses to playing companies. Throughout the 1590s Henslowe leased the Rose to the company that, emerging from an amalgamation of the Admiral's Men and Strange's Men, was led by his son-in-law the actor Edward Alleyn, with whom he maintained a close and profitable professional association (he also opened the Fortune Playhouse in 1600 and the Hope in 1613). During this period, following the allocation in 1594 of exclusive rights to public performance in London to two companies, the Lord Admiral's Men's activities at the Rose formed one half of what became a virtual industry duopoly in London, staging the work of a stable of writers that included Marlowe, Thomas Dekker (c.1572–1632), Thomas Heywood (c.1574–1641), George Chapman (c.1559–1634) and Ben Jonson (1572–1637).

The other party in the duopoly was the company which was formed from the remnants of Lord Strange's, Lord Pembroke's and the Queen's Men in 1594, and which operated under the patronage of Henry Carey (1526–96), Queen Elizabeth's Lord Chamberlain since 1583. Lord Hunsdon's company, the Lord Chamberlain's Men, who were briefly known as the Chamberlain's Men when his son George (1547–1603) succeeded him as patron in 1596, became the Lord Chamberlain's Men again in 1597 when he assumed the post vacated as a result of the death of Hunsdon's successor, William, Lord Cobham. They became the King's Men on the accession of James I in 1603. The company was based first at the Theatre in the north London borough of Shoreditch, and then, when its lease

Philip Henslowe (c.1555–1615)

Theatrical entrepreneur

Born in Sussex, Henslowe was first apprenticed to the Dyers' Company in London, before moving on to manage an extensive and diverse investment portfolio, not untypical of entrepreneurship in the period, that included trading in both timber and real estate, starch making and acting as a pawnbroker. In 1587 he erected the Rose playhouse on the site in Southwark that he had acquired some three years previously; from 1592, the year in which he refurbished and expanded the capacity of the playhouse, then home to Lord Strange's Men, he began to keep detailed accounts of receipts and expenditures, as well as inventories of his assets, pertaining to his theatrical and other business activities. In the same year his stepdaughter Joan Woodward married the leading Lord Strange's Men actor Edward Alleyn, and from that point on the two men acted as business partners, extending their interests to the playhouse in Newington Butts and to the Beargarden in Bankside. In 1600 Henslowe and Alleyn contracted Peter Street, the master carpenter who had built the Globe playhouse the previous year, to construct the Fortune in St Giles Cripplegate. Henslowe's entertainment business activities included bear-baiting: in 1604 he and Alleyn were awarded the patent as Masters of 'the Royal Game of Bears, Bulls and Mastiff Dogs', and in 1613 he demolished the old Beargarden and replaced it with a new dual-purpose arena, the Hope, on the same site. Henslowe sustained a close connection with the court throughout his career, being appointed a Groom of the Chamber and, in 1603, Gentleman Sewer to James I.

Edward Alleyn (1566–1626)

Actor

A member of the Earl of Worcester's Men in 1583 and of the Lord Admiral's Men between 1592 and 1597, he married Philip Henslowe's stepdaughter Joan Woodward on 22 October 1592; following a three-year retirement he joined forces with Henslowe to build the Fortune Playhouse, which opened in 1600. Playing Marlowe's Tamburlaine, Barabas and Faustus, Orlando in Greene's *Orlando Furioso* and Muly Mahomet in Peele's *The Battle of Alcazar*, Alleyn was known for his imposing stature and for a grand style that was subsequently unfavourably compared with that of Burbage.

expired in 1597, at the nearby Curtain, and finally, from 1599 until 1613, at the newly built Globe in Southwark.

By dividing London's theatre industry into two officially sanctioned companies, one north of the city, one south, and each with its own playhouse, star performer and repertoire of plays, Hunsdon and the Lord Admiral, his son-in-law Charles Howard (1536–1624), were not acting purely as high-minded cultural philanthropists; the scheme was an act of centralisation and control, which involved the delicate balancing of competing political, civic and commercial interests. The players' companies were afforded the support of the Crown on the understanding that they were available to perform at court as required, with the business of performing to paying audiences regarded as a form of public rehearsal; by positioning them on the suburban outskirts, Hunsdon and Howard hoped to placate the Lord Mayor by keeping them out of the city centre and in particular out of the traditional haunts of the itinerant touring companies, the taverns.

Thomas Dekker (c.1572–1632)

Prose writer and playwright

Dekker first appears in the records as one of the most prolific and energetic members of the group of dramatists engaged by Philip Henslowe to supply scripts for the Lord Admiral's and Earl of Worcester's Men during the 1590s; in the four-year period between 1598 and 1602 alone, Dekker contributed to over forty plays (only six of which made their way into print), and he remained active as a playwright throughout the Jacobean and well into the Caroline periods. Chiefly remembered today for his 1599 comedy *The Shoemakers Holiday*, which was published with the announcement that it has been performed for the queen's New Year celebrations, and for his co-authored treatment of the folk-hero petty criminal and cross-dresser Mary Frith, known as Moll Cutpurse, *The Roaring Girl* (1611, with Thomas Middleton), Dekker wrote history plays, tragedies and civic pageants, as well as prose reportage on London life. Tolerant, broad-minded and sympathetic to the vicissitudes of his city's underdogs, misfits, losers and outsiders, Dekker was himself repeatedly afflicted by poverty and debt.

Thomas Heywood (c.1573–1641)

Poet, player, playwright and essayist

Claiming that he had had 'an entire hand, or at least a main finger' in more than two hundred plays, the consummately professional Heywood regarded himself as one of early modern London's most prolific writers, though only one-tenth of these plays were published; in addition, he acted with the Lord Admiral's Men between 1588 and 1589, and with Worcester's (who became Queen Anne's) Men from 1601 to 1619. Hailed by Francis Meres in *Palladis Tamia* (1598) as one of the 'best for comedy', Heywood had a penchant for romantic adventure stories, as represented by the picaresque *The Four Prentices of London* (1600), *Fortune by Land and Sea* and *The Fair Maid of the West* (written between 1601 and 1609). He produced popular hagiographical works tapping into the cult of Elizabeth I, notably the two-part *If You Know Not Me, You Know Nobody* (1605), whose first part was reprinted eight times, a five-part mythological saga consisting of *The Golden Age* (1611), *The Silver Age* (1613), *The Brazen Age* (1613) and two instalments of *The Iron Age* (published 1632), and the domestic tragedy *A Woman Killed with Kindness* (1603). Heywood published poetry, a widely read translation of Ovid's *Ars amoratia* (1608) and an important defence of the theatre profession, *An Apology for Actors* (published 1612).

The Lord Chamberlain's Men's occupancy of the Theatre marked the beginning of their ascendancy among the Elizabethan companies, a position which was confirmed by the move to the Globe. In common with the Rose and other playhouses that were built south of the River Thames from the 1570s through to the 1590s (including the first Beargarden, the Hope and the Swan), the Theatre was situated in one of the suburban border regions known as the Liberties, which were technically outside of the jurisdiction of the city authorities, whose opposition to the theatre on both religious and commercial grounds was frequently, and stridently, audible. Licensed by the Crown and enjoying the benefits of exemption from the vagrancy laws, playing companies conducted their business in areas already renowned for immorality and profanity: alongside the playhouses stood brothels, drinking dens and gaming houses, as well as the sporting arenas and lazar-houses (where those afflicted with leprosy were accommodated). Associated by moralists with deceit, pretence, falsehood and disregard for social hierarchy, as well as with lewd and deviant practices such as transvestism, playing was regarded not only as wicked and seditious but as a scandalously profitable form of idleness.

Nearly twenty years old when the Chamberlain's Men assumed residency, the Theatre was the longest-established of London's permanent playhouses. In 1576, while the twelve-year-old William Shakespeare was laboriously parsing Latin phrases in Warwickshire, the actor, builder and entrepreneur James Burbage (1531–97) erected it as a successor to the first permanent commercial playhouse built in England, the Red Lion, which had opened in 1567; in the same year, the first indoor Blackfriars playhouse opened, as well as another open-air arena in Newington Butts. James Burbage thus created the conditions in which his son Richard, founder member and sharer in the Chamberlain's Men, rose to the position of lead actor; assuming ownership of the Blackfriars playhouse in 1596 with the plan of refurbishing it as a base for the company, James also provided the new company with what they would a decade later use as a technologically sophisticated, coterie-audience base for its winter activities, and one which, like the Globe, concentrated ownership in the hands of its actors rather than those of a landlord.

Making a name

There was another factor at play in the Chamberlain's Men's dominance of the theatre scene after 1594, which was its reliance on the work of one playwright, also an actor and a sharer: William Shakespeare. The Lord Admiral's Men had their own core repertoire in the form of the plays of Marlowe, which were repeatedly revived throughout the 1590s and into the seventeenth century, and yet, since Shakespeare had the advantage over Marlowe of not having been stabbed to death in mysterious circumstances in 1593, he was in a better position to deliver new work; from the outset, the Lord Chamberlain's Men were shaping the theatre's future, whilst their chief rival looked to its past. As has already been mentioned, Shakespeare may have been involved with Lord Strange's Men and his first works were possibly staged at Henslowe's Rose; according to the standard practices of the theatre of the time, his earliest experience as a playwright is likely to have been that of a contributor to works written on a collaborative basis, often divided piecemeal into scenes and speeches assigned on the basis of aptitude or specialism.

An entry in Henslowe's accounts dated 3 March 1591 (that is, 1592 new style) refers to a new play he entitles 'Harey the vj' (Foakes and Rickert 1961: 16). If this documents a performance of one of the *Henry VI* plays, it is one that is likely to have been co-authored by Shakespeare and, it has been speculated, various combinations of Marlowe, Nashe, Greene and Peele (*Titus Andronicus* has recently been confidently attributed to Shakespeare and Peele). Evidence of Shakespeare's collaborative activities at this time is provided by what have been identified as his contributions to the manuscript of the unpublished play *Sir Thomas More* (1592–95), written by Anthony Munday (1560–1633), Henry Chettle (c.1560–c.1607) and possibly Dekker, for Lord Strange's Men at the Rose playhouse, and his authorship of a number of scenes of *King Edward III* (published in 1596).

In *Sir Thomas More*, identified by scholars as 'Hand D', Shakespeare is responsible for the scene in which More persuades a group of rioters not to vent their fury on immigrant traders, and which is notable both for its compassionate evocation of the 'wretched strangers,/ Their babies at their backs, with their poor luggage/ Plodding to th' ports and coasts for transportation' and for the force with which it urges 'obedience to authority', to the

Sir Thomas More

Date, text and authorship

1592–93. Never performed or published; MS held in British Library. First draft conjectured as by Anthony Munday and possibly Henry Chettle, revised by Thomas Dekker, Thomas Heywood and Shakespeare in 1603–04.

Sources and influences

Raphael Holinshed, *Chronicles of England, Scotland and Ireland* (second edition, 1587); Foxe, *Actes and Monuments* (1583); Nicholas Harpsfield, *The Life and Death of Sir Thomas More, Knight* (c. 1557)

On stage

Nottingham Playhouse, 1964 (More: Ian McKellen); RSC, 2005 (dir. Robert Delamere; More: Nigel Cooke).

Criticism

Gabrieli, Vittorio and Giorgio Melchiori (eds) (1990) *Sir Thomas More*. The Revels Plays. Manchester: Manchester University Press.
McMillin, Scott (1987) *The Elizabethan Theatre and 'The Book of Sir Thomas More'*. Ithaca, NY and London: Cornell University Press.

king, who is styled 'god on earth' (ADD.II.D.81–83, 102, 113). In *Edward III*, Shakespeare contributes the story of the unrequited passion of the King for the Countess of Salisbury. Shakespeare returned to collaboration towards the end of his writing career, probably with George Wilkins for *Pericles* (1609), and certainly with John Fletcher (1579–1625) on *All Is True* (printed in the 1623 Folio as *The Life of Henry VIII*), which was staged at the Globe in 1613, and *The Two Noble Kinsmen*, published as the work of 'the memorable Worthies of their time' in 1634 and probably written and first performed around 1612–13. Other works solely attributed to Shakespeare in the Folio (*Measure for Measure, Macbeth* and *Timon of Athens*) have also been identified as the product of multiple authorship, in the sense of their having been co-authored, revised or adapted by his colleague and eventual successor as pre-eminent playwright of his age, Thomas Middleton (1580–1627).

It is evident, however, that Shakespeare established a name for himself as major or sole author of playscripts for the Lord Chamberlain's Men from a relatively early stage and, moreover, that his sole authorship was a factor in the marketability of his work in its published form as well as on the stage. The first of his plays to appear in print did so, not unusually for plays of the time, anonymously. The second and third parts of *Henry VI* appeared as *The First Part of the Contention of the Two Famous Houses of York and Lancaster* and *The True Tragedy of Richard Duke of York and the Good Henry the Sixth* in 1594 and 1595, *Titus Andronicus* in 1594, *Romeo and Juliet*, *Richard II* and *Richard III* in 1597, and the first part of *Henry IV* in 1598. At this point Shakespeare emerges into visibility as a named author, an established player and the bearer of a growing literary reputation. In 1598, *Love's Labour's Lost* appeared in quarto, advertised as 'Newly corrected and augmented by W. Shakespere' on the title page; in the same year, according to the list included in its 1601 printing, Shakespeare was one of the 'principal Comedians' in *Every Man in His Humour* at the Curtain, an early success from his associate and rival, Ben Jonson.

King Edward III

Date, text and authorship

Q1 1596. Conjectured as co-written by Shakespeare and unknown collaborator(s).

Sources and influences

Raphael Holinshed, *Chronicles of England, Scotland and Ireland* (second edition, 1587); Jean Froissart, *Chronicles* (English translation by Lord Berners, 1523).

On stage

RSC, 2002 (dir. Anthony Clark; King Edward: David Rintoul; Countess: Caroline Faber; Prince Edward: Jamie Glover).

Criticism

Melchiori, Giorgio (1994) *Shakespeare's Garter Plays: 'Edward III' to 'Merry Wives of Windsor'*. Newark, DE: University of Delaware Press.
Melchiori, Giorgio (ed.) (1998) *King Edward III*. New Cambridge Shakespeare. Cambridge: Cambridge University Press.

In the same year Shakespeare was also mentioned in the clergyman-critic Francis Meres's (1565–1647) compendium of quotations and commentaries, *Palladis Tamia, Wit's Treasury*:

> As *Plautus* and *Seneca* are accounted the best for Comedy and Tragedy among the Latines: so *Shakespeare* among ye English is the most excellent in both kinds for the stage; for Comedy, witnes his *Gētlemē of Verona*, his *Errors*, his *Loves labours lost*, his *Loves labours wonne*, his *Midsummer night dreame*, & his *Merchant of Venice*: for Tragedy his *Richard the 2. Richard the 3. Henry the 4. King John*, *Titus Andronicus* and his *Romeo* and *Juliet*.
>
> (Meres 1973: 282)

Meres had heard of, seen, or read in print or in manuscript, at least a dozen of Shakespeare's plays, including two that appeared in quarto shortly afterwards (*A Midsummer Night's Dream* and *Merchant of Venice*, both published in 1600) and three that remained unpublished until the first Folio of 1623. Elsewhere, an early performance of *The Comedy of Errors* is confirmed by a reference in *Gesta Grayorum* (which documents the Christmas revels at London's Gray's Inn law school, and was written in the 1590s but not published until 1688), which reports that on 28 December 1594, after a boisterous evening's entertainment of 'Dancing and Revelling with Gentlewomen', 'a Comedy of Errors (like to *Plautus* his *Menechmus*) was played by the Players' (Greg 1914: 22).

Meres also makes a tantalising reference to Shakespeare's *Loves labours wonne*, which has been conjecturally identified as either a sequel to *Love's Labour's Lost* or, less plausibly, an alternative title for one of the other comedies. This is one of two lost plays attributed to Shakespeare by his contemporaries, the other being *The History of Cardenio*, a play entered in the Stationers' Register on 9 September 1653 and identified as the work of 'Mr Fletcher and Shakespeare', which is likely to be the 'Cardenno' performed by the King's Men at court in 1613. Shakespeare has also been speculatively identified as the author, or part-author, of various plays published anonymously, under initials or fraudulently under his own name: *Locrine*, published in 1595, was advertised on the title page as 'Newly set foorth, overseene and corrected, By *W.S.*', which may indicate that he had a hand in its revision; other apocryphal texts (generally not now accepted as Shakespearean) include *The Life of Sir John Oldcastle* (1600), *The London Prodigal* (1605) and *The Puritan Widow* (1607). One thing suggested by these false attributions is that the appropriation of Shakespeare's name was considered a good marketing ploy.

Plays in print

Shakespeare was not the only playwright to have written plays which, for various reasons, have disappeared: of roughly 3,000 plays known by their titles to have existed between the 1570s and the 1640s, just over 500 found their way into print; of these, a mere 18 have survived in manuscript form (Long 1999). Given the conditions under which early modern plays were written and produced, however, what seems more remarkable is not how few have come down to us but how many. Whether working singly or as part of a collaborative team, the playwright initially wrote, by candlelight, with a quill pen on paper (an expensive commodity). The evidence of Hand D in *Sir Thomas More* suggests that Shakespeare followed the standard practice of composing the spoken text first, adding in stage directions and speech headings later; the more firmly embedded the writer in the company for which the script was intended, the less specific and consistent these needed to be. The writer's copy, complete with deletions and marginal and interlineal additions and revisions, then passed to a professional scribe (in the case of Shakespeare's company this was most frequently Ralph Crane) to be copied for the individual members of the playing company, each of whom would receive only his own part (or parts, as multiple doubling was standard practice) and cues, in the shape of a roll of paper (from which derives the term 'role'), and which he would be required to rapidly memorise alongside the dozens he might be called upon to perform at short notice.

A copy of the play was also submitted to the state censor and member of the royal household, the Master of the Revels, for licensing, and should he insist upon cuts or alterations for political reasons or, following the introduction in 1606 of the 'Act to Restrain Abuses of Players', on the grounds of profanity, these would need to be incorporated into the working script. The Revels Office could order the excision of entire scenes (including, apparently, the deposition scene [4.1] in *Richard II*, which was omitted from the

Love's Labours Won

Francis Meres's reference to a play of this title in *Palladis Tamia* in 1598 is the source of one of the most enduring, and in this instance genuine, Shakespearean literary mysteries. Although it has been suggested that this is merely an alternative title (along the lines of *Twelfth Night, or What You Will*) for one of the comedies likely to have been written by 1598 but not mentioned by Meres (*The Taming of the Shrew*, however, being the only halfway plausible candidate), the case for the independent existence of a play of this name, in all likelihood a sequel to *Love's Labour's Lost* (a work which seems to positively cry out for one) is strengthened by the corroborating evidence of a bookseller's list, dating from 1603 and discovered by one Mr Solomon Pottesman in 1953, which includes 'loves labor won' alongside 'loves labor lost', 'marchant of vennis', 'taming of a shrew' and plays by Shakespeare's contemporaries. Reasons for the play's total disappearance, despite apparently having been published in quarto, can only be guessed at.

Cardenio

On 20 May 1613, the leading player of the King's Men, John Heminges, received £20 from the Revels Office in payment for the performance of six plays at court, including one 'Cardenno'. Less than two months later, on 9 July, he was paid £6 13s. 4d. for another performance of what was presumably the same play, 'called Cardenna'. Thereafter there is no trace of the play until 9 September 1653, when the publisher Humphrey Moseley placed an entry for *The History of Cardenio, by Mr Fletcher and Shakespeare* in the Stationers' Register. One of his era's most productive publishers of pre-Restoration drama (he was jointly responsible for the Beaumont and Fletcher Folio of 1647), Moseley could not have known about the court performances, though he did have a history of making fraudulent entries attributing lost, possibly non-existent, or non-canonical, works to Shakespeare: on the same date, he also entered under Shakespeare's name *The Merry Devil of Edmonton* (possibly written by Thomas Dekker or Michael Drayton), which had been published in quarto anonymously in 1607 and which was one of the plays performed by the King's Men during the 1612–13 court festivities, as well as *Henry the First* and *Henry the Second*, identified as the work of Shakespeare and the dramatist Robert Davenport (a *Henry I* had been licensed for the King's Men on 10 April, eight years after Shakespeare's death; it was not published). On 29 June 1660 Moseley made a further three entries: *Duke Humphrey, a Tragedy*, *The History of King Stephen* and *Iphis and Iantha, or a marriage without a man, a Comedy*. None of these is extant, though the existence of *Duke Humphrey* (if not its Shakespearean authorship) is possibly confirmed by its inclusion in a list of manuscripts compiled by the antiquary John Warburton in the eighteenth century (tragic-comically, Warburton's manuscript collection was largely destroyed when his cook used it as a source of scrap paper for fire-lighting). The case of *Cardenio* experienced a further twist in 1727, when the writer and editor Lewis Theobald presented his play *Double Falsehood: or, The Distressed Lovers* at the Theatre Royal, Drury Lane. Published the following year billed as 'Written Originally by W. SHAKESPEARE; and now Revised and Adapted to the Stage by Mr. THEOBALD', it contained a preface in which he claimed that it was based on a previously unknown Shakespearean manuscript, of which he had no less than three copies in his possession. Theobald's play is based on the Cardenio episode in Cervantes's *Don Quixote*, which was translated into English in 1612; given that he was seemingly unaware either of the evidence of court performances of a play of this title in 1613 or of the later Stationers' Register entry, it seems unlikely that he was making it up. Most readers have found *Double Falsehood* predominantly Fletcherian rather than Shakespearean, and Theobald, to do him justice, declares an interest, confessing that 'my partiality for Shakespeare makes me wish that everything that is good, or pleasing, in our tongue has been owing to his pen'. Since Theobald's *Double Falsehood* is itself a text fashioned to the tastes of early eighteenth-century theatre audiences, it is one in which Shakespeare and Fletcher's original is at best discernible in outline, or as distant echo. In March 2010, it was published in its first-ever scholarly edition, edited by Brean Hammond, as part of the Arden Shakespeare third series.

first three quarto printings) and, on occasion, impose an outright ban. In August 1597, for example, as the doctored version of *Richard II* was entered in the Stationers' Register (the official record of all works projected for publication), the scurrilous topical satire *The Isle of Dogs*, co-authored by Nashe and Jonson, and performed by the Earl of Pembroke's Men at the Swan playhouse, was suppressed for containing seditious material, and its authors imprisoned.

Playscripts, which were accounted the property of the playing companies, not their authors, were adjustable commodities, liable to amendment, adaptation and revision subject to the dictates of censorship and audience taste; to the vagaries of players' memories and of their propensity to introduce interpolations of their own, and to local circumstances and conditions of performance, in the public playhouses, at court, on tour; performed and revived as part of the daily repertoire of the company and as demanded to mark particular festivities or special occasions. The primary medium of the drama was performance, wherein lay its major commercial potential, not print, and there was usually no compelling reason for the companies to release plays for publication; indeed, with copyright belonging to the printer or publisher rather than the company or the writer, and with fewer enforceable legal sanctions against unauthorised reproduction, there were good reasons not to do so. Should a script (designed as a working document for a playhouse's use rather than as private reading material) make its way into print, in cheap quarto or octavo editions, its text, already liable to the multiple processes of alteration endemic to the medium, underwent further transformation through the transcription, compositorial and proof-reading activities involved in the preparation and production of copy in the printing-house, each pair of hands it passed through introducing the possibility of errors, revisions and improvements.

As is still the case, the readership for plays was fairly select and the market for publication small. Plays hardly registered as 'literature' in the sense in which later generations of readers would come to understand them. The founder of Oxford University's Bodleian Library, Sir Thomas Bodley (1545–1613), classed plays alongside other 'idle books and riff-raffs' (Bentley 1971: 52); and their title pages usually promoted the companies that had performed them, not their writers. The first edition of the second part of *Henry VI* in 1595 announced that it was presented 'as it was sundrie times acted by the Right Honourable the Earle of Pembrooke his servants', and *Titus Andronicus* was offered in 1594 'As it was Plaide by the Right Honourable the Earle of *Darbie*, Earle of *Pembrooke*, and Earle of *Sussex* their servants'; after 1597, when Shakespeare was attached to the Lord Chamberlain's, and subsequently King's, Men, the quartos continued to prioritise the company over the writer, drawing attention to the venue in which it was performed or to special circumstances of the play's performance: *Love's Labour's Lost* in 1598 appeared 'As it was presented before her Highnes this last Christmas'; the fourth (1608) quarto of *Richard II* 'As it hath been lately acted by the Kinges Majesties servantes, at the Globe', and the first (1622) quarto of *Othello* 'As it hath beene diverse times acted at the Globe, and at the Black-Friers, by his Majesties Servants'.

Already several stages removed from the authorial manuscripts that were presumably in the safe keeping of Shakespeare's company, the earliest printed texts of his plays derive from the medium of performance, but the extent to which they can be regarded as a record of what was said and done in the playhouses and elsewhere is debatable. The idea that Shakespeare's plays are texts for performance has been part of a widespread scholarly consensus for decades, but to designate either the quartos or the Folio versions in these terms is to risk conflating the scripts that he generated for his fellow actors (which we do not have) with published documents intended not to be performed, but read, although it appears that the embedded memory of the plays' performance was a vital constituent of the reading experience. When the Prologue to *Romeo and Juliet* speaks of the 'two-hours' traffic of our stage' (l. 12) the timing may be nominal rather than chronologically precise, but even taking into account the rapidity of Elizabethan stage recitation, the majority of quarto and Folio versions of the plays are probably too long to be comfortably accommodated in a performance schedule that, in the public playhouses, commenced at two o'clock in the afternoon and ended before dark. The quartos which have often been viewed as particularly close to performance, *Romeo and Juliet* (1597), *Henry V* (1600), *The Merry Wives of Windsor* (1602) and *Hamlet* (1603), are significantly shorter than the authorised editions that succeeded them; and although their reliability has been challenged on the basis that they allegedly represent fraudulently obtained, abbreviated, pirated or memorially reconstructed versions of the plays, they may provide more direct evidence of theatrical practice than do later, fuller inscriptions.

Shakespeare's own attitude towards the publication of his plays is unknowable. It is routinely asserted that he had no interest in seeing them in print, a position which seems to be supported by the intermittent pattern of quarto publication: seventeen of the thirty-seven plays attributed to him were published during his lifetime, leaving the majority, including those which posterity would consider his greatest achievements, to the mercy of posthumous publication. Among the quartos, fifteen were printed between 1594 and 1603, after which date the rate of output of new Shakespearean works (as distinct from reprints of earlier successes) sharply drops: there is a five-year gap between the first quarto of *Hamlet* and the 1608 quarto of *King Lear*, which was followed a year later by *Pericles, Prince of Tyre* and *Troilus and Cressida*.

Both are problematic. *Pericles* is often seen as textually corrupt, disjointed and incomplete, and its publication probably unauthorised, its doubtful provenance apparently confirmed by the fact that it was the only Shakespearean play already extant in quarto not to be included in the 1623 Folio; described by Ben Jonson in 1629 as a 'mouldy tale', which he characterised as a generic ragbag of 'scraps out of every dish', it was nonetheless a popular stage success and was revived and reprinted numerous times up until the 1630s. *Troilus and Cressida* was entered in the Stationers' Register 'as yt is acted by my lo: Chamberlens Men' in 1603 but it was six years before a quarto emerged with a title-page bearing the legend 'As it was acted by the Kings Maiesties servants at the Globe'. Simultaneously, a second quarto version was published which eradicated the reference to performance (of which there is no record), and which incorporated a prefatory epistle from a 'never writer' to the 'ever reader' which advertised a 'new play, never stal'd with the Stage, never clapper-clawed with the palmes of the vulger' and which defined the play (identified on the title-pages of both quartos as a history and included as a late insertion in the Folio among the tragedies) as a comedy.

Poetry and patronage

Beyond the textual indeterminacies of the last new plays attributed to Shakespeare to appear in print while he was still alive, the attitude of their author is unreadable. He may or may not have had anything to do with their publication, and he may or may not have endorsed what is presumably the publisher's anti-theatricalism, though the widely cited view that he was indifferent (or even opposed) to seeing his plays in print has been vigorously challenged in recent years (Erne 2003). Unlike later seventeenth-century colleagues, he did not include in the quarto editions the kind of dedicatory, vindicatory or self-promoting verses and epistles that served to recommend the work to a patron or more general readership; nor did the printers and publishers perform these actions on his behalf.

Addressing 'Gentlemen and courteous readers', the 1590 octavo of Marlowe's anonymously issued *Tamburlaine the Great* contains a declaration by the printer 'R[ichard]. J[ones].' that he hoped the works 'will be no less acceptable unto you to read … than they have been, lately, delightful for many of you to see'; the second quarto of Francis Beaumont's (1584–1616) *The Knight of the Burning Pestle* (1635) advises 'the Readers of this

Comedy' that 'the author had no intent to wrong anyone in this comedy, but as a merry passage ... which he hopes will please all, and be hurtful to none'; and Jonson persistently insinuates his personal presence into his works, for example signing the dedicatory epistle to *Volpone or The Fox* (performed by the King's Men in 1605) 'From my house in the Black-Friars this 11. of February, 1607'. *Troilus and Cressida* excepted, there is none of this in the Shakespearean quartos; and although, as we have seen, the role of the writer was generally not promoted, or even acknowledged, in early modern printed playtexts, Shakespeare remains distinctly elusive, even evasive, continuing to offer his plays without apology or explanation even after his name is prominently attached to them.

This was not the case, however, with his other earliest published works, the narrative poems, which also provide better evidence that here, at least, he *was* concerned about publication, and that he, or at least his publisher, wanted them produced stylishly, and with care. Predating *The First Part of the Contention* by a year, Shakespeare's first published work was the erotic narrative poem *Venus and Adonis*, entered in the Stationers' Register on 18 April 1593 and in circulation by the summer. The publisher and printer was Shakespeare's contemporary from Stratford-upon-Avon Richard Field (1561–1624), whose forte was sumptuous editions of high-class literary works, and whose output included very few plays; the edition is among the best presented of Shakespeare's early texts. It was followed in 1594 by the quarto of the narrative poem *Lucrece*, also published by Field, alongside the first reissue of *Venus and Adonis* (which proved to be Shakespeare's most popular work for nearly half a century, undergoing a succession of reprints until 1636). It was also scrupulously printed, and ran to eight editions until 1640. Direct evidence of Shakespeare's formal professional association with Field ends here, though the fact that Field was involved in the publication of the second editions of Raphael Holinshed's (d. c.1582) *Chronicles* (1587) and of Sir Thomas North's (c.1535–c.1603) translation of Plutarch's *Lives* (1595 and 1603) suggests that the relationship was sustained, possibly affording Shakespeare access to these key sources for his English and Roman history plays.

The other important relationship that is textually manifest in these two poetic works is that of the poet to his patron. Like most sixteenth-century English poets not possessed of aristocratic means themselves, Shakespeare may at this point in his career have been financially dependent upon the favour of wealthy and well-connected sponsors: in return for material support and protection, writers incorporated flattering allusions to their benefactors into their work, or dedicated it to them in effusive terms. Shakespeare's decision to launch his career as a poet may have been a pragmatic one. Having enjoyed some success seeing Lord Strange's Men performing *Titus Andronicus* and parts of *Henry VI* at Henslowe's Rose in the early 1590s, he would have found his playhouse activities, if not his writing, brought to a halt by one of the deadliest of occupational hazards endemic to the early modern theatre profession: bubonic plague. Between June 1592 and June 1594, in response to a particularly lethal outbreak (which in 1593 resulted in more than 15,000 deaths, or approaching 10 per cent of the capital's population), the London civic authorities ordered the closure of the playhouses, located amongst the most densely populated and insanitary regions of the city, as a precaution against the spread of infection.

During this twenty-four-month hiatus, the playing companies struggled to maintain a living through provincial touring; whether or not he went on the road with Strange's Men or with some other outfit, and presumably unable to make a living from script commissions, Shakespeare meanwhile secured (or at least solicited the attention of) a patron who was also one of Queen Elizabeth's most fashionable, charismatic and well-connected

Ben Jonson (1572–1637)

Poet and playwright

Educated at Westminster School, Jonson was apprenticed as a bricklayer to his stepfather (he remained a paid-up member of the Bricklayers' Guild at least until his late thirties), spent some time in the early 1590s on military service in the Netherlands and then joined the theatre profession as a player in the Earl of Pembroke's Men. Later described as 'never a good Actor, but an excellent Instructor', Jonson soon relinquished acting for playwriting, supplying Pembroke's company with *The Case Is Altered* in 1597, and contributing, along with Thomas Nashe and others, to the lost satirical drama *The Isle of Dogs*. The play landed Jonson in trouble with the authorities: the Privy Council ordered the immediate closure of the playhouses and Jonson himself was briefly imprisoned. On his release, his services were engaged by Philip Henslowe, for whom he supplied contributions to various plays now lost; within a year, he was in prison again, charged with the manslaughter of his fellow actor Gabriel Spencer, whom he killed during a duel in September 1598. Jonson escaped the gallows by the time-honoured ruse of claiming benefit of clergy (he converted to Catholicism whilst incarcerated). For the Lord Chamberlain's Men Jonson wrote *Every Man in His Humour* in 1598 and *Every Man Out of His Humour* the following year; it was followed by comedies and tragedies for the King's Men (*Sejanus*, 1603–04; *Volpone*, 1606; *The Alchemist*, 1610; *Catiline*, 1611), and works for the boys' companies: *Cynthia's Revels* (Children of Queen Elizabeth's Chapel, 1600–01), *Poetaster* (Children of Her Majesty's Chapel, 1601) and *Eastward Ho!* (Children of Her Majesty's Revels, 1605). Written in collaboration with John Marston and George Chapman, the last of these provided further evidence of Jonson's habit of falling foul of the political establishment (two years previously, *Sejanus* had caused him to be hauled before the Privy Council charged with sedition): the play's anti-Scots satire led to his temporary imprisonment. A final comedy for the Children of Her Majesty's Revels, *Epicene, or, The Silent Woman*, was performed during the winter festivities at court in 1609–10, but was again the occasion of controversy, when the king's cousin Arabella Stuart took exception to what she regarded as the libellous portrayal of her in the play; the play was suppressed. *Bartholomew Fair* was performed at the Hope in 1614; the King's Men presented *The Devil Is an Ass* (1616), *The Staple of News* (1626), *The New Inn* (1629) and *The Magnetic Lady* (1632). Jonson was sufficiently shrewd not to allow his talent for picking fights and troublemaking to jeopardise his parallel career as a scriptwriter for royal masques: the first of his collaborations with the architect and scene designer Inigo Jones, *The Masque of Blackness*, was lavishly mounted at court on 6 January 1605, and was followed by a succession of similarly extravagant entertainments that ended with *Chloridia* on 22 February 1631, by which point, inevitably, Jonson and Jones had spectacularly fallen out. One colleague with whom Jonson seems to have sustained consistently cordial relations was Shakespeare, who appears on the cast list of *Every Man In*, though as a rigorous classicist who prided himself on his erudition and his adherence to the rules of unity of time, place and action, Jonson periodically sniped at the freer craft of his fellow writer. Jonson's *Works*, published in 1616, collected his plays and poems in a handsome Folio volume that created the precedent for the posthumous publication of Shakespeare's dramatic works seven years later; he was among the most fulsome of the contributors to the edition's dedicatory and prefatory materials.

courtiers, Henry Wriothesley (1573–1624), the third Earl of Southampton, to whom both *Venus and Adonis* and *Lucrece* are dedicated. How and when (and even if) Shakespeare came into contact with Southampton is not known, but it was clear by the time the two narrative poems were published that the nineteen-year-old Earl was a man already much sought after. A keen consumer of theatre, literature and the arts, he acted as patron to fellow Cambridge graduate Nashe (who dedicated his prose work *The Unfortunate Traveller* to him in 1594) and to his tutor, the translator John Florio (c.1554–c.1625), attracted scores of minor verses from admirers and, next to Elizabeth, was the most popular subject of portraiture of his time.

Acting as a patron to poets and artists was, for an Elizabethan aristocrat, one among many duties as a distributor of favour and support to a network of companions, associates, retainers and liveried servants; as a system for maintaining a household as well as securing political advancement, patronage was a reflection of prestige, but it could be, and often was, ruinously expensive. In Southampton's case, his own personal circumstances at the time of Shakespeare's approach saw him under particular financial, as well as social, pressure. A royal ward, Southampton was under the guardianship of one of the most powerful men in England, Elizabeth's Lord Treasurer and trusted advisor William Cecil, Lord Burghley (1520–98). In 1589, as was his prerogative, Burghley decided that the interests of the Wriothesley dynasty as well as his own would be best served by marrying the seventeen-year-old earl to his granddaughter, Lady Elizabeth Vere (d. 1626); when Southampton refused, he became legally liable on attaining his majority to pay his guardian a sum equivalent to the dowry that would have been earned from the marriage (somewhere in the region of £5,000, an enormous sum).

Those who paid tribute to Southampton might have had little more to expect than promises and the not inconsiderable benefit of his endorsement, but they did so nonetheless. The dedication to Southampton attached to *Venus and Adonis* is formulaically fulsome: addressing the recipient of his verses as 'Right Honourable', Shakespeare confesses that 'I know not how I shall offend in dedicating my unpolisht lines to your Lordship', whilst indicating that these are but a taste of what is to follow and issuing a 'vow to take advantage of all idle hours, till I have honoured you with some graver labour'. The tone is appropriately deferential, and not necessarily indicative of personal familiarity, though the Ovidian tenor of the poem perhaps indicates that Shakespeare was aware enough of his patron's literary tastes; but the dedication of *Lucrece* to Southampton the following year suggests either a greater degree of intimacy or an intensification of hyperbole on Shakespeare's part: declaring that the 'love I dedicate to your Lordship is without end', he indicates that he has already benefited from the earl's favour or, at least, from the assurance of it: 'The warrant I have of your honourable disposition, not the worth of my untutord Lines makes it assured of acceptance'; and offers both himself and the poem in rather more extravagant terms: 'What I have done is yours, what I have to doe is yours, being part in all I have, devoted yours'.

The significance of these lines in terms of what they reveal about Shakespeare's relationship with Southampton has been much scrutinised by biographers. Even by the standards of Elizabethan dedicatory rhetoric, this appears to be a passionate, even ecstatic, declaration, not just of friendship, but of love; a love, moreover, that can be read as not merely platonic but fiercely sexual. Southampton's own preferences are a factor here. Although it is not known why he refused the proposed match with Lady Vere, speculation about the sexuality of the narcissistic earl began in his own lifetime and has continued to this day: according to the malicious reporting of one contemporary, when on campaign in Ireland he liked to sleep with a fellow officer, 'cole and huge him in his armes and play wantonly *with* him' (Honan 1999: 177); while Nashe's *Unfortunate Traveller* dedication mischievously praises Southampton as 'A dere lover and cherisher … as well of the lovers of Poets, as of Poets themselves'. However, to attempt to determine whether this constitutes evidence that Southampton (or, for that matter, Shakespeare) was homosexual is to invoke anachronistic categories of sexual identity and orientation that would have been unthinkable in early modern England.

Rather than being understood as the distinguishing element of a homosexual identity distinct from, and opposed to, heterosexuality, same-sex desire was regarded by Shakespeare's contemporaries as something to which all men were potentially liable; sodomy, which included not only buggery but all manner of non-procreative activities between men, between men and women, and between men, women and beasts, was a capital offence; but Elizabethan culture also valued and celebrated intense, overtly homoerotic male friendships, and cultivated the literary and visual arts that idealised them. To be accused of sodomy was to be marked as deviant, but the judgement was upon a man's acts, not his identity; moreover, it was equated not just with sexual behaviour but with other, equally pernicious, transgressive acts: atheism, treason, witchcraft, murder, currency fraud. Thus the Marlowe who was alleged by the informer Richard Baines (b. c.1566) to have opined that 'all they that love not Tobacco and Boies were fooles' was posthumously styled a comprehensive sodomite, deriding both biblical and state authority by declaring that 'Moyses was but a Jugler … That the first beginning of Religioun was only to keep men in awe' and that 'he has as good Right to Coine as the Queen of England' (MacLure 1979: 36–38).

As the author of plays and poems that celebrated the cult of classical pederasty, Marlowe was in Baines's slanderous testimony an openly vilified member of an all-male theatre profession which, employing an apprentice system that involved boys, domiciled in the households of their master-actors, dressing as women, courted accusations of sexual irregularity both onstage and off. As the outraged moralist Philip Stubbes (c.1555–c.1610) put it in his comprehensive and richly imagined catalogue of Elizabethan depravity, *The Anatomie of Abuses* (1583), 'these goodly pageants being done, every mate sorts to his mate, everyone brings another homeward of their way verye freendly, and in their secret conclaves (covertly) they play the *Sodomits*, or worse' (Chambers 1923, 4: 223–24). As with every other aspect of experience in Elizabethan England, divisions of rank and class were also a powerful factor in the definition of licit and illicit sexual activity: intense bonds between men of the same elite rank might be tolerated, but desire between masters and servants (or, say, between an earl and a provincial tradesman's son-turned-player-and-poet) might well not. And then, as now, an individual's sexual preferences could be acted upon, denied or suppressed, and could be multiple, fluid and subject to change: Southampton subsequently secretly married one of the queen's maids of honour, Elizabeth Vernon (1573–1655), whom he had made pregnant (an action which led to their temporary imprisonment by the furious monarch).

The passionate language of Shakespeare's second dedication, the only such document of its kind that survives, may be evidence of a sexual liaison between Southampton and himself, and it may not. Speculation about the possibility of such a relationship, or of one with another, variously identified 'Fair Youth', has been further fuelled by the efforts that have been made by generations of biographers and critics to determine the autobiographical significance of Shakespeare's other substantial poetic output, the sonnets. If the provenance of the narrative poems is relatively straightforward, in that they can be dated with some precision, were published with Shakespeare's co-operation and are dedicated to a clearly identifiable individual, that of the sonnets, on all of these counts, is not. Published by Thomas Thorpe in 1609, the same year as *Troilus and Cressida* and *Pericles*, as *Shake-Speares Sonnets. Never before Imprinted*, the cycle of poems appears to have been commenced in the early 1590s.

Referring in 1598 to 'his sugred Sonnets among his private friends' (1973: 282), Francis Meres indicates that Shakespeare was engaged in the practice of circulating sonnets in manuscript, and thus participating in the vogue for courtly sonneteering that had been given a fresh impetus by the posthumous publication of Sir Philip Sidney's (1554–86) *Astrophil and Stella* in 1591. Two at least can be certainly dated to the 1590s: versions of Sonnets 138 ('When my love swears that she is made of truth … ') and 144 ('Two loves I have, of comfort and despair … ') were included in the second edition of the unauthorised collection *The Passionate Pilgrim* (1599), a set of twenty poems attributed (mostly falsely) to Shakespeare by its publisher William Jaggard (d. 1623). Others have been conjecturally dated on stylistic grounds between the 1590s and the early 1600s, which is also considered to be the date of the other work included in the 1609 edition of the sonnets, 'A Lover's Complaint'.

Like the quartos of *Venus and Adonis* and *Lucrece*, *Shake-Speares Sonnets* contains a dedication, but on this occasion it is intriguingly enigmatic:

TO. THE ONLIE BEGETTER OF.

THESE ENSUING. SONNETS.

MR. W.H. ALL HAPPINNESS.

AND. THAT. ETERNITY.

PROMISED

BY.

OUR. EVER-LIVING.POET.

WISHETH.

THE WELL-WISHING.

ADVENTURER.IN.

SETTING.

FORTH.

T.T.

'T.T.' is the bookseller and publisher Thomas Thorpe, the 'well-wishing adventurer' who has set forth the work in print, but the identities of 'the only begetter', of 'Mr. W.H.' and of the 'ever-living poet', despite centuries of speculation, remain a mystery. 'W.H.' may be, relatively straightforwardly (and most probably), a simple misprint of the initials of the author, 'W.S.' (or 'W.SH.'); but it may also signal teasing or subterfuge on the part of the composer of the dedication (whether Shakespeare or Thorpe), implying that the 'only begetter' of the sonnets is the person who inspired or solicited them. The prime candidates for the identity of this figure are the Earl of Southampton (Henry Wriothesley, initialised in reverse) and William Herbert (1580–1630), the third Earl of Pembroke, one of the great literary patrons of the early seventeenth century, who, with his brother Philip, the Earl of Montgomery (1584–1650), was subsequently the dedicatee of the 1623 Folio.

Southampton was in his late teens in the early 1590s, and thus, for subscribers to the theory that the sonnets were composed at this time, a plausible model for the 'Fair Youth' that the first poems in the sequence encourage to marry and sire a successor ('So thou, thyself outgoing in thy noon/ Unlooked on diest unless thou get a son' [7: 13–14]). For those who hold to a later date, the poems' exhortations connect with Pembroke's very similar behaviour in refusing to enter into arranged marriages with Elizabeth Carey (1576–1635) in 1595 and Burghley's granddaughter Bridget Vere in 1597. Initially focussing on the young man's reluctance to reproduce, the sequencing of the sonnets seems to reveal a deepening and intensification of a desire on the part of their author that is clearly homoerotic; and the intimacy that has been attributed to the poet's attachment to the male addressee of just

Sir Philip Sidney (1554–86)

Poet, courtier, diplomat and soldier

As well as pursuing a high-ranking political, diplomatic and military career that took him to France in 1572 as a member of the delegation sent to conclude the Treaty of Blois, an agreement that finally put an end to centuries of enmity and united the kingdoms against Spain, into a marriage in 1583 with Frances Walsingham, daughter of Elizabeth's head of espionage, and finally to the battle of Zutphen, the Netherlands, in 1586, where he died of gangrenous infection of a minor wound (earning him the honour of a state funeral), Sidney was regarded by many of his contemporaries as one of the most significant literary figures of his time. A leading exponent of the values of Renaissance humanism, his impact upon English letters contemporaries was largely owed to three works, none of which was published during his lifetime: the prose romance *Arcadia* (published 1590), written for his sister Mary Herbert, the Countess of Pembroke (an important patron of the arts, whose son William later became the subject of the dedication of the first Folio), the sonnet sequence *Astrophil and Stella* (published 1591), and a work of literary and dramatic theory, *An Apology for Poetry* (published 1595). *Astrophil* seems to have stimulated the sonnet-writing revival of the 1590s that included Shakespeare's own interventions on the form; the *Apology* constructs an eloquent neo-Platonic case for the validity and worth of poetry whilst also launching a fierce attack on the popular drama of the English stage, and in particular on its indiscriminate mixing of 'kings and clowns' and its ignorance of the classical unities of time, place and action. With the exception of Ben Jonson, few dramatists took much notice of Sidney's complaints; it would probably have pained him to discover his *Arcadia* would go on to act as a fertile source of plot material for the industry whose products he so despised – among them Shakespeare's *King Lear*, which reworks Sidney's narrative of the King of Paphlagonia and his two sons as the Gloucester sub-plot.

over three-quarters of the sonnets has been seen as part of their narrative of passionate involvement, rivalry and betrayal, between two men, a woman characterised as 'dark' and a rival poet, in which their begetter oscillates between hope and despair, desire and self-loathing, and veneration and disgust.

The candidature of the dark woman and of the rival poet has been subject to extensive speculation, with the former variously identified as Mary Fitton (1578–1647), one of Queen Elizabeth's maids of honour, who in 1600 was impregnated and then abandoned by Pembroke; as Emilia Lanier (1570–1654), mistress both of the Chamberlain's Men's patron Henry Carey and of the court physician and astrologer, and eyewitness of early Shakespearean performances, Simon Forman (1552–1611); and as a Clerkenwell prostitute who went by the name of Lucy Negro. Nominations for the rival poet have included Chapman, Marlowe and the Welsh poet John Davies (c.1565–1618). Nonetheless, attempts to render the sonnets as exercises in autobiography, whether by construing them as directly or codedly confessional, by reducing their cast of characters to real-life counterparts or by reconfiguring their multiple and fluid sexualities into stable and singular patterns of attraction and repulsion, invariably leave us none the wiser about the secrets which modern criticism and biography continue to yearn to unlock.

Apparently conceived as part of a courtly game that involved highly intricate mechanisms of disclosure and concealment, distancing and enticement, Shakespeare's sonnets were unprecedented in their capacity to generate the effect of a personal and immediate speaking voice, whilst also creating a series of brilliantly compressed micro-dramas inhabited by personae who may well be entirely fictive. Whatever their designs may have been upon their original reader or readers, the sonnets have artfully and triumphantly succeeded in drawing successive generations into their, and what they have assumed to be Shakespeare's, world of romantic and erotic fantasy (see *Works*, pp. 216–25, *Criticism*, pp. 383–84).

One sonnet alone has been generally acknowledged as directly autobiographical, because it appears to pun on the maiden name of the only woman that Shakespeare is known, rather than merely conjectured, to have been involved with. Sonnet 145 begins by referring to a female lover whose lips 'Breathed forth the sound that said "I hate"/ To me that languished for her sake', and ends by happily recording that '"I hate" from hate away she threw/ And saved my life, saying "not you"' (145: 1–2, 13–14): Andrew Gurr was the first to suggest that 'hate away', in Elizabethan pronunciation, would have sounded very much like 'Hathaway'. The (allegedly) clumsy contrivance of the wordplay, and the facts that the poem is anomalously written in octosyllabics rather than iambic pentameter and that it has no connection with the sonnets placed either side of it have encouraged the view that it is a very early work, perhaps Shakespeare's earliest, dating from 1582, the year of his hasty marriage to Anne Hathaway; as Gurr surmises, the really extraordinary thing about what he calls 'arguably the worst of all the Shakespeare sonnets' is the fact that it 'survived in the author's possession through twenty-six years of travel and change, until it joined the hundred and twenty-six to the Young Man and the twenty or so to the Dark Lady in Thorpe's publication of 1609' (Gurr 1971: 221, 226). For Gurr, the anomaly may hint at a biographical context: 'Perhaps Shakespeare kept it for sentimental reasons' (226); but whether he did so, and indeed whether he ever showed this (or any other of his work) to its presumed addressee either at the time of its composition or when it appeared in print, must remain a matter for speculation.

Making history

Venus and Adonis and *Lucrece* established Shakespeare's name as a poet; by the end of the 1590s his name was appearing on the title-pages of plays published in quarto; and Francis Meres was acknowledging his command of the range of theatrical genres and his peerless facility as a playwright of the vernacular: 'the Muses would speak with *Shakespeares* fine filed phrase, if they would speak English' (Meres 1973: 282). Though some of the plays Meres mentions belong to the period prior to the closure of the playhouses during the 1592–93 plague outbreaks, the bulk of the work upon which Shakespeare's reputation was beginning to be built dates from the first years of his long, and mutually beneficial, association with the Lord Chamberlain's Men. Shakespeare was one of three payees named for performances by the company at court at the end of 1594, and during the course of the next five years he supplied his colleagues with a steady output of tragedies and comedies.

For Meres, Shakespeare's facility within both literary modes is impressive; he includes within his list a number of works that have subsequently been categorised as histories, a genre which provides evidence of Shakespeare's ambition and major early achievement in that he was to a large extent responsible for its reinvention as a coherent, recognisable and relatively respectable new dramatic form. At the time of Shakespeare's intervention, the English chronicle history play, as part of the output of a popular stage that traced its inheritance back to the medieval mystery, miracle and morality dramas, was characterised by a lively eclecticism and vigorous, often xenophobic, patriotism that consorted well with the nationalistic sentiments of the late 1580s (especially following the rout of the Spanish Armada in 1588). In plays such as *The Famous Victories of Henry V* (1586), Robert

Wilson's (d. 1600) *The Three Lords and Three Ladies of London* (1588) and Greene's *Friar Bacon and Friar Bungay* (1589), audiences could relish the combination of materials drawn from myth and folklore, the legendary events of the English history narrated by the Tudor chroniclers Holinshed, Polydore Vergil (c.1470–c.1555) and Edward Halle (d. 1547), the interplay between the Christian providentialist and secular, Machiavellian accounts of history and politics, and the virtuoso display of highly wrought rhetoric, all offering compelling lessons for the present.

Shakespeare's (and others') *Henry VI* plays utilise this format, as well as contributing to the genre's project of carnivalising orthodoxy. In 1592, Thomas Nashe, alluding to the (then unpublished) first part, wrote of how its staging of the exploits of Lord Talbot during the 1420s war with France served as a 'reproof to these degenerate effeminate days of ours', and speculated that

> How it would have joyed brave *Talbot* (the terror or the French) to thinke that after he had lyne two hundred yeares in his Tombe, he should triumphe againe on the Stage, and have his bones newe embalmed with the teares of ten thousand specators at least (at severall times), who, in the Tragedian that represents his person, imagine they behold him fresh bleeding.
>
> (McKerrow 1958: 212)

Nashe is hardly a dispassionate evaluator of the play's impact in performance (having very probably been one of those contributing to its authorship), and his chronology and his figures are as cheerfully approximate as the play's. The historical Lord Talbot, the first Earl of Shrewsbury, died in 1453 (just less than one hundred and fifty years previously, not two hundred), and the play represents Talbot and one of his chief antagonists, Joan La Pucelle (Jeanne d'Arc) as contemporaries, whereas in reality she had been burned at the stake as an heretic over twenty years earlier; and ten thousand spectators is something in the order of five capacity houses at Henslowe's Rose. But he nonetheless provides an indication of what it was thought the chronicle history play ought to achieve: the manly 'reproof' it offered to the 'degenerate effeminate' present was that 'our forefathers valiant actes (that have line long buried in rustie brasse and worme-eaten bookes) are revived, and they themselves raised from the Grave of Oblivion' (McKerrow 1958: 212).

Imagining Talbot imagining himself surrogated in the hide of a player from an unknown futurity, Nashe magnifies the impact of his historical personage by identifying the histrionic

---

Thomas Nashe (1567–1601)

Playwright and pamphleteer

Graduating from Cambridge University in 1586, Nashe's first publication was the preface he contributed to Robert Greene's *Menaphon* (1589), which contains an early allusion to the *Hamlet* play, possibly written by Thomas Kyd, that predated Shakespeare's; it was followed by *Pierce Penniless His Supplication to the Divell* (1592), which offers a glowing account of the first part of *Henry VI*, a work to which he may have contributed, and by *The Unfortunate Traveller* (1595). His theatrical collaborations included, with Christopher Marlowe, *Dido, Queen of Carthage* (published 1594) and, with Ben Jonson and others, the suppressed satire *The Isle of Dogs* (1597), a venture that led to Jonson's imprisonment.

agent as a *tragedian*. Whereas many of the chronicle plays engage extensively with the comic mode (as indeed do *Henry VI* and Shakespeare's successive histories), Nashe defines a space for the performance of history closely allied to tragedy in its more didactic guises. As Meres's cataloguing understood, and as the title-pages of a number of the early quartos confirm, it was as tragedies that Shakespeare's first history plays for the Lord Chamberlain's Men were initially presented: *3 Henry VI* was issued in octavo in 1595 as *The True Tragedy of Richard Duke of York and the Good Henry the Sixth*; the 1597 printings of *Richard III* and *Richard II* label both as tragedies; however, the first and second parts of *Henry IV* (1598 and 1600), at least one of which is also referred to by Meres, were respectively entitled *The History of Henry the Fourth* and *The Second Part of Henry the Fourth*. Dramatic genres were fluid, flexible and subject to reinvention, and plays could be re-designated over time. The 1608 quarto of *King Lear* was published as a 'True Chronicle History', and *Troilus and Cressida* appeared to defy categorisation by appearing in the 1609 quartos as a history but as a tragedy in the 1623 Folio, whose compilers also organised the history plays into a coherent sequence, chronologically ordered by reign and subjected to a degree of standardisation by title yet still retaining a dual generic identity (*Richard II* and *Richard III* are still entitled tragedies).

This lay in the future: in the early 1590s, the genres of both tragedy and history play were open to opportunistic experimentation. Having attempted to out-Plautus the Plautus he had studied in grammar school in *The Comedy of Errors* (Question: what is twice as funny as a comedy of mistaken identity involving a set of twins? Answer: a comedy of mistaken identity involving *two* sets of twins) and to out-Seneca the Roman tragedian Seneca in *Titus Andronicus* (Question: how to emulate an oeuvre that combines high verbal style with the depiction of extreme mental and physical anguish, including sexual obsession, madness, murder, rape, torture, dismemberment and cannibalism? Answer: put all of these ingredients in one play), Shakespeare now turned back to the historical material of the *Henry VI* plays to capitalise upon the diabolic appeal of the figure who dominates the closing scenes of *True Tragedy*, Richard Plantagenet, Duke of Gloucester (1452–85), whose last act in that play is the murder of the deposed Henry VI.

Richard played a key role in Tudor mythology as a usurper and tyrant whose bloody reign was blessedly (and, according to orthodox historiographers, providentially) brought to an end with his overthrow by Queen Elizabeth I's grandfather, Henry, the Earl of Richmond (1457–1509), subsequently the first of the Tudors, King Henry VII. Dramatising the period of English history that stretched from the immediate aftermath of the defeat of the House of Lancaster at the Battle of Tewkesbury in 1471 to Richard III's demise at the Battle of Bosworth in 1485, *Richard III* staged a century-old series of events whose import was both immediate and very real for its first audiences. Providing a satisfactory resolution to the historical narrative encompassing the chaos and nightmare violence of the Wars of the Roses, which incorporated civic insurrection in the form of the comic-grotesque popular revolt led by the demagogue Jack Cade as well as dynastic conflict, the play invited its viewers to reflect upon the parallels, and the dissimilarities, between its time and their own, as well as upon the balance between the rights and wrongs of usurpation, and the duty of obedience.

Poet and player

The primary value of *Richard III* for the Chamberlain's Men, however, was as likely to lie in the stellar role that it offered the company's leading player, Richard Burbage, as in its efficacy as a piece of Tudor propaganda, and it is in this sense that the play marks the inauguration of the unique alliance between Shakespeare and the company. The part might not have been originally written for Burbage (the play may have been first performed by either Lord Strange's Men or the Earl of Pembroke's Men between 1591 and 1593), but once it entered the possession of the Chamberlain's Men he made it very much his own. At just over a thousand lines in the quarto (bearing in mind the proviso that what was published may not have precisely matched what was actually said onstage), Richard was a part almost unprecedented in terms of length in the theatre at the time, and certainly unprecedented in terms of range and scope: only Marlowe's Barabas in *The Jew of Malta* and Kyd's Hieronymo in *The Spanish Tragedy*, at 1,138 and 1,018 lines respectively, come close; subsequently, Hamlet, at 1,507 lines, would exceed it.

Richard Burbage (1568–1619)

Actor

Son of the actor and builder of the Theatre, James Burbage, Burbage was the lead actor in the Lord Chamberlain's, then King's, Men, from the company's formation in 1594 until his retirement sometime after 1610. Named as one of the 'principal comedians' in Ben Jonson's *Every Man in His Humour* (1598) and *Every Man Out of His Humour* (1599), Burbage is conjectured to have played Richard III, Hamlet, Othello, King Lear, Hieronimo in Kyd's *The Spanish Tragedy*, Ferdinand in John Webster's *The Duchess of Malfi* (1613) and Malevole in John Marston's *The Malcontent* (1604). A sharer in the first Globe playhouse, 1599, in 1608 Burbage resumed control of the Blackfriars property that had been partially converted into an indoor playhouse by his father in 1596, and from 1609 onwards he led the King's Men's dual commercial operations there and at the Globe, which had opened in 1599. After his death, he was praised by Richard Flecknoe as 'a delightful Proteus, so wholly transforming himself into his part, and putting off himself with his clothes, as he never (not so much as in the Tiring-house) assumed himself again until the play was ended' (Chambers 1923, 4: 370).

Thomas Kyd (1558–94)

Playwright

Kyd was born in London and attended the Merchant Taylor's school from 1565 until about 1575. He was identified by Thomas Dekker as having written for the Queen's Men between 1583 and 1585, but his earliest work to have survived is *The Spanish Tragedy*, possibly written around 1589 and performed by Lord Strange's Men at the Rose on 23 February 1592. A bloody revenge tragedy that mixes Senecan stylistics with an ingenious multiple-frame, metatheatrical structure (it culmimates in a performance-within-a-performance in which a staged massacre turns out to be real), it was one of the most popular and influential plays of its time: recorded by Philip Henslowe as performed twenty-nine times between 1592 and 1597, it was reprinted eleven times, the last quarto appearing in 1633. Kyd published his translation from the French of the tragedy *Cornelia* in 1594 and has been attributed as author of *Soliman and Perseda* (1592). A retrospective prequel by an unknown author, *The First Part of Jeronimo*, was published in 1605. In May 1593 Kyd was implicated in the allegations of sodomy and atheism against Christopher Marlowe; under arrest, and, probably, under torture, he dissociated himself from his former room-mate whilst protesting his own innocence. Released from custody, he died the following year.

The core of a script that combined the narrative resources of the English chronicle play with the ritual formalities of Senecan tragedy, the role demanded a performer simultaneously capable of sustaining a compromising complicity with the audience closely modelled upon that of the medieval Vice whilst incarnating the evils of tyranny within his hyperbolically disfigured body, and of moving from tyrannical self-assertion to despairing introspection. The immediate and enduring popularity of the play (which ran to eight quarto editions by 1634), and the close association between the actor and the role in a number of contemporary accounts, suggest that Burbage triumphantly rose to the challenge. In his satirical take on contemporary manners *The Letting of Humours Blood in the Head-Vaine* (1600), the pamphleteer Samuel Rowlands (d. 1628) conflates Burbage with Richard by describing what appears to be his physicalisation of the role, referring his 'Gentleman Readers' to 'Gallants', flamboyant and assertive performers who 'like Richard the usurper, swagger/ That had his hand continuall on his dagger' (ll. 5–6). Richard Corbet's (1582–1625) poem *Iter Boreale*, published in 1647, a quarter-century after Burbage's death, tells the story of a guided tour of the site of the Battle of Bosworth, wherein the drunken host 'mistook a player for a king': 'For when he would have said, "King Richard died/ And called, 'A horse! A horse!'" he "Burbage" cried' (Nungezer 1968: 77).

A similar moment of ellipsis between history, performance and charismatic personality is found in an apocryphal piece of gossip recorded by the lawyer John Manningham (c.1576–1622) in his diary on 13 March 1602:

> Upon a tyme when Burbidge played Rich[ard] 3. there was a citizen grewe soe farre in liking with him, that before shee went from the play shee appointed him to come that night unto hir by the name of Ri[chard] the 3. Shakespeare, overhearing their conclusion, went before, was intertained, and at his game ere Burbidge came. The message being brought that Richard the 3d was at the dore, Shakespeare caused returne to be made that William the Conqueror was before Rich[ard] the 3. Shakespeare's name William.
>
> (Sorlien 1976: 75)

The anecdote need not be literally true to be significant: if on one level it indicates that Burbage and Shakespeare both enjoyed sufficient celebrity status to generate prurient interest in their sexual adventures and in the showcasing of their ready wit, it also enacts a scenario of rivalry between player and playwright, manoeuvring for the favours of a female fan who is in actuality an object of barter between them, that taps into a more pervasive cultural preoccupation with what Robert Weimann (2000) has described as the competing discourses of writing and playing, which are also potentially opposed loci of power and authority, or of 'author's pen' and 'actor's voice' (citing *Troilus and Cressida*, Prologue, l. 24).

Shakespeare, in this incident, displays an opportunism and a talent for improvisation worthy of his own theatrical creation, whose charismatic force is, nonetheless, most visibly manifest in the work of the player upon whom his writing is dependent. He was also not averse to playing personal name-games in print himself: Sonnets 134, 135 and 136, notably, play emphatically upon the multiple connotations of the word 'Will' as a name and as synonym for intention, desire and both male and female sex organs; he himself might have been amused to contemplate how much mightier was Will's quill than Dick Burbage's property sword.

Perhaps Manningham is thinking of Shakespeare less as a writer here than as a player: pointing out that William the Conqueror is a part in *Fair Em*, first performed by Sussex's

Men at Henslowe's Rose in 1594, Rosalyn L. Knutson has suggested that this script was among those acquired by the Chamberlain's Men (1999: 349) and that Shakespeare might have played this role. Although the evidence for this is at best circumstantial, the speculation is tempting insofar as it acknowledges that a degree of self-conscious trade-off between stage roles and players' personalities was intrinsic to the theatrical experience. It also serves to remind us not only that Shakespeare's scripts were designed for the known and familiar colleagues of his company, that they were composed to exploit and perhaps extend the individual quirks, talents and potentialities of those performers, but also how thoroughly implicated his craft was within its conditions of actualisation.

A more elaborate working-out of the drama's self-referentiality is seen in the Induction (possibly provided by John Webster [1571/7–1634/8]) to the revised version of John Marston's (c.1575–1634) *The Malcontent* (printed in 1604), a play written for the Children of the Queen's Revels at the Blackfriars playhouse and subsequently appropriated by the King's Men for the Globe. It has Burbage and fellow players Henry Condell (c.1562–1627) and John Lowin (1576–1653) appearing as themselves, and William Sly (d. 1608) and John Sinklo (or Sinckler) impersonating members of the play's onstage audience; in a dazzling metatheatrical moment, Sly asks after 'Harry Condell, Dick Burbage, and Will Sly' and demands to speak with himself (Ind. 15–16).

This was not the first time that Will Sly thus presented himself; he was a member of the Earl of Pembroke's Men, the troupe that toured the anonymous play *The Taming of a Shrew* sometime between 1592 and 1594 (it was published in 1595), and with which Shakespeare may have been connected prior to his joining the Chamberlain's Men. It may be a coincidence that the drunken tinker of the play's frame narrative, who serves as an intermediary between the taming drama and the audience, is named Sly, or it may be an instance of the name of the player being substituted for that of the role (as occurs in various printed plays of the period, for example the second quarto of *Romeo and Juliet* [1599], in which the entry of the part identified in the dialogue as the servingman 'Peter' [4.4.126] is marked as '*Enter Will Kemp*' [Sig. C4v]). It may also suggest that the boundary between performer and the part was at such moments, and probably others, fluid and permeable: 'Sly' is a hybrid figure, both within and outside the play's fiction.

The relationship between *A Shrew* and Shakespeare's *The Taming of the Shrew,* a play generally thought to date from his first years with the Chamberlain's Men though unpublished until the 1623 Folio, has been much discussed (*A Shrew* was once regarded as the source of *The Shrew* but has been more recently described as a memorial or pirated reconstruction of it); one of the more provoking enigmas of this textual history is the fact that the most distinctive, and accomplished, aspect of the anonymous quarto, the Sly framework, is in the Folio version abandoned halfway through the first act. In these shifting and ambiguous scriptural circumstances, the mock-heroic claims of the figure generically identified as 'Begger' that 'I am Christophero Sly' and 'Am not I Christopher Sly – old Sly's son of Burton Heath?' (Ind. 2.5, 16–17) might conceivably contain a metatheatrical joke that would have been very immediate to its auditors pressed around the platform of the Theatre, the Curtain or the Globe, as would the same speaker's earlier boast (uncannily echoing Manningham) that he 'came in with Richard Conqueror' (Ind. 1.4).

Sly's self-identifications are embedded within a passage that is, for Shakespeare, unusually localised in its references. 'Burton Heath' refers to Barton-on-the-Heath, a village fifteen miles to the south of Stratford-upon-Avon, while Sly's suggestion that his companions 'Ask Marian Hacket, the fat ale-wife of Wincot, if she know me not' (Ind. 2.19–20) invokes a variant spelling of the village of Wilmcote, four miles north of the town, and the location of the house of Shakespeare's mother, Mary Arden. Both places held significance for Shakespeare: resident in Barton-on-the-Heath was Edmund Lambert (c.1525–87), his father's brother-in-law and one of his most serious creditors: in 1578 John Shakespeare had mortgaged his wife's property at Wilmcote to him for £40, and when two years later he was unable to repay the debt, Lambert finalised his claim on the estate, which neither John Shakespeare nor his son ever recovered.

But if the combination of playhouse in-joking, gossip and autobiographical reminiscence (which flaunts the rustic background scorned by the University Wits) seems momentarily to draw aside a curtain on Shakespeare's private and professional life, it was one just as swiftly closed. Shakespeare (as) himself does not appear in the *Malcontent*'s Induction; perhaps by this stage he was considerably more valuable to the company as a sharer and writer than for his playing abilities. He is listed in the cast of Jonson's *Every Man in His Humour* (1598) and *Sejanus His Fall* (1603), and at the head of the list of 'The Names of the Principall Actors' in the Folio, above 'Richard Burbadge': the ornate typographical elaboration of the enlarged initial 'W' in 'William' and the insetting of both names seems to bracket them as legendary coequals.

Nowhere, however, can he be positively identified with specific roles, either in his own works or in those of others, though he has been conjecturally, and sometimes sentimentally, assigned the parts of the Ghost in *Hamlet*, Adam in *As You Like It*, the King in *Henry IV*, Chorus in *Henry V* and the Poet in *Timon of Athens*. Often such identifications stem from a desire to find in the work either self-portraiture or the voice of their author (or both), and as such must remain suspect. Largely absent from his own plays, Shakespeare is a periodic offstage presence in those of his contemporaries, including the anonymously authored trilogy comprising *The Pilgrimage to Parnassus* and the two parts of *The Return from Parnassus*, performed by students at Cambridge University between 1599 and 1603. Featuring scenes in which Kempe and Burbage visit the university to audition students for their company (one of them tries his hand at the opening monologue of *Richard III*, prompting Burbage to judge it 'Very well I assure you' [4.4.1840]), *Part 2* has the critic Judicio declare of Shakespeare that 'His sweeter verse contaynes hart robbing lines' whilst wishing that 'Could but a graver subject him content/ Without loves foolish lazy languishment' (1.2.303–04).

The title-page of the first quarto of *Hamlet*, which advertises the play as having been acted 'in the two Universities of Cambridge and Oxford', conceivably indicates that the Lord Chamberlain's Men had visited Cambridge at the turn of seventeenth century, but whatever the advantage this was intended to confer upon the company and the work, it was not appreciated by the *Parnassus* author, whose contempt for the visiting players, and for his fellow undergraduates vulgar enough to pander to them, is palpable. Burbage and Kempe are presented as a pair of illiterate clowns, practitioners of 'the basest trade' who are described as 'leaden spouts/ That nought doe vent but what they do receive' (*2 Return*, 4.4.1846–48).

In the first part of *The Return* the equally idiotic double act of Ingenioso and Gullio are seen trading Shakespearean quotations in a fashion not, apparently, designed to reflect their good taste. 'We shall have nothinge but pure Shakspeare', says Ingenioso, 'and shreds of poetrie that he hath gathered at the theators', and Gullio responds by reciting chunks of *Venus and Adonis* and garbled fragments of *Romeo and Juliet*: 'Pardon mee moy mittressa, ast am a gentleman the moone in comparison of thy bright hue a mere slutt, Anthonies Cleopatra a blacke browde milkmaide, Hellen a dowdie' (3.1.986–91); compare Mercutio's account of Romeo's Petrarchan affectations: 'Laura to his lady was a kitchen wench … Dido a dowdy, Cleopatra a gypsy, Helen and Hero hildings' (2.3.35–37).

This was evidently to the liking of the university audience, though at some point during the period in which the *Parnassus* plays were staged the retired Cambridge scholar and poet Gabriel Harvey (c.1550–1631), who had some years earlier been embroiled in a literary spat of his own in the form of a vicious war of words with Nashe, scribbled in the margins in his copy of Thomas Speght's recently published edition of Chaucer that 'The younger sort takes much delight in Shakespeares Venus & Adonis: but his Lucrece, & his tragedie of Hamlet, Prince of Denmarke, have it in them, to please the wiser sort' (Stern 1979: 127). Ben Jonson, who was fulsome in his praise of Shakespeare after his death, at least in his dedicatory verse for the Folio, ventured a few barbs at his rival whilst he was alive, including the allusion to the *Henry VI* plays and the Chorus of *Henry V* in the Prologue to *Every Man in His Humour*, which derides poets who 'with three rusty swords,/ And help of some foot-and-half-foot words,/ Fight over York and Lancaster's long jars', and offers a play 'as other plays should be./ Where neither Chorus wafts you o'er the seas' (Prologue, 9–11, 14–15), and the inclusion in *Every Man Out of His Humour* (a play also commissioned by the Chamberlain's Men, and first acted at the Globe at the end of 1599) of the clown Sogliardo, who pays £30 to acquire a coat of arms bearing the motto 'Not without Mustard'.

As Jonson and Shakespeare's fellow players might have been aware (perhaps to their amusement), Shakespeare had in 1596 paid to secure a coat of arms for his father, whose motto was rendered three times on the draft grant document: as 'non, sanz droict' ('no, without right'), scored out and repeated as 'Non, Sanz Droict', and, at the head of the page, 'NON SANZ DROICT' ('not without right'). The accidentally (or mischievously?) interpolated comma matters, as it effectively disqualifies the application; and although the arms were granted, the emphatic capitalised correction is shadowed by the spectre of its converse, a potentially humiliating rebuff. Shakespeare has recently been detected elsewhere in Jonson's work: as the absentee householder Lovewit in *The Alchemist*, performed at Blackfriars in 1610 (Gurr 1999), and in the considerably less benign guise of the raving Fitzdottrell at the end of *The Devil Is an Ass* (1616), who has been interpreted by Katharine Duncan-Jones as a spiteful portrait of Shakespeare on his deathbed (2001: 276–77).

The Lord Chamberlain's Men

1596 was also the year of another significant recorded event in Shakespeare's personal life: on 11 August, the register of the Holy Trinity Church in Stratford-upon-Avon recorded the burial of his eleven-year-old son Hamnet. The impact of this upon Shakespeare, though presumably considerable, can only be guessed at, but, whatever his sorrows, Shakespeare's efforts to establish gentlemanly status for his family reflected the social ambitions of an increasingly prosperous businessman. The year after he petitioned the College of Arms, he paid about £120 for one of the largest houses in Stratford-upon-Avon, New Place, on Chapel Lane; this was the first of a series of property acquisitions that included the purchase, in 1602, of 107 acres of land in Stratford's Old Town for £320 as well as a cottage in Chapel Lane, and, in 1613, of the Gatehouse in Blackfriars.

Shakespeare's documented activities are those of a shrewd, occasionally litigious, successful professional playwright and company member. He was evidently better with his money than some of his colleagues (when Burbage died in 1619 he was recorded as being worth around £300, a fraction of Shakespeare's substantial estate of assets and property interests), and his success was built upon that of the company in which he was a sharer. Shakespeare exclusively supplied the scripts that constituted the core of a repertory varied and flexible enough to appeal both to the socially mixed and volatile crowds drawn to the open-air playhouse during the summer months and to the courtiers and visiting dignitaries in attendance at the Queen's Revels at Christmastime. *Richard III* was among a number of loosely historical dramas in the hands of the Lord Chamberlain's Men in 1594, along with the anonymous *King Leir*, *The Troublesome Reign of King John* and *The Famous Victories of Henry V*. It was followed by a further historical tragedy, *Richard II* (published 1597), in which Shakespeare turned his attention to the events that initiated what he and his contemporaries regarded as the distinctly calamitous phase of English history that concluded with the defeat of Richard III.

Composed entirely in verse, and bereft of the comic elements that characterised *Richard III*, it appears to have been in the repertoire, and in demand, by 1595. On 7 December, the diplomat and parliamentarian Sir Edward Hoby (1560–1617) wrote to his uncle, Lord Burghley, to invite him to supper the following evening, adding as an enticement that he would have the opportunity to see 'K. Richard present him self to your vewe' (Chambers 1930, 2: 320–21). As son-in-law to the Lord Chamberlain, Hoby was able to call Burbage's Men away from the Theatre to give a private performance of a play that might well have commanded the attention of the man who would become Queen Elizabeth's most trusted advisor: in 1601, famously but possibly apocryphally, the queen is reported to have said (in circumstances to which we shall return on pp. 41–42), to the historian William Lambarde (1536–1601), 'I am Richard II, know ye not that?' (Chambers 1930, 2: 237).

If one takes the view that *Richard II* was, whether opportunistically or by design, the first instalment of an epic sequence of history plays conceived and executed on a scale which no English dramatist had hitherto attempted, it seems as though Shakespeare once again considered the achievements of his mentors, rivals and influences and determined to surpass them. In this instance, these included the stable of playwrights, to which he had himself belonged, that produced the *Henry VI* plays and, perhaps most challengingly, Marlowe, whose *Edward II* (published 1594) provided a model of lyrical tragic history, a narrative of the deposition and assassination of a king, and an epic part for Alleyn at the Rose.

Around the same time Shakespeare provided his company with another historical drama which is out of sequence with his others in the genre, *King John*, before continuing with the historical narrative opened in *Richard II* in the play published in 1599 as *The History of Henrie the Fourth*. Although this subsequently became known (from the Folio onwards) as the first part of the diptych of *Henry IV* plays, the play as originally published shows no indication of having been conceived as such; as contemporary filmgoers will know, the contingencies and opportunistic circumstances that generate series, serials and sequels (and prequels) do not necessarily confirm prior or forward thinking, or long-range planning, though in retrospect these can appear to be inherent in the works in question.

Richard II was in some respects an attempt at a classically purer tragedy, with another substantial role for Burbage (and *King John* a tonally ambiguous study in *Realpolitik* that may have left its initial audiences, if it had any, as uncertain as subsequent ones). The first *Henry IV* play is more heterogeneous, its appeal lying, according to the title-page of the first quarto, in the historical narrative of the conflict between the regicide-by-association, Henry, and the rival factions epitomised by the legendary 'Henry Percy, surnamed Henry Hotspur of the North', but also in 'the humorous conceits of Sir John Falstaffe'. Richard is the undoubted centre of his play, speaking over one-quarter of the play's lines, but the eponymous monarch of *1 Henry IV* is afforded barely more than 10 per cent of his; the largest part in the play (in every sense) is the one written for the Lord

Christopher Marlowe (1564–93)

Playwright and poet

Educated on scholarships at the King's School, Canterbury, and at Corpus Christi, Cambridge, which he left in 1587, Marlowe (also variously known, according to the flexible naming and spelling conventions of the time, as Marlow, Marlo, Marloe, Marley, Morley, Marlin and Merling) is rumoured to have become involved in espionage on behalf of the English Crown during his final years at university, being reported by the Privy Council as having 'done her Majesty good service' whilst at the Catholic seminary in Rheims. At the same time he is likely to have completed his first literary works, translations of Ovid's *Amores*. His collaboration with Thomas Nashe, *Dido, Queen of Carthage* (published 1594), has often been assigned to this period, though this dating has recently been convincingly contested (Wiggins 2008). His first play for the commercial stage was the bloody and majestic first part of *Tamburlaine*, performed by the Lord Admiral's Men at the Rose in 1587. It was followed by a hastily composed sequel in 1588, thus initiating the vogue for multi-part play sequences that included the three parts of *Henry VI* (to which Marlowe has occasionally been conjectured as having contributed) in the early 1590s and the two *Henry IV*s towards the end of the decade. In the Prologue to *Tamburlaine*'s first part, its author promised to steer clear of 'jigging veins of rhyming mother-wits/ And such conceits as clownage keeps in pay' (that is, the antics of popular comedians such as Richard Tarlton and Will Kempe), but, as the texts of *The Jew of Malta* (1592) and *Doctor Faustus* (c.1593) demonstrated, the rebarbative juxtaposition of tragedy, high style and low comedy was the hallmark of much of Marlowe's output. Following this with *The Massacre at Paris* (performed 1593) and *Edward II* (published 1594) and the narrative poem *Hero and Leander* (c.1592), Marlowe had also acquired a reputation as an atheist and sodomite. He was alleged to have been behind a poster campaign in May 1593 inciting violence against London's Dutch immigrant community; implicated by his fellow spy and informer Richard Baines and sometime room-mate and playwright colleague Thomas Kyd, Marlowe was accused of circulating blasphemous and seditious opinions and of advocating pederasty, though whether their testimony was reliable is open to doubt. Still under surveillance by the authorities, Marlowe was stabbed to death in Deptford at the end of May 1593.

Chamberlain's clown, Will Kempe, who as the humorously conceited, lying, cheating, boozing, lecherous, cowardly Falstaff is given double this amount.

Dangerous games: Falstaff and Essex

The Second part of Henrie the fourth was published in 1600: Falstaff, again, is the dominant part, with one-fifth of the play's lines. In these plays, Shakespeare turns to Holinshed's *Chronicles* and to Samuel Daniel's (1562–1619) epic poem *The First Four Books of the Civil Wars* (1595) for a sober account of the civic conflicts between the house of Henry Bolingbroke and those of the Earls of Northumberland and Mortimer, but he also subjects these events to the alternative perspective that is offered by the story of the lowlife exploits of the monarch's son, Prince Hal.

This material had been dramatised in the popular potboiler *The Famous Victories of Henry V* (c.1588), and Falstaff, or as he is named in that play, Sir John Oldcastle, is at the centre of Shakespeare's treatment. Initially, it appears, Shakespeare followed his source, thereby opting, for reasons best known to himself, to give the fat knight the name and title of the revered ancestor of the man who in August 1596 became Lord Chamberlain, William Brooke (1527–97), the tenth Lord Cobham. The historical Sir John Oldcastle (c.1378–1417) was involved in the radical anti-clerical movement led by renegade preacher John Wycliff (c.1324–84) known as Lollardry; following an abortive attempt in 1413 to lead an uprising against the newly crowned Henry V, he was charged with heresy and treason, and in December 1417 executed and burned. His story had been resuscitated in the 1560s by the Protestant chroniclers of martyred forbears, notably by John Foxe (1516–87), whose *Acts and Monuments* (1563) – one of the books that was instrumental in the formation of Elizabethan Protestant consciousness – had rehabilitated Oldcastle by denying his participation in the treasonous rebellion and emphasising his credentials as a martyr.

For Brooke's family, their ancestor was hardly a figure to be joked about. Quite why Shakespeare and his company would have chosen to slander the name of such a powerful and potentially dangerous figure at court as Lord Cobham is difficult to fathom, but unsurprisingly Brooke failed to see the funny side of the depiction of Oldcastle as a fat, lying, drunk; and the name was changed. Shakespeare retrieved the name of the cowardly Sir John Fastolf from *1 Henry VI* (who in historical fact was a decent knight who served his king honourably), but Oldcastle refused to completely lie down, lingering somewhat insolently in such textual traces as Prince Henry addressing Falstaff as 'my old lad of the castle' (1.2.37), and in the rather over-emphatic reminder at the end of *2 Henry IV* that 'Oldcastle died a martyr, and this is not the man' (Epilogue, l. 27). The name also seems to have been implicated in the long-running feud between the Brookes and Shakespeare's patrons, the Careys: when George Carey commissioned the Lord Chamberlain's Men to give a private performance of *1 Henry IV* at his Blackfriars house in March 1600, he mischievously instructed them to revert to the Oldcastle nomenclature (Gurr 2004b: 170).

The Epilogue to *2 Henry IV* promises a further instalment of the saga initiated in *1 Henry IV*, 'with Sir John in it' (l. 24), clearly pointing towards *Henry V* (the historical fact that Oldcastle would have been in no position to have accompanied Henry on his French campaign in 1415, being at that time on the run after the failed rebellion, was neither here nor there). The plan did not come to fruition, for by the beginning of 1600 Kempe had danced his way out of the Lord Chamberlain's Men and on his legendary way to Norwich, and Sir John's only appearance in *Henry V* is in the form of the reports of his sickness and death (2.1, 2.3). Published in quarto in 1600, *Henry V* is generally agreed to date from 1599 on the basis of what seems to be one of the few directly topical allusions in Shakespeare's oeuvre:

William Kempe (d. c.1603)

Comedian and dancer

First heard of with the Earl of Leicester's Men in the mid-1580s, Kempe succeeded Richard Tarlton (who died in 1588) as the leading comic actor on the English stage during the 1590s. An accomplished jig-maker as well as stage clown, Kempe joined the Lord Chamberlain's Men in 1594, and it was for him that Shakespeare wrote the parts of Peter in *Romeo and Juliet*, Dogberry in *Much Ado* and Falstaff in *Henry IV* and *Merry Wives*. In 1599 Kempe was one of the sharers in the Globe playhouse, but he sold his stake in the enterprise to dance the one hundred and thirty miles from London to Norwich, an achievement chronicled in his *Kempe's Nine Days Wonder* (1600). Having previously toured the Netherlands between 1585 and 1586, Kempe now took himself across Germany and Italy, though he was back in London at the end of 1601 and with the Earl of Worcester's Men in 1602.

> Were now the General of our gracious Empress –
> As in good time he may – from Ireland coming,
> Bringing rebellion broachèd on his sword,
> How many would the peaceful city quit
> To welcome him!
>
> (*Henry V*, 5.0.30–34)

The 'General', it is generally agreed, is the charismatic Robert Devereux (1566–1601), the second Earl of Essex, who in March 1599 set off to Ireland from London with an expeditionary force, carrying with him high hopes that he would rapidly crush the latest wave of insurgency against English rule led by Hugh O'Neill (c.1540–1616), the Earl of Tyrone. By the end of September, with the costs of the campaign escalating and his forces worn down by fierce resistance from the Irish rebels, Essex had agreed a truce with Tyrone and, against the express wishes of an empress who was less gracious than furious, returned to London. If penned in an optimistic mood at the start of the year, the flattering allusion to the queen's former favourite was nonetheless not without risk; by the end of 1599, with Essex banished from court and his career in ruins, such a public declaration of support was positively dangerous. Equally touchy was the implied comparison of Essex with warrior-king and national hero Henry V, which has been seen by some as a gesture of solidarity towards a man who harboured his own ambitions for the Crown.

Essex himself would soon involve the Lord Chamberlain's Men in an even more hazardous enterprise. Placed under house arrest and smarting from the plotting of his enemies at court, Essex pondered his grievances through the winter; though he was granted his liberty in August 1600, his political career was over and he was in dire financial straits. In February 1601, convinced that rival factions in court were prevailing with the queen to strike a treacherous deal with Spain over the succession, and accompanied by a group of disaffected aristocratic supporters, he attempted to launch a coup. As a way of rallying his supporters, he arranged for the Lord Chamberlain's Men to be paid £2 to revive *Richard II* on 7 February, which, whether or not it included the deposition scene that was omitted from the 1597 quarto, was, in the circumstances, incendiary material. The rebellion the next day, which saw Essex riding through the streets of London at the head of a contingent of around three hundred lightly armed men, was a resounding failure; swiftly arrested and tried for treason, the earl went to the executioner's block in the Tower of London just over a fortnight later. The Lord Chamberlain's Men were hauled before the Queens' Council and called to account for their part in the insurrection; managing to persuade the authorities that they had acted for commercial rather than political motives (Phillips declared that they had responded to the incentive of 40s over and above 'their ordinary'), they were released without further action being taken. Perhaps as the beneficiaries of someone's black sense of humour, they were called back to perform at court on 24 February, the night before Essex's execution.

Phillips's oral testimony on behalf of the Lord Chamberlain's Men is the only such statement to have been preserved in the public records, and the author of the play is nowhere to be seen. Phillips, perhaps in order to play down the significance of the revival, took the opportunity to claim in the company's defence that it had taken Essex's money in part because it was a welcome return on a play 'so old and so long out of use' (Honan 1999: 217). It was only four years since *Richard II* had been published, and a year since the publication of *Henry V*, the play that announced the conclusion of the cycle (if that was what it was) that it commenced, but it appeared that the vogue for historical drama was over. Not until 1613 would Shakespeare, in collaboration with John Fletcher, return to the subject of English history, in the very different form of the life of King Henry VIII, in *All Is True*. History plays dominated Shakespeare's output between 1594 and 1599, but he also supplied the company with a popular tragedy, *Romeo and Juliet* (published 1597), presented on the title-page of the first quarto 'As it hath been often (with great applause) plaied publiquely, by the L. of Hunsdon his Servants', which possibly places the date of its first performances between July 1596 and April 1597, when the company was temporarily known as Lord Hunsdon's Men. Other than histories, Shakespeare's main output was in comedy: in addition to *Two Gentlemen of Verona* (noted by Meres), *The Comedy of Errors* (performed at the Gray's Inn Christmas revels in 1594), *Love's Labour's Lost* (published in 1598 and advertised as having been performed at court 'this last Christmas'), this period also produced *A Midsummer Night's Dream*, *The Merchant of Venice*, *Much Ado about Nothing* and *The Merry Wives of Windsor* (all published in quarto between 1600 and 1602), as well as, conjecturally, *The Taming of the Shrew* and *As You Like It*.

Courting comedy

Dream and *Merry Wives* were both published with the statement that they had been publicly performed (the latter 'Both before her Majestie, and else-where'), and both have been speculatively identified as pieces commissioned, as befitted Burbage's men's duties as servants of the Lord Chamberlain, to mark specific occasions. Despite the absence of any direct evidence to support the theory, *Dream* has long been seen as a play commissioned to be performed at an aristocratic wedding, at which the queen herself was guest of honour. Nominated candidates for the happy couple have included the ageing Sir Thomas Heneage (1533–95) and Mary Browne (c.1552–1607), widow of the second Earl of Southampton and the mother of Shakespeare's (presumed) patron, Henry Wriothesley, who married on 2 May 1594; William Stanley (1548–1630), the Earl of Derby, and the Earl of Oxford's daughter, Lady Elizabeth Vere, married on 26 January 1595; and, most plausibly, Thomas Berkeley (1575–1611) and Elizabeth Carey, granddaughter of the Lord Chamberlain's Men's patron, Lord Hunsdon, who married on 19 February 1596. The case for this wedding being the occasion of *Dream* appears to be strengthened by association by the fact that its venue, the house of Sir George Carey, the bride's father, was in Blackfriars, close by the disused Dominican monastery acquired by James Burbage for £600 just two weeks previously, which he would later that year begin to convert into the company's second playhouse.

Anecdotal tradition has also traced the presence of Queen Elizabeth in *Merry Wives*, who was alleged by the editor of an adaptation of the play published in 1702 to have ordered Shakespeare to write the play in a fortnight; more plausibly, it has also been argued that the play (or at least what is represented of it by the 1602 quarto) was staged as part of the Garter festivities on 23 April 1597 (Shakespeare's thirty-third birthday), when Sir George, now the Lord Chamberlain's Men's second patron following the death of his father, was elected as a Knight of the Garter, thus joining the ranks of an elite cadre, membership of which was a mark of especial favour personally bestowed by the monarch herself. Lack of solid evidence for the occasional provenance of these and other plays neither confirms nor negates its likelihood; what is evident, from the way in which they were subsequently marketed in print, is that their significance, and audience appeal, is by no means hermetically limited to the circumstances of their conjectured premieres. Here, as always, the Lord Chamberlain's Men knew that the viability of their business depended upon their work being robust and accessible enough to live on the stage of the public playhouse as well as in coterie performance.

The appearance of *Merchant* in the repertoire, alongside *Much Ado* and possibly *As You Like It*, is also indicative of another aspect of the company's good fortunes during this period: the presence within it of at least one unusually, perhaps exceptionally, talented boy player capable of taking on the longest and most challenging female roles yet devised for the English stage. Regarded just in terms of raw numerical evidence of line counts, Shakespeare had already written a number of substantial women's roles: the part of Joan La Pucelle in *1 Henry VI*, at 255 lines, is second to that of Talbot, at 407; Queen Margaret in *2* and *3 Henry VI* is given 599 lines across the two plays, just behind King Henry (680) and ahead of Richard Plantagenet (557), Edward IV (436), Warwick (572) and Richard of Gloucester (385); the *Two Gentlemen*'s Julia has 322, against 442 and 385 lines for the respective male leads, Proteus and Valentine; Juliet has 541 lines to Romeo's 615. With *Merchant*, however, there is a quantum leap: at 578 lines, Portia's part is by far the longest in the play, well ahead of Shylock's 355 lines and Bassanio's 336; speaking more than one-quarter of its total lines, Portia, statistically at least, dominates the spoken action, delivering 117 speeches (seventeen of which are longer than ten lines) and appearing in nine of its eighteen scenes.

Again with the proviso that the published texts almost certainly contain more than what was actually spoken on stage, this is impressive, and almost unprecedented. Only one previous play offers a comparable female part, the domestic tragedy *Arden of Faversham*, published anonymously in 1591, whose murderous adulteress Alice is afforded a part, at 558 lines, which is nearly twice that of both the eponymous protagonist (296 lines) and her lover and accomplice Mosby (285 lines); this play has now been convincingly identified as part-authored by Shakespeare (Jackson 2006). Samuel Daniel's closet drama *The Tragedy of Cleopatra* (published 1591) allocates its heroine 362 lines, one-fifth of its total, and Marlowe's and Nashe's *Dido, Queen of Carthage* (published 1594) affords Dido 532 (nearly one-third of the total), but neither play was seen on the public stage: Daniel's was designed for private reading and Marlowe's was performed by a juvenile company, the Children of Her Majesty's Chapel, at some point during the late 1580s or early 1590s.

The challenges posed by Shakespeare's women's parts are a matter not simply of length, of course, but also of range and depth; in the case of *Merchant*, Shakespeare recycled a device that he had put to good use in *Two Gentlemen* by setting his company's leading boy player the intricate task of playing a woman masquerading as a young man, in this instance a lover in the guise of a lawyer's clerk. Whether or not the unknown youth pulled it off is impossible to determine, but Shakespeare and his colleagues had sufficient confidence in the abilities of their apprentice (or apprentices) to repeat the transvestite turn in *As You Like It* and *Twelfth Night* (reported by Manningham as performed at Middle Temple in February 1602), as well as affording the comic heroines a dominant role in each (for Rosalind, 677 lines, one-quarter of the play's total). Further still, these plays contain scenes which rest upon the skills not only of a leading boy but also of another boy in a substantial subsidiary role (Jessica, Celia and Olivia). If in Burbage Shakespeare had found a player who made Richard, Hamlet, Lear, Othello and Shylock possible, at some point in the 1590s he was lucky enough to be able to employ the talents of the first of a succession of young men that would enable him to write Cordelia, Isabella and Helena, and such scenes as those between Viola and Olivia, Rosalind and Celia, and Desdemona and Emilia.

There was nothing in the repertoire of the Lord Chamberlain's Men's chief rivals, the Admiral's Men, to match this, as perhaps both organisations were aware, one to its benefit, the other to its cost. *Merchant* also provides one among the many pieces of evidence that each company was keenly conscious of what the other was doing, and that on occasions they set themselves in direct competition with each other. Published in 1600, *Merchant* was entered in the Stationers' Register two years previously, in July 1598, as 'a booke of the Marchaunt of Venyce or otherwise called the Jewe of Venyce'. The implication is that the latter title was how it was known on stage, and as such it appeared to directly allude to one of the staples of the Rose's repertoire, Marlowe's *The Jew of Malta*, a play dating from the late 1580s, whose recorded performance was by Lord Strange's Men in February 1592, with Edward Alleyn in the lead role of Barabas (the 'Jew' of the title). It was staged another nine times between February and June of that year, and between the periodic outbreaks of plague that forced the closure of the playhouses. It was revived again in January 1593 and regularly between April and December 1594, possibly in the wake of the trial and very public execution of the queen's physician, the Portuguese-born assimilated Jew Roderigo Lopez (d. 1594) that summer, whom the Earl of Essex had implicated in an alleged assassination plot against the queen.

Now in the hands of the Admiral's Men, it was seen again throughout the first half of 1596, bringing the total number of performances to thirty-six in four years; Henslowe's prop and costume inventories indicate that it was still in service half a decade on. Its appeal is not hard to fathom. An obsessive preoccupation within popular mythology, actual Jews were all but invisible in early modern England (having been expelled from the country by order of Edward I in 1290, over three hundred years earlier); the portrayal of Barabas in *The Jew of Malta* conforms in every aspect to the malignant anti-Semitic stereotype: conniving, bloodthirsty, avaricious and rapacious, utterly bereft of scruple and conscience, he openly boasts about his villainy; his only redeeming feature being that, within the play's blackly comic, and generally misanthropic, scheme of things, he is no worse than the play's Christians.

The play's evident popularity during the 1590s may be due to its audience's recognition that it was, as has been claimed, 'a play about racism, not a racist play' (Shepherd 1986: xi). If they had anything in common with the crowds that gathered around the base of the scaffold at Tyburn on 7 June 1594 to jeer and laugh at Lopez, even as with his last breath he declared his loyalty to the queen and his faith in Jesus Christ, the Rose's audiences probably had a rather less finely tuned sense of comic irony. By conspicuously evoking the spirit of one of their competitor's biggest hits, the Lord Chamberlain's Men might have hoped to cash in on its success, and perhaps to suggest that the new play shared its predecessor's style and outlook, irrespective of whether this mis-sold what Shakespeare had actually written (though perhaps not what was performed). If the title-pages of the quartos are any guide (and Tiffany Stern [2006] has recently argued that these provide a record of what might have been put upon the playbills that were circulated and posted around the city in advance of performances), playhouse publicity would have emphasised the lurid, sensational and excessive qualities of the work it promoted.

Q1 *Merchant* thus announces that it features 'the extreme crueltie of Shylocke the Jew towards the sayd Merchant, in cutting a just Pound of his Flesh', and the fact that the action of the play thwarts the bloody scenario that this describes is, for marketing purposes, a triviality. As Stern concludes, 'Just because this summary of *Merchant* is viciously reductive does not mean that it was not effective, and does not mean it was not authorial' (2006: 30). By these standards, the title-page of the earliest quarto of *The Jew of*

Malta (published much later, in 1633) is a model of restraint, referring merely to 'The famous Tragedy of the Rich Jew of Malta'. Spectators drawn into the playhouses to witness the 'extreme cruelty' of Shylock may or may not have found themselves revising their preconceptions; out on the streets and on the bookstalls, the play as advertised reinforced them.

It is thanks to Henslowe's scrupulous book-keeping that we have as much information as we do about the stage history of Marlowe's play; and it is one of the crueller tricks of theatrical history that whereas there is a wealth of detail about his transactions as proprietor of the Rose, documented between his activities as a pimp and as a loan shark, the public playhouse activities of the Lord Chamberlain's Men during the same period are largely a matter of guesswork. The records of the Revels Office with respect to court performances are slightly more informative. From the end of 1594 to the start of 1603, Burbage's company gave between two and six performances during the Christmas festivities, though which plays were presented is a matter of conjecture: presumably they usually took to court works that had already been tested before the wider paying public. As we shall see in a later section (pp. 57–61), from the winter of 1603 onwards, after the Lord Chamberlain's Men had been taken under the patronage of James himself and become the King's Men, the records are fuller, though better in some years than others, with plays both by Shakespeare and by others clearly identified.

Lord Hunsdon had attempted to mollify civic opposition to the establishment of the Admiral's–Chamberlain's duopoly in 1594 by proscribing these and other companies from playing within London but also by claiming that playhouse performance was a form of rehearsal for the more prestigious court engagements. This did not convince the new Lord Mayor, John Spencer (c.1535–1610), who wrote to Burghley, the Lord Treasurer, on 3 November 1594 to complain that the playhouses were 'the ordinary places of meeting for all vagrant persons and maisterles men that hang about the Citie, theeves, horsestealers, whoremoongers, coozeners, coneycatching persones, practizers of treason, and other such lyke' (Chambers 1923, 4: 317) and to demand their demolition. Spencer objected in particular to the plans of the moneylender Francis Langley (d. 1601) to build a playhouse on a site in Bankside's Paris Garden that he had purchased in 1589; his plea was not heard, and in 1595 the Swan playhouse opened.

The importance of this building for theatre history lies in the fact that it furnishes us with the sole piece of visual evidence of the layout of the interior of an Elizabethan theatre. In 1596, the Dutch humanist scholar and traveller Johannes de Witt (c.1566–1622) visited London and recorded in his diary his impressions of the city's four playhouses. Especially notable was the Swan, 'the largest and most magnificent', which accommodated 'three thousand persons', was built 'of a mass of flint stones' and was 'supported by wooden columns painted in such excellent imitation of marble that it is able to deceive even the most cunning'. For de Witt, the interesting aspect of the Swan was its emulation of the precedent of classical theatre architecture: 'Since its form resembles that of a Roman work', he continued, 'I have made a sketch of it above' (Schoenbaum 1977: 138–39).

As copied by his friend Aernout van Buchell (1565–1641), de Witt's sketch shows a circle of tiered galleries surrounding an open stage; two columns support a thatched roof which projects halfway over the stage platform; two doors are set either side into the rear wall, and a gallery overlooks the stage at the rear. Ambiguous, of questionable accuracy and probably poorly executed, the sketch has proven notoriously difficult to interpret: since de Witt's aim was to emphasise the Romanesque aspect of the playhouse, its details reinforce this scheme; and whereas it may indicate some features that the open-air amphitheatres held in common, it may equally well document the unique configuration of the Swan, as de Witt claims not that the Swan is typical, but that it is distinctive. In any case, the Swan's moment of glory proved relatively brief: in July 1597, following the Earl of Pembroke's Men's staging there of Nashe and Jonson's lost play *The Isle of Dogs*, the Privy Council issued a restraining order on playing and ordered the closure of the playhouses; when the ban was lifted in October the Lord Admiral's Men at the Rose and the Lord Chamberlain's at the Theatre were alone permitted to resume operations.

The Lord Chamberlain was himself party to the playing profession's active flouting of the law. Three years earlier, following an unsuccessful attempt to persuade the Lord Mayor to allow his men to take up residency for the winter of 1594 at the Cross Keys Inn in Gracechurch Street, Hunsdon backed James Burbage's acquisition of the site that would become the Blackfriars playhouse, the former Dominican priory close by St Paul's Cathedral. Positioned in one of the few London Liberties to benefit from a central rather than suburban location, it thus evaded the jurisdiction of the city authorities. But the work that Burbage began in the summer of 1596, to convert the great hall of the priory into London's first purpose-built indoor theatre, was brought to a halt by the end of the year: in November, thirty-one residents of Blackfriars wrote to the Privy Council to object to this 'comon playhouse', which, they complained, would 'grow to be a very great annoyance and trouble … by reason of the great resort and gathering togeather of all manner of vagrant and lewde persons that, under cullor of resorting to the playes, will come thither and worke all manner of mischeefe' (Chambers 1923, 4: 320). These were familiar charges, repeatedly levelled at both the indoor and open-air amphitheatres by godly and respectable citizens, and on this occasion they were heard sympathetically; the Privy Council upheld the petition and imposed a ban upon the building's use as a playing space. James Burbage died at the beginning of 1597; having banked upon moving the Lord Chamberlain's Men into a venue in a well-off district in which they might expect their future to be reasonably secure, he left behind a company that would soon find itself in need of a new theatre.

In April 1597, the twenty-one-year lease on the land on which the Theatre had been built in 1576 expired, and its owner, Giles Allen (d. 1608) refused to renew it. Allen conceded the Lord Chamberlain's Men's continued use of the site for a further year, but by September 1598 the Theatre was reported to be 'unfrequented' and 'in dark silence' (Egan 2003: 37). Possibly the company assumed temporary occupancy of the nearby Curtain, while the Burbage clan launched what turned out to be a fairly protracted lawsuit against Allen. Towards the end of 1598 Richard Burbage and his brother Cuthbert (1567–1636) took the law into their own hands by reclaiming what they regarded as rightfully theirs, dismantling the timber frame of the Theatre and carting it off the site to be placed in storage for the rest of the winter. On 21 January 1599, the Burbages, along with John Heminges (d. 1630), Thomas Pope (d. 1604), Phillips, Kempe and Shakespeare, signed the lease for a plot of land in Southwark (for which they paid £1,000), the site for the Globe playhouse. Organised as a syndicate of sharers (or, to use the contemporary term, 'housekeepers') in the venture, the Lord Chamberlain's Men were now in the uniquely strong position of owning their own theatre building.

Everyday entertainments

Fashioned from the thriftily recycled timbers of the Theatre, the Globe was, like the Swan, constructed to make a strong visual impression and to invoke classical precedent. The naming of the Theatre has been conceived to associate its playmaking activities both with the medieval figure of the *theatrum mundi* (the world-as-stage; the stage as the world; 'theatre' was a term cognate with 'atlas' in editions of early modern maps) and with the performance arenas of antiquity: a point which had been noted with some sarcasm back in 1578, by the Puritan preacher John Stockwood, who wrote witheringly of 'the gorgeous Playing place erected in the fieldes … as they please to have it called, a Theatre' (Chambers 1923, 4: 200). The naming of the Globe, a playhouse situated close by a waterway that opened a gateway to empire, signified the yet larger ambitions of the company.

It appears to have been in operation by the end of 1599. In September, a Swiss physician and traveller, Thomas Platter (1574–1628), visited London and recorded his generally favourable impressions of his encounters with, amongst other things, English architecture, cuisine, medical care and tobacco-smoking. Apparently unable to speak English, Platter also documented his experiences of playgoing, including a visit to Bishopsgate, where he witnessed the zany tale of

> various nations with whom each time an Englishman fought for a maiden, and overcame them all, except the German, who won the maiden in fights, sits down beside her, and hence got himself and his servant very fuddled, so that they both became drunk, and the servant threw his shoe at his master's head, and they both fell asleep. Meanwhile the Englishman went [or, possibly, 'climbed'] into the tents and carries off the German's prize, and so he outwits the German too.
>
> (Schanzer 1956: 466)

Perhaps Platter had lunched particularly well that day; elsewhere he recorded his appreciation of the cheapness and ready availability of the wine and beer that almost everyone in England, regardless of age, rank or gender, drank daily in significant quantities, from early in the morning onwards. Platter's account of tobacco-taking likewise confirms that playgoing was, at least for those gallants that could afford the indulgence, pleasantly linked with narcotic inhalation:

> In the ale-houses tobacco or a species of woundwort are also obtainable for one's money, and the powder is lit in a small pipe, the smoke sucked into the mouth, and the saliva is allowed to run freely, after which a good draught of Spanish wine follows … they always carry the instrument with them, and light up on all occasions, at the play, in the taverns or elsewhere … and it makes them riotous and merry, and rather drowsy, just as if they were drunk, though the effect soon passes – and they use it so abundantly because of the pleasure it gives.
>
> (Razzell 1995: 32)

Platter went on to note that 'some types are stronger than others' and that 'they perform queer antics when they take it' (Razzell 1995: 32).

Platter's account of the dubious marvels of tobacco is echoed by that of another foreign visitor, Orazio Bursino, the chaplain to the Viennese Embassy: calling the substance imported from Virginia (the colony named after the celibate monarch) the 'queen's weed', he wrote in 1618 that it was 'an affair of vanity and smoke and his Majesty therefore abhors it … it enters cities with vapouring ostentation and then … departs loaded with gold, leaving the purses of its purchasers empty and their wits addled' (Razzell 1995: 132–33). King James's well-known dislike of smoking (his *Counteblaste to Tobacco* was published in

1604, the year in which he increased the tax levy on the substance by 4,000 per cent) was shared by those who regarded the indispensable component of playhouse practice as not only unhealthy and antisocial but potentially seditious: stupefying, effeminising and profane. Baines's testimony against Marlowe, for example, takes pains to associate his love of tobacco with his other sodomitical tendencies.

At 'about two o'clock' on 21 September 1599, again after dinner, Platter joined a party for a wherry journey across the Thames to visit 'the straw-thatched house', where he witnessed

> the tragedy of the first Emperor Julius Caesar, very pleasingly performed, with approximately fifteen characters; at the end of the play they danced together admirably and exceedingly gracefully, according to their custom, two in each group dressed in men's and two in women's apparel.
>
> (Schanzer 1956: 466)

It is generally thought that Platter refers to a performance of *Julius Caesar* at the Globe, which seems likely, though not certain (just conceivably, he may have seen an unknown play on the same subject at Henslowe's Rose); and since his diary is written in what has been described as 'a slovenly form of sixteenth century Alemannic' (Schanzer 1956: 465) it presents translation difficulties that generate significant ambiguities in his evidence which have been differently interpreted by theatre historians: 'ohnegefahr 15 personen' has been taken to refer both to the number of characters in the play and to the number of actors in the company, while the account of the transvestite dance, 'ye zwen in mannes vndt 2 in weiber kleideren angethan', usually understood as two pairs of two men and boys, might also suggest 'more than a total of four dancers ... in fact several groups of dancers, each consisting of two actors in male and two in female attire' (Schanzer 1956: 467).

Whatever the arithmetic, Platter's eyewitness account reports on the custom of ending performances (even, as in this instance, of the most solemn of classical tragedies) with a dance; perhaps, we may speculate, the play that ends with Octavius inviting his victorious companions on the corpse-strewn fields of Philippi to 'part the glories of this happy day' (*Julius Caesar*, 5.5.80) properly concluded with the bodies, led by Burbage as Brutus, rising to their feet to launch into what Platter recalls from the Bishopsgate show as a dance 'in the English and the Irish mode'; though, as Bruce R. Smith cautions, the assumption that 'the dancing Platter describes was a comic jig' needs rethinking in the light of 'his qualifier "*überausz zierlich*" (extremely dainty)', which 'sorts oddly with the rollicking jig texts that have survived' (2004: 133).

As Richard Wilson puts it, the collision between the apparently decorous milieu of classical tragedy and the dance consorts with the anachronistic qualities of a play which contains 'chimney-pots, feather hats, bound books and chiming clocks' (1993: 47); a contemporary illustration of Shakespeare's earlier Roman drama, *Titus Andronicus* (by Henry Peachum, on a manuscript sheet that dates from between 1595 and 1614), which shows an eclectic mix of Roman and Elizabethan costuming, togas and swords, halberds and doublet and hose, may provide a glimpse of a similarly hybrid stage practice.

One other detail of Platter's account is worth noting: his reference to the 'streüwine Dachhaus', which translates as either 'the straw-thatched house' (Schanzer 1956: 465) or 'the house with the thatched roof' (Razzell 1995: 27). If the thatched roof was that of the Globe, not the Rose, then Burbage and company were knowingly handling dangerously incendiary material: following a succession of disastrous fires in London, thatching had been banned by an ordinance as long ago as 1212, though this was not consistently enforced, particularly in the Liberties, where the playhouses, with their hardcore clientele of ardent smokers, were situated. The use of thatch rather than the considerably more expensive tiles was probably due to cost; but it was an economy which the company would live to regret, fourteen years later, when in May 1613 the playhouse burned to the ground during a performance of *All Is True*. The lesson was learned: as the Long View of London drawn by the Prague-born engraver Wenceslas Hollar (1607–77) in 1647 shows, the building that replaced it, the second Globe, had a tiled roof.

This distracted Globe

Whether or not *Julius Caesar* was written specifically for the Globe (perhaps even for its opening – though *Henry V*, with its invocation in the Folio-text-only Chorus passages of 'this cockpit' and 'this wooden O' [Prol. 11, 13], has also been nominated for this) – its Roman content seemed to resonate strangely within a building that was simultaneously new and old, both rooted in the present and harking back to a venerated past, the model for England's own nascent imperial aspirations. It also manifested a new self-consciousness about the immediate environment, context and location of its own performance. Shakespeare's previous work had exhibited a heightened and sophisticated metatheatrical awareness through such devices as the inset performances in *Love's Labour's Lost*, *Dream* and *Henry IV, Part 1*, the Sly framework of *Shrew*, the play-acting of Richard III, Richard II, Falstaff, Henry V and many others, the imagery of the player king threaded through the history plays; in *Twelfth Night* (c.1601), he has Fabian joke about how 'If this were played upon a stage, now, I could condemn it as an improbable fiction' (3.4.114–15).

Many of these touches serve as pleasurable, sometimes deeply searching, reminders of the nature and circumstances of the medium in which the plays have their life. In one brief, highly charged and extraordinarily proleptic moment, *Julius Caesar* takes these explorations into another dimension. Lingering at the scene of Caesar's assassination, an event that profoundly haunted the Renaissance imagination, the conspirators are suddenly confronted with their uncanny doubling as ghosts from their own future, rendered on the Globe's stage as the bodies of the Lord Chamberlain's players in time present, as Cassius invites them – and the audience – to think of 'How many ages hence/ Shall this our lofty scene be acted over/ In states unborn and accents yet unknown!' (*Julius Caesar*, 3.1.112–14), prompting Brutus in turn to reflect on 'How many times' Caesar, perhaps like the baited bulls or bears seen in the amphitheatres alongside the Globe, would 'bleed in sport' (115). Prising apart history and theatrical representation and repatriating the action from the pre-Christian Mediterranean to an autumn afternoon in Southwark, the moment counterpoints the lofty ideals of the conspirators with both the banality and the brutality of the here and now; and as the fiction turns inside out, in a move designed (though not guaranteed) to negate the republican project, credibility drains from the assassins even as the stage blood oozes from play-dead Caesar spread out by their feet.

It is a remarkable *coup de théâtre*, but one that seems almost rudimentary compared to the metatheatrical games played in what was probably the next of Shakespeare's plays to premiere at the Globe, which was also his last Elizabethan tragedy, and his most sustained reflection upon the medium of performance itself. Published in what is generally regarded as an unauthorised quarto edition in 1603, and in an enlarged and modified form in 1604, *The Tragicall Historie of Hamlet, Prince of Denmark* was presented on the title page of the former 'As it hath beene diverse times acted by his Highnesse servants in the Cittie of London' (as well as at Oxford and Cambridge Universities, 'and else-where'); the year before, the Stationers' Register recorded an entry on 26 July for 'A booke called the Revenge of Hamlett Prince of Denmarke' which had been 'latelie Acted' by the Lord Chamberlain's Men. In this play, Shakespeare turned to the narrative, which was presumably also the subject of a lost play possibly dating from the 1580s, which is first alluded to in 1589 by Nashe, who wrote that 'English Seneca read by candlelight yields many good sentences, as *Blood is a beggar* and so forth; and if you entreat him fair in a frosty morning he will afford you whole Hamlets, I should say handfuls, of tragical speeches' (McKerrow 1958, 3: 315).

Henslowe's accounts for June 1594, the period in which a restraining order enforcing the temporary closure of the Rose and the Theatre led to the two companies sharing the stage at Newington Butts, record a performance of a *Hamlet* play alongside *The Taming of a Shrew*, *The Jew of Malta*, *Titus Andronicus* and the since-lost (but on this occasion most lucrative) *Cutlacke* and *Bellendon*; in 1596, Thomas Lodge's (1558–1625) *Wit's Miserie* referred to a figure who 'looks as pale as the vizard of the ghost who cried so miserably at the Theatre like an oyster-wife, *Hamlet, revenge!*' (Bullough 1957, 7: 24). This may point to the existence of a version of *Hamlet* in the repertoire of the Lord Chamberlain's Men from the very outset, but the fact that Nashe's quibbling allusion predates Shakespeare's first publications (*Venus and Adonis*, *Lucrece*) by nearly half a decade suggests that this source play, if that is what it was, had nothing to do with him.

What cannot be avoided, though its significance must remain conjectural, is the coincidence between the name of the play's protagonist and that of the eleven-year-old son that Shakespeare lost to unknown causes in 1596, particularly when we remember that 'Hamnet' (very probably named after the family friend Hamnet Sadler [d. 1624], who would eventually act as signatory to Shakespeare's will) was, as Park Honan points out, 'interchangeable with "Hamlet"' (1999: 90). The story of a son grieving for a dead father, as a kind of mirrored or inverted autobiography, may have had a very personal immediacy indeed for Shakespeare. Shakespeare's play is considered in more detail in the 'Works' section of this book (pp. 190–202); here, I wish not only to draw attention to certain aspects of the play that place it in its particular moment in the history of the Lord Chamberlain's Men but also to suggest that the significance of this lay in its particularly close, and manifestly self-aware, involvement in the circumstances of its own production.

For a play set in Denmark which ostensibly derives from an ancient Norse legend (recorded by Saxo Grammaticus in 1200 and subsequently rendered into French by François de Belleforest [1530–83] as part of his *Histoires tragiques*, published between 1559 and 1582), it seems strongly, and as anachronistically, preoccupied with the Roman world that is the subject of the play that the company quite possibly performed immediately prior to it. In a play in which Hamlet, anglicised from the source's Amleth, contends with the Danish-sounding Rosencrantz and Guildenstern, the Germanic Gertrude and the Francophone Fortinbras, Latinate names proliferate: Claudius (Feng in Saxo's telling of the tale, Fengon in Belleforest's), Polonius (Corambis in the first quarto), Marcellus, Lucianus; to complicate matters still further, Laertes takes his name from the father of Odysseus in Homer's *Odyssey*. In the first scene, Horatio, whose naming aptly evokes Horace, the renowned poet of ancient Rome, recounts tales of the portents seen 'In the most high and palmy state of Rome' (*Hamlet*, 1.1.106.6) prior to Caesar's assassination; the same speaker ends the play by declaring himself 'more an antique Roman than a Dane' (5.2.283) as he attempts to wrest the poisoned cup from Hamlet's grasp.

Hamlet himself, confronting his own capacity for murder, pleads to 'Let not ever/ The soul of Nero enter this firm bosom' (3.2.363–64); later, musing by the graveside on the passing of the greatest of mythical figures, he reduces the most tragic of Roman emperors to two lines of derisive, faintly scatological, doggerel: 'Imperial Caesar, dead and turned to clay,/ Might stop a hole to keep the wind away' (5.1.196–97). Burbage, who was subsequently acclaimed as the 'English Roscius' by the historian William Camden (1551–1623), making him the first English player to receive the accolade of being compared with the legendary Roman actor, is given an equally scornful riposte in 2.2 to Polonius, who, entering with news of the arrival of a troupe of players for whom 'Seneca cannot be too heavy, nor Plautus too light' (382–83), is met with the bogus promise of a report that begins 'When Roscius was an actor in Rome' (373–74).

Several scenes later, in what is to turn out to be their penultimate, and on this occasion relatively amicable, exchange, the prince and the counsellor trade recollections of playing that combine memories of a dramatised Rome with intimations of Polonius's impending demise: prompting his colleague with the observation that 'you played once i'th'university', Hamlet solicits from him the news that he 'did enact Julius Caesar' and that 'Brutus killed me' (3.2.89–94). As well as foreshadowing Polonius's own fate at Hamlet's hands, the exchange seems irresistibly to suggest a metatheatrical dimension, with Burbage and his fellow master player self-referencing the roles they had recently exhibited on the same stage.

Shortly before Polonius's entry bearing news of the arrival of the players, there is an exchange (in the Folio, but not in the second quarto) between Hamlet and Rosencrantz in which the decline in the fortunes of the 'tragedians of the city' (2.2.316) is ascribed to fashionable allure of 'an eyrie of children, little eyases', whose attention-seeking facility for bitter satire has reportedly created an unwelcome competitor for the 'common stages' (326–29). This is an unmistakeable reference to the boys' companies that had, after a hiatus during the 1590s, assumed a new vigour and visibility at the turn of the century: in 1599, the Children of St Paul's resumed operations in the quarter-century-old performance space in the cathedral, and in 1600 Burbage himself leased the Blackfriars playhouse to the Children of the Chapel, who were managed by the scrivener Henry Evans. It is also, for Shakespeare, an uncharacteristically direct engagement with contemporary entertainment industry affairs, perhaps prompted by the evident appeal of the new and innovative forms of drama that the boys' companies were offering, which in the first decade of the seventeenth century increasingly dominated the market in playbooks. These companies attracted the talents of writers who had previously contributed to the output of the public playhouses, including Jonson, Dekker and Marston; Jonson in turn was sufficiently taken with at least one of the child actors, Solomon Pavy (1588–1602) of the Children of the Queen's Revels, to compose an elegy in response to his premature death at the age of thirteen (Pavy is listed in the casts of Jonson's *Cynthia's Revels* and *Poetaster* [both 1601]), calling him 'The stages jewell' and claiming that he 'did act ... old men so duely,/ As, sooth, the *Parcae* thought him one,/ He plai'd so truly' (Steggle 2004: 259).

Little eyases

Jonson's affection and respect for at least one of these boy players is not shared by Hamlet: 'little eyases' may sound light-hearted, charming or patronising to modern ears but for the eagle-eyed Prince who reminds Guildenstern that he knows 'a hawk from a handsaw' (*Hamlet*, 2.2.362), the diminutive songbirds, actually highly trained predators, are a real menace. And for Shakespeare and company, the topic might have had some urgency. Recent scholarship has questioned the much-recycled narrative of the 'War of the Theatres' between the children's and adult companies that is supposed to have taken place at the turn of the century (a myth that largely rests, as Rosalind L. Knutson argues [1995], on a couple of references in *Poetaster* and Dekker's *Satiromastix*, staged at the Queen's Chapel and the Globe, respectively, in 1601), but it is apparent that the Lord Chamberlain's Men were at this time faced with a potential weakening of their prime position in the established London theatre duopoly. Additionally to the emergence of the chorister companies, adult companies were drawing audiences to the refurbished Boar's Head in Whitechapel, an inn which had been the site of performances prior to 1561 and which was in operation as a playhouse from 1599 onwards (as was, possibly, the Curtain).

On 22 June 1600, after a great deal of wrangling, the Privy Council issued an order which reasserted the exclusive rights of the Lord Chamberlain's and Admiral's Men in the city, and which acknowledged that a recent proliferation of playhouses and performances 'is daylie occasion of the ydle ryotous and dissolute livinge of great nombers of people that doe meete and assemble there and of many particular abuses and disorders that doe there upon ensue' whilst offering the standard defence that 'some order is fitt to bee taken for the allowance and maynetenance of suche persons as are thoughte meetest in that kinde to yeald hi Maiestie reacreation and delighte and consequently of the howses that must serue for publike playinge to keepe them in exercise' (Rutter 1984: 192).

By such means did the Privy Council manage to balance the demands of the Lord Mayor, the entertainment needs of the court and the commercial interests of the companies that several of its members patronised, with fears of both real and imagined civic disorder, as well as of more generally defined profane, immoral and dissolute behaviour. In practice, the Council's orders were interpreted with rather more flexibility. The company at the Boar's Head was led by the actor Robert Browne (d. 1603) and patronised by William Stanley, the Earl of Derby, who was also a key supporter of the Children of St Paul's; they performed at court in 1600 and after 1602 spent much of the rest of their time on provincial tour. In 1602, an amalgamation of Lord Oxford's Men and the Earl of Worcester's Men took up residency at Henslowe's Rose; their personnel included Will Kempe, returned from his morris dance to Norwich, and Christopher Beeston (c.1580–1638), another former member of the Lord Chamberlain's Men. Their patron, Edward Somerset (c.1550–1628), was a powerful figure in Elizabeth's court, and of comparable stature to the Lord Admiral and the Lord Chamberlain; the apprehender and chief witness against the Earl of Essex following the failed coup of 1601, he was appointed as the Queen's Master of Horse and as Privy Councillor.

The Admiral's Men had moved out of the ageing Rose in 1600, to the newly built Fortune playhouse in the north London suburb of St-Giles-without-Cripplegate; employing Burbage's builder, Peter Street, Henslowe issued him with a building contract that in a number of points of detail stipulated a repeat performance of his work on Bankside the previous year: thus it was to be 'doen according to the manner and fashion of the saide howse Called the Globe Saveinge only that all the princypall and maine postes of the saide ffarme and Stadge forwarde shalbe square and wroughte pal*asterwise* *w*ith carved proporcions' (Rutter 1984: 176). As well as providing valuable material for future theatre historians of the Globe as well as the Fortune (the contract for the former has not survived), Henslowe showed that he was both ready to take account of the successes of his competitors and willing to learn from their mistakes; perhaps a shrewder long-term investor than Burbage (or one at that moment with access to more ready cash), he ensured that the roof of the Fortune was tiled, not thatched; although this did not prevent it from being destroyed by fire in 1621.

Shakespeare could not have known in 1600 (or in 1603) that the Blackfriars satirists' inability to know where to draw the line would by 1606 have caused Samuel Daniel to lose his post as licenser of the Queen's Revels for his authorship of *Philotas* (1604), Jonson and Chapman's imprisonment for *Eastward Ho!* (1605), and the loss of the queen's patronage that resulted in the Children of the Queen's Revels' demotion to Children of the Black-friars. Nor could he have foreseen that, two years later, their persistence in causing offence (especially with Chapman's two-part *Byron* plays) would result in the company's demise and an opportunity for Shakespeare and Burbage's company to finally occupy the indoor venue that James Burbage had converted twelve years previously. Whether the 'little eyases' passage was provoked by the events of around 1600 or of 1606–08, however, one aspect of it could have been prompted at either moment: Hamlet's musings on the projected pro-fessional futures of the juvenile performers, who 'should grow themselves to common players – as it is like most will, if their means are not better' (*Hamlet*, 2.2.333–35). Knutson, who argues for the later date, suggests that this seems to be prompted by the recognition that the boys are on the cusp of adulthood, and thus an immediate potential rival to the adult companies: at the earlier date, 'Shakespeare and the Chamberlain's Men might have anticipated that the troublesome children would become adult players, but in 1606–8 that eventuality was imminent' (1995: 24).

There is a further dimension to this, which is connected with the self-referentiality of the play as a whole and of this passage in particular, and which pertains to the approaching maturity not only of the members of the boys' companies but also of the boys who were the members of Shakespeare's own company. Probably by 1600, and certainly by 1606, the boys who were apprenticed to the Lord Chamberlain's sharers sometime around 1594 would have been close to, at the end of or out of their periods of indenture; with no guarantee that any of these unknown young men would remain with the Lord Cham-berlain's Men company beyond their apprenticeship, succession planning would have been one of the company's priorities. Alexander Cooke (d. 1614), who was included in the Folio list of actors as well as in the cast lists in Jonson's 1616 *Works* and of Beaumont and Fletcher's *The Captain* (performed at court in 1612), and who became a sharer in 1604, was apprenticed to Heminges in 1597, and presumably progressed from female to male adult roles when his voice broke, though it has also been suggested that Cooke's appearance at the bottom of a number of these lists indicates that he continued to play women as an adult. Christopher Beeston (d. 1638), conversely, was apprenticed to Phillips (the senior player named him as his 'servant' in his will), performed in *Every Man in His Humour* after 1598 (when he would have been at least eighteen years of age), but by 1602 was with Worcester's Men.

The documented performances at court of *Merchant*, *Merry Wives*, *Measure for Measure* and *Othello* during the Christmas season of 1604–05, in the midst of what McMillin describes as 'a long period of disruption in the London commercial theatre' (2004: 2439), suggest that by then a new generation of talented boys had been secured by the company. In the years immediately following 1599 the outlook may have seemed less secure. From this perspective, the comparatively restricted nature of the women's roles in the two Globe plays we have been considering may be partly attributable to the limitations of neophyte boy actors, rather than solely to the patriarchal and misogynist inclinations of Shake-spearean tragedy. In this light the 'inordinate interest', as Knutson calls it (1995: 24), that Hamlet takes in the career trajectories of the juveniles is complemented by the intrusive-ness (perhaps compounded by anxiety) with which he hails the boy who is to play the Queen, of whom he expresses the pious hope that his voice, 'like a piece of uncurrent gold, be not cracked within the ring' (2.2.411–12). It has been widely recognised that the simile associates the prospect of a broken voice both with the debasement of coinage (by clipping or cracking) and the surrendering of virginity; what we may also register here is an association with the loss of a rare and valuable investment or commodity, which, perhaps, is what the boy player represents. In passing, we might also wish to note that clipping or currency fraud was one of the misdemeanours that was categorised in the period under the umbrella term of sodomy; its conjunction with sexual defloration brings to mind the lurid scenarios of players and boys envisaged by the likes of Stubbes.

All this is, necessarily, speculative. Hamlet's apparent digression from the narrative into the world of the London theatres in the early 1600s is a moment where the fictional fabric of Denmark's nominally feudal Elsinore parts to offer a glimpse of the stages and streets, and the personalities that surround it, a move likewise performed by Robert Armin (c.1570–1615), lead clown in the graveyard scene, where he sends his companion off to a local tavern to ask 'Yaughan' (Johan? Joan?) for a 'stoup of liquor' (5.1.55–56). As such, it is seemingly extraneous to the action of the play; yet in another way its preoccupations are very much in tune with the world in which they are anachronistically and anatopically implanted. Condemning the satirical little voices that 'exclaim against their own succession' (2.2.336), Hamlet reiterates what is, of course, not only one of the play's key terms but an extremely current professional, political, and perhaps on Shakespeare's part personal, preoccupation.

The death of Hamnet would have made Shakespeare, as a member of a society in which patrilineage was fundamental to both the perpetuation of patriarchal privileges and authority and the orderly transmission of inheritance rights and property (generating, amongst other things, the paranoid fear of cuckoldry that drives both comedy – *The Merry Wives* – and tragedy – *Othello*), keenly aware of his own lack of a male heir. Not only that: William was also the last male Shakespeare of Stratford to bear his father's name. His brothers Gilbert and Richard died in 1612 and 1613 respectively, both without issue, and his youngest brother Edmund was buried in London in 1607 after a brief career as an actor and an even briefer one as a parent (his son Edward was baptised in July of that year and buried the following month).

Robert Armin (c.1568–1615)

Comic actor

Prior to joining the Lord Chamberlain's Men in 1599, as the successor to William Kempe, Armin had been apprenticed as a goldsmith and had, alongside his clowning, carved out a modest career as a balladeer and pamphlet-writer. Under the *nom de plume* 'Clonnico de Curtanio Snuffe' (Snuff, the Clown of the Curtain) he published a collection of anecdotes, *Fool upon Fool*, in 1600; this was reissued in 1605 as the work of 'Clonnico del Mondo Snuffe' (Snuff, the Clown of the Globe), and again in 1608 under his own name. Listed as one of the players in the 1623 Folio, Armin's talents and temperament encouraged a shift in Shakespeare's writing away from the physical clowning of his exuberant predecessor and towards a more introspective, verbally dexterous, style of comedy: among the parts written for him were Touchstone, Feste, Thersites, Lear's Fool, Autolycus and Abel Drugger in Jonson's *The Alchemist*. Armin also wrote plays: *The Two Maids of More-Clacke*, published in 1609, depicted its author on the title-page.

By the time the new century dawned, whatever concerns Shakespeare may have had about his individual legacy might have found echoes in the growing unease that surrounded the question of Queen Elizabeth's succession. Having throughout her reign used the attentions of potential suitors, whilst guarding her unmarried status, as a key, and very effective, instrument of policy, the ageing Elizabeth (she turned sixty-seven in 1600) continued to refuse to nominate her successor. The failed Essex rebellion of 1601 was a symptom of discontent and potential instability in a country suffering from price inflation and food shortages caused by a series of poor harvests throughout the 1590s, and the protracted and costly on–off war with Spain, which had begun in 1585, weighed heavily on the exchequer; Elizabeth herself was in declining health and increasingly short tempered. If *Hamlet* voiced uncertainty and anxiety about the future, the last but one of Shakespeare's plays to be recorded in the Stationers' Register during Elizabeth's reign expressed the prevailing mood of cynicism. Entered on 7 February 1603, *Troilus and Cressida* satirically represented the legendary icon of femininity and cause of the Trojan wars, Helen of Troy, as an ageing roué, the seemingly endless conflict itself as a squalid and futile squabble. Finally, on 24 March 1603, the queen died, having at last consented to the succession passing to James Stuart, King of Scotland since 1567, who on 25 July (the feast day of St James the Apostle) rode through the plague-stricken streets of London to Westminster, to be crowned James I of England.

James VI and I (1566–1625)

King of England, Scotland and Ireland

When he offered his patronage to the Lord Chamberlain's Men shortly after his accession to the English throne in 1603, James I not only assigned the company a uniquely advantageous position within London's theatre economy, formalising and revitalising the mutually supportive relationship between the Crown and the players that had been sustained from the earliest years of Elizabeth's reign; he also elevated the social status of the members of Burbage's troupe to that of gentlemen. Crowned king of Scotland in his infancy, James had strongly supported the arts and drama in his native country, hosting visits from English companies in the context of a nation that enjoyed considerably more developed cultural ties with the European mainland than its English neighbour; his own impressive literary output included the masque that he devised for the marriage of the Marquess of Huntley in 1588, and he may have sponsored a company of players in Edinburgh towards the end of the sixteenth century. Regarding himself as a conciliator in the field of foreign policy, James was, domestically, almost permanently in conflict with the Commons throughout his reign, largely as a consequence of his extreme profligacy. If James's talent for spending money that he did not have meant that the King's Men were the beneficiaries of a largesse that saw them regularly performing at court from 1603 onwards, his other major contribution to the performance culture of the early seventeenth century was his cultivation of the court masque, which, in the hands of Ben Jonson and Inigo Jones, became one of the most preposterously extravagant vehicles ever devised for the glorification of monarchical authority. Whereas the plays that Shakespeare possibly presented before Queen Elizabeth rarely seem to evoke the monarch directly (Oberon's reference in *Dream* to the 'fair virgin thronèd by the west' [2.1.158] is exceptional), those of the Jacobean era are, perhaps quite sensibly, much more concerned to accommodate their patron's tastes and preoccupations, whether in the form of *Measure for Measure*'s apparently flattering representation of a benevolently self-effacing, yet ubiquitous, ruler; in the diplomatic handling of James's ancestor Banquo in *Macbeth*; or in the same play's treatment of witchcraft, a subject on which the king had written a learned treatise.

The King's Men

The final years of Elizabeth's reign had been ones of uncertainty, professional as well as political, for the Lord Chamberlain's Men. The company continued to perform at court during the Christmas season (three times in 1599–1600 and 1600–01, four times in 1601–02 and twice in 1602–03), which favoured them over the Lord Admiral's Men, who played there five times over the same period; however, the Lord Chamberlain's Men's ageing and sick patron, George Carey, was in no position to promote their cause. With the accession of James, the company's fortunes underwent a considerable improvement. Within two months of Elizabeth's demise, on 19 May 1603, James issued the command which turned the Lord Chamberlain's servants into his own, licensing and authorising

> theise our Servauntes Lawrence Fletcher, William Shakespeare, Richard Burbage, Augustyne Phillippes, John Heninges, Henrie Condell, William Sly, Robert Armyn, Richard Cowly, and the rest of their Assosiates freely to use and exercise the Arte and faculty of playinge Comedies, Tragedies, histories, Enterludes, morals, pastoralls, Stage-plaies, and Suche others like as theie have alreadie studied or hereafter shall use or studie, aswell for the recreation of our lovinge Subjectes, as for our Solace and pleasure when wee shall thincke good to see them, during our pleasure.
>
> (Chambers 1923, 2: 208)

The king's patronage was immediately reflected in his Men's new status as Grooms Extraordinary of the Chamber, a position usually conferred upon men of aristocratic birth, and in their being supplied with four hundred yards of red cloth to fashion their livery for James's triumphant procession through London on 15 March 1604.

The support afforded to the company could hardly have been more opportune, as on 26 May an outbreak of plague enforced the complete closure of all London playhouses, which did not reopen until April the following year. The King's Men took to the road, performing in Oxford, Coventry, Bridgnorth and Bath. In November they returned to London to rest up at the house that Augustine Phillips had recently bought in Mortlake, then were summoned to Wilton House in Wiltshire, home of William Herbert, the Earl of Pembroke, for 2 December, for which Heminges was paid £30 'for the paynes and expences of himself and the rest of the company in comming from Mortelake in the countie of Surrie unto the courte aforesaid and there p'senting before his ma*j*estie one playe' (Chambers 1923, 4: 168).

The play performed on this occasion is not known (*As You Like It* has been suggested); at the end of the month, the King's Men performed at Hampton Court, and the plays included the anonymous *The Fair Maid of Bristow*, published in 1605 and recorded in the Stationers' Register (8 February) as 'plaide at Hampton, before the King and Queenes most excellent majesties'; a letter sent by the diplomat Dudley Carleton (1573–1632) to the dilettante and gossip-monger John Chamberlain (1554–1628) recording that on 1 January 1604 'we had a play of Robin Goodefellow' at the Great Hall at Hampton Court strongly suggests *A Midsummer Night's Dream* (Barroll 1991: 120). The company gave seven performances in total between 26 December and 19 February; tided over by a 'free gift' from the Crown of £30 to Burbage for 'mayntenaunce and reliefe' while the playhouses remained shut (Chambers 1923, 2: 168), the company resumed public playing when they were permitted to reopen in April.

Whatever sense of privilege royal patronage conferred upon the King's Men, however, it did not make them particularly rich. Though the £30 that they received for performing at

Wilton House, the £30 'free gift' and the £80 they were paid for performing at court at the end of the year represented an overall increase on the Elizabethan rate of £10 per court performance, it still amounted to a small fraction of what could be earned in the course of a public playhouse season: Gurr estimates that, on the basis of the figures provided in Henslowe's accounts, the Rose had a turnover of around £1,377 per annum during the period between 1594 and 1599, and conjectures that the Lord Chamberlain's/King's Men earned significantly more (2004b: 106–11).

Court dramatists

By comparison with the other form of performance art favoured by James, the court masque, the King's Men's performances were laughably cheap: although £10 seems not inconsiderable when one is reminded that this was in the early 1600s the average annual wage of a skilled labourer, it pales into insignificance next to the phenomenal £3,000 that was lavished on the single performance of *The Masque of Queens* in 1609. Sumptuous and sycophantic, and performed by a joint cast of courtiers and professional players, the masques combined the spoken word, music, song, dance and mechanised scenic displays in entertainments, devised to mark specific state occasions, that both allegorised and enacted the king's munificence. Orazio Bursino, whose disapproving account of the evils of early modern tobacco-taking was cited above, provides an equally detailed report of one of these events that took place on 6 January 1618, the occasion of *Pleasure Reconciled to Virtue*, a long evening which ended with the drunk and rowdy courtiers attacking the post-performance refreshments 'like so many harpies … at the first assault they upset the table and the crash of glass platters reminded me precisely of a severe hailstorm at mid-summer smashing the window glass'. Anticipating that his readers might well 'writhe on reading or listening to this tediousness', Bursino concludes that they might like to 'imagine the weariness I felt in relating it' (Razzell 1995: 143–44).

In November 1604 the King's Men were back before the court, at Whitehall, and for the first time the Revels Accounts provide details of the plays performed. The season opened on 1 November with *The Moor of Venis* (i.e. *Othello*); this was followed by *Merry Wives* on 4 November, *Measure for Measure* (26 December), *Comedy of Errors* (28 December), both attributed to 'Shaxberd', *Henry V* (7 January), Jonson's *Every Man Out of His Humour* and *Every Man in His Humour* (8 January and 2 February), *Merchant* (10 February and again on the 12th), and the lost *The Spanish Maze* (11 February). As well as indicating Shakespeare's dominance of the King's Men's repertoire at this stage, the list shows that this ascendancy was characterised by the judicious combination of revivals and new works. It suggests that if Shakespeare's company had been hampered by a shortage of talent amongst its boy apprentices during the preceding years, the situation had now been rectified: evidently they now had boys capable of at least making a decent fist of Mistress Page, Mistress Ford, Mistress Quickly, Portia, Desdemona, Emilia and Isabella. Some company personnel changes are documented: the inclusion of Lawrence Fletcher (d. 1608) on the 1603 Royal Patent saw the – probably temporary – drafting into the King's Men's ranks of one of James's favoured actors from Scotland; Nicholas Tooley (c.1575–1623) and Cooke, respectively apprentices of Burbage and Heminges, became sharers in 1603; and Lowin, defecting from Worcester's Men in 1603, joined them as a sharer around 1605.

The plays themselves also provide evidence that the company's new status as royal servants carried with it the responsibility to deliver material to their patron's taste. It has often been observed that the theologically minded Duke in *Measure for Measure*, who declares that 'I love the people/ But do not like to stage me to their eyes' (1.1.67–68), shares with the king an aversion to public appearances that was in marked contrast to the practices of his predecessor; and although it is reductive to interpret the Duke as a flattering image of the most important spectator in its first audience, *Measure* seems to have been contrived to offer tactfully worded support for the new monarch. Though James was presumably sufficiently sharp to recognise that the play's formally harmonious resolution hinges upon a number of fairly preposterous contrivances, including two bodily substitutions (Mariana for Isabella, Ragozine for Barnardo), with respect to the latter we must assume that Burbage was professional enough to keep a straight face when declaring that it was 'an accident that heaven provides' (4.3.69). *Othello*, similarly, engages at least one of James's areas of interest with its background of conflict between the Venetian Republic and the Turk. James prided himself on being a peacemaker rather than a war leader (the formal ratification of his successful efforts to bring to an end hostilities between England and Spain in August 1604 included requiring members of the King's Men, in their capacity as Grooms of the Chamber, acting in attendance upon the Spanish Ambassador when he visited Somerset House): the appearance of the Elizabethan war play *Henry V* at court on 7 January 1605 was a throwback to a previous era.

Othello was presumably also of interest to James and his court for its representation of a noble Moor turned wife-murderer in Burbage's blackfaced protagonist. Black men and women were starting to become visible on the streets of London towards the end of the sixteenth century, often in their capacity as servants and prostitutes, and were the subject of often malevolent stereotyping, in plays such as Peele's *The Battle of Alacazar* (1594), a dramatisation of recent history in which the figure of Muly Mahamet, played at the Rose by Edward Alleyn, is the full-blooded incarnation of what Virginia Mason Vaughan calls 'the equation between blackness and the demonic' (2005: 39), and Shakespeare's own *Titus Andronicus*, in which the Moor Aaron gleefully confesses to acts of rape, murder and mutilation (and yet who also displays humane tenderness towards his own baby son). Peachum's sketch of the play depicts Aaron in a short-sleeved tunic and skirt that reveal and emphasise blackness as grotesque spectacle in the form of full-body makeup; in this respect, the representation accords with elements of other court entertainments that employed images of racial difference and otherness to convey a sense of the exotic. On 30 August 1594, at the baptismal feast of his son Henry, Prince of Wales (1594–1612), at the Scottish court, James himself had been amused by the sight of a 'blackamoor' hauling a chariot (a last-minute substitution for the planned lion, which has been taken by some as the source of the mechanicals' circumspection in *Dream*).

The Christmas season of 1604–05 included, on Twelfth Night (6 January), the first of Jonson's collaborations with the architect and stage designer Inigo Jones, *The Masque of Blackness*, which was written at the request of the king's consort, Queen Anne: in it, the queen and her ladies-in-waiting play the twelve daughters of Niger, who travel to England in search of the 'sun' (i.e. James) whose rays will 'cure' them of their negritude. The decision to use body makeup rather than masks was not universally appreciated; Dudley Carleton wrote of the Queen and her ladies that 'instead of Vizzards, their Faces, and Arms up to the Elbows, were painted black, which was a Disguise sufficient, for they were hard to be known … *and you cannot imagine a more ugly Sight, then a troop of lean-cheek'd Moors*' (Orgel and Strong 1973, 1: 89). If Shakespeare wrote *Othello* with an eye on contemporary events, he might also have been aware of a rather different image of the Moor in the shape of the Moroccan ambassador Abd-el-Oahed ben Massaood, who had been entertained at Elizabeth's court in 1600 with a view to creating an alliance between

Protestant England and Muslim North Africa against Catholic Spain, and who was the subject of a portrait by an unknown artist dating from the turn of the century (see Harris 2000 [1958]). From this perspective, the Moor is marked by religious rather than racial difference.

Jonson's second career as a writer of masques perhaps compensated for the ill judgement that had led him, in 1603, to produce the Roman tragedy *Sejanus His Fall*, a play whose obvious parallels with the factional and intrigue-ridden world of the Jacobean Court resulted in him being called before the Privy Council accused of 'Popery and treason'. Jonson escaped serious consequences on this occasion, but the indignity was compounded by the failure of the play when the King's Men brought it to the stage of the Globe later in 1604, whose audiences reportedly 'screwed their scurvy jaws and looked awry/ Like hissing snakes, adjudging it to die' (Ayres 1999: 20). Shakespeare is listed by Jonson as one of the actors of this play; it was to be one of his last documented appearances as a performer. By the middle of the first decade of the seventeenth century, Shakespeare's own pace of production had nearly halved: having supplied the Lord Chamberlain's Men with at least eighteen plays in the six-year period from 1594 to 1601, the figure after 1603 was fifteen over the course of a decade.

The writing changed in other ways. In *Hamlet*, Shakespeare had not only written for Burbage the longest, most varied and most demanding part yet written for the English stage; he had also, by setting down more than could feasibly be spoken, created one impossible to accommodate within the two to three hours of public performance. *Hamlet* is 3,668 lines in quarto; *Troilus and Cressida* 3,291; *King Lear* 3,092 and *Othello* 3,055; and while the first three of these are slightly shorter in the Folio, *Othello*, at 3,222 lines, is even longer; the Folio-only texts of *Coriolanus* (3,279 lines), *Antony and Cleopatra* (3,016) and *Cymbeline* (3,264) are equally expansive (Erne 2003: 141). The actors' parts themselves became increasingly taxing, and it is perhaps worth citing the actor's perspective here: Lawrence Olivier, after attempting Othello, joked that this was a play of which Shakespeare had said to Burbage, 'Now, I'm going to write a part that you really can't play' (Burton 1967: 22).

Shakespeare continued, first and foremost, to produce work that kept in mind the dual demands of command performance and the public stage, but the impression that emerges particularly after 1600 of his writing in excess of the theatrical capacities of his own time indicates that by now he was testing the limits of the possible: a Roman tragedy whose action moves between two continents, a romance that wanders around the Mediterranean over a course of decades, a play that begins with '*A tempestuous noise of thunder and lightning*', a character who both falls and does not fall off Dover Cliff, another given an exit '*pursued by a bear*'. He may have been harbouring longer-term literary ambitions, though the drop in quarto publication during this period suggests that he may have envisaged their realisation in other forms (manuscript circulation, perhaps) than print.

Jacobean tragedy

Following the 1604–05 season, the King's Men gave ten performances at court in 1605–06, and twelve in 1606–07; among the latter was the next Shakespeare play to be entered in the Stationers' Register (on 27 November 1607), *King Lear*; the entry recorded that it had been played on St Stephen's Night (26 December) in 1606. Shakespeare was accustomed to the standard playhouse practice of recycling existing works for plot material; here he turned to an old, anonymously authored play that had been in the possession of the Lord

Chamberlain's/King's Men since the 1590s (and which was published in quarto in 1605), *The True Chronicle Historie of King Leir and His Three Daughters*, and gave it a drastic overhaul. Some historians have sensed a topical connection between the material of Shakespeare's tragedy and the sad story of the Kent landowner and former Gentleman Pensioner to Queen Elizabeth Brian Annesley (d. 1604), the father of three daughters, Grace, Christian and Cordell (d. 1636), who in late 1603 was the subject of an attempt by Grace's husband, Sir John Wildgoose, to take control of his estate on the grounds that he had 'fallen into such imperfection and distemperature of mind and memory' as to render him 'altogether unfit to govern himself or his estate'. Annesley's will (made aptly enough on All Fools Day, 1 April, 1600) had named Cordell as his prime beneficiary, and it was she who stepped in to defend her father against her sisters' alleged depredations, arguing that his years of service to the recently deceased queen meant that he deserved better 'than at his last gasp to be recorded and registered a lunatic' (Duncan-Jones 2001: 186).

Whether or not Shakespeare knew of the case, and whether its uncanny resonances with the *Leir* story prompted the publication of the chronicle play in 1605, his transformation of the familiar narrative of Lear and his three daughters into his bleakest and most brutal tragedy yet was both innovative and, one must assume, unexpected. The generic designation of the quarto as *The True Chronicle Historie of King Lear* suggests that the play was originally presented – perhaps with a wilful intent to mislead – as a reworking of the old chronicle play. In some respects, Shakespeare was only restoring some of the harsher aspects of the narrative that *Leir* suppressed (in Geoffrey of Monmouth's account, Cordilla outlives her father but is imprisoned and eventually commits suicide), but by confronting his Lear with the death of his own beloved child he not only introduced into the story an unexpected, and devastating, twist but also, perhaps, drew upon the anguish of bereavement; a pain that was possibly intensified by his witnessing of Burbage's Lear rehearsing and performing opposite a young man not much older than his own son at the time of his death. What James made, as Christmas entertainment, of a piece which showed, amongst other things, the torture of a loyal councillor and the ranting of a mad king accompanied only by a courtier masquerading as a lunatic beggar and a terminally acrid Fool can only be wondered at; as can the response of the scandalously profligate king to Lear's acknowledgement of the 'Poor naked wretches' whose condition of abject poverty was not far removed from that of a substantial number of James's own subjects, and to his injunction to 'Take physic, pomp' and to 'Expose thyself to feel what wretches feel' in the rather forlorn hope that this might 'show the heavens more just' (*King Lear*, 3.4.34–37).

If James did hear this message, he chose not to act upon it; as mentioned above, his increasingly lavish expenditure included the colossal sums assigned to the single performance of *The Masque of Queens* in 1608. And if Shakespeare registered any sense of conflict, compromise or contradiction in the idea of incorporating such a potentially radical, levelling message into the play, he kept it to himself. Nor did James appear to take any offence at it, if the continuing attendance of the King's Men at court is any guide: between the end of 1607 and the beginning of 1611, they performed fifty-three times during the holiday festivities, far more frequently than any of their potential rivals. Prior to and following the documented performance of *King Lear* in 1606, Shakespeare is generally understood to have written a number of plays of which no record of original performance exists and which remained unpublished until the 1623 Folio: *All's Well that Ends Well* (1603–06), *The Life of Timon of Athens* (1604–06), *The Tragedy of Macbeth* (c.1606) and *The Tragedy of Antony and Cleopatra* (1606–07).

For one of these, *Timon*, Shakespeare was again working in collaboration, this time with, probably, the younger dramatist Thomas Middleton; it has recently been argued by the editors of the Oxford edition of the complete works of Middleton that the versions of *Macbeth* and *Measure for Measure* printed in the Folio are his later adaptations, dating from around 1616 and the early 1620s respectively, of the pieces that were performed at court in the early years of the seventeenth century (Taylor and Lavagnino 2007a). As far as *Timon* is concerned, the collaboration was not a success: there is no evidence that the play was ever performed in its time, either publicly or at court, and a long critical tradition has regarded the play as incomplete or unfinished; its story of a recklessly profligate aristocrat (nominally an ancient Greek but a type no doubt instantly recognisable from James's court) who turns on his false friends, exiles himself from his city and eventually dies showering curses on humankind was perhaps just too relentlessly misanthropic (and too crudely schematic) for the King's Men to risk.

Macbeth was an altogether more successful venture. Here Shakespeare provided his Scots king with a Scottish play, one which featured material on which he had written a tract, *Demonology* (1597), and which traced the back story of his own claim to the Scottish

---

Thomas Middleton (1580–1627)

Poet, playwright and prose writer

Leaving Oxford University for London just after 1600 without completing his studies, Middleton began his writing career as a poet, having already published three volumes of verse, starting with *The Wisdom of Solomon Paraphrased* (1597) and including a homage to Shakespeare's much-read narrative poem *The Ghost of Lucrece* (1600). He soon moved into writing for the theatre, first providing scripts co-written with Thomas Dekker (a long-term collaborator), Michael Drayton, Anthony Munday and John Webster (Henslowe records paying the team £8 for *Caesar's Fall, or, Two Shapes* on 22 May 1602) for the Lord Admiral's Men, and then establishing himself in his own right as sole author of a series of comedies for the Children of St Paul's, all written and performed between 1603 and 1606: *The Phoenix, Michaelmas Term, A Trick to Catch the Old One, A Mad World, My Masters* and *The Puritan Widow*. In 1606 Middleton provided the King's Men with *The Revenger's Tragedy*, a play in which the emblematic figure of the revenger, Vindice (a part devised for Richard Burbage), carries around the skull of his murdered lover in a black parody of the Prince of Denmark. He also wrote for them *A Yorkshire Tragedy* (c.1605), which was published in 1608 attributed to 'W. Shakespeare'; Middleton collaborated with Shakespeare on *Timon of Athens* (1604–06) and later revised parts of *Measure for Measure* and *Macbeth*. Combining his career as a commercial dramatist with pamphlet-writing and the provision of scripts for civic entertainments, Middleton was second only to Shakespeare among his contemporaries in his theatrical range: equally adept in city-based comedy (*A Chaste Maid in Cheapside*, 1613; and *The Roaring Girl*, co-authored with Dekker, 1611), tragicomedy (*The Witch*, c.1615) and tragedy: notably *Women Beware Women* (1621) and *The Changeling* (1622). This last was jointly written with William Rowley, another long-term colleague. Middleton's final play, *A Game at Chess*, was performed by the King's Men at the Globe in 1624, achieving what was, for its time, a phenomenal run of nine performances before the Privy Council, unnerved by its satirical portrayal of the Spanish Court, ordered the closure of the playhouse. *A Game at Chess* addressed contemporary power politics with audacious and unprecedented directness; whatever their genre, and whether sole- or jointly authored, Middleton's plays are characterised by the frankness with which they address matters of sex, power, class and religion.

throne in highly flattering terms. No trace of a court performance, if there was one, survives; but the play is the subject of one of the handful of eyewitness accounts of public playhouse performance. In 1611 the quack physician and astrologer Simon Forman (1552–1611) documented a performance of *Macbeth* at the Globe on 20 April, in which he appears to inveigle memorable details of the staging into his synopsis of the plot; thus 'ther was to be obserued, firste, howe Mackbeth and Bancko, 2 noble men of Scotland, Ridinge thorowe a wod, the[r] stode before them 3 women feiries or Nimphes'; 'when Mack Beth had murdred the kinge, the blod on his handes could not be washed of by any means, nor from his wiues handes which handled the bloodi daggers in hiding them'; and, during the banquet scene, as Macbeth stood up

> to drincke a Carouse to him, the ghoste of Banco came and sate down in his cheier be-hind him. And he turning A-bout to sit down Again sawe the goste of banco, which fronted him so, that he fell in-to a great passion of fear and fury, Vtteringe many wordes about his murder, by which, when they hard that Banco was Murdred they Suspected Mackbet.
>
> (Chambers 1930, 2: 237–38)

As a doctor himself, taking notes on the spectacle of a doctor taking notes, Forman took an interest in the sleepwalking scene: 'Obserue Also howe mackbetes quen did Rise in the night, in the night in her slepe, & walke and talked and confessed all & the doctor noted her wordes' (Chambers 1930, 2: 237–38).

Forman's testimony has been questioned, though it is now accepted as authentic; one of its implications is that the scenes which he does not mention (such as Macbeth's return to the witches and the Hecate dialogue [4.1.]) were yet to be added by Middleton. As well as telling us that the Globe staging had Banquo's ghost sit in Macbeth's chair and Macbeth and his Lady washing their hands after Duncan's murder onstage, the account has Macbeth and Banquo first enter 'Riding'. Scholars have been quick to accuse Forman of confusing what he saw on stage with Holinshed's account (and with the woodcut that illustrates it), but if we assume that he knew what he was documenting then this can be interpreted in three ways: that Macbeth and Banquo actually did enter the playhouse on horseback (presumably through the yard); that they used props or hobbyhorses; or that there was a recognised, non-mimetic convention for representing riding that did not involve real horses at all. According to Alan C. Dessen and Leslie Thompson's *A Dictionary of Stage Directions in English Drama, 1580–1642*, the latter two options appear to have been the most commonly used, with horses generally signified by offstage sound-effects or by characters entering wearing riding clothes (1999: 117, 181).

At one level, Foreman's account serves as a useful reminder of how ambiguous and partial is the evidence of actual staging practices presented by early modern playtexts; at another, this particular effect might also give us pause to reflect on the vitality and immediacy of the theatre's engagement with its own world. A strange, and perhaps unsettlingly anomalous, moment (they can never bring in a *horse*), the equine incursion would have been not just a spectacular entry (and perhaps, given the crowding in the yards, a potentially hazardous one) but also one which disrupted the play's field of performance with the corporeal reality of one of early modern England's central and most powerful cultural tokens, simultaneously commodity, beast of burden, war machine and symbol of prestige.

Blackfriars

Forman also provides eyewitness accounts of *The Winter's Tale* on 15 May 1611 and of *Cymbeline*, confirming that these were in the repertory by then; the first of these was subsequently performed at court in November 1611. *Antony and Cleopatra* is generally dated between 1606 and 1607; entered in the Stationers' Register on 20 May 1608, it appears to have been read or seen by the poet Barnabe Barnes (1571–1609) some time before this, as some of the phrasing in his play *The Devil's Charter*, staged at court by the King's Men on 2 February 1607 and published later in the year, recalls the action and imagery of Shakespeare's play. Shakespeare's last Roman play, and what we would regard as his final tragedy (though *Cymbeline* was designated as such in the Folio), *Coriolanus*, was probably written around 1608, though it was not printed until 1623.

The dating is suggested by theatrical and political factors as well as by the play's style. This is the first of Shakespeare's plays to show signs of having been conceived for performance at the Blackfriars (though there is no record of this). The King's Men recovered the playhouse from the Children of the Queen's Revels in 1608. One of the innovations brought about by the move to the indoor playhouse was the necessity of introducing *entre-acte* intervals in order to tend to the candles; the play has a clear five-act structure that is evidently of the period of the play's composition rather than retrospectively imposed by the Folio editors (as is the case with the Folio texts of plays written prior to 1608). The editor of the Oxford edition also finds aspects of the play's style cognisant with the ambience of the private playhouse: its 'sardonic tone, long passages of constitutional debate, and heavy use of legal terminology are well suited to a sophisticated audience with a high proportion of Inns of Court men' (Parker 1994: 88); Lucy Munro has recently argued (2007) that *Coriolanus* can also been seen as the King's Men's riposte to the satirical drama purveyed by the juvenile company that had recently vacated the building.

At the same time, the play also contains features which seem to strain against the confines of the Blackfriars: it is a large-scale public play punctuated by public (and potentially riotous) assemblies and pitched battles, presented before an audience of between five and six hundred, drawn from a much narrower social catchment than the two and a half thousand who might attend the Globe. In addition to its scenic machinery, one of the most important aspects of the Blackfriars was the quality of its musical facilities: having been occupied by a troupe of trained choristers performing work with a significant and sophisticated musical component, the Blackfriars distinguished itself from the Globe in terms of the extended range, variety and subtlety of the musical textures that it could accommodate.

Performances in the outdoor playhouses, punctuated by the sounds of drums, trumpets, gunfire, fireworks and thunder-effects, were bold, brash and, to respectable citizens' ears, disruptive and offensive (Bruce R. Smith writes that 'To popular imagination, brass and percussion seem to have been what these playing places were all about' [1999: 218]); the warmer and more intimate acoustic of the indoor playhouses nurtured the more melliflu-ous sounds of soprano voices, strings and woodwind: organ, flute, mandolin, viol, recorder and hautboy (oboe). Yet *Coriolanus* is a play that in a climactic crowd scene specifies that '*Trumpets, hautboys, drums, beat all together*' (5.4.44.s.d.): if this was heard within the walls of the Blackfriars, rather than at the Globe, the aural effect must have been shattering; generating, like the image of mutinous citizens gathered on the small stage in the opening scene, a sense of danger as well as excitement.

Perhaps this was in keeping with the play's topicality. It is generally agreed that the grain shortage that motivates the plebeian uprising at the start of the play was inspired by events in the Midlands in the summer of 1607, which saw a serious and prolonged outbreak of rioting prompted by food shortages; one of the matters at issue was whether this was a consequence of bad weather and poor harvests or of hoarding and inflationary price-fixing. This local dispute, also fuelled by popular opposition to land enclosures (whereby small-holders and tenant farmers were frequently dispossessed by rich landowners consolidating and converting arable land to pasture), reverberated on a national level: insurrection was always a source of worry, especially for the elite spectators at the Blackfriars, but the instability it augured resonated with other sources of anxiety, including the widespread opposition to King James's increasingly forceful attempts to assert his prerogative against Parliament.

The goodwill that had greeted James on his accession (and that had temporarily revived after the thwarting of the Gunpowder Plot in 1605) had evaporated, squandered by a king who had already unsuccessfully attempted to impose the unification of Scotland and England as Great Britain (the background to both *Macbeth* and *Lear*) upon a resistant Commons. He was also finding himself forced into ever more desperate revenue-gathering expedients in an attempt to deal with the rapidly escalating royal debt, which had stood at £300,000 at Elizabeth's death but had reached £1 million by the time her long-standing confidante and trusted advisor, William Cecil, Lord Burghley, took up the post of Lord Treasurer in 1608. To add to the sense of malaise, the first decade of the seventeenth century was one ravaged by recurrent plague outbreaks, resulting in frequent closures of the playhouses (78 out of 120 months between 1603 and 1613) and a casualty rate in London that reached nearly two hundred deaths a week in August to September 1609 (Barroll 1991: 217–26).

For Shakespeare, events in the Midlands may have been something experienced at close quarters: the landowner William Combe (d. 1610), who had sold him 107 acres of land in Old Stratford for £320 in 1602, wrote to the king's spymaster Robert Cecil (1563–1612), the Earl of Salisbury, on 2 June 1608 to report the 'dearth of corn in Warwickshire' and to report that 'the common people threaten to resist turning arable land into pasture' (Green 1857: 436–44). Following a period between 1602 and 1604 which he spent lodging with the family of the French Huguenot refugee Christopher Mountjoy in Silver Street, Cripplegate (and his involvement in 1612 as a witness in a lawsuit between Mountoy and former landlord's son-in-law; see Nicholl 2007), Shakespeare appears to have spent some time in Stratford-upon-Avon dealing with important family business.

In July 1605 he committed £440, a very substantial sum of money, to a half-interest in a property lease that secured him tithe income from land around Stratford-upon-Avon; two years later, on 5 June 1607, his elder daughter Susanna married the Stratford-based doctor John Hall (1575–1635), receiving a dowry that included over a hundred acres of family land. Susanna had been among those listed (as 'Susannam Shakespeere') by Stratford's ecclesiastical court at Easter the previous year as failing to receive Holy Communion, which has kindled suspicions of the persistence of a strain of recusancy within the Shakespeare family; Hall, however, was firmly Protestant and an active church-man, so presumably whatever Catholic sympathies Susanna might have harboured were dismissed, suppressed or silently accommodated. In February 1608 Susanna gave birth to a daughter, Elizabeth (whose death in 1670 marked the end of Shakespeare's family line), and the following September his mother died in Stratford at the age of sixty-eight.

Collaborations and departures

A grandfather, approaching his mid-forties in an age where the average man could expect to live into his early fifties, Shakespeare was now in the final phase of his professional association with the King's Men. In 1609, his sonnets were published, with or without his authorisation. Although, as Forman indicates, the King's Men continued to make dual use of the Globe and the Blackfriars, and to transfer plays between the two venues as well as to court, the indoor playhouse, in which Shakespeare had a one-seventh share, seems to have solicited from him work designed to make use of its scenic machinery and musical facilities, and also to engage in generic and formal experimentation, which was further encouraged by his entry into new collaborative partnerships.

The first of these was with the playwright, and reputed pimp and petty criminal, George Wilkins, whom Shakespeare may have encountered whilst lodging with the Mountjoys (Wilkins was another of the witnesses in the 1612 court case). Wilkins supplied the King's Men with *The Miseries of Enforced Marriage* in 1607, a play which represented what was for the King's Men a new foray into the territory of citizen comedy, and had co-authored the picaresque drama of *The Travels of the Three English Brothers* with John Day and William Rowley for Queen Anne's Men at the Red Bull in the same year. This play, which takes the eponymous siblings on a tour of Asia and Europe (and which incidentally includes a character appearance by the Lord Chamberlain's Men's departed clown, Will Kempe), was a response to the new interest in foreign travel that was being shown by young men of fashion. *Pericles*, published in 1609, is a product of co-authorship between Wilkins, responsible for the first third of the play, and Shakespeare, who wrote the remainder. Regarded with horror by Shakespearean scholars as loose and episodic in structure, meretricious and implausible in content, this retelling of a medieval romance (which Wilkins turned into a prose narrative from the play *The Painful Adventures of Pericles, Prince of Tyre*, published in 1608) was one of the King's Men's most successful plays: the quarto stated that it had been 'divers and sundry times acted by his Majesties servants, at the Globe on the Banck-side'.

Shortly after this came the two plays seen by Forman, *The Winter's Tale* and *Cymbeline*, both in 1611, and *The Tempest* (the closest Shakespeare comes to the masque format), which was performed at court on 1 November the same year. In these plays we see an enhanced use of music integrated with scenic spectacle, represented by such moments as the awakening of Hermione's statue, the visions encountered by Posthumous that culminate in the descent of Jupiter on an eagle, and the banquet in *The Tempest* that appears and, '*with a quaint device*' (3.3.53.s.d.), disappears. As ventures in tragicomedy, these late plays experiment with a genre whose early seventeenth-century format was defined by Francis Beaumont and John Fletcher, in works such as *Cupid's Revenge* (Queen's Revels, 1608) and *Philaster*, acquired by the King's Men in 1609.

Shakespeare's older plays continued to enjoy revivals at court, whose records for 1613 document total payments of £153 6s. 8d. to Heminges for fourteen plays, including, in addition to *Cardenio*, *Much Ado*, *The Tempest*, *The Winter's Tale* and *Othello*, and others identified as 'Sir John Falstaffe' and 'the Hotspur' (probably *1* or *2 Henry IV*).

The Two Noble Kinsmen, according to the title-page of the 1634 quarto, was performed 'at the Blackfriers ... with great applause', probably in the winter season of 1613–14. Its prologue ends a conventional plea for the audience's indulgence with the rueful observation that 'If this play do not keep/ A little dull time from us, we perceive/ Our losses fall so thick we must needs leave' (Prol. 30–33), a remark that has often been seen as an allusion to the misfortune that befell the King's Men at the Globe on 29 June 1613, when the playhouse burned down during a performance of *All Is True*. The event is documented in some detail by the poet and diplomat Sir Henry Wotton (1568–1639):

The Kings Players had a new Play called *All is True*, representing some principal pieces of the Reign of Henry 8, which was set forth with many extraordinary circumstances of Pomp and Majesty, even to the matting of the stage; the Knights of the Order, with their Georges and Garter, the Guards with their embroidered Coats, and the like: sufficient in truth within a while to make greatness very familiar, if not ridiculous. Now, King *Henry* making a masque at Cardinal *Wolseys* House, and certain Canons being shot off at his entry, some of the Paper, or other stuff wherewith one of them was stopped, did light on the Thatch, where being more attentive to the show, it kindled inwardly, and ran round like a train, consuming within less then an hour the whole House to the very grounds.

(Pearsall Smith 1907, 2: 32)

Miraculously, the disaster resulted in no serious casualties ('only one man had his Breeches set on fire, that would perhaps have broyled him, if he had not by the benefit of a provident wit put it out with bottle ale'); as another eyewitness, John Chamberlain, wrote to Ralph Winwood, the occupants managed to escape even though 'having but two narrow doores to get out' (McLure Thomson 1965: 1, 467).

Wotton's account is significant not only for its record of the Globe's demise but also for the evidence it furnishes of the playhouse's staging practices, and for the critical stance

John Fletcher (1579–1625)

Playwright

Educated at Eton and Cambridge University (which he entered at the age of eleven in 1591), Fletcher co-wrote his first play, *The Woman Hater*, in 1606. His collaborator was Francis Beaumont, with whom he wrote another dozen plays; in total, he authored or contributed to more than fifty plays, and counted among his co-authors the former child star Nathan Field, Philip Massinger, Thomas Middleton and Shakespeare. The nature of Beaumont and Fletcher's partnership has fuelled personal speculation: they were reported by John Aubrey as having 'lived together on the Bankside, not far from the playhouse, both bachelors; lay together ... had one wench in the house between them, which they did so admire; the same clothes and cloak, &c., between them', which implies that their closeness had a sexual as well as professional component. In the preface to the published edition of his first sole-authored work, *The Faithful Shepherdess* (performed by the Children of the Queen's Revels in 1607–08, published 1610), he offered his readers a definition of the new and perhaps for some baffling genre of tragicomedy, 'not so called in respect of mirth and killing, but in respect it wants deaths, which is enough to make it no tragedy, yet brings some near to it, which is enough to make it no comedy'. As a form that could legitimately accommodate both gods and 'mean people', Fletcherian tragicomedy offered a template for the Shakespearean romances that followed. Beaumont and Fletcher produced further collaborative works for the King's Men (*The Maid's Tragedy*, 1610; *A King and No King*, 1611; *Love's Pilgrimage*, 1616). He collaborated with Shakespeare on his last plays. Having written a sequel to *The Taming of the Shrew* entitled *The Tamer Tamed: Or, the Woman's Prize* (1611–12), a play in which Petruccio remarries after Kate's death and finds the tables turned on him, and which appears to have been designed to appeal to the substantial female component in the Blackfriars audience, Fletcher joined forces with Shakespeare to write the lost *Cardenio*, recorded as performed at court during the festive season of 1612–13 and again on 8 June 1613; *All Is True* (published in the Folio under the title *The Life of Henry VIII*); and *The Two Noble Kinsmen* (1613–14). After Shakespeare's retirement Fletcher assumed the role of the King's Men's principal dramatist.

that it adopts towards them: the narrative dwells upon the extraordinary and, it implies, somewhat excessive detail of the King's Men's staging, and indicates that making greatness 'familiar', apparently, carried with it the risk of breeding contempt. Even the king's own company, presenting a play which is, on the face of it, an unapologetic hagiography, was liable to the suspicion of offering potentially seditious material. The Globe was soon up and running again; almost a year to the day after the burning of the first building, on 30 June 1614, Chamberlain wrote to report that a friend had 'gone to the new Globe, to a play'; rebuilt on the same site with a tiled roof, it remained standing until, following the parliamentary ordinance that closed down the playhouses in 1642, it was demolished to make space for tenement housing in 1644. The Blackfriars playhouse experienced the same fate a decade later.

4 Final years

Welcombe

The Globe was rebuilt at the expense of the sharers, who each initially contributed £50–£60 towards the costs, but it appears that Shakespeare was not among them. In March 1613, Shakespeare had paid £140 for a property in London, the Blackfriars Gatehouse, entering into a trustee partnership with John Heminges, William Johnson and John Jackson which ensured that his wife would not have been entitled to a claim on the property after he died, though it is not known whether this was by design or by default. He may have been in Stratford-upon-Avon, or in London, during the course of the next year or so.

Whether or not he settled into the life of quiet retirement that biographical tradition has rather fondly imagined for him, his final years were not without personal incident. Shakespeare was peripherally involved in a local dispute over land enclosures that began in 1614 and lasted until 1615. William Combe (1586–1667) was the son of the man who had sold Shakespeare 107 acres in Old Stratford in 1602; working in league with Arthur Mainwaring (the steward to Thomas Egerton [1540–1617], the first Lord Ellesmere) and the lawyer William Replingham, he announced his intention of enclosing common land in Welcombe, a move that was opposed by Stratford council as an infringement of the rights of townspeople and tenant farmers. Shakespeare earned tithe income from his freeholds, and enclosure could have resulted in a reduction in it from the conversion of arable land into pasture, and his name was among the list of those compiled by the town council's clerk, Thomas Greene (c.1578–1641), as liable to be affected by the proposed move.

At the same time, Shakespeare secured an agreement (dated 28 October 1614, a month after Stratford council had unanimously voted to oppose the scheme by whatever legal means necessary) that promised recompense 'for all such loss, detriment and hindrance' suffered 'by reason of any enclosure or decay of tillage there meant and intended by the said William Replingham' (Schoenbaum 1977: 283). The charitable interpretation of Shakespeare's actions is that he positioned himself as a neutral party in the affair; but it is evident that he expended rather more energy in securing his own financial interests than in supporting the cause of the Stratford residents. In January 1615, determined to thwart Combe's plans, the local people (including a large contingent of women) took to the fields to fill in the ditches that he had started digging on the common land; when Combe responded with violence, the Stratford councillors obtained an injunction from Warwick Assizes preventing Combe from proceeding further. Replingham and Mainwaring accepted the terms of the ruling, but Combe persisted with a campaign of violent intimidation against the tenant farmers of Welcombe and the surrounding area, persisting with his attempt to enclose land even in the face of further court orders, finally conceding defeat in

1617. What Shakespeare made of all this is unknowable: the author of *King Lear* may have felt deeply for the plight of the poor whom Combe was robbing, imprisoning and rendering homeless; he might not have cared at all.

One sequence of personal events that he presumably did care about, since it may have played a part in his revisions to his will, occurred in early 1616. On 10 February his younger daughter Judith, aged thirty-one, married the local vintner Thomas Quiney (1589–c.1662); since the wedding took place illegally during the season of Lent, both were summoned before the consistory court at Worcester Cathedral. When Quiney failed to appear, he was excommunicated, as possibly was Judith also. Worse, on 26 March Quiney was hauled before Stratford's Church Court, which had jurisdiction over matters of sexual impropriety, charged with 'incontinence' (fornication) with one Margaret Wheeler (d. 1616), whom the parish register recorded as having been buried along with her child on 15 March. Compared to the fate suffered by Margaret Wheeler, Quiney's penalty was relatively mild: 'ordered to stand in a white sheet on three Sundays at church, he was quickly allowed instead to give 5 *s.* to the poor of the parish' (Honan 1999: 393). Whether Shakespeare forgave him so readily for the dishonour done to his daughter is another matter. In January 1616, before Quiney's misdemeanours were made public in what was known as the 'bawdy court', Shakespeare called in his lawyer, Francis Collins (d. 1616), to begin drafting his will; on 25 March, Collins returned to New Place to finalise it.

Will and testament

Peter Holland observes that probably 'nothing in Shakespeare's plays has provoked as much commentary' as this heavily revised document laced with deletions and interlineations (2004: 954), and there is little to add to this immense body of speculation here. Its first provision is to bequeath Judith £150, subject to stringent provisions; notably, while the initial draft also nominates 'my sonne in Law' (who is not named), this is deleted. A further legacy of £150 to Judith is guaranteed for three years later, again subject to provisions, and provided that 'such husbond as she shall att thend of the saied three yeares by marryed unto' is prepared to match the amount with lands of equal value. Shakespeare also provided for his sister Joan and her sons, and for Burbage, Heminges and Condell to buy memorial rings. The bulk of his estate went to his daughter Susanna Hall, who together with her husband was appointed as executor.

Anne Shakespeare is, notoriously, afforded one brief mention, in what appears to be a late addition inscribed towards the end of the final page: 'Item I gyve unto my wief my second best bed with the furniture'. Biographers have worried over the seemingly curt tone and derisory terms of this bequest, which has been interpreted as a calculated insult, perhaps born of terminal bitterness; though it has also been rather optimistically interpreted as a final token of affection, on the grounds that the second-best bed was the one the Shakespeares slept in, the best bed being reserved for guests. It has been suggested that Shakespeare made no specific provision for Anne because custom dictated that there was no need to, since as his widow she would have been entitled to one-third dower rights of the estate; however, this right was not universally available to exercise, and in some regions actively denied. Shakespeare offers no terms of endearment towards his spouse ('loving wife' was a standard formulation), but then he offers none to any other of his legatees. Shakespeare's will might offer evidence of a lifetime of marital unhappiness; it may encode a long history of intimacy, mutual affection and shared understanding; or it may signify a combination of elements of both. As with so much else to do with Shakespeare's life, we are finally left with what we want to believe about him, rather than with what can possibly be known.

Two monuments

On 23 April 1616, according to biographical consensus, Shakespeare was dead; he was buried two days later in the chancel of Holy Trinity Church. Legend has it that his death was brought on by a prodigious drinking bout with Jonson and the poet and dramatist Michael Drayton (1563–1631), though its actual cause is unknown. The grave was inscribed with the epitaph with which Part I began (see p. 4–5). A couple of years later, it is thought, a funerary monument was erected and set into the north wall of the chancel. This is generally identified as the work of Gheerart Janssen (who was also known as Garret Johnson), a sculptor of Dutch extraction whose father had set up a business in Southwark near by the Globe in the 1590s; Janssen had previously been paid £60 to erect a comparable monument in Holy Trinity for Shakespeare's acquaintance and Stratford's wealthiest resident John Combe (c.1561–1614). The half-length Cotswold limestone bust, set within an arch and flanked by perpendicular columns, shows a neatly moustached and goateed, bald and rather fleshy Shakespeare dressed in the garb of a well-to-do small-town worthy, holding a quill pen in one hand and a blank sheet of paper in the other.

Though it was commissioned by those who knew him in his lifetime and thus probably as accurate a likeness as we can expect, the bust has dismayed those who have hoped that Shakespeare might have looked more, well, like *Shakespeare*; whether this means a figure with the stature of a national hero or the romantic image of artistic genius. John Dover Wilson (1881–1969), the editor of the New Cambridge Shakespeare, described the Janssen bust as having the demeanour of a 'self-satisfied pork-butcher' (Schoenbaum 1977: 309), and the phrase stuck. For those who prefer a Shakespeare less redolent of chops and sausages, a range of images from the period compete for the claim of depicting Shakespeare as a leaner, younger and altogether sexier man, including, notably, the Chandos portrait, dating from 1610, and, in the most recent case, the Cobbe portrait, also identified as dating from this time. Such attributions continue to generate both excitement and scepticism.

The Stratford monument, disappointing – or refreshingly down-to-earth – as it is as an incarnation of Shakespeare, occupies a place in the history of Shakespearean iconography alongside the only other portrait of the writer that can be provisionally trusted to have received the endorsement of his colleagues: the engraving that adorns the title-page of what most would consider his more fitting memorial, the First Folio of 1623. For a long time this was attributed to Martin Droeshout (1601–51), whose connections with Janssen (they were members of the same Dutch refugee church congregation) may have led him to the commission; more recently, it has been persuasively argued (Edmond 1991) that the engraving was made by his uncle, Martin Droeshout the elder (c.1565–1642), a freeman of the Painter-Stationers' Company. This (for its time) old-fashioned and relatively crude representation postdates Shakespeare's death, though it presumably met with the approval of the compilers of the volume it fronts. Dominated by an immense forehead looming out of the page, the head served on a platter-like stiff collar that seems to disengage it from the disproportioned body, the visage has the iconic status of a global trademark; to observe that it has been reproduced on everything from banknotes to tea-towels is almost as much of a cliché as the use of the image itself.

An accompanying poem in the Folio by Ben Jonson claimed of the engraver that 'could he but have drawne his wit/ As well in brasse, as he hath hit/ His face', then 'the Print would then surpasse/ All that was ever writ in brasse', which endorses the accuracy of the portrait whilst acknowledging the gap between the man and what Jonson and the other Folio editors were already constructing as the myth. The story of the production of the first Folio is itself one of monumental and exceptional achievement, and its outcome is a book which assembled in one place all but two of the plays in the accepted canon (*Pericle*s was left out, though included in the second printing of the third edition of the Folio published in 1663–64; *The Two Noble Kinsmen* was published in quarto in 1634), including eighteen previously unpublished (amongst them *The Tempest*, *King John* and *Macbeth*).

In sixteenth- and seventeenth-century England the expensive, high-quality Folio format was for prestige publications, works of theology, philosophy or history; the undertaking to print the collected works of an English playwright was a bold, though not unprecedented, one. In 1616, Ben Jonson personally saw through the press his own *Works*, a book that included nine previously published plays, non-dramatic poems and masques and entertainments. It was meticulously crafted both to secure and promote Jonson's authorial status and, with its carefully worded and targeted dedications and acknowledgements, to embed his output within a network of patronage favours and obligations. Jonson and his publisher, William Stansby (d. 1638–39), presented the contents of the volume with a maximum of neoclassical and Latinate orchestration and embellishment, including a frontispiece which implanted the title within a representation of a monumental façade not unlike the arches which King James had passed through during the triumphal civic procession of 1604, and which incorporated the figures of Apollo and Bacchus, the muses of tragedy and comedy, panpipe-toting satyrs and a Roman amphitheatre; Jonson is depicted crowned with a poet's laurels and flanked by his library. This literary production attracted sceptical commentary. An anonymous wag in *Wits Recreations* (1640) posed the question, 'Pray tell me Ben, where does the mystery lurk,/ What others call a play you call a work', providing an answer that will perhaps ring true for many a subsequent reader or spectator of his plays: 'Ben's plays are works, when others works are plays.' Nonetheless, it represents a landmark in the history of modern literary authorship as an attempt to fashion Jonson's output into a singular, coherent and sequentially organised oeuvre that is firmly attached to a named and pictured originator who is everywhere a forceful presence within its pages.

The 1623 Folio bears some comparisons with Jonson's but departs from it in many important respects. Just as the earlier work sought to retrieve a literary corpus from the compromising and contaminating affiliations of playhouse practice and to effect a new conjunction of authorship and authority, so, too, the editors of Shakespeare's plays aimed to put into circulation a complete and authorised version of their former colleague's scripts that would be both definitive and robust enough to stand the test of time. A key difference here, though, is that while Jonson's *Works* were published while he was still very much alive, Shakespeare had no say in the construction of his posthumous literary identity. The performance and publication of Shakespeare's plays had not ended either with his retirement or with his death: the court accounts document performances of *Twelfth Night* and *Winter's Tale* in 1618 and *Pericles* in 1619, and *Twelfth Night* again in 1623; and quartos continued to be issued: *Richard II* (Q5, 1615), followed in 1622 by Q6 *1 Henry IV*, Q6 *Richard III*, Q4 *Hamlet*, Q4 *Romeo and Juliet* and, nearly twenty years after its first performances, the first quarto of *Othello*.

The publisher of this last work, Thomas Walkley, prefaced the text with an epistle which (contrary to the practice of every one of the previous Shakespeare quartos except *Troilus*) declared that 'To let forth a booke without an Epistle, were like to the old English proverbe, A blew coat without a badge'; so, 'the Author being dead', Walkley announced, 'I thought good to take that piece of worke upon mee'. The burden of the epistle, simply, is that 'the Authors name is sufficient to vent his worke'. It is significant that this rash of quarto publications just pre-empted the First Folio; and they were preceded by the unauthorised publication in 1619, by the bookseller Thomas Pavier (d. 1625), of ten plays (including four to which he owned the copyright). Four of these appeared in the first quarter of 1619: *The First Part of the Contention* and *The Second Part of the Contention* (i.e. *2* and *3 Henry VI*), *Pericles* and *A Yorkshire Tragedy*; however, the King's Men intervened, persuading the Lord Chamberlain, William Herbert, to write to the Stationers' Company to request that further publications be forestalled. The Company responded with the order that 'no playes that his Matyes playes do play shalbe printed wth out consent of som*me* of them' (Jackson 1957: 110; see also Berger and Lander 1999: 403–04); Pavier managed to put out quartos of *Merchant*, *Merry Wives*, *A Midsummer Night's Dream*, *King Lear*, *Henry V* and *The First Part of the Life of Sir John Oldcastle*, whilst rather clumsily trying to cover his tracks by falsifying the name of the publisher and altering some of the dates of publication to those of earlier editions, but if he had plans for a more ambitious collection (the ten plays were evidently designed as a set) these were now thwarted.

Their author being dead, the responsibility for putting the plays into Folio publication was jointly that of Shakespeare's actor colleagues John Heminges and Henry Condell, on behalf of the King's Men, and a syndicate of printers and publishers comprising William Jaggard (c.1568–1623), his son Isaac (1597–1627), John Smethwick (d. 1641), Edward Blount (d. 1632) and William Apsley, who between them owned the rights to the plays. The story of the laborious and lengthy process of printing the First Folio has been told by Charlton Hinman (1963), as has the Folio's subsequent fortunes as a commodity in the early modern book market (West 2001); here we will simply take account of some of the more salient features of the enterprise. Jonson's *Works* is structured chronologically as well as in terms of distinctions between his playhouse output and his court commissions. *Mr William Shakespeares Comedies, Histories, & Tragedies* is a feat of generic organisation (whose middle term formalises a new Shakespearean genre, the English history play), cataloguing the plays not, to the eternal frustration of scholars, according to their order of composition or performance but within three distinct categories that result in *The Tempest*, probably Shakespeare's last sole-authored play, being placed first and *The Tragedy of Cymbeline* (a play generally thought of as a tragicomedy) last, and the histories ranged chronologically. The comedies and tragedies seem, as Holland puts it, 'fairly randomly sequenced' (2004: 957), though it is perhaps worth noting, even as a happy accident, that the ordering means that the body of work that opens with the stage direction '*A tempestuous noise of thunder and lightning heard*' (*Tempest*, 1.1.0.s.d.) closes with the phrase ' … with such a peace' (*Cymbeline*, 5.6.485).

But the Folio's creators probably had far too many local challenges to deal with to contemplate such a grand design. Assembling the Folio involved the collation of a diverse range of written and printed materials which were, in a variety of senses, in multiple hands: quarto editions of previously published works, manuscripts, scribal transcripts, which between them represented inscriptions of the plays at different stages in their life. As well as undertaking the task of collating, and selecting between, these variants in order to produce what could be offered as definitive versions of the works, the Folio's compilers took pains to emphasise that these were *authoritative*. As Heminges and Condell reassured their 'great variety of readers', whereas they had previously been 'abused with divers stolen and surreptitious copies, maimed and deformed by the frauds and stealths of injurious impostors that expos'd them' (possibly a reference to Pavier's quartos), their publication offered Shakespeare's plays 'cured and perfect of their limbs, and all the rest absolute in their numbers, as he conceived them'. The prefatory materials, in addition to the appropriately fulsome joint dedication to the King's Men's key supporters, 'the Most Noble and Incomparable Pair of Brethren, William Earl of Pembroke etc.' and 'Philip Earl Montgomery etc.' (to whom they 'consecrate ... these remains of your servant Shakespeare'), eulogise the dead author, 'the happy imitator of nature' and 'most gentle expresser of it', and claim for him an instinctive fluency, such that 'His mind and hand went together: And what he thought, he uttered with that easinesse, that wee have scarce received from him a blot in his papers'. 'Would that he had blotted a thousand' was Jonson's later retort to this; though in the pages of the Folio he has nothing but praise for its author.

We have already noted his commentary upon the Droeshout engraving of Shakespeare on the title-page; what we might further note here is how unusual was this presentation of the author's relation to, and presence within, the work. In comparable books of the period – Jonson's *Works*, the King James Bible (1611), Sir Walter Ralegh's *History of the World* (1614) – the recto frontispiece provides an opportunity to display an emblematic conspectus of the contents; where the author is figured, as in Jonson's text, it is on the preceding verso. In the Folio, Shakespeare occupies the place where one might expect to see a visual summation of the world of his creation. Fortuitously or not, it reinforces Heminges and Condell's imagining of Shakespeare as a creative mind, and hand, at one with his work. And, as Jonson insisted, in some of the most straightforwardly generous writing of his entire career, it was a monument built to last, reflecting the transcendent genius in whose honour it was erected; coining the phrase that would echo throughout posterity, Jonson declared that his 'beloved' colleague was 'not of an age, but for all time'.

What happened next is too vast and rich a story to tell here. The First Folio sold well enough on its first printing to warrant a second edition in 1632 and a third in 1663, by which time Shakespeare's works had begun to establish a foothold in the newly re-opened English theatre, and the beginnings of a presence beyond it, that they have yet to relinquish. As Jonson put it to Shakespeare, 'Thou art a Moniment, without a tombe,/ And art alive still, while they booke doth live'. Shakespeare may have been laid to rest in 1616, but in 1623 his afterlife was only just beginning.

Chronology
1564–1644

1564	William Shakespeare (WS) born (baptised 26 April) in Stratford-upon-Avon, eldest son of John and Mary Shakespeare.
1570	Pope Pius V excommunicates Queen Elizabeth I and encourages her assassination.
1576	James Burbage erects London's first purpose-built permanent public playhouse, the Theatre, in Shoreditch.
1577	The Curtain built in Shoreditch.
1582	Licence issued to WS to marry Anne Hathaway (27 November).
1583	Birth of WS's daughter Susanna (baptised 26 May).
1584	Birth of WS's twins, Hamnet and Judith; the Rose built on Bankside; WS possibly begins association with Lord Strange's and Lord Admiral's Men.
1587	Execution of Mary, Queen of Scots.
1588	Defeat of the Spanish Armada.
1592	WS attacked in Robert Greene's *Groats-Worth of Wit*; Philip Henslowe's accounts list performances of 'Harey the vj' and 'Titus & Vespacia' (possibly a variant of *Titus Andronicus*); London playhouses close in response to recurrent outbreaks of plague and do not re-open until June 1594.
1593	*Venus and Adonis* published.
1594	*The Rape of Lucrece* published, dedicated to Henry Wriothesley, Earl of Southampton; Henslowe lists *Titus & Ondronicus*; Stationers' Register records *The Tamynge of a Shrowe*; *Titus Andronicus* and *The First Part of the Contention of the Two Famous Houses of York and Lancaster* published; *Comedy of Errors* performed at Gray's Inn; WS becomes a sharer in the Lord Chamberlain's Men.
1595	The Swan opens on Bankside; *The True Tragedy of Richard Duke of York and the Good King Henry the Sixth* published.
1596	John Shakespeare acquires a coat of arms and the title of 'gentleman'; WS's son Hamnet dies.
1597	First quartos of *Richard II*, *Richard III* and *Romeo and Juliet* published; Blackfriars playhouse built; Lord Chamberlain's Men perform at the Curtain.
1598	*Love's Labour's Lost* and *The Life of King Henry IV* published; WS listed as one of the 'principal comedians' in the cast list for Ben Jonson's *Every Man in His Humour*; WS praised in Francis Meres's *Palladis Tamia, Wit's Treasury*, which lists in addition to plays already published *The Two Gentlemen of Verona*, *The Comedy of Errors*, *A Midsummer Night's Dream*, *The Merchant of Venice* and the lost *Love's Labour's Won*.

1599	Lord Chamberlain's Men open the Globe playhouse, built from recycled materials of the demolished Theatre; Thomas Platter records performance of *Julius Caesar* at the Globe; second quarto of *Romeo and Juliet* published; Robert Devereux, Earl of Essex, leads an expeditionary force to Ireland to suppress uprising led by Hugh O'Neill, Earl of Tyrone; he returns at the end of the year in disgrace.
1600	Publication of *The Second Part of King Henry IV*, *The Merchant of Venice*, *The Life of Henry V*, *Much Ado about Nothing* and *A Midsummer Night's Dream*; Fortune playhouse built by Philip Henslowe and Edward Alleyn.
1601	Death of John Shakespeare; 'Let the bird of loudest lay' published; Earl of Essex leads an abortive uprising against the queen, fails and is executed.
1602	*The Merry Wives of Windsor* published; *Hamlet* entered in Stationers' Register. WS acquires substantial property interests in Stratford-upon-Avon; *Twelfth Night* performed at Middle Temple.
1603	Death of Queen Elizabeth I (24 March) and accession of James I; Lord Chamberlain's Men become the King's Men; first quarto of *Hamlet* published.
1604	The Revels Accounts record court performances of *Othello*, *The Merry Wives of Windsor*, *Measure for Measure* and *The Comedy of Errors*; second quarto of *Hamlet* published; James secures peace treaty with Spain.
1605	Revels Accounts record performances of *Love's Labour's Lost*, *Henry V* and *The Merchant of Venice*; Gunpowder Plot discovered and its perpetrators arrested and executed.
1606	'An Act to Restrain Abuses of Players' passed.
1607	Death of WS's brother Edmund; WS's daughter Susanna marries John Hall; grain shortages provoke rioting in the Midlands.
1608	The King's Men assume occupancy of the Blackfriars playhouse.
1609	*Sonnets*, *Troilus and Cressida* and *Pericles* published.
1610	James dismisses Parliament.
1611	King James Bible published; Revels Accounts record court performances of *The Tempest* and *The Winter's Tale*; Simon Forman records performances of *The Winter's Tale*, *Cymbeline* and *Macbeth* at the Globe.
1612	Women accused of witchcraft executed in Lancashire.
1613	The Globe playhouse is destroyed by fire during a performance of WS and John Fletcher's *All Is True* (*The Life of Henry VIII*); WS acquires the Gatehouse in Blackfriars.
1614	The rebuilt (second) Globe opens; Henslowe builds the Hope playhouse on Bankside; James calls and dismisses the 'Addled' Parliament; WS involved in disputes over William Combe's attempts to enclose common land around Stratford-upon-Avon.
1616	WS's daughter Judith marries Thomas Quiney; WS dies (23 April); Ben Jonson publishes his *Works* in Folio.
1619	Thomas Pavier attempts unauthorised publication of ten plays attributed to WS; black slavery instituted in Virginia.
1622	*Othello* published.
1623	*Mr William Shakespeares Comedies, Histories & Tragedies* published in Folio; death of Anne Shakespeare.

1625	Death of James I; accession of Charles I.
1632	Second Folio published.
1634	*The Two Noble Kinsmen* published.
1642	Outbreak of English Civil War enforces the closure of the playhouses.
1644	Second Globe playhouse demolished.

Part II
Works

A catalogue

Among the many challenges faced by John Heminges and Henry Condell in constructing the first Folio, not the least was deciding not only what materials to incorporate, what to exclude, but also how to order, organise and categorise them. With regard to the former, Shakespeare's first editors included eighteen plays that had previously been issued in quarto (or, in one instance, octavo) and eighteen previously unpublished; they chose not to include the narrative poems, the sonnets, two works written in collaboration (*Pericles* and *The Two Noble Kinsmen*), two plays now lost (*Love's Labours Won* and *Cardenio*) and the minor poems published in various turn-of-the-seventeenth-century anthologies. Thus, the Folio compilers conferred a semblance of unity and coherence upon a heterogeneous body of playscripts by regularising their texts and distributing them according to the tripartite generic division between comedies, histories and tragedies.

By so doing, they established the fundamental contours of a canon that, supplemented by the works that Heminges and Condell opted to overlook, continues to define the Shakespearean reading experience and its associated critical and performance activities. The Folio's 'catalogue' of 'the severall Comedies, Histories, and Tragedies contained in this Volume' yields some anomolies: *Troilus and Cressida*, as a late addition, is not listed, and it appears in the generic interstices between the histories and the tragedies; *Cymbeline* is placed as the last of the tragedies. Its distinctions have also been modified and disputed, as scholars, editors, readers and theatre practitioners have refined and problematised Shakespeare's genres, subdividing the comedies into, for example, romantic comedies, problem plays and Late Romances; querying the positioning of *Henry VIII* at the end of a group with which it has less in common than with the last plays; and wondering whether *The Life of Timon of Athens*, as its title suggests, should really be located (as it is in the Folio) between *Romeo and Juliet* and *Julius Caesar*. For readers habituated to the chronological ordering of Shakespeare's works, the Folio's sequencing may seem odd and even arbitrary: the first play, *The Tempest*, is the one that is generally assumed to be Shakespeare's last sole-authored work, and this is followed by *The Two Gentlemen of Verona*, equally widely regarded as one of his earliest. The histories are printed in order of reign, not of composition and publication. The final Roman tragedy, *Coriolanus*, which deals with the historically earliest events, is followed by *Titus Andronicus*, a play nominally set in the fourth century AD but comprised of sheer fantasy.

Editorial and critical tradition has responded to the Folio's ordering of Shakespeare by re-ordering strategies of its own, usually in combinations of the generic and the chronological. With the exception of the RSC-sanctioned *Complete Works*, which claims to edit the Folio 'in its own right' (Bate and Rasmussen 2007: 53) for the first time in three centuries (and yet which includes the non-Folio plays and poems), and the single-volume edition of the Arden Shakespeare (which prints the plays alphabetically, *All's Well* to *The Winter's Tale*), many of the widely used modern editions of Shakespeare organise the canon chronologically, sometimes subdividing by form and genre (between comedies, histories, tragedies, romances and poems in the case of the Riverside Shakespeare [second edition, 1997]; between plays and poems for the Signet Classic Shakespeare [1972]). The conjectural order of the works' composition, performance and publication also structures the Oxford and Norton editions to which the current volume refers, though in this instance plays and poems are jointly accommodated, and this accordingly provides the broad shape for this section.

What needs to be borne in mind, however, is that the ordering or dating of a significant number of Shakespeare's plays – especially those not printed until 1623 – is at best conjectural. The twenty-five sections that comprise Part II of this book address the plays and poems individually and in groups, and from a variety of angles, on the basis of Oxford's dating, beginning with the earliest works and concluding with the last; but they do so on the understanding that the works could be grouped, ordered and combined in very different ways. For the Oxford editors, *The Two Gentlemen of Verona* is Shakespeare's earliest work and the keynote entry to their edition; for the Riverside and Signet, it is *The Comedy of Errors*; for Oxford and Riverside, *Titus Andronicus* is the first tragedy; for Signet, *Richard III*. Oxford broke with editorial tradition by placing *The First Part of Henry the Sixth* after Parts 2 and 3 (and after *Titus*), reflecting their view that its was composed as a 'prequel' after the success of the earlier plays. Such differences matter because they help to shape perceptions of the relations between the works, as well as, more contentiously, of their maker's progression or development (or perhaps even decline) as a creative artist.

Each section addresses a work or group of works, offering, in most cases, an overview and account of the play (though the emphases vary from case to case), identifying key characteristics, idiosyncrasies, issues and controversies. Inset boxes detail relevant factual information and reliable conjecture, listing dates of composition, early performance and publication; authorship (whether sole or collaborative); and likely sources and influences. Also listed are significant modern stage productions and screen versions, together with their important personnel (directors, lead actors), and a sample of the offshoots, spin-offs and adaptations that the work has generated. Each section concludes with a short, indicative list of further reading. In order to avoid undue repetition, I have avoided multiple citations of critical works that are relevant across works, genres and groups of plays. With a few exceptions, I have also not listed individual entries in widely used series of guides, companions, textbooks, critical anthologies, and stage and screen histories, assuming that these, together with the critical introductions and apparatus of the major scholarly editions of Shakespeare's works, will be an obvious first port of call for readers wishing to take their investigations further.

The following sections can be read in – almost – any order.

Henry VI, Parts 1, 2 *and* 3

Date, text and authorship

'Harry the vi' performed at Rose 3 March 1592; *Part 1*, c.1590; F 1623; *Part 2,* c.1590, as *The First Part of the Contention of the Two Famous Houses of York and Lancaster,* Q1 1594; Q2 1600; Q3 1619; F 1623; *Part 3*, c.1590; as *The True Tragedy of Richard, Duke of York,* O, 1595; Q2 1600; Q3 1619; F 1623. Conjectured as co-authored with George Peele, Robert Greene and Thomas Nashe.

Sources and influences

Edward Hall, *The Union of the Two Noble and Illustre Famelies of Lancastre and Yorke* (1548); Raphael Holinshed, *Chronicles of England, Scotland and Ireland* (1577; second edition 1587); Geoffrey of Monmouth, *Historia Regum Britanniae* (c.1136); Robert Fabyan, *New Chronicles of England and France* (1516); Jean Froissart, *Chronicles* (trans. Lord Berners, 1523–25); John Stow, *Chronicles of England* (1580).

On stage

SMT (Shakespeare Memorial Theatre), 1906 (dir. Frank Benson); Birmingham Repertory Theatre, 1951–53 (dir. Barry Jackson and Douglas Seale); *The Wars of the Roses,* RSC, 1963 (dir. Peter Hall and John Barton; Henry: David Warner; Margaret: Peggy Ashcroft; Richard: Ian Holm); *Il gioco del potenti,* Piccolo Teatro di Milano, 1965 (dir. Giorgio Strehler); RSC, 1977 (dir. Terry Hands; Henry: Alan Howard; Margaret: Helen Mirren; Richard: Anton Lesser); *The Wars of the Roses,* English Shakespeare Company, 1987 (dir. Michael Bogdanov; Henry: Paul Brennan; Margaret: June Watson; Richard: Andrew Jarvis; Cade: Michael Pennington); *The Plantagenets,* RSC, 1988 (dir. Adrian Noble; Henry: Ralph Fiennes; Margaret: Penny Downie; Richard: Anton Lesser); RSC, 2000 (dir. Michael Boyd; Henry: David Oyelowo: Margaret: Fiona Bell; Richard: Aidan McArdle); *Rose Rage,* Propeller, UK, 2001 (dir. Edward Hall; Henry: Jonathan McGuinness: Margaret: Robert Hands; Richard: Richard Clothier); RSC, 2006, 2008 (dir. Michael Boyd; Henry: Chuk Iwuiji; Margaret: Katy Stephens; Richard: Jonathan Slinger).

On screen

An Age of Kings, BBC TV, UK, 1960 (dir. Michael Hayes; Henry: Terry Scully; Margaret: Mary Morris; Richard: Paul Daneman; Joan la Pucelle: Eileen Atkins); *The Wars of the Roses,* BBC TV, 1965 (dir. Michael Bakewell; broadcast version of 1963 RSC production); BBC Television Shakespeare, UK, 1983 (dir. Jane Howell; Henry: Peter Benson; Queen Margaret: Julia Foster; Richard: Ron Cook; Talbot/Cade: Trevor Peacock); *The Wars of the Roses,* English Shakespeare Company, UK, 1990 (dir. Michael Bogdanov; video record of 1987 English Shakespeare Company stage production).

Alarums and excursions

When the great Victorian Shakespearean actor-manager Frank Benson added to his company's repertoire the third part of *Henry VI* in order to stage the three parts of *Henry VI* together as part of what was billed as a 'Week of Kings' at the Shakespeare Memorial Theatre, Stratford-upon-Avon, in May 1906, he was venturing upon an undertaking that was unprecedented in English – and, indeed, world – theatre. Infrequently revived even individually since the seventeenth century (and then invariably in heavily cut and adapted forms), the plays collectively had been ignored or dismissed by critics as immature hackwork; on this occasion, although the season was put together at such speed that there was only enough rehearsal time to run through the last act of *Henry VI, Part 3*, the plays were met with surprised acclaim. The texts were still drastically edited, for reasons of length but also to accommodate the demands of the scenic theatre – so much so that the *Athenaeum*'s reviewer complained that the productions 'suffered so much from cutting, contraction, and transposition in order to give intervals long enough to permit the changing of scenery and costumes … Many might have wished to have less scenery and more Shakespeare' (Trewin 1960: 156). Even so, Benson had sufficient confidence in his material to announce to his audience at the final curtain call that the performances had communicated Shakespeare's 'philosophy of History and his patriotic desire to point out the evils of civil war' (Hattaway 1990: 39).

By presenting the three parts as a sequence and by laying claim, in this instance, to a liberal-nationalist agenda that also ascribed to the plays a coherent intellectual and moral purpose, Benson anticipated their subsequent stage history in the later twentieth and early twenty-first century, though it would be nearly half a century before they would be seen as a group again, in Sir Barry Jackson and Douglas Seale's staging at the Birmingham Repertory Theatre in 1953. This time, Jackson and Seale had the scholarly backing, and subsequent endorsement, of the historicist critic E. M. W. Tillyard (see 'Criticism', pp. 303–11), whose *Shakespeare's History Plays* had a decade earlier advanced the case for treating the works as a planned sequence, solely authored by Shakespeare, that articulates a clear political vision rooted in order and degree, arguing that

> Behind all the confusion of civil war, and the more precious and emphatic because of the confusion, is the belief that the world is part of the eternal law and that earthly mutability … is itself a part of a greater and permanent pattern.
>
> (Tillyard 1962: 150)

Jackson and Seale's reading was bleaker than Tillyard's; though the second and third parts had been staged under the auspices of the Festival of Britain in 1951, and the complete cycle as part of the Coronation celebrations two years later, the tone was sombre: *Part 3* ended not with King Edward's

> Sound drums and trumpets – farewell, sour annoy!
> For here, I hope, begins our lasting joy.
>
> (5.7.45–46)

but with the interpolated opening lines of the play whose action would prove this hope desperately short lived: 'Now is the winter of our discontent … ' (*Richard III*, 1.1.1.).

Timed to coincide, though somewhat ambivalently, with two moments of national self-definition, the Birmingham Rep's *Henry VI* cycle established the postwar British theatre's pattern of staging these works in terms of large-scale events in which Shakespeare's earliest works were reconceived as a whole larger than its disparate constituent parts, serving as an opportunity to engage questions of national history and identity on an epic scale. It was followed in 1963 by Peter Hall and John Barton's three-part adaptation of the *Henry VI* plays and *Richard III*, *The Wars of the Roses*, for the Royal Shakespeare Company, productions which were instrumental in defining the company's identity (the following year the cycle was revived and presented in sequence with the second tetralogy); in 1977 by Terry Hands's virtually uncut trilogy also for the RSC, which performed a similar function for the company in the 1970s; in 1987 (as *The Wars of the Roses*) by the English Shakespeare Company under the direction of Michael Bogdanov, and again, a year later, by the RSC's *The Plantagenets*; and in 2000 by *Rose Rage*, a two-part adaptation for Edward Hall's Propeller Company, as well as by the productions that formed part of the RSC's *This England* cycle in the same year. The director on this occasion was Michael Boyd, who was also responsible for what is at the time of writing the latest staging of these histories, the RSC's in 2007–08, when for the first time since 1964 they were offered as part of a complete History Cycle that began with *Richard II* and ended with *Richard III*.

What the plays have lacked in terms of both frequency of productions and individual prestige has been more than compensated for by these productions' institutional significance and critical and popular impact; and, given that ventures on this scale would be impossible to mount professionally outside of the environment of a large-scale, state-funded theatre organisation like the RSC, this tradition is uniquely definitive of the dominant mode of English Shakespearean history in performance. The plays have been filmed for BBC Television three times: as *An Age of Kings* in 1960, for the televised version of the RSC's *Wars of the Roses* in 1965 (a feat described by its director as 'one of the most ambitious enterprises' ever undertaken by the Corporation, akin to the televising of 'the Coronation or the World Cup' [Bakewell 1970: 231]) and for the BBC Television Shakespeare in 1983, and broadcast as many times on BBC radio. There have been some fairly recent instances of the plays being staged singly (in 1992, *Henry VI, Part 3* was presented at Stafford Castle in repertory with *Richard III*, and a touring production of the same play – subtitled *The Battle for the Throne* – was directed by Katie Mitchell for the RSC in 1994), but these have been infrequent; as far as the modern British – or, more precisely, English – theatre is concerned, the plays work best supersized.

The theatrical logic of presenting the *Henry VI* plays cyclically (and florally, colour-coded in relation to the familiar historical referent of the Wars of the Roses) is entirely comprehensible; but in relation to their original circumstances of composition and performance it is anachronistic. Cyclical and sequential staging is textually mandated in the sense that it follows the order in which the plays are presented in the Folio, where *The Second Part of Henry VI* is preceded by *The First Part of Henry VI* and succeeded by *The Third Part of Henry VI*. However, the chronological sequence that Heminges and Condell devised for the Folio did not reflect the plays' order of writing. The 1623 publication of *Part 1* was the play's first appearance in print, and the textual evidence points to the likelihood that it postdated the second and third parts, which were published, respectively in quarto and octavo, in 1594 and 1595.

Whereas the Folio titles, centralising the role of the reigning monarch, confer continuity upon the three works as well as integrating them into the full run of histories, the title pages of the earlier editions advertised plays with different, and diverse, sources of interest and appeal. *Henry VI, Part 2* in quarto is *The First Part of the Contention of the Two Famous Houses of York and Lancaster, with the Death of the Good Duke Humphrey*, its subtitles also promising the banishment and death of the Duke of Suffolk, the demise of the Cardinal of Winchester, the Jack Cade rebellion and the Duke of York's bid for the Crown. *Part 3* was offered as *The True Tragedy of Richard, Duke of York*, featuring the death of Henry VI (a figure not mentioned on the title page of *Contention*), and promoted as having been played 'sundrie times' by the Earl of Pembroke's Men. Both texts are considerably shorter than the Folio versions, *Contention* by one-third, *True Tragedy* by about a thousand lines, and show significant variations; their authority and provenance remain disputed. For some editors, including those of the Oxford edition (on which the Norton edition cited in this volume is based), both are pirated texts memorially reconstructed by rogue players from an abridgement of the manuscripts that eventually formed the basis for the Folio; for others, they are early drafts of works that Shakespeare subsequently revised.

However, they appear to be fairly directly derived from performance: in places, players' names are offered as speech prefixes instead of those of characters ([George] Bevis and [John] Holland in *Contention*, 4.2; Gabriel, Sinklo and Humfrey in *True Tragedy*, 1.2 and 3.1), and the stage directions are often particularly full:

> *Enter at one door* [HORNER] *the armourer and his* NEIGHBOURS, *drinking to him so much that he is drunken; and he enters with a drum*[mer] *before him and* [carrying] *his staff with a sandbag fastened to it ...*
>
> (*Contention*, 2.3.58.s.d.)

> *Enter the* DUCHESS, *Dame Eleanor Cobham, barefoot,* [with] *a white sheet about her, written verses pinned on her back,* [and carrying a] *wax candle in her hand;* [she is] *accompanied with the* [two] SHERIFFS *of London ...*
>
> (*Contention*, 2.4.17.s.d.)

> *Alarums within, and the chambers be discharged like as it were a fight at sea. And then enter the* CAPTAIN *of the ship ...*
>
> (*Contention*, 4.1.1.s.d.)

> *Three suns appear in the air*
>
> (*True Tragedy*, 2.1.21.s.d.)

> *Enter* KING HENRY, *disguised, with a prayer-book*
>
> (*True Tragedy*, 3.1.12.s.d.)

> GEORGE OF CLARENCE *Father of Warwick, know you what this means?*
>   [He] *takes his red rose out of his hat and throws it at* WARWICK
>
> (*True Tragedy,* 5.1.84.s.d)

The theatrical vocabulary is iconic and emblematic, the plays' incident-packed narrative of civil feud and insurrection realised through sharply visualised confrontations and moments of baroque violence; in which the seemingly endless succession of severed heads paraded onstage provides both a prop counterpart to the pitch-preserved remnants of executed traitors adorning the city gates and river bridges of Shakespeare's London and a compellingly graphic figuration of the disintegrating body politic of fifteenth-century England.

Let's kill all the lawyers

The Folio editors' decision to re-entitle the two previously published *Henry VI* plays suggests that their narrative focus, and, in theory, England's ultimate locus of regal authority, lies in the figure who is the, at least, nominal monarch for their duration. In practice, as the earlier titles suggest, the plays are characterised by proliferating storylines and shifting centres of gravity, amidst which King Henry, who is from one perspective a kind of saint and from another a holy fool, is mostly a passive, reactive presence. *Contention* shows the King progressively weakened both by the manoeuvring of his prime antagonist, Richard, Duke of York, and by that of dissenting factions within his own House of Lancaster, including the ambitious Duke of Suffolk, secret lover of his new French Queen, Margaret of Anjou, and his ally the scheming Bishop of Winchester. In the course of the play, Suffolk has the King's saintly Lord Protector, the Duke of Gloucester, murdered in his bed (an incident staged in a typically sensational discovery scene [3.2.]), is exposed, banished and, while en route to France, captured by pirates and executed; out of consideration for the Queen, his companion retrieves Suffolk's head and returns it to her as a grisly keepsake; the next time she appears, she is seen cradling it, mourning her dead lover and openly contemptuous of her timid husband.

The breadth of the plays' historical canvas is such that the in-fighting is not confined to the nobility; disorder is seen to extend to every corner and level of society. When Richard, Duke of York, decamps to Ireland to suppress a rebellion there, he leaves in place plans for an uprising led by the plebeian Jack Cade. Cade is a clownish demagogue who, declaring himself the descendent of Edmund Mortimer, harnesses what the text presents as a rather arbitrary and vaguely defined sense of popular grievance (the source of which, as an opening exchange between two nameless rebels reveals, is little more than that 'Virtue is not regarded in handicraftsmen' and that 'the King's Council are no good workmen' [4.2.8–12]), promises the overthrow of the aristocracy and the liquidation of class enemies ('The first thing we do', announces his right-hand man Dick the Butcher, 'let's kill all the lawyers' [4.2.68]: the line usually gets a big laugh in the theatre), declares literacy a capital crime and predicts the imminent transformation of England into a festive utopia:

> There shall be in England seven halfpenny loaves sold for a penny, the three-hooped pot shall have ten hoops, and I will make it felony to drink small beer. All the realm shall be in common, and in Cheapside shall my palfrey go to grass.
>
> (4.2.58–61)

Comic though this may seem at the outset (Cade's claims are manifestly both preposterous and contradictory, combining radically democratic rhetoric with an equally radical self-aggrandisement), things soon turn ugly.

First the mob executes the hapless, mild-mannered Clerk of Grantham for the crime of being able to write his own name ('hang him with his pen and inkhorn about his neck' [4.2.96]), then takes on the King's forces led by Sir Humphrey Stafford, who, though one of Henry's most able and experienced soldiers, is somewhat lacking in diplomatic skills:

> Rebellious hinds, the filth and scum of Kent,
> Marked for the gallows, lay your weapons down,
> Home to your cottages ...
>
> (4.2.109–11)

Slain in a fight which sees Dick, the butcher of Ashford, applying the skills of his trade to the targets of the Commons' wrath ('thou behaved'st thyself as if thou hadst been in thine own slaughterhouse' [4.3.3–5]), Stafford, along with his brother, is subjected to the posthumous degradation of being dragged at Cade's horse's heels to London while his vanquisher sports his armour.

The presence of the butcher as violent agent and sardonic intermediary between the rebels and the audience is key here: carnivalesque in the sense that it involves a dark inversion of the hierarchal relations between the rulers and the ruled that recalls the holiday rituals of traditions of popular festivity extending back to the Roman Saturnalia, Cade's rebellion also invokes carnival's etymological connection with slaughter and meat production. Arriving in the capital, Cade pronounces himself lord of the city and, in another festive gesture that epitomises the rebellion's ghastly carnivalesque spirit, declares that the 'Pissing Conduit' (a water fountain in Cheapside used by poorer Londoners) shall 'run nothing but claret wine this first year of our reign' (4.6.3–4). Cade's beneficence, here figured in terms of an incontinence that is both proverbial and mythical, is bottomless, and without foundation; as the carnage escalates, so too his malevolence assumes ever more absurd and sadistic forms.

As a denizen of Kent (incidentally one of the handful of English counties to this day still retaining a selective secondary education system), Cade is comically well placed to condemn his captive Lord Saye for having 'most traitorously corrupted the youth of the realm in erecting a grammar school' (4.7.27–28), but he becomes altogether less amusing when, interpreting Saye's palsy-induced quivering as insolence, he orders his decapitation in order to see 'if his head will stand steadier on a pole or no' (4.7.86). The episode culminates in a piece of macabre puppetry:

Enter two with the Lord Saye's head and Sir James Cromer's upon two poles.

CADE But is this not braver? Let them kiss one another, for they loved well when they were alive.
[*The two heads are made to kiss*]
Now part them again, lest they consult about the giving up of some more towns in France.

(4.7.137–41)

The violation of the noblemen is a kind of posthumous sexual assault, manipulated in death into a perverse homoerotic tryst that couples illicit intimacy with treachery, and immediately follows a short sequence, printed in the quarto but not in the Folio, in which Dick the butcher leeringly recounts his rape of a sergeant's wife; the episode ends with Cade urging the rebels to begin a campaign of mass rape whilst promenading his victims' heads through the streets.

It is here, at the very point that the street party is about to become very nasty indeed, as the aggression and sexual violence seem set to spiral completely out of control (Cade's own orders having degenerated into mere ranting – 'Up Fish Street! Down Saint Magnus' Corner! Kill and knock down! Throw them into the Thames!' [4.7.145–46]), that order is restored, in the form of the intervention of the Duke of Buckingham and Lord Clifford, who, simply by invoking the patriotic shade of the revered Henry V, effortlessly persuade Cade's followers to forsake their allegiance to their erstwhile leader and return to the fold of loyal citizenry. And it is also at this point, unexpectedly, that the blackly comic monster Cade affords a realistic but also quietly subversive perspective upon the restoration of official governance and the rebels' surrender to authority: if there is some justice in his recognition of the mob's fickle self-interest when he asks, 'Was ever feather so lightly blown to and fro as this multitude?', there is also a wry recognition of the dangerously manipulative potential of state propaganda in his observation that 'The name of Henry the Fifth hales them to an hundred mischiefs' (4.7.197–99).

Cade ends the play in a surprisingly sympathetic light. When he next appears, he is starving, and a fugitive; digging for herbs in the garden of a member of the minor gentry, Alexander Iden, he is discovered, challenges his discoverer to single combat and, in his weakened state, is killed. For the conservative Tillyard, Iden is 'the symbol of degree' and the embodiment of 'blameless orderliness' (1962: 175, 159), and thus Cade's fate at his hands is a fair and apt act of closure; yet there is something a touch excessive, or obsessive, in his repeated stabbing of a Cade who is already dead and in his statement that he will drag the body 'Unto a dunghill, which shall be thy grave' (4.9.78). Despite his claim at the start of the scene that he seeks 'not to wax great by others' waning' (4.9.18), he is quick enough to profit from his action, and to join the ranks of Henry's noblemen. Cade, meanwhile, is dignified and rather courageous, and can legitimately claim that he is 'vanquished by famine, not by valour' (4.9.72).

Iden's presentation of Cade's head to Henry in the following scene provides a narrative bridge between the Commons rebellion and the Yorkist revolt; no sooner has the newly knighted Iden risen from his knees than the Queen appears with York's sworn enemy, the Duke of Somerset. It is the cue for the outraged York to finally lay explicit claim to the Crown, a speech act which instantly is afforded a visual correlative: one of the core items in the plays' visual repertoire is the use of opposing entry doors to map forces in contention, and in this scene the entry on the one side of '*York's sons* EDWARD *and crookback* RICHARD *with [a] drum[mer] and soldiers*' is immediately mirrored by Henry's ally 'CLIFFORD *and his son, with [a] drum[mer] and soldiers*' (5.1.119–20). The opposition of a pair and a trio of father and sons is both schematic and prescient, for this is the starting round in a conflict that by the end of the play has led to the death of Clifford at York's hands and the discovery of his body by his own son, the defeat of Henry at the battle of Saint Albans and York apparently poised to take the throne, and, by the end of the play that follows, to the descent of the country into a civil war whose apocalyptic dimensions are limned by Young Clifford as he stands and declaims over his father's corpse:

> O, let the vile world end,
> And the premisèd flames of the last day
> Knit earth and heaven together.

(5.3.40–42)

To catch the English Crown

The cycle of retribution, driven by the actions of murdered and murdering fathers and sons, provides the narrative spine of the *True Tragedy*, a play in which the intensification of viciousness is accompanied by the abandonment of even the residual veneer of the chivalric code professed, if not adhered to, in the previous play. It opens in a state of emergency: where *Contention* had started with a relatively stately '*Flourish of trumpets, then hautboys*' (1.1.s.d.), *True Tragedy* crashes into life with a warlike '*Alarum*' (1.1.s.d.), the King and his entourage on the run, a display of bloodied swords and a severed head (the Duke of Somerset's), and the kingmaker, the Earl of Warwick, urging the Duke of York to assume the throne. In the confrontation between the houses of Lancaster and York that follows, in which the relative legitimacy of their respective claims to the Crown is contested, it is very evident that power resides less in the royal word than in the blade, the mailed fist and, here, the boot:

> Do right unto this princely Duke of York,
> Or I will fill the house with armèd men
> And over the chair of state, where now he sits,
> Write up his title with usurping blood.
>   *He stamps with his foot and the soldiers show themselves.*

(1.1.167–70)

What follows is a total collapse of both regal and patriarchal authority, as Henry agrees to disinherit his son Edward in return for being permitted to retain the title of king.

It is an act of political and personal emasculation, symbolically even a kind of rape of the royal body ('Pardon me, Margaret; pardon me, sweet son', Henry pleads, 'The Earl of Warwick and the Duke enforced me' [1.1.229–30]) that provokes the Queen to 'divorce myself/ Both from thy table, Henry, and thy bed' (248–49); and it is then she who assumes the position of hyper-aggressive masculinity that Henry is so conspicuously incapable of occupying. Leading the forces of revolt against York, she captures, sadistically tortures and finally kills her husband's antagonist, though not before displaying a macabre sense of humour that sees her offering him a napkin soaked in his son Rutland's blood to wipe away his grieving father's tears, and subjecting him to a mock coronation with a toytown crown (possibly of paper, though if Shakespeare had followed Holinshed's reference to a 'crowne … made of sedges or bulrushes' [1965, 3: 269], there might also be a ghastly echo of the thorny coronation of Christ). As a figure whose monstrosity is multiply figured in terms of bestiality, foreignness and sexual deviance, Margaret, the 'She-wolf of France', an 'Amazonian trull' with a 'tiger's heart wrapped in a woman's hide' (2.1.112, 115, 138), is Plantagenet England's darkest threat, and the incarnation of her culture's deepest misogyny, even if she is in her words and deeds no worse than the men who surround her.

With York's sons Edward and Richard now in open contention for the throne, the pace of events accelerates into nightmare, in a series of battlefield confrontations that culminate in the emblematic spectacle of the scene – fatalistically witnessed by the plays' ultimate failed father, King Henry, settled on a molehill to momentarily contemplate the prospect of the 'happy life' of 'a homely swain' (2.5.21–22) – in which, as the Folio stage directions stipulate, there enter at opposite doors 'a Son that hath kill'd his Father' and 'A Father that hath kill'd his Son'; an image whose horrific symmetries elegantly encapsulate both the full horrors of civil war and the extremity of the violation of the filial bond: 'I'll bear thee hence, and let them fight that will', declares the Father as he exits bearing his son's body, 'For I have murdered where I should not kill' (2.5.121–22). If Henry's response to this scenario is little more than pious hand-wringing ('Sad-hearted men, much overgone with care', he pleads, 'Here sits a king more woeful than you are' [2.5.123–24]; his appeal falls on deaf ears), there are others more than ready to seize the initiative afforded by chaos, not least Richard of Gloucester, who is introduced by Queen Margaret as 'a foul misshapen stigmatic/ Marked by the destinies to be avoided,/ As venom toads or lizards' dreadful stings' (2.2.136–38), and, like her, presents a monstrous and perverse conjunction of the demonic, the bestial and the ruthlessly self-preserving.

Viewed from one angle, Richard is the diabolic embodiment of the evil that has descended upon England, an agent of disorder as well as a force of retribution; from another, he is the most proficient and accomplished exponent of the values of a society founded in violence. Announcing that 'I am myself alone' (5.6.84), Richard borrows from the self-sufficiency of the Morality play Vice, but also adopts the pragmatic self-interestedness ascribed by sixteenth-century Englishmen to the political philosophy of Machiavelli:

boasting that he will 'set the murderous Machiavel to school' (3.2.393), Richard is a pro-totype of the conniving and shape-shifting protagonist of *Richard III*, a man for whom the arts of violence and of performance are effortlessly one and the same ('Why, I can smile, and murder whiles I smile' [3.2.182]), and for whom ambition knows no limits:

> I'll drown more sailors than the mermaid shall;
> I'll slay more gazers than the basilisk …
> Can I do this, and cannot get a crown?
> Tut, were it farther off, I'll pluck it down.

(3.2.186–95)

Regardless of the titles of Octavo and Folio, it is Richard of Gloucester, rather than Richard of York or Henry of Lancaster, who dominates the latter action of the play.

A Talbot

One of the factors lending support to the argument that the second and third parts of *Henry VI* were originally two instalments of a narrative to which *Part 1* was added after-wards is that neither *Contention* nor *True Tragedy* assumes the spectator's familiarity with the events of the play that in the Folio precedes them. That *Henry VI* had been performed, probably by Lord Strange's Men at Henslowe's Rose, in the early 1590s is evident from Thomas Nashe's reference to one of its central characters, the warrior Lord Talbot, trium-phantly soliciting 'the teares of ten thousand spectators at least' (McKerrow 1958: 212; see 'Life and contexts', pp. 32–3), and from the records in Henslowe's accounts of a play he calls 'harey the vj', first performed on 3 March 1592 (1591 old-style) and revived more than a dozen times in the space of just less than a year. However popular it may have been, the play remained unpublished until the 1623 Folio; the assumption that it postdated the second and third parts is strengthened by the fact that Talbot, whose exploits form *Part 1*'s moral and patriotic core and which account for a large part of its popular theatrical appeal, is subsequently not once mentioned.

Acting in the fashion of what we would now term a prequel, *Part 1* establishes backstories for some of the key players in the chronologically later plays (including King Henry, Mar-garet of Anjou, the Earls of Warwick and Suffolk, Richard Plantagenet), as well as the feud between the King's Protector, the Duke of Gloucester, and the Bishop of Winchester; in a key scene, set in London's Temple Garden, both the conflict and the symbolism of the Wars of the Roses are traced to source in a confrontation between the Yorkists and the Lancas-trians in which the opponents pluck the white and red blooms that formalise their allegiance to incompatible claims to the throne, in gestures that are both momentous and irreversible:

> RICHARD PLANTAGENET
>   … If he suppose that I have pleaded truth,
>   From off this briar pluck a white rose with me.
>   [*He plucks a white rose*]
> SOMERSET Let him that is no coward nor no flatterer,
>   But dare maintain the party of the truth,
>   Pluck a red rose from off this thorn with me.
>   [*He plucks a red rose*]

(2.4.29–33)

The actions set in motion a train of events whose conclusion is reached at the end of *Richard III*, when the victorious Earl of Richmond, and new King Henry VII, declares that he 'will unite the white rose and the red' (5.7.19), thus establishing the House of the Tudors.

Representing the political conflicts of Shakespeare's first set of history plays in boldly schematic, as well as starkly iconographic, terms, the scene is pure invention; throughout *Part 1*, Shakespeare and his co-authors mingle historical fact and fantasy, as well as compressing or altering chronology and eliding events and incidents for dramatic convenience, economy and immediacy of effect. The play opens with the funeral of the hero-king Henry V, on a note of high tragic solemnity ('Hung be the heavens with black! Yield, day, to night' [1.1.1]), and immediately degenerates into squabbling as quarrels ignite and insults are traded over the coffin; the body is not even in the ground when news arrives of the loss of French territories that the late king had only recently succeeded in conquering. Historically, it took nearly seven years from the death of Henry V for his acquisitions to slip from English rule; in the play, it takes fewer than a hundred lines.

In action that alternates between scenes of domestic division and battles abroad, the play presents a précis of Anglo-French conflicts from 1428 (the siege of Orléans) to 1453 (the death of Talbot), manipulating its timelines so that, for example, Talbot and Joan of Arc (in the play, Joan la Pucelle) are depicted as contemporaries (her actual martyrdom took place in 1431), and so that Henry appears before Parliament to resolve the dispute between Gloucester and Winchester at a point when in actuality he was five years old. The play concludes by conjoining events separated by seven years: the peace negotiations that resulted in the Treaty of Arras in 1435, when Henry was thirteen; and the proxy wooing (by the Earl of Suffolk) of Margaret of Anjou, which took place in 1442.

As Gary Taylor (1995) and others have argued, one possible inference to be drawn from this aspect of the play's chronological flexibility is that the part of Henry was written for a juvenile, for one of Lord Strange's boys. In this respect, the fact that Henry makes his first entry at the start of the third act is indicative of his relative status in the action: despite his nominal position as the play's title character, he features in only five of its thirty-five scenes; far from acting as a locus of authority, he is a marginal and ineffectual presence, acted upon, not acting. Performatively, this projected casting associates Henry with the group of characters certainly played by boys: the play's women.

In the casting chart appended to his third series Arden edition (2000), Edward Burns proposes a distribution of roles between two boys that allocates Joan la Pucelle and Talbot's other chief female antagonist, and would-be seducer, the Countess of Auvergne, to one, and the King and his intended bride, Margaret, to another; as he suggests, the casting might well have offered scope for 'thematic' pairings and juxtapositions, positing holy innocent king against the sexually assertive princess, French peasant-saint (a whore and witch masquerading as a virgin) alongside an enchantress with a taste for bondage ('I will chain these legs and arms of thine' [2.3.38]). The combination of eroticism, deadliness and foreign guile reflects the gender politics of a play in which nationhood and sexuality freely and often explicitly interpenetrate: if Frenchness is of its very nature degenerate, treacherous and destructive (that is, effeminate), the essence of Englishness, best represented by Talbot, lies in the warrior masculinity for which his very name is a byword (as one unnamed soldier says, 'The cry of "Talbot" serves me for a sword' [2.1.81]).

The point of Talbot is not only what he is and does in himself ('Frenchmen, I'll be a Salisbury to you', he boasts, '*Pucelle* or pucelle, Dauphin or dog-fish,/ Your hearts I'll stamp out with my horse's heels/ And make a quagmire of your mingled brains' [1.6.85–88]), but what he embodies and represents, which is the collective, hence invincible, spirit of English patriotism; ensnared by a Countess of Auvergne (in another fabulously fabricated scene not in the chronicle sources) who hopes to belittle him as 'a child, a seely dwarf', a 'weak and writhled shrimp' (2.3.21–22), he laughs in her face:

> my substance is not here.
> For what you see is but the smallest part
> And least proportion of humanity.

(2.3.51–53)

At Talbot's summons, as if magically or miraculously, the corporate body of the English army materialises on the stage:

> How say you, madam? Are you now persuaded
> That Talbot is but shadow of himself?
> These are his substance, sinews, arms, and strength,
> With which he yoketh your rebellious necks …

(2.3.61–64)

The reversal is triumphant but also comic, the scene ending with the captive turned captor enjoining the acquiescent countess to feast his men.

But Talbot's ultimate fate at the hands of the French is (as Nashe emphasised) tragic – and a direct consequence of what happens in the Temple Garden scene that immediately follows. Of all of the deaths in this play and in those it followed (which include those of Talbot's son, Joan la Pucelle, the Duke of Gloucester, the Bishop, later Cardinal, of Winchester, the Dukes of Suffolk, Somerset, Buckingham and York, Lord Clifford and his son, Sir Humphrey and William Stafford, the Earls of Mortimer, Westmorland and Rutland, Lord Saye, King Henry himself, Jack Cade and countless unnamed common soldiers), it is a measure of his potency on the early modern stage that it was, for Nashe, Talbot's that left the most powerful and abiding memory.

Further reading

Bogdanov, Michael and Michael Pennington (1990) *The English Shakespeare Company: The Story of the Wars of the Roses, 1986–1989*. London: Nick Hern.

Brockbank, J. P. (1961) 'The Frame of Disorder – *Henry VI*', in *Early Shakespeare*, ed. John Russell Brown and Bernard Harris. London: Edward Arnold, 73–99.

Jackson, Gabriele Bernhardt (1988) 'Topical Ideology: Witches, Amazons, and Shakespeare's Joan of Arc', *English Literary Review (ELR)*, 18: 40–65.

Rackin, Phyllis (1990) *Stages of History: Shakespeare's English Chronicles*. Ithaca, NY: Cornell University Press.

Shaughnessy, Robert (1994) *Representing Shakespeare: England, History and the RSC*. Hemel Hempstead: Harvester Wheatsheaf.

Taylor, Gary (1995) 'Shakespeare and Others: The Authorship of *Henry the Sixth, Part One*', *Medieval and Renaissance Drama in England*, 7: 145–205.

The Two Gentlemen of Verona, Love's Labour's Lost *and* The Comedy of Errors

The Two Gentlemen of Verona

Date, text and authorship

c.1590; listed by Francis Meres, 1598; F 1623. Solely Shakespearean.

Sources and influences

Giovanni Boccaccio, *Decameron* (1353; English translation by William Painter, 1566); Jorge de Montemayor, *Diana Enamorada* (1559; English translation by Bartholomew Young, 1598); Arthur Brooke, *Romeus and Juliet* (1562); Ovid, *Metamorphoses* (English translation by Arthur Golding, 1567); Richard Edwards, *Damon and Pithias* (1571); John Lyly, *Euphues* (1578).

On stage

RSC, 1960 (dir. Peter Hall; Proteus: Derek Godfrey; Valentine: Denholm Elliott); RSC, 1970 (dir. Robin Phillips; Proteus: Ian Richardson; Valentine: Peter Egan; Silvia: Estelle Kohler); RSC, 1991 (dir. David Thacker; Silvia: Saskia Reeves); Shakespeare's Globe, 1996 (dir. Jack Shepherd; Proteus: Mark Rylance); RSC, 2004 (dir. Fiona Buffini; Sylvia: Rachel Pickup).

On screen

BBC Television Shakespeare, UK, 1984 (dir. Don Taylor; Proteus: Tyler Butterworth; Valentine: John Hudson; Julia: Tessa Peake-Jones).

Offshoots

Two Gentlemen of Verona, musical, New York, 1971 (book by John Guare and Mel Shapiro; music by Galt MacDermot); *Dawson's Creek*, Season 4: *Two Gentlemen of Capeside*, USA, 2000.

Love's Labour's Lost

Date, text and authorship

c.1595; listed by Francis Meres, 1598; Q1 1598; F 1623. Solely Shakespearean.

Sources and influences

No direct sources identified; influenced by works of John Lyly and conventions of *commedia dell'arte*.

On stage

Westminster Theatre, 1932 (dir. Tyrone Guthrie); SMT, 1946 (dir. Peter Brook); NT (National Theatre), 1968 (dir. Laurence Olivier); RSC, 1965, 1977 (dir. John Barton); RSC, 1984 (dir. Barry Kyle; King: Kenneth Branagh; Biron: Roger Rees; Rosaline: Josette Simon); RSC, 1990 (dir. Terry Hands; King: Simon Russell Beale; Biron: Ralph Fiennes; Rosaline: Amanda Root); NT, 2003 (dir. Trevor Nunn; Biron: Joseph Fiennes); RSC, 2008 (dir. Gregory Doran; Biron: David Tennant); Shakespeare's Globe, 2007 (dir. Dominic Dromgoole).

On screen

BBC Television Shakespeare, UK, 1985 (dir. Elijah Moshinsky; King: Jonathan Kent; Biron: Mike Gwilym; Rosaline: Jenny Agutter); UK, 2000 (dir. Kenneth Branagh; Biron: Kenneth Branagh; Dumaine: Adrian Lester).

The Comedy of Errors

Date, text and authorship

c.1594; performed at Gray's Inn, 28 December 1594; F 1623. Solely Shakespearean.

Sources and influences

Plautus, *Menaechmi* (trans. William Warner, 1595) and *Amphitruo*; John Gower, *Confessio Amatis* (1390).

On stage

SMT, 1938 (dir. Theodore Komisarjevsky); RSC, 1960 (dir. Clifford Williams; Antipholus of Epheseus: Ian Richardson; Antipholus of Syracuse: Alec McCowen: Adriana: Diana Rigg); RSC, 1976 (dir. Trevor Nunn; Antipholus of Epheseus: Mike Gwilym; Antipholus of Syracuse: Roger Rees; Dromio of Epheseus: Nickolas Grace; Dromio of Syracuse: Roger Williams; Adriana: Judi Dench); RSC, 1983 (dir. Trevor Nunn; Adriana: Zoë Wanamaker); RSC, 1990 (dir. Ian Judge; Antipholus of Epheseus/Antipholus of Syracuse: Desmond Barrit; Dromio of Epheseus/Dromio of Syracuse: Graham Turner; Adriana: Estelle Kohler); RSC, 2005 (dir. Nancy Meckler; Antipholus of Epheseus: Christopher Colquhoun; Antipholus of Syracuse: Joe Dixon; Dromio of Epheseus: Forbes Masson; Dromio of Syracuse: Jonathan Slinger; Adriana: Suzanne Burden).

On screen

ATV, UK, 1978 (dir. Philip Casson; screen version of 1976 RSC production); BBC Television Shakespeare, UK, 1983 (dir. James Cellan Jones; Antipholus of Epheseus/Antipholus of Syracuse: Michael Kitchen; Dromio of Epheseus/Dromio of Syracuse: Roger Daltrey; Adriana: Suzanne Bertish).

Offshoots

Twice Two, USA, 1933 (dir. James Parrott; Stan Laurel and Oliver Hardy play themselves, each other's wives and their own identical twins); Richard Rogers and Lorenz Hart, *The Boys from Syracuse*, New York, 1938; film version USA, 1940 (dir. A. Edward Sutherland; Antipholus of Epheseus/Antipholus of Syracuse: Allan Jones; Dromio of Epheseus/Dromio of Syracuse: Joe Penner; Adriana: Irene Hervey).

The letter very orderly

These three comedies are generally agreed to date from the earliest years of Shakespeare's career as a professional playwright: *Two Gentlemen* and *The Comedy of Errors* were not published until the 1623 Folio but both are included in Francis Meres's list of his comedies in 1598, and there is a record of a performance of *Errors* at Gray's Inn in 1594; *Love's Labour's Lost*, also mentioned by Meres, was issued in quarto in 1598. As Shakespeare's first attempts at comedy, the plays reveal the benefits as well as the risks of bringing the fruits of a sixteenth-century grammar school education to the popular stage. All three demonstrate the familiarity with classical literature and drama, and fluency in the techniques of classical rhetoric, that characterised the cultural accomplishment of the courtier, the bourgeois professional and the aspiring playwright; all are to varying degrees self-conscious exercises in style and technique.

The Two Gentlemen of Verona has not been particularly well favoured by critics or by theatregoers: rarely seen throughout the nineteenth and twentieth centuries, it has been revived more frequently in recent years (it was chosen for the prologue season at Shakespeare's Globe in London in 1996); it also features in the film *Shakespeare in Love* (1998) as an example of the kind of laboured apprentice work that the author soon learns to transcend, and where it is chiefly notable for providing opportunities for a running gag about a dog. The play is generally regarded as an uneven attempt to adapt the materials of romance to drama, limited in its ambitions and technique: the presentation of parallel sets of lovers is seen as too obviously schematic; characterisation, plotting and use of setting are inconsistent; rarely does it manage to orchestrate scenes with more than two speakers. Indeed, the naming of the dramatis personae suggests predictability: 'Valentine' designates an ideal lover; 'Silvia' is associated with woodland and hence with the idealised world of pastoral; while the danger that Proteus poses to this pair is manifest in a name which is taken from the shape-shifting Greek god, and which in the period was notoriously synonymous with guile and deception. The play's language is equally formalised. Consider, for example, this early exchange between Proteus and Valentine:

> PROTEUS So by your circumstance you call me fool.
> VALENTINE So by your circumstance I fear you'll prove.
> PROTEUS 'Tis love you cavil at. I am not love.
> VALENTINE Love is your master, for he masters you,
>   And he that is so yokèd by a fool
>   Methinks should not be chronicled for wise.
> PROTEUS Yet writers say 'As in the sweetest bud
>   The eating canker dwells, so doting love
>   Inhabits in the finest wits of all.'

(1.1.36–44)

The duologue, which is not untypical of the play, diligently employs a range of rhetorical devices: the duplication of 'So by your circumstance' in successive verse lines (*anaphora*), as well as the parallel phrasing (*isocolon* and *parison*); the repetition and echoing of 'love' in lines 38–39 (*anadiplosis*); the personification of love as a figure to be derided, respected and feared; the metaphor of 'yoking'; the antithesis between folly and wisdom at the end of the final two lines; the literary quotation which shifts from the specific experience to the general via a commonplace. The difficulty is not that Shakespeare does not make use of such formal techniques throughout his writing (quite the reverse), but that their application here, particularly to modern readers and theatregoers attuned to 'naturalistic' speech, seems heavy handed, predictable and formulaic. Later on, Proteus is afforded a soliloquy, in which he evaluates his emerging disloyalty to both his male friend and his lover, Julia, and his desire for Valentine's lover, Silvia:

> Even as one heat another heat expels,
> Or as one nail by strength drives out another,
> So the remembrance of my former love
> Is by a newer object quite forgotten.

(2.4.185–88)

Readers looking for distinctiveness or originality of expression, or for speech which characterises its speaker in terms of psychological nuance, depth and complexity, are likely to be disappointed. The ideas are proverbial, and the means of delivery thoroughly conventional: arguably, the images of fire and nails simply reiterate, in a slightly different format, the idea of new love supplanting the old rather than expanding or developing it. What the passage does reveal is Shakespeare's talent for creative borrowing, in that it is a close paraphrase of Arthur Brooke's 1562 poem *Romeus and Juliet*, ll. 203–10:

> And whilest he fixd on her his partiall perced eye,
> His former love, for which of late he ready was to dye,
> Is nowe as quite forgotten, as it had never been.
> The proverb saith, unminded oft are they that are unseene
> And as out of a planke a nayle a nayle doth drive,
> So novell love out of the minde the auncient love doth rive.
> This sodain kindled fyre in time is wox so great,
> That onely death and both theyr bloods might quench the fiery heate.
>
> (Bullough 1957, 1: 291)

Shakespeare's version of this, even if it improves upon its source in terms of economy, precision and elegance of expression, is close enough to its source to look suspiciously like plagiarism to modern eyes, but for early modern readers and auditors with a rather different sense of literary property rights and of creative originality, the successful remodelling of an existing text was to be commended rather than condemned: the play's appeal lies in the familiarity of the sentiments and the generic mode of their articulation.

The play's alleged crudities of style, characterisation and construction may account less for its critical and theatrical neglect than the difficulties posed by its subject matter, in particular its problematic sexual politics. Dealing with the inconstancy and duplicity of male desire, and with the tensions and conflicts between male friendships and male–female relationships, *Two Gentlemen* traces a series of deceptions and betrayals on the part of Proteus, culminating in his attempted rape of Silvia, an assault witnessed both by Julia (disguised as a page) and by Valentine, who intervenes to denounce the attacker in terms which focus exclusively upon the breach of friendship: 'Thou common friend, that's without faith or love/ For such is a friend now. Treacherous man,/ Thou hast beguiled my hopes' (5.4.62–64). Even more problematically, Valentine responds to Proteus's immediate declaration of remorse by offering to confirm his friendship by relinquishing Silvia to him:

> And that my love may appear plain and free,
> All that was mine in Silvia I give thee.
>
> (5.4.82–83)

Previous generations of critics dealt with this difficult moment in ways which both resisted and evaded the misogynist implications of Valentine's largesse; Sir Arthur Quiller-Couch, editor of the 1921 Cambridge edition, was so appalled by the business that he suggested that the text must be corrupt, 'a piece of theatre botchwork patched upon the original' (Quiller-Couch and Wilson 1921: xviii), since he found it hard to imagine that gentle Shakespeare could have conceived such an ungentlemanly pair of gentlemen.

The perspective afforded by more recent feminist criticism recognises in this offer a patriarchal imperative which, underwriting the primacy of the homosocial bond, defines women within it as objects in a system of barter: this, as Jean E. Howard concludes, reminds us 'of the different ways in which Shakespeare is and is not our contemporary' (Greenblatt *et al.* 1997: 83). What most readers will find conspicuous is that Silvia remains silent from this moment to the end of the play. It may be that it is Shakespeare's theatrical inexperience (or his and his audience's sense of who the priority speakers are) that leaves Silvia without a final reply to either of her would-be lovers; but, as with Isabella's silence in response to the Duke's proposal at the close of *Measure for Measure*, imaginative speculation, and theatrical practice, can work to make it unusually eloquent.

Too long for a play

The spoken word is also something of a problem in *Love's Labour's Lost*. Citing Hazlitt's frequently quoted view that 'if we were to part with any of the author's comedies, it should be this' (Furness 1904: 357), a recent editor acknowledges the play's traditionally poor reputation, and that what he believes to be one of Shakespeare's 'cleverest and funniest plays' is nonetheless 'odd and difficult', a piece concerned with 'fantastic and strange figures whose language is at times almost impossible to understand' (Woudhuysen 1998: 1). Some aspects of the play, such as plot and characterisation, are relatively straightforward. The King of Navarre, in the company of three courtiers (Biron, Longueville, Dumaine), declares his intention of forswearing the company of women for three years and turning his court into 'a little academe,/ Still and contemplative in living art' (1.1.13–14); almost immediately the vow is undermined by the arrival of the king of France's daughter and three attendant ladies, with whom the King and his companions instantly and symmetrically fall in love.

The pursuit of higher learning surrenders to the business of penning sonnets and *billets-doux*; the aristocrats' courtship games are paralleled and parodied by those of the Spaniard, Armado, a figure modelled upon the stage stereotype of the Braggart (as he is designated in the 1598 quarto and – inconsistently – in the 1623 Folio); and their intellectual pretensions are satirised in the stock figures of Holofernes and Sir Nathaniel. The pair are identified in the quarto and Folio as Pedant and Curate respectively; here, as throughout Shakespeare's work, the early speech-prefixes that modern editors prefer to regularise as character names are more representative of type and function than they are of individual personality (McCloud 1991: 88–96; Orgel 2002). The cast is completed by a Clown (Costard), Constable (Dull), Page (Mote) and Maid (Jaquenetta).

As in Shakespeare's other early comedies, the method is taken from the highly conventionalised theatrical form of *commedia dell'arte*; the self-consciousness of the work is further emphasised in the final act, which works through a sequence of metatheatrical conceits, as the King and lords attempt to seduce the French princess and her ladies through performance, first with a masque in which they place themselves at the limits of the exotic by appearing costumed as Russians, and accompanied by '*blackamoors with music*' (5.2.156), and then with the Masque of the Nine Worthies, in which Pedant, Page, Clown, Braggart and Curate heroically attempt to impersonate the great figures of classical mythology – a project which is utterly sabotaged by their courtly audience's persistent interruptions (prompting the Pedant to comment that this is 'not generous, not gentle, not humble' [5.2.617]), and then, more decisively, by the entry of a messenger, Mercade (glossed by the Oxford editors as a combination of 'Mercury' and 'Mar-Arcadia'), bringing news of the king of France's death, and effecting an instantaneous and unexpected shift of tone. The anticipated romantic denouement is deferred as the new Queen announces a year of mourning; the comedy ends by self-reflexively invoking its own conventions:

BIRON Our wooing doth not end like an old play.
    Jack hath not Jill. These ladies' courtesy
    Might well have made our sport a comedy.
  KING Come, sir, it wants a twelvemonth and a day,
    And then 'twill end.
  BIRON   That's too long for a play.

(5.2.851–55)

The action of the play, then, is little more than a pretext: as advertised on the title page of the quarto, which describes it as 'A Pleasant Conceited Comedy', the primary concern is with language, or rather, as Keir Elam puts it, with discourse, which he defines as 'language in *use*' and characterises as 'a tangible presence possessing imposing qualities … active and self-advertising' (Elam 1984: 1). The various courtships are conducted through ornate, highly formalised verbal and textual games, in which the participants manipulate rhetoric in order to seduce, impress, dazzle and persuade, but also indulge in wit as an end in itself.

Language does the work of the body and its desires and, in its exuberant and relentless punning, both spirals away from and rebounds upon its speakers:

BIRON Lady, I will commend you to mine own heart.
ROSALINE Pray you, do my commendations. I would be glad to see it.
BIRON I would you heard it groan.
ROSALINE Is the fool sick?
BIRON Sick at the heart.
ROSALINE Alack, let it blood.
BIRON Would that do it good?
ROSALINE My physic says 'Aye'.
BIRON Will you prick't with your eye?
ROSALINE *Non point*, with my knife.
BIRON Now God save thy life.
ROSALINE And yours from long living.
BIRON I cannot stay thanksgiving.

(2.1.179–92)

The rules of exchange are those of a verbal fencing match, with each rhymed rejoinder offered as an attack which demands and receives an apt counter-manoeuvre: Biron's initial offer of the bleeding heart of the conventional lovesick suitor is parried by Rosaline's macabre vision of his evisceration and bleeding; in response, Biron plays upon 'prick' and 'eye' (penis and vagina), only to back off when Rosaline shows her steel.

Language games are not the sole preserve of the aristocrats, of course; among the play's multiple forms of speech is that of Costard the Clown, who in words and deeds serves to parody both the amorous aspirations and verbal pretensions of his social superiors (much the same function is fulfilled by Lance and Speed in *Two Gentlemen*). Costard's introduction in the first scene effects a shift of tone and register, in that he has been caught in the act of attempted intercourse with Jacquenetta; rather than attempting to evade the King's edict of celibacy, he simply ignores it, and in the process incarnates the recalcitrance of physical appetites which simply refuse to recognise the law's punitive rigour. Costard carnivalises the discourse of courtship by indulging the body rather than deferring its gratifications (and as a result is afforded a suitably Lenten punishment of fasting upon 'bran and water' [1.1.292]), but his set-piece routines are equally prone to teasing out a turn of phrase for the sake of comic or rhetorical ingenuity.

Quizzed by Biron about the contents of Don Armado's written report on his misdemeanours, Costard plays upon the text's 'matter' (content) and 'manner' (form):

> The matter is to me, sir, as concerning Jacquenetta. The manner of it is, I was taken with the manner.
>
> (1.1.199–200)

The joke may well be lost on most modern audiences: to be taken 'with the manner' plays upon the legalese 'mainoure', or hand-work, which is, evidently, what Costard and Jacquenetta have been practising. Pressed by Biron ('In what manner?'), Costard takes the conceit several stages further:

> In manner and form following, sir – all those three. I was seen with her in the manor house, sitting with her upon the form, and taken following her into the park; which put together is 'in manner and form following'.
>
> (1.1.202–06)

Costard employs the principles and formulae of disputation ('in manner and form following') as material props and actions in a narrative of seduction which takes the lovers from the manor house to the form, or park-bench, to the parkland scene of interrupted pursuit: a thwarted act of sex assumes the characteristics of a formal text. Here, and throughout the play, speech and writing become as seductive as the work of wooing they are ostensibly meant to accomplish.

Like brother and brother

The Comedy of Errors is another work which relies upon its original audience's familiarity with a known theatrical prototype, in the *Menaechmi*, by the Roman playwright Plautus. The play typifies Shakespeare's use of source material, in that it appropriates the situation and dramatis personae from an existing, possibly well-known, work and then proceeds to outdo it in terms of the audacity and complexity of its plotting and set-pieces. Plautus's play deals with a pair of identical twins, the sons of a Syracusan merchant, one living in the town of Epidamnus, the other arriving there as a visitor and taken for his sibling in a series of encounters with his family and his lover; his brother is incarcerated as a lunatic, but released when the real identity of his twin is revealed at the end. Adopting this basic scenario, Shakespeare added a second set of twins (the servant Dromios); from Plautus, he also acquired an intricate calculus of entrances, exits and encounters, contriving an accelerating sequence of misrecognitions, misapprehensions and perceived betrayals that culminates in the final scene in which the two sets of twins are finally brought together onstage; adhering to the classical unities of time, place and action, *Errors* observes the spatial constraints of the Roman comic stage: the action requires only three sets of doors (denoting the houses of the Courtesan, Antipholus of Epheseus and the Priory) to accommodate all of the action's set-pieces and situations.

Whereas the *Menaechmi* is set in the relatively neutral environment of Epidamnus, the prime location of Shakespeare's play is provided by the undifferentiated streets of Epheseus itself, a city defined by its lively but dangerous marketplace, a realm, according to Antipholus of Syracuse, of 'cozenage', and the haunt of

> nimble jugglers that deceive the eye,
> Dark-working sorcerers that change the mind,
> Soul-killing witches that deform the body,
> Disguisèd cheaters, prating mountebanks,
> And many suchlike liberties of sin.
>
> (1.2.97–102)

To step into this perfidious domain is, this Antipholus senses, to expose oneself to the risk not only of moral contamination and the likelihood of being duped, but also of the loss of one's own sense of identity. Initially savouring the prospect of idly loitering in an Epheseus in which he can 'go lose myself' (1.2.30), Antipholus of Syracuse goes on to reflect that his epic quest to find his own twin involves the possibility of a rather less congenial experience of aimless dispersal:

> I to the world am like a drop of water
> That in the ocean seeks another drop,
> Who, falling there to find his fellow forth,
> Unseen, inquisitive, confounds himself.
>
> (1.2.35–40)

What Antipholus does not yet realise is that this threatened loss of self will be precipitated not by what he imagines to be the immense distance between himself and his twin but by their proximity.

Hailed by his Ephesian counterpart's wife as her own husband, Antipholus questions the veracity of his memory:

> What, was I married to her in my dream?
> Or sleep I now, and think I hear all this?
> What error drives our eyes and ears amiss?
>
> (2.2.182–84)

Farcically oblivious to the adjacency of their fraternal others, the two Antipholuses act as each other's unwittingly malevolent doppelgangers, so that their every well-intentioned word and action multiplies and intensifies the mutual damage done to reputation, physical well-being and sense of sanity. The compounding of errors is also a consequence of the master–servant relationship upon which the play and its principal figures are dependent, in that the system of commands, obligations and displaced responsibilities which constitute this contract supplies the opportunity for faithfully executed instructions to seemingly turn into acts of defiance, and for innocent candour to read as insolence or disobedience. The Antipholuses' equally unwitting partners in this action are the paired Dromios, whose masters' psychological misfortunes are mirrored in the form of repeated physical assaults, which they carry with the stoic fortitude that is the comic servant's lot (although at one point Dromio of Ephesus ominously warns his master that 'I should kick being kicked, and, being at that pass,/ You would keep from my heels, and beware of an ass' [3.1.17–18]).

The pattern of domination and submission that is articulated through the overt brutality of the master–servant relationship is echoed, but contested, in the play's central marital relationship, that of Antipholus of Epheseus and his wife, Adriana. One of the significances of Epheseus for Shakespeare's contemporaries was that its inhabitants were recipients of one of St Paul's biblical epistles, which offered advice, in particular, on the proper conduct of the relation between husband and wife:

> Wives, submit your selves vnto your owne husbands, as vnto the Lord: For the husbande is head of the wife, even as Christ is ye head of the Church … But as the Church is subject vnto Christ, like wise, the wiues of their owne husbands in all things.
>
> (Epehesians 5, 22–25)

Rehearsing concerns which would be explored more substantially in *The Taming of the Shrew*, the play employs the opportunity of domestic farce to touch upon the question of the balance of power between genders.

Answering Adriana's complaint (2.1.14) that 'There's none but asses will be bridled so' (that is, by their husband's exercise of superior will), Luciana sets forth the orthodox view, which naturalises male dominion by invoking hierarchical analogies in the animal world:

> The beasts, the fishes, and the wingèd fowls
> Are their males' subjects and at their controls.
> Man, more divine, the master of all these,
> Lord of the wide world and wild wat'ry seas,
> Indued with intellectual sense and souls,
> Of more pre-eminence than fish and fowls,
> Are masters to their females, and their lords.
> Then let your will attend on their accords.
>
> (2.1.18–25)

This earns a tart response from Adriana ('This servitude makes you to keep unwed' [2.1.26]) and a hint of resistance:

> A wretched soul bruised with adversity,
> We bid be quiet when we hear it cry.
> But were we burdened with like weight of pain,
> As much or more we should ourselves complain …
>
> (2.1.34–37)

The extent to which these grievances are real or imagined, and whether they can be exorcised through the symmetrical partnerings of a resolution which pairs Antipholus of Syracuse with Luciana and reconciles his twin to Adriana, remains an open question; it is not insignificant here that this closure is effected through the intervention of the matriarchal *deus ex machina* figure of the Abbess (who is also, according to the logic of romance, Egeon's long-lost wife).

Female power is imagined in the play as, amongst other things, a jealous regard of time, enforcing both business and desire to heed the imperatives of the domestic routine. Dromio of Epheseus earns a beating first from Adriana, who, the clock having 'strucken twelve upon the bell', is 'so hot because the meat is cold' (1.2.45–47), and then from Antipholus of

Syracuse when he attempts to fetch 'from the mart' the man he thinks his master ('Home to your house, the Phoenix, sir, to dinner' [1.2.74–75]); Antipholus of Epheseus subsequently makes his excuses to the goldsmith and the merchant by confessing that 'My wife is shrewish when I keep not hours' (3.1.2). This is just one of the instances in which time and time-keeping are characterised in terms of pressure and obligation: the comedy rests upon the making and breaking of a rigorously precise schedule of transactions and appointments.

Shakespeare affords the unities of time, place and action a particular intensity by framing the comedy with the narrative of Egeon's impending execution; as a consequence, time is experienced in the play as a pressure and preoccupation with what the audience knows to be mortal consequences. One of the purposes of the frame, in this respect, is to accommodate the pagan material of Roman comedy within an Elizabethan Christian worldview, in that cryptic references to judgement, blood and redemption (1.1.8–9) allude to a pattern of fall, sin and salvation, which shapes and makes sense of the relentless forward movement of time towards death: 'by fusing Plautus' rambunctious plot with the life-and-death romance of Egeon's quest, and both with allusions to St Paul ... Shakespeare's hybrid tests their respective modes of narration, as though asking "Which kind of story, if any, can help us stave off death?"' (Bishop 1996: 74–75). This story, at least, does that work – for the time being.

Further reading

Barber, C. L. (1959) *Shakespeare's Festive Comedy: A Study of Dramatic Form and Its Relation to Social Custom*. Princeton, NJ: Princeton University Press.

Bishop, T. G. (1996) *Shakespeare and the Theatre of Wonder*. Cambridge: Cambridge University Press.

Carroll, William C. (1985) *The Metamorphoses of Shakespearean Comedy*. Princeton, NJ: Princeton University Press.

Elam, Keir (1984) *Shakespeare's Universe of Discourse: Language-Games in the Comedies*. Cambridge: Cambridge University Press.

Parker, Patricia (1996) *Shakespeare from the Margins: Language, Culture, Context*. Chicago, IL: University of Chicago Press.

Salingar, Leo (1974) *Shakespeare and the Traditions of Comedy*. Cambridge: Cambridge University Press.

Smith, Bruce R. (1991) *Homosexual Desire in Shakespeare's England: A Cultural Poetics*. Chicago, IL: University of Chicago Press.

Weimann, Robert (1969) 'Laughing with the Audience: *The Two Gentlemen of Verona* and the Popular Tradition of Comedy', *Shakespeare Survey*, 22: 35–42.

Titus Andronicus

Date, text and authorship

Q1 1594; Q2 1600; Q3 1611; F 1623. Conjectured as partly co-authored with George Peele.

Sources and influences

Seneca, *Hercules Furens, Troades, Thyestes* (trans. Jasper Heywood, 1559–61); Ovid, *Metamorphoses* (trans. Arthur Golding, 1567); Thomas Kyd, *The Spanish Tragedy* (c.1589).

On stage

SMT, 1955 (dir. Peter Brook; Titus: Laurence Olivier; Lavinia: Vivien Leigh; Aaron: Antony Quayle); RSC, 1987 (dir. Deborah Warner; Titus: Brian Cox; Tamora: Estelle Kohler; Lavinia: Sonia Ritter); NT/Market Theatre, Johannesburg, 1995 (dir. Gregory Doran; Titus: Antony Sher); Ninagawa Company, Tokyo, 2004 (dir. Yukio Ninagawa; Titus: Kotaro Yoshida).

On screen

BBC Television Shakespeare, UK, 1985 (dir. Jane Howell; Titus: Trevor Peacock; Lavinia: Anna Calder-Marshall; Aaron: Hugh Quarshie); *Titus*, USA/Italy, 1999 (dir. Julie Taymor; Titus: Antony Hopkins; Tamora: Jessica Lange; Saturninus: Alan Cumming).

A wilderness of tigers

Few of Shakespeare's works have enjoyed as drastic a turn-around in critical reputation as *Titus Andronicus*, seen for many years as his first and, for many commentators, undoubtedly worst play. It was evidently popular in its time: the first recorded performances took place, according to Henslowe's accounts, at the beginning of 1594, when it was the season's highest-earning play; published in quarto in 1594 'As it was Plaide by the Right Honourable the Earle of *Darbie*, Earle of *Pembrooke*, and Earle of *Sussex* their Servants', there followed two further quartos in 1600 and 1611. It was also the stimulus for the only surviving six-teenth-century illustration of a Shakespeare play, by Henry Peachum in a manuscript tran-script of lines from 1.1 and 5.1, which is captioned 'Enter Tamora pleadings for her sonnes going to execution' and which depicts the queen of the Goths and two sons kneeling before the protagonist, flanked on the right by the moor Aaron and on the left by two halberdiers. The mix of Roman costume and Elizabethan dress in the picture has prompted speculation that it records the eclectic and anachronistic conventions of early modern staging, though it is unknown whether the sketch records performance or merely imagines it.

The play's popularity did not outlive its initial moment; the Restoration playwright Edward Ravenscroft, who adapted the play as *The Rape of Lavinia* in 1687, described it as 'a heap of rubbish', and though his version was staged intermittently during the first quarter of the eighteenth century it disappeared from the repertoire after 1725; the play was next seen, again in a heavily adapted form, in London in 1852 and 1857, when it served as a bowdlerised, melodramatic vehicle for the black American-born actor Ira Aldridge (who played Aaron, and who was styled the 'African Roscius' for his portrayal of Othello). The first time *Titus* was seen in London in anything like its original form was in 1923, when it was staged, as it were through gritted teeth, as part of the Old Vic's commitment to presenting the entire canon. The production failed to win over the play's critics: T. S. Eliot spoke for most when he called it 'one of the stupidest and most uninspired plays ever written' (1932: 82), and theatre continued to avoid it.

Editing the play for the New Cambridge Shakespeare in 1948, John Dover Wilson contrived the grandest of guignol images to characterise an 'absurd' drama which 'seems to jolt and bump along like some broken-down cart, laden with bleeding corpses from an Elizabethan scaffold, and driven by an executioner from Bedlam dressed in cap and bells' (1948: xii). It is obvious enough what Wilson and others are objecting to: written in conscious imitation of Seneca, the play lurches between highly formalised verbal artifice, Ovidian pastiche and extreme violence, sometimes conjoining both in the same moment, and includes madness, rape, dismemberment, miscegenation, cannibalism and a seemingly endless relentless round of killings – including, notoriously, an episode in which the deranged Titus and his brother Marcus expostulate upon the casual killing of a household fly:

> MARCUS Alas, my lord, I have but killed a fly.
> TITUS 'But'? How if that fly had a father, brother?
> How would he hang his slender gilded wings
> And buzz lamenting dirges in the air!
> Poor harmless fly,
> That with his pretty buzzing melody
> Came here to make us merry – and thou hast killed him!
>
> (3.2.59–65)

The changing status of the play can be gauged from the differences between the respective editions for the second and third series Arden Shakespeare. The first of these, published in 1953 (reprinted in 1961), was the work of J. C. Maxwell, and was the sole contribution to the series of a scholar who, as a patron of lost causes, seems to have specialised in the largely thankless job of editing marginal or unloved texts. For the New Shakespeare he edited *Pericles* (1956), *Timon of Athens* (1957), *Henry VIII* (1962) and the *Poems* (1966). In the first of these, Wilson wrote in a preface that the play 'offers the editor a task of extreme perplexity in return for which he can expect little gratitude', while assuring Maxwell and his readers that 'in generously undertaking it he has earned the sincere thanks of one man at least' (Wilson 1956: vii); in the second that in *Timon* Maxwell was 'confronted with something textually better but dramatically scarcely less baffling' (Wilson 1957: vii); and in the third that he was 'again indebted' to Maxwell for 'relieving me of a burden', that is, of dealing with 'a play I find less interesting than any other in the Folio' (Wilson 1962: vii).

The Arden second series General Editors' appreciation of Maxwell's efforts with *Titus* is not on record, but his own view of the play is evident enough from the fact that he begins his critical overview with the admission of 'its inferiority to all Shakespeare's other tragedies' (Maxwell 1961: xxxvi). Bearing in mind that the Arden introductions lengthened along with publication schedules as the series progressed (reaching an end in the 160-page monster – supplemented by a further 150 pages of 'Longer Notes' – for Harold Jenkins's 1982 *Hamlet*), Maxwell's for *Titus*, at just under fifty pages, is the still shortest in the series; and a mere seven of those pages deal with matters of critical interpretation, the remainder being given over to issues of text, sources and authorship (by way of fairly direct comparison, even *Pericles*, in F. D. Hoeniger's edition of 1963, merits a ninety-page introduction). Maxwell is less dismissive of the play than Wilson, in part because he is readier to credit Shakespeare with majority authorship, and, since it would be hard to live with the play for as long as it takes to produce an Arden edition without learning to love it at least a little, he is driven to conclude that 'the very fact that we can point to so many things that are wrong with *Titus* is itself evidence of dramatic life: no one dwells on defects, and suggests improvements, in the irremediably dull and worthless' (Maxwell 1961: xlii).

If this seems either like damnation with faint praise or special pleading, it is in marked contrast to the position adopted by the Arden third series editor, Jonathan Bate, who begins by referring to the play's 'complicated and sophisticated' aesthetics and politics, and its 'intricate structure and innovative use of theatrical resources', and who proceeds from the premise that '*Titus* is an important play and a living one' (Bate 1995: 2–3). It is not incidental that Bate, at the time of the edition's publication the King Alfred Professor at the University of Liverpool, was and is one of the profession's highest-profile Shakespearean scholars, or that (alongside T. W. Craik's *Henry V*) *Titus* was one of the first third series editions to appear: far from treating the play as a marginal embarrassment, this *Titus* was a prestige publication that could, at the end of an introduction of 121 pages, proclaim with confidence the play's 'greatness' (Bate 1995: 121).

Bate does not share Maxwell's view that '*Titus* is neither a play with a complicated staging nor one which will ever be widely read' (Maxwell 1961: xvii); and if the numerous borrowings documented by the date stamps in the three copies held by my own university library are any guide, he is right on the latter count at least (Maxwell's *Titus* was called out on loan less than once a year on average between 1972 and 2008). Bate's enthusiasm for the play is shared to varying degrees by a number of other recent editors: though the Oxford editor, Eugene M. Waith, cautiously averred that despite its inferiority in relation to the rest of Shakespeare's oeuvre, 'it moves, unevenly at times, but often powerfully, toward a disaster for which the cause is established in the first minutes of action' (1984: 69), the New Cambridge Shakespeare editor, Alan Hughes, declared that, as a product of Shakespeare's 'genius', it is 'the work of a brilliant stage craftsman' (2006: 32–33); while the Norton editors suggest that it is 'a daring experiment ... that nonetheless provides fascinating insight into his development as a dramatist' (Greenblatt *et al.* 1997: 377).

It is Bate, however, who is most ardent, and lengthily eloquent, in his defence of the play, and he presents this on the basis of two major, interrelated, grounds. The first is indicated by the structure and organisation of his introduction, which pointedly reverses the order in which Maxwell approaches the play. The 1953 edition, according to the systematic protocols of the Arden second series, begins with bibliographical matters, issues of date and authorship, and sources, ends with a critical assessment and survey, and mentions performance not at all. Significantly, for Bate's and our purposes, the supplement to the 1961 reprint outlining recent critical work on the play makes no acknowledgement of the one event to have occurred since the edition's first publication that might have impinged upon Maxwell's judgement: the stage production, starring Laurence Olivier as Titus, Antony Quayle as Aaron and Vivien Leigh as Lavinia, and directed by Peter Brook, that was mounted at the Shakespeare Memorial Theatre in Stratford-upon-Avon in 1955.

Bate, conversely, deliberately begins with this landmark production, the first professional one of the play in the United Kingdom since the Old Vic's in 1923, and the first ever in Stratford, in order to highlight a stark antithesis between the play's execrable critical reputation and its theatrical power, progressing by means of Brook's solemn, ritualised and formalised staging, a conjectural reconstruction of original performance at Henslowe's Rose, and Deborah Warner's viscerally memorable production in the RSC's Swan in 1987, to construct the case, familiar to proponents of stage-centred criticism, that modern performance is uniquely able to activate or reveal the latent strengths of a text in ways that reading and criticism cannot. In the process, aspects of the play that have been regarded as flaws, grotesque liabilities or serious misjudgements are re-evaluated as positives: seen in the light of Artaud's Theatre of Cruelty, the Theatre of the Absurd, Edward Bond's theatre of political violence and (postdating Bate's edition) the more recent dramaturgy of Sarah Kane, Antony Neilson, Mark Ravenhill and other 1990s British 'New Brutalists', the conjuncture of verbal artifice, intense realism and grisly comedy seems neither shocking nor incomprehensible (the edition was published before the 1999 release of Julie Taymor's stylishly macabre, Pasolini-influenced film *Titus*). Bate cites contemporary media culture (and in particular the mid-1980s moral panic in the United Kingdom over graphically violent 'video nasties') as another point of reference; since his edition, a new wave of violent mainstream movies, as well as the proliferation of readily accessible images of abuse and suffering on the internet, have situated the play's cruelties even more firmly within the realms of the gruesomely familiar.

It has become a reviewer's commonplace that for a generation weaned on the films of Quentin Tarantino and the like, movies about movies that consider violence to be funny and cool, the blood and rhetoric of *Titus* are readily digestible; and this connects with the other argument that has been advanced in favour of the play: that it has been our exposure to the atrocity exhibition of the late twentieth century that has enabled us to catch up with it: as Bate puts it, 'in its willingness to confront violence, often in ways that are simultaneously shocking and playful, our culture resembles that of the Elizabethans' (1995: 1); and as Sue Hall-Smith writes in a supplement to the updated New Cambridge edition, '[t]he frequency with which the play is now performed across the globe demonstrates its relevance to contemporary concerns' (2006: 45). It is here, I suggest, that we need to recognise that the play's representational strategies, and the acts of witnessing in which it implicates its audiences, involve deeply problematic ethical as well as aesthetic considerations. One of the key debates within *Titus* criticism with respect to its depiction of violence has been whether this is 'gratuitous' or whether it serves a serious literary, theatrical and, it is sometimes implied, sometimes argued, moral function. The tendency of recent criticism, we have seen, has been to construct rationales which, as Bate puts it, 'do justice to the play's sustained artfulness' (1995: 34), so that the apparently gratuitous is rehabilitated within schema that are considered, purposeful and responsible; viewed with the apparent advantage of hindsight, the dismissive responses of earlier critics can themselves be discarded either as indicative of a misguided sense of decorum, a failure or inability to appreciate the richness, subtlety and power that theatrical performance, especially, has discovered in the play, or, more simply, as mere fastidious wincing.

Baked in that pie

There is no shortage of modern critical writing for the reader to consult that positively values the play, but I will conclude by positing an alternative perspective, one that returns to the views articulated by earlier twentieth-century commentators and attempts to put them in a different kind of context, not in order to suggest that they were right about it, but that they were less wrong than many have assumed. First, differences of opinion about whether the play is artful or gratuitous can obviously not be separated from consideration of their and our respective attitudes to real-life violence. It is easy enough to suspect previous generations of squeamishness, and late twentieth- and early twenty-first-century critics, readers and spectators have been very ready to assume a position of sophistication and superiority (which affords them the maturity and insight to genuinely appreciate a play like *Titus*); but to do so, I suggest, both patronises our critical forbears and does them a potentially grave disservice.

Wilson's New Shakespeare edition was published in 1948, Maxwell's Arden in 1953; and although I have no way of knowing whether the younger of these men saw military service (Wilson certainly did not, being in his late fifties when the Second World War broke out), the dating surely indicates a frame of reference for their judgements that, though the gentlemanly circumspection appropriate to English scholarship of the time discouraged them from articulating it, deserves acknowledgement. For those that had supped full of the horrors of the war, even from the remove of the home front, the problem with *Titus* was not the nature of its content but the callow and juvenile way Shakespeare appeared to treat it; 'what is wrong', Wilson found, 'is not the character of the material ... but uncertainty of taste and lack of skill in the handling of it' (1948: x); while for Maxwell what the play lacked was 'spiritual depth and imaginative significance' (1953: xxxv). Violence is considerably more amusing for those who have not experienced it at first hand than for those who have; I want to suggest that these editors might be considered historically better placed to judge whether or not the play is or is not in poor taste than those whose experience of violence derives primarily, if not exclusively, from media representations of it.

Finally, we should address the implication that earlier commentators might have thought differently about *Titus* had they had the opportunity to experience it in performance, an issue which is connected with the play's contemporary currency as a limit case for performance practice and criticism, an instance of where, as Alan Dessen contends, 'given the right conditions, the "unplayable" can become the theatrically potent' (1989: 69). The point is worth labouring a little as it raises performance issues of a more general nature. Brook's 1955 production, as has already been mentioned (p. 106), was almost universally hailed as a theatrical triumph, an event of singular lyricism, grotesque beauty and intense tragic power. Yet it was also almost equally unanimously identified as a spectacular *mis*representation of what Shakespeare wrote: 'The play was "twaddle", they said – a crude Elizabethan pot-boiler, a "horror comic" without "poetic characterization", a "preposterous melodrama" and a "bloody awful play"' (Hughes 2006: 30–31).

It is tempting to see such responses as evidence of the persistence of reviewers' prejudices – for did not the production prove the play otherwise? – but to do so is actually to undervalue and indeed devalue the power and integrity of performance itself. The reviewers were right: Brook's production worked on the terms that it did, not because it respected, realised or was pre-authorised by the text, but because it transformed, transcended and occasionally violently transfigured it: when, famously, he staged the entry of the raped and dismembered Lavinia with scarlet ribbons trailing from her wounds, accompanied by 'the slow plucking of harp-strings, like drops of blood falling into a pool' (David 1957: 127), he also completely cut Marcus's descriptive monologue (2.4.11–57).

What was at work in this production was less Shakespeare's genius than Olivier's and Brook's; and the experience was immeasurably stronger as a consequence. Deborah Warner's 1987 production, which, even more than Brook's, has been celebrated not only as the one which finally validated the play but as 'the most highly acclaimed Shakespearean production of the 1980s' (Bate 1995: 1), seems to provide even stronger vindication of Dessen's thesis, even more so because it was played (unlike Brook's) entirely uncut. For Bate, this 'textual fidelity' was 'remarkable' (62); for Dessen, a welcome instance of 'trust in the script' (57). Both critics, ostensibly proffering 'performance-centred' criticism, actually present an essentially literary judgement: what the show really proved – and what authorised the show – was the worth and integrity of the *text*. But what if, as in Brook's production, its terrible beauty and power derived not primarily from the play but from its articulation within a whole set of factors quite independent of it: a deeply committed ensemble cast, inspired direction, space and context of performance, the particular place and time in which these converged, conversed and agreed to disagree? What if the production worked not because of the play, but in spite of it?

To suggest this is to rub against the grain of every critical commentary on the production of which I am aware, and, indeed, of my own experience: I was one of those in 1987 who sat transfixed, moved and stunned by the performance, which remains one of the highpoints of my theatregoing life. Yet, re-reading the play, I cannot convince myself that it was by trusting the uncut script that its affect was secured. There were too many factors, too many brilliant actors, in this production to take account of here, but, above all, it was the presence of the unforgettable Brian Cox in the role of Titus that demanded and sustained my attention: craggy, imposing, capable in this production of moving in an instant from psychotic rage to deep tenderness, Cox is both a dangerous actor and a charming one, and, crucially, one with the power to project utter conviction in his material. As his long and successful career as a commercial voiceover artist attests, he has an unerring knack of investing even the most banal and thankless of texts with authority, human warmth and psychological interest. The voice of frozen fish; the voice of early Shakespeare: Cox's compelling surrogation of the central dilemma of Shakespearean performance – how to render the unplayable the theatrically potent – assumed the clearest, simplest and most immediate of forms. It's called acting.

Further reading

Aebischer, Pascale (2004) *Shakespeare's Violated Bodies: Stage and Screen Performance*. Cambridge: Cambridge University Press.

Barker, Francis (1993) *The Culture of Violence: Essays on Tragedy and History*. Manchester: Manchester University Press.

Dessen, Alan C. (1989) *Titus Andronicus*. Shakespeare in Performance. Manchester: Manchester University Press.

Little, Arthur L. Jr (2000) *Shakespeare Jungle Fever: National-Imperial Re-Visions of Race, Rape, and Sacrifice*. Stanford, CA: Stanford University Press.

Miola, Robert S. (1992) *Shakespeare and Classical Tragedy: The Influence of Seneca*. Oxford: Clarendon Press.

The Taming of the Shrew

Date, text and authorship

c.1590; F 1623. Solely Shakespearean.

Sources and influences

George Gascoigne, *Supposes* (1566); *The Taming of a Shrew* (1594) is debatably either a source or a derivative. The shrew-taming story is widespread in medieval and early modern folklore.

On stage

RSC, 1960 (dir. John Barton; Kate: Peggy Ashcroft; Petruccio: Peter O'Toole); RSC, 1978 (dir. Michael Bogdanov; Kate: Paolo Dionisitti; Petruccio: Jonathan Pryce); RSC, 1987 (dir. Jonathan Miller; Kate: Fiona Shaw; Petruccio: Brian Cox); RSC, 1995 (dir. Gale Edwards; Kate: Josie Lawrence; Petruccio: Michael Siberry); RSC, 2003 (dir. Gregory Doran; Kate: Alexandra Gilbreath; Petruccio: Jasper Brittan); Propeller, 2006 (dir. Edward Hall; Kate: Simon Scardifield).

On screen

USA, 1929 (dir. Sam Taylor; Kate: Mary Pickford; Petruccio: Douglas Fairbanks); USA/Italy, 1967 (dir. Franco Zeffirelli; Kate: Elizabeth Taylor; Petruccio: Richard Burton); BBC Television Shakespeare, UK, 1980 (dir. Jonathan Miller; Kate: Sarah Badel; Petruccio: John Cleese).

Offshoots

Cole Porter, *Kiss Me Kate*, USA, 1948 (film version, USA, 1953, dir. George Sidney); *A Shrew*, Open Space, 1975 (adapt. and dir. Charles Marowitz); *Shakespeare: The Animated Tales: The Taming of the Shrew*, UK/Russia, 1996 (dir. Aida Ziablikova); *10 Things I Hate About You*, USA, 1999 (dir. Gil Junger); *Shakespeare Retold: The Taming of the Shrew*, BBC TV, UK, 2005 (adapt. Sally Wainwright).

Anyone contemplating performing *The Taming of the Shrew* today finds herself confronted with a number of dilemmas. The first and most obvious (and it is not necessarily an issue exclusive to this play) is the question of whether a play that appears to rely for laughs on the spectacle of an assertive woman, belittled as a kind of rodent by the entertainment's title and demonised – by her own father, no less – as a 'hilding of a devilish spirit' (2.1.26), being progressively taunted, verbally and perhaps physically abused, ridiculed, humiliated, starved, sleep-deprived and ultimately psychologically coerced into utter capitulation to her fortune-hunting husband (or rather, as she herself terms him to her sister-wives in the final scene, 'thy lord, thy king, thy governor' [5.2.142]) continues to deserve to be regarded as in any sense a comedy. Viewed from this angle, the challenge posed by the play is not just a matter of how it should be performed but whether, given its underlying misogyny and the sadistic quality of its humour, it should be performed at all. The change in the play's status from a boisterous frolic which, if critically undervalued, has nonetheless been consistently popular on stage, to a problem comedy to be treated at the very least with considerable caution (revived over fifty times at Stratford-upon-Avon in the period between the opening of the Shakespeare Memorial Theatre and the establishment of the Royal Shakespeare Company in 1960, it has been seen there little more than a dozen times since) is of course partly attributable to the rise of feminism, and of feminist criticism, which from the outset adopted a robust approach to its gender politics, but disquiet about the play has been in evidence for at least a century.

During Shakespeare's own lifetime, John Fletcher (who would subsequently become his late collaborator) composed a sequel, *The Tamer Tamed; or, The Woman's Prize* (1611), which takes up Petruccio's story after Kate's death and reverses the comic stakes by altering the balance of power so that it is his second wife, Maria, who eventually emerges on top; adapted by David Garrick in the eighteenth century as the afterpiece *Catherine and Petruchio* (1754), a version which works assiduously to reassure its audiences that the taming business is all a game, the play as written was tucked tactfully away from sight until the late nineteenth century, when it was revived under the direction of Augustin Daly in New York, in 1887, and subsequently in London, with his star comedienne Ada Rehan in the lead. As rescripted by Garrick, Kate is afforded a crucial aside: 'I'll marry my Revenge, but I will tame him'.

It is the equivalent of the wink to Bianca (and, almost, to camera) that is performed by Mary Pickford at the end of Kate's submission speech in the 1929 movie version (the first full-length Shakespearean 'talkie'), a clear sign that she, and we, should take neither words nor actions at face value. Credited as 'based on the play by William Shakespeare, with additional dialogue by Sam Taylor', the film copies Garrick's cuts and interpolations, notably at this moment: in Pickford's hands, the homily (which ends on the promise to 'serve, love, and obey' [5.2.168]) is a mischievous, artfully ironic performance, pandering to the infantile vanity and self-delusion of her husband (the previous scene saw her tossing the prop that had become iconic of Petruchio's role, the whip, on the fire – though not before she has eyed it, and him, with a sly salaciousness that hints at the altogether more adult fun to come after the credits have rolled).

That the film deemed such tactics necessary in order to secure a commodiously comic finale congruent with the values of 1920s Hollywood slapstick is indicative of the play's already problematic status: over thirty years earlier, in 1897, George Bernard Shaw, champion of the new European drama that had brought to England's shores, amongst others, Ibsen's Nora (in *A Doll's House*, 1879) and *Hedda Gabler* (1881), wrote: 'No man with any decency of feeling can sit it out in the company of a woman without being extremely ashamed of the lord-of-all-creation moral implied in the wager and the speech put into the woman's own mouth' (1961: 198). Shaw's liberal conviction that 'men of decency' would be repelled by the play's ideology was not universally shared: the year before the release of Taylor's *Shrew*, the editor of the New Cambridge edition, Sir Arthur Quiller-Couch, confessed, 'a little wistfully' that he could not 'help thinking ... that the Petruchian discipline had something to say for itself' (Quiller-Couch and Wilson 1928: xvi). Quite what the sixty-five-year-old, thirty years married Cambridge professor meant by this is best known to himself, though it seems in character for the man warmly described by his successor as English Chair as 'intensely and even sentimentally patriotic; unobtrusively but sincerely Christian; a passionate believer in liberal education, liberal politics, and the idea of the gentleman' (Willey 1968: 20).

Even at the time of writing, as Pickford's wink testified, Quiller-Couch's perhaps rather elegiac patriarchalism was recognisable even to himself as a relic of a former age, as harmless fantasy (in any case, academic shrew-tamers have tended to favour subtler weaponry than that wielded by Petruccio), though as late as 1960 the self-proclaimed progressive and *Observer* theatre critic Kenneth Tynan thought it amusing to write in his review of John Barton's RSC production that Peggy Ashcroft's delivery of the final speech 'almost prompts one to regret the triumph of the suffragette movement' (*Observer*, 26 June 1960).

Despite the ingenuities of a tradition, popularised if not inaugurated by Pickford, of playing Kate's final speech, and sometimes the whole play, ironically, the play seemed to many by the 1970s, according to the *Guardian*'s Michael Billington, 'totally offensive … barbaric and disgusting' (*Guardian*, 5 May 1978), a conclusion that was forcibly prompted by the brutally direct alignment of the play's taming plot with contemporary gender inequalities and male violence seen in Michael Bogdanov's modern-dress RSC production of 1978.

Billington's indignation represented one strand of feminist response to the play and to Shakespeare's perceived misogyny more generally, and it coincided with the emergence of a variety of feminist approaches to Shakespeare that, while often asking broadly similar critical, historical and political questions about its subject-matter, offered divergent answers as to what attitudes the play, Shakespeare and its readers and audiences might adopt towards it. The argument that the play connives in the male supremacism that is explicitly expounded in the final scene ('Such duty as the subject owes the prince,/ Even such a woman oweth to her husband' [5.2.159–60]), that confidently underwrites Petruccio's treatment of his wife as commodity, and as an animal to be broken and domesticated, and that is articulated in both verbal and physical terms, has been well made, and occasionally staged: it was the perspective that, for example, informed Charles Marowitz's furious reworking of the play as *A Shrew* at the Open Space in 1975, which (in a scene in equally its own way deeply questionable in terms of its sexual politics) showed Kate brutalised, drugged and raped by Petruccio, and reduced to catatonia at the end; as well as, more recently, Conall Morrison's 2008 production for the RSC.

An alternative view is that male supremacism and misogyny, far from uncritically informing the play, are in actuality subverted and satirised by it. By this light, the play's most overt demonstrations and articulations of patriarchal dominance are self-evidently not to be taken at face value. When Petruccio declares that he 'will be master of what is mine own' –

> She is my goods, my chattels. She is my house,
> My household-stuff, my field, my barn,
> My horse, my ox, my ass, my anything …

> (3.3.100–103)

the litany is so extreme that, far from nodding their approval, audiences are invited to laugh at its preposterousness. The spectator's scepticism could be said to be encouraged by the shrew-taming story's knack of qualifying or interrogating itself as it unfolds. Developing the trope of 'supposes' that Shakespeare borrows from the 1575 play of that name by George Gascoigne that provided him with the source for the Bianca sub-plot, *Shrew* is throughout preoccupied with pretence, role-play, disguise, transformation, and the relations between the real and the counterfeit.

Its first scene involves the exchange of garments between a master and his servant, the first of a series of clothing-related incidents that includes Petruccio's arrival at his wedding decked out in a carnivalesque inversion of a groom's finery ('an old jerkin, a pair of old breeches thrice-turned, a pair of boots that have been candle-cases' [3.2.41–43]), Kate's thwarted acquisition of a new gown (4.3) and Petruccio's final-scene assertion of his mastery when he tells his wife that 'that cap of yours becomes you not' and orders her to 'throw it underfoot' (5.2.125–26); swapping clothes, Tranio and Lucentio are also involved in a temporary trading of power and status, wherein the dominator may become the dominated, and vice versa (Tranio, of course, ends the play completely under the dominion of his new wife). There is, perhaps, a clue here as to how the taming narrative might be interpreted: Petruccio and Kate may be at no point in the play what they appear to be; all may be pretence, all performance.

This is particularly so in the scene which apparently stages Kate's final capitulation:

> PETRUCCIO Come on, i'God's name. Once more toward our father's.
>   Good Lord, how bright and goodly shines the moon!
> KATHERINE The moon? – the sun. It is not moonlight now.
> PETRUCCIO I say it is the moon that shines so bright.
> KATHERINE I know it is the sun that shines so bright.
> PETRUCCIO Now, by my mother's son – and that's myself –
>   It shall be moon, or star, or what I list
>   Or ere I journey to your father's house.
>
> (4.6.1–8)

It is at this point, confronted with the implacably irrational force of Petruccio's will, that Kate realises the futility of continuing to cleave to what she knows and believes to be objective truth. Regardless of the claims of the real, true obedience can only be demonstrated by capitulating to her husband's caprice, irrespective of how demonstrably absurd this may be:

> Then God be blessed, it is the blessèd sun,
> But sun it is not when you say it is not,
> And the moon changes even as your mind.
> What you will have it named, even that it is,
> And so it shall be still for Katherine.
>
> (4.6.19–23)

Extracted from its farcical context, this is a chilling, even heartbreaking passage: reminiscent of the moment in George Orwell's *Nineteen Eighty-Four* when Winston Smith, under torture, finally agrees that he will assent to the proposition that two and two make five if Big Brother says so, it suggests that Kate has, in the interests of survival, surrendered the last vestiges of resistance, and dignity, to pander to the whims of a man who is quite possibly a lunatic. But who is manipulating whom here? Ironically, it is Petruccio who displays the irrationality and the (lunar) inconstancy assigned to womanhood; it is hard to see how even the most complacent patriarch in Shakespeare's audience could have claimed this incident as a victory. Moreover, the scene leaves unresolved the question of whether it is, actually, the sun or the moon that 'shines so bright': though common sense tells us that Kate is very probably in the right here, common sense, as the play has repeatedly indicated, is the one thing that is absolutely not to be trusted. On Shakespeare's open-air, daylight stages, or in his candle-lit indoor theatres, suns and moons come and go in the words of the actors and the imaginations of the spectators.

Complicating the picture even further, the shrew-taming story is itself partly framed by another level of narrative, that of the drunken tinker Christopher Sly, who appears at the beginning of the play in the two scenes of the Induction, and who acts as audience for the performance of what is described as 'a kind of history' (Ind. 2. 135). The Induction scenes, which begin with Sly collapsing in an alcoholic stupor following an argument with the Hostess of a Warwickshire inn, have him discovered by a passing aristocrat, who decides to 'practise on this drunken man' (Ind. 1. 32) by tricking him into believing that he is himself 'nothing but a mighty lord' (Ind. 1. 61) rather than a beggar. Persuading Sly that his former existence was nothing but a dream, the Lord and his attendants embroil Sly within a scenario whose dynamics of metamorphosis evidently mirror those of the shrew-story. Not insignificantly, Sly is supplied with a suitably subservient wife, in the form of the Lord's page, Bartholomew:

> Such duty to the drunkard let him do
> With soft low tongue and lowly courtesy,
> And say 'What is't your honour will command
> Wherein your lady and your humble wife
> May show her duty and make known her love?'

> (Ind. 1. 109–13)

Sly's fantasy-wife, it is clear, is the paragon imagined by Kate in the final scene; she is also a fake, a parody of pliable femininity performed by a boy in drag.

Treated as a frame narrative that renders the action of *Shrew* as a play-within-a-play, the Sly story distances, and ironises (and inoculates us against) it: since what we are seeing we see at least doubly, as an entertainment and lesson (and perhaps a wish-fulfilment fantasy) for Sly, it cannot be taken straight. One problem, however, is that the Sly framework is not sustained; at the end of the first scene of the shrew-story, Sly, who is already drifting off, is nudged awake by his companions to remark to his stage-bride that ''Tis an excellent piece of work … Would 'twere done' (1.1.246–47), but then is neither heard nor seen again. There are numerous ways of dealing with the indeterminacies that this generates: one has been to cut the Induction altogether (an option favoured by the three major screen versions), another to find an unobtrusive means of removing Sly from the scene so that the frame dissolves into the main narrative.

The third option, which has been particularly in favour since the 1960s, has been to make use of the anonymously authored *The Taming of a Shrew*, published in 1594, a play which has been variously seen as the source of *The Shrew*, a reported version of Shakespeare's text and a descendent from the original from which *The Shrew* also derives. What *A Shrew* has to offer is a complete Sly framework that can be deployed to fill in the gaps in the Folio text: not only does Sly intervene with comments at several points; he is also given an epilogue scene in which, having been re-dressed in his own clothes and returned penniless to the alehouse ditch where the start of the play found him, he vows to the Tapster (it is perhaps significant that Shakespeare reassigns the gender of Sly's antagonist) that, having absorbed the message of the play he has seen, he now knows 'how to tame a shrew':

> I'll to my
> Wife presently and tame her too,
> An if she anger me.

Ending the play with Sly's dreams of domination is a neat way of undermining whatever cocksure male triumphalism may be found in the final scene, and it provides more of a sense of closure than the Folio does. To the very end, the question of what is real and what is not remains in play, and so does the question of what marriage has in store for Petruccio and Kate. 'Come on, and kiss me, Kate' (5.2.184) is the invitation (order? solicitation?

entreaty?), but it has been the actors, and the editors, that have matched the deed to the word by supplying the stage direction, and stage action ('[*They kiss*]'), that the Folio does not. 'Come, Kate, we'll to bed' (5.2.188): the Folio marks an exit for Petruccio, but not for Kate, though editors and actors, almost without exception, have added one, for her, with him. The demands of comedy suggest that they have generally been right to do so; but what should not be forgotten is that this continues to be a matter of choice rather than textual inevitability.

Further reading

Hating-Smith, Tori (1985) *From Farce to Metadrama: A Stage History of 'The Taming of the Shrew'*. Westport, CT: Greenwood Press.

Hodgdon, Barbara (1998) 'Katharina Bound: or Play(K)ating the Strictures of Everyday Life', *The Shakespeare Trade: Performances and Appropriations*, Philadelphia, PA: University of Pennsylvania Press, 1–38.

Korda, Natasha (2002) *Shakespeare's Domestic Economies: Gender and Property in Early Modern England*. Philadelphia, PA: University of Pennsylvania Press.

Maguire, Laurie E. (1992) '"Household Kates": Chez Petruchio, Percy, and Plantagenet', in *Gloriana's Face: Women, Public and Private, in the English Renaissance*, ed. S. P. Cerasano and Marion Wynee-Davies. Detroit, MI: Wayne State University Press.

Marcus, Leah (1992) 'The Shakespearean Editor as Shrew-Tamer', *ELR*, 22: 177–200.

Schafer, Elizabeth (1998) *Ms-Directing Shakespeare: Women Direct Shakespeare*. London: The Women's Press.

Richard III

Date, text and authorship

1592–93; Q1 1597; Q2 1598; Q3 1602; Q4 1605; Q5 1612; Q6 1622; Q7 1629; Q8 1634; F1623. Solely Shakespearean.

Sources and influences

Sir Thomas More, *History of King Richard III* (c.1513); Edward Halle, *The Union of the Two Noble and Illustre Famelies of Lancastre and Yorke* (1548); Raphael Holinshed, *Chronicles of England, Scotland and Ireland* (1577; second edition 1587); *The Mirror for Magistrates* (1559 and 1563).

On stage

Staatliches Schauspielhaus, Berlin, 1920 (dir. Leopold Jessner); Old Vic, 1944 (Richard: Laurence Olivier); RSC, 1963 (dir. Peter Hall; Richard: Ian Holm); Rustaveli Company of Tbilisi, Georgia, 1979 (dir. Robert Strurua; Richard: Ramaz Chkhikvadze); RSC, 1984 (dir. Bill Alexander; Richard: Antony Sher); NT, 1990 (dir. Richard Eyre; Richard: Ian McKellen); RSC, 1992 (dir. Sam Mendes; Richard: Simon Russell Beale); RSC, 1995 (dir. Steven Pimlott; Richard: David Troughton); Satirikon, Moscow, 2004 (dir. Yuri Butusov; Richard: Konstantin Raikin); RSC, 2006 (dir. Michael Boyd; Richard: Jonathan Slinger).

On screen

UK, 1911 (photography: Will Barker; Richard: Frank Benson; included in *Silent Shakespeare*, BFI, 2000); UK, 1955 (dir. Laurence Olivier; Richard: Laurence Olivier; Lady Anne: Claire Bloom; Clarence: John Gielgud; Buckingham: Ralph Richardson); *An Age of Kings,* BBC TV, UK, 1960 (dir. Michael Hayes; Richard: Paul Daneman; Queen Margaret: Mary Morris); BBC Television Shakespeare, UK, 1983 (dir. Jane Howell; Richard: Ron Cook; Queen Margaret: Julia Foster; Lady Anne: Zoë Wanamaker); *The Wars of the Roses*, English Shakespeare Company, UK, 1990 (dir. Michael Bogdanov; Richard: Andrew Jarvis); UK/USA, 1995 (dir. Richard Loncraine; Richard: Ian McKellen).

Offshoots

Bertolt Brecht, *Der aufhaltsame Aufstieg des Arturo Ui* (*The Resistible Rise of Arturo Ui*), 1941; David Hare and Howard Brenton, *Pravda*, NT, 1985; *Looking for Richard*, USA, 1996 (dir. Al Pacino; Richard: Al Pacino); *Shakespeare: The Animated Tales: Richard III*, UK/Russia, 1996 (dir. Natalia Orlova).

Although it is positioned in the Folio as the final instalment in the group of history plays that the editors of the volume assembled in chronological sequence (beginning with *The Life and Death of King John*), *Richard III* has often been seen as a reasonably autonomous work which is not necessarily disadvantaged by being treated in isolation from the histories that precede it. During the first part of the twentieth century, the play's performance tradition was divided: on the one hand, 'ranting Richards on scenic sets continued to dominate the theatres of Stratford-upon-Avon, London, and New York' (Jowett 2000: 98), while, on the other, experimentalists such as Leopold Jessner in 1920s Berlin applied the tortured scenographies of expressionism. It was not until 1963, when the play was staged as part of the Royal Shakespeare Company's *The Wars of the Roses* cycle in conjunction with a two-part adaptation of the three parts of *Henry VI*, that the play was definitively offered as the culmination of a dramaturgical and historical sequence; in this respect, theatrical innovation reflected a shift of scholarly emphasis that had been initiated by E. M W. Tillyard in his influential *Shakespeare's History Plays* (1962 [1944]). More immediate to the production's concerns was Jan Kott's *Shakespeare Our Contemporary* (1964; English translation, 1965), which turned Tillyard's providentialism inside out, placing the play within the deterministic scheme of the brutal, relentless Grand Mechanism, an 'implacable roller of history' which 'crushes everybody and everything', the human face of which is Richard himself: 'the mastermind ... its will and awareness' (Kott 1965: 39, 35).

The play's fluctuating capacity to operate in and out of sequence within the theatre reflects at one level the shifting nature of theatrical taste and critical fashion, but it also points towards a degree of mobility and ambivalence in its own relation to both history and genre. In the Folio, the play's captioning affords it a dual identity: although it is designated on the contents page and in the running titles as 'The Life & Death of Richard the Third', it is headed 'The Tragedy of Richard the Third' (and, alerting its readers to the climactic events of the play, subtitled 'with the Landing of Earle Richmond, and the Battell at Bosworth Field'); and although the generic flexibility of the history play format was one of its defining characteristics, the distinction between a chronicle-style 'life and death' and classical 'tragedy' suggests a range of possible attitudes to the fate of the protagonist, to the play's own use of history, and to the kind of moral, ethical and political lessons that might be drawn from it.

All eight of the quarto editions published between 1597 and 1634 were also designated as tragedies, although the subtitling of Q1 also took care to establish Richard as the political criminal, tyrant and usurper of Tudor mythology: 'Containing His treacherous Plots against his brother Clarence; the pittiefull murther of his innocent nephews; his tyrannicall usurpation; with the whole course of his detested life, and most deserved death.' As advertised, this sensationalist account of Richard was that of the Tudor chronicles, Halle and Holinshed, and of popular myth: as an icon of the diabolic villainy that was graphically figured in his own grotesquely deformed body, Richard is the necessary demon of the Tudor version of English history, whose defeat (treated as a kind of exorcism) seals the legitimacy of the succession. For Halle, especially, the end of Richard was key to securing the 'union' that his historical narrative is intended to ratify, a point which Shakespeare seems to endorse in the newly crowned Richmond's final speech:

> We will unite the white rose and the red.
> Smile, heaven, upon this fair conjunction,
> That long have frowned upon their enmity.
> What traitor hears me and says not 'Amen'?

> (5.7.19–22)

Just prior to this, Richard has been summarily dispatched as a 'bloody wretch' and 'bloody dog' (5.7.5, 5.7.2), in what is the final manifestation of a vituperative register that persistently associates him with the demonic and the animalistic. Hailed by Lady Anne as a 'lump of foul deformity' (1.2.57), Richard is addressed or described as a 'hedgehog' (1.2.102), 'swine' (5.2.10), 'wolf' (4.4.22), 'toad' (1.2.147, 4.4.145), 'dog' (1.3.213, 1.3.287, 4.4.49, 4.4.78, 5.7.2), 'boar' (3.2.8, 3.2.25–26, 3.2.70, 3.4.82, 5.2.7), and twice characterised as a 'bottled spider' (1.3.240, 4.4.81).

No other Shakespearean character is so relentlessly, and indiscriminately, bestialised. The vilification of Richard is in keeping with the spirit of the chronicles, and Shakespeare extends and amplifies the invective; conversely, his own usurper, Richmond, is depicted as 'virtuous and holy', visited by friendly ghosts on the eve of the Battle of Bosworth with assurances that 'the wronged souls/ Of butchered princes fight on thy behalf', and that, uniquely, as 'offspring of the house of Lancaster', he is the one whom ' the wronged heirs of York do pray for' (5.4.100–16). Shakespeare also follows the chronicles by charging Richard with the murder of the Princes in the Tower (as the title page of Q1 advertises, although it is not actually dramatised in the play), although the evidence for this was, historically speaking, less than conclusive.

This is the politically orthodox scheme of Richard's rise and fall, one which (in keeping with the homiletic tradition of tragedy) would seem to present a straightforwardly didactic message concerning the tyrannical misappropriation of rule. But the play's relation to its source narratives is complicated not only by the fact that there were other versions of Richard's history in circulation (including the anonymous play *The True Tragedy of Richard III*, published in 1594), but also by the divisions, variations and shifting viewpoints offered by the chronicles themselves. Both Halle and Holinshed were anthologists, assembling narratives not necessarily in agreement with each other: the material relating to Richard in the *Union* is a reproduction of Sir Thomas More's *History of Richard III*, written around 1513 and published in 1543; the *Chronicles* in turn reprint Halle's account taken from More, as well as including material from the new edition of More's works which had appeared in 1557. It is to More that Shakespeare owes the impression of Richard as physically deformed: in Halle, he is 'eivill featured of limnes, croke backed' (Bullough 1960, 3: 253); in Holinshed, however, in a small but significant move from the metaphysical to the secular, More's Latin is translated as 'ill-featured of limbs'.

It is also More who supplies Shakespeare with the outlines of a theatrical frame of reference for Richard's history, one which qualifies and complicates the simple dichotomies of Tudor propaganda (Halle entitles the section dealing with Richard 'The Tragical Doings of King Richard the Third'). As well as showing an interest in Richard's guilty conscience (emblematised by 'his hand ever upon his dagger'), and thus anticipating one of the dramatic concerns of the play, More refers directly to the popular stage in his discussion of the histrionic basis of Richard's journey to power:

> And in a stage play, all the people know right well that one playing the sultan is percase a souter ... And so they said that these matters be kings' games, as it were stage plays, and for the more part played upon scaffolds, in which poor men be but the lookers on.
>
> (Jowett 2000: 396)

The sultan played by the souter (or cobbler), like the king portrayed by a common player, is an apt enough analogy for the dissembling and illegitimate monarch, although the general recognition of the transparency of the deception is accompanied by a warning against 'poor men' straying into an arena of political theatre in which they are best advised not to intervene.

In *Richard III*, as throughout the history plays, the strong connection between political advancement, kingship and performance is repeatedly articulated. There is a straightforward sense in which most of Richard's actions and interactions on the route to the throne are based upon deceit and pretence, by saying one thing while intending another; his most memorable scenes are those in which he is clearly role-playing, whether in the part of the wooer of Lady Anne (2.1) or as the pious, reluctant contender for the Crown (3.7). This performance dimension is also embedded within the verbal texture of the play. In his opening speech, before telling of the 'Plots have I laid, inductions dangerous' (1.1.32), Richard imagines himself having 'no delight to pass away the time/ Unless to spy my shadow in the sun' (1.1.25–26), and thus initially invokes an impotent and insubstantial theatrical double ('shadow' being a synonym for player), who reappears much strengthened at the end of the scene of his seduction of Lady Anne: 'Shine out, fair sun – till I have bought a glass,/ That I may see my shadow as I pass' (1.2.247–48).

This dark figure replicates the diabolism which (strangely oblivious to the abuse directed at him by his opponents) Richard seems to believe he can conceal through the adroitness of his acting, declaring 'thus I clothe my naked villainy'

> With old odd ends, stol'n forth of Holy Writ,
> And seem a saint when most I play the devil.
>
> (1.3.335–36)

Richard's self-dramatising tendencies are endorsed by others, for instance by Buckingham, who in 3.4 alerts him to Hastings's attempt to politically upstage him:

> Had not you come upon your cue, my lord,
> William Lord Hastings had now pronounced your part –
> I mean, your voice for crowning of the king.
>
> (3.4.28–30)

The metadramatic dimension of the play is most explicitly articulated in 3.5, the scene of Richard and Buckingham's appearance before the Lord Mayor, which has them enter costumed 'in rotten armour, marvellous ill-favoured' and launch into a parody of the acting conventions of the medium within which the play itself is operating:

> RICHARD GLOUCESTER Come, cousin, canst thou quake and change thy
>   colour?
>   Murder thy breath in middle of a word?
>   And then again begin, and stop again,
>   As if thou wert distraught and mad with terror?
> BUCKINGHAM Tut, I can counterfeit the deep tragedian,
>   Tremble and start at wagging of a straw,
>   Speak, and look back, and pry on every side,
>   Intending deep suspicion; ghastly looks
>   Are at my service, like enforcèd smiles,
>   And both are ready in their offices
>   At any time to grace my stratagems.
>
> (3.5.1–11)

The repertoire of gestures, facial expressions and verbal tics that stereotypically characterise the tragic actor provide the means for the cynical manipulation of the Lord Mayor in the scene that follows; in conjunction with Richard's semblances of piety, the arts of performance are those of the stage machiavel, who is able to exploit both the hypocrisy and the gullibility of those around him. Richard and Buckingham are themselves, of course, played by tragic actors, and in this respect the metaphor of the player king works to remind spectators of the mechanisms of the dramatic fiction itself, here opened up to a momentarily comic perspective that transforms tragedy into the joke of shoddy and meretricious theatricality.

In 3.1, in a characteristic instance of verbal double-dealing in his dialogue with the Prince Edward, Richard offers a self-reflexive comment upon his theatrical ancestry:

> Thus like the formal Vice, Iniquity,
> I moralize two meanings in one word.
>
> (3.1.82–83)

The reference is to one of the personae of the medieval Morality drama, the Vice, renowned for his talent for trickery, disguise, equivocation and duplicity, but also liable to enjoy a particularly close and complicit relationship with his audience. One of the defining characteristics of the Vice was his freedom to move in and out of the world of the play, and to manipulate the boundaries between the fictional and the real: in the terms supplied by Robert Weimann, the Vice is able to comment (humorously, sceptically or satirically) upon the *locus* of theatrical illusion from the permeable space of the *platea*, the haunt of both devils and clowns (Weimann 1978). As the culminating embodiment of the retributive, destructive energies of the Wars of the Roses, Richard occupies a theatrical position which allows him, for the first part of the play at least, not quite to believe in the history he is energetically shaping. In the second part, however, he finds himself having to drop the act, discovering that it is history, after all, that has the last word, as his past, in the shape of the ghosts of his victims, and his present, in the form of Richmond's forces, finally catch up with him.

Further reading

Charnes, Linda (1993) *Notorious Identity: Materializing the Subject in Shakespeare*. Cambridge, MA: Harvard University Press.

Garber, Marjorie (1987) *Shakespeare's Ghost Writers: Literature as Uncanny Causality*. London: Methuen.

Kott, Jan (1964) *Shakespeare Our Contemporary*, trans. Boleslaw Taborski. London: Eyre Methuen.

Maus, Katherine (1995) *Inwardness and Theater in the English Renaissance*. Chicago, IL: University of Chicago Press.

Ornstein, Robert (1972) *A Kingdom for a Stage: The Achievement of Shakespeare's History Plays*. Cambridge, MA: Harvard University Press.

Rossiter, A. P. (1989 [1961]) *Angel with Horns: Fifteen Lectures on Shakespeare*, ed. Graham Storey London: Longman.

Venus and Adonis *and* Lucrece

Venus and Adonis

Date, text and authorship

1593; Q1 1593; Q2 1594; Q3 1595; Q4 1596; Q5 1599; Q6 1599; Q7 1602; Q8 1607–08; Q9 1608–09; Q10 1610; Q11 1617; Q12 1620; Q13 1627; Q14 1630; Q15 1630–36; Q16 1636. Solely Shakespearean.

Sources and influences

Ovid, *Metamorphoses* (English translation by Arthur Golding, 1567); Thomas Lodge, *Scilla's Metamorphosis* (1589).

On stage

RSC, 1987 (dir. Stephen Rayne; Narrator: Oliver Ford-Davies; Venus: Imelda Staunton; Adonis: Douglas Hodge); Citizens Theatre, Glasgow, 1992 (dir. Matthew Radford and Malcolm Sutherland); Young Vic, 1995 (dir. Mark Rylance); Shakespeare's Globe, 2002; RSC, 2004 (dir. Gregory Doran; Narrator: Michael Pennington); RSC, 2007 (dir. Gregory Doran; Narrator: Harriet Walter).

Lucrece

Date, text and authorship

1594; Q1, Q2 1594; Q3, Q4 1600; Q5 1607; Q6 1616; Q7 1624; Q8 1632; Q9 1655. Solely Shakespearean.

Sources and influences

Ovid, *Fasti*; Livy, *Ab urbe condita libri* (English translation by William Painter, 1566); Geoffrey Chaucer, *The Legend of Good Women* (c.1385–94); *The Mirror for Magistrates* (1559).

On stage

Almeida, London, 1988 (dir. Bardy Thomas); Shakespeare's Globe, 1996; RSC, 2006 (dir. Gregory Doran; Lucrece: Jane Lapotaire).

Desire sees best of all

As a grammar school boy in Stratford-upon-Avon in the 1570s, William Shakespeare would have found himself faced with a daunting array of set reading, exposing him to formalities of the prescribed primer in Latin grammar, the sonorous verse and prose of the *Book of Homilies*, *Book of Common Prayer* and Geneva Bible; but if there was one work that appeared to have left a profound and lasting impression upon him it was the one which provided the direct source for his first published work, which was printed and distributed by his fellow Stratfordian, Richard Field, in 1593. *Venus and Adonis* takes its narrative from the *Metamorphoses* (completed in 8 AD), the epic collection of mythical stories of transformation by the Roman poet Ovid that was studied in Latin as part of the school curriculum and widely read in Arthur Golding's English translation of 1567; as an episode in a compendium of tales of shape-shifting that sees gods, humans and beasts trading shapes and places, exchanging identities, passions and desires, the story of the thwarted encounter between the legendary epitome of youthful male beauty and the goddess of love occurs in the tenth of the work's fifteen books, where it is among the most lurid, perverse and pornographic scenarios of all. It illustrates, as Golding observes, 'chiefly one kynd of argument/ Reproving most prodigious lusts as have been bent/ Too incest most unnatural' (Rouse 1961: 5).

For Shakespeare, in his late twenties at the time of the poem's publication, the tale of a young man offered sexual initiation at the hands of a worldly older woman (a cultural narrative that has appealed to generations of schoolboys) provided an opportunity to demonstrate at length his mastery, in particular, of the arts of *copia* and *amplifactio* (copiousness and amplification). As a dazzling exercise in the art of linguistic manipulation, *Venus and Adonis* is also a virtuoso act of literary seduction, flirting with and teasing its readers (and especially its explicitly intended reader, dedicatee and would-be patron, the Earl of Southampton) by provoking, arousing and deferring the desire for closure, engaging in sexual power games and role-play (the poem's comedy lies in its depiction of the woman as sexual aggressor), alternating passivity and activity, tumescence and dilation, and toying with gender reversals whereby the male hunter, the ironic icon of chastity, becomes the hunted prey, the female the one who experiences the unsatiated desire of the Petrarchan lover ('She red and hot as coals of glowing fire;/ He red for shame, but frosty in desire' [ll. 35–36]).

In Golding's version, Venus's pursuit of Adonis, a chase which culminates in the youth's death (according to the familiar early modern double sense of the term, a moment metonymic of sexual release) beneath the tusks of a wild boar, is told in a hundred lines: the pair are introduced ('the beawty of the lad/ Inflamed her'), her infatuation briskly summarised; warned by Venus not to try his chances with those who 'bear thunder in theyr hooked tusks', Adonis heads straight into a confrontation with a beast that results in it 'hyding in his codds his tuskes as farre as he could thrust' (Rouse 1961: 217). The erotic and sadistic connotations of Adonis's impalement upon what appears to be the externalisation of the force of desire (ambiguously, both his repressed own and Venus's) would not have been lost on Golding's (and Ovid's) Elizabethan readers; for Shakespeare, however, the relatively straightforward linear exposition offered the potential for an audaciously ambitious early experiment in which the pressures of narrative and the pleasures of rhetoric – or, alternatively, the imperative to get through it, get it over and done with, and the desire to linger, indulge, expand and digress – are placed in counterpoint.

Retaining the narrative core of Venus's pursuit of Adonis while he is attempting to engage in some woodland hunting, and occupying a classically compressed two-day time-scheme that generates within it a succession of dilatory moments in which temporality is extended and suspended, Shakespeare's expansion of the episode takes it to nearly 1,200 lines. In the first section, consisting of just over 250 lines, we see Venus insistently attempting to force her attentions ('Backward she pushed him, as she would be thrust' [l. 41]) upon the unwilling Adonis, her overtures culminating in an evocation of her body as the terrain of the hunt, the landscape of an aristocratic country estate: 'I'll be a park, and thou shalt be my deer' (l. 231):

> Graze on my lips, and if those hills be dry,
> Stray lower, where the pleasant fountains lie.

(ll. 233–34)

As a form of enclosed, managed wilderness that is partway between nature and culture, and that both harbours and nurtures its inhabitants and solicits the play of their death, the parkland is both a fertile source of innuendo and an epitome of the poem's topography of sex, which is envisaged as ecstatic, transformative and deeply destructive.

If for the poem's first readers its witty novelty lay in the reversal of male–female, active-passive gender roles, wherein Adonis repels Venus's salacious advances ('"In night", quoth she, "desire sees best of all"' [l. 720]) with a prim lecture on chastity ('Love surfeits not; lust like a glutton dies./ Love is all truth, lust full of forgèd lies' [803–04]), its nature imagery also provides a comic perspective and context for their thwarted coupling. Heralded by a couplet that would not have shamed the author of *Pyramus and Thisbe* ('"Pity", she cries, "Some favour, some remorse!"/ Away he springs, and hasteth to his horse' [ll. 257–58]), the episode which succeeds the poem's first phase, in which Adonis's outrageously priapic stallion ('His ears up-pricked, his braided hanging mane ... now stand on end' [ll. 271–72]) romps off into the woods with a lusty mare, is one of the more striking of Shakespeare's embellishments of Golding's narrative: presenting Adonis with animal passions that pose a reproof of his own recalcitrance, it simultaneously enhances and parodies the desires of human lovers, rendering sex and courtship both celestial and absurd. In this instance, the female party is the reluctant one: nonetheless, the interlude ends with the equine couple thundering into a nearby copse to consummate their romance: 'As they were mad unto the wood they hie them,/ Outstripping crows that strive to overfly them' (ll. 323–24).

Venus and Adonis, of course, experience a considerably less happy end. In Shakespeare's hands, the murderous, castrating boar that is the male protagonist's nemesis is witnessed not in the throes of killing, as in Golding, but in the deadly consequences of that act: once Adonis disappears from the scene at line 816 (the theatrical terms of reference are singularly apt to a piece, at least in its use of dialogue, so dramatically conceived), he is not seen alive again; as in classical tragedy, the climactic act of violence occurs offstage. As in Golding, Adonis's demise conflates desire and death: in Shakespeare's poem, via the fractured, anguished vision of Venus herself, who, imaginatively trading places with the boar sinking his head into her beloved's groin, draws from the spectacle of the mangled corpse the perverse, oxymoronic (but also, the poem implies, true) inference that the act of 'the loving swine' is the corollary of her own desire, expressed here as a fellatio fantasy with added bite:

> 'Had I been toothed like him, I must confess
> With kissing him I should have killed him first ...

(ll. 1117–18)

It is the poem's last reference but one to Venus's seemingly insatiable demand for kissing (marked with an obsessive orality, Venus is perverse, devouring mother as well as frustrated lover): in the penultimate stanza, following Adonis's magical transformation into an anemone, she promises that 'There shall not be one minute in an hour/ Wherein I will not kiss my sweet love's flower' (1187–88); the ironic outcome of her attempted deflowerment is what might be called a kind of enflowerment.

Graver labour

The polymorphous, playful eroticism of *Venus and Adonis* contrasts markedly with what in his dedication to the poem Shakespeare termed the 'graver labour' intended for the Earl of

Southampton's eyes (see 'Life and contexts', pp. 29–31): *The Rape of Lucrece*, which was published, again by Richard Field, in 1594. Ovid again provided the source of a story (set in 509 BC) which was of legendary significance to Shakespeare's readers: over the course of two thousand lines, *Lucrece* narrates the rape of Lucretia, chaste wife of the Roman nobleman Collatine, by Tarquin, the son of the last king of Rome, Tarquinus Superbus ('The Proud'), and her subsequent suicide. The act had important political as well as personal consequences, since it provoked Collatine's allies to rise up against the tyrannical Tarquins, depose the monarchy and establish the Roman republic, events which are summarised in the poem's 'Argument', but only briefly alluded to in the main body of the work itself, which focuses on the personal dimensions of the rape, first from the point of view of the rapist and second from that of his victim.

Tarquin's share of the poem runs from the opening lines, where he is dramatically evoked in breathless, lust-fuelled motion, 'Borne by the trustless wings of false desire', bearing (in what is one of the poem's key images) a 'lightless fire', and seeking to 'girdle with embracing flames the waist/ Of Collatine's fair love' (ll. 2–7), to just over one-third of the way through, when he slinks away after the rape, creeping 'like a thievish dog' that 'faintly flies, sweating with guilty fear' (ll. 736–40). The lines between track Tarquin's transit from the besieged city of Ardea to Collatine's household, and from his own sleeping quarters to Lucrece's bedchamber, each stage of the journey featuring external and internal obstacles, in terms both of the physical barriers that interpose between the rapist and his target and of the vacillations in his consciousness, which the poem vividly dramatises. Warmly welcomed by the trusting Lucrece on his arrival, Tarquin (whose lust has been aroused by her husband's praise of her) talks with her long into the night before taking himself to a sleepless bed.

There he lies 'revolving/ The sundry dangers of his will's obtaining' (ll. 127–28) for sixty lines, 'madly tossed between desire and dread' (l. 171), before he leaps from the bed, lights a torch (like the sword with which he strikes its light, 'a symbol for his penis' [Duncan-Jones and Woudhuysen 2007: 254]), resolving that 'As from this cold flint I enforced this fire,/ So Lucrece must I force to my desire' (ll. 181–82). Yet the firmness of purpose immediately dissipates, as 'he doth premeditate/ The dangers of his loathsome enterprise' (ll. 183–84) for nearly one hundred lines, oscillating between self-reproach, shame and disgust ('he doth despise/ His naked armour of still-slaughtered lust' [ll. 188–89]), appalled recognition of the dishonour of the deed, contemptuous dismissal of the pangs of conscience and aggressive self-justification; embracing the freethinking stance of the Marlovian hedonist ('Who fears a sentence or an old man's saw/ Shall by a painted cloth be kept in awe' [ll. 244–45]), he finally determines that 'Desire my pilot is, beauty my prize./ Then who fears sinking where such treasure lies?' (ll. 279–80).

The next section follows Tarquin on his way through the house, via a series of symbolically charged 'locks between her chamber and his will,/ Each one by him enforced' (ll. 302–03), and thus through a succession of rape images, all the while internally torn between condemnation and legitimation of the intended act; and, as 'each unwilling portal yields him way' (l. 309), even the rogue gusts of air that emit 'Through little vents and crannies of the place' (l. 310) and momentarily extinguish his torch, cannot quell the 'hot heart' (l. 314) which reignites it. The flare reveals Lucrece's embroidery, a glove penetrated by a needle, an emblem of her virtue which, rather than deterring the attacker, stimulates his appetite all the more. Arriving at Lucrece's chamber, he finds her, 'like a virtuous monument' (l. 391), lying asleep. It is here that it is made clear that the ramifications of Tarquin's act extend well beyond the violence that it inflicts upon Lucrece herself: by possessing the chaste wife (whose breasts are described as 'A pair of maiden worlds unconquerèd' that 'Save of their lord no bearing yoke they knew' [ll. 408–09]) of Collatine, the 'thievish' (l. 736) Tarquin is committing a crime against what is, according to Roman and early modern patriarchal prerogative, his property (though a self-defeating one: later, in the aftermath of the rape, the poem reports that 'Pure chastity is rifled of her store,/ And lust, the thief, far poorer than before' [ll. 692–93]); not only that, but his action is that of a 'foul usurper' intending 'From this fair throne to heave the owner out' (ll. 412–13).

Ironically transposed upon the behaviour of the son of the king, the terminology of rebellion and regicide anticipates the political outcome of the story that the poem otherwise downplays; and at this point Tarquin forfeits the semblance of nobility, the mutinous constituents of his desire dissolving into 'straggling slaves for pillage fighting' (l. 428) as he launches an assault on his victim imaged in precisely militaristic terms: a hand grabbing her breast is a 'Rude ram, to batter such an ivory wall' (l. 464), as he prepares 'To make the breach and enter this sweet city' (l. 469). Employing the classic rapist's manoeuvre of blaming his victim for having 'provoked' his attack ('The fault is thine/ For those thine eyes betray thee unto mine' [ll. 482–83]), Tarquin informs Lucrece that he will have his way or kill her, sophistically arguing that it will be the better for her to acquiesce to 'A little harm done to a great end' (l. 528) than to bequeath to her husband and children 'The shame that from them no device can take' (l. 535). In vain, she appeals, over the course of nearly a hundred lines, to his sense of honour, to his obligations to her husband, to her hospitality and to his own royal position ('kings' misdeeds cannot be hid in clay … This deed will make thee only loved for fear' [ll. 609–10]), her pleas culminating in an emphatic reiteration of the figure of insurrection:

> So shall these slaves be king, and thou their slave;
> Thou nobly base, they basely dignified;
> Thou their fair life, and they thy fouler grave;
> Thou loathèd in their shame, they in thy pride.
> The lesser thing should not the greater hide.
>
> (ll. 659–63)

The actual rape is dealt with relatively briefly and circumspectly: the poem jump-cuts from the nastily vivid detail of Tarquin swathing Lucrece's head in her own linen to the stained sheets of her bed. The deflated and dejected Tarquin quits the scene well aware that 'through the length of times he stands disgraced' (l. 718), and the poem thereafter focuses on Lucrece's tragedy.

If the Tarquin-dominated part of the poem derives momentum from its sense of internal conflict and its itinerary of penetration, the latter section is necessarily more static, its scope for movement circumscribed by Lucrece's incarceration at the scene of the crime and within the more limited options available to the role of victim: whereas 'He runs, and chides his vanished loathed delight', she stays, 'exclaiming on the direful night' (ll. 741–42). Lengthily addressing herself to night ('image of hell,/ Dim register and notary of shame' [ll. 764–65]), to time ('Thou ceaseless lackey to eternity' [l. 967]) and to opportunity ('Thou ravisher, thou traitor, thou false thief' [l. 888]), Lucrece laments her state and calls upon the fates to 'Devise extremes beyond extremity' (l. 969) to inflict upon Tarquin; resolves to kill herself, then decides to call back Collatine to confess what has occurred and to incite him to vengeance. Throughout, her concern is more with the impact of the rape upon her husband's honour (and, in particular, with the prospect of illegitimate offspring – 'This bastard graft' [l. 1062] – that will contaminate the bloodline) than with herself, her urge to self-sacrifice a violent introjection of patriarchal proprietorial rights over her body.

This position is resisted both by the poem and by her husband and his male companion. The poem sententiously shifts the burden of rape onto the perpetrator:

> O, let it not be held
> Poor women's faults that they are so full-filled
> With men's abuses. Those proud lords, to blame,
> Make weak-made women tenants to their shame.

(ll. 1257–60)

Accepting the distinctions between the body, mind and will that vindicate her of any complicity in the crime ('Her body's stain her mind untainted clears' [l. 1710]), the assembled lords attending Lucrece's public avowal are unanimous in declaring her guiltless; nonetheless, they are powerless to prevent the suicide which for her seems the only way of resolving the unbearable conflict between innocence and shame, as well as the definitive spur to the vengeance that results in the overthrow of the Tarquins. The action of anything but a 'weak-made' woman, Lucrece's self-administered death displays a strength, determination and singularity of purpose that, whilst seeming to affirm gender hierarchy, paradoxically reframes it by presenting masculinity with its proper model: 'My resolution', she declares to Collatine, 'shall be thy boast,/ By whose example thou revenged mayst be' (ll. 1193–94).

Both *Venus and Adonis* and *The Rape of Lucrece* were much read by Shakespeare's contemporaries, the former running to ten reprints by 1620, the latter reissued six times up until 1616. They were considerably less popular with readers and critics up until the end of the twentieth century, though their subject-matter has lent them some interest to feminist criticism during the past few decades. Both narratives have relatively recently attracted the attention of theatre practitioners, most notably in the puppet version of *Venus and Adonis*, directed by Gregory Doran for the Royal Shakespeare Company in 2004, which was revived for the company's Complete Works festival in 2007.

Further reading

Bate, Jonathan (1993) 'Sexual Perversity in *Venus and Adonis*', *Yearbook of English Studies*, 23: 80–92.

Berry, Philippa (1992) 'Woman, Language, and History in *The Rape of Lucrece*', *Shakespeare Survey*, 44: 33–39.

Cheney, Patrick (2004) *Shakespeare, National Poet-Playwright*. Cambridge: Cambridge University Press.

Kolin, Philip C. (ed.) (1997) *Venus and Adonis: Critical Essays*. New York: Garland.

Maus, Katherine Eisaman (1986) 'Taking Tropes Seriously: Language and Violence in Shakespeare's *Rape of Lucrece*', *Shakespeare Quarterly*, 37: 66–82.

Smith, Peter J. (2000) 'A "Consummation Devoutly to Be Wished": The Erotics of Narration in *Venus and Adonis*', *Shakespeare Survey*, 53: 25–38.

Ziegler, G. (1990) 'My Lady's Chamber: Female Space, Female Chastity in Shakespeare', *Textual Practice*, 4: 73–100.

A Midsummer Night's Dream *and* Romeo and Juliet

A Midsummer Night's Dream

Date, text and authorship

1594–96; Q1 1600; Q2 1619; F 1623. Solely Shakespearean.

Sources and influences

Plutarch, *Lives of the Noble Grecians and Romans* (trans. Thomas North, 1579); Geoffrey Chaucer, *The Knight's Tale* (c.1392–95); Ovid, *Metamorphoses* (English translation by Arthur Golding, 1567); Apuleius, *The Golden Ass* (English translation by William Adlington, 1566); John Lyly, *Gallathea* (1585) and *Edimion* (1588).

On stage

Savoy Theatre, 1914 (dir. Harley Granville Barker); Old Vic, 1937, 1951 (dir. Tyrone Guthrie); SMT, 1954 (dir. George Devine); RSC, 1962 (dir. Peter Hall; Theseus: Tony Steedman; Hippolyta: Yvonne Bonnamy/Rosemary Frankau; Oberon: Ian Richardson; Titania: Judi Dench/Juliet Mills); RSC, 1970 (dir. Peter Brook; Theseus/Oberon: Alan Howard; Hippolyta/Titania: Sara Kestelman; Bottom: David Waller); RSC, 1977 (dir. John Barton); RSC, 1981 (dir. Ron Daniels); RSC, 1989 (dir. John Caird); Renaissance Theatre Company, 1990 (dir. Kenneth Branagh); NT, 1992 (dir. Robert Lepage); RSC, 1994 (dir. Adrian Noble; Theseus/Oberon: Alex Jennings; Hippolyta/Titania: Lindsey Duncan; Bottom: Desmond Barrit; Philostrate/Puck: Finnbar Lynch); Shakespeare's Globe, 2002 (dir. Mike Alfreds); RSC/Dash Productions, 2006 (dir. Tim Supple); Rose Theatre, Kingston, 2010 (dir. Peter Hall; Titania: Judi Dench).

On screen

USA, 1935 (dir. Max Reinhardt and William Dieterle; Puck: Mickey Rooney; Bottom: James Cagney); ITV, UK, 1964 (dir. Joan Kemp-Welch; Oberon: Peter Wyngarde; Titania: Anna Massey; Bottom: Benny Hill); UK, 1968 (dir. Peter Hall; Oberon: Ian Richardson; Titania: Judi Dench; Puck: Ian Holm; Bottom: Paul Hardwick); BBC Television Shakespeare, UK, 1981 (dir. John Gorrie; Puck: Phil Daniels); UK/Spain, 1984 (dir. Celestino Coronado); UK, 1995 (dir. Adrian Noble; Theseus/Oberon: Alex Jennings; Hippolyta/Titania: Lindsey Duncan; Bottom: Desmond Barrit; Philostrate/Puck: Finnbar Lynch); USA, 1999 (dir. Michael Hoffman; Bottom: Kevin Kline).

Offshoots

George Balanchine, *A Midsummer Night's Dream*, New York City Ballet, 1962; Frederick Ashton, *The Dream*, Royal Ballet 1964; *A Midsummer Night's Sex Comedy*, USA, 1982 (dir. Woody Allen); *Shakespeare: The Animated Tales: A Midsummer Night's Dream*, UK/Russia, 1992 (dir. Robert Saakianz); *Shakespeare Retold: A Midsummer Night's Dream*, BBC TV, UK, 2005 (adapt. Peter Bowker).

Romeo and Juliet

Date, text and authorship

1595–96. Q1 1597; Q2 1599; Q3 1609; Q4 1622; F 1623. Solely Shakespearean.

Sources and influences

Arthur Brooke, *The Tragicall Historye of Romeus and Juliet* (1562); Matteo Bandello, *Le novelle di Bandello* (1560; trans.William Painter as *The Palace of Pleasure*, 1567); Chaucer, *The Parliament of Fowls* (c.1383).

On stage

New Theatre, 1935 (dir. John Gielgud; Romeo/Mercutio: John Gielgud/Laurence Olivier; Juliet: Peggy Ashcroft); Shakespeare Memorial Theatre, 1947 (dir. Peter Brook; Romeo: Paul Scofield); Old Vic, 1960 (dir. Franco Zeffirelli; Romeo: John Stride; Juliet: Judi Dench); Prague, 1963 (dir. Josef Svoboda); RSC, 1973 (dir. Terry Hands; Romeo: Ian McKellen; Juliet: Estelle Kohler); RSC, 1985 (dir. Michael Bogdanov; Romeo: Sean Bean; Juliet: Amanda Root); Montreal, 1991 (dir. Robert Lepage); RSC, 1997 (dir. Michael Attenborough; Romeo: Ray Fearon; Juliet: Zoë Waites); NT, 2000 (dir. Tim Supple; Romeo: Chiwetel Ejiofor; Juliet: Charlotte Randle); RSC, 2000 (dir. Michael Boyd; Romeo: David Tennant; Juliet: Alexandra Gilbreath); Vesturport/Old Vic, Reykjavik/ London, 2003 (dir. Gísli Örn Gardarsson); Shakespeare's Globe, 2004 (dir. Tim Carroll); RSC, 2008 (dir. Neil Bartlett).

On screen

USA, 1936 (dir. George Cukor); UK/Italy, 1954 (dir. Renato Castellani); Italy/UK, 1968 (dir. Franco Zeffirelli; Romeo: Leonard Whiting; Juliet: Olivia Hussey; Mercutio: John McEnery); BBC Television Shakespeare, UK, 1978 (dir. Alan Rakoff; Romeo: Patrick Ryecart; Juliet: Rebecca Saire; Tybalt: Alan Rickman; Nurse: Celia Johnson; Chorus: John Gielgud); *William Shakespeare's Romeo + Juliet*, USA, 1996 (dir. Baz Luhrmann; Romeo: Leonardo Di Caprio; Juliet: Claire Danes).

Offshoots

Arthur Laurents, Leonard Bernstein and Stephen Sondheim, *West Side Story*, New York, 1957 (film version, USA, 1961, dir. Robert Wise and Jerome Robbins); *Shakespeare Wallah*, USA, 1965 (dir. James Ivory); *China Girl*, USA, 1987 (dir. Abel Ferrara); *Shakespeare: The Animated Tales: Romeo and Juliet,* UK/Russia, 1992 (dir. Efim Gambourg); *Tromeo and Juliet,* USA, 1996 (dir. Lloyd Kaufmann); *Shakespeare in Love*, UK, 1998 (dir. John Madden; Shakespeare: Joseph Fiennes; Viola: Gwyneth Paltrow); *Romeo Must Die*, USA, 2000 (dir. Andrzej Bartkowiak); Ben Power, *A Tender Thing*, Northern Stage, Newcastle, 2009.

A dream past the wit of man

Mentioned by Francis Meres in 1598 as evidence of Shakespeare's excellence as a comic dramatist, and first printed in quarto in 1600, *A Midsummer Night's Dream* has long been a feature of the school syllabus, theatrical repertoire (there have also been four mainstream film versions), musical and literary culture; it is also one of the handful of Shakespeare's plays to have established a secure foothold within popular culture. The play's standing as the occasion for many a primary encounter with Shakespeare, in the classroom, within the worlds of the school play and amateur performance, has meant that it has been regarded with particular affection and nostalgia. The introductions to three widely used modern editions of the play begin by invoking memories of innocent pleasure and desire: Harold Brooks's preface to his Arden text records his (enviable) 'first experience of the theatre: a matinee of Granville Barker's famous production, to which at the age of seven I was taken by my aunts' (Brooks 1979: ix); Peter Holland notes that *Dream* was 'the first Shakespeare play that I can remember seeing ... Peter Hall's production at Stratford in 1959 when I was eight' (Holland 1994: v); more guardedly, Stanley Wells recalls that 'during the interval of a performance ... of one of Shakespeare's other plays, I once heard a schoolboy say plaintively "I wish it was *A Midsummer Night's Dream*"' (Wells 1995: 7).

Rarely does scholarship place itself so candidly within the scene of childhood, which is an indication of the singularity of the play's appeal, but also a clue as to why it has been regarded by some as an embarrassment; such nostalgia cannot be entertained without a degree of ambivalence. The play has been admired for the precision of its plotting, the juxtaposition of broad comedy and delicate lyricism, the complex interplay between aristocratic, artisan and fairy realms; for its explorations of the relations between dream, reality and performance; and it has been mined for evidence of its implication within darker Elizabethan fantasies of sex and power, race and empire. At a basic level, though, the play's potential as a source of pleasure and wonder relies upon what seems to be a wilfully (or childishly) naïve capacity to believe in fairies and theatrical magic; and it is upon the test of this belief that the play may stand or fall. Returning from a performance of 1662, Samuel Pepys recorded in his diary that it was 'the most insipid ridiculous play that ever I saw in my life' (Odell 1966, 1: 40–41); and subsequent witnesses to stage productions have declared themselves particularly unconvinced by overly literal attempts to depict the fairy kingdom: in 1816, drawing a distinction between the play of the imagination and that of the stage, William Hazlitt complained of Frederick Reynolds's production that 'fancy cannot be represented any more than a simile can be painted ... fairies are not incredible, but fairies six feet high are so' (Hazlitt 1957: 274–76).

Hazlitt's warning went unheeded for much of the nineteenth century: the play was the occasion for spectacularly authentic realisations of classical Athens and lush English woodland (populated, in Beerbohm Tree's 1900 production at Her Majesty's, by real live rabbits), for *corps de ballet* fairies (ninety of them for the final scene of Charles Kean's 1858 staging at the Princess's Theatre) and for musical embellishment, most famously in Mendelssohn's overture and incidental music. The combination of romanticism and earnest literalism in turn earned the censure of the theatrical modernists: in a ground-breaking version at the Savoy Theatre in 1914, Harley Granville Barker replaced fake marble, grass and gauze with a post-impressionist scheme of non-representational silk curtains, and orientalised and mechanised his sprites as 'heavy little idols of gold with shiny yellow faces ... ormulu fairies ... detached from some fantastic, bristling old clock' (Griffiths 1996: 41–42). But it was not until 1970, and Peter Brook's legendary production for the Royal Shakespeare Company at Stratford, that the play was finally stripped of its Victorian legacy: famously, and controversially, Brook defoliated the stage space, framing the action within a gymnasium-like white box, and treating the magic as metaphor, realised through circus skills, acrobatics and conjuring tricks. The apotheosis of modernist theatrical Shakespeare, Brook's *Dream* defined a performance identity for the play which, over thirty years on, continues to haunt theatrical practice.

If its performance history – at least for many of its adult spectators – has been shadowed by persistent problems of belief, this is a concern anticipated within the play itself. At the beginning of Act 5, with all four sets of human and fairy lovers successfully paired off, Theseus responds to Hippolyta with an abrupt dismissal of the 'strange' stories 'that these lovers speak of' (5.1.1):

> More strange than true. I never may believe
> These antique fables, nor these fairy toys.

(5.1.2–3)

For Hippolyta, the 'strange' events of the lovers' narratives may lie beyond the scope of rational explication, but can nonetheless gather towards 'something of great constancy' (5.1.26); for Theseus, the strange is defined in a simple binary opposition to the true. Stating his disbelief in 'antique fables', Theseus dismisses classical mythology, but also invokes a sense of the 'antic': lunacy, the grotesque, the performative. In the speech that follows, Theseus triangulates the figures of 'the lunatic, the lover, and the poet' (5.1.7) to map the 'shaping fantasies' (5) of madness, desire and art. Theseus's strategy is, simply, to demonise that which cannot be accommodated within a rationalist worldview. Distinguishing the chaotic sensory apprehension of the lover and the madman from the comprehension afforded by 'cool reason' (6), and hence the body from the intellect, he evokes an imaginative landscape of the afflicted populated by 'more devils than vast hell can hold'; a place where desire scandalously erases racial markers, locating 'Helen's beauty's in a brow of Egypt' (10–11); that is, confusing the classical image of female whiteness with its racialised antithesis.

Theseus's account is a caricature, of course, but it is to a certain extent borne out by the experience of the lovers in the play itself. Even before the couples have entered the liminal zone of the forest, their desires, and desire itself, are characterised in terms of strange and arbitrary attachments and reversals, as forces capable of radically unsettling boundaries and hierarchies. Theseus's own military-political erotic alliance with Hippolyta is announced via an oxymoron:

> I wooed thee with my sword,
> And won thy love doing thee injuries.
>
> (1.1.16–17)

If the generic Petrarchan conjunction of love-conquest and warfare is here disconcertingly close to the language of rape and violent assault, the arrival of Egeus a few lines later introduces a parallel account of wooing in which coercion is coupled with deceit, as he accuses Lysander of having 'bewitched the bosom of my child', of moonlight visits to sing

> With feigning voice verses of feigning love,
> And stol'n the impression of her fantasy ...
>
> (1.1.32–33)

Egeus's account of necromantic seduction conducted through an exotic trading of relics and artefacts, 'bracelets of thy hair, rings, gauds, conceits,/ Knacks, trifles, nosegays, sweetmeats' (33–34), is explicable as the lurid imaginings of a paranoid patriarch, but the combination of the tangible and the immaterial, the corporeal and the manufactured, points emphatically towards the dangerously mobile, evasive and excessive character of erotic desire (moreover, Egeus's charge that Lysander's professions of love are depthless, duplicitous and inconstant is, given subsequent events in the forest, not without substance).

Love and incipient madness are visibly combined in the unfortunate person of Helena, who 'dotes,/ Devoutly dotes, dotes in idolatry' (108–09) upon the (as Lysander has it) worthless Demetrius; later on, Hermia and Helena exchange stichomythia whose brutal symmetries reveal a pattern of rejection, misrecognition and masochistic abjection that accords well with Theseus's vision of the lover's deluded fancy:

HERMIA I frown upon him, yet he loves me still.

HELENA O that your frowns would teach my smiles such skill!

HERMIA I give him curses, yet he gives me love.

HELENA O that my prayers could such affection move!

HERMIA The more I hate, the more he follows me.

HELENA The more I love, the more he hateth me.

(1.1.194–99)

In the forest, a space which, rather like the outskirts of the city of London, seems beyond the jurisdiction of the law, the association of love with deception, devilry and madness is unambiguous. Oberon's 'forgeries of jealousy' (2.1.81) implicate the Fairy King and Queen, Titania and Theseus, in lurid scenarios of infidelity and betrayal, as well as spawning a 'progeny of evils' (2.1.115), the nightmare of rotting crops, famine, flooding, plague, decay and death. Stung by Titania's refusal to relinquish the exotic eastern figure of the Indian 'changeling boy' (2.1.120), Oberon conjures up a 'little western flower', the 'love-in-idleness' whose juice has the power to make 'man or woman madly dote/ Upon the next live creature that it sees' (2.1.166–72).

In the crudest of Freudian terms, the love-juice is a means of releasing the restraints that the super-ego places upon the id, unleashing the full force of undifferentiated desire which potentially acknowledges no distinctions of gender or species, which switches arbitrarily from one love-object to another, and which can transform revulsion to passion, affection to disgust and murderous aggression. The Demetrius who had declared to Helena, 'I am sick when I do look on thee', and threatens to 'do thee mischief in the wood' (2.1.212–37) hails her as 'goddess, nymph, perfect, divine', and as 'This princess of pure white, this seal of bliss' (3.2.138–45); the Lysander who had promised Hermia 'my heart unto yours is knit,/ So that but one heart we can make of it' (2.2.53–54) abuses her as an 'Ethiope', railing at her as 'thou cat, thou burr; vile thing'; 'serpent', 'tawny Tartar', 'loathed med'cine, hated potion' (3.2.257–65).

The ease with which the language of devotion trades places with that of insult and invective and the absolute quality of the *volte-face* that the lovers undergo are components of the play's farcical machinery, and are no more or less credible than the magical milieu in which they operate, but the comic-lunatic extremity of the feelings laid bare in the dream space of the wood invites us to wonder whether eros can ever be trusted, despite Lysander's optimistic invocation of 'true love' (1.1.134) and Robin's jingling, formulaic promise, on redirecting the lovers' desires to their proper paths:

Jack shall have Jill,
Naught shall go ill,
The man shall have his mare again, And all shall be well.

(3.3.45–47)

The play's erotic equations are balanced in the interests of the conventions of romantic comedy, but the muted quality of the lovers' final waking at the end of the fourth act suggests that the experiences in the wood have left their mark. The sense of unreality persists: for Hermia, vision is distorted, as she sees 'with parted eye,/ When everything seems double' (4.1.186–87), which is not an unapt phrase in view of the multiple desire-paths of the male lovers; Helena finds Demetrius 'Mine own and not mine own' (189),

Demetrius wonders whether 'yet we sleep, we dream' (190). Leading the two pairs of lovers from the stage, he invites them to 'recount our dreams' (195), and thus to fashion narratives that are also attempts at retrospective rationalisation of events which might otherwise be fairly painful to contemplate. Oberon has predicted that the lovers will 'think no more of this night's accidents/ But as the fierce vexation of a dream' (4.1.65–66), and it is left ambiguous just how far the 'story of the night' acknowledges the cruelty and pain endemic within the hallucinogen-fuelled 'accidents' of misrecognition, rejection, vilification and threatened violence that have formed the substance of the play's central action.

The capriciousness of the desires of the male characters, which operate along a spectrum of objectification which situates the idealised white female lover at one end and the despised and feared dark woman at the other, is an only partially satirical depiction of the reckless inconstancy of masculine sexuality; Oberon's treatment of Titania reflects a view of female desire founded upon suspicion and mistrust. In order to punish Titania for an alleged promiscuity that, according to his account, violates the boundary between the mortal and fairy worlds (which raises a concern with cross-border sexual traffic which is prevalent throughout the play, as well as identifying her as a kind of succubus), Oberon attempts to subject her to the degradation of union with an animal: 'lion, bear, or wolf, or bull ... meddling monkey, or ... busy ape' (2.1.180–81); 'ounce, or cat, or bear,/ Pard, or boar with bristled hair' (2.2.36–37). The proliferating bestiary supplies a comprehensive iconography of danger, lawlessness and insatiability that taps into masculine fears of rampant and indiscriminate female sexuality; Oberon's wish to see his queen mated with 'some vile thing' (2.2.40) is to be enacted as a cruel parody of her refusal to submit to his lawful authority.

The actual result, thanks to Robin's act of subsidiary mischief-making with the mechanicals that equips Bottom with an ass's head, is even better (that is, perverse) than Oberon hoped: the encounter between translated weaver and aristocratic fairy unsettles discriminations of rank as well as species; as Gail Kern Paster and others have suggested, the coupling offers the potentially subversive fantasy scenario of 'the forbidden mating of a queen with the grotesque body of the populace' (Paster 1993: 127). Such a spectacle offers scope for the entertainment of cultural anxiety as well as pleasure, particularly if we consider Bottom as a substitute for the Indian Boy, and his metamorphosis as a means of negotiating the discourses of racial integrity and difference, miscegenation and hybridity that were beginning to define the emergent English culture of empire at the end of the sixteenth century (Hendricks 1996). If the transformation of Bottom into an ass is a manifestation of the class antagonism towards the 'hempen homespuns', who make the mistake of 'swagg'ring here/ So near the cradle of the Fairy Queen' (3.1.65–66), an antagonism that also emerges in wedding-party laughter at their presumption in rendering *Pyramus and Thisbe*, his entanglement with Titania ('So doth the woodbine the sweet honeysuckle/ Gently entwist; the female ivy so/ Enrings the barky fingers of the elm' [4.1.39–41]) undoubtedly leaves her the more foolish and degraded, as she coos over his 'sleek smooth head' and offers to 'kiss thy fair large ears, my gentle joy' (4.1.3–4).

Waking to an Oberon fully satisfied that his punishment has done its work, Titania cries 'what visions I have seen!'; an obvious keyword in the play, the 'vision' is here grounded within the prosaic comedy of imagining herself 'enamoured of an ass' (4.1.73–74). The idea that visionary experience, like dreaming, may both contain a truth beyond the empirically observable and be variously ephemeral, misleading, harmless and worthless is elaborated in a variety of forms throughout the play, including its own mechanics of representation. The status of the *Dream* as a fantastic and essentially disposable fiction is explicitly addressed in the valedictory solicitation of the epilogue:

> If we shadows have offended,
> Think but this, and all is mended:
> That you have but slumbered here,
> While these visions did appear;
> And this weak and idle theme,
> No more yielding but a dream ...

(Epilogue, 1–6)

The mock-apology directly addressed to the audience is entirely conventional, a gestural humility calculated to solicit applause, but the explicit equation of two kinds of 'shadow' being, the fairy and the performer ('shadow' being a common synonym for 'player'), definitively reiterates the connection between magic and theatre-making that has been sustained throughout (and that has been extensively elaborated in the modern performance history of the play). Reminiscent of John Lyly's prologue to his *Sapho and Phao*, which, for a performance at court in 1584, entreated the queen to excuse its tediousness by imagining 'yourself to be in a deep dream, that staying the conclusion, in your rising your Majesty vouchsafe but to say, *And so you awaked*' ('The Prologue at the Court', 15–16), Robin's epilogue aims to pre-empt criticism by pretending to trivialise it as innocuous fantasy.

The trick of transforming the material event of a just-witnessed performance into an airy nothing has a certain cogency: this utterance at the close of the play reveals Robin to be a sophisticated theorist of performance ontology, well aware, as Peggy Phelan has it, that performance 'honors the idea that a limited number of people in a specific time/ space frame can have an experience of value which leaves no visible trace afterward'; and that, once it is over, it 'disappears into memory, into the realm of invisibility and the unconscious where it eludes regulation and control' (Phelan 1993: 148–49). But the self-abnegation, however light hearted, also voices a caution over the possibility of giving 'offence' that tacitly acknowledges that theatre has a dangerous, and unpredictable, power; a power that needs to be carefully managed. This is simply a reflection of the prevailing conditions of performance. The working practices of the professional theatre in sixteenth-century London were a matter of ongoing and complex negotiations with a range of court and city systems and institutions of licence, regulation and control; in *Dream*, this is replayed in parodic form in the comically excessive circumspection of Quince's troupe.

Much of the comedy of the mechanicals' scenes is metatheatrical: here are highly skilled professional players taking the parts of inept amateur performers who have a touchingly misplaced faith in their own histrionic proficiency, cheerfully oblivious to the established conventions and techniques of contemporary stage practice, and operating in a spirit of earnest literalism that finds them bringing on a wall and finding a figure to personify moonshine. Here is a troupe of players rehearsing within an imagined woodland which, in witty theatrical inversion, is re-imagined as playhouse architecture: 'This green plot shall be our stage, this hawthorn brake our tiring-house, and we will do it in action as we will do it before the Duke' (3.1.3–5). As Holland notes, generations of commentators have read this in terms of illusionistic literalism, suggesting property thickets and the like, covering the stage-floor with green carpet and thus 'making Quince's line even more directly referential'

(Holland 1994: 178), which, of course, entirely misses the point of the gag, which is that there is neither 'green plot' nor 'hawthorn brake' upon the platform stage.

But the problems posed by Wall and Moonshine are relatively minor compared to what Bottom identifies as the elements 'in this comedy … that will never please': first, 'Pyramus must draw a sword to kill himself, which the ladies cannot abide'; second, there is the matter of the lion, 'a most dreadful thing; for there is not a more fearful wild fowl than your lion living' (3.1.8–9, 29–30). These concerns have already been aired in the previous mechanicals' scene. Responding to Bottom's offer to roar the lion's part, Quince cautions, 'An you should do it too terribly you would fright the Duchess and the ladies that they would shriek, and that were enough to hang us all'; and the point is echoed by the entire company: 'That would hang us, every mother's son' (1.2.61–64). Although we are routinely cajoled to laugh at what seems to be an exaggerated fear of the Athenian state's willingness to apply the death penalty for a relatively minor theatrical misdemeanour, the mechanicals' trepidation points, quite reasonably, towards the authorities' nervousness about performance; the spectacle of an artisan wielding a sword and roaring in aristocratic company is, potentially, a deeply threatening one (Patterson 1989: 52–70; Montrose 1996: 179–99). As a consequence, the company devise elaborate framing tactics calculated to neutralise the power of their show: Bottom promises to roar 'as gently as any sucking dove … an 'twere any nightingale' (1.2.67–78), then proposes that Snug's face 'must be seen through the lion's neck' (3.1.33); in the event, Snug declares, 'Then know that I as Snug the joiner am … For if I should as Lion come in strife/ Into this place, 'twere pity on my life' (5.1.218–21). This method of theatrical prophylaxis is also practised in Quince's prologue ('If we offend, it is with our good will' [5.1.108]) and at the playlet's end, as Bottom springs up to assure his audience that 'the wall is down that parted their fathers' (5.1.337–38).

Bottom's offer of an epilogue prompts another joke, from Theseus, on the subject of hanging: 'for when the players are all dead there need none to be blamed. Marry, if he that writ it had played Pyramus and hanged himself in Thisbe's garter it would have been a fine tragedy' (341–44). It appears that Bottom and company are right to exercise discretion; theatrical mimesis in Theseus's Athens is a serious business, and an implicitly political one. For Theseus, expounding upon the lunatic, the lover and the poet, the artistic imagination (like love and madness) is another potential source of trouble for the well-ordered city-state: the poet is caught in the throes of a 'fine frenzy' which profanely parodies ecstatic religious experience as his rolling eye oscillates between heaven and earth (5.1.12–13); uncertainly poised between matter and spirit, poetic fancy yields a monstrous birth as it 'bodies forth/ The forms of things unknown' (14–15). The charge that poetry (or art, or, in this instance, theatre) 'gives to airy nothing/ A local habitation and a name' (16–17) appropriates Sir Philip Sidney's defence of the autonomy of the creative imagination as a way of improving upon the mundane material world, 'in making things either better than Nature bringeth forth, or, quite anew, forms such as never were in Nature' (Sidney 1966: 53); but it does so in order to interrogate it. Less of a revisionist Platonist than Sidney, Theseus echoes that section of *The Republic* in which the philosopher declares that there is no room for the poet in the ideal state because 'he awakens and encourages and strengthens the lower elements in the mind to the detriment of reason, which is like giving power and political control to the worst elements in a state' (Plato 1974: 373).

Theseus concludes his catalogue of delusions with a proverbial summation which neatly reiterates much of the action of the play:

Or in the night, imagining some fear,
How easy is a bush supposed a bear!

(5.1.21–22)

If the concern here is the ease with which imagination can play tricks upon perception, the enactment of the mechanicals' play in the scene which follows demonstrates the opposing problem: none of the best efforts of Quince's company can prevail upon the collective imagination of their courtly audience to permit them to transcend their trade identities as Bottom the Weaver, Snug the Joiner, Flute the Bellows-Mender. As if to compensate for their previous excessive imaginative receptiveness, the new-married lovers ostentatiously refuse to acknowledge the efficacy of the *Pyramus and Thisbe* performance; for Hippolyta, it is simply 'the silliest stuff that ever I heard' (5.1.207).

The burlesque idiom in which the play-within-the-play is conducted ('O night which ever art when day is not' [169]; 'Quail, crush, conclude, and quell' [276]) and the manifold opportunities for displays of comic ineptitude and theatrical hubris that the play in performance has traditionally afforded make this a reasonable judgement, and invite us to echo the wedding party's laughter, if not to entirely approve of their persistent ill-mannered disruptions of the artisans' efforts. But perhaps there is also a defensive edge, as well as an element of relief, to the laughter which is intended to signal their sophistication. There are clear parallels between the tragic narrative of *Pyramus and Thisbe* and the scenario of the *Dream*, particularly in the pattern of parental thwarting of 'true love'; in the latter case, comic resolution is ultimately secured through the arbitrary over-ruling of what had earlier been identified as a 'law of Athens' which 'by no means we may extenuate' (1.1.119–20). There is, in the final scene, much to be relieved about; however much it is played broadly for laughs, *Pyramus and Thisbe* stages the pain and violence that are latent in the play by offering a version of what might have been: the nightmare inside the dream.

Death-marked love

If *A Midsummer Night's Dream* can be regarded as one of the plays that pre-eminently tells the story of Shakespeare in the modern theatre, *Romeo and Juliet* has served equally well as a bellwether of his shifting status within modern popular culture. As the source of adaptations, reinventions, derivatives and spin-offs in a wide variety of media that range across the visual and performance arts, from symphonic, operatic and ballet treatments (Berlioz, 1839; Gounod, 1867; Prokofiev, 1934) to musicals (*West Side Story*, 1957, filmed 1961) to narrative updates (*China Girl*, 1987), the play has had a consistent visibility beyond the confines of stage, page and screen that perhaps only *Hamlet* can match. In particular, the play's focus on a pair of young lovers has provided popular culture (and, since the 1950s in particular, popular music) with the iconic imagery of youthful passion. The spectacle of Juliet on the 'balcony', which, in the play, is never mentioned, is archetypal: whether singly or as a pair, Romeo and Juliet are name-checked in countless pop songs, in references that have been, variously, sly (Peggy Lee's cover of 'Fever', 1958) streetwise (Lou Reed, 'Romeo Had Juliette', 1989), vapid (Taylor Swift, 'Love Story', 2008) and staggeringly erudite (*The Juliet Letters*, a 1992 collaboration between singer-songwriter Elvis Costello and the classical string ensemble the Brodsky Quartet, which managed to successfully alienate the fan bases of both). The inspiration for two of the most successful Shakespearean movies of all time, Baz

Lurhmann's *William Shakespeare's Romeo + Juliet* and John Madden's *Shakespeare in Love*, both released in the mid-1990s, *Romeo and Juliet* is, alongside *Dream*, the play most likely to define most readers' and viewers' first (and perhaps only) experience of Shakespeare.

The play's evident durability both as material for reading and performance and as a source of quotations and allusions within popular culture appears to testify to its universality; in an obvious sense, it would clearly be counter-intuitive to argue that it has not, in ways that are both important and trivial, transcended its moment of origin and the culture that produced it. Its template will fit, as well as shape, cultural narratives of desire, of loss and of intergenerational conflict as long as there are people prepared – or not prepared – to fall in love with those who, for familial, cultural or other reasons, they shouldn't fall in love with. While its potent conjuncture of sex and premature death continues to exercise its perennially morbid grip upon, particularly, teenaged sensibilities (which are also especially responsive to the message that *it's just so unfair*), other aspects of the play resonate with contemporary concerns, and find local referents and analogues: the feuding Montagues and Capulets recast as the protagonists in urban gang wars (a tradition that extends from *West Side Story* to Luhrmann's *Romeo + Juliet* and beyond) and, almost as frequently, opposed across an ethnic and racial divide; Juliet's arranged marriage, which, after multiculturalism, seems no longer the anomaly that it once appeared to be. As a consequence, what was once seen as a tragedy of fate, of 'star-crossed lovers' (Prologue 6), has become a tragedy of social rather than cosmic circumstance, and in the process the assurance that their demise 'Doth. ... bury their parents' strife' (8) has seemed less than altogether convincing.

Of course, the narrative alone hardly accounts for the play's extraordinary emotional power, which is also the effect of the passionate lyricism that affords Romeo and Juliet some of the most radiant and expansive love poetry in the English language:

> But soft, what light through yonder window breaks?
> It is the east, and Juliet is the sun.
>
> (2.1.44–45)

> speak again, bright angel; for thou art
> As glorious to this night, being o'er my head,
> As is a wingèd messenger of heaven ...
>
> (2.1.68–70)

> My bounty is as boundless as the sea,
> My love as deep. The more I give to thee
> The more I have, for both are infinite.
>
> (2.1.175–77)

> Come night, come Romeo; come, thou day in night,
> For thou wilt lie upon the wings of night
> Whiter than snow on a raven's back ...
>
> (3.2.17–19)

The lovers' discourse is shaped by complementary principles of mutuality and reciprocity: initially a parody of the Petrarchan lover, mooning disconsolately over his cruel mistress

Rosaline, Romeo finds his feet as a true lover in a first encounter with Juliet that is conducted in the format of a shared sonnet that culminates in a kiss:

> ROMEO If I profane with my unworthiest hand
> This holy shrine, the gentler sin is this
>   My lips, two blushing pilgrims, ready stand
>   To smooth that rough touch with a tender kiss.
> JULIET Good pilgrim, you do wrong your hand too much,
>   Which mannerly devotion shows in this.
>   For saints have hands that pilgrims hands do touch,
>   And palm to palm is holy palmer's kiss.
> ROMEO Have not saints lips, and holy palmers, too?
> JULIET Ay, pilgrim, lips that they must use in prayer.
> ROMEO O then, dear saint, let lips do what hands do:
>   They pray; grant thou, lest faith turn to despair.
> JULIET Saints do not move, though grant for prayers' sake.
> ROMEO Then move not while my prayer's effect I take.
>
> (1.5.90–103)

Matching quatrain for quatrain, coupling couplet with couplet, the passage offers an exquisite synergy of voices, minds, bodies and spirits, shaped by an elegant verbal choreography that is commensurate with the dance from which it emerges.

Framed in the language of devotion and of the sacred, love is here exalted, celestial, and transcendent. Elsewhere in the play, it is profane, resolutely carnal, and occasionally perverse; and its most eloquent spokesperson is Mercutio, whose task (shared with Juliet's Nurse) is repeatedly to bring matters of desire down to earth. Fresh from the balcony scene, Romeo becomes entangled in a prose exchange with Mercutio that reprises their chaste *pas de deux* in rather more graphic terms:

> MERCUTIO Nay, I am the very pink of courtesy.
> ROMEO Pink for flower.
> MERCUTIO Right.
> ROMEO Why, then is my pump well flowered.
>
> (2.3.51–54)

The *double entendres* hardly need translating; as an example of the kind of macho banter that men like to indulge in when out of earshot of the women they have pedestalised, it is representative not only of one of the play's alternative registers to Petrarchanism but also of the sexualised aggression that informs their homosocial bonding.

Relentless in its pursuit of an obscene quibble, Mercutio's imagination runs riot in the preamble to Romeo and Juliet's moonlight meeting:

> Now will he sit under a medlar tree
> And wish his mistress were that kind of fruit
> As maids call medlars when they sit alone.
> O Romeo, that she were, O that she were
> An open-arse, and thou a popp'rin pear.
>
> (2.1.34–38)

As in most modern editions, the Norton editors helpfully gloss 'medlar' (nicknamed 'open-arse') as a 'fruit thought to resemble the female sex organs' and 'popp'rin pear' as a pomacious variety 'from Poperinghe in Flanders' that affords a pun on 'popper-in' or 'pop her in' (Greenblatt *et al.* 1997: 890). As an imaging of heterosexual coitus this is conventional enough, if graphic; but we might also wish to note that Mercutio's fruity speculations extend someway further than this: if an open-arse is a vagina it is also, not to put too fine a point on it, an anus. Within Mercutio's polymorphously pornographic imaginings, at least, the repertoire of penetrative sex encompasses the sodomitical as well as the normative. Sex in Verona is not just vanilla-flavoured.

The element of brutality in Mercutio's calculated defilement of Juliet, his fetishistic reduction of Romeo's mistress to her sexual anatomy, reflects one of the attitudes to women and to sex prevalent throughout the world of the play. In the play's opening moments, fuelled by self-aggrandising fantasies of rape and murder ('when I have fought with the men I will be civil with the maids – I will cut off their heads' [1.1.18–20]), Capulet's men cut a certain swagger by projecting themselves as the agents of the 'ancient grudge' broken 'to new mutiny' (Prologue, 3); however, the bluster instantly evaporates when the ironically named Samson and Gregory actually confront their opponents, as macho posturing degenerates into rapid-fire legalistic quibbling over who exactly is challenging whom.

The tone of this opening is farcical rather than alarming: armed with bucklers (carried by servants, not noblemen), the serving-men incarnate the spirit of the feud in comically degraded form, while appearing to treat the opportunities for violence that it affords as a kind of sporting activity. The sense of comedy is enhanced when the warring factions' most senior exponents, who also happen to be the most distinguished embodiments of Veronese patriarchy, take to the stage to participate in the melee: entering in his nightgown whilst calling for his 'long sword' (1.1.68), 'old' Capulet is, like 'old' Montague, reminiscent of the impotent *senex* of classical comedy: as his wife sarcastically reminds him, he would be better off asking for his crutch (1.1.69).

The power that Old Capulet exercises is financial rather than physical: in this respect, the context of the tragedy is less a feud that no one apart from Tybalt appears to take particularly seriously (Capulet is singularly relaxed about Romeo's would-be incognito appearance at his ball) than a marriage-market in which Juliet is plainly an object of barter between the city's established dynasties. Modern readers and spectators tend to align themselves with the young and against the old. The play's sympathies, however, are not quite so one-sided: although we are rightly repelled by the heavy-handed patriarchy that attempts to enforce Juliet's union with the Count Paris, appalled by the violent, near murderous, fury her refusal provokes in her father, and moved by a cluster of deaths (of not only the lovers but also Mercutio, Tybalt and Paris) that seem arbitrary, undeserved and preventable, the play also reminds us of the children's duty to obey their parents, though less to lend endorsement to parental authority than to confirm the tragic cost of transgressing it.

If there is a model of the good father in the play, it is found in Friar Laurence, who is addressed as such by Romeo on their first encounter in the play. Both cleric and, as the expert minister of 'the powerful grace that lies/ In plants, herbs, stones, and their true qualities' (2.2.15–16), early modern scientist, Friar Laurence has, for a man of the cloth, a notably realistic and non-judgemental attitude to sex, teasing rather than chiding Romeo for having supposedly slept with Rosaline, sufficiently romantically inclined to agree to sanctify the lovers' union but also sober enough to acknowledge, even as he does so, that

'These violent delights have violent ends' (2.5.9). A voice of moderation, but also of optimism and idealism, in a society torn between brutal commercial pragmatism and adolescent rage, the Friar is nonetheless one of the unwitting instruments of the catastrophe that his well-intentioned plotting is intended to avert.

The impression that the outcome of the drama is determined by what once might have been thought of as fate, but which strikes many of us now as more like bad luck, unfortunate timing or the failures of the postal service, has for some readers diminished the play's status as tragedy, but it could equally be seen as an integral part of a pattern of misdirected actions, well-meaning interventions and their unintended consequences that runs throughout the play that begins with Benvolio's interference in the street brawl in the first scene, continues through the attempt by Romeo to protect Mercutio from the swordthrust that results in his death, and culminates in Romeo's fatally pre-emptive self-poisoning.

Viewed dispassionately, the chain of coincidences that leads to the deaths of the protagonists of *Romeo and Juliet* is as tendentious as the plotting of the play's burlesque alter-image, *Pyramus and Thisbe* (whose denouement likewise turns upon a lover's misconception that results in a double suicide, and which equally effects a familial reconciliation as 'the wall is down that parted their fathers' [*Dream*, 5.2.337–38]); and its conclusion as trite, formulaic and reductive ('For never was a story of more woe/ Than this of Juliet and her Romeo' [5.3.308–9]) as anything penned by Peter Quince. And yet: if the joy of Quince's '*Most Lamentable Comedy*' (1.2.) lies in its magnificent failure to transcend its own narrative limitations and representational conventions, the power of Shakespeare's *Most Excellent and Lamentable Tragedy* diametrically inheres in its enduring capacity to persuade actors and audiences to countenance its improbabilities and absurdities, in the name of love.

Further reading

Calderwood, James L. (1992): *A Midsummer Night's Dream*. Harvester New Critical Introductions to Shakespeare. Hemel Hempstead: Harvester Wheatsheaf.

Garber, Marjorie (1997) *Coming of Age in Shakespeare*. London and New York: Routledge.

Halio, Jay L. (ed.) (1995) *Shakespeare's Romeo and Juliet: Texts, Contexts, and Interpretation*. Newark, DE and London: Associated University Presses.

Kahn, Coppélia (1981) *Man's Estate: Masculine Identity in Shakespeare*. Berkeley and Los Angeles, CA: University of California Press.

Lehmann, Courtney (2002) 'Strictly Shakespeare? Dead Letters, Ghostly Fathers, and the Cultural Pathology of Authorship in Baz Luhrmann's *William Shakespeare's Romeo + Juliet*', in *Shakespeare Remains: Theater to Film, Early Modern to Postmodern*. Ithaca, NY and London: Cornell University Press, 130–60.

Montrose, Louis A. (1983) '"Shaping Fantasies": Figurations of Gender and Power in Elizabethan Culture', *Representations*, 1: 61–94.

Williams, Gary J. (1997) *Our Moonlight Revels: A Midsummer Night's Dream in the Theatre*. Iowa City, IA: University of Iowa Press.

The Merchant of Venice

Date, text and authorship

c.1596; entered Stationers' Register (SR) 22 July 1598; mentioned by Francis Meres, 1598; Q1 1600; Q2 1619; F 1623. Solely Shakespearean.

Sources and influences

Giovanni Boccaccio, *Decameron* (1353; trans. William Painter, 1566); John Gower, *Confessio Amantis* (1390); *Gesta Romanorum* (trans. Richard Robinson, 1577); Christopher Marlowe, *The Jew of Malta* (c.1589).

On stage

Habimah, Tel Aviv, 1936 (dir. Leopold Jessner); Queen's, London, 1938 (Shylock: John Gielgud); SMT, 1948; Old Vic, 1956 (dir. Michael Benthall; Shylock: Robert Helpmann); Freie Volksbühne, Berlin, 1963 (dir. Erwin Piscator); RSC, 1965 (dir. Clifford Williams; Shylock: Eric Porter; Portia: Janet Suzman); NT, 1970 (dir. Jonathan Miller; Shylock: Laurence Olivier; Portia: Joan Plowright); RSC, 1978 (dir. John Barton; Shylock: Patrick Stewart); RSC, 1987 (dir. Bill Alexander; Shylock: Antony Sher); Phoenix, New York, 1989 (dir. Peter Hall; Shylock: Dustin Hoffman); RSC, 1993 (dir. David Thacker; Shylock: David Calder; Portia: Penny Downie); Goodman, Chicago, 1994 (dir. Peter Sellars); Shakespeare's Globe, 1998 (dir. Richard Olivier; Shylock: Norbert Kentrup); NT, 1999 (dir. Trevor Nunn; Shylock: Henry Goodman; Portia: Derbhle Crotty); RSC, 2008 (dir. Tim Carroll).

On screen

ATV, UK, 1974 (dir. Jonathan Miller; screen version of 1970 NT production); BBC Television Shakespeare, 1980 (dir. Jack Gold; Shylock: Warren Mitchell; Portia: Gemma Jones); BBC TV, UK, 2000 (dir. Trevor Nunn and Chris Hunt; screen version of 1999 NT production); USA/Italy/Luxembourg/UK, 2004 (dir. Michael Radford; Shylock: Al Pacino; Portia: Lynn Collins; Antonio: Jeremy Irons; Bassanio: Joseph Fiennes).

Offshoots

Arnold Wesker, *The Merchant*, 1976.

> Which is the merchant here, and which the Jew?
>
> (4.1.169)

Among the multiple challenges facing the actor playing Portia, who has just arrived in the Venetian civil court cross-dressed in the guise of the 'young doctor of Rome' (151), Balthasar, in defence of the merchant Antonio against the Jew Shylock, is whether this is actually a question; that is, whether it is possible, or not, to identify who's who by visual means alone. As far as the stage and screen history of the play is concerned, Portia's question, which might have been contrived to foster an impression of impartiality, is somewhat redundant, even naïve: at its worst extreme, the anti-Semitic caricature of the stage Jew variously equipped with red wig, hooked nose, gabardine and lisp renders it laughable and grotesque. But even in the more realistic, sympathetic and liberal-minded productions that we have long been used to, the actor playing Shylock will usually display sufficiently conventional signs of the role's ethnic and religious identities as to make the question more rhetorical than real.

According to a long but not very reliable tradition, Shylock on Shakespeare's stage was played as a malign figure in a red wig, kin to the monstrous Barabas of Marlowe's *The Jew of Malta* (c.1590; entered in the Stationers' Register 1594; published 1633), who would have been regarded by audiences presumed to have been almost uniformly racist as a figure of hatred and derision; and although efforts had been made to challenge stereotyping almost from the beginning of the post-Restoration stage history of the play (beginning with Charles Macklin's celebrated 'Jew that Shakespeare drew' – a couplet attributed to Alexander Pope – at Drury Lane in 1741), it took the crimes of the Holocaust in the mid-twentieth century to force the reassessment that not only transformed Shylock from the play's (albeit complex) villain to its victim but also led many to question whether the play, as a document of anti-Semitism or an anti-Semitic document, ought to be performed at all. If the response of performance makers has been to find ways of deepening the role of Shylock whilst often also painting the Christians of Venice and Belmont in a less than flattering light, production history focuses the issue of whether the play is offensively and irredeemably anti-Semitic or a critique and exposé of such attitudes by posing the challenge of how to mark Shylock's difference, visually and vocally, from his Venetian compatriots in ways that are plausible and readable without being demeaning and stereotypical.

A small part of the spectrum of approaches to the play is suggested by three relatively recent stage and screen productions. As powerfully, sympathetically yet unsentimentally played by the Jewish actor Henry Goodman in Trevor Nunn's 1930s-set National Theatre production of 1999 (subsequently filmed for the BBC and widely available), Shylock wore a yarmulke beneath his Homburg, signifying both his efforts to conform and his proud retention of difference, shared Hebrew prayers with Jessica and exited the play dignified in defeat. At Shakespeare's Globe on Bankside a year earlier, in 1998, Richard Olivier directed German-speaking Norbert Kentrup to play a grey-bearded Shylock in a red gown and cap in a production which was received by many in its audiences as an opportunity to indulge in what they imagined to be an authentically Elizabethan response to the play by hissing and booing, pantomime-style, whenever he appeared on stage. And in 2004, disproving Charles Edelman's conclusion of two years earlier that 'There has never been a major feature film of *The Merchant of Venice*, and given the sensitivity of the play's subject-matter, it is very unlikely that one will ever be made' (2002: 86), non-Jewish actor Al Pacino, starring in Michael Radford's cinematic rendering of the play set in Renaissance Venice, offered a tragically abused, sympathetic figure who was, sartorially at least, difficult to distinguish from the Christians that surrounded him; as Samuel Crowl observes, by making the merchant and the Jew both maligned outsiders, Radford 'makes us understand the natural confusion Shakespeare has built into the play's title' (2006: 119).

The ambiguity inscribed within Portia's/Balthasar's opening question is more pointed than it first appears, and is underlined by a principle of interchangeability that permeates the play's narrative and representational frameworks. When *Merchant* was entered in the Stationers' Register in July 1598 it was given two alternative titles: 'the Marchaunt of Venyce or otherwise called the Jewe of Venyce'; as well as possibly alluding to (and capitalising upon the succcess of) Marlowe's play, this indicates that either the merchant or the Jew could be accounted its centre of interest. According to the title-page of the first quarto of 1600, which may reflect the wording of the playbills that advertised it (see 'Life and contexts', pp. 45–6), the Christian 'Merchant' was clearly distinguishable within the play's moral economy from '*Shylocke* the Jewe', who was characterised by his 'extreame crueltie towards the sayde Merchant, in cutting a just pound of his flesh'. But the spectator or reader lured by this scenario finds that it envisages an event that, in actuality, does not happen: Shylock's 'extreme cruelty' is, it turns out, virtual or aspirational, a matter of intent rather than execution.

For Shakespeare and his contemporaries, moreover, differentiating the Jew from the Christian may, on a number of levels, have been less straightforward than received wisdom about stage tradition would have us believe. Theologically speaking, the Jew presented a paradox to early modern Christian culture, in that he was defined simultaneously by difference and sameness, in that Judaism could be perceived both in opposition to Christianity and as its progenitor, and Jews 'understood not only to be inveterate opponents of Christians but also imminent coreligionists' (Shapiro 1996: 34). Reflecting this, some of the more fundamentalist early seventeenth-century Puritan sects even went so far as to adopt Judaic practices such as circumcision and observance of kosher regulations.

As James Shapiro points out, the dual image of the Jew as the Christian's antithesis and double is represented in visual terms in the frontispiece to Hugo Grotius's *True Religion Explained and Defended* (1632), which features four inset panels illustrating the Christian, Jew, Pagan and Turk. The latter two are clearly marked by their ethnic difference, the Turk by turban and scimitar and the Pagan by his feathered headdress and bare feet, but the Christian and Jew, placed in opposition on either side of the page, nearly identically dressed and represented as equally devout, are virtual mirror-images, the key difference being that the Christian man, bathed in the light of salvation, prays to the heavens, while the Jew fixes his unconverted gaze on the tablets of the law. Unlike the Turk or Pagan, whose otherness seems more stubbornly retrograde, the Jew has the potential to convert. This seems relatively benevolent; but the proximity between the Jew and the Christian could also be perceived as more insidious and threatening: if the condition of being a Jew in an early modern England from which one was nominally excluded involved a certain amount of concealment and masquerade, then it created difficulties in differentiating the 'true' Jew or (English) Christian from the false or counterfeit. If the Jew was liable to conversion to Christianity, so too was the Christian vulnerable to 'turn Jew', with potentially devastating theological, cultural and racial consequences.

The idea that Portia's question hinges upon a general principle of convertibility connects with the two acts (one aborted) that are instrumental to the trial scene: Shylock's attempt to reclaim in lieu of Antonio's fiscal obligation one 'equal pound' (operating at an exchange rate of one pound to 3,000 ducats) of his 'fair flesh' (1.3.145–46), and his enforced conversion to Christianity towards the end. Confronted with Antonio's demand that he 'presently become a Christian', the Duke's ultimatum that he accept the condition or forfeit his right to a pardon, and Portia's interrogation, 'Art thou contented, Jew?', Shylock is afforded the briefest and most perfunctory of answers: 'I am content' (4.1.382–89) (that Portia is driven to add 'What dost thou say?' to her question may suggest that it is met with silence). The violation of both Shylock's faith and his ethnic loyalties is one of the most troublesome aspects of the play to modern audiences, although it has been argued that Elizabethan spectators would have regarded this offer as a generous one conducted in a spirit of Christian forgiveness; and Shylock's response and the monosyllabic lines that precede his final exit leave it open as to how positively the offer is received. But Shylock's forcible conversion merely mirrors his own attempt to carry out a symbolic circumcision of Antonio, wherein the 'flesh' that he seeks to separate from his victim's body is, via another of the play's mechanisms of displacement and substitution, transplanted from the penis to the place 'Nearest the merchant's heart' (4.1.228) (see Shapiro 1996; Parker 2008).

For many Elizabethans, the practice of circumcision, perceived as physical mutilation, was hardly distinguishable from castration; and in this respect Antonio's self-description as the 'tainted wether' (castrated ram) of the flock (4.1.113) marks him as an ironically apt target for Shylock's vengeful ire. But Antonio's use of the term 'tainted' also carries implications of disease, degeneration or corruption, and in modern performance this miasma of negativity has informed his transformation from melancholy outsider to passive-aggressive, self-hating gay man ('The weakest kind of fruit' [4.1.114]), hopelessly besotted with Bassanio and tragically excluded from the last-act marital couplings. Dealing with irreconcilable asymmetries of desire that result in the uneasy pairing of Christian Lorenzo and converted Jewess Jessica, whose romantic and religious salvation is secured through a betrayal of her filial bond, and whose marriage is inaugurated by an ominous recital of legendary lovers' deaths and betrayals (5.1.1–22), and in Bassanio's acquisition of Portia by the fortuitously correct 'choyce of three chests', the resolution of both main plot and romantic sub-plot is effected through a transvestite masquerade that, in the final act, becomes the pretext for a micro-drama of sexual deception. If the fact that Portia's standing as the voice of the law is complicated yet further by her adoption of a persona, Balthasar, whose name invokes the 'Moor among the Wise Men of the East' (Parker 2008: 111), whilst also associating him/her with Portia's unsuccessful, possibly Muslim, suitors, Morocco and Aragon, the assumption of a masculine alter ego by the female lead (who is herself played by an adolescent boy) provides another instance of the play's economy of conversion, substitution, exchange and interchange.

Technically a device which links *Merchant* with the other cross-dressing romantic comedies with which it is contemporaneous, it here generates little, if any, of the charged eroticism that is elsewhere produced by the dynamics of sexual ambiguity and concealed identity; indeed, apart from functioning as Portia and Nerissa's means of entry to the trial, its chief purpose is to serve as an opportunity for the women to test, and find wanting, their new husbands' fidelity, and to stimulate a sequence of deeply uneasy jokes about betrayal and the availability of women's 'rings' (vaginas), culminating in a concluding couplet in which Graziano conjoins death, the paranoid fear of cuckoldry, physical discomfort and a public announcement about the state of his wife's genitalia: 'while I live I'll fear no other thing/ So sore as keeping safe Nerissa's ring' (5.1.305–06). It has become customary for modern productions of the play to end on an ominous note: the 1980 BBC Television version ended with Jessica staring stricken to camera, having read the contents of a letter which, we cannot but assume, carries the news of her father's death; while Trevor Nunn's National Theatre version closed with the bright young things of his Weimar-era production gazing apprehensively into a future which we, and perhaps they, knew was soon to darken. The play remains one of Shakespeare's most unsettling.

Further reading

Drakakis, John (2000) 'Jew. Shylock is my name: Speech Prefixes in *The Merchant of Venice* as Symptoms of the Early Modern', in *Shakespeare and Modernity*, ed. Hugh Grady. London: Routledge, 105–21.

Engle, Lars (1993) 'Money and Moral Luck in *The Merchant of Venice*', in *Shakespearean Pragmatism: Market of His Time*. Chicago, IL: University of Chicago Press, 77–106.

Holmer, Joan Ozark (1995) *The Merchant of Venice: Choice, Hazard and Consequence*. Basingstoke: Macmillan.

Parker, Patricia (2008) 'Cutting Both Ways: Bloodletting, Castration/Circumcision, and the "Lancelet" of *The Merchant of Venice*', in *Alternative Shakespeares 3*, ed. Diana E. Henderson. London: Routledge, 95–118.

Shapiro, James (1996) *Shakespeare and the Jews*. New York: Columbia University Press.

Woodbridge, Linda (ed.) (2003) *Money and the Age of Shakespeare*. New York: Palgrave.

King John *and* Richard II

The Life and Death of King John

Date, text and authorship

c.1595; mentioned by Francis Meres, 1598; F 1623. Solely Shakespearean.

Sources and influences

Raphael Holinshed, *Chronicles of England, Scotland and Ireland* (1577; second edition 1587); *The Troublesome Reign of King John* (1591).

On stage

Birmingham Rep, 1945 (dir. Peter Brook); RSC, 1974 (dir. John Barton; John: Emrys James); RSC, 1988 (dir. Deborah Warner; John: Nicholas Woodeson); RSC, 2001 (dir. Gregory Doran; John: Guy Henry); RSC, 2006 (dir. Josie Rourke; John: Richard McCabe).

On screen

Extract from 5.2, John's death scene, from Sir Hebert Beerbohm Tree's Her Majesty's Theatre production, 1899, UK, 1899 (dir. William Kennedy; John: Sir Herbert Beerbohm Tree; included on *Silent Shakespeare*, BFI, UK, 2000); BBC Television Shakespeare, UK, 1984 (dir. David Giles; John: Leonard Rossiter; Bastard: George Costigan; Constance: Claire Bloom; Hubert: John Thaw).

King Richard II

Date, text and authorship

1595; Q1 1597; Q2, Q3 1598; Q4 1608; Q5 1615; F 1623. Solely Shakespearean.

Sources and influences

Raphael Holinshed, *Chronicles of England, Scotland and Ireland* (1577; second edition 1587); *The Mirror for Magistrates* (1559 and 1563); Christopher Marlowe, *Edward II* (c.1592); *Thomas of Woodstock* (c.1592).

On stage

Avignon Festival, 1947–53 (dir. Jean Vilar); SMT, 1951 (dir. Anthony Quayle; Richard: Michael Redgrave; Bolingbroke: Harry Andrews); RSC, 1964 (dir. Peter Hall and John Barton; Richard: David Warner; Bolingbroke: Eric Porter); Prospect Theatre, 1968 (dir. Richard Cottrell; Richard: Ian McKellen; Bolingbroke: Timothy West); RSC, 1973 (dir. John Barton; Richard/Bolingbroke: Richard Pasco/Ian Richardson); Théâtre du Soleil, Paris, 1980 (dir. Ariane Mnouchkine); English Shakespeare Company, 1986 (dir. Michael Bogdanov; Richard: Michael Pennington); NT, 1995 (dir. Deborah Warner; Richard: Fiona Shaw); RSC, 2000 (dir. Steven Pimlott; Richard: Sam West; Bolingbroke: David Troughton); Shakespeare's Globe, 2003 (dir. Tim Carroll; Richard: Mark Rylance); RSC, 2007 (dir. Michael Boyd; Richard: Jonathan Slinger; Bolingbroke: Clive Wood).

On screen

An Age of Kings, BBC TV, UK, 1960 (dir. Michael Hayes; Richard: David William); BBC TV, UK, 1970 (dir. Richard Cottrell and Toby Robertson; Richard: Ian McKellen; Bolingbroke: Timothy West; screen version of 1968 Prospect Theatre production); BBC Television Shakespeare, UK, 1978 (dir. David Giles; Richard: Derek Jacobi; Bolingbroke: Jon Finch; John of Gaunt: John Gielgud); BBC TV, UK, 1997 (dir. Deborah Warner; Richard: Fiona Shaw; screen version of 1995 NT production); English Shakespeare Company, 1999 (dir. Michael Bogdanov; video record of ESC production); BBC TV, UK, 2003 (dir. Sue Judd; live broadcast of Shakespeare's Globe production on 7 September).

Beginnings

Probably written within a year of each other, the plays published in sequence in the Folio as *The Life and Death of King John* and *The Life and Death of King Richard II* represent the extremities of the Shakespearean English history play. The latter, published in quarto in 1597, reprinted four times in Shakespeare's own lifetime, alluded to by Elizabeth I and revived by the supporters of the Earl of Essex on the eve of his failed coup in 1601, presents an account of the events that precipitated the century of political unrest that ended with the establishment of the Tudor dynasty under Henry VII in 1485, with a clear narrative line which centres upon the political mismanagements of Richard II, his deposition by the Duke of Hereford, Henry Bolingbroke, and his assassination whilst imprisoned in the Tower of London. Composed entirely in verse, predominantly lyrical in tone and marked by elaborate linguistic and ceremonial artifice, carefully attentive to the particularities of the feudal world it depicts, mindful of the profound historical reverberations of its action and largely bereft of comic relief, *Richard II*, advertised in quarto as a tragedy (and identified by Francis Meres as such in 1598), treats what was not only, for Shakespeare and his contemporaries, a foundational moment in the history of their nation, but also a matter of political urgency: the legitimacy of resistance, even rebellion, against tyranny.

King John, which was not published until 1623, likewise draws upon the second edition of Raphael Holinshed's *Chronicles of England, Scotland, and Ireland* (1587) for its dramatisation of a sequence of sometimes seemingly arbitrarily connected incidents from a reign that lasted from 1199 to 1216.

Despite being set two centuries prior to what seems like the self-consciously archaic *Richard II*, *King John* is, in Elizabethan terms, aggressively, often jingoistically, contemporary, harnessing the strident patriotism of the war years but also subjecting the political manoeuvrings depicted in the play to a witheringly satirical critique. History in *Richard II* appears to have dignity and purpose, its agents motivated both by self-interest and by lofty principle; history in *King John* is a matter of chance, coincidence, expediency, opportunism and accident. *Richard II*'s controlling register is one of stately grandeur, in which the political process is imagined to operate within a larger cosmic context, as represented by the Earl of Salisbury's choric commentary upon the king's imminent fall:

> Ah, Richard! With the eyes of heavy mind
> I see thy glory, like a shooting star,

Fall to the base earth from the firmament.
Thy sun sets weeping in the lowly west,
Witnessing storms to come, woe, and unrest.
Thy friends are fled to wait upon thy foes,
And crossly to thy good all fortune goes.

(2.4.18–24)

In *King John*, the privileged viewpoint is that of the Bastard, Philip Falconbridge, the illegitimate son of King John's dead hero father, Richard I (the Lionheart), a sardonic commentator semi-detached from the action whose summation after witnessing the brokering of a particularly squalid territorial settlement – 'Mad world, mad kings, mad composition!' (2.1.562) – concisely encapsulates the spirit of scepticism, verging on nihilism, that animates the play.

For the Bastard, who declares that 'Since kings break faith upon commodity,/ Gain, be my lord, for I will worship thee' (2.1.598–99), brutal self-interest, or 'commodity', is the perverse, corrupting basis of society, politics and history. The Bastard is initially the play's greatest cynic, and initiator of some of its sharpest jokes, which include his satirical suggestion, during the siege of Angers, that the English and French join forces against the defiant 'scroyles' (2.1.373) of the town before resuming battle with each other, prompting King John, whether out of stupidity or sarcasm, to invite his French opponent to

knit our powers,
And lay this Angers even to the ground,
Then after fight who shall be king of it?

(2.1.398–400)

But, by the end, it is the Bastard, whose tirades against commodity implicitly conceal outraged idealism, who comes to stand for honesty, honour and integrity; to him, as the illegitimate but nonetheless true heir to the Lionheart's throne, is given the patriotic affirmation of the play's finale:

This England never did, nor never shall,
Lie at the proud foot of a conqueror
But when it first did help to wound itself.
Now these her princes are come home again,
Come the three corners of the world in arms
And we shall shock them. Naught shall make us rue
If England to itself do rest but true.

(5.7.110–18)

The different ways in which these two plays work can be discerned by comparison of the expectations set by the opening scenes. Both involve a scenario whereby the king is called to judgement in a confrontation between two noblemen. In *Richard II*, the issue is between Bolingbroke and Thomas Mowbray, Duke of Norfolk, who is accused of disloyalty to the Crown, corruption and, most seriously, the murder of the Duke of Gloucester, Thomas of Woodstock, a crime in which Richard himself was implicated, and an event which precedes the action of Shakespeare's play but which had been dramatised in the anonymous chronicle play *Thomas of Woodstock* (1592–93).

The political stakes could not be higher; the scene is stately, formal, marked by ceremonial rhetoric and ritual professions of loyalty, charge and counter-charge:

> BOLINGBROKE Many years of happy days befall
>   My gracious sovereign, my most loving liege!
> MOWBRAY Each day still better others' happiness,
>   Until the heavens, envying earth's good hap,
>   Add an immortal title to your crown!
>   KING RICHARD We thank you both. Yet one but flatters us,
>   As well appeareth by the cause you come ...

(1.1.20–26)

Richard's ostensibly even-handed mediation of the dispute, which escalates through the ritual gesture of throwing down gauntlets to his declaration that it will be settled in trial by combat, operates within an historically specific judicial system, whereby the power of the king is circumscribed by the enablements and restraints of feudalism.

Richard is as much mandated to remain within the law as his subjects; yet, as the scene uncomfortably reminds us, he is already guilty at least by association of one murder and, according to the historical record, of which Shakespeare was well aware, compromised by his own ineffectiveness as a ruler who had ascended the throne as a juvenile under the wardship of his uncles, including John of Gaunt, the 'time-honoured Lancaster' (1.1.1), to whom he addresses the play's first words. Outwardly, at least, Richard's Court is defined by its observance of due process and its monarch securely invested with divinely sanctioned authority: 'We were not born to sue, but to command' (1.1.196), Richard pronounces at the end of the scene, and will later insist, even as he is on the point of losing his throne, that 'Not all the water in the rough rude sea/ Can wash the balm from an anointed king' (3.2.50–51). The tragedy of the play is that he is both right, in that his rule is legitimate, and catastrophically wrong, in that the fantasy of being God's earthly deputy is not in itself enough to prevent his deposition by an opponent who is not only better supported politically and militarily but also more single-minded and ruthlessly pragmatic in his pursuit, and retention, of power. Nonetheless, at the outset, Richard appears to be at the height of his powers, even if only to establish how far he is to fall.

Compare the opening of *King John*, which from the very beginning casts its nominal protagonist's authority comically in doubt. The majority of the scene is given to John's hearing of the inheritance dispute between the Bastard and his half-brother, Robert Falconbridge, but it opens with a short audience with the French ambassador, regarding the king of France's attempts to claim Ireland and a swathe of English-controlled territories in France. Within seconds, the ambassador insults the King, referring to his 'borrowed majesty' (1.1.4), prompting an interjection from the monarch's domineering mother, Queen Eleanor:

> QUEEN ELEANOR A strange beginning: 'borrowed majesty'?

(1.1.5)

Defensively intended, perhaps, the reiteration compounds the indignity by drawing attention to the slight, as well as immediately placing John in a position of filial subjection; metadramatically, also, this is indeed a 'strange beginning' to an action, likened by the Bastard to 'industrious scenes and acts of death' whose witnesses 'As in a theatre ... gape and point' (2.1.375–76), which culminates in a death scene in which the King imagines himself as a merely textual entity, 'a scribbled form, drawn with a pen/ Upon a parchment'

(5.7.32–33). The assertion of authority is, moreover, patently unsafe; for, as Eleanor briskly reminds John when he attempts to appeal to 'Our strong possession and our right' (1.1.39), his claim to power is primarily based on the former.

Richard has evidently been well briefed for his hearing, and conducts it with careful regard for feudal protocols and with a watchful eye on his own interests; John, apparently, is presented with the Falconbridges without warning, decisively resolves a tricky, finely balanced case, and awards the Bastard a knighthood in return for him surrendering his claim to his half-brother's inheritance. Legally, the Bastard is entitled to the estate, but morally, perhaps, the issue is less clear cut; there are parallels here between this domestic dispute and both the rival territorial claims of England and France and those of the contenders for the English throne, John, and Richard I's other brother, Geoffrey. With John's rule established as precarious from the beginning, the tone and verbal texture of the play's opening scene create an appropriately very different kind of world to Richard's. In lieu of elaborate circumlocution, deadly courtesies, ritualised deference and formal ceremonial, the dialogue is comically combative, displaying the energies of improvisation and spontaneous response: commended by John as a 'good blunt fellow' (1.1.71), the Bastard addresses the sovereign with a directness and candour that would be unthinkable in Richard's court.

As ironic commentator, he is also afforded the privilege of a close rapport with the audience, in this scene and elsewhere, in the form of soliloquies and sardonic asides, spoken from the *platea* space occupied in the theatre Shakespeare inherited by the licensed fool, the clown and the medieval Vice: in the liminal zone of the legitimate illegitimate, the Bastard has one foot in, one out, of the play's fictional world. Little escapes the Bastard's satirical eye, whether courtly affectation:

> 'Good e'en, Sir Richard' – 'God-a-mercy fellow';
> And if his name be George I'll call Peter,
> For new-made honour doth forget men's names …

> (1.1.185–87)

the rhetoric of warfare:

> Ha, majesty! How high thy glory towers
> When the rich blood of kings is set on fire!
> O, now doth Death line his dead chaps with steel;
> The swords of soldiers are his teeth, his fangs …

> (2.1.350–59)

or the hypocrisy of the opportunist:

> Well, whiles I am a beggar I will rail,
> And say there is no sin but to be rich,
> And being rich, my virtue then shall be
> To say there is no vice by beggary.

> (2.1.594–97)

The Bastard nonetheless remains the defender of the seemingly indefensible John, who vacillates between the role of national hero in his defiance of the French and of the Papacy, and that of villain and victim.

Endings

In *Richard II*, the soliloquy is mainly the preserve of the King, who is positioned within the *locus* space of high tragedy. If Richard is the play's most eloquent generator of his own regal mythology when in power, he becomes an accomplished tragic self-dramatist when he surrenders it. His first response to the news that his supporters have abandoned him is solipsistic fatalism:

> Of comfort no man speak.
> Let's talk of graves, of worms and epitaphs,
> Make dust our paper, and with rainy eyes
> Write sorrow on the bosom of the earth …
> For God's sake, let us sit upon the ground,
> And tell sad stories of the death of kings …
>
>   (3.2.140–52)

Rendering his immediate situation one that is caught within an endless cycle of deposition and assassination, Richards fashions a timeless fable of political and personal mortality, invoking a medieval conception of tragedy, wherein death, the real king of kings, is the great leveller. But the mood of resignation is soon displaced by the effort of securing Richard's legacy, realised via his canny seizure of the ideological initiative even as power drains away from him.

This is achieved through a series of brilliantly stage-managed moments in which Richard reframes the actions of the rebels within his own terms, compelling them to accommodate his own self-glorifying iconography and to participate within his own rituals for the ceremonial surrender of power. Cornered and outnumbered by Bolingbroke's forces at Flint Castle, Richard places himself on the walls, symbolically high above the stage, entrapping the otherwise prosaic Bolingbroke within his favoured solar rhetoric by prompting him to observe that 'King Richard doth himself appear,/ As doth the blushing discontented sun' (3.3.61–62); when he assents to descend to the 'base court', it is as 'glist'ring Phaethon' (3.3.177–79), the son of the Greek sun god. Arraigned before Bolingbroke's show trial, in which he is commanded to surrender the crown, he begins by comparing himself to Christ ('Did not they sometime cry "All hail!" to me?' [4.1.160]), and delivers a ritual incantation which is designed to insist that he alone remains the author of his own dethronement:

> With mine own tears I wash away my balm,
> With my own hands I give away my crown,
> With my own tongue deny my sacred state,
> With my own breath release all duteous oaths.
>
>   (4.1.196–99)

The transfer of power is enacted with priestly solemnity, reflecting the gravity of the historical moment; it is possible that the reason the scene was omitted from the first three quartos was that it was too politically sensitive.

Finally, in a move which looks towards the psychological explorations of the final act, and which reiterates the motif of the player king that resonates throughout the histories, Richard calls for a mirror, expostulates upon the reflected image of his own face and shatters the glass. Richard suggests a 'moral' to the 'silent king': 'How soon my sorrow hath destroyed my face'; Bolingbroke is unmoved, cryptically observing that

The shadow of your sorrow hath destroyed
The shadow of your face.

(4.1.280–83)

'Shadow' is a synonym for actor: for Bolingbroke (who will in turn come to be seen as an equally pretend-king by his opponents), Richard is merely play-acting, presenting a mimicry of grief. Richard nonetheless turns the remark to his advantage, appropriating and exploiting the opposition between show and substance to lay claim to an interior sovereignty that lies beyond Bolingbroke's command.

The claim is, however, doubtful; as it remains in his prison scene, in which, in a lengthy soliloquy, Richard seeks to map the microcosm of his solitary, incarcerated consciousness upon the macrocosm of the imaginatively peopled globe, in an attempt to 'play in one person many people/ And none contented' (5.5.31–32). Deprived of power, the king who had relied above all on the manipulation of language to keep him in office finds that language is all that he has left, and that the only person left to play to is himself. Even so, he sustains the fiction that he is touched by divinity to the end, his final words laying claim to the celestial throne he considers truly his whilst also pronouncing a curse upon his killers that will reverberate through the history plays that succeed him:

Exton, thy fierce hand
Hath with the King's blood stained the King's own land.
Mount, mount, my soul; thy seat is up on high,
Whilst my gross flesh sinks downward, here to die.

(5.6.109–12)

He could not have asked for a better exit.

Further reading

Braunmuller, A. L. (1988) '*King John* and Historiography', *English Literary History* (*ELH*), 55: 309–32.

Cavanagh, Dermot, Stuart Hampton-Reeves and Stephen Longstaffe (eds) (2006) *Shakespeare's Histories and Counter-Histories*. Manchester: Manchester University Press.

Curren-Aquino, Deborah T. (ed.) (1989) *King John: New Perspectives*. Newark, DE: University of Delaware Press.

Howard, Jean E. and Phyllis Rackin (1997) *Engendering a Nation: A Feminist Account of Shakespeare's English Histories*. London: Routledge.

Kastan, David (1999), '"Proud Majesty Made a Subject": Representing Authority on the Early Modern Stage', in *Shakespeare after Theory*. London and New York: Routledge, 109–20.

Pugliatti, Paolo (1996) *Shakespeare the Historian*. Basingstoke: Macmillan.

Womersly, David (1989) 'The Politics of Shakespeare's *King John*', *Review of English Studies*, 40: 497–515.

Henry IV, Parts 1 *and* 2

Date, text and authorship

Part 1 1596–97; Q1 1598; Q2 1598; Q3 1599; Q4 1604; Q5 1608; Q6 1613; Q7 1622; F 1623. *Part 2* 1597–98; Q1 1600; F 1623. Solely Shakespearean.

Sources and influences

Raphael Holinshed, *Chronicles of England, Scotland and Ireland* (1577; second edition 1587); Samuel Daniel, *The First Four Books of the Civil Wars* (1595); *The Famous Victories of Henry the Fifth* (c.1588).

On stage

Old Vic Company at the New Theatre, 1945 (dir. John Burrell; Falstaff: Ralph Richardson; Henry: Nicholas Hannen; Hal: Michael Warre; Hotspur/Justice Shallow: Laurence Olivier); SMT, 1951 (dir. Anthony Quayle; Falstaff: Anthony Quayle; Henry: Harry Andrews; Hal: Richard Burton); RSC, 1964 (dir. Peter Hall and John Barton; Falstaff: Hugh Griffith; Henry: Eric Porter; Hal: Ian Holm); RSC, 1975 (dir. Terry Hands; Falstaff: Brewster Mason; Henry: Emrys James; Hal: Alan Howard); RSC 1982 (dir. Trevor Nunn; Falstaff: Joss Ackland; Henry: Patrick Stewart; Hal: Gerard Murphy); English Shakespeare Company, 1985 (dir. Michael Bogdanov; Falstaff: John Woodvine; Henry: Patrick O'Connell; Hal: Michael Pennington); NT, 2005 (dir. Nicholas Hytner; Falstaff: Michael Gambon; Henry: David Bradley; Hal: Matthew MacFadyen); RSC, 2007 (dir. Michael Boyd; Falstaff: David Warner; Henry: Clive Wood; Hal: Geoffrey Streatfeild).

On screen

An Age of Kings, BBC TV, UK, 1960 (dir. Michael Hayes); *Chimes at Midnight* (a.k.a. *Falstaff*), Spain/Switzerland, 1966 (dir. Orson Welles; Falstaff: Orson Welles; Henry: John Gielgud); BBC Television Shakespeare, UK, 1979 (dir. David Giles; Falstaff: Antony Quayle; Henry: Jon Finch; Hal: David Gwillim); BBC TV, UK, 1995 (dir. John Caird; Falstaff: John Calder; Henry: Ronald Pickup; Hal: Jonathan Firth)

Offshoots

My Own Private Idaho, USA, 1991 (dir. Gus Van Sant).

Shakespeare's output includes a relatively durable core of works that are internationally known, that are taught and studied at every level of the educational system, that have been repeatedly filmed and that are performed in the professional theatre, including its commercial sector, with dependable (for some, predictable) regularity (and that also feature in the general culture of semi-professional and amateur performance): most obviously, *A Midsummer Night's Dream*, *Twelfth Night*, *Hamlet* and *Macbeth*. The plays that comprise the centre of the second historical tetralogy, by contrast, have for some time now rarely been seen other than under the auspices of the major subsidised theatre companies, and even more rarely beyond the borders of the nation whose distant prehistory they dramatise. At the time of writing, the most recent of the half-dozen major productions of the two parts of *Henry IV* to have been mounted in the United Kingdom since 1951 was presented by the Royal Shakespeare Company in its Courtyard Theatre, and subsequently at the

Roundhouse in London, over the course of 2007–08; this was the seventh time the company had staged the plays in the course of a near fifty-year history that has, over the same period, seen fifteen productions of *Hamlet*, twelve *Macbeth*s, thirteen *Dream*s and eighteen *Twelfth Night*s.

The National Theatre, which unlike the RSC is not constrained by the centrality of Shakespeare to its repertoire, has been rather less compelled to reflect the range of the canon in its Shakespearean programming: the two parts were staged there for the first time in 2005, when they served chiefly as an opportunity to showcase Michael Gambon's tremendous Falstaff, the seventh time (out of a total in the order of sixty Shakespeare productions) the National had attempted any of the histories since 1964. Beyond the two national institutions, the plays have occasionally surfaced in the commercial sector: for Michael Pennington and Michael Bogdanov's English Shakespeare Company in 1986, for the English Touring Company in 1996; and in the open air at Chepstow Castle in 1994, Regents Park in 2004 and Shakespeare's Globe in 2010. Outside the United Kingdom, the plays are intermittently performed in the Anglophone world (the plays are a regular feature of the regional American Shakespeare festivals, and were staged at New York's Lincoln Center in 2003 and by the Chicago Shakespeare Theatre in 2006) and, very rarely, as part of the English companies' touring activities: the last time a Stratford production of *Henry IV, Part 1* toured the United States was in 1931. In translation, the plays have been memorably directed by Roger Planchon (Lyon, 1957) and by Ariane Mnouchkine (Paris, 1984).

The comparative infrequency with which the plays have been staged has, however, generally been counterbalanced by the larger significance that these productions have carried as cultural and institutional events, and the RSC in particular has not only developed ways of making them particularly its own, but also constituted them as important markers of institutional history and identity. The *Henry IV* plays marked the opening of the rebuilt Shakespeare Memorial Theatre in 1932, as well as the RSC's move to the Barbican Centre in London fifty years later; they were at the heart of the Shakespeare Memorial Theatre's contribution to the 1951 Festival of Britain, and of the RSC's to the Shakespeare quatercentenary of 1964. For the RSC they have also operated, sometimes within the larger framework of the histories performed entire, as a means of defining a company aesthetic or ethos, and of marking directorial succession. Run in conjunction with the adaptation of the three parts of *Henry VI* as *The Wars of the Roses*, the second tetralogy, in 1964–65, under the direction of Peter Hall and John Barton, both established the company's Brecht-influenced house style and sealed its case for substantial, long-term public funding.

Ten years later, Terry Hands's productions prepared the way for his assumption of joint Artistic Directorship of the RSC with Trevor Nunn, a ritual repeated in 1991, when the plays formed Adrian Noble's first production as Hands's successor. Presented thus, the *Henry* plays have provided the occasion for a company like the RSC to demonstrate what it can, uniquely, do best and what the commercial Shakespearean theatre can do only rarely. Unmatched in their social and narrative range, and tonal variety, the plays have been seen as combining star opportunities, in the parts of Falstaff and Prince Henry, with ideal material for ensemble building; moving between the tavern, the court and the battlefield, and from the personal to the political, they encompass the comic, the historical and the tragic, inhabiting in modern performance the timeframes of the medieval, the early modern and the contemporary.

If the sense of historical momentousness that is an important part of the theatrical texture of *Henry IV* in performance derives in part from the auspices under which the plays have generally been presented, an important constituent of these events has been their durational quality. Since the *Henry IV* plays are rarely presented in isolation, they tend to be encountered in the theatre as marathon undertakings, a full day rather than a mere afternoon or evening, in which the bond that develops between performers and audiences over many hours of talking and fighting, watching and listening (and, perhaps just as importantly, over multiple intervals of eating, drinking, conversation and comfort breaks) appears by the end to have forged a unique sense of collective endeavour, of communal achievement, pride in having witnessed and endured. The presentation of the two parts in tandem is, however, a relatively recent phenomenon.

For the first three centuries of their theatrical afterlife, *Part 1* and *Part 2* were often presented independently. In Shakespeare's lifetime, *Part 1*, whose quarto title, 'The History of Henrie the Fourth', gave no indication that it was not a self-contained play, seems to have been more popular: mentioned by Francis Meres in 1598 (as an example of Shakespeare's facility for tragedy), it prompted the Lord Chamberlain's Men's rivals, the Lord Admiral's Men, to stake their own claim to the material with the multiply authored *First Part of Sir John Oldcastle* a year later; the quarto was reprinted six times between 1598 and 1622. *Part 2* was not reprinted in quarto but was one of the plays presented at court between 1612 and 1613, and again in 1619; *Part1* was offered under the title 'The Hotspur' at court during the 1612–13 season, as 'The First Part of Sir John Falstaff' at Whitehall at the end of 1625 and as 'ould Castel' at the Cockpit in 1638. After the Restoration, *Part 1* entered the repertoire as a secure fixture within the half-dozen stock Shakespeare plays to be regularly produced between 1660 and the early eighteenth century; *Part 2*, however, had to wait until 1720 for its first post-Interregnum revival, and for the next two hundred years managers generally saw little need to programme the two together. At the Shakespeare Memorial Theatre, for example, Frank Benson staged *Part 2* nine times between 1894 and 1915 but *Part 1* only twice; and only once (in 1905) did the two parts coincide in the same season.

In London between 1906 and 1940, there were in total fifteen productions of the two plays, which included eight of *Part 1* and two of *Part 2* as stand-alone pieces. The plays have also from a fairly early stage been treated as material for abridgement and adaptation. The first of these was Sir Edward Dering's version, for a private amateur performance at his house in Kent in 1622, which, combining elements of both parts into a single work of some three and a half thousand lines, consists of most of *Part 1* and about one-quarter of *Part 2*; during the Interregnum, the Gadshill robbery incident was the basis of the short sketch, or 'droll', *The Bouncing Knight, or the Robbers Robbed*, which was published as part of the anthology *The Wits, or Sport upon Sport* in 1662, a volume whose frontispiece is dominated by the figures of Sir John Falstaff and the Hostess. Throughout the eighteenth and nineteenth centuries, the plays were recurrently raided and revisited, usually for the comic possibilities afforded by the Falstaff material: 1760 saw the publication of W. Kenrick's *Falstaff's Wedding*, a work dedicated to the eighteenth-century London stage's definitive fat knight, James Quin; in 1829 Charles Short compiled episodes from both parts to produce *The Life and Humours of Falstaff*; with the *Merry Wives*, the plays also provided additional material for Verdi's opera *Falstaff* (1893). The tradition of adaptation continued into the twentieth century, notably in Orson Welles's *Chimes at Midnight* (1965; released in the United States as *Falstaff*), and in the BBC Television version broadcast in 1995 as part of its *Performance* season, which conflated both parts as a three-hour film.

Both screen redactions did rather more than edit and abbreviate the existing texts for the purposes of economy and concision: in both cases, scenes and incidents were selected, shaped and rearranged in order to create unity of focus and narrative and thematic coherence. Emphasising the Eastcheap material over the political narrative, Welles's film ensures that its two hours are dominated by his melancholy Falstaff (whether or not he is on screen), who here is a tragic figure cruelly abandoned by Henry; the BBC *Performance* version streamlines the plotlines of the two parts so that the Battle of Shrewsbury (the conclusion of *Part 1*) is concurrent with Falstaff's rejection at the end of *Part 2*. Both are substantial interventions in the existing scripts that might well be seen to alter and perhaps distort the concerns and emphases of the plays as written, and as such, we might suppose, operate on different terms to the stage productions referred to above, which explicitly or implicitly offer themselves as recovering the cumulative power and narrative progression that is missing when the plays are presented in isolation or in adaptation. Yet to present the *Henry IV* plays in sequence, and whole, as if they were instalments of a single work, is also to confer a chronological and developmental logic that is itself a retrospective theatrical and critical imposition (though, as with the *Henry VI* plays, it was one initiated as early as 1623, when the histories were first subjected to a standardised chronology).

As outlined in the 'Criticism' section (pp. 303–11), one of the important legacies of the historicist criticism of the 1940s (and this fed directly into the theatre productions that immediately followed) was its treatment of the history plays not as relatively discrete episodes but as components of a grand providentialist design, whose artistic and political project was to work through the consequences of Bolingbroke's usurpation of Richard II's throne, in a dialectic of order and disorder, rebellion and retribution, and crime and punishment, that achieves a temporary synthesis in the glorious but brief reign of Henry V, and a final resolution in the enthronement of the Tudor dynasty at the close of *Richard III*. Bracketed by *Richard II* and *Henry V*, the *Henry IV* plays contribute to this argument, in the view of the founding father of this critical movement, E. M. W. Tillyard, by presenting Prince Henry with a schematically clear 'Morality-fashion' choice 'between Sloth or Vanity', represented by Falstaff and his crew, and 'Chivalry', identified by his father and brothers; it is only when we 'treat the two parts as a single play' that the political coherence of the whole, encapsulated in 'the theme of England', can become visible, so that it 'grows naturally till its full compass is reached when Henry V, the perfect English king, comes to the throne' (Tillyard 1962: 265, 299).

Read or staged sequentially, the plays can be seen not only to trace the education of the king but to prepare the ground from an early stage for the rejection of Falstaff (who over the course of the drama 'goes from the harmlessly comic Vice to the epitome of the Deadly Sins at war with law and order' [Tillyard 1962: 287]), an action which, Tillyard considered, was both inevitable and unquestionably just: 'The school of criticism that furnished him with a tender heart and condemned the Prince for brutality in turning him away was deluded' (291). Tillyard's conservative politics were enthusiastically adopted in some theatrical quarters; John Dover Wilson, who had in 1943 shifted the plays' balance of sympathies and priorities by stating that their 'technical centre' is 'not the fat knight but the lean prince' (1943: 117), wrote of the 1951 Stratford production that the 'measure of unity and coherence' that was afforded by serial presentation of the tetralogy enabled its message of a 'united and harmonious commonweal' to emerge with clarity and force (Wilson and Worsley 1952: 4, 22).

Though the appeal of this orthodoxy dwindled fairly rapidly as the latter part of the century progressed, the other important opportunity created by sequential presentation of the *Henry* plays, that is, the possibility of seeing them as *Bildungsdramen*, as a study in the moral, political and emotional education of Prince Henry, did not. For Henry to be played as a dynamic rather than static character, and as one who merits at least a degree of audience sympathy, the difference between the Henry who finishes his first scene in *Part 1* by declaring of his tavern companions that 'I know you all ... ' (1.2.173) and the Henry who announces to Falstaff at the end of *Part 2* that 'I know thee not, old man' (5.5.45) marks an emotional journey, a progression towards self-understanding as well as towards the assumption of responsibility, that is, usually, mirrored by the trajectory of Falstaff's decline. Often, in performance, Henry's story has been represented as a three-cornered Oedipal contest between himself, Bolingbroke and Falstaff, with the conflicted royal son finding himself divided in his emotional loyalties between real and symbolic fathers, between the king who is the embodiment of duty (and who is frequently played as cold, inhibited and distant) and the king of misrule who, however corruptly, is able to proffer warmth and affection.

An alternative approach, argued, for example, by the editor of the New Cambridge edition of *Part 2*, is to regard the relation between the two plays as a matter of opportunism rather than design; 'merely a "sequel"', the second part was written as a blatant attempt to cash in on the perhaps unexpected success of *Part 1*, involving 'the introduction of a host of new characters to support the central figure responsible for the success of the original play, the parallelism in structure with the "parent" production, and even the explicit promise at the end of further instalments' (Melchiori 1989: 1). The projected appeal of *Part 2*, according to this account, lay in its repetition of, and variation upon, the formula that had proved so winning for *Part 1*. The repetition can be found, for example, in the structure: both plays begin in the turmoil of revolt (seen, in *Part 1*, from Henry Bolingbroke's perspective; in *Part 2*, from that of his rebel antagonists) before moving to Falstaff; both include crucial encounters between Falstaff and Henry during the second act (*Part 1*, 2.5; *Part 2*, 2.4); and both lead to a fifth-act confrontation between the Crown and the forces of opposition, the difference being that in the first play the outcome is settled by force of arms, and in the second by the power of words.

The two parts share a common dramatis personae, not only the clear principals but their comrades and hangers-on; but *Part 2* adds a number of important new figures that, given their historic and dramaturgical significance, seem to have been unaccountably left out of *Part 1*: Lord Bardolph, a key member of the rebel faction whose name had already been attributed to one of Falstaff's gang in *Part 1*, and whose namesake, confusingly, remains on the payroll until the end of the play; Ancient Pistol, who crashes into Falstaff's tavern in the middle of the second act, thereby stealing his thunder as the role of braggart; and the Lord Chief Justice, who is kept offstage for the entirety of *Part 1*, but who in *Part 2* takes the place of Hotspur as Henry's chief antagonist. The quarto title-page of *Part 2* had signalled both the continuity and the shift of emphasis: where the earlier play had recommended itself in part for its historical and political narrative, and for its inclusion of Hotspur, this time the selling point was 'the humours of Sir John Falstaff, and swaggering Pistol'. This is history played the second time, at least intermittently, as farce.

A double man

Despite the critical and theatrical emphasis during much of the postwar period on Prince Hal, the plays' centre of gravity has for much of their history been the figure originally known as Oldcastle (see 'Life and contexts', pp. 40–41), Sir John Falstaff, a character who has absconded from the confines of the drama to enter a cultural afterlife even larger than his role in the play. An aristocrat who keeps company with both the Prince and cutpurses, who is entrusted with the command of a company of the king's infantry only moments after he has been yet again exposed as a liar, drunk and thief, and who moves effortlessly through the London underworld of taverns and brothels, Falstaff is the bridge between the plays' different social worlds. In *Part 1*, Falstaff's star is in the ascendant, and it is in this play, which ends with his comically miraculous resurrection on the battlefield ('FALSTAFF *riseth up*', as the stage direction has it, in response to Hal's promise to disembowel him, with the Eucharistic answer 'I'll give you leave to powder me, and eat me too, tomorrow' [5.4.110–11]), that he is at his most fantastically inventive, exuberantly quick witted and energetic.

Pre-eminently a scamster, bon viveur, raconteur and comic fantasist, the Falstaff of *Part 1* occupies a world in which the responsibilities of history are consistently evaded, spending much of his, the play's and our stage time either engaged in acts of larceny or re-performing a self-aggrandising version of his own fictitious heroics, conjuring out of nowhere legions of buckram-clad assailants ('if I fought not with fifty of them, I am a bunch of radish' [2.5.170–71]) and just as deftly manufacturing an even more spurious rationale for his own deceptions:

> POINS Come, let's hear, Jack; what trick hast thou now?
> FALSTAFF By the Lord, I knew ye as well as he that made ye ... Was it for
> me to kill the heir-apparent?

> (2.5.245–48)

Accomplished as he is as a teller of palpably untrue tales and serial liar ('if I tell thee a lie, spit in my face, call me horse' [2.5.177–78]), Falstaff is also one of the play's most self-conscious performers (Henry and Hal, in their own ways, being the others), nowhere more so than in the inset episode of the 'play extempore' in which he and Hal trade places as the Prince and his father. The metadramatic ramifications of this vignette – in which Falstaff, or on Shakespeare's original stage Will Kempe, who (exclaims the Hostess, his 'tristful Queen' [2.5.359]) attacks the task of playing 'as like one of these harlotry players as ever I see' (2.5.361–62) – are personal and political: playing, or 'stand[ing] for' (342), Hal's father at the Prince's own invitation, Falstaff engages in an act of surrogate parenting that mirrors, perhaps painfully, his role in relation to the Prince, who stands in the place of the 'thousand sons' (*Part 2*, 4.2.109) that (like the 'thousand pounds' of which he repeatedly dreams) he longs for but will never have.

Playing the king with a joint-stool for a throne, a leaden dagger for a sceptre and a cushion for a crown (2.5.344–45), he is also the final travesty of the counterfeit, play-acting kings that rule the England of the histories. Playing his part in turn as Hal while Hal plays his own father, he seems to invite upon himself what most modern readers and spectators experience as an intimation of his eventual nemesis at the end of *Part 2*, when, hailing his 'sweet boy' (5.5.40), he is brutally warned ('on pain of death') 'Not to come near our person by ten mile' (5.5.61–63):

> as he is,
> old Jack Falstaff,
> Banish not him thy Harry's company,
> Banish not him thy Harry's company.
> Banish plump Jack, and banish all the world.
> PRINCE HARRY I do; I will.

> (2.5.434–39)

Accustomed to serial presentation of the *Henry* plays, actors and audiences invariably invest this exchange with grim, proleptic seriousness, which makes a good deal of sense in terms of the projected arc of Hal's character development, but it also, perhaps prematurely, darkens the mood of a play that, considered as a work whose sequel was supplied retrospectively rather than anticipated in its original design, works towards a primarily comic conclusion.

The Shakespearean creation that in the late eighteenth century provided the impetus for character criticism itself (in the shape of Maurice Morgann's 1777 *Essay on the Dramatic Character of Sir John Falstaff*), Falstaff is imagined by means of a vocabulary of excess that itself breaks the bounds of the mimetically decorous. At once shamelessly true to his own self-interest and inherently duplicitous, cowardly and evasive, the Falstaff of *Part 1* in particular is the embodiment of carnality and appetite, fantastically defined by his iconic belly as an insatiable, omnivorous machinery of consumption profanely transubstantiated into the materials of his own gratifications, 'that huge bombard of sack, that stuffed cloak-bag of guts, that roasted Manningtree ox with the pudding in his belly' (2.5.411–13), whose leaky lack of integrity is figured in a body that obscenely violates distinctions between inside and outside, matter and spirit, and solid and liquid: a 'greasy tallow-catch' (2.5.210–11), a constitutionally incontinent 'globe of sinful continents' (*Part 2*, 2.4.258) who, when he sweats, 'lards the lean earth as he walks along' (2.3.17). There is, Hal tells him, 'no room for faith, truth, nor honesty in this bosom of thine; it is all filled up with guts and midriff' (3.3.142–43); as absolute body, Falstaff is impervious to morality and oblivious to shame.

A creature determined to inhabit a perpetual present in pursuit of pleasure, he is also, in *Part 1*, almost entirely immune to introspection and regret; and part of his instinct for self-preservation is a profound disregard for the abstractions that especially motivate the rebel faction. The most explicit articulation of Falstaff's radical scepticism is the characteristically dialogic 'honour' monologue, in which the concept is subjected to a catechistic interrogation that ruthlessly exposes its essential emptiness:

> What is honour? A word. What is in that word 'honour'? What is that honour? Air. A trim reckoning! Who hath it? He that died o'Wednesday. Doth he feel it? No. Doth he hear it? No.
>
> (5.1.133–36)

Falstaff's perspective is placed in obvious counterpoint to that of the honour-driven Hotspur, who, inflamed by 'Imagination of some great exploit', thinks it 'an easy leap/ To pluck bright honour from the pale-faced moon' (1.3.197–200), and also to the actions of Hal, whose action on the battlefield at Shrewsbury acquits him of the alleged dishonours of his previously dissolute lifestyle. To an extent, then, Falstaff's subversive antipathy to the martial code of this England offers a critical perspective on it; as a Vice figure occupying the *platea*-space between the play-fiction of medieval history and its early modern (and modern) audiences, he is both its inhabitant and its semi-detached observer, in and out of its time, his time and ours.

Yet Falstaff's position, attractive as it is to those of us who are less than convinced that honour and bloodshed are somehow complementary, is not unequivocally that of the plays. To be sure, Falstaff finds corroboration of his stance when he stumbles across the body of Sir Walter Blunt, one of Henry's battlefield stunt doubles killed at the hands of a rebel who mistakenly believes him to be the king: 'There's honour for you', he sarcastically reports, 'I like not such grinning honour as Sir Walter hath' (5.3.32, 57–58); but Blunt's self-sacrifice, the consequence of a courageous selflessness that is alien to Falstaff's nature, can hardly be dismissed as trivial or futile. Nor, indeed, should be the deaths of the conscript company, the 'food for powder' that Falstaff has pressed into service for his own financial gain, and that he callously reports as having been led to 'where they are peppered' (5.3.35). Hal's anger when he calls upon Falstaff for his sword only to be dealt a bottle of sack and an excruciating pun ('There's that will sack a city' [5.3.53]) is, in the circumstances, entirely understandable and legitimate; whatever else Falstaff might be, he is not a good man to have around in a crisis.

For all his expressed contempt for it, Falstaff betrays no scruples about appropriating the fruits of honour when they become available; presented with the opportunity to post-humously mutilate Hotspur's corpse and thus to claim his killing for himself, Falstaff con-cludes the play with a final act of deceit that, while it may be particularly ingenious, is degrading rather than amusing. Much as we may marvel at and delight in Falstaff's effrontery, we also feel disquieted by his ruthlessness. Risen as from the dead at the play's end, he lives not to fight another day; but like every other of his accomplishments, it is as a result of a monstrous, and magnificent, lie.

Hal and Falstaff's first exchange in the play offers a concise anatomy of the scope and scale of his abuses. In response to an atypically bland enquiry from Falstaff about the time of day, Hal lets rip:

> What a devil hast thou to do with the time of the day? Unless hours were cups of sack, and minutes capons, and clocks the tongues of bawds, and dials the signs of leaping-houses, and the blessed sun himself a fair hot wench in flame-coloured taffeta, I see no reason why thou shouldst be so superfluous to demand the time of the day.
>
> (1.2.5–10)

Considered pathologically, the condition that Hal surreally ascribes to Falstaff is an eroto-maniac, obsessive-compulsive relationship to food, drink and sex that treats *everything* as material to be consumed, ingested and taken; such is the obscenely infectious power of Falstaff's lust and gluttony that it virally transforms the regulatory mechanisms that mea-sure out and order the worlds of the quotidian, and of work, sobriety and sexuality into the signs of their delinquent others, cocks in the place of clocks, heedless pleasure in the place of responsibility, idleness in the place of industry.

On the face of it, Falstaff stands condemned by Hal's vituperation; and yet in the nar-rative scheme of a play that begins with Henry's breathless plea to 'Find we a time for frighted peace to pant' (1.1.2), it is Falstaff's time, rather than that of the sun, of the king or of the relentless juggernaut of history, that governs much of the action. Beginning in the midst of what appears to be a national emergency, *Part 1* is a work in which surprisingly little actually happens in the political sphere, other than meetings, talk and plotting, until the final act; in the meantime, it is the practical jokes, play-acting and backchat that account for much of the play's interest.

Chimes at midnight

If *Part 1* depicts a world in which there is plenty of time to kill, *Part 2*, in marked contrast, is one in which what becomes progressively more apparent is that it is time to die. 'We have heard the chimes at midnight' (3.2.197), says Falstaff to Master Shallow, two-thirds of the way into a scene which began with the aged justices swapping reminiscences of youthful misdemeanours and news of the deaths of former friends, including, in a pre-sentiment of the eventual fate of the man who at the end of *Part 1* had denied himself a 'double man' (5.5.134), one 'old Double' (3.2.37). Sonorously intoned by Orson Welles as the keynote for his own movingly elegiac treatment of the Falstaff story, the line epitomises the balancing of nostalgia and incipient mortality that is central to the play's second- (and last-) time round effect. From the outset, *Part 2* is preoccupied by time and its passing ('We are time's subjects', says Hastings [1.3.110]; Hal worries that 'thus we play the fools with the time' [2.2.120]), and haunted by sickness, decay, ageing and death, which afflict both the deteriorating bodies of an increasingly venerable, and vulnerable, dramatis personae and the body politic of England, a place that, at its close, has become no country for old men.

In terms of the sheer number of lines, speeches and scenes for which he is present, Falstaff's dominance of *Part 2* replicates that of *Part 1*, and, being 'not only witty in myself, but the cause that wit is in other men' (1.2.8–9), he continues both to generate and to activate a language of characterisation that is itself characterised by extremity and excess. 'I do here walk before thee', he tells his diminutive page, 'like a sow that hath o'erwhelmed all her litter but one' (1.2.9–10); the man Doll Tearsheet calls her 'whoreson little tidy Bartholomew boar-pig' has 'a whole merchant's venture of Bordeaux stuff in him' (2.4.206, 54–55); the Prince, for whom he is a 'candlemine' (2.4.273; i.e. a fatty supply of tallow, material for making candles), cannot resist the urge, even as he is enacting Falstaff's banishment, to issue a grim joke about his bulk, warning him to 'Leave gormandizing' since 'the grave doth gape/ For thee thrice wider than for other men' (5.5.51–52), a quip that also reminds him of his accelerating mortality. Falstaff retains his capacity for wit and verbal inventiveness, in the magnificent prose arias that, whether mercilessly exposing Master Shallow's shamming about his wild youth ('I do remember him at Clement's Inn, like a man made after supper of a cheese paring. When a was naked, he was for all the world like a forked radish, with a head fantastically carved upon it with a knife' [3.2.280–84]), discoursing on the literally heart-warming properties of 'your excellent sherry' (4.2.92) or prevaricating with the Lord Chief Justice (1.2), sent to rebuke him for his part in the petty crimes of *Part 1* (whom he even attempts to touch up for a loan of – inevitably – a thousand pounds), continue to confirm his verbal command of the stage.

The Falstaff of *Part 2* is, however, a markedly older man than the nimble trickster of the previous play, and is, moreover, plagued by unwelcome reminders of the fact: by the Lord Chief Justice, who describes him as 'blasted with antiquity' (1.2.168), but also by Doll, who rather tactlessly tails her luscious coaxing of the 'Bartholomew boar-pig' with the passion-killing 'when wilt thou leave fighting o'days, and foining o'nights, and begin to patch up thine old body for heaven' (2.4.206–08); small wonder that Falstaff, urging her to 'not speak like a death's-head' (209), is happy to change the subject and slander the Prince and Poins, who, disguised as drawers, are at that moment waiting upon him.

Just as Falstaff's first entry in *Part 2* reprises that of *Part 1* by assigning him a companion and a question – though this time, more ominously, it is to enquire after the doctor's verdict on a urine sample – this tavern scene reruns its earlier counterpart but takes it into darker territory; prepared at the end of *Part 1*, 2.5 to cover for the man he had just theatrically banished, Hal is no longer prepared to see the funny side of Falstaff's deceits; and neither, perhaps, should we. Having finalised the project initiated in *Part 1* of infiltrating the hearts and minds of his commoners by sounding 'the very bass-string of humility' (2.5.5–6), Hal needs no longer 'to profane the precious time' (2.4.331); the curt 'Falstaff, good night' (335) which concludes their last scene together before the play's end marks a parting of the ways far more decisive, and far harsher, than the play-acting of *Part 1*.

If Falstaff's fate is an inevitable betrayal, he is, at least, not alone. King Henry, himself a sick man throughout, is cheated of his dream of a crusade to the Holy Land, an action that he hoped might have expiated the guilt over King Richard's murder, when he realises that his prophesied death in Jerusalem will actually take place no further from home than the so-named Chamber in Westminster Palace. Henry's exit forms the conclusion to a final encounter with his son, at the end of a scene which sees Hal prematurely appropriating the crown from the pillow of the father he believes to be at the point of death. Confronted with what he believes to be Hal's ultimate misdemeanour, Henry identifies it as a subconscious act of parricidal treachery; when Hal protests that he 'never thought to hear you speak again', the king's response is: 'Thy wish was father, Harry, to that thought' (4.3.219–20).

Though father and son are reconciled, Henry dies haunted by thoughts of the 'bypaths and indirect crook'd ways' by which he acquired the Crown, of the turmoil that his actions unleashed and of his own guilt: 'How I came by the crown, O God forgive!' (4.3.312, 346). Hoping against hope that the criminal taint of usurpation (the 'soil of the achievement' [317]) might go to the grave with him, Henry nonetheless knows that the loyalty of Hal's Earls cannot be counted upon; confessing that his planned crusade was a cunning conjuncture of pious aspiration and *Realpolitik* ('rest and lying still might make them look/ Too near unto my state' [339–40]), he sets the tone for his son's reign: counselling him to 'busy giddy minds/ With foreign quarrels' (341–42), he points to the way for his successor to at least temporarily unify his faction-riven, divided kingdom by targeting its aggressive energies against an external enemy.

The ground is already prepared for the events of *Henry V*; and before the play is out the reformed Hal, now King Henry, has given us a clear foretaste of the new regime, in the shape of the newly discovered and very public religiosity that is a defining characteristic of the Henry of the subsequent play ('God consigning to my good intents,/ No prince or peer shall have just cause to say,/ "God shorten Harry's happy life one day"' [5.2.143–44]), as well as in the law-and-order crackdown that is manifested not only in the rejection of Falstaff (who, relatively speaking, fares not too badly, given that he is allowed 'competence of life' so that 'lack of means enforce you not to evils' [5.5.64–65]) but also in the incident that immediately precedes it, where for the first time in the two plays the officers of the law are seen actually exercising their duties: taken into custody by parish Beadles, Mistress Quickly and Doll Tearsheet are on their way to a whipping (a standard, and notably vicious, penalty for prostitution) and also, possibly ('for the man is dead that you and Pistol beat amongst you' [5.4.16]), to the gallows. For Hal, for Falstaff and for Eastcheap, the party is well and truly over.

Further reading

Bradley, A. C. (1965 [1909]) 'The Rejection of Falstaff', in *Oxford Lectures on Poetry*. London: Macmillan, 245–75.

Calderwood, James L. (1979) *Metadrama in Shakespeare's Henriad: Richard II to Henry V*. Berkeley, CA: University of California Press.

Callow, Simon (2002) *Henry IV*. London: Faber.

Greenblatt, Stephen J. (1988) 'Invisible Bullets', in *Shakespearean Negotiations: The Circulation of Social Energy in Renaissance England*. Berkeley, CA: University of California Press, 21–65.

Hodgdon, Barbara (1991) *The End Crowns All: Closure and Contradiction in Shakespeare's History*. Princeton, NJ: Princeton University Press.

Holderness, Graham (1985) *Shakespeare's History*. Dublin: Gill and Macmillan.

Knowles, Ronald (ed.) (1998) *Shakespeare and Carnival: After Bakhtin*. Basingstoke: Macmillan.

Tillyard. E. M. W. (1962 [1944]) *Shakespeare's History Plays*. Harmondsworth: Penguin.

Traub, Valerie (1989) 'Prince Hal's Falstaff: Positioning Psychoanalysis and the Female Reproductive Body', *Shakespeare Quarterly*, 40: 456–74.

Twelfth Night, Much Ado about Nothing *and* As You Like It

Twelfth Night, or What You Will

Date, text and authorship

c.1601; performed at Middle Temple, 2 February 1602; F 1623. Solely Shakespearean.

Sources and influences

Plautus, *Menaechmi*; Matteo Bandello, *Novelle* (1554–73; trans. Geoffrey Fenton as *Certain Tragical Discourses*, 1567).

On stage

Savoy Theatre, 1912 (dir. Harley Granville Barker); Old Vic, 1937 (dir. Tyrone Guthrie; Sir Toby: Laurence Olivier); SMT, 1955 (dir. John Gielgud; Malvolio: Laurence Olivier; Viola: Vivien Leigh); SMT, 1958 (dir. Peter Hall); RSC, 1969 (dir. John Barton; Viola: Judi Dench); RSC, 1974 (dir. Peter Gill); Théâtre du Soleil, Paris, 1982 (dir. Ariane Mnouchkine); RSC, 1987 (dir. Bill Alexander; Malvolio: Antony Sher; Viola: Harriet Walter); Renaissance Theatre Company, 1987 (dir. Kenneth Branagh; Malvolio: Richard Briers; Viola: Frances Barber); RSC, 1994 (dir. Ian Judge; Malvolio: Desmond Barrit); Propeller, UK, 1999 (dir. Edward Hall); Shakespeare's Globe, 2002 (dir. Tim Carroll); Donmar Warehouse, 2002 (dir. Sam Mendes; Malvolio: Simon Russell Beale); Maly Theatre, St Petersburg, 2003 (dir. Declan Donnellan); RSC, 2007 (dir. Neil Bartlett); Donmar Warehouse, 2008 (dir. Michael Grandage; Malvolio: Derek Jacobi); RSC, 2009 (dir. Gregory Doran; Olivia: Alexandra Gilbreath).

On screen

Dvenadtsataya Noch, USSR, 1955 (dir. Yakow Fried); ATV, UK, 1970 (dir. John Dexter; Malvolio: Alec Guinness; Viola: Joan Plowright; Sir Toby: Ralph Richardson; Feste: Tommy Steele); BBC Television Shakespeare, UK, 1980 (dir. John Gorrie; Viola: Felicity Kendal; Olivia: Sinead Cusack; Malvolio: Alec McCowen); Thames TV, UK, 1988 (dir. Paul Kafno; Viola: Frances Barber; Olivia: Caroline Langrishe; Malvolio: Richard Briers); UK, 1996 (dir. Trevor Nunn; Viola: Imogen Stubbs; Olivia: Helena Bonham Carter; Malvolio: Nigel Hawthorne); Channel 4, UK, 2003 (dir. Tim Supple; Viola: Parminder Nagra; Malvolio: Michael Maloney).

Offshoots

Shakespeare: The Animated Tales: Twelfth Night, UK/Russia, 1992 (dir. Marcia Muat); *She's the Man*, USA, 2006 (dir. Andy Fickman).

Much Ado about Nothing

Date, text and authorship

c.1598; Q1 1600; performed at Court May 1613; F 1623. Solely Shakespearean.

Sources and influences

Matteo Bandello, *Novelle* (1554–73; trans. Geoffrey Fenton as *Certain Tragical Discourses*, 1567); George Whetstone, *The Rock of Regard* (1576); Ariosto, *Orlando Furioso* (trans. Sir John Harrington, 1591); *A History of Ariodante and Genevra* (1583).

On stage

Old Vic, 1931, SMT, 1950, 1955 (Benedick: John Gielgud; Beatrice: Peggy Ashcoft); NT, 1965 (dir. Franco Zeffirelli; Benedick: Robert Stephens; Beatrice: Maggie Smith); RSC, 1968 (dir. Trevor Nunn; Benedick: Alan Howard; Beatrice: Janet Suzman); RSC, 1976 (dir. John Barton; Benedick: Donald Sinden; Beatrice: Judi Dench); NT, 1981 (dir. Peter Gill; Benedick: Michael Gambon; Beatrice: Penelope Wilton); RSC, 1982 (dir. Terry Hands; Benedick: Derek Jacobi; Beatrice: Sinead Cusack); Renaissance Theatre Company, 1988 (dir. Judi Dench; Benedick: Kenneth Branagh; Beatrice: Samantha Bond); Cheek by Jowl, 1998 (dir. Declan Donnellan; Beatrice: Saskia Reeves); RSC, 2002 (dir. Gregory Doran; Benedick: Nicholas Le Provost; Beatrice: Harriet Walter); NT, 2007 (dir. Nicholas Hytner; Benedick: Simon Russell Beale; Beatrice: Zoë Wanamaker).

On screen

BBC Television Shakespeare, UK, 1984 (dir. Stuart Burge; Benedick: Robert Lindsay; Beatrice: Cherie Lunghi); UK/Italy, 1993 (dir. Kenneth Branagh; Benedick: Kenneth Branagh; Beatrice: Emma Thompson).

Offshoots

Shakespeare Retold: Much Ado about Nothing, BBC TV, UK, 2005 (adapt. David Nicholls).

As You Like It

Date, text and authorship

c.1599; entered SR 4 August 1600; F 1623. Solely Shakespearean.

Sources and influences

Thomas Lodge, *Rosalynde* (1590); Ariosto, *Orlando Furioso* (English translation by Sir John Harrington, 1591).

On stage

SMT, 1957 (dir. Glen Byam Shaw; Rosalind: Peggy Ashcroft); RSC, 1961 (dir. Michael Elliott; Rosalind: Vanessa Redgrave); NT, 1967 (dir. Clifford Williams; Rosalind: Ronald Pickup); RSC, 1973 (dir. Buzz Goodbody; Rosalind: Eileen Atkins); Schaubühne, Berlin-Spandau, 1977 (dir. Peter Stein); NT, 1979 (dir. John Dexter; Rosalind: Sara Kestelman); RSC, 1985 (dir. Adrian Noble; Rosalind: Juliet Stevenson; Celia: Fiona Shaw); Cheek by Jowl, 1991 (dir. Declan Donnellan; Rosalind: Adrian Lester); RSC, 1996 (dir. Steven Pimlott); RSC, 2000 (dir. Gregory Doran; Rosalind: Alexandra Gilbreath); Shakespeare's Globe, 2009 (dir. Thea Sharrock; Rosalind: Naomi Frederick); RSC, 2009 (dir. Michael Boyd; Rosalind: Katy Stephens).

On screen

UK, 1937 (dir. Paul Czinner; Orlando: Laurence Olivier; Rosalind: Elisabeth Bergner); BBC Television Shakespeare, UK, 1978 (dir. Basil Coleman; Rosalind: Helen Mirren); UK, 1992 (dir. Christine Edzard; Rosalind: Emma Croft), UK, 2006 (dir. Kenneth Branagh; Rosalind: Bryce Dallas Howard).

Offshoots

Shakespeare: The Animated Tales: As You Like It, UK/Russia, 1996 (dir. Alexei Karakov).

Cakes and ale

On 2 February 1602, the law student John Manningham took part in a feast at Middle Temple. As he recorded in his diary, the evening's festivities included 'a play called *Twelve night or what you will*'; noting that it was 'much like the commedy of errores or Menechmi in Plautus, but most like and near to that in Italian called Inganni', Manningham also wrote that it was 'a good practise in it to make the steward beleeve his lady widowe was in love with him' (Sorlien 1976: 48). This is the only mention of the play during Shakespeare's writing life, and it was not published until the First Folio of 1623. The occasion of the lawyers' celebratory feast was Candlemas Day (Twelfth Night, or the Feast of the Epiphany, was marked on 6 January), and the play was subsequently revived by the King's Men on Easter Monday (6 April) 1618 and Candlemas (2 February) 1623; taken in conjunction with the first part of the play's title, the timing of the play's early performances has prompted speculation that *Twelfth Night* was designed for a performance to mark a specific festive event (which might account for its non-appearance in print). It is also possible that Shakespeare took his name for the Duke from the visit of the Tuscan nobleman Don Virginio Orsino, who was the guest of Queen Elizabeth a year before the Middle Temple performance, and for whom the Lord Chamberlain's Men performed at Whitehall on Twelfth Night 1601, though Leslie Hotson's speculation (1954) that the play was composed in his honour – given its presentation of Orsino as a narcissist and poseur – has long been discredited.

The play's seasonal significance or topical relevance is, however, ambiguous. The reference to Twelfth Night invokes the climactic moment of the festive season, a work-free period of licensed misrule given over to music, dancing, feasting and drinking, in which, in imagination at least, masters and servants may trade places, exchanges of identity, disguise and cross-dressing become temporarily permissible, and in which scapegoats are targeted: all of which aptly suits the design and sentiments of the play. By this reckoning, the vaguely located Illyria of *Twelfth Night* is a fantasy playground, a world in which a transvestite female aristocrat can briefly transcend the impositions of rank and gender by cross-dressing as a page, becoming thus an object of hetero- and homoerotic desire for both Duke and Lady alike (and played before the all-male audience at Middle Temple by a boy player in drag); and in which the killjoy steward, the would-be prohibitionist of cakes and ale, is exposed as a pompous and humourless sham, and mercilessly exposed for the temerity of his social aspirations. At the same time, Twelfth Night marks the festive season's end, the moment when (as experienced in 2.3 by Sir Toby, Sir Andrew and Feste) boozy camaraderie evaporates in the cold, hungover light of early morning, when the clock is set ticking again and the world returns to the business of the everyday.

The play is shot through with an exquisite melancholy, and shadowed by death (Olivia is in mourning for her brother at the start of the play, as – mistakenly – is Viola). Although the season of festive misrule is one in which the rules of work, courtship and social etiquette become temporarily renegotiable, the play is full of dark reminders, not least from Feste, that the idyll is not to last: as he remarks to Orsino, when the Duke offers to pay his pleasure, 'pleasure will be paid, one time or another' (2.4.69–70); he sings of how 'Youth's a stuff will not endure' (2.3.48), and concludes the play with a melancholy bawdy song in which the only constant in life is 'the wind and the rain', for 'the rain it raineth every day' (5.1.376–95). Other references in the play complicate the wintry ambience of the title by invoking other periods of seasonal frivolity and disorder: Sir Andrew's carefully worded letter of insults to Viola is 'more matter for a May morning' (3.4.127) and Malvolio's overtures to Olivia are 'very midsummer madness' (3.4.52).

As Shakespeare had shown in *A Midsummer Night's Dream*, published in 1600, a year or so before *Twelfth Night* was composed, midsummer was proverbially the period in which madness was experienced at its most heated, but it might also be viewed optimistically as a temporary phase, cyclical and transient in nature like the period of misrule itself. Although this further suggests that a spirit of sunny benevolence hovers over the proceedings, which end with the Duke looking forward to the 'golden time' (5.1.369) of romantic union and general harmony, the vindictive ferocity of the gulling of Malvolio, the brutality of his incarceration in a dark house, and his all-too-evident sense of injustice and humiliation threaten to sour the holiday mood; as he leaves, accompanied by Feste's taunt, 'thus the whirligig of time brings in his revenges' (5.1.364), he casts a dark shadow across the scene of general harmony by promising to be 'revenged on the whole pack of you' (5.1.365), and thus throwing his tormentors' hunting conceits back in their faces. The comically imposed madness of Malvolio (rather than the love plot) was recorded by Manningham as note-worthy, and the impression made by the figure in this early performance has been echoed throughout the play's performance history: the part has attracted actors of the calibre of Charles Macklin (1741), Laurence Olivier (1955), Antony Sher (1987), Nigel Hawthorne in Trevor Nunn's film version (1996) and Derek Jacobi (2008).

For most post-seventeenth-century audiences, Malvolio is a part which invites sympathy, and accommodates pathos and even tragedy as well as broad comedy. It is, at least, debatable whether the play's original audiences would have shared these sympathies. Writing in the 1630s, Leonard Digges, the author of a commendatory poem to a volume of Shakespeare's poetry, dismissively referred to Malvolio as 'that cross-gartered gull'; and while the play is happy to entertain the erotic games of aristocrats whose polymorphous sexual desires and identities are eventually requited by the quasi-magical, uncanny twinning of Viola and Sebastian as differently sexed solutions to the problematics of same-sex desire, its tolerance does not extend to the middle-class parvenu who dares to dream that his lady loves him. The play, setting fantasies of social mobility against those of sexual ambiguity, remains one of Shakespeare's most dependably popular comedies.

A kind of merry war

Twelfth Night's alternative title, *What You Will*, has a take-it-or-leave-it quality that suggests that we might not want to take its proceedings too seriously; *Much Ado about Nothing*, similarly, carries a sunny inconsequentiality that implies that, however painful its content, there is really 'nothing' to worry about, that all will in the end be well. Published in 1600 and probably written two years earlier, *Much Ado* strikes a similar balance between romance and melancholy. The 'much ado' alluded to in the title concerns the misfortunes of one of the play's two pairs of lovers, Claudio and Hero: maliciously framed as unfaithful by the play's villain, Don John (a prototype for Iago), on the eve of her wedding, Hero is publically and viciously humiliated at the altar by both her husband-to-be and her enraged father, Leonato; taken into hiding, she feigns her own death; when the plot is exposed thanks to the fortuitous intervention of the local Watch, Claudio is stricken with grief and remorse. Making atonement at the family tomb in which she is supposedly buried, Claudio agrees to wed the woman who is offered to him as Leonato's niece; in the final scene, she is revealed as Hero and the lovers are reconciled.

Thus is Hero's alleged betrayal confirmed as what it was all along: a baseless fabrication, non-existent, to be forgotten as easily (or not) as Claudio's brutal reaction to it is forgiven, with any potentially lasting, and damaging, consequences neutralised in the interests of comic closure. In common with a number of Shakespeare's other comedies, the ending is doubly festive because it consists of two weddings; the other, on this occasion, being that of Claudio and Hero's older, wiser and sadder counterparts, Benedick and Beatrice, whose pairing has also come about as a result of intrigue and deception, though in this instance of a benevolent variety. The play that begins with the good news of the successful completion of a military campaign that saw the loss of 'But few of any sort, and none of name' (1.1.6) ends with a dance, and not even the news that the architect of Hero's misfortunes has been apprehended in flight, and is to be returned under guard to face the music, is allowed to sour the party atmosphere. 'Think not on him till tomorrow', urges Benedick, 'I'll devise thee brave punishments for him'. Justice, and retribution, can wait; for now, 'Strike up, pipers' (5.4.121–22).

The determinedly feelgood conclusion reflects the holiday world of a play in which doing nothing, or at least doing nothing that might be accounted anything like work, is the favoured pursuit of the leisured elite who inhabit it. Prior to the crisis of Hero's shaming, Messina is, under Leonato's initially easygoing governance, a slow-paced, convivial place whose daily round is defined by an endless cycle of eating, drinking, music, dance and talk, and which considers itself sufficiently safe to entrust its security to a volunteer constabulary (seconded to the Mediterranean from deepest rural Warwickshire) whose approach to the maintenance of law and order could hardly be more hands off:

> DOGBERRY … You are to bid any man stand in the Prince's name.
>
> FIRST WATCHMAN How if a will not stand?
>
> DOGBERRY Why then take no note of him, but let him go and, and, and presently call the rest of the watch together, and thank God you are rid of a knave.
>
> (3.3.22–7)

As one of the founding fathers of the great English comic tradition of the verbally infelicitous, ostensibly slow-witted, but terrier-determined policeman who in the end always gets his man, Dogberry is, in his touchingly pompous belief in the dignity of his own office ('Though it be not written down, yet forget not that I am an ass' [4.2.69–70]), a figure of fun, but he and his men are nonetheless the play's ablest instruments of justice, whose intervention secures the outcome by means that seem semi-providential in their fortuitousness. If it is a matter of both luck and comic inevitability that the Watch happen to be on hand to overhear Don John's henchmen expounding a full disclosure of the Hero plot, it is an even happier anomaly that the Watch appear for once to decide to ignore the laissez-faire principles of Messinian policing by actually making the effort to take their suspects into custody.

In the overall scheme of things, Dogberry's complacent sense of community seems well founded. The play depicts a tightly knit network of kinship and affective relationships in which everyone is known to everyone else (and where the eavesdropping scenarios that advance the narrative are entirely at home in a world of gossipy intrigue and mutual surveillance) and where outsiders are rare (though Claudio, for example, is as a Florentine apparently a stranger in town, he nonetheless has 'an uncle here in Messina' [1.1.15]). Roles and relationships are clearly defined, with the importance of ties of family and kinship signalled in stage directions and dialogue: the very first entrance has Leonato accompanied by 'HERO *his daughter*, and BEATRICE *his niece*' (1.1.0.s.d.; the quarto text also intriguingly includes 'Innogen his wife', a ghost character invariably erased by the play's editors), designations repeated at the beginning of the second act, with the entrance of 'LEONATO, [ANTONIO] *his brother*, HERO *his daughter*, BEATRICE *his niece* (2.1.0.s.d.), and in the play's second scene he enters in the company of Antonio, '*an old man brother to Leonato*' (1.2.0.s.d.; in the quarto, Antonio's speech-prefixes vary between 'Old', 'Antonio' and 'Brother').

Antonio himself is assigned a son at the beginning of this scene (though later in the play [5.1.274] Leonato indicates that he is actually childless), in an apparently gratuitous reference to Leonato's 'cousin', the 'son' that 'Hath provided this music' (1.2.1–2); at the end of a scene of some twenty lines (which takes pains to report that 'the Prince discovered to Claudio that he loved my niece, your daughter' [1.2.9–10]), Leonato addresses the musicians preparing for the evening's festivities as 'Cousins' (1.2.21), a term of address which occurs with striking frequency throughout the play. Within an elite community bound by ties both of blood and of social obligation, Don John's malcontented alienation both from the commonality and from his brother's network of favours ('I had rather be a canker in a hedge than a rose in his grace' [1.3.21–22]), manifested in his degradation of Hero, is an assault upon the entire social body, which, as Don John's bastard sibling, he is at once both part of and excluded from. The successful achievement of comic closure, which is physically figured in the rhymed bodies that dance the play to its real conclusion, depends on the one hand upon his exclusion from the finale, on the other on his projected re-incorporation (as the recipient of Benedick's 'brave punishments') beyond it.

Perhaps *Much Ado* could be regarded as a family-centred play in another sense: by the time it was written, Shakespeare had been embedded in the Lord Chamberlain's Men for four years, as its chief provider of scripts closely tailored to the strengths and idiosyncrasies of his fellow players. In this respect, the speech prefixes in the quarto that assign Dogberry's part to (Will) Kempe and that of Verges to (Richard) Cowley not only provide direct evidence of original casting but also suggest that consciousness of the player in the role was never far from the surface, and indeed may have been part of the play's texture; the connotations of Benedick's naming (*bene dicte*, or well spoken) seem apt for a role taken by Burbage, and, out of many possible in-jokes now lost to us, I find it hard not to read Benedick's references to 'Hero, Leonato's short daughter' (1.1.172–73) as a jibe at a diminutive boy player (perhaps the one who had also played Hermia a year or so earlier). Shakespeare's company was one which, Andrew Gurr has noted, was remarkably closely knit by marriage as a family business (2004b: 20–22); additionally, within an apprenticeship system that involved adult sharers tutoring boy players as members of their own households, the onstage dynamics between male and female, as well as senior and junior, characters might also have been suffused with the dynamics of affective, and power, relationships that were as much those of father and son as of master and apprentice.

The emphasis upon kinship, and upon established relationships, contributes to the impression (unusual for a Shakespearean comedy) that the participants in the drama have shared personal histories that extend beyond, and significantly predate, the events of the play. Though they are conventional lovers in some respects, the partnering of Claudio and Hero has less of the love-at-first-sight aspect than does that of, say, Viola and Orsino, Claudio having already set his eye on her prior to his departure to fight Don Pedro's war. The sense of a back story is even more pronounced with Benedick and Beatrice; and if the play's primary appeal from the outset of its stage history has resided less in Claudio and Hero's narrative than in the brilliant verbal sparring of the maturer leads (advertised in quarto as 'sundrie times publikely acted', the play was twice recorded in the Revels accounts for 1613, both under its own title and as *Benedicte and Betteris*), part of the roles' attraction for modern actors has resided in their potential to suggest that their banter is as much defensive as it is witty, that it masks the pain of a previous betrayal.

Responding to Don Pedro's accusation that she has 'lost the heart of Signor Benedick', Beatrice replies (often, as it has been played in recent years, with a sense of hurt or regret): 'Indeed, my lord, he lent it me a while, and I gave him use for it, a double heart for his single one. Marry, once before he won it of me, with false dice' (2.1.242–44). In a similar vein, the extremism of Benedick's denunciations (should he ever become a fool for love, he vows, he will invite his comrades to 'pick out mine eyes with a ballad-maker's pen and hang me up at the sign of a brothel house for the sign of blind Cupid' and to 'hang me in a bottle like a cat, and shoot at me' [1.1.205–11]) offers ample comic opportunities for the portrayal of a man in denial, who needs only to hear of Beatrice's supposed passion for himself to instantly declare that 'it must be requited' (2.3.199). For modern actors and audiences, it is the impression the play creates that Benedick and Beatrice's love is hard earned, and, moreover, tested to the limit by her injunction that he 'Kill Claudio' (4.1.287), that makes us feel that it is more substantial, more worthwhile and more enduring than most.

It needs to be; for both Benedick's macabre solicitations and the 'merry war' (1.1.50) that rages between himself and Beatrice (who 'speaks poniards', and whose 'every word stabs' [2.1.216]) belong to a society in which violence and conflict seem endemic and systemic. The association of wooing and warfare is recurrent: for Claudio, seducing Hero means taking 'her hearing prisoner with the force/ And strong encounter of my amorous tale' (1.1.272–73), a sentiment echoed by Don Pedro, who wonders that 'her spirit had been invincible against all assaults of affection' (2.3.106–07); and there are repeated references to shooting and hanging (Cupid, visualised as the deadliest of archers, is a 'little hangman' [3.2.9]), and even, in the course of some lighthearted banter around Benedick's toothache, to the grisly public spectacle of drawing and quartering (3.2.19–20). Seen in this light, the nothingnesss about which the play creates much ado is neither light nor trivial, since 'nothing' (a homophone for 'noting' in Elizabethan English, appropriately enough for a play full of songs and structured around observation, spying, overheard conversations) is not only that of the void that beckons from beyond the comedy's horizon but also, as slang for women's genitals, the play's ultimate locus of both desire and terror.

No clock in the forest

As You Like It: another almost whimsically insouciant title (in contemporary teen parlance: whatever) for a comedy that anthologises a range of structural and plot components from Shakespeare's other forays into the genre: a cross-dressed female lead (*Merchant, Twelfth Night*) who undertakes a risky outing into the rural wilds (*Two Gentlemen*) and becomes romantically involved with a man prone to producing lousy love poetry (*Love's Labour's Lost*); a dangerous and corrupt court contrasted with a freer, life-enhancing and more authentic green world (*A Midsummer Night's Dream*). Entered in the Stationers' Register on 4 August 1600 alongside *2 Henry I V, Much Ado* and Jonson's *Every Man in His Humour*, but unpublished until the 1623 Folio, it is tonally the lightest, most unambiguously pleasurable and most straightforwardly festive of the comedies considered in this section.

The play's insouciant spirit is reflected in its casual disregard for Shakespeare's own rules of comic plotting: in order to get through the business of establishing character, situation and narrative as briskly as it can, it begins with one of the most excruciatingly expository 'conversations' in the entire Shakespearean canon. 'As I remember, Adam', begins Orlando to his ageing servant, 'it was upon this fashion bequeathed me by will but poor a thousand crowns, and, as thou sayst, charged my brother on his blessing to breed me well – and there begins my sadness.' (1.1.1–4): over twenty densely packed prose lines of background information about a situation with which the listener is already quite familiar. This is immediately followed by a meeting between Orlando and Oliver (as Adam helpfully points out on his entrance, 'my master, your brother' [22]) that, having allowed the younger sibling to reiterate his grievances in person, rapidly escalates from verbal to physical confrontation that in turn just as rapidly collapses when Oliver fobs his assailant off with the promise that 'You shall have some part of your will' (65–66).

The introduction of Charles, the Duke's wrestler, one of whose implausible tasks is to provide the answer to Oliver's arbitrary query as to whether 'Rosalind, the Duke's daughter, be banished with her father' (91–92), another to report on the Duke's exile in the forest of Ardenne (or, as the Folio spells it, Arden, thus referring its readers to the woodlands neighbouring Stratford-upon-Avon), where he and his 'merry men' besport themselves 'like the old Robin Hood of England' (100–01), and yet another to inform Oliver that he will the next day face a challenge from Orlando in disguise, contributes to the breathless, switchback effect of a scene that seems to wish to trail as many characters and plotlines as is comically possible in fewer than one hundred and fifty lines. Having established Oliver's mistreatment of Orlando, the tyrannical, despotic and arbitrary nature of Duke Frederick's court, and a network of filial and interfamilial rivalries and loyalties that include the banishment of 'the old Duke' by 'his younger brother, the new Duke', and the friendship between Rosalind and Celia, 'being ever from their cradles bred together' (87–88, 94), things are no less hectic in the second scene, which opens with a brain-twisting exposition from Celia ('If my uncle, thy banished father, had banished thy uncle, the Duke my father, so thou hadst been still with me I could have taught my love to take thy father for mine' [1.2.7–9]), moves with casual serendipity, in response to Celia's injunction to her cousin to 'be merry' (19), to the 'sports' of the *ars amorata*, embraced by Rosalind in the most whimsical of spirits: 'Let me see, what think you of falling in love?' (20–21).

Though the wrestling match that follows, in which Orlando duly vanquishes the Duke's champion, may not be the 'sport' that Rosalind had in mind, its staged falls and enforced submissions graphically and energetically physicalise the rapidity and the force with which the lovers fall in love; 'Sir, you have wrestled well', Rosalind tells Orlando, 'and overthrown/ More than your enemies' (1.2.220–21), and Orlando responds to himself in kind: 'Thou art overthrown./ Or Charles or something weaker masters thee' (226–27). By the end of the scene, Orlando is condemned to exile from court, 'from the smoke to the smother,/ From tyrant Duke unto a tyrant brother' (254–55), as well as being provided with further evidence of the Duke's capriciousness, in that he has 'ta'en displeasure 'gainst his gentle niece' (1.2.245); by the end of the following scene and of the first act, Rosalind and Celia, accompanied by the clown, Touchstone, have followed him. In a further twist, they do so in male disguise, under the psuedonyms of, respectively, Ganymede (in classical mythology, the name of the pederastic Jupiter's boy lover) and Aliena:

> Were it not better,
> Because that I am more than common tall,
> That I did suit me all points like a man,
> A gallant curtal-axe upon my thigh,
> A boar-spear in my hand, and in my heart,
> Lie there what hidden woman's fear there will.

(1.3.108–13)

The pretext for the women's cross-dressing, as in previous comedies, is pragmatic, but, as previously, the move releases Rosalind, in particular, from the constraints of gender and of courtly femininity. Ardenne awaits.

It is at this point, as the setting shifts from court to forest, and the play settles decisively into pastoral mode, that the main action of the play begins. If the play's first half-hour is characterised by its frantic pace and exposition-crammed succession of incident, the transition marks not only a profound change of tempo and mood but also a drastic, and surprising, shift of dramatic priorities, as the narrative proceeds to modify or thwart the expectations generated by the events of the first three scenes, as well as to suppress their more damaging implications. The play begins in violent fraternal conflict, and indicates that Orlando and Oliver's feuding will be a major narrative strand; but Oliver is forgotten until the beginning of the third act, at which point he is in his turn expelled by Duke Frederick for allegedly conspiring with Orlando; when he next appears, it is to tell of his rescue by his brother from the jaws of a lioness (a beast not particularly plausibly native to the forests of either Ardenne or Arden) and to undergo a semi-miraculous volte-face: 'I do not shame/ To tell you what I was, since my conversion/ So sweetly tastes, being the thing I am' (4.3.134–36).

Duke Frederick, the malign patriarch of the first act, who briefly reappears during the second and third acts as a reminder of the world that the protagonists have fled, likewise disappears from view until he is unexpectedly revived forty lines from the play's end, when Jaques de Bois, 'the second son of old Sir Rowland' (5.4.141), makes his first appearance in the play with the news that the Duke, while en route to Ardenne with the aim of putting his brother to the sword, has fortuitously encountered 'an old religious man', and

> After some question with him was converted
> Both from his enterprise and from the world,
> His crown bequeathing to his banished brother,
> And all their lands restored to them again
> That were with him exiled.

(5.4.150–54)

As Jaques insists (and one can almost hear his author's tongue wedging itself firmly in his cheek), 'This to be true/ I do engage my life' (154–55); as an almost derisorily perfunctory resolution of the seemingly irreconcilable contradictions of the primogeniture system that had initiated the fraternal conflicts in the first place, it represents Shakespeare's mid-period comic dramaturgy at its most willfully magical.

If this is one of those moments in Shakespeare's comedies where credibility is visibly tested (and this moment immediately succeeds the arrival of Hymen, god of marriage, to finalise the distribution of wedded alliances between the play's couples), it is one that answers to a need for closure that is perhaps more formal than felt, given that the inhabitants of Ardenne appear to have long stopped worrying about the forces that were instrumental in sending them there in the first place. Though it harbours its occasional hazards (bestial – lions and snakes – and meteorological – 'the icy fang/ And churlish chiding of the winter's wind' [2.1.6–7]), Ardenne is an extremely congenial alternative to the world of the court, as observed by Duke Senior:

> Hath not old custom made this life more sweet
> Than that of painted pomp? Are not these woods
> More free from peril than the envious court?

(2.1.2–4)

The sentiments are conventional: the rural world is both idyllic and, set against the artificiality of court life, naturally authentic; while the natural world offers itself as a kind of meaningful and morally instructive language, a compendium of 'tongues in trees, books in the running brooks,/ Sermons in stones, and good in everything' (2.1.16–17).

It is also, importantly, a place where nothing much happens, where, for vast stretches of the play's action, time appears to dilate, or to stand still. As part of the role-playing game in 3.2 Rosalind enquires of Orlando, playing the part of a forester, what time it is by the clock. His reply, in character, might serve as a keynote for the play:

> You should ask me what time o' day. There's no clock in the forest.
>
> (3.2.275–76)

In the absence of clocks, time in Ardenne is measured diurnally and seasonally, allowing ample space for its lords and lovers to masquerade as outlaws, to hunt, to poeticise and philosophise, and to sing; a play unusually rich in songs and notable for set-speech, literally show-stopping speeches (notoriously, the 'seven ages of man' [2.7.138–65], a near-impossible challenge for any modern Jaques wishing to make Shakespeare's words his own), *As You Like It* is punctuated by material that, rather than advancing its narrative, deliberately slows or pauses its forward movement, encouraging audiences and performers alike to linger in the moment, to take in the scenery and enjoy the view. Falling in love in this environment is not so much a matter of consummation as of elaborate delaying tactics, of idealisation, sublimation and deferral. The play's temporal and dramaturgical rhythms are contrary to the speed imperatives of the customary – if not literal – 'two-hours' traffic' (*Romeo and Juliet*, Prol. 12) both of Shakespeare's stage and of the modern theatre. My dream production, aiming to do justice to this durational aspect, would stage it over many hours or even days, with scenes played repeatedly and in different orders, actors swapping parts between them, and audiences free to come and go as they pleased.

Much virtue in 'if'

Perhaps the play's most virtuosic exponent of the arts of evasion and hedonistic procrastination is its clown, Touchstone, whose name is itself symptomatic of his place within the drama's libidinal economy. Designated throughout the Folio text as 'Clowne', he is identified as 'Touchstone' at the beginning of 2.4 in a stage direction ('*Clowne,* alias *Touchstone*') that might suggest that this is an alter ego or pseudonym of the same order as Rosalind's Ganymede and Celia's Aliena. An allusion has been identified here to Robert Armin, the Lord Chamberlain's Men's new clown and Kempe's successor, who prior to taking to the stage had been apprenticed to a goldsmith (a tool of whose trade is the smooth mineral of that name, used to test the quality of precious metal alloys); and the name certainly fits his role as a comical sceptic philosopher, or 'tester' of values. But the conjunction of touching and stones (early modern slang for testicles) suggests another dimension that makes this touch-stone a particularly fitting travelling companion for Jupiter's catamite; the compulsive, verbally self-pleasuring wordsmith also stands for the art of non-productive, indulgently recreational sex, the kind of fantasy activity that finds 'much virtue in "if"' (5.4.92).

With these, his last words in the play, Touchstone brings to an end a tirade that represents both himself and the play at their most dilatory, the ornately circumlocutory and parodically repetitive elaboration of the seven stages of challenge that escalate from the Retort Courteous, via the Quip Modest, Reply Churlish, Reproof Valiant, Countercheck Quarrelsome and Lie with Circumstance, to the Lie Direct. Epitomising the play's temporising method, this is in essence a sixty-line segment of blatant filler, which at one level serves no purpose other than to allow Rosalind and Celia to effect the quick offstage change that sees them out of their boys' clothes and into their wedding gowns. But that is the point: going nowhere at great length, this gloriously pointless piece of dramaturgic lead-swinging is a shaggy dog story lacking even the excuse of a proper punchline. And, as Touchstone makes clear, the 'virtue' in 'if' lies in its capacity as a peacemaker, as a means of conciliation and conflict resolution: 'one of them thought but of an "if" … and they shook hands and swore brothers' (5.4.89–91).

For a play that so conspicuously flouts the norms of Shakespearean comedy *As You Like It* has been a consistently popular theatre work; a large measure of its appeal has been attributed to Rosalind. Speaking one-quarter of its lines and dominating every scene in which she appears, Rosalind is the shrewdest and most resourceful of Shakespeare's comic lovers (male and female), who gives voice both to the play's most joyous articulations of passion ('O coz, coz, coz, my pretty little coz, that thou didst know how many fathom deep I am in love' [4.1.175–76]) and to the reasoned scepticism that balances the Petrarchan idealism of Orlando, the carnality of Touchstone and the melancholy of Jaques: 'men are April when they woo, December when they wed' (4.1.124–25). 'The audience of *As You Like It* falls in love with Rosalind', writes Juliet Dusinberre (2006: 13), and it is hard to disagree: venerated by nineteenth-century commentators as Shakespeare's ideal of femininity, her appeal for more recent commentators and spectators, as a woman who conducts the affairs of the play mostly dressed as a man (or boy), lies in her capacity to interrogate and transgress gender roles and categories.

Beloved of Orlando, Celia and Pheobe, Rosalind, like Viola, excites desires across the gender divide; unlike Viola, who diagnoses her situation as a predicament that fate alone can 'untangle' as 'It is too hard a knot for me t'untie' (*Twelfth Night*, 2.2.38–39), and who is largely acted upon rather than active, Rosalind controls the initiative almost throughout, to the extent of playing the thrillingly dangerous game of the mock-marriage ceremony, an incident sufficiently shocking for Celia to angrily denounce her 'coz' for having 'simply misused our sex in your love-prate' (4.1.172). The delirious conundrums of the gender identity of a part conceived for a boy (playing a woman playing a boy), who teasingly both conceals and discloses himself as such in the Epilogue ('If I were a woman … '), encompass a homoerotics that would not have been lost on the play's first audiences, occluded though it may be by modern conventions of cross-gender casting. As *you* like it: it is this playfully polymorphous inclusivity, that can entertain the love of women for men and men for women, of men for men and of women for women, and that invites each and every one of us to imagine ourselves wherever, and however, and with whomever we might desire or hope to be in love, that lies at the heart of the play's enduring charm.

Further reading

Barber, C. L. (1959) *Shakespeare's Festive Comedy: A Study of Dramatic Form and Its Relation to Social Custom*. Princeton, N.J.: Princeton University Press.

Belsey, Catharine (1985) 'Disrupting Sexual Difference: Meaning and Gender in the Comedies', in *Alternative Shakespeares*, edited by John Drakakis. London: Routledge, 166–90.

Billington, Michael (ed.) (1990) *Directors' Shakespeare: Approaches to Twelfth Night*. London: Nick Hern.

Callaghan, Dympna (2000) *Shakespeare Without Women*. London: Routledge.

Gay, Penny (1994) *As She Likes It: Shakespeare's Unruly Women*. London: Routledge.

Girard, René (1991) *A Theatre of Envy: William Shakespeare*. Oxford: Oxford University Press.

Laroque, François (1991) *Shakespeare's Festive World*, trans. Janet Lloyd. Cambridge: Cambridge University Press.

Neely, Carol (1985) *Broken Nuptials in Shakespeare's Plays*. New Haven, CT: Yale University Press.

Traub, Valerie (1992) *Desire and Anxiety: Circulations of Sexuality in Shakespearean Drama*. London and New York: Routledge.

Young, David (1972) *The Heart's Forest: A Study of Shakespeare's Pastoral Plays*. New Haven, CT: Yale University Press.

The Merry Wives of Windsor *and* Henry V

The Merry Wives of Windsor

Date, text and authorship

1597–98; Q1 1602; Q2 1619; F 1623. Solely Shakespearean.

Sources and influences

No known single source; Henry Porter's *The Two Angry Women of Abingdon* (1599) bears some similarities.

On stage

RSC, 1968 and 1975 (dir. Terry Hands; Falstaff: Brewster Mason); RSC, 1979 (dir. Trevor Nunn; Falstaff: John Woodvine); RSC, 1985 (dir. Bill Alexander; Falstaff: Peter Jeffrey); Northern Broadsides, 1993 (dir. Barrie Rutter; Falstaff: Barrie Rutter); NT, 1995 (dir. Terry Hands; Falstaff: Denis Quilley); Shakespeare's Globe, 2008 and 2010 (dir. Christopher Luscombe; Falstaff: Christopher Benjamin).

On screen

BBC Television Shakespeare, UK, 1982 (dir. David Jones; Falstaff: Richard Griffiths; Mistress Ford: Judy Davis; Mistress Page: Prunella Scales; Ford: Ben Kingsley; Mistress Quickly: Elizabeth Spriggs; Justice Shallow: Alan Bennett).

Offshoots

Merry Wives – The Musical, RSC, 2006 (dir. Gregory Doran; Falstaff: Simon Callow; Mistress Quickly: Judi Dench).

Henry V

Date, text and authorship

1599; Q1 1600; Q2 1602; Q3 1619; performed at Court 7 January 1605; F 1623. Solely Shakespearean.

Sources and influences

Raphael Holinshed, *Chronicles of England, Scotland and Ireland* (1577; second edition 1587); *The Famous Victories of Henry V* (c.1586; published 1598).

On stage

Old Vic, 1937 (dir. Tyrone Guthrie; Henry: Laurence Olivier); SMT, 1951 (dir. Anthony Quayle; Henry: Richard Burton; Chorus: Michael Redgrave); RSC, 1964 (dir. Peter Hall and John Barton; Henry: Ian Holm; Chorus: Eric Porter); RSC, 1975 (dir. Terry Hands; Henry: Alan Howard; Chorus: Emrys James); RSC, 1984 (dir. Adrian Noble; Henry: Kenneth Branagh; Chorus: Ian McDiarmid); English Shakespeare Company, 1985 (dir. Michael Bogdanov; Henry: Michael Pennington; Chorus: John Woodvine); RSC, 1994 (dir. Matthew Warchus; Henry: Iain Glenn; Chorus: Tony Britton); Shakespeare's Globe, 1997 (dir. Richard Olivier; Henry: Mark Rylance); RSC, 2000 (dir. Edward Hall; Henry: William Houston); NT, 2003 (dir. Nicholas Hytner; Henry: Adrian Lester; Chorus: Penny Downie); RSC, 2007 (dir. Michael Boyd; Henry: Geoffrey Streatfeild; Chorus: Forbes Masson).

Ashore at Windsor

At the close of *2 Henry IV*, the Epilogue promised its audiences a further instalment of the historical narrative, specifically, if they were 'not too much cloyed with fat meat', with 'Sir John in it'; one that would take the action to France, where, perhaps, 'Falstaff shall die of a sweat' (*2 Henry IV*, Epilogue, 22–26). Possibly as a consequence of Will Kempe's abrupt departure from the Lord Chamberlain's Men early in 1599, this in the event proved not to be the case: Falstaff is absent in person from *Henry V*, though the report of his death extends his shadow over at least the first part of the play. The grim denouement of the second of the *Henry IV* plays, which saw Falstaff decisively rejected by the new king and sent to the Fleet prison by the Lord Chief Justice was not, however, the fat knight's last contemporary appearance on stage or in print, for in 1602 there appeared in quarto *The Merry Wives of Windsor*, the title-page of which announced a 'Most pleasaunt and conceited Comedie of Syr Iohn Falstaffe'.

A legend that first surfaced in the early eighteenth century has it that the play was written to order in a few weeks at the behest of Queen Elizabeth, who reportedly had been so taken with the Falstaff of *Henry IV* that she commanded his creator to devise a new work with the fat knight in it, this time in love. The Tudor connection with the solidly bourgeois town of Windsor, home to the oldest of the royal residences in the form of the park and castle which the queen favoured as a retreat in times of plague (and which she had recently equipped with a gallows to deal with any wanderers from the capital unwise enough to bear with them the threat of infection), was strong; there is evidence that the play, or some version of it, was first performed as part of the entertainments commissioned to mark the Order of the Garter ceremony, over which the queen presided, on 23 April 1597.

Although, in addition to Falstaff, *Merry Wives* carries over a number of names and figures from the *Henry* plays (Bardolph, Pistol, Nim, Justice Shallow and Mistress Quickly) and is nominally set in the reign of Henry IV (Fenton is said to have 'kept company with the wild Prince and Poins' [3.2.61]), neither their characterisation nor their biographical trajectories are consistent with those of their counterparts; moreover, Shakespeare's only specifically English-set comedy is one with a strongly local and contemporary feel (akin to the city and citizen comedies of Shakespeare's contemporaries and it is written almost entirely in prose, as is appropriate to its largely non-aristocratic cast of characters). We find Falstaff at the start of the play in rather more comfortable circumstances than those anticipated at the end of *2 Henry IV* and reported in *Henry V*: domiciled at Windsor's Garter Inn on an income sufficiently substantial for him to lodge at £10 a week and to be able to bail his companions on a number of occasions, he nonetheless shares with his namesake in the histories a keen eye for a scam; which, in this instance, takes the form of the simultaneous, would-be adulterous, wooing of Mistresses Page and Ford, the 'merry wives' of the play's title, who prove to be his nemesis.

If Queen Elizabeth had expected to see Falstaff in love, however, she would have been disappointed: his pursuit of the women seems neither erotic nor romantic but blatantly mercenary. Despatching his lieutenants, Nim and Bardolph, with identically worded love-letters to the two wives, he declares that Mistress Page

> bears the purse too. She is a region in Guiana, all gold and bounty. I will be cheaters to them both, and they shall be exchequers to me. They shall be my East and West Indies, and I will trade to them both.
>
> (1.3.58–62)

Falstaff's conceit of himself as global trader commanding the wealth of Orient and Occident in the form of a pair of burghers' wives is comically incongruous and characteristically self-aggrandising; it is also a touch disproportionate in the context of a play which generally maintains more restricted and carefully demarcated horizons. The town's topography is evoked in such details as the tolling of the clock that provides Ford with the 'cue' to go in pursuit of the philandering Falstaff in his own house (3.2.38), and that sounds the midnight hour for Falstaff himself (5.5.1), in the Host's offer to lead the citizens 'about by the fields' and 'through the town to Frogmore' (2.3.65–68), in the ooze of the river banks at Datchet Mead, where Falstaff is deposited, and in Herne's Oak in the Great Park itself, where the play's lovers and schemers ultimately converge; the chiming clock reminds us of the play's neatly circumscribed timeframe, with its action unfolding over a period of days. The play is strong on the domestic detail of everyday provincial life: from the 'hot venison pasty' promised by Mistress Page (1.1.163) to her houseguests and the 'pippins and cheese' that tempt the Welsh parson Sir Hugh Evans back to the dinner table (1.2.10), to, finally, the 'country fire' that draws the adventurers home to 'laugh this sport o'er by' (5.5.219).

It is entirely fitting that Falstaff, the counterfeit hero of Gad's Hill and the field of Tewkesbury, makes his humiliating exit from his thwarted assignation with Mistress Page in a laundry basket, a conveyance which serves as an epitome of the everyday and the mundane; and it is his immersion first in soiled laundry and then in the Thames that provides his greatest occasion for verbal inventiveness: 'in the height of this bath, when I was more than half stewed in grease like a Dutch dish, to be thrown into the Thames and cooled, glowing-hot, in that surge, like a horseshoe' (3.5.101–4).

In some ways, the Sir John Falstaff of *Merry Wives* is conceived on the gargantuan scale of the figure that dominates *Henry IV*: musing upon the 'tempest' that 'threw this whale, with so many tuns of oil in his belly, ashore at Windsor' (2.1.55–57), Mistress Ford suggests both a sense of physical bulk and the monstrosity of the presence of the man Mistress Page terms 'this greasy knight' (2.1.94) as an aristocratic interloper within the town's respectably bourgeois community. Yet when compared to the legendary liar and dreamer of *Henry IV*, this Falstaff, gone to earth and partly gone to seed, is a markedly less eloquent, diminished figure: the dispute with Shallow that activates the first scene seemingly little more than an act of petty, unmotivated vandalism ('you have beaten my men, killed my deer, and broke open my lodge' [1.1.93–94]), the product of spite or perhaps boredom.

The threat that Falstaff hopes to pose to the sanctity of companionate small-town marriage is never more than minor, since Mistresses Ford and Page have the better of him –

and of their own husbands – from the outset. Manipulated first into the laundry basket, second into the borrowed clothes of the Old Woman of Brentford (a subterfuge that earns him a beating from the misogynist Ford) and third into the horned guise of Herne the hunter that leads to his ambush by a troupe of children, led by Mistress Quickly dressed as sprites and fairies, Falstaff is subjected to a succession of ordeals that culminate in the ritual expatiation of the 'sinful fantasy' and 'lust and luxury' (5.5.90–91) which he incarnates, in the form of the ordeal by fire of the mock-fairies' burning tapers.

A suitably chastened man, Falstaff is re-integrated into the community on its own terms, and his is not the only one of the play's male characters to be firmly put in his place by the end of the play; as the title indicates, this is a work in which power and agency are afforded to the citizenry rather than to noblemen, and to wives rather than husbands. Mistress Ford and Mistress Page have the upper hand not only over Falstaff but also over their ostensible lords and masters.   As far as Mistress Ford is concerned, the gulling of Falstaff is as much an opportunity to teach a few lessons in marital good sense to her pathologically jealous and possessive spouse. Alerted to Falstaff's plans by the disgruntled Nim and Bardolph, Ford secures an audience with the aspiring seducer by visiting him in disguise as 'Master Brooke', to hear of how Falstaff will arrange for him to 'enjoy' his own wife; left alone, he rages both against the 'damned epicurean rascal' that aims to pimp his spouse and, even more vehemently, against 'the hell of having a false woman' (2.2.225–57); for Ford, his wife's alleged infidelity is simultaneously an assault upon property rights and upon social status ('My bed shall be abused, my coffers ransacked, my reputation gnawn at' [2.2.257–58]), whose impact is measured at least as much in terms of Ford's rivalry with Page as in terms of his own marriage.

Projecting himself catching Falstaff, Mistress Ford and Mistress Page in a *ménage à trois*, Ford sadistically imagines that he will 'take' the miscreant knight, 'then torture my wife, pluck the borrowed veil of modesty from the so-seeming Mistress Page' and, perhaps most importantly, 'divulge Page himself for a secure and willful Actaeon' (3.2.33–36); it is almost as if the satisfaction of exposing his neighbour as a cuckold and dupe is worth the price of the wives' adultery. The violence and invective ('A witch, a quean, an old, cozening quean … you witch, you rag, you baggage, you polecat, you runnion!' [4.2.149–62]) that Ford unleashes upon Falstaff in the guise of 'Mother Prat' (4.2.158; slang for 'arse') serves as a displacement of the barely suppressed rage that is directed against his wife; at the same time, the comic-grotesque effeminisation of Falstaff as an aged witch re-engenders the transgressions of the sexual saboteur by subjecting him to a demeaning gender reversal that is also, Valerie Traub (1989) has argued, the accumulation of the running thread of associations, throughout the *Henry IV* plays, between Falstaff ('a sow that hath o'erwhelmed all her litter but one' [*Part 2*, 1.2.9–10]) and the female, and specifically maternal, body.

Falstaff's public exposure at Herne Oak in the final scene, one in which the realist texture of the play is touched by the ritualistic, the magical and the uncanny in the form of Falstaff's assumption of the mantle of Herne the hunter, and the spectacle of characters costumed as satyrs, fairies and hobgoblins, coincides with the resolution of the play's other primary plot component, which has centred on the wooing of Page's daughter Anne by the rival suitors Masters Slender and Fenton. It is this narrative strand that demonstrates Mistress Page's exercise of 'the warrant of womanhood' (4.2.179–80) in order to confirm that 'Wives may be merry, and yet honest too' (4.2.89). Utilising one of the plot staples that citizen comedy borrowed from Roman New Comedy, Anne is pursued by three men: the first, Slender, an egregious fop favoured, on social and financial grounds, by her father; the second, Doctor Caius, a comedy Frenchman preferred by her mother, who is prone to duelling, oaths ('By Gar') and pidgin English ('Vat is you sing?' to Mistress Quickly on his first entrance, 'I do not like dese toys' [1.4.38]); the third, Fenton, a raffish adventurer who at first courts her with an eye for gain but subsequently discovers, or affects to discover, genuine affection ('I found thee of more value/ Than stamps in gold or sums in sealèd bags;/ And 'tis the very riches of thyself/ That now I aim at' [3.4.15–18]). Like Mistress Ford, Mistress Page engineers a disguise plot in order to outwit her husband (a somewhat milder patriarch than Ford, but one who nonetheless has to yield some of his authority by the end), arranging for Caius to smuggle her away from the scene at Herne Oak to secretly marry (and thus hoping to sabotage Page's own plan of having Anne elope with Slender); both Pages, however, fall victim to a further disguise plot contrived by Fenton, who, with the aid of the Garter Inn's genial Host, sets both of his rivals up with mock-brides, boys in disguise (inevitably calling to mind the conventions of Shakespeare's own stage), while he secures his own match with Anne.

The play's finale, as comprehensive as any in Shakespearean comedy, is not only a masterly example of a plot resolution that manages to bring on stage practically the entire town, but also the opportunity for the social tensions latent within the community, its customary hierarchies temporarily relaxed, to be equally momentarily eased. Fenton, who not unlike Falstaff starts off as an aristocratic chancer on the trail of citizen money, and apparently redeemed by the discovery that what he wins is love as well as (modest) wealth, is given the opportunity to demonstrate the meaning of true nobility by admonishing the Pages for attempting to manoeuvre Anne into a forced union (Anne, meanwhile, says nothing other than to ask her parents' pardon); the now-reformed Ford, in response, reiterates the triumph of romantic love over financial gain, sententiously insisting that 'In love the heavens themselves do guide the state;/ Money buys lands, and wives are sold by fate' (5.5.209–10).

Contributing to the general sense of bonhomie, neutered Falstaff, the symbolic target against which the town unites in a ritual act of expiation, is himself readmitted into the fold, invited by Mistress Page to join in the festivities which will continue when the play is over. Whether or not it was composed for an aristocratic audience, as a celebration of bourgeois virtues, *Merry Wives* may be complacent, even utopian, in its vision of the accommodating capacities of the middle class, but as the play's consistent popularity on stage, both in its own shape and in the form of operatic and musical adaptations, attests, it is one that continues to exercise considerable appeal.

Star of England

If Falstaff is better served in *Merry Wives* than auditors of the Epilogue to *2 Henry IV* would have had reason to expect, his fleeting offstage presence in *Henry V* traces a darker outcome for a character who, despite the hopes aroused by the Epilogue, really has no place in the new world of this play. First published in an abbreviated form in quarto in 1600, *Henry V* takes as its subject the brief and brilliant military career of 'warlike Harry', the 'star of England' (Prologue, 5, Epilogue, 6), the monarch regarded by many of Shakespeare's English contemporaries (and, indeed, many of their descendents) as the greatest of national heroes. In outline, Henry's is a success story: the play shows him lead a unified national army, accommodating Scots, Irish and Welsh soldiers alongside English lowlife and nobility, against one of the nation's oldest enemies, subject it to a crushing defeat, against the odds, on the fields of Agincourt with a miraculously scant loss of English lives, negotiate a truce which secures considerable swathes of mainland European territory for the English Crown, and win the hand of the French Princess Catherine, thus cementing a dynastic alliance wherein, as the Queen of France prophesies,

> God, the best maker of all marriages,
> Combine your hearts in one, your realms in one.
> As man and wife, being two, are one in love,
> So be there 'twixt your kingdoms such a spousal
> That never may ill office or fell jealousy,
> Which troubles oft the bed of blessèd marriage,
> Thrust in between the paction of these kingdoms
> To make divorce of their incorporate league;
> That English may as French, French Englishmen,
> Receive each other, God speak this 'Amen'.

> (5.2.331–40)

Investing the oaths of loyalty sworn by the subjugated French nobility with the sanctity of the marriage bond, and equating the alliance between England and France with that of husband and wife, Henry redoubles the sentiment: 'Then shall I swear to Kate, and you to me,/ And may our oaths well-kept and prosp'rous be' (5.2.345–46).

Coupling a peace treaty with a wedding (and thus providing closure to an action which has throughout disturbingly conjoined conquest with both the imagery and the actuality of rape), *Henry V* essays a generic confluence of comedy and chronicle history, hoping to sound a note of resolution to the narrative of revolt and conflict of which it is the concluding instalment. This is the version of the play that has for centuries served as a vehicle for straightforward and vigorous English patriotism (and not-so-occasional jingoism), the play that, as John Dover Wilson, editor of the New Cambridge edition published just after the Second World War, remarked, 'men of action have been wont silently to admire, and literary men, at any rate during the last hundred and thirty years, volubly to contemn' (1947: vii; Wilson pointedly dedicated the edition to the '"Star of England" in her darkest night', Field Marshall the Viscount Wavell, distinguished wartime commander-in-chief of British forces in the Middle East and Burma, and editor of the popular poetry anthology *Other Men's Flowers* [1944]). This is the play that, supported by lavish resources of pageantry and spectacle, was mounted by Charles Kean at London Princess's Theatre in 1859, in which Henry's triumphant return to London was greeted by six hundred cheering supers; and the play that provided the basis for the last gasp of that nineteenth-century tradition, Laurence Olivier's morale-boosting film of 1944.

This is, up to a point, the version of the play represented by parts of those passages, preceding each act, that are designated in the Folio as Prologue and Choruses. Shakespeare is a fairly infrequent user of prologues and epilogues, and their style and function varies: of the thirty-seven plays, five have epilogues but no prologue (*A Midsummer Night's Dream, As You Like It, Twelfth Night, All's Well that Ends Well, The Tempest*), one a prologue but no epilogue (*2 Henry IV*), and five both (*Romeo and Juliet, Troilus and Cressida, Pericles, The Two Noble Kinsmen* and *Henry V*). Assigned in the text or in performance either to the character who speaks the final lines of the play (Puck, Feste, Pandarus, Prospero), to its star (Rosalind) or to a chorus or narrator who stands apart from the action (Rumour, Gower), they vary in the degree to which they reproduce, are integral to or are essential to the plays: whereas Robin's epilogue emerges smoothly from the final scene in which he features, linking the shadow identities of the fairies with those of the players and imaging the reciprocity of the actor–audience relationship through the joining of hands, that of *The Two Noble Kinsmen* is oddly tentative and ambivalent: 'I would now ask ye how ye like the play,/ But, as it is with schoolboys, cannot say' (Epilogue, 1–2).

In the manner of *Romeo* and *Troilus*, *Kinsmen*'s Epilogue formally completes the frame that its prologue initiates, though the connections between the two passages of text are nominal; in *Pericles*, the only (part-authored) Shakespeare play other than *Henry V* to make sustained and systematic use of a choric narrator, the device is employed both to confer a sense of literary archaism and to fill the gaps in the play's sprawling story. At its most straightforward, this is the role of Chorus in *Henry V*, which defines itself as enabling and supplementary, 'jumping o'er times,/ Turning th'accomplishment of many years/ Into an hourglass' (Prologue, 29–31), paraphrasing the historical record 'Of time, of numbers, and due course of things,/ Which cannot in their huge and proper life/ Be here presented' (5.0.4–6), and, in the Epilogue, locating Henry's achievement in the context of subsequent English history, and of the disasters that befell the reign of a successor 'Whose state so many had the managing/ That they lost France, and made his England bleed' (Epilogue, 11–12).

Remembered as events 'Which oft our stage has shown' (13), *Henry V*'s future lies in its theatregoing audience's past, as dramatised by Shakespeare and others in the *Henry VI* plays performed and published the best part of a decade earlier. According to the Chorus, whose key temporal marker is 'now' (Prologue, 28; 2.0.1; 4.0.1; 5.0.6), the present tense of this play would be a mythic and heroic one, purporting to celebrate the exploits of the most exemplary of English warrior-kings in a coherently and unambiguously patriotic narrative. Calling, hyperbolically, for nothing less than 'A kingdom for a stage, princes to act' and monarchs for its spectators, to do justice to its subject-matter (Prologue, 3) the Chorus repeatedly insists upon the nobility and valour of the 'warlike Harry' (5) and his comrades, upon the 'inward greatness' of the England of 'little body with a mighty heart' (2.0.16–17), upon the unity of nation and army ('who is he … that will not follow/ These culled and choice-drawn cavaliers to France?' [3.0.22–24]), and upon the rightness of the cause, the scale of the victory and the glory of the triumph of the play's 'conqu'ring Caesar' (5.0.28).

The personification of England, the Chorus's Henry is the embodiment of war itself, who, truly depicted, would 'Assume the port of Mars' (Prologue, 6); but, being 'free from vainness and self-glorious pride' (5.0.20), he is also the bearer of 'a largess universal, like the sun', his 'liberal eye' bestowing upon men of all ranks and classes 'A little touch of Harry in the night' (4.0.43–47). The Chorus likewise protests modesty about the play's own accomplishments, apparently apologising for the rudimentary conditions in which it is staged ('this unworthy scaffold … this cock-pit … this wooden O' [Prologue, 10–13]), urging its auditors to 'Piece out our imperfections with your thoughts' (22) or to use their imaginations to flesh out the bones of the story, and, repeatedly, labouring the terminology of the 'quick forge and working-house of thought' (5.0.23), issuing injunctions to 'think' (Prologue, 26), to 'Linger your patience' (2.0.31), to 'Suppose' (3.0.3, 28), to 'entertain conjecture' and to 'Behold' (4.0.1, 46). Nowhere else does Shakespeare so emphatically draw metatheatrical attention to the apparatus of a play's construction (even in *Pericles*, which arguably poses far greater problems of dramatic credibility, Gower's interventions are restricted to straightforward narration); and nowhere else is the audience so relentlessly solicited, cajoled, bargained and pleaded with.

On the face of it, the repeated drawing of the audience's attention to the disparity between what should be shown and what the play and the stage are capable of serves its patriotic purpose, its humble apologetics a genuine expression of national pride that is all the more affecting because low key rather than brashly triumphalist. To be sure, the Chorus's panegyric is at many points endorsed by ample testimony as to the potency of his impact upon those around him: recounting his sudden conversion from hooligan to regal paragon, the Archbishop of Canterbury talks of 'his body as a paradise/ T'envelop and contain celestial spirits':

> Hear him but reason in divinity
> And, all-admiring, with an inward wish
> You would desire the King were made a prelate ...
> List his discourse of war, and you shall hear
> A fearful battle rendered you in music ...

(1.1.39–45)

To his Archbishop, the king is a holy warrior; to his noblemen, he is a monarch 'Never ... better feared and loved' (2.2.25), who, unlike his predecessors, has 'cause; and means and might' (1.2.125); to his common soldiers, he is 'a good king' (2.1.114), 'a bawcock and a heart-of-gold ... of fist most valiant', a 'lovely bully' (4.1.45–49). Even such internal dissent as there is in the play is no sooner brought into contention than neutralised: not only are the trio of Cambridge conspirators effortlessly entrapped into securing their own executions, but they confess their own guilt with an alacrity worthy of the victims of Stalin's show trials: 'Our purposes God justly hath discovered', says one; 'God be thankèd for prevention', echoes the second; 'Never did faithful subject more rejoice/ At the discovery of most dangerous treason', confirms the third (2.2.146–57).

Yet, as generations of readers and theatregoers could not fail to notice, there is something about the Chorus's combination of hyperbole and exaggerated deference that does not quite ring true. It is, of course, quite possible to read the Chorus's 'apologies' as ironic or disingenuous, as a supremely eloquent articulation of the play's self-confessed inarticulacy, that is even more oxymoronic than its author envisaged when transferred to the kinds of performance media that are more than adequate to the task of holding 'The vasty fields of France' (Prologue, 12). But it is not just that its adoption of the manner of an over-enthusiastic tour guide or real estate agent is likely to arouse suspicions in the minds of contemporary audiences that something or someone might be being oversold or spin-doctored; it is that, however successfully the Chorus's account encapsulates the Harry, and the Agincourt, of sixteenth-century mythology, it is one that is in places significantly at odds with the play. It is not just poverty of resources that generates the gap between the ideal Henry, armed with 'famine, sword, and fire' (Prologue, 7), and the player king that the audience encounters on stage; it is the play's recurrent habit of diverging from the script that the Chorus is determined to establish, to qualify, modify and often contradict its version of events with its own, rather more ambivalently rendered, history of the French campaign.

Rather than providing a reliable index of events, the Choruses create expectations that, scene by scene, the action struggles to fulfil or actively subverts: Act 2, which begins with the boast that 'all the youth of England are on fire' and that 'honour's thought/ Reigns solely in the breast of every man' (2.0.1–4), is mired first in Eastcheap, where the only incendiaries on show are between the brawling Nim and Pistol (whose 'cock is up,/ And flashing fire will follow' [2.1.46–47]; before the act is out, Pistol urges his companions onwards to France 'like horseleeches ... To suck, to suck, the very blood to suck!' [2.3.46–47]), and then in Southampton. Act 3, in which the much-anticipated military campaign finally swings into action with the English navy bearing gloriously down upon the port of Harfleur, a roar of cannons and the arrival of soldiers with scaling ladders, sees the English in retreat. Act 4, which promised to show Henry the benefits of a 'little touch of Harry in the night' (4.0.43–47), has him on the eve of Agincourt attempting an undercover encounter with the troops on the ground that is sufficiently hamfisted as to embroil him in an unseemly row with the one speaker in the play to suggest that the legitimacy of the war might be open to dispute and that the king might be culpable ('if the cause be not good, the King himself hath a heavy reckoning to make' [4.1.128–29]). And although the Chorus has pre-empted its audience's disappointment by warning that Agincourt will be represented by 'four or five most vile and ragged foils,/ Right ill-disposed in brawl ridiculous' (4.0.50–51), the reduction of the conflict to a single one-word stage direction ('*Excursions*' [4.4.0.s.d.]) and a queasily comic stand-off between a ransom-hunting Pistol and a terrified French Soldier, who mistakes his vanquisher as '*le gentilhomme de bon qualité*' and finds himself answered with a scrap of Irish balladry, '*Calin o custure me*' (4.4.2–4), is a battlefield re-enactment for which the term 'vile and ragged' seems quaintly overstated.

Despite the assertions of the Chorus, aspects of the king's character and behaviour undercut the idea that the play is in any straightforward sense pro- (or indeed anti-) Henry. Among the many troubling and morally debatable incidents in the play, Henry's ordering of the slaughter of the French prisoners in 4.6 is one of the most disturbing, not only because of its expedient ruthlessness (Shakespeare chooses not to follow the sources' emphasis on its military necessity), but also because it is a moment where, in a war play that seems more concerned with the anticipation of conflict, its aftermath and its consequences than with actual fighting, the force of arms, rather than of words, is the arbiter. For all his forward publicity as a warmaker, the power that Henry exerts in the play and on the stage is primarily verbal; indeed, he achieves his most impressive results when he plays as much upon imaginary forces as military ones: thus it is in the end the devastating vividness of his imaging of the horrors of rape and infanticide before the walls of Harfleur, rather than the repeated, failed assaults on the besieged town, that secures its capitulation.

Here, as throughout, Henry proves himself the histories' most consummate actor, and one who knows better than any that war is nothing if not theatre:

> imitate the action of the tiger.
> Stiffen the sinews, conjure up the blood,
> Disguise fair nature with hard-favoured rage.
> Then lend the eye a terrible aspect ...

> (3.1.6–9)

Armoured with the terminology of display, dissimulation and mimetic reproduction, the speech encapsulates the terrible energies of the play, representing soldiering as histrionic excess, as transformative Artaudian performance that makes men into beasts or machines. In a work that demands that we 'force – perforce – a play' (2.0.32), this and others of Henry's addresses work as much upon the spectator as on those on stage; one does not have to share the views of Wilson to feel stirred by convictions ('No king of England, if not king of France' [2.2.189]), sentiments ('We few, we happy few, we band of brothers' [4.3.60]) and exhortations to action ('Cry "God for Harry! England and Saint George!"' [3.1.34]) that, considered dispassionately, most peace-loving types would regard with deep suspicion, even abhorrence.

Pacifist and republican though he was, William Hazlitt recognised this two centuries ago: acknowledging the very considerable faults of the king, who, 'because he did not know how to govern his own kingdom, determined to make war on his neighbours' and whose heroism consisted of being 'ready to sacrifice his own life for the pleasure of destroying thousands of other lives', he nonetheless concluded that 'We like him in the play' as 'a very amiable monster, a very splendid pageant. As we like to gaze at a panther or a young lion in their cages' (Hazlitt 1957: 286). Though some of us today might take rather less pleasure in the contemplation of caged animals, the point retains its force. Whether we choose to see the play as a celebration of the myth of Henry or a subversion of it is a matter of politics and attitudes to warfare; what cannot be denied is the fiendish energy and eloquence of the means by which we are embroiled in the doings of those for whom, to quote the common soldier who dares to voice his opposition to the whole business, 'blood is their argument' (4.1.136).

Further reading

Barton, Anne (1975) 'The King Disguised: Shakespeare's *Henry V* and the Comical History', in *The Triple Bond: Plays, Mainly Shakespearean, in Performance*, ed. Joseph Price. University Park, PA: Pennsylvania State University Press, 92–117.

Erickson, Peter (1987) 'The Order of the Garter, the Cult of Elizabeth, and Class–Gender Tension in *The Merry Wives of Windsor*', in *Shakespeare Reproduced: The Text in Ideology and History*, ed. Jean E. Howard and Marion F. O'Connor. London: Methuen, 116–42.

Knowles, Ronald (2001) *Shakespeare's Arguments with History*. Basingstoke: Palgrave.

Marcus, Leah (1988) *Puzzling Shakespeare: Local Reading and Its Discontents*. Berkeley, CA: University of California Press.

Parker, Patricia (1987) *Literary Fat Ladies: Rhetoric, Gender, Property*. London: Methuen.

Rabkin, Norman (1977) 'Rabbits, Ducks, and *Henry V*', *Shakespeare Quarterly*, 28: 279–96.

Smith, Emma (ed.) (2004) *Shakespeare's Histories*. Oxford: Blackwell.

Julius Caesar

Date, text and authorship

c.1599; performed at the Globe 21 September 1599; F 1623. Solely Shakespearean.

Sources and influences

Plutarch, *Lives of the Noble Grecians and Romans* (trans. Thomas North, 1579); Samuel Daniel, *Musophilus* (1599); Sir John Davies, *Nosce Teipsum* (1599).

On stage

Death of a Dictator, Mercury Theatre, New York, 1937 (dir. Orson Welles); SMT, 1950 (dir. Anthony Quayle); RSC, 1972 (dir. Trevor Nunn); NT, 1977 (dir. John Schlesinger); RSC, 1983 (dir. Ron Daniels); RSC, 1993 (dir. David Thacker); RSC, 1995 (dir. Peter Hall); *Guilio Cesare*, Societas Raffaello Sanzio, Teatro Fabbricone, Prato, 1997 (dir. Romeo Castelluci); Shakespeare's Globe, 1999 (dir. Mark Rylance); RSC, 2001 (dir. Edward Hall); Barbican, 2005 (dir. Deborah Warner); RSC, 2009 (dir. Lucy Bailey); *Roman Tragedies*, Toneelgroep Amsterdam, 2008 (dir. Ivo van Hove).

On screen

USA, 1953 (dir. Joseph L. Mankiewicz; Brutus: Marlon Brando; Cassius: John Gielgud); *The Spread of the Eagle*, BBC TV, 1963 (dir. Peter Dews; Brutus: Paul Eddington); UK, 1969 (dir. Stuart Burge); BBC Television Shakespeare, UK, 1979 (dir. Herbert Wise; Caesar: Charles Gray; Brutus: Richard Pasco).

Offshoots

Shakespeare: The Animated Tales: Julius Caesar, UK/Russia, 1994 (dir. Yuri Kulakov).

Over one weekend in November 2009, London's Barbican Centre hosted a visit by the leading Dutch theatre company Toneelgroep Amsterdam, who brought with them their production *Roman Tragedies*, a deftly edited composite of *Coriolanus*, *Julius Caesar* and *Antony and Cleopatra* that, running to nearly six hours, was one of the largest-scale ventures yet to be mounted under the auspices of the BITE (Barbican International Theatre Events) festival programme. If Shakespeare spoken in Dutch (for the first time on the London professional stage since 1916) was for many in the audience one of the 'accents yet unknown' (3.1.114) that *Julius Caesar* itself anticipates as phrasing its theatrical afterlife, the political vocabulary that constituted this 'Roman' world was nonetheless very familiar indeed.

Occupying an indeterminate, anonymised zone somewhere between a television studio, the lobby of a corporate hotel and an airport departure lounge, this was the society of the media spectacle, a (non)place packed with computer screens, television monitors and cameras, in which radio-miked actors in sharp suits argued and fought and died according to the dictates of the twenty-four-hour news cycle, their words and deeds doubled and dispersed across screens and refracted through PA systems, and in constant competition with all sorts of other media noise: sports coverage (Olympic swimming, for example, as a sardonic accompaniment to Cassius's account of his dip with Caesar in the Tiber

[1.2.102–30]), weather reports, children's cartoons, footage of contemporary and not-so-contemporary politicians (Obama, Hussein, Blair, Nixon, Kennedy), children's cartoons, music videos. On the back wall hung a row of clocks, set in real time to Amsterdam, London, New York, San Francisco, Sydney: by the end of *Antony and Cleopatra* we had taken the equivalent of a flight between continents that nonetheless left us in exactly the place where we began. What was nowhere to be seen, other than in the odd clip of pop-cultural kitsch (a screen shot of the Coliseum, a snippet of gladiator movie), was anything reminiscent of the historic Republican or Imperial Rome; in the course of a production whose temporal range of reference extended only so far back as the 1960s (Bob Dylan's 'The Times They Are a-Changin'' framed the performance at the beginning and end), the Rome of Toneelgroep's Roman tragedies was only visible, if at all, as the most oblique and indistinct of reference points.

None of this was surprising. For all its undoubted impact as an event, and the ambition, wit and ingenuity of its staging, *Roman Tragedies* was only making very effective use of a contemporised and, increasingly, mediatised performance idiom that has become globally ubiquitous, in connection with Shakespeare's political dramaturgy in general. But the currency of the contemporary has been particularly germane to the *Julius Caesar* performance tradition for longer than most, a tendency which began with one of the landmark productions of the prewar mid-twentieth century. In 1937, Orson Welles directed a radically edited and rapidly paced production, which he entitled *Death of a Dictator*, at the Mercury Theatre in New York. Running for an unprecedented 157 performances on Broadway, the show targeted what Welles saw as the specific, urgent relevance of the text, by setting the action in what looked unmistakeably like fascist Italy and by presenting the play as a dire warning about the dangers posed by totalitarianism. For Welles and his audiences, the power and immediacy of the play lay in its diagnosis of tyranny; for Toneelgroep and its spectators, in its recognition that politicians are media-savvy performers. The two strands are, of course, interrelated.

As discussed elsewhere in this book, Rome for Shakespeare and his contemporaries was a source of fascination in a wide variety of ways: as the source of the imaginative and discursive literature, and the art and architecture, that constituted the core of artistic, educational, political and legal culture; as an agent of imperialism whose history was both exemplary and cautionary, and which offered to both Queen Elizabeth and King James a model of aspiration for their own world-encompassing ambitions; as the cradle of institutional Christianity; and as an imaginary space of decadence and cruelty beyond limits. Just as Shakespeare is for us at once both immediate and familiar, because we hope to make it so, and alien and distant, so the Romans for Shakespeare might be seen as both neighbours and strangers.

Whether or not it depicts the conventions of early modern performance, the sketch that Henry Peachum made on his copy of excerpts from *Titus Andronicus* at some point between 1590 and 1620 eloquently encapsulates this double perspective. Depicting a Romanesque Titus, a medieval Tamora, Aaron and Titus's sons as Roman-Elizabethan, and halberdiers in Jacobean livery (a line-up that does not correspond to any moment in the actual play), the drawing articulates past and present in terms of sameness and difference that are co-existent without being identical. The effect is one of dis-location: like the jet-lagged international traveller who finds herself physiologically out of phase with her new environment even as she is relentlessly solicited to re-adjust, to feel at home (everywhere, and thus nowhere), the modern and the early modern spectator may encounter Shakespeare's Roman world as a disorienting combination of the known and the unfamiliar, a place which harbours, within the threat of the incomprehensible, the possibility of the pleasures of imaginative escape.

Though we should probably exercise caution when applying the attributes of the Peachum sketch to *Julius Caesar* as text or performance, its longitudinal diachronisms (which locate Rome on the meridian, the present tense westwards, to the left, and the geographically and temporally alien to the east) indicate some of the play's imaginative latitude. Anachronism is, of course, a well-recognised attribute of Shakespearean drama and of early modern theatre in general: to the disgust of Sir Philip Sidney, the popular theatre was indiscriminate in its mixing not only of kings and clowns, and modes and genres, but of periods and timeframes. Performed, according to the evidence of Peachum, Henslowe and the works themselves, in contemporary dress occasionally augmented with period markers, Shakespeare's plays characteristically oscillate between their then and their now, between the imagined moment of representation and the material actuality of its realisation, producing, for example, a Danish clown within an enactment of a thirteenth-century Norse legend who asks his sidekick to pop round to a local Southwark alehouse to fetch him a pint, and a Cleopatra who calls for her waiting-women to cut the lace on her Jacobean-style bodice (1.3.71). *Julius Caesar*, a play written for a new building that, designed to appear monumental, classical and consciously Romanesque, was the first house that the Lord Chamberlain's Men could have regarded as truly their own, seems not only acutely self-conscious of its own positioning within a particular time and place (Bankside, 1599, as documented with some precision by Thomas Platter [see pp. 48–50]) but also, within its representational field of 'strange-disposèd time' (1.3.33), significantly attentive to the disruptive potentialities of anachronism.

Though Shakespeare was not bound by the strictures of accuracy and consistency that pertain to the realisms of the nineteenth century and after, meaning that the occasional time-slip is casual or unconscious rather than pointed and deliberate, the accumulation of anachronistic details in *Julius Caesar* seems to suggest that, far from being incidental, they are integral to the play's design. Within seconds of the opening, one of the holidaying artisans, a carpenter, has been interrogated about the whereabouts of the sign of his profession, the 'leather apron' (1.1.7) customarily displayed by practitioners of the Elizabethan trade; he is joined by an equally indigenous cobbler, a proud maker of shoes of 'neat's' (that is, English, rather than Spanish) leather; and when the tribune imagines these 'men of Rome' clambering 'up to walls and battlements,/ To towers and windows, yea to chimney-tops' (1.1.37–38) to catch a glimpse of Pompey, he evokes the topography not of ancient Rome but of the London beyond the playhouse. In the second scene, Caesar is reported as wearing a doublet and Cassius urges Brutus to 'pluck Casca by the sleeve' (1.2.180); the emperor is regally presented with 'one of these coronets' (1.2.237–38) rather than, as in Plutarch's account, a laurel headband, to which the mob respond by hurling aloft 'their sweaty nightcaps' (244).

Non-Roman headgear is also sported by the conspirators who turn up at Brutus's house (2.1.73) with 'their hats … plucked about their ears' (a solecism that so disgusted Alexander Pope that he bowdlerised the line in his edition of 1723–25 as 'Their – are pluckt … '). Caesar's Rome provides the conspirators with preachers' pulpits from which to perform and to proselytise in the immediate aftermath of the assassination; Caesar's Italy is the home of adders and 'knotty oaks' (1.3.6); and when Brutus, dressed in a nightgown with pockets, turns to his bedtime reading it is in the codex format, a book with 'the leaf turned down/ Where I left reading' (4.2.324–25). Most strangely of all, at a key moment (2.1.191) the play features the striking of a clock, more than a millennium before the invention of mechanised timekeeping. Marking the crucial point when the conspiracy shifts from speculation (and prevarication) to commitment to action, its chimes sound across the centuries between 44 BC and 1599, momentarily linking mythic and historical time to the rhythms of the diurnal. What Brutus hears, as the clock strikes three times, is the sound of futurity.

The time that is out of joint in *Julius Caesar* is calendrical as well as horological. The scene that is punctuated by the proleptic striking of an Elizabethan timepiece begins with Brutus (evidently at this stage lacking access to artificial chronometry, and already a man out of time) fretting that he 'cannot by the progress of the stars/ Give guess how near to day' (2.1.2–3), and then, according to the Folio, asking his servant Lucius whether tomorrow is 'the first of March'. Noticing the glaring discrepancy between this, Lucius's reply, nineteen lines later, that 'March is wasted fifteen days' (2.1.59), and the action that ensues on the Ides (that is, the fifteenth) of March, and refusing to believe that Brutus has somehow lost track of two weeks, most editions (including the Oxford and Norton) follow the emendation proposed by Lewis Theobald in his edition of 1733, by changing 'first' to 'Ides'.

Though this makes sense realistically, it tends to obscure an aspect of the play's treatment of time that, though largely invisible to later readers and spectators, may well have been considerably more pressing for Shakespeare's own audiences: the disparity between the Julian and Gregorian calendars that had resulted, by 1599, in Protestant England finding itself five whole weeks out of line with Catholic Europe (Burkhardt 1968). At a time when the precise dating of holy days (or holidays) was a matter not only of deeply divisive theological dispute but of lived daily experiences, Brutus's question is neither trivial nor incidental. Whether, as some have maintained, it offers the key to the play is more debatable. In the broader sense, the connection that it posits between late sixteenth-century arguments over the calendar and the temporal indeterminacies that surround a pivotal event in Roman history serves to enable its first spectators to engage in a kind of analogical thinking that treats anachronism both as a way of making the past accessible and familiar on the terms of the present and as a means of rendering the present strange on those of the past.

The play's capacity for imaginative projection beyond both the historical limits of its narrative and those of its own contexts and conditions of articulation is central to its work of political speculation. Part of the fascination exerted by Rome, and especially the assassination of Caesar, upon early modern Europeans was that it offered a compelling case of the rights and wrongs of resistance to tyranny, and of regicide: intensely debated throughout the period, Caesar's death could be regarded as both a legitimate response to dictatorship and an act of criminal insurrection (Shakespeare's play admits both perspectives). To an extent unthinkable even in the English history plays, *Julius Caesar* entertains, relatively dispassionately, possibilities of radical thought and deed, carefully weighting the cases for and against the conspirators' actions, acknowledging that they may be motivated by something more than self-interest or malignity, and admitting of doubt and division. At least, that is, until the scene of the assassination itself; for the minute that Brutus invites his blood-drenched fellow assassins to venture forth to the marketplace, waving 'our red weapons o'er our heads' and proclaiming 'peace, freedom, and liberty' (3.1.111), the play's own imaginative freedoms evaporate, the heavy-handed (or perhaps red-handed) irony being sufficiently weighty to sink the vessel of radical republicanism before it is barely afloat.

In this respect, it is noticeable that the bulk of the anachronistic touches that we have identified are planted in the part of the play leading up to Caesar's death; once the hands of history strike, time begins to move in one direction only. As the insomniac Brutus, having heard the knocking that announces the arrival of Cassius and his colleagues at his house, reflects,

> Between the acting of a dreadful thing
> And the first motion, all the interim is
> Like a phantasma or a hideous dream.
> The genius and the mortal instruments
> Are then in counsel, and the state of man,
> Like to a little kingdom, suffers then
> The nature of an insurrection.

(2.1.63–69)

The micro–macro–cosmic correspondence is an Elizabethan commonplace, the 'insurrection' encompassing Brutus's own mental turmoil, meteorological disorder and the chaos of civil war that is to follow, but it also limns a space of radical imaginative possibility in which the play's disordering of time and place maps the exhilarating, and terrifying, unknown territory between contemplation and execution. If the events that follow the funeral orations and the atavistic mob fury that is calculatedly unleashed by rhetorically pitch-perfect Mark Antony in their wake seem anti-climactic, it may be because the play has of necessity to close down the anarchic possibilities that its own speculations have invited for consideration.

Further reading

Burkhardt, Sigurd (1968) *Shakespeare's Meanings*. Princeton, NJ: Princeton University Press.
Drakakis, John (1992) '"Fashion it Thus": *Julius Caesar* and the Politics of Theatrical Representation', *Shakespeare Survey*, 44: 65–73.
Kahn, Coppélia (1997) *Roman Shakespeare: Warriors, Wounds, and Women*. London: Routledge.
Miola, Robert S. (1983) *Shakespeare's Rome*. Cambridge: Cambridge University Press.
Ripley, John (1980) *Julius Caesar on Stage in England and America, 1599–1973*. Cambridge: Cambridge University Press.
Wilson, Richard (1993) '"Is this a holiday?": Shakespeare's Roman Carnival', in *Will Power: Essays on Shakespearean Authority*. Hemel Hempstead: Harvester Wheatsheaf, 47–65.

Hamlet

Date, text and authorship

c.1600; Q1 1603; Q2 1604; F 1623. Solely Shakespearean.

Sources and influences

Saxo Grammaticus, *Historiae Danicae* (published 1514; trans. François de Belleforest as *Histoires Tragiques*, 1559–80); Thomas Kyd, *The Spanish Tragedy* (c.1589)

On stage

Moscow Art Theatre, 1911 (dir. Konstantin Stanislavsky); Sam H. Harris Theatre, New York, 1922 (dir. Arthur Hopkins; Hamlet: John Barrymore); Kingsway Theatre, 1925 (dir. H. J. Ayliff; Hamlet: Colin Keith-Johnston); Old Vic, 1930 (dir. John Gielgud; Hamlet: John Gielgud); Old Vic, 1937 (dir. Tyrone Guthrie; Hamlet: Laurence Olivier); Old Vic, 1938 (dir. Tyrone Guthrie; Hamlet: Alec Guinness); SMT, 1948 (dir. Michael Benthall; Hamlet: Paul Scofield/Robert Helpmann); Phoenix, London, 1955 (dir. Peter Brook; Hamlet: Paul Scofield); Lunt-Fontanne, New York, 1964 (dir. John Gielgud; Hamlet: Richard Burton); RSC, 1965 (dir. Peter Hall; Hamlet: David Warner); Taganka, Moscow, 1971 (dir. Yuri Lyubimov; Hamlet: Vladimir Vyostsky); RSC, 1975 (dir. Buzz Goodbody; Hamlet: Ben Kingsley); NT, 1975 (dir. Peter Hall; Hamlet: Albert Finney); Bochum, West Germany, 1977 (dir. Peter Zadek; Hamlet: Ulrich Wildgruber); Royal Court, 1980 (dir. Richard Eyre; Hamlet: Jonathan Pryce); National Theatre, Prague, 1982 (dir. Josef Svoboda); RSC, 1988 (dir. Ron Daniels; Hamlet: Mark Rylance); Stary Theatre, Kraków, 1989 (dir. Andrzej Wajda; Hamlet: Teresa Budzisz-Kryzyżanowksa); RSC, 1992 (dir. Adrian Noble; Hamlet: Kenneth Branagh); Schauspielhaus, Hanover, 2000 (dir. Peter Zadek; Hamlet: Angela Winkler); Shakespeare's Globe, 2000 (dir. Giles Block; Hamlet: Mark Rylance); NT, 2001 (dir. John Caird; Hamlet: Simon Russell Beale); Théâtre du Bouffes Nord, Paris, 2001 (dir. Peter Brook; Hamlet: Adrian Lester); The Wooster Group, New York, 2007 (dir. Elizabeth LeCompte); RSC, 2008 (dir. Gregory Doran; Hamlet: David Tennant); NT, 2010 (dir. Nicholas Hytner; Hamlet: Rory Kinnear).

On screen

UK, 1913 (dir. Hay Plumb; Hamlet: Johnston Forbes-Robertson); Germany, 1920 (dir. Svend Gade and Heinz Schall; Hamlet: Asta Nielsen); UK, 1948 (dir. Laurence Olivier; Hamlet: Laurence Olivier; Claudius: Basil Sydney; Gertrude: Eileen Herlie; Ophelia: Jean Simmons); USSR, 1964 (dir. Grigori Kozintsev; Hamlet: Innokenti Smoktunovsk); UK, 1969 (dir. Tony Richardson; Hamlet: Nicol Williamson; Claudius: Antony Hopkins; Gertrude: Judy Parfitt; Ophelia: Marianne Faithfull); BBC Television Shakespeare, UK, 1980 (dir. Rodney Bennett; Hamlet: Derek Jacobi; Claudius: Patrick Stewart; Gertrude: Claire Bloom; Ophelia: Lalla Ward); UK, 1990 (dir. Franco Zeffirelli; Hamlet: Mel Gibson; Claudius: Alan Bates; Gertrude: Glenn Close; Ophelia: Helena Bonham-Carter); UK, 1996 (dir. Kenneth Branagh; Hamlet: Kenneth Branagh; Claudius: Derek Jacobi; Gertrude: Julie Christie; Ophelia: Kate Winslet); USA, 2000 (dir. Michael Almereyda; Hamlet: Ethan Hawke; Claudius: Kyle McLachlan; Gertrude: Dianne Venora; Ophelia: Julia Stiles); BBC TV, UK, 2009 (dir. Gregory Doran; screen version of 2008 RSC production).

Offshoots

To Be or Not to Be, USA, 1942 (dir. Ernst Lubitsch); *Warui Yatsu Hodo Yoku Nemuru* (*The Bad Sleep Well*), Japan, 1960 (dir. Akira Kurosawa); Tom Stoppard, *Rosencrantz and Guildenstern Are Dead*, NT, 1966 (film version, UK 1990, dir. Tom Stoppard); Tom Stoppard, *Dogg's Hamlet*, 1979; *Hamlet liikemaailmassa* (*Hamlet Goes Business*), Finland, 1987 (dir. Aki Kaurismäki); *Shakespeare; The Animated Tales: Hamlet*, UK/Russia, 1992 (dir. Natalia Orlova); Peter Brook, *Qui est là*, Théâtre du Bouffes Nord, Paris, 1995; *In the Bleak Midwinter*, UK, 1996 (dir. Kenneth Branagh); Robert Lepage, *Elsinore*, Ex Machina, Québec, 1997; Charlotte Jones, *Humble Boy*, NT, 2001.

Who's there?

When, on 26 July 1602, the printer James Roberts entered 'A booke called the Revenge of Hamlett Prince Denmarke as yt was latelie Acted by the Lord Chamberleyne his servants' in the Stationers' Register, he could hardly have dreamed that he was inaugurating the documented cultural history of a play that would become one of western literature's most celebrated, quoted, avidly discussed and imitated texts. Nor, one suspects, would he have imagined that its titular hero would become a universally familiar theatrical icon, the reluctant keeper of the conscience of sensitive intellectuals during the eighteenth, nineteenth and twentieth centuries; a figure whose progress as a secular Everyman has seen him in the successive guises of romantic poet, ineffectual man of inaction and anti-establishment rebel, as each age, holding Shakespeare's mirror up to nature, has found in it, and in him, a uniquely sharp and eloquent image of current conflicts and anxieties.

No discussion of *Hamlet* can begin without recognising the sheer scale of cultural interest that has, historically, been vested in it; as witnessed by its consistently secure position within the theatrical and cinematic repertoire, and by the volumes of commentary that have been provoked by a text (or rather, a set of texts) whose enigmas and problems belie the straightforward designation of the genre piece ('the Revenge of Hamlett Prince Denmarke') blandly announced by Roberts's Register entry. As early as 1607, the future global dominion of the play, and its exemplary status (and Shakespeare's imperial mission as an agent of pacification and moral instruction), was indicated by a shipboard performance off the coast of Sierra Leone, of which the captain gratefully recorded that he 'had *Hamlet* acted abord me' since it discouraged his crew 'from idlenes and unlawful games, or sleepe' (Chambers 1930, 2: 335).

A century later, the Earl of Shaftesbury identified *Hamlet*'s particular capacity to get beneath the skin of its receptors, praising it as the Shakespearean work 'which appears to have most affected English hearts', and locating its appeal in its reiteration of 'one continued moral: a series of deep reflections, drawn from *one* mouth' (Vickers 1974: 2, 264). Shaftesbury pointed towards the direction of subsequent commentary and theatre practice, asserting that the play has 'only one character or principal part'; and while more hardheaded eighteenth-century writers regarded this singularity with a degree of coolness, his privileging of the figure which would itself become central to the development of theories of Shakespearean character was enthusiastically taken up by early nineteenth-century commentators keen to enlist the prince in the cause of Romanticism. Writing towards the end of the eighteenth century, Goethe eulogised Hamlet's 'beautiful, pure, noble, and most moral nature' (Furness 1877, 2: 273); a nature which was inevitably, and impotently, at odds with the brutal contingencies of life and history.

In 1827 Hamlet took a decisive step towards the identity that would become synonymous with the modern condition of Shakespearean tragic heroism, when Coleridge wrote of his 'great, enormous, intellectual activity, and a consequent proportionate aversion to real action' and, essaying a self-identification that would become a critical reflex, bashfully admitting that 'I have a smack of Hamlet myself, if I may say so' (Hawkes 1974: 154). In 1817 Hazlitt drove the point home, characterising Hamlet's utterances as 'as real as our own thoughts', and concluding that 'It is *we* who are Hamlet' (Hazlitt 1957: 232). During the Victorian period Hamlet was regarded with a mixture of veneration and suspicion as a poet and thinker temperamentally incapable of adopting the avenging role demanded by the play. In the twentieth century the hero's inexplicable inertia acquired a new rationale in the application of pyschoanalytic method to a textual construct already understood to be a complex human individual whose psychopathology was both recognised and shared, even universal. Following an aside in Freud's *The Interpretation of Dreams* (1900), Ernest Jones (1949) elaborated the case for Hamlet's Oedipus complex, explaining the delay in killing Claudius as a symptomatic paralysis, a consequence of his denial of his own hostile feelings towards his father, his unwitting identification with his usurping uncle, and his secret desire for his mother.

Jones's reading of one of the key texts in the Shakespearean canon was controversial, and it heralded the emergence of a collaboration between literary criticism and psychoanalysis that has proved to be as contested as the individual disciplines themselves; it was popu-larised by Olivier's 1948 film, which notoriously declared itself to be 'the tragedy of a man who could not make up his mind', the image of the self-divided, exquisitely sensitive hero has remained the Hamlet of both stage and screen tradition and popular mythology. Visualised as a melancholy, black-clad figure contemplating the mysteries of life and death in the shape of a graveyard skull, the received image of Hamlet is of a lonely but charis-matic figure, as instantly recognisable as an ambassador for theatrical high culture as he is a target for quotation, appropriation and parody.

If the special status of *Hamlet* as a work of genius and a landmark of world culture is unquestionable, it is nonetheless complicated by its proliferating, and apparently insoluble, mysteries and problems. T. S. Eliot may have gone further than most by branding the play 'an artistic failure', but he articulated a long-standing concern that there was a damaging disparity between the philosophical and psychological complexities of the play and the oddly thwarted demands of its narrative: 'nothing that Shakespeare can do with the plot can express Hamlet for him'. For Eliot, this ineffability connected with an equally funda-mental artistic and emotional disequilibrium, in that Hamlet's violent feelings towards his mother (which he took to be the real concern of the play) seem 'in *excess* of the facts as they appear' (Eliot 1951: 143–45). Eliot's description of *Hamlet* as a failure is calculated to provoke; nonetheless, the play which opens with a question of identity ('Who's there?') has continued to trouble its readers with unanswered challenges.

Hamlet's delay in executing his first-act promise to his father's ghost that he would 'with wings as swift/ As meditation or the thoughts of love/ May sweep to my revenge' (1.5.29–31) is only the most obvious of these. Is the Ghost what he claims to be, or, as Hamlet spec-ulates at one point, 'a devil' who plays upon 'my weakness and my melancholy' and 'Abuses me to damn me' (2.2.576–80)? How is it that the Ghost is visible to all on his appearances in the first act (1.1, 1.4, 1.5) but seen by Hamlet alone in the closet scene with Gertrude ('Alas, how is't with you,/ That you do bend your eye on vacancy/ And with th'incorporal air do hold discourse?' [3.4.107–9]). When Hamlet refers to death as 'The undiscovered country from whose bourn/ No traveller returns' (3.1.81–82), has he forgotten the evidence of the Ghost, who is, evidently, just such a traveller? Why does Claudius not respond to the dumbshow of *The Murder of Gonzago* (or *The Mousetrap*), when it depicts the murder of Old Hamlet just as graphically as the spoken text? How are we to reconcile the legendary sensitive intellectual, the 'sweet prince' invoked by Horatio in the hero's dying moments (5.2. 338), with the figure who boasts (3.2.360–62) that 'Now could I drink hot blood/ And do such bitter business as the day/ Would quake to look on'? Or with the man who dis-patches Rosencrantz and Guildenstern to their deaths with ruthlesss efficiency?

These local difficulties raise larger issues. The riddle of Hamlet's 'character' is a matter to which I will return below; the contexts in which this takes shape and operates are them-selves shifting, volatile and uncertain. The doubtful status of the Ghost indicates a theolo-gical schism between a residual sixteenth-century Catholicism and the varieties of

Protestantism that repudiated the notion of Purgatory which might have afforded the Ghost some credibility, but the play as a whole occasions more searching questions about the existence, or otherwise, of a theological framework for its cycle of death and retribution. The play offers some comforting traces of the official Christian script in Hamlet's 'There's a divinity that shapes our ends,/ Rough-hew them how we will' (5.2.10–11), in his 'There's a special providence in the fall of a sparrow' (5.2.157–58) and in Horatio's call for 'flights of angels' to 'sing thee to thy rest' (5.2.339). But Hamlet's own dying words (5.2.337) merely evoke a bleak void: 'the rest is silence' (and, in the Folio version, the final sundering of eloquence with an agonised 'O, o, o, o'). Nor does the conclusion of the play persuasively suggest that any kind of justice – divine, poetic or otherwise – has been done as a consequence of Hamlet's belated accomplishment of his father's injunction to revenge. Technically speaking, Old Hamlet's death has been answered by that of Claudius, but it has also led to the deaths of Polonius, Ophelia, Gertrude, Rosencrantz and Guildenstern, Laertes and Hamlet himself.

Politically, the consequences are even more disastrous. As an incentive for his pursuit of Claudius, the Ghost urges that Hamlet must 'Let not the royal bed of Denmark be/ A couch for luxury and damnèd incest' (1.5.82–83); but Hamlet's execution of his filial duty to punish this personal transgression leads to the state of Denmark being annexed by the warlord Fortinbras, who steps into the bloody shambles of the final scene to assume 'some rights of memory in this kingdom,/ Which now to claim my vantage doth invite me' (5.2.368–69). Whether he is guilty of the death of Old Hamlet or not, Claudius is a careful and diplomatic ruler who is largely successful in his efforts to disengage Denmark from the wasteful military skirmishing which had characterised his predecessor's reign. The conclusion of the play leaves us with an open question of whether the completion of the action of revenge justifies the price of the political consequences.

Hamlet's transformations

Underlying all of these questions is the even more radical indeterminate nature of the play's textual identity, an issue which has in recent decades returned to haunt scholars of the play with renewed vigour. There are three versions of the play dating from the early seventeenth century, each with its own distinctive characteristics and its own claim to authority. The first of these appeared in quarto format in 1603 (hereafter referred to as Q1), the year after Roberts's entry in the Stationers' Register. Entitled *The Tragicall Historie of Hamlet Prince of Denmarke*, this was attributed to 'William Shake-speare', and advertised as 'as it hath beene diverse times acted by his Highnesse servants in the Cittie of London: as also in the two Universities of Cambridge and Oxford, and else-where'.

The allusions to the play's peripatetic progress around the two university towns and its 'diverse times acted' in London may indicate that the publication aimed to exploit a popularity that was already established; it also suggests a version closely related to performance. Q1 is by far the briefest of the three versions (it is 2,154 lines, as compared to the 3,674 lines of the Second Quarto and 3,535 lines of the Folio); character names differ (Polonius here is Corambis, Laertes is Leartes, Gertrude is Gertred, Hamlet's partners Rossencraft and Gilderstone) and key speeches are presented in significantly altered form: 'To be or not to be … ' (3.1.58ff) becomes 'To be, or not to be, I there's the point … '; 'O what a rogue and peasant slave am I' (2.2.527ff) is offered as 'Why what a dunghill idiot slave am I?' Such difficulties as might arise in attempting to align these variants with the received version of the play have largely been contained by the tendency of editors and critics to question (or deny) the legitimacy of this text. Often identified as the 'Bad' quarto, Q1 has been stigmatised as an abbreviated, corrupt and unreliable pirated text, reconstructed from memory and published without the sanction of either the author or the playing company, and as such of a different order to the Second Quarto and Folio versions, which have been the foundation of all subsequent editions of the play.

A year later, James Roberts printed, for Nicholas Ling, the Second Quarto (Q2), entitled *The Tragicall Historie of Hamlet, Prince of Denmarke* and ascribed to 'William Shakespeare', which proclaimed that it was 'Newly imprinted and enlarged to almost as much againe as it was, according to the true and perfect Coppie'. Generations of editors have been content to accept this assertion (corroborated by such evidence as can be gleaned from the physical characteristics of the published text about the processes of transmission, compositorial intervention and printing) as confirmation that Q2 is based upon Shakespeare's manuscript; in short, that it is a legitimate, authorised version of the play. But not, it seems, the final version: in the form in which it appears in the 1623 Folio, *Hamlet* is altered again: shorter than Q2 by some one hundred and fifty lines, *The Tragedie of Hamlet Prince of Denmarke* (F) omits 222 lines found in Q2 (including most of 5.5) but adds 83 new ones. Most readers, critics and theatre practitioners have maintained their sanity in the face of this potentially disorienting indeterminacy by accepting eclectic editions pieced together from Q2 and F as representative of Shakespeare's *Hamlet*, even though the material history of its texts suggests that no such singular entity ever existed.

Moreover, the ambiguities surrounding the relationship between the texts of *Hamlet* and the version (or versions) of the play as Shakespeare is imagined to have conceived it open up larger critical questions about what 'legitimacy' and 'authority' actually mean in this context. At one extreme is the view of the play's New Cambridge editor that 'the nearer we get to the stage, the further we are getting from Shakespeare'; and that the processes of preparing the work as originally conceived by its author for the contingencies of performance is a business of 'what one can only call degeneration' (Edwards 1985: 32). The more recent turn towards Shakespeare's scripts as performance texts has fostered a different view: as Stanley Wells, editor of the Oxford Shakespeare edition, declared, the editorial priority became, 'when possible, to print the more theatrical version of each play', since 'the theatre of Shakespeare's time was his most valuable collaborator' (Wells and Taylor 1988: xxxv, xxix). Either position leaves the reader with the unfinished task of hypothesising the relationship between the texts of the play and its various identities as it underwent alteration, adjustment and revision, whether for performance or for publication (the Norton edition, to which the current volume refers, modifies the tactics of the Oxford edition upon which it is based by printing Q2-only passages in italic type).

The ultimate source of *Hamlet* lies in feudal legend, in the story of Amleth, a twelfth-century Danish prince whose pursuit of vengeance against his uncle, Feng (who has openly assassinated Amleth's father and married his mother, Gerutha) is narrated in Saxo Grammaticus's *Historiae Danicae*, published in Latin in 1514. Saxo's lively tale of brutality contains key features of Shakespeare's play: in order to deflect his uncle's suspicions, Amleth assumes a pose of madness; he casually slaughters an eavesdropper placed in his mother's chamber (but here cuts the body of the unfortunate interloper into pieces which he deposits in a sewer to be eaten by pigs); he travels to Britain with a pair of retainers whom he tricks into their own deaths in place of his own; and returns, as if from the dead, to Denmark, where he dispatches Feng in his own bed, burns down the palace and, to the acclaim of his countrymen, becomes king. Closer to hand for Shakespeare was François de

Belleforest's French translation of Saxo, which appeared in his *Histoires tragiques* in 1570. Although he retained the main elements of Saxo's narrative, Belleforest assuaged his own unease about the decidedly unChristian character of Amleth's revenge by proposing an adulterous affair between Geruthe and Fengon, and by moralising the killing of Fengon as the operation of Divine justice.

Revenge

Here was suitably lurid material for treatment within the conventions of revenge tragedy, which emerged at the turn of the seventeenth century as a stylistically inventive and ingeniously bloody popular genre. At its head was Thomas Kyd's *The Spanish Tragedy*, published in 1592, reprinted numerous times and a firm staple of the repertoire until well into the seventeenth century. A key source for subsequent plays for imitation, quotation and parody, *The Spanish Tragedy* can also be identified as a prototype for Shakespeare's play. Constructed around four interlocking revenge plots, Kyd's drama is initiated by the injunction of a ghost, depicts a father's efforts to avenge the murder of his son, includes an episode of madness which may be feigned or genuine and achieves an intricate, Pirandellian denouement in the violent implementation of a play-within-the-play. Shakespeare had previously made his own intervention in this mode in *Titus Andronicus*, early in the 1590s; *Hamlet* was contemporaneous with works such as John Marston's *Antonio's Revenge* (c.1600), George Chapman's *Bussy D'Ambois* (1604) and Thomas Middleton's *The Revenger's Tragedy* (1606); later examples include Cyril Tourneur's *The Atheist's Tragedy* (1611) and John Webster's *The Duchess of Malfi* (c.1613).

These plays concern the actions of a disaffected or malcontent member of court (invariably within a contemporary European setting), and characteristically deal with the private vengeance of individuals who have been denied access to official mechanisms of justice within a compromised, corrupt or actively oppressive state. They are heavily indebted to the Roman playwright Seneca, who supplied the rhetorical and oratorical verbal style, the stage ghosts and tyrant princes, and the preoccupation with extremity and violence; philosophically, they weld Seneca's stoicism to the pragmatic and secular scepticism of contemporary thinkers such as Machiavelli and Montaigne. The pursuit of the revengers' schemes usually entails the perpetration of intricate, and sadistically apt, acts of violence: *Antonio's Revenge* opens with the emblematic spectacle of the diabolically eloquent villain Piero entering 'unbraced, his arms bare, smeared in blood, a poniard in one hand, bloody, and a torch in the other', followed by his accomplice Strotzo 'with a cord' (1.1.1), and ends with a choreographed bloodbath in which masked dancers rip out Piero's tongue, serve him a dish of his son's mangled limbs and then stab him; prompting the Ghost of Antonio's father to sententiously announce that 'now my soul shall sleep in rest./ Sons that revenge their father's blood are best' (5.5.81–82). Revenge drama was characterised by a ghoulishness that frequently tilted over into black comedy. By the time of *The Revenger's Tragedy*, the form has achieved a level of parodic self-consciousness that is signalled by the antiheroic protagonist's name, Vindice ('vengeance') and by an openly derisory attitude to the moral orthodoxy to which the genre is nominally held to pay lip-service. Like Hamlet (perhaps deliberately so), Vindice makes an appearance holding a skull; in his hands, however, it becomes not an opportunity for reflection upon mortality but an instrument of torture, which he uses to trick the principal villain into a sadistically grotesque death.

Whether Roberts's initial entry in the Stationers' Register ('the Revenge of Hamlett') was only an approximation of the billing under which the Lord Chamberlain's Men initially offered the play or an indication of its original working title, it is an indication that the immediate audience appeal lay in its apparent conformity to generic expectations. Allusions to what is generally presumed to be a lost prototype *Hamlet* dating from the 1580s (Henslowe's accounts record that he made 8*s*. from a performance of the play at Newington Butts on 9 June 1594 [Foakes and Rickert 1961: 21]), possibly written by Kyd (and usually referred to as the Ur-*Hamlet*) strengthen the Senecan connection. In 1589, the prose satirist Thomas Nashe wrote that 'English Seneca read by candlelight yields many good sentences, as *Blood is a beggar* and so forth; and if you entreat him fair in a frosty morning he will afford you whole Hamlets, I should say handfuls, of tragical speeches' (McKerrow 1958, 3: 315); in 1596, Thomas Lodge's *Wit's Miserie* referred to a figure who 'looks as pale as the vizard of the ghost who cried so miserably at the Theatre like an oyster-wife, *Hamlet, revenge!*' (Bullough 1975, 7: 24).

In Thomas Dekker's *Satiromastix* (1601) the declaration by the blustering Captain Tucca that 'my name's Hamlet revenge' (4.1.121) suggests that the conjunction was already a catchphrase; as does a later reference in Dekker and Webster's *Westward Ho!* (1605): 'when light wives make heavy husbands, let these husbands play mad Hamlet, and cry revenge' (5.4.50–51). Nashe's reference invokes a Hamlet play which adheres far more closely to the Senecan formula than does Shakespeare's, and the Hamlet/handful wordplay hints that for him at least the title had become a byword for superfluous verbiage with classical pretensions. Lodge's and Dekker's allusions indicate that the titular hero had already entered theatrical mythology as a figure associated with decisive, and bloody, vengeful action.

Such may have been the expectations of first audiences; if this were the case, they would have found themselves confronted with a play which repeatedly evokes the conventions of the genre in which it is working only to frustrate and interrogate them. As in *The Spanish Tragedy* and *Antonio's Revenge*, the action of *Hamlet* is initiated by a ghost, who urges the living protagonist towards his duty of avenging a murder committed before the play's start. On his first appearance, Hamlet conforms to the disaffected type of the malcontent, pointedly clad in mourning black in the court at Elsinore, which, like the claustrophobic, rancid settings of Spain, France and Italy, is characterised as dangerous, perverted and corrupt:

> Something is rotten in the state of Denmark.
>
> (1.4.67)

> one may smile and smile and be a villain
> At least I'm sure it may be so in Denmark.
>
> (1.5.109–10)

> Denmark's a prison.
>
> (2.2.239)

Confronted with his father's ghost, and his account of Claudius's crime, Hamlet initially embraces the identity of the Senecan revenger, declaring a resolve that will lead to instant justice:

> with wings as swift
> As meditation or the thoughts of love
> May sweep to my revenge.
>
> (1.5.29–31)

And shall I couple hell? O fie! Hold, hold my heart,
And you, my sinews, grow not instant old,
But bear me stiffly up.

(1.5.93–95)

At this point, Hamlet displays the grim determination of the Hieronymo of *The Spanish Tragedy* confronted with the body of his murdered son:

Seest thou this handkercher besmeared with blood?
It shall not from me till I take revenge.
See'st thou those wounds that yet are bleeding fresh?
I'll not entomb them till I have revenged.
Then will I joy amidst my discontent,
'Till then my sorrow never shall be spent.

(2.5.51–56)

In *Hamlet*, there are no doubts at this stage about the status of the revenant: 'it is an honest ghost' Hamlet tells Horatio (1.5.142), as he urges his companions to swear to silence and pledges to 'put an antic disposition on' (1.5.173). So far, the combination of decisiveness and strategic guile is true to the spirit of the play's sources and to the protocols of revenge drama: by assuming the pose of madness, Hamlet is both practising a necessary subterfuge and biding his time, waiting for the most expedient (and theatrically apt) moment to strike. For the Jacobean spectator familiar with *The Spanish Tragedy* (or, perhaps, Hamlet's previous theatrical incarnations), it would have been reasonable to anticipate a gradual but inexorable gathering of momentum, with the plot unfolding according to a clear logic of action and retribution, the hero steadfast in his task, the villain unmasked, honour satisfied and a satisfyingly violent denouement. Instead, of course, the play offers something rather different.

Mad in craft

In what is to prove only the first of a sequence of diversions, prevarications and reversals of the expectations that would have aroused by the play's generic status, the scenes that follow Hamlet's ringing – but ambivalent – affirmation 'O cursèd spite/ That ever I was born to set it right!' (1.5.189–90) all but bury the revenge imperative. Hamlet's madness is introduced as promised, but it already appears to run away from his declared scheme: as reported by Ophelia, the 'antic disposition' takes the form of a painstaking enumeration of the stock gestures of a crazed stage lover:

He took me by the wrist and held me hard,
Then goes he to the length of all his arm,
And with his other hand thus o'er his brow
He falls to such perusal of my face
As a would draw it.

(2.1.88–92)

For Polonius, the signs of 'the very ecstasy of love' (2.1.103) sufficiently explain the prince's erratic behaviour and prompt him to confidently report to Claudius that he has found 'The very cause of Hamlet's lunacy' (2.2.49); and there is potential comedy in the complacent literalism of his misreading and a prescient tragic irony in the fact that Hamlet's pretended insanity is a factor in Ophelia's descent into the genuine variety. The spectator may already have cause to wonder whether the assumed madness has taken on a life beyond its ostensible strategic function; particularly for the modern reader alert to symptoms of depth and complexity in Hamlet's 'character', the form in which he chooses to display his madness signifies more than it immediately appears, and perhaps more than the protagonist himself intends to reveal.

Denied access to Ophelia as commanded by her father, Hamlet appears to her in a guise reminiscent of the spectre he has himself encountered ('As if he had been loosèd out of hell/ To speak of horrors' [2.1.84–85]), to ritually enact a silent parting that is both entreaty and punishment. Already, it seems, the progress of the revenge plot is being obstructed by the uncertain operations of emotional loyalties much more tangled than those of murdered father and avenging son. When (in Q2 and F) Hamlet himself encounters Polonius soon after, he inhabits a persona which is hardly consistent with the account of melancholy lover that has preceded his entrance: brandishing a book written by a 'satirical slave' (2.2.196), he himself adopts the arch, sardonic voice of the satirist, insulting his venerable interlocutor by quoting his reading matter, 'old men … have a plentiful lack of wit, together with most weak hams' (196–99), and deploying the language of topsy-turveydom: 'you yourself, sir, should be old as I am – if, like a crab, you could go backward' (201–02). Again, Hamlet's posture is subject to comic misreading, as Polonius interprets the vicious directness of his wit as fortuitous aptness, the 'happiness that often madness hits' (207); imagining ourselves as privileged by our complicity with the prince's deception, and believing that we have the measure of both, we are tempted to laugh at the old man's misplaced confidence in his diagnostic skills.

Our confidence might well be misjudged. Unlike *King Lear*'s Edgar, another Shakespearean aristocrat who simulates lunacy for reasons of self-preservation, Hamlet signally fails to observe the distinction between role and actor that is maintained, in Edgar's case, by the methodical consistency of his performance (itemised in his account of the 'proof and precedent/ Of Bedlam beggars … with roaring voices' [*Lear*, 2.3.13–14]) and by his reassuring asides that he is not what he seems: 'My tears begin to take his part so much,/ They'll mar my counterfeiting'; 'Poor Tom, thy horn is dry' (3.6.55–56, 69); 'I cannot daub it further' (4.2.53). Although Hamlet issues a coded warning (or threat) to Rosencrantz and Guildenstern that he is 'but mad north-north-west' (2.2.361), and later insists to Gertrude that 'I essentially am not in madness,/ But mad in craft' (3.4.171–72), the boundary between masquerade and inner man is not just difficult to locate; it is doubtful that it is there to be found at all.

Traditionally, this ambiguity has generated critical speculation about whether Hamlet's madness is feigned or genuine (which in turn prompted Oscar Wilde to wonder whether *Hamlet*'s commentators were really mad or only pretending to be so); the terms of this debate nonetheless suppose that Hamlet's behaviour and motivation pertain to a self characterised, however complexly, by both continuity and integrity. The search for the true self behind Hamlet's multiple roles is invited by the play itself: 'I have that within which passeth show' (1.2.85), Hamlet proclaims in his first scene, and, later, 'I could be bounded in a nutshell and count myself a king of infinite space' (2.2.248–49); and subsequent readers and performers have been happy to take him at his word. In more recent criticism, however, the legitimacy of this approach to *Hamlet* has been seriously challenged, particularly within the new historicist and cultural materialist readings operating under the aegis of post-structuralism.

One difficulty – enthusiastically exploited, in different ways, in post-structuralist criticism and the stage-centred readings which preceded it – is that both the playtext and the circumstances of the medium for which it was originally designed tend to undermine the opposition between being and seeming ('Seems, madam? Nay, it *is*. I know not "seems"' [1.2.76]) upon which Hamlet's (and his critics') avowals of integrity depend. Categorising the conventions of gesture, costume and expression that constitute 'all forms, moods, shows of grief', Hamlet proudly dispatches them as 'actions that a man might play', as 'but the trappings and the suits of woe' (1.2.84, 86); but the status of this discrimination is, in the context of performance, more questionable, since it is offered by a speaker who is himself 'playing', engaged in 'seeming', presenting the shadow of woe rather than the substance. Assuming the mantle of madness is but the addition of a further tier of role-playing to the already multi-layered and many-voiced construct that goes under the name of the Prince of Denmark.

Such a figure seems an unlikely candidate for the heroic (or anti-heroic) role of revenger, and as Polonius exits to contrive a meeting between Hamlet and Ophelia, it appears that Hamlet has slipped back into the suicidal inertia that the ghost's provocation had temporarily displaced:

> My lord, I will take leave of you.
> HAMLET You cannot, sir, take from me anything that I will more willingly part withal –
> except my life, my life, my life.
>
> (2.2.210–13)

This is the tenor of the subsequent encounter with Rosencrantz and Guildenstern: declaring that he has 'lost all my mirth', Hamlet invokes the earth as a 'sterile promontory' and, alluding also to the *mise-en-scène* of the Globe playhouse itself, describes 'this most excellent canopy, the air ... this majestical roof fretted with golden fire' as 'a foul and pestilent congregation of vapours' (2.2.288–93). The revenge narrative has stalled or even gone into reverse, and it takes what looks like an even more drastic detour with Rosencrantz's announcement of the arrival of a company of players, 'the tragedians of the city' (315–16), at Elsinore. Not only does Hamlet himself suddenly spring to life, but the play itself unexpectedly shifts its temporal and geographical ground. Prompted by Hamlet's enquiry as to why the players are on the road, Rosencrantz raises the spectre of the 'late innovation' of the 'eyrie of children, little eyases' (320–26); that is, the company of boy actors who occupied the Blackfriars playhouse from 1600 to 1608 and who fashionably gave vent to Ben Jonson's diatribes against the public stage (see 'Life and contexts', pp. 52–4). As Hamlet picks up this cue to indulge in topical theatrical chat, the fabric of Elsinore, already a hybrid of Renaissance court and feudal epic, parts to reveal the London of the here and now, and the play briefly inhabits the *pièce-à-clef* world of Jonson's *Poetaster* and Dekker's *Satiromastix*.

For the remainder of the second act, and for much of the third, the progress of the revenge plot hinges upon the staging of *The Murder of Gonzago*, while Hamlet's attention is upon ethical questions of action and acting, as the relationship between being and seeming informs his reflections upon the disparity between the authentic and achieved performance of the First Player's recital of the death of Hecuba and his own failure to act: 'What would he do/ Had he the motive and the cue for passion/ That I have?' (2.2.337–39). Berating himself for his inactivity, Hamlet self-consciously tries on the mantle of the stage revenger:

> ... ere this
> I should 'a' fatted all the region kites

With this slave's offal. Bloody, bawdy villain!
Remorseless, treacherous, lecherous, kindless villain!
O, vengeance!—

(2.2.355–59)

As if embarrassed or unconvinced by his own bombast, Hamlet breaks off: 'Why, what an ass am I?' This fustian ranting is no way for a theatre-loving intellectual to behave; and so, prompted by new doubts about the Ghost's own reliability ('The spirit that I have seen/ May be the devil ... ' [575–76]), he concocts an appropriately theatrical means of securing the conviction of Claudius: 'The play's the thing/ Wherein I'll catch the conscience of the King' (581–82).

Once again, the plot twist is generic. The device of employing an inset performance to bring about the exposure and demise of the villain had been established by Kyd in *The Spanish Tragedy*, and was repeated in *The Revenger's Tragedy*; in a related vein, Shakespeare had already explored the comic possibilities of the play-within-a-play in *A Midsummer Night's Dream* and *Love's Labour's Lost*. What is different (and, for its original audiences, perhaps unexpected) about its use in *Hamlet* is the position of the play within the narrative: in all of the examples cited, the inset drama occupies a climactic position which, in the case of the revenge tragedies, leads to a bloodily decisive outcome.

In Kyd's and Middleton's texts, the staging of the court performance is exploited by the protagonist as a means of wreaking havoc, with simulated bloodshed turning real. Hieronimo casts his son's murderers in the play of *Solimon and Persida* (whose narrative replicates key elements of *The Spanish Tragedy* itself) and then, apparently in jest, slaughters them in full view of the court; in *The Revenger's Tragedy* the group presenting the 'masque of revengers' turn their swords first on the banqueting spectators and then on themselves. If early seventeenth-century audiences of *Hamlet* were expecting the eponymous hero to have a similar trick up his sleeve they would have been disappointed; the play is cut short, Claudius quits the stage and Hamlet is free to conclude that the Ghost's testimony is reliable: 'I'll take the Ghost's word for a thousand pound' (3.2.263–64). The last remaining obstacle in the way of Hamlet's pursuit of his filial duty has been removed; yet again, however, the anticipated denouement is deferred.

The readiness is all

The next scene (3.3) brings Hamlet and Claudius alone together for the first and last time, as the nephew discovers the uncle, having now admitted his guilt to the audience, at prayer; here, Hamlet recognises, is the opportunity to match the motive and means for Claudius's killing: 'Now might I do it pat, now a is praying,/ And now I'll do't' (3.3.73–74). In a move which has disquieted many of Hamlet's staunchest admirers, he pauses for thought, realises that to kill Claudius at prayer will ensure that 'a goes to heaven', a fate which would be 'hire and salary, not revenge' (74, 79), and stays his hand, deciding to carry out his sentence at a more diabolically appropriate moment:

When he is drunk asleep, or in his rage,
Or in th'incestuous pleasure of his bed,
At gaming, swearing, or about some act
That has no relish of salvation in't ...

(3.3.89–92)

Although many have felt that Hamlet has exceeded his brief as a righter of wrongs by attempting to determine the fate of Claudius's soul as well as his body, he is merely displaying his generic inheritance; as the New Cambridge editor notes, such vicious ingenuity is 'familiar to students of Elizabethan revenge fiction' (Edwards 1985: 52). In the event, it is a misjudgement. In the closet scene which follows, Hamlet's next decisive action, performed under the catastrophically mistaken apprehension that he has finally cornered Claudius, is the quasi-farcical stabbing of Polonius:

> POLONIUS [*behind the arras*] What ho! Help, help, help!
> HAMLET How now, a rat? Dead for a ducat, dead.
> [*He thrusts his sword through the arras.*] *Kills* POLONIUS
>
> (3.4.21–22)

If Hamlet's first killing is a blunder, it activates a new cycle of action and retribution that leads to the death of Ophelia, the return of a rather more straightforward revenge hero in the shape of Laertes (who needs no ghost from the grave to instruct him in his duty) and his own messy demise; at the end, the death of Claudius is accomplished almost as an incidental after-effect of the king's own intrigues.

As if making a concerted attempt to set the play back on its original track, the Ghost makes a reappearance, this time, according to the Q1 stage direction, in the altogether less majestical (and potentially bathetic) habit of '*his nightgown*'. This time, however, he is seen and heard by Hamlet alone. In the first act, the visual presence of the Ghost, if not the authority of his testimony, is corroborated by the witness of the sentinels and Horatio; here Gertrude responds to Hamlet's entreaties by asserting that

> This is the very coinage of your brain.
> This bodiless creation ecstasy
> Is very cunning in.
>
> (3.4.128–30)

Various explanations have been advanced for the Ghost's invisibility to Gertrude, often drawing upon Jacobean views about the capacity of spirits to exercise selectivity over whom they choose to reveal themselves to, but most have agreed with Hamlet's indignant response that 'It is not madness/ That I have uttered' (132–33) and rejected Gertrude's supposition that his vision is an hallucination born of madness ('ecstasy').

But we may also entertain the possibility that Gertrude is, actually, right; that the Ghost's appearance is a delusion visible only to her son and, possibly, the audience. The inconsistency with the first act can now be seen as part of the shifting representational tactics, as well as the generic mobility, of the play. If *Hamlet* is a play in which a composite of twelfth- and sixteenth-century Denmark can intermittently morph into seventeenth-century London, and in which the lineaments of theatre architecture are insistently visible behind the arras, it is one in which a ghost which seems real enough on its first appearance has been reduced to a strangely mute theatrical device at its last. The Ghost urges Hamlet to speak to Gertrude, and then falls silent; despite the prince's earlier solemn vow never to forget 'while memory holds a seat in this distracted globe', he is mentioned again only once, when Hamlet refers to Claudius as 'He that hath killed my king and whored my mother' (5.2.65).

From the moment of the arbitrary slaughter of Polonius onwards, Hamlet's agency as an instrument of retribution for his father's death is effectively subordinated to the task of survival; indeed, he barely reflects upon the responsibility reluctantly assumed as a result of the Ghost's initial injunction (the one extended instance of such reflection, the 'How all occasions do inform against me' soliloquy [4.4.9.22], in which the word 'revenge' is heard for the last time from Hamlet's mouth, is present in Q2 but omitted from the Folio). Exiled to England and, in the Folio version, absent from the stage for most of the fourth act, Hamlet is apprehended by report rather than seen in action, while the play proceeds to unfold the consequences of his action in Gertrude's closet. His return in the final act sees the initial revenge scheme subordinated to the secondary revenge plot which duplicates and displaces it, as the avenger's imperative embodied in Laertes allies with the expedient state-craft practised by Claudius to effect Hamlet's removal. Following his death, there is one final attempt to retrospectively re-order the events of the play as generically coherent tragic narrative:

> So shall you hear
> Of carnal, bloody, and unnatural acts,
> Of accidental judgements, casual slaughters,
> Of deaths put on by cunning and forced cause;
> And, in this upshot, purposes mistook
> Fall'n on th'inventors heads.

(5.2.324–29)

The reprise is strangely formulaic, an attempt to force the play back into the generic mould which it has persistently interrogated and resisted; as is the triumphant warlord Fortinbras's epitaph for the Hamlet who is to be borne, incongruously, 'like a soldier to the stage', a passage which is marked by 'The soldier's music and the rites of war' (340–43). But it is Fortinbras, nonetheless, who has the last word, and who cues the concluding effect. Opening with a question that is also a challenge, the play ends with a funerary tribute which silences opposition and enquiry: the sound of gunfire.

Further reading

Bradley, A. C. (2007[1904]) *Shakespearean Tragedy*. Fourth edition. Basingstoke: Palgrave.
Charnes, Linda (2006) *Hamlet's Heirs: Shakespeare and the Politics of a New Millennium*. London and New York: Routledge.
de Grazia, Margreta (2007) *'Hamlet' without Hamlet*. Cambridge: Cambridge University Press.
Foakes, R. A. (1993) *Hamlet versus Lear: Cultural Politics and Shakespeare's Art*. Cambridge: Cambridge University Press.
Greenblatt, Stephen J. (2001) *Hamlet in Purgatory*. Princeton, NJ: Princeton University Press.
Hawkes, Terence (1986) 'Telmah', in *That Shakespeherean Rag*. London: Methuen, 92–119.
Jones, Ernest (1949) *Hamlet and Oedipus*. London: Gollancz.
Neill, Michael (1997) *Issues of Death: Mortality and Identity in English Renaissance Tragedy*. Oxford: Clarendon Press.
Rosenberg, Marvin (1992) *The Masks of 'Hamlet'*. Newark, DE: University of Delaware Press.
Worthen, W. B. (2010) 'Performing Writing: *Hamlet*', in *Drama: Between Poetry and Performance*. Oxford: Wiley-Blackwell, 94–138.

Troilus and Cressida, All's Well that Ends Well *and* Measure for Measure

Troilus and Cressida

Entered SR 7 February 1603; Q1, Q2 1609; F 1623. Solely Shakespearean.

Sources and influences

Geoffrey Chaucer, *Troilus and Criseyde* (c.1385); William Caxton, *Recuyell of the Histories of Troy* (1475); John Lydgate, *Troy Book* (1412–20); Robert Greene, *Euphes his Censure to Philatus* (1587); George Chapman, *Seven Books of the Iliad of Homer* (1598); Thomas Elyot, *The Book of the Governor* (1531).

On stage

Old Vic, 1956 (dir. Tyrone Guthrie); RSC, 1960, 1962, 1968, 1976 (dir. John Barton); RSC, 1985 (dir. Howard Davies; Cressida: Juliet Stevenson); RSC, 1990 (dir. Sam Mendes); Tara Arts, Manchester, 1993 (dir. Jatinder Verma); NT, 1998 (dir. Trevor Nunn); Shakespeare's Globe, 2009 (dir. Matthew Dunster).

On screen

BBC Television Shakespeare, UK, 1981 (dir. Jonathan Miller; Troilus: Anton Lesser; Cressida: Suzanne Burden; Pandarus: Charles Gray; Thersites: 'The Incredible Orlando' [Jack Birkitt]).

All's Well that Ends Well

Date, text and authorship

c.1605; F 1623. Solely Shakespearean.

Sources and influences

Giovanni Boccaccio, *Decameron* (trans. William Painter as *Palace of Pleasure* [1566–67]).

On stage

Shakespeare Festival Theatre, Stratford, Ontario, 1953 (dir. Tyrone Guthrie; Helena: Irene Worth; King: Alec Guinness); SMT, 1959 (dir. Tyrone Guthrie; Countess: Edith Evans); RSC, 1981 (dir. Trevor Nunn; Helena: Harriet Walter; Countess: Peggy Ashcroft); RSC, 1992 (dir. Peter Hall); RSC, 2004 (dir. Gregory Doran; Countess: Judi Dench), NT, 2009 (dir. Marianne Elliott).

On screen

BBC Television Shakespeare, UK, 1981 (dir. Elijah Moshinsky; Helena: Angela Down; Bertram: Ian Charleson; Parolles: Peter Jeffrey; Countess: Celia Johnson; King: Donald Sinden).

Measure for Measure

Date, text and authorship

c.1604; performed at court 26 December 1604; F 1623. Shakespeare's text adapted by Thomas Middleton in early 1620s.

Sources and influences

Cinthio, *Hecatommithi* (1565); *Epitia* (1573); George Whetstone, *Promos and Cassandra* (1578).

On stage

Old Vic, 1933 (dir. Tyrone Guthrie; Angelo: Charles Laughton); SMT, 1950 (dir. Peter Brook; Angelo: John Gielgud; Isabella: Barbara Jefford); RSC, 1970 (dir. John Barton; Duke: Ian Richardson; Isabella: Estelle Kohler); RSC, 1978 (dir. Barry Kyle; Duke: Michael Pennington); NT, 1981 (dir. Michael Rudman; Duke: Norman Beaton; Isabella: Yvette Harris); RSC, 1983 (dir. Adrian Noble; Isabella: Juliet Stevenson); RSC, 1987 (dir. Nicholas Hytner; Duke: Roger Allam; Isabella: Josette Simon); RSC, 1994 (dir. Stephen Pimlott; Duke: Alex Jennings); Cheek by Jowl, 1994 (dir. Declan Donnellan); Complicite/NT, UK, 2004, 2006 (dir. Simon McBurney; Duke: David Troughton [2004], Simon McBurney [2006]; Isabella: Naomi Frederick); Shakespeare's Globe, 2004 (dir. John Dove; Duke: Mark Rylance).

On screen

BBC Television Shakespeare, UK, 1979 (dir. Desmond Davis; Duke: Kenneth Colley; Isabella: Kate Nelligan; Angelo: Tim Piggot-Smith); BBC TV, UK, 1994 (dir. David Thacker; Duke: Tom Wilkinson; Isabella: Juliet Aubrey; Angelo: Corin Redgrave); BBC TV, UK, 2004 (dir. Janet Fraser Cooke; live broadcast of Shakespeare's Globe production on 4 September).

Offshoots

Bertolt Brecht, *Die Rundeköpfe und die Spitzköpfe* (*Roundheads and Pointed Heads*), Copenhagen, 1936; Charles Marowitz, *Measure for Measure*, Open Space, London, 1975.

Bifold authority

Among the many insistent, but apparently unanswerable, questions posed in *Hamlet* is that of whether one should trust the evidence of one's own eyes, a concern that is perhaps most intricately rehearsed in the multiple acts of looking and watching involved in the staging of the court performance of *The Murder of Gonzago*, wherein the audience is invited to consider themselves watching Hamlet studying a Claudius who scrutinises player kings and queens performing a drama which is very close to a set of events which we have heard about but not seen. In the second scene of Act 5 of *Troilus and Cressida*, a play written around the same time as *Hamlet* (1601–02), a comparably complex and ambiguous scenario of surveillance, spectatorship and interpretation is created. The action of the play, taken from Homer's *Iliad*, takes place seven years into the Greek siege of Troy: Cressida, daughter to the Trojan defector Calchas, has just been sent to join her father in the Greek camp as part of a hostage exchange in return for the release of the Trojan commander Antenor; Troilus, son of Priam, the king of Troy, and her lover of only one day, has followed. Standing concealed alongside the Greek war hero Ulysses, Troilus looks on with dismay and disbelief as Cressida is seduced by the man who will subsequently become his battlefield opponent, Diomedes, her every word and move the subject of close scrutiny and appalled commentary.

At the end of the episode, with Cressida having given the appearance of having pledged herself to Diomedes and betrayed Troilus, she exits, though not before she has uttered a final speech that is both valedictory and self-convicting; bidding farewell to the lover that she is unaware of watching her, she declares:

> One eye yet looks on thee,
> But with my heart the other eye doth see.
> Ah, poor our sex! This fault in us I find:
> The error of our eye directs our mind.
> What error leads must err. O then conclude:
> Minds swayed by eyes are full of turpitude.

(5.2.107–12)

What is Cressida confessing to or accusing herself of here? Depending upon whether they are played as, at one extreme, a frank admission of sexual collusion or, at the other, as the desperate pleading of a terrorised victim (a number of modern productions have staged the scene of Cressida's arrival in the Greek camp, the result of a brutal piece of bartering, as one of macho bullying and intimidation, and Diomedes's seduction as near-rape), the lines can provide a crucial index of how a production, or a performer, wishes an audience to interpret and judge her character.

In themselves, the lines do not make the task of decoding Cressida's behaviour in this scene any more straightforward. Cressida speaks of herself as split, her gaze divided between Troilus and someone or something else, her rational higher faculties subverted by the baseness of her vision. In the circumstances of its original performance, there is a further cleavage at work, between the player and the woman's part; spoken by a boy player, the commentary is distanced, a man's perspective on female weakness and inconstancy rather than a personal confession, and the mechanical quality of the parting couplet reflects the pat nature of the conclusion. But it is more than enough for Troilus: left behind on stage with Ulysses, he finds himself undergoing an epistemological and ontological crisis enmeshed in a kind of madness; unable to reconcile the evidence of what he has just witnessed with his own idealised view of the object of his desires, he imagines her as impossibly doubled and dispersed, simultaneously present and absent, and what he has seen as having both happened and not happened:

> Was Cressid here?
> ULYSSES   I cannot conjure, Trojan.
> TROILUS She was not, sure.
> ULYSSES   Most sure, she was.
> TROILUS Why, my negation hath no taste of madness.

(5.2.124–27)

For Troilus, the agony of betrayal is an affront to reason that feels like nothing less than a division and dissolution of meaning, order and authority themselves: 'The bonds of heaven are slipped, dissolved, and loosed' (156) and 'If there be rule in unity … This is not she' (141–42):

> Bifold authority, where reason can revolt
> Without perdition, and loss assume all reason
> Without revolt! This is and is not Cressid.

(5.2.144–46)

This is, to say the least, a difficult passage, some of the difficulty hinging on the ambiguity of the Shakespearean coinage 'bifold', and some on the neatly antithetical, yet also bafflingly tautological, shape of the argument. 'This is and is not Cressid' is, on the face it, much clearer: yet in another sense the paradox that Troilus confronts is as much that of the spectator in the audience as that of the spectator onstage, for whom Cressida seems, simultaneously (and in a variety of senses of the terms) knowable and impenetrable.

By having Ulysses as his companion, Troilus has at least chosen the right man to talk to about authority, order and revolt, for these are topics apparently very close to his inter-locutor's heart. In the first scene set in the Greek camp, the commander-in-chief, Aga-memnon, holds a council of war in which he debates with his generals the reasons for the current military stalemate, and Ulysses, in a set-piece oration which has been appropriated by conservative-minded readers as an expression of Shakespeare's own political viewpoint, takes the floor to deliver, at sixty-three lines, one of the lengthiest speeches in the canon, whose argument is that the Greek army's failure of nerve stems from its lack of respect for the order, degree and hierarchy that are held to operate at every level of creation, from the cosmic to the familial:

> The heavens themselves, the planets, and this centre
> Observe degree, priority, and place,
> Infixture, course, proportion, season, form,
> Office and custom, in all line of order.

(1.3.85–88)

Once order is disrupted or disregarded, Ulysses urges, chaos ensues ('Strength should be lord of imbecility/ And the rude son should strike his father dead' [114–15]); bereft of loyalties and obligations and driven only by self-interest, man surrenders himself to 'appetite' the 'universal wolf' (121) that is possessed of a will-to-power so destructive and all-consuming that in the end it 'Must make perforce a universal prey,/ And last eat up himself' (123–24).

The fact that Ulysses's diagnosis of the Greek malaise is endorsed rather than disputed by his listeners does not necessarily mean that the audience is expected to agree with the ideology it articulates, of course; and within the dramaturgy of the scene and the play it is evident enough that Ulysses has sound Machiavellian reasons for framing the situation in this way: as his next speech clearly reveals, the moral panic instigated by his account of social breakdown is a part of his ongoing feud with his rival commander Achilles, whom he sarcastically recounts as skulking in his quarters with his male lover Patroclus, breaking 'scurrile jests' and, 'like a strutting player', performing satirical impersonations of his superiors (148–58). But it is an indication of the distinctive, peculiarly intellectual and satirical character of a play in which a betrayed lover's anguish is treated as a philosophical conundrum concerning the nature of knowledge that the core of the scene is a lengthy, rhetorically complex, frequently abstract and, for many recipients of the play, frankly tedious debate.

The two narratives that comprise the major strands of the plot, that of the military conflict between the Greeks and Trojans and that of the lovers, seem to compete for priority rather than complement each other, and both end in irresolution: the final battle towards which the action has been building is a messy montage of alarums and excursions, in which the Trojan warrior-hero Hector, surrendering the advantage by revealing himself to be unarmed, is crudely slaughtered by Achilles's henchmen, and in which the expected stand-off between the rival lovers ends inconclusively and anti-climactically with Troilus chasing Diomedes off stage. Bizarrely, when Troilus confronts his

Greek antagonist he makes no mention of Cressida but taunts him to 'pay the life thou ow'st me for my horse' (5.6.7); nor does he refer to her when he returns to deliver his final speech, when all the weight of the scene lies upon the death of Hector. It is a death that seems to achieve nothing: the war continues, as pointlessly as ever, while the play's estranged protagonists are denied the dignity of being united in death afforded to Romeo and Juliet, Pyramus and Thisbe, and Antony and Cleopatra. At the end of a play which seems, as the Norton editors put it, to have an urge 'to provide philosophical rationales for even the most trivial of actions' (Greenblatt *et al.* 1997: 1828), we are left wondering whether its ramshackle plot is, indeed, barely more than a pretext for such intellectual speculation.

The characteristic of the play that we have already seen to be richly demonstrated in the scene in which Troilus witnesses Cressida's alleged infidelity, the multiplication of sightlines and perspectives that is accompanied by a unsettling interrogation of their trustworthiness, is also manifested in the presence in that scene of another watcher, who offers another point of view which is radically incommensurate with that of both Troilus and Ulysses: Thersites, Ajax's Fool, scabrously ironic commentator and professional cynic. A figure who has been played as a manservant, draftee, camp follower and war correspondent, who is frequently made up to appear diseased or disfigured, and who tends to enjoy a stand-up or vaudeville relation to his audiences, Thersites's first words consist of a grotesque fantasy about the Greek army's commander-in-chief: 'Agamemnon – how if he had boils, full, all over, generally? … And those boils did run? Say so, did not the General run then? Were not that a botchy core?' (2.1.2–6); his perspective on the action is one of relentless, levelling misanthropy, effectively encapsulated in his declaration that the entire campaign is nothing but 'Lechery, lechery … wars and lechery' (5.2.193).

Contemptuously contemplating Troilus's convoluted agonising over Cressida in 5.2, Thersites punctuates the scene with a string of obscene comments, acting as an intermediary between the observed, their observers and the observing audience, and rounding off his own rancid imaginings with the announcement, as she exits, that 'A proof of strength she could not publish more/ Unless she said, "My mind is now turned whore"' (5.2.113–14). It is tempting to see Thersites's scepticism about the war, and his decidedly unheroic view of its participants, as the voice of the play; certainly his charge that it is a 'war for a placket' (2.3.17), that is, Helen of Troy's vagina, is not one that is seriously countered. The play is, clearly, a response to the satirical drama, performed by the boys' companies, that was in vogue at the turn of the seventeenth century; as a drama which consistently cuts the heroes of classical antiquity down to size by reducing them to squabbling rival platoons of thugs, prigs and bores, it has something of the spirit of works by Chapman, Marston and others, whose comic and satiric appeal derived in part from the incongruity between the legendary dramatis personae and the diminutive figures presenting them. But in other respects, and especially in the scene of Cressida's defection, Thersites's position is no more privileged than any other: he may be right both about the squalid and absurd motives that have led to the conflict and about the vanity and stupidity of Ajax, Achilles and the rest, but the insistence with which he determines to prostitute the reputation of Cressida may repel as much as it convinces.

'This is and is not Cressid': the bewilderment that afflicts Troilus in his attempts to classify and comprehend what he sees before him mirrors that of many readers of a play which, right from the start of its life, has seemed to be possessed of a divided or multiple identity, making it elude definition. Its provenance and circumstances of publication are mysterious: the play was entered in the Stationers' Register early in 1603, where it was reported as having been performed by the Lord Chamberlain's Men, but not printed until 1609, when a further Stationers' Register entry noted 'The Historie of Troylus and Cresseida' but made no reference to performance. Two quartos of the play appeared in 1609, one bearing the title *The Historie of Troylus and Cresseida. As it was acted by the Kings Maiesties servants at the Globe*, the other *The Famous Historie of Troylus and Cresseid*, which also includes an introductory epistle conveying 'Newes' from 'A never writer, to an ever reader' which explicitly states that this 'new' play is 'never stal'd with the Stage, never clapper-clawed with the palmes of the vulger'.

The disparities defy explanation, though it has been suggested that the unforgivingly cerebral and cynical tone of the work points towards private, coterie performance (perhaps at one of the Inns of Court); possibly the play was a failure on the public stage, or never even offered on it. The narrative is complicated yet further with the first Folio: although it was planned for inclusion at the end of the tragedies section, after *Romeo and Juliet* (to which it would perhaps have provided a fittingly antipathetic counterpart), the printing stopped after three pages, possibly as a result of problems over copyright. These must have been resolved as the play was eventually included in the volume, but between the histories (after *Henry VIII*) and the tragedies (before *Coriolanus*), where it is generically re-categorised, as *The Tragedy of Troilus and Cressida*; it was entered too late, however, to be included on the Folio's contents page. The Folio version also introduces a number of significant variations: the play ends not with the epilogue in which the lovers' sleazy go-between, Pandarus, addresses himself to the syphilitic 'Good traders in the flesh' (5.11.31.14) of early modern London's sex trade, and promises to 'sweat and seek about for eases/ And at that time bequeath you my diseases' (31.23–24), but with Troilus's rather more dignified invitation to his comrades: 'To Troy with comfort go:/ Hope of revenge shall hide our inward woe' (5.11.30–31). The change is more in keeping with the conclusion of a tragedy than the satirical comedy of the quartos, and the tonal shift is reinforced by the addition of an epic Prologue, which introduces the narrative of 'The princes orgulous, their high blood chafed' and which alerts its 'fair beholders' to the fact that this narrative 'Leaps o'er the vaunt and firstlings of those broils' to confines itself 'To what may be digested in a play' (Prologue, 2, 27, 29). Possibly intended as a jab (albeit a rather belated one) at Ben Jonson's pugilistic prologue to his satire *Poetaster* (1601), its high style cannot necessarily be taken seriously, and whether it and the other revisions that were made for Folio publication count sufficiently to locate the play more decisively within the generic realm of tragedy is open to question.

Generations of readers and theatregoers have generally not been convinced: presented a few times in heavily adapted form after the Restoration, the play dropped out of the repertory entirely at the beginning of the eighteenth century and did not surface again until the start of the twentieth. Unsurprisingly, its subject-matter did not recommend itself to the Victorians (preparing the text for inclusion in the *Henry Irving Shakespeare*, its editor found Troilus and Ulysses admirable but Cressida 'utterly shallow … the type of all disloyalty' [1888: 5, 253]); but early in the twentieth century a combination of the rise of pacifist activism and revived interest in both neglected early modern texts and Elizabethan-style staging finally found the play a more sympathetic audience. The pioneer in this respect was William Poel, who in 1912 and 1913 anticipated the outbreak of the war to end wars with a production under the auspices of his modernist-antiquarian Elizabethan Stage Society; this was followed by others by university and amateur groups and the first English professional production of the unadapted text at the Old Vic in 1923. Thereafter the play has featured sporadically in the programmes of the major national theatres, its action often transposed to more recent scenes of conflict and tending to tap into contemporary anti-war sentiments (notably as directed by Tyrone Guthrie at the Old Vic in 1956, where it coincided with the Suez crisis; by John Barton for the RSC in 1968 and 1976, with the Vietnam War in the background; and by Sam Mendes for the RSC at the Swan in 1990, on the eve of the First Gulf War); more recently, it was staged with a multi-ethnic cast at the National Theatre in 1999 (directed by Trevor Nunn) and, in a production seemingly indifferent to the Second Gulf War, the so-called War on Terror, or any other contemporary conflict, in an 'original practices' staging at Shakespeare's Globe in 2009. It has been broadcast and televised a number of times (the most readily available version being the BBC Television Shakespeare production, directed by Jonathan Miller, of 1981), but not as yet commercially filmed. The play's indeterminate placement between history and tragedy, both in and not in the Folio, remains vexingly appropriate.

All yet seems well

Like *Troilus and Cressida, All's Well that Ends Well* left no trace of performance in its own time. Generally agreed on the basis of stylistic evidence and of thematic resemblances with the other problem comedies of the turn of the seventeenth century to have been written somewhere between 1603 and 1606, the play is not mentioned anywhere until it was entered in the Stationers' Register in 1623, prior to publication in the First Folio, which furnishes its only text. Along with *Troilus* and *Measure for Measure*, it has been classed as a 'problem play', a generic coinage of George Bernard Shaw's, who saw in these works an affinity with the socially aware and, for its time, sexually frank dramaturgy of the works by Ibsen and himself (Shaw's *Mrs Warren's Profession* [1894], which, without once naming the 'profession', deals with prostitution; Ibsen's *Ghosts* [1881; London premiere 1891], which dramatises the scandal of syphilis), which in twentieth-century critical tradition was extended to incorporate recognition of its tonal ambiguities, the qualified and uncertain nature – despite the apparent optimism of the reiterated title – of its resolution and, more recently, the uneasy quality of its sexual and class politics.

As a woman prepared to defy gender hierarchies, social convention and barriers of rank in pursuit of her desire, its heroine's appeal to Shaw as a prototype of the suffrage-seeking New Woman is readily understandable; but the bare outlines of the main plot are themselves sufficient to indicate why he might also have classified it alongside his 'Plays Unpleasant'. Helen, an upwardly mobile, educated young woman, travels to the court of the king of France in pursuit of the son of the widowed Countess her protector, Bertram, a man who is her social superior and who shows no interest in returning her love; deploying the quasi-magical medical art that she has learned from her dead doctor father to cure the king of a life-threatening fistula, she is rewarded with her choice of a husband.

When Bertram publicly and humiliatingly spurns her advances, the king imposes his will and enforces the marriage, upon which Bertram announces that he is off 'to the Tuscan wars and never bed her' (2.3.257) and that, for good measure, he will 'Acquaint my mother with my hate to her' (271); writing to Helen from the front, he tells her that 'When thou canst get the ring upon my finger, which never shall come off, and show me a child begotten of thy body that I am father to, then call me husband' (3.2.55–57). Taking him at his word, Helen travels to Italy in the guise of a pilgrim, seizes the opportunity presented by Bertram's own pursuit of Diana, the virtuous daughter of another widower, and offers herself to him in bed in her place. The play concludes with the revelation of her deception, Helen confronting Bertram with the exposure of his would-be infidelity and his own written ultimatum, and Bertram acceding to the terms of the marriage contract:

There is your ring.
And, look you, here's your letter. This it says:
'When from my finger you can get this ring,
And are by me with child,' et cetera. This is done.
Will you be mine now you are doubly won?
BERTRAM [*to the* KING] If she, my liege, can make me know this clearly,
   I'll love her dearly, ever ever dearly.

                                                                    (5.3.307–13)

In a related sub-plot, Bertram's braggart companion, Parolles, is tricked by his fellow officers into exposing himself as a sham and a coward; the witty and amusing companion of the first acts is transformed shamefully, into a broken man, abjectly dependent on charity, and yet a figure not of ridicule but of sympathy, by the last. Although there is perhaps little here to unsettle a regular viewer of *EastEnders*, it is hardly surprising that a drama that appears to depend upon coercion, manipulation and deceit, that has as its nominal leading man a character whose behaviour is snobbish, dishonourable, devious and disloyal, and whose heroine, for all her undoubted strengths, appears to have few good reasons other than masochistic ones to want to possess him (although in a way she has little alternative) has been one of Shakespeare's most unpopular comedies.

It is unwise to argue with the facts of a stage history that, beginning with the yawning silence that surrounds the play in the early seventeenth century, sees its profile decline from fifty-one performances in the eighteenth century (in Garrick's adaptation) to seventeen in the nineteenth, the last in 1852 at Sadler's Wells under Samuel Phelps; when it did appear, the text had to be so heavily cut and rephrased in the interests of propriety that its denouement barely made sense. Rather than ascribing the play's unpopularity to the malign aftermath of nineteenth-century repression, as does the Oxford editor, who suggests that it testifies to 'the tenacity of Victorian distaste for the indecencies of the play's plot' (Snyder 1993: 26), we might need to acknowledge that when as distinguished a critic as Tillyard labelled the play as a 'failure' he was worth taking seriously. The increased number of productions in the second half of the twentieth century (notably, Tyrone Guthrie's at the Festival Theatre in Stratford, Ontario, in 1953, and Trevor Nunn's for the RSC in 1981) prompted claims that this is a play that speaks particularly well to modern and more liberated sensibilities; moreover, its pivotal position as the play that, in Guthrie's production, launched the postwar open stage movement has seen it connected with the rediscovery of non-illusionist stagecraft (Styan 1977; Shaughnessy 2002).

But in some ways the 'problems' that the play presented to twentieth-century readers and audiences were of their own making. To accept the outcome of the comedy, one must assent to both the plausibility and the probity of the bed-trick: within the patriarchal barter economy of the play's source, Boccaccio's *Decameron*, and perhaps on Shakespeare's all-male stage, the exchangeability of women as sexual objects is unexceptional, but for audiences accustomed to ascribing to female characters even a modicum of autonomy the subterfuge seems not only fantastic but degrading. One must also be prepared, in the interests of comic closure, to accede to the formally happy ending of a marriage that appears to be built on the most precarious of foundations, and that rewards the seemingly unrepentant hero with a wife he patently does not deserve. Were these the two-dimensional figures of a folk tale, we would be less worried about the moral and emotional implications of these actions and outcomes, but, given that the other major legacy of Victorianism is a realist dramaturgy that generally compels us to interpret Shakespeare's stage personae as more complex and conflicted than narrative requirements might need them to be, it is perhaps impossible for us to react without empathy. Nor, indeed, would it be desirable to attempt to do so: even if it is a form of anachronistic back-projection to take the side of a heroine whose original audiences, if there were any, might have viewed her as a sexual transgressor, and who might have cared little about her feelings as party to a marriage of anything but equals, our desire to do so is perhaps an indication that the real problem with this play today is not, as it may have been for our immediate forbears, that it is too modern, but that it is too early modern.

Like doth quit like, and measure still for measure

Measure for Measure is the one play in this group for which there is a definite record of early performance: it is documented in the Revels Accounts as having been presented at court on St Stephen's night, 26 December, 1604, as one of the fourteen plays staged by the King's Men over the festive season. The play remained unpublished until the First Folio of 1623, where, according to recent scholarship, it appeared as adapted by Thomas Middleton (Taylor and Lavagnino 2007a). As noted elsewhere ('Life and contexts', pp. 58–9), aspects of the play seem contrived to appeal to the Christmas performance's principal spectator, King James, in particular the Duke's expressed distaste for displaying himself in public (1.1.67–68) and the play's involvement in theological debate, which linked it with the spirit of the 1604 Hampton Court conference, which James convened and in which he enthusiastically participated. Nominally set in Catholic Vienna, the action of the play is in some respects closer to the contemporary London depicted in the comedies of Middleton than to the Mediterranean or mythical worlds of previous Shakespearean comedies: set in the brothels and prisons that, in Shakespeare's own world, were adjunct to the playhouses on the Thames's South Bank, *Measure* poses sharp and immediate questions about the nature and exercise of authority, and about the relations between principles and practice, between the abstract and absolute rigours of the law and actualities of human fallibility.

The prime concern is with the regulation of sexual behaviour, and the play begins by conjuring a situation, as expounded by Vienna's ruler, Duke Vincentio, which might have had the more moralistically inclined members of its early 1600s audiences nodding in recognition:

> We have strict statutes and most biting laws,
> The needful bits and curbs to headstrong weeds,
> Which for this fourteen years we have let slip;
> Even like an o'ergrown lion in a cave
> That goes not out to prey.

(1.3.19–23)

Invoking a scenario of insubordination and incipient chaos that echoes Ulysses's account of local and cosmic disorder in *Troilus* ('Liberty plucks Justice by the nose,/ The baby beats the nurse, and quite athwart/ Goes all decorum' [1.3.29–31]), the Duke indicates that it is, in particular, the flouting of statutes against fornication that is responsible for breeding disrespect and unrest.

For reasons that are never satisfactorily explained (this is, perhaps, a fable after all), the Duke decides to go under cover, adopting the guise of a mendicant Friar, ceding responsibility to his deputy, the puritanical Angelo, to ensure that the laws that have been allowed to slacken are applied with renewed, and it seems extreme, rigour. In certain respects the central plot of *Measure* recapitulates elements of *All's Well*, notably the use of the bed-trick: what was in the (possibly) earlier play an act of entrapment performed by Helen to secure her marriage with an unwilling husband, here is contrived by the 'Duke of dark corners' in order to manoeuvre Angelo, who intends to rape the novice nun Isabella in return for pardoning her brother Claudio, under sentence of death for fornication, into consummating his betrothal to the woman he, Bertram-like, has abandoned. In this instance, the stakes are considerably higher, for the dilemma confronted by Isabella is one of a choice between the enforced surrender of her virginity and her brother's life, and one of the play's most distinctive features is the skill with which it balances the competing claims and counter-claims of its dramatis personae upon the audience's sympathies.

Persuaded by the libertine Lucio to petition Angelo on behalf of her brother, Isabella presents a powerful argument for exercising leniency, presenting him with a version of the biblical injunction to 'Judge not, that ye be not judged' (Matthew 7):

> Go to your bosom;
> Knock there, and ask your heart what it doth know
> That's like my brother's fault. If it confess
> A natural guiltiness, such as is his,
> Let it not sound a thought upon your tongue
> Against my brother's life.
>
> (2.2.139–44)

Animating the Christian Gospels' condemnation of hypocrisy ('why see'st thou the mote, that is in your brother's eye, and perceivest not the beam that is in your own eye?') and the central New Testament principle of mercy, by realising them in terms of a desperate human situation, the plea seems unassailable. Yet when Angelo responds by presenting Isabella with his ultimatum, her defence of her chastity assumes as absolute a character as the Duke and Angelo would (at least at this stage in the play) prefer the law to exhibit. Having cleverly managed to get Isabella to concede that there might 'be a charity in sin/ To save this brother's life' (2.4.63–64), Angelo's own attempt to ensnare her is met with defiance: 'Better it were a brother died at once/ Than that a sister, by redeeming him,/ Should die for ever' (2.4.107–09).

Quite a few modern readers, taking a generally more relaxed attitude to virginity, have been appalled by this, seeing the choice that Isabella is making as selfish, hysterical or perverse (it has been observed that the fantasy of mortification which precedes this assertion – 'Th' impression of keen whips I'd wear as rubies,/ And strip myself to death as to a bed … ere I'd yield/ My body up to shame' [101–04] – has a strong erotic and masochistic dimension). How the play's contemporary audiences might have reacted is hard to know: on the one hand, a woman's chastity was considered by some as something to be defended with her life; on the other, the specifically Catholic aspect of Isabella's vow was something audiences in Protestant England might have regarded with scepticism. Facing Claudio in the expectation that he will offer his full backing to her position ('Isabel live chaste, and brother die;/ More than our brother is our chastity' [2.4.184–85]), she is appalled when he pleads with her to consent to Angelo's demand to save his life, accusing him even of contemplating 'a kind of incest' in hoping 'to take life/ From thine own sister's shame' (3.1.140–41). At the beginning of this scene, the Duke in the guise of the Friar seems to have reconciled Claudio to his fate by persuading him of the vanity, pain and worthlessness of earthly existence ('What's in this/ That bears the name of life? [3.1.38–39]), but when confronted with the possibility of escaping the seemingly inevitable, Claudio's fatalism evaporates as he articulates the equally compelling case for staying alive: 'The weariest and most loathèd worldly life … is a paradise/ To what we fear of death' (3.1.129–32).

Presented with such finely balanced antimonies, the audience may find its responses impossibly divided, since Isabella and Claudio are, in their own respective ways, both right and wrong, sympathetic and unsympathetic at the same time. Offering a stark polarity between death and dishonour, at the very moment that a tragic outcome seems unavoidable, the play stages a series of interventions that ultimately enable a formally comic resolution. The first of these, engineered by the Duke, is the bed-trick, the substitution of Mariana for Isabella: 'by this', or so runs the plan, 'is your brother saved, your honour untainted, the poor Mariana advantaged, and the corrupt deputy scaled' (3.1.244–45). With an abundance of happy outcomes compacted into one improbable sentence, it seems too good to be true; what is worth noticing is that by making Isabella's defence of her virginity so unconditional Shakespeare seems to have deliberately made more difficult for himself, and for the audience, a situation which in the play's source narratives is resolved when the Isabella-figure relents and sleeps with the magistrate. Not only is the bed-trick an innovation made necessary by Shakespeare's sharpening of the moral and emotional stakes; it doesn't work, as, having had Mariana, Angelo orders the execution to proceed anyway.

Again, the play seems destined to end inevitably in tragedy; and it is this that generates the second, literally quite incredible, plot intervention, this time even more visibly a piece of narrative and theatrical legerdemain, where the hand at work is that of the author himself. Angelo has ordered that Claudio's head be sent to him at dawn; the Duke and the Provost of the prison agree to thwart the order while appearing to conform to it by planning to send in its place the head of Barnadine, another prisoner scheduled to be executed later that day: a bed-trick is capped with a head-trick. Yet when Barnadine does appear on stage, in what is one of the briefest but best cameo parts in the Shakespearean canon, he flatly refuses to accept the role that has been scripted for him, declaring that 'I have been drinking all night. I am not fitted for't' (4.3.36–37), and forcing the Duke to concede that, as a condemned man defiantly unprepared to meet maker, 'to transport him in the mind he is/ Were damnable' (4.3.60–61).

The situation seems irresolvable without someone paying an intolerable price; and yet again Shakespeare seems to have deliberately contrived a situation impossible to resolve within the framework of a comedy (plenty of Shakespeare's comic characters face the threat of execution, but no one ever actually dies as a result of another's action). Then, as if plucked forth from his sleeve or out of a conjurer's hat, the Provost supplies the solution:

> Here in the prison, father,
> There died this morning of a cruel fever
> One Ragusine, a most notorious pirate,
> A man of Claudio's years, his beard and head
> Just of his colour.

> (4.3.61–65)

'O', cries the Duke, ' 'tis an accident that heaven provides' (4.3.69), a line which I have never heard delivered in the theatre without it earning one of the biggest laughs in the play.

Whether this is simply a moment where Shakespeare is unable to get away with the kind of plot manipulation whereby, in earlier comedies, disaster was averted by a hair-splitting legalism (*Merchant*) or by the fantasy doubling of the beloved of both man and woman (*Twelfth Night*), or one in which the play is in collusion with our own sense of its preposterousness is hard to say; but it decisively, and both pleasurably and disturbingly, complicates still further our response to an already challenging and unsettling play. Does Shakespeare's apparently flagrant exposure of the mechanics of his craft advertise his scepticism about the happy ending which the comedy is compelled to enforce, despite everything in the play that seems to pull in the opposite direction? Placing desire, the law, justice, mercy and human fallibility in such lethal opposition, the play is at once all too real and, at such moments especially (to borrow the designation of the hedonist Lucio, upon whose labours the outcome of the play ultimately depends), fantastic. The issues technically balance out at the end of the play, via the formal closure of its contracted marriages.

The realism of the play lies not only in the subtlety of its psychological investigation, wherein characters such as Isabella and Angelo may be seen to have complex, divided and sometimes unconscious motives (as latterly the birthplace of psychoanalysis, the Viennese setting seems inadvertently apt for a play itself intent on repressing its own implications), but also in its candid depiction of the world of prostitution and petty crime that Angelo's moral crackdown is intended to regulate and reform. Isabella's refusal of Angelo is afforded particular moral and theatrical force not only because her brother's death hinges upon it, but because hers is a city in which the walls of the convent and courthouse abut those of the prison and brothel, and in which the pimp Pompey presents the magistrate Escalus with the painful but compelling truth that the only way to make his 'trade' cease to exist would be 'to geld and spay all the youth of the city' (2.1.201–06).

Exemplary execution for fornication is one thing, but even Angelo's government would appear to draw the line at mass castration and hysterectomy; and there is in Pompey's animalistic vocabulary a resigned sense of human sexual desire as an inevitable, and per-haps ugly and shameful, fact of nature, an impression the play, emanating from the same stable as that which produced Shakespeare's *Sonnets*, does not much qualify. In these cir-cumstances, justice in Vienna is not just ineffective but riven with contradictions. When Pompey is driven out of his trade, he finds ready re-employment as a gaoler, a volte-face that in this instance indicates not so much the opposition of as the interdependence between the law and deviance; as Escalus exclaims in exasperation, as Pompey traps the constable Elbow into ever more self-incriminating malapropisms, 'Which is the wiser here, justice or iniquity?' (2.1.154): the question goes unanswered.

It is within this substratum of his metropolis that the Duke conducts his experiment in purportedly benevolent, invisible government. The action of a ruler who prefers stealth to display, the Duke's unmotivated but potentially rather sinister tactic of moving amongst his subjects in the guise of their confessor (and not even Henry V, under cover on the eve of Agincourt, thought of that one) enacts the new, more appropriately Jacobean, relationship between religion and statecraft that Elizabeth I at least, who made it known that it was not her wish to 'make windows into men's hearts and secret thought', had forsworn. As a depiction of a surveillance society in which the exercise of social and political control is implicated within mechanisms of exposure and concealment of the ruler's person, and conducted in the policing, both public and covert, of sexuality, and in which the cell and the scaffold afford different sites upon which justice can be seen to be done, the play may be said to prefigure some of the central preoccupations of new historicist, cultural materialist and feminist criticism (see 'Criticism', pp. 314–19).

In particular, its conjunction of sex, the law and death recalls the work of one of these critical movements' most important influences, Michel Foucault, whose studies of the pro-duction of transgression, of the evolution of the modern penal system in terms of a move from the punitive display of state power to internalised systems of self-correction, and of the invention of the history of sexual repression the play seems proleptically to anticipate. As with the other plays discussed in this group, *Measure*'s status as a 'problem' has led many to ascribe to it an astonishing modernity; although many of us would like to consider what passes between consenting adults in private to be none of the law's business, the persistence of both private and state coercion in the field of sexual behaviour will ensure that it will continue to find audiences. Staged after the Restoration and during the eighteenth century only in a heavily cut and adapted form, the play was rarely seen during the nineteenth century and only sporadically in the first part of the twentieth; the play became a settled part of the repertoire after the Second World War, in particular following Peter Brook's revelatory 1950 production at the Shakespeare Memorial Theatre, Stratford-upon-Avon.

Further reading

Charnes, Linda (1993) *Notorious Identity: Materializing the Subject in Shakespeare*. Cambridge, MA: Harvard University Press.

Desens, Merliss C. (1994) *The Bed-Trick in English Renaissance Drama*. Newark, DE: University of Delaware Press.

Dollimore, Jonathan (1994) 'Transgression and Surveillance in *Measure for Measure*', in *Political Shakespeare: Essays in Cultural Materialism*, ed. Jonathan Dollimore and Alan Sinfield. Second edition. Manchester: Manchester University Press, 72–89.

Escolme, Bridget (2005) '"Bits and Bitterness": Politics, Performance, *Troilus and Cressida*', in *Talking to the Audience: Shakespeare, Performance, Self*. London: Routledge, 24–51.

Grady, Hugh (1996) *Shakespeare's Universal Wolf: Studies in Early Modern Reification*. Oxford: Clarendon Press.

McGuire, Philip C. (1984) *Speechless Dialect: Shakespeare's Open Silences*. Berkeley, CA: University of California Press.

Parker, R. B. (1984) 'War and Sex in *All's Well that Ends Well*', *Shakespeare Survey*, 37: 99–113.

Shakespeare's Sonnets *and* A Lover's Complaint

Date, text and authorship

Sonnets mentioned by Francis Meres, 1598; Q1 1609. Solely Shakespearean.

Sources and influences

Petrarch, *Trionfi, sonetti e canzoni* (1490); Sir Thomas Wyatt and Sir Henry Howard, *Tottel's Miscellany* (1557); Sir Philip Sidney, *Astrophil and Stella* (1591, 1598).

On stage

Lyric, Hammersmith, London, 1990; South Bank Centre, London, 1990; Berliner Ensemble, Berlin, 2009 (dir. Robert Wilson; music by Rufus Wainwright); *Love Is My Sin*, Théâtre des Bouffes du Nord, Paris, 2009 (dir. Peter Brook; perf. Michael Pennington and Natasha Parry).

On screen

The Angelic Conversation, UK, 1985 (dir. Derek Jarman; read by Judi Dench).

Offshoots

George Bernard Shaw, *The Dark Lady of the Sonnets* (1910); Anthony Burgess, *Nothing Like the Sun* (1964), *Enderby's Dark Lady* (1984); William Boyd, *A Waste of Shame*, BBC TV, 2005 (dir. John McKay); Rufus Wainwright, *All Days are Nights: Songs for Lulu* (2010).

Whereas the publication of Shakespeare's first poetic works (and those over which he apparently took most care), *Venus and Adonis* and *Lucrece*, appears to have been conducted under his supervision and close scrutiny, the volume that appeared in 1609 under the title *Shakespeare's Sonnets* did so in circumstances that generations of critical commentators, and biographers, have considered intriguing, mysterious and suspicious (see 'Life and contexts', pp. 24–31). As we have seen, much of the intrigue has been generated by the enigmatic dedication to 'Mr W. H.', named as the 'onlie begetter' of the sonnets (my own view is that the initials are a tease, most probably inserted by the printer, Thomas Thorpe: 'Who He?' [Burrow 2002: 103]; 'Whoever He (may be)' [Blakemore Evans 2006: 6]), and widely identified with the 'Fair Youth' of the first two-thirds of the total of 154 sonnets, which, coupled with the alleged presence of a shadowy supporting cast of Rival Poet and so-called 'Dark Lady', has fuelled speculation about Shakespeare's sexuality, his personal and literary rivalries, and the supposedly autobiographical orientation of the work.

The questions that the sonnets have generated (which perhaps should be properly seen as intrinsic to the practice of early modern sonneteering per se, which frequently involved the cultivation of mystery around the supposed or conjectured identities of its subjects of address), will never be definitively resolved, and probably no one would want them to be. If Shakespeare's sonnets seem, uniquely within his ouevre, to allude to the deepest secrets of his private life, they also offer a sharp contrast with his creative practice as a playwright generally content to bend and break the established rules of the dramaturgy he inherited in that they operate – with a few notable and deliberate exceptions – within the strict conventions of a verse form established in the fourteenth century by the Italian poet Petrarch, introduced to England in the early seventeenth century by Sir Thomas Wyatt and revived during the 1590s in the wake of the posthumous publication of Sir Philip Sidney's *Astrophil and Stella* (1591). The sonnet, as Shakespeare crafted it, is a poem of fourteen lines of ten syllables, organised as three quatrains of alternately rhymed lines followed by a concluding rhyming couplet (ababcdcdefefgg): within these constraints, which, far from inhibiting his creativity, seem to have profoundly enabled it, Shakespeare succeeded in transforming what in his poetic predecessors' hands had often been a studiedly artificial genre devoted to variations upon the formulae of unrequited love and the worship of idealised mistresses into an artform which employs the most conventionalised of poetic forms to convey with uncompromising realism the ecstasies and agonies of desire.

Lovers of codes and cryptograms have also found the sonnets a happy hunting-ground. Developing the work of Alastair Fowler (1970) and T. P. Roche (1989), Katherine Duncan-Jones, editor of the Arden third series edition, identifies at least five numerological systems at work in the sonnet (1997: 97–101). The first seventeen correspond to the years of minority, eighteen being the age thought best for young men to marry. If we take the step of subtracting number 126 (technically not a sonnet, but an 'envoi', consisting of twelve lines in six couplets), the total of 108 sonnets which form the central group (sonnets 18–125) equals that of Sidney's *Astrophil and Stella*. This is followed by 28 poems, all addressed to a woman, a total which matches the number of days in the lunar month and in the menstrual cycle. The tripartite structure echoes the division of the Holy Trinity; if we subtract number 126 (or, alternatively, treating 153 and 154 as a single unit), the grand total of 153 has biblical resonances, being the number of fishes miraculously caught in the fishermen's nets in St John's Gospel (John, 21.11). The placement of individual sonnets can also be read as numerically pointed: sonnet 12, in which the poet counts 'the clock that tells the time' (12: 1) evokes twelve hours in the day; sonnet 60 ('so do our minutes hasten to their end' [60: 2]), the number of seconds in a minute and minutes in an hour; sonnet 144 (or twelve multiplied by twelve), which deals with the poet's conflicted desires for a male 'better angel' and female 'worser spirit' (144: 3, 4), represents the limit of the multiplication table, and the number termed a 'gross'; sonnet 52, reflecting on 'the long year set' (52: 6), refers to the weeks in the calendar year; sonnet 71, beginning 'No more mourn for me when I am dead' (71: 1), is one on from the traditional number of years a man was supposed to live. No doubt, given enough of the time that the sonnets repeatedly remind us we do not have, and ingenuity, many more correspondences could be found. At the very least, the intricate care with which the collection appears to have been assembled, in which presentation, form and content are thoughtfully and wittily matched, is strong evidence against the argument that the publication of the sonnets neither involved Shakespeare nor was authorised by him.

Beauty's rose

If we take the view that the principal means of sequencing and structuring the sonnets is the individuals, whether real or fictitious, to whom they are apparently addressed, the cycle can be seen to fall into three distinct parts. The first, a homogenous sequence comprising sonnets 1–17, target a young man, urging him to marry and produce an heir. In the second part, sonnets 18–126, what may or may not have been a Platonic and disinterested concern for the youth's reproductive future takes a more intense and explicitly homoerotic turn, as the sonnets chart the vicissitudes of a love affair, or alternatively a succession of entanglements with a series of possibly multiple or overlapping partners, most if not all of whom are male. In the final part, sonnets 127–54, the poet directs his attentions to a woman, or to women; the series concludes with a pair of linked poems which are addressed to no one in particular but, in a coda that meditates on the venereal legacy of the preceding narrative of enacted desires, plunge the iconography of Cupid's 'heart-inflaming brand' (154: 2) into the 'seething bath' (153: 7) of the sweating tubs used for the treatment of syphilis. Modelled on fifth-century Greek epigrams, the final sonnets are at once the most overtly conventionalised and formulaic exercises in the group and, as figurations of what desire comes to in the end, among its most pornographically frank confrontations of the relationship between love and sex; yet the final words of the sonnets are not despairing or dismissive, but affirmative: 'and this by that I prove:/ Love's fire heats water, water cools not love' (154: 14).

The elegant sophistry of the concluding couplet, which disputatiously summarises the argument of not only Sonnet 154 but of the entire sequence, returns us, in one sense, to the point at which it began. If the first seventeen poems form a unified set in terms of an emphatically iterated imperative and subject-matter that directly concerns a single individual, they are also characterised both by the explicitness of their presentation as exercises in persuasion and by the variety and sophistication of the logic that they employ in the process. In the absence of any conclusive evidence that the intended or implied reader of the procreation sonnets was the real-life counterpart of his literary surrogate, the reproductively averse 'fair youth', it is impossible to say whether their instrumental function (their efforts, that is, to get him to agree that nature 'carved thee for her seal, and meant thereby/ Thou shouldst print more, not let that copy die' [11: 13–14]) is in some way grounded in the imperative actualities of dynastic succession (which might conceivably have been the case had Shakespeare's talents been commissioned by the Wriothesley or Herbert families to tackle the problem of their respective sons' resistance to marriage) or merely a literary game. What is undeniable, however, is the consistency, the ingenuity and the force with which the argument, which is explicitly constructed in order to solicit its recipient to *do* something, to make a decision, to perform an act, is presented. The project of the subset is direct, explicit and uncompromising: get married, produce an heir; in this respect what Duncan-Jones calls the 'eugenic proposition' of the keynote sonnet and of those that follow (1997: 112) is not at all incompatible with (indeed, actively produces) the values of an aristocratic procreative economy geared towards the maintaining of the security and stability of succession and orderly transmission of land and property via the carefully managed interbreeding within its own class.

Recalling a range of contemporary texts which reflect on the desirability of aristocratic marriage (Erasmus's 'Epistle to persuade a young man to marry', passages in Sidney's *Arcadia*), the sequence scripts dynastic obligation in terms calculated to exploit their reader's narcissism:

> From fairest creatures we desire increase,
> That thereby beauty's rose might never die.

(1: 1–2)

> Look in thy glass, and tell the face thou viewest
> Now is the time that face should form another …

(3: 1–2)

> Those hours that with gentle work did frame
> The lovely gaze where every eye doth dwell …

(5: 1–2)

Elsewhere the sonnets perform a form of mirror-work by inversion and reversal, whereby where the verse appears most to attack, it most insistently flatters: the youth's solipsism is turned inside out, to become selflessness ('Is it for fear to wet a widow's eye/ That thou consum'st thyself in single life' [9: 1–2]); his masturbatory self-absorption ('traffic with thyself alone'), characterised as a form of ungentlemanly niggardliness, serves as a means of reiterating the 'bounteous largesse' of his 'Unthrifty loveliness' (4: 9, 6, 1).

Extravagant praise is one component within the poems' rhetorical armoury; the necessary corollary of the emphasis upon beauty is the counterpointed insistence upon its transience, its vulnerability to the ravages of time and ageing:

> When forty winters shall besiege thy brow
> And dig deep trenches in thy beauty's field,
> Thy youth's proud livery, so gazed on now,
> Will be a tattered weed, of small worth held ...
>
> (2: 1–4)

> Then of thy beauty do I question make
> That thou among the wastes of time must go ...
>
> (12: 9–10)

> wasteful time debateth with decay
> To change your day of youth to sullied night
>
> (15: 11–12)

Siring a son, as far as these sonnets are concerned, is itself a narcissistic act: the child that will result from the hoped-for union with the youth's unspecified bride (represented as merely a receptacle for propagation) will be both a perfect copy, or mirror-image, of his father and an indefinite perpetuation of his own self. Written by a man in his late twenties to mid-thirties (if they were composed for Wriothesley's or Herbert's benefit) addressing a man ten years younger, the poems reinforce their argument that reproduction is a way of cheating time by playing upon their reader's sense of mortality, insistently infiltrating images of beauty with those of death, climactically positioned at the end of the sonnets in which they recur: 'die single, and thine image dies with thee' (3: 14); 'thou art much too fair/ To be death's conquest and make worms thine heir' (6: 13–14); 'thyself outgoing in thy noon,/ Unlooked on diest' (7: 13–14); 'nothing 'gainst time's scythe can make defence/ Save breed to brave him when he takes thee hence' (12: 13–14).

The series concludes with a bravura gesture whereby, turning its gaze upon itself, the verse becomes its own mirror. Sonnet 16, musing on the relations between the respective (and for Shakespeare's readers, competing) arts of visual and literary portraiture and the art of physical reproduction itself, compares the incapacity of its 'pupil pen' to capture the likeness of its subject when compared to the 'lines of life' (descendents) that are his true image, fusing the patience of the sitter who has become a timeless work of art, the reciprocity of erotic surrender and the prospect of immortality:

> To give away yourself keeps yourself still,
> And you must live drawn by your own sweet skill.
>
> (16: 13–14)

It is followed by a sonnet which, conceding that there is no more to be said on the topic of procreation, and reflexively wondering, 'Who will believe my verse in time to come' (yes, gentle reader, this means us), doubles its final offer of reproductive immortality by declaring that 'were some child of yours alive that time,/ You should live twice: in it, and in my rhyme' (17: 13–14). Shorn of its conditional offspring, this promise is reiterated in later sonnets: sonnet 63 concludes with the assurance that 'His beauty shall in these black lines be seen,/ And they shall live, and he in them still green' (63: 13–14); and sonnet 81, likewise, that 'You still shall live – such virtue hath my pen–/ Where breath most breathes, even in the mouths of men' (81: 13–14). The enticing prospect of eternal fame is presumably offered in the confidence that its intended recipient, had he existed, would be happy to accept the paradox of celebrity in anonymity.

Master-mistress

Treated as a relatively self-contained group, the narrative of sonnets 1–17 performs a kind of surrogated wooing, in which the poet's articulations of desire operate strategically in the interests of others (family, a prospective partner). But while this keeps the sonnets – just – on the side of heterosexual propriety, there are indications enough even in this relatively chaste material that the passion that is expressed for the youth goes beyond the Platonic, the quasi-paternal or the tactically effusive. The youth's womanly qualities, for one, are insistently stressed: addressed at the outset as 'beauty's rose' (1: 2; the word is capitalised throughout the 1609 text and here also italicised for additional emphasis), a term often associated with women and with female genitals; praised as 'his mother's glass', that 'she in thee/ Calls back the lovely April of her prime' (3: 9–10), he is associated with flowers and fragrance, and with sweetness. Bearing in mind the consideration that in the aristocratic culture of early modern England the eroticised language of praise and courtship was an everyday and accepted component of male friendship as well as of the patronage system, and that the distinctions between homosociality and homosexuality (in any case a term largely meaningless when applied to sexual identities and orientations during the period) were by no means clear cut (see 'Life and contexts', pp. 25–31; 'Criticism', pp. 384–7), it is impossible to definitively determine whether the rapturous register of the first seventeen sonnets is indicative of sexual desire or not.

At sonnet 18, however, there is a distinct shift of register. 'Shall I compare thee to a summer's day?' (18: 1) is a question that might be asked of a lover of either gender, and there is nothing in this sonnet to fix its subject as male or female, but the next two sonnets launch a narrative in which the poetic voice's lover is male, and in which any sex that is imagined is recreational rather than reproductive. Pleading with 'Devouring time' not to inflict the devastation of ageing on his lover in sonnet 19, the poet asks him to 'carve not with thy hours my love's fair brow' but 'Him in thy course untainted do allow' (19: 9, 11), and reminders of the lover's masculinity are threaded throughout: he is variously addressed as 'Lord of my love' (26: 1); 'beauteous and lovely youth' (54: 13); 'fair friend' (104: 1); and 'sweet boy' (108: 5) and 'lovely boy' (126: 1); the poet depicts himself as 'your slave' (57: 1) and 'your vassal' (58, 4); asks whether 'it his spirit … that struck me dead?' (86: 5–6); declares that 'him as for a map doth nature store' (68: 13); laments that 'if he thrive and I be cast away,/ The worst was this: my love was my decay' (80: 13–14); and likens him to a 'stern wolf' in the guise of a lamb (96: 9–10).

In sonnet 20, homoeroticism is directly addressed:

A woman's face with nature's own hand painted
Hast thou, the master-mistress of my passion ...
But since she pricked thee out for women's pleasure,
Mine be thy love and thy love's use their treasure.

(20: 1–2, 13–14)

This represents the artistry of the sonnets at its most seductively double edged: at once an explicit confession of sexual desire and a statement that actual sex is (morally if not physically) an impossibility, the poem represents the beloved as both beguilingly effeminate and incontrovertibly masculine, active and passive, a woman endowed with a prick, an impossible androgyne capable of dispensing physical pleasure to women whilst preserving his higher feelings for a man. In their attempts to determine the sexual secrets that the sonnet seems both to reveal and conceal, readers have struggled with its delirious slippages between gendered roles and anatomies: the master-mistress's 'thing' that is 'nothing', that is, of no use, but also, according to vernacular, a vagina; the love between men that is simultaneously alike and utterly unlike that between a man and a woman; the object of desire that seems to oscillate polymorphously between manhood and femininity. In the conundrums that it generates, the sonnet should perhaps be read as the keynote for the sequence it serves to initiate.

Treated less as a continuous narrative than an anthology of poems that might well have been composed over a period of at least a decade, the sonnets might equally suggest a succession of sexual partners or of desires consummated or unconsummated, both male and female; in this sense, the overtly homoerotic strand operates within a spectrum of sexuality considerably more fluid and flexible than positionings of hetero- and homosexuality that postdate the sonnets' moment of writing. He – or maybe sometimes she – is variously ecstatic, abject, fierce and tender in desire, but, like his or their beloveds, the voices of the sonnets are not monogamous; if we must have narrative, then most readers have discerned in the progression towards sonnet 126, the final poem addressed to the 'lovely boy', stories of betrayal and infidelity on both sides.

Sonnet 78 introduces a 'rival' for the youth's affections, or patronage, initiating a sequence in which the author of the sonnets witnesses the waning of his artistic and poetic potency by 'the proud sail of his great verse' (86: 1), gradually surrendering his claim on the youth, as 'too dear for my possessing' (87: 1), he expresses his doubts about his fidelity whilst acknowledging his continuing abjection to him ('O, in what sweets dost thou thy sins enclose' [95: 4]), protests the continuance of his devotion in absence and separation ('O never say that I was false of heart,/ Though absence seemed my flame to qualify' [109: 1–2]), denies or confesses to alleged infidelities of his own ('What potions have I drunk of siren tears' [119: 1]), and finally takes his leave, reminding him for the last time of his mortality by referring him to his ultimate 'mistress', nature, whose 'audit, though delayed, answered must be,/ And her quietus is to render thee' (126: 11–12). Seemingly truncated (though metrically complete and, if 'render' is read in the legal sense of 'surrender', semantically sound, the conclusion also hints at something unspoken: 'render thee –'), the final stanza of this twelve-line poem is followed, in the quarto, by two pairs of empty brackets, enclosing an expected, but absent, final couplet. Bearing in mind the anatomical resonances of 'nothing' as alluded to in sonnet 20, if the signification of nothingness suggests the end of the affair and probably also the youth's life, it perhaps also defines a change of focus: from here onwards the sonnets' attentions turn to a woman, or women, and their prevailing mood changes to one of self-loathing and often toxic disgust.

Nothing like the sun

'His beauty shall in these black lines be seen,/ And they shall live, and he in them still green' (63: 13–14): the antithesis between the youth's fairness and the black ink of print is a nicely, if conventionally, parodoxical conceit, but it also indicates one of the key oppositions of the entire cycle. Gendered as well as colour coded, its co-ordinates are defined by, on the one hand, the fair youth and, on the other, the mistress, who is almost invariably identified with ugliness, deceit and the demonic. Although popularly known as Shakespeare's 'dark lady', she is described as 'dark' only once (147: 14, where the term is coupled with 'black as hell') and as a 'lady' never. But she is, repeatedly, termed 'black':

> In the old age black was not counted fair,
> Or if it were, it bore not beauty's name;
> But now is black beauty's successive heir …
> Therefore my mistress' eyes are raven-black …
>
> (127: 1–3, 9)

> If hairs be wires, black wires grow on her head …
>
> (130: 4)

> Thy black is fairest in my judgment's place.
>
> (131: 12)

> Then will I swear beauty herself is black,
> And all they foul that thy complexion lack.
>
> (132: 13–14)

Much ink has been spilt over the significance of 'black': from the mid-nineteenth century to the present, opinions have divided over whether it is operative as a racial marker (which has in turn fuelled biographical speculation), whether it signifies dark hair or eyes rather than skin, whether it is indicative of the woman's (more likely, women's) class rather than racial difference, or whether it is primarily metaphorical: blackness, the traditional mark of devilry, providing the link between female sexuality, death and the demonic.

Initiated within a discourse of praise by dispraise, where it seems at first to trump the duplicitous fairness produced by the 'bastard shame' of cosmetic enhancement (127: 4), the idea that black is beautiful is offered by the sonnets not, as we might hope, as an affirmative, but as self-evidently oxymoronic; and the sonnets seem riven by contradictory impulses of desire and misogynistic hostility, divided between eulogy and scorn:

> My mistress' eyes are nothing like the sun …
> If snow be white, why then her breasts are dun;
> If hairs be wires, black wires grow on her head …
> And in some perfumes is there more delight
> Than in the breath that from my mistress reeks.
>
> (130: 1, 3–4, 7–8)

The satirical targets (eyes like suns, lips like coral, hair like wires: the clichés of contemporary love poetry) are obvious enough, though well chosen; a benign reading of this sonnet might see it as a reasoned plea for realism as well as a teasingly affectionate tribute to a mistress who, so earthbound that 'when she walks' she 'treads on ground' (130: 13, 12), is yet as 'rare' as the women falsely idealised by rival poets; alternatively, the sonnet is a string of insults and inflicted humiliations.

In the preceding sonnet, the lust that women incite is characterised in terms of degradation, loss, violence and madness ('Th' expense of spirit in a waste of shame' [129: 1]):

> Had, having, and in quest to have, extreme;
> A bliss in proof and proved, a very woe …
>
> (129: 10–11)

The irregular yet relentless movement towards the 'extreme' of 'bliss', the moment of ecstatic suspension and successive dying fall, sarcastically replicates the physical rhythms of intercourse; yet even as the sonnet bitterly concludes with the recognition that the lust's final destination is, in another synonym for vagina, 'hell', it recognises that no man can 'shun the heaven' that led him there (14). If love for another man appears to bring out the best in a man, desire for a woman solicits his worst: contrasted with the exquisite suffering of sonnets 18–126, the agonies of love and lust explored in sonnet 127 bring scant joy and little hope. Dealers in disease and death, women exercise monstrous power; and while there is justice and propriety in the poet's submission to the youth's whims in the preceding section, the indignities and betrayals accounted in the latter part of the cycle yield shame, disgust and anger: she is 'tyrannous', 'cruel' (131: 1, 2), a torturer (133) and a sadist. Inherently duplicitous ('When my love swears that she is made of truth/ I do believe her though I know she lies' [138: 1–2]), the lover incites him to connive in his and her self-deceit: 'I lie with her, and she with me,/ And in our faults by lies we flattered be' (138: 13–14). And she is not even beautiful ('I do not love thee with mine eyes … 'tis my heart that loves what they despise' [141: 1–3]).

Rich in Will

Nonetheless, the fact that the final section is not without elements of playfulness suggests that unrelieved sourness may not be its sole aftertaste. Sonnet 145, sandwiched oddly between 144's account of the poet's conflicted desire for his 'better angel, 'a man right fair' and the 'female evil' of 'a woman coloured ill' (3–5) and 146's address to his 'Poor soul' (1), both metrically and tonally anomalous, provides a momentary, startling (and, many readers have thought, startlingly trite) relief from the prevailing cynicism and hatred, sweetly depicting the beloved as an agent of pity, redemptive mercy, one in whom hatred is transformed to forgiveness:

> 'I hate' she altered with an end
> That followed it as gentle day …
> 'I hate' from hate away she threw,
> And saved my life, saying 'not you.'
>
> (145: 9–10, 13–14)

Critics have considered the sonnet an embarrassment as well as an enigma, finding it superficial, juvenile and contrived (some have questioned its authorship); as recounted in 'Life and contexts', one explanation that has been offered is that it was rather sentimentally preserved as a tribute to Anne Hathaway (see 'Life and contexts', p. 31).

Given the care with which *Shakespeare's Sonnets* was compiled, it seems hard to believe that the inclusion was fraudulent, thoughtless or arbitrary, though it is perhaps impossible to work out what its purpose in the scheme might be, other than to cast a sudden and unexpected shaft of light across the darkness. One thing that might be worth noting is that it is positioned in relatively close proximity to a trio of sonnets in which Shakespeare is briefly seen in self-referential, even quasi-autobiographical mode, as, in what seems an almost parodically virtuoso act of authorial unmasking, he quibbles elaborately and ingeniously upon the word 'will' as forename, legal term and synonym for desire, determination and both male and female sex organs:

> So thou, being rich in Will, add to thy Will
> One will of mine to make thy large Will more ...
>
> (135: 11–12)

> Will will fulfil the treasure of thy love,
> Ay, fill it full with wills, and my will one.
>
> (136: 5–6)

> So will I pray that thou mayst have thy Will
> If thou turn back and my loud crying still.
>
> (143: 13–14)

Confronted with the John of Gaunt who, though at death's door, puns with comparable wit and audacity on his surname, King Richard finds it both amusing and astonishing that a sick man can 'play so nicely' with his name (2.1.84); his one-liner injecting a note of facetiousness that momentarily undercuts the solemnity of high tragedy; perhaps here, too, the wordplay works to situate the sonnets' theatre of passion and obsession within a framework of affectionate intimacy, where lovers exchange pet names for their parts (Mr W.H.?) and where the bedchamber, the scene of death and ecstasy, is also the space of affectionate, healing laughter.

This double voice

The 1609 quarto of the *Sonnets* also included the short narrative poem (just under three hundred and fifty lines) *A Lover's Complaint*, a work that has until relatively recently been disregarded by readers of the work to which it provides an addendum, coda or supplement. Long regarded as an interpolation of doubtful Shakespearean authorship, the poem was identified as canonical during the 1960s and has since attracted a degree of favourable attention (Jackson 1965; Kerrigan 1991; Burrow 2002), though its provenance is still liable to dispute (Vickers 2007). Composed in a seemingly consciously archaic style, and utilising the conventional form of female complaint, the poem tells the story of an unnamed woman seduced and betrayed by a 'maiden-tongued' (l. 100) young man, whose androgynous appeal recalls that of the sonnets' fair youth:

> His browny locks did hang in crookèd curls,
> And every light occasion of the wind
> Upon his lips their silken parcels hurls
> Small show of man was yet upon his chin;
> His phoenix down began but to appear ...
>
> (ll. 85–87, 92–93)

The narrative, presented via the medium of a succession of interlocking voices in which quotation is embedded within quotation, wherein the woman relays her predicament by repeating her lover's words to an aged rustic interlocutor, both observed by the poem's narrator, carries echoes of the triangular scenarios of the sonnets, as does the sense of being trapped in an endless cycle of erotic obsession, in which love's victims are doomed forever to repeat their mistakes.

At the poem's end, which yields neither resolution nor closure, the woman confesses that, regardless of his duplicity, she would be only too ready to again succumb to the charms of the 'infected moisture' of his eye, the 'false fire' of his cheek and the 'forced thunder' of his heart; his 'borrowed motion seeming owed'

> Would yet again betray the fore-betrayed,
> And new pervert a reconcilèd maid.

> (ll. 328–29)

If the poem's treatment of the woman's sorrows casts new light on the sonnets by offering the female perspective that they conspicuously lack, it also serves to remind the reader that the most powerful instruments of seduction are words themselves: it is as much the young man's eloquence as his beauty that beguiles and confounds, and that ensnares the young woman in self-abjection. A consummate wordsmith and performer, the young man is poet, playwright and player, whose 'passion, but an art of craft' (l. 295), is as irresistible as it is counterfeit. There is a warning for women here, but perhaps there is one for the reader too: bearing in mind the preoccupations with the staged and the authentic, and the auto-biographical and the fictive, that have continued to haunt the sonnets' reception and interpretation, the woman's entanglement within a lover's discourse that she knows to be untrue even as she desires it to be otherwise remains ours also. Seduced by the indeterminately gendered power of Shakespeare's words, we are always already betrayed by them, and yet we know that it is to them, once again, that we will return.

Further reading

Booth, Stephen (ed.) (1977) *Shakespeare's Sonnets*. New Haven, CT: Yale University Press.

Callaghan, Dympna (2007) *Shakespeare's Sonnets*. Oxford: Blackwell.

de Grazia, Margreta (1994) 'The Scandal of Shakespeare's Sonnets', *Shakespeare Survey*, 47: 35–49.

Edmondson, Paul, and Stanley Wells (2004) *Shakespeare's Sonnets*. Oxford Shakespeare Topics. Oxford: Oxford University Press.

Kerrigan, John (ed.) (1991) *Motives of Woe: Shakespeare and 'Female Complaint'*. Oxford: Clarendon Press.

Fineman, Joel (1986) *Shakespeare's Perjured Eye: The Invention of Poetic Subjectivity in the Sonnets*. Berkeley, CA: University of California Press.

Pequigney, Joseph (1985) *Such Is My Love: A Study of Shakespeare's Sonnets*. Chicago, IL: University of Chicago Press.

Roberts, Sasha (2003) *Reading Shakespeare's Poems in Early Modern England*. Basingstoke: Palgrave.

Smith, Bruce R. (1991) *Homosexual Desire in Shakespeare's England: A Cultural Poetics*. Chicago, IL: University of Chicago Press.

Vickers, Brian (2007) *Shakespeare, A Lover's Complaint, and John Davies of Hereford*. Cambridge: Cambridge University Press.

Othello

Othellophobia

Introducing a collection of essays on the topic of Shakespeare and race published in 2000, Margo Hendricks writes that her interest in the question was first aroused by the experience, as an undergraduate, of reading G. E. Bentley's introduction to *Othello* in the 1958 Penguin edition. What she found striking, she recalls, is Bentley's 'near total inattention to Othello's skin colour', a seemingly odd and possibly evasive move given that 'so much has been made of Othello's hue' both before and since. Hendricks records that in retrospect she came to recognise Bentley's silence as 'an astute stratagem to redirect the reader's attention and gaze away from Othello's colour and to his status as a warrior, and to the complex moral dimension that status entails in Shakespeare's tragedy' (2000: 1); what she does not pursue is the question of why Bentley found it appropriate to engineer such a deflection of attention.

Reference, however, to the other edition of the play published in the same year as Bentley's, M. R. Ridley's for the Arden Shakespeare, furnishes the outlines of an answer. Surveying the long and shameful history of both conscious and inadvertent racism that extends from Thomas Rymer, writing in 1693 of how Othello's charming of Desdemona 'was sufficient to make the Black-amoor white', down to A. C. Bradley's attempts to assuage Coleridge's horror of Desdemona 'falling in love with a veritable negro', which nonetheless suggests that 'if we saw Othello coal-black with the bodily eye, the aversion of our blood … would overpower our imagination' (Bradley 2007: 151), Ridley evokes a personal memory:

> Now a great deal of the trouble arises, I think, from a confusion of colour and contour. To a great many people the word 'negro' suggests as once the picture of what they would call a 'nigger', the woolly hair, thick lips, round skull, blunt features, and burnt-cork blackness of the traditional nigger minstrel … There are more races than one in Africa, and that a man is black in colour is no reason why, even to European eyes, he should look sub-human. One of the finest heads I have ever seen on any human being was that of a Negro conductor on an American Pullman car … He was coal-black, but he might have sat to a sculptor for a statue of Caesar, or, so far as appearance went, have played a superb Othello.
>
> (Ridley 1958: li)

It is a passage which, as Lena Cowen Orlin says, 'has become thoroughly notorious', reflecting an 'unforgivable' attitude to race (2004: 12, 250); as Karen Newman comments, 'What are we to make of a widely used scholarly edition of Shakespeare which, in the very act of debunking, canonizes the prejudices of Rymer and Coleridge?' (1987: 144).

Perhaps the attitudes voiced here may now strike us as a relic of, as Newman (1987) puts it, 'a long ago past of American Pullman cars and dignified black conductors'; of an age where it was entirely acceptable for white actor Laurence Olivier to transform himself into Othello through the cosmetic application of 'Max Factor 2880, then a lighter brown, then Negro No. 2, a stronger brown. Brown on black to give a rich mahogany' (Olivier 1986: 158) for the 1964 National Theatre production; and of a period before the advent of the Civil Rights Movement in the United States. But before mercifully consigning it to history we need to bear in mind that Ridley's edition stayed in print for nearly forty years (it was superseded by E. A. J. Honigman's for the Arden third series in 1997) and, moreover, that it remained the standard text worldwide, including, as Martin Orkin and Ania Loomba have respectively testified, in the universities of South Africa and the Indian subcontinent (Orkin 1987; Loomba 1989). Neither Ridley nor Olivier register any awareness of the implications of their attitudes; both, indeed, seem to consider themselves innocent of prejudice, and one of the sadder aspects of all this is that Ridley seems to be congratulating his own liberalism.

As Orkin has shown, Ridley's gaffe is illustrative of the long-standing tendency, even amongst the most well-intentioned critics, to inhabit a racist frame of reference when discussing this play and its protagonist (as, for example, when they draw upon the language of 'primitive' passions, savagery, darkness and so on). The difficulties experienced by the generations of, predominantly, white male commentators have, of course, been exacerbated by a text which constructs the 'Moor' from disparate, contradictory and unreliable markers of ethnic and cultural difference, perceptions of others which map uncertainly onto Elizabethan and Jacobean definitions of and presuppositions about the term – which in turn themselves cannot be easily disentangled from the subsequent cultural history of race. Of course, similar concerns are pertinent to the portrayal of Aaron in *Titus Andronicus* and of the Prince of Morocco in *The Merchant of Venice*, and yet the (until relatively recently) marginal status of a largely unperformed play, in the first instance, and the incidental quality of what has been viewed as merely a minor cameo, in the second, have meant that they have had a lesser impact; with *Othello*, the passions and the anxieties that circulate around the matter of race are registered, both critically and theatrically, with particular intensity. Most critics agree that the portrayal of Aaron the Moor in *Titus Andronicus*, who orchestrates rape, mutilation and murder, and boasts that he has 'done a thousand dreadful things/ As willingly as one would kill a fly' (5.1.141–42), conforms to the stereotyping that is found in other plays of the period, but *Titus Andronicus* can be sidelined as a less than canonically central text. *Othello* cannot, and thus disturbs its audiences in a more unsettling way. Bentley's brief reference to Othello's 'exotic colour and background' (1958: 17; quoted in Hendricks 2000: 1), rather than indicating simple evasiveness, seems to demonstrate masterly circumspection.

Hendricks does not specify when her first undergraduate encounter with Bentley took place; but for the reader who might have wanted to take the question of Othello's exoticism further (or who wished to take issue with Ridley's version of the same), there was, in the decades following both editions, little in the way of sustained commentary to consult. Marvin Rosenberg's *The Masks of Othello* (1961) devoted just seven of its three hundred-plus pages to the question of Othello's ethnicity, most of which were concerned with Paul Robeson's 1943 portrayal of the role (and which it described as 'socially conscious' [151]); surveying what he regarded as inconclusive evidence regarding Elizabethan attitudes to race, Rosenberg found that the tension and unease that this performance generated 'implied a special audience mood totally unlike that of Shakespeare's time, when none of the uneasiness inherited from the master–slave relationship, or the guilt, anger and fear of the oppressor–oppressed, would have discolored [sic] the romantic love between heroine and stranger-hero' (152).

In 1965, Eldred Jones published *Othello's Countrymen*, the first systematic attempt to place Shakespeare's representation of Othello in the context of other stage Moors, and of Elizabethan beliefs and fantasies about black Africans; two years later, G. K. Hunter devoted the British Academy Shakespeare lecture to the topic of '*Othello* and colour prejudice' (the essay has recently been reprinted; Hunter 2004). For Hunter, in his 1964 essay on Elizabethan attitudes to 'strangers' – which included Jews and Moslems, Turks and other Europeans, Moors, Orientals, Africans and American Indians – frequently furnished 'material for caricature, but hardly for character'; acting as 'part of a process of *vulgarization*', popular prejudice worked 'to deprive those who were known from close contact with English life of any status save that of failed Englishmen. And the more intimately these strangers are known, the less their *strangeness* seemed intriguing, the more it seemed despicable' (Hunter 2000: 45, 47). 'The word "Moor"', writes Hunter, 'had no clear racial status', and the qualities associated with the term 'are hardly at all affected by Elizabethan knowledge of real Moors from real geographical locations' (2004: 252–53). At the beginning of *Othello*, Shakespeare trades in the stereotypical identification of the black man with pagan wickedness and unbridled sexuality; yet the play proceeds to challenge this view, invoking 'careless assumptions about "Moors"' in order to 'abandon these as the play brings them into focus and identifies them with Iago' (256). The outcome is that Iago succeeds in 'making the deeds of Othello at last fit in with the prejudice that his face at first excited' (259).

Commenting on the 2000 reprint of 'Elizabethans and Foreigners', Margo Hendricks observes that it is an essay considerably ahead of its time, being reminiscent of 'the type of scholarship typical of New Historicism', in that it attempts the kind of 'thick description' of Elizabethan culture characteristic of 'the type of intertextual analyses generated by New Historicists' (Hendricks 2000: 4). The birth of this movement in 1980 in the form of Stephen Greenblatt's *Renaissance Self-Fashioning*, found *Othello* in attendance; but although the protagonist is described in passing as a 'warrior and alien', the subject of race is peripheral to Greenblatt's discussion of 'violence, sexual anxiety, and improvisation' (1980: 245, 232); and the figure of the Jew in Marlowe's work receives more detailed attention. The 1980s saw the publication of a number of works addressing both the black presence in early modern drama and black performance history: assessing the representation of black men in works ranging from 1550 to 1688, Eliott H. Tokson (1982) finds much evidence to confirm Hunter's account of relentless stereotyping (Othello is excluded from the survey); Anthony Barthelemy (1987) extends the field of investigation to consider the incorporation of black figures in court masques and the Lord Mayor's Pageants as well as the drama; while Errol Hill, in *Shakespeare in Sable: A History of Black Shakespearean Actors* (1984), documents a previously overlooked aspect of the nineteenth- and twentieth-century American theatre.

The late 1980s also saw the publication of a cluster of important essays on *Othello* (Neill 1989; Newman 1987; Orkin 1987) which debated the possibility that Shakespeare's text might itself be complexly complicit with, or actively productive of, the sexual and racial stereotyping which older generations of critics had indulged, and more liberal modern critics had attempted to explain away, ignore or ameliorate. Both Orkin and Karen Newman argue that Shakespeare's text is, basically, liberal and progressive; the former proposing that 'in its rejection of human pigmentation as a means of identifying worth, the play, as it had always done, continues to oppose racism' (Orkin 1987: 188); the latter that 'The union of Desdemona and Othello represents a sympathetic identification between femininity and the monstrous which offers a potentially subversive recognition of sexual and racial difference' (Newman 1987: 151–52). Ania Loomba's *Gender, Race, Renaissance Drama* (1989) furthers the investigation of the interactions of sexuality, gender and race, emphasising the reciprocal and the historically differentiated quality of these interactions: 'The processes by which women and black people are constructed as the "others" of white patriarchal society are similar and connected, and they also reflect upon other sorts of exclusion such as that based on class'; however, race 'problematises feminist efforts to make analogies between or intertwine different aspects of women's subordination; the *specificity* of each emerges more clearly' (Loomba 1989: 2).

In the case of *Othello*,

> no simple mapping of racial difference on to the sexual is possible precisely because Othello's colour and gender make him occupy contradictory positions in relation to power ... firstly, Othello's blackness is central to any understanding of male or female sexuality or power structures in the play; secondly, the filtering of sexuality and race through each other's prism profoundly affects each of them.
>
> (Loomba 1989: 41)

Loomba also registers that the indeterminate nature of Othello's 'blackness' is itself, historically speaking, a product of the homogenising tendencies of colonial discourse: 'Debates over whether Othello was black, brown or mulatto anxiously tried to recover the possibility of his whiteness from this ambiguity which, on the contrary, alerts us to the very construction of the "other" in Orientalist and colonial discourses' (Loomba 1989: 49). Thus 'to consider Othello as a black man' is 'to concur with Fanon that colonial discourse itself erases differentiation between its various subjects and treats all outsiders as black' (50). In this context, Desdemona is as contradictory a figure as her husband; on the one hand, the agent of a desire that is 'especially transgressive because its object is black' (56); on the other, a woman initially secure in a power which bespeaks 'the confidence of both race and class' (57).

Loomba's central concerns, from a cultural materialist perspective, are the connections between history and the present, and, in particular, the implications of reading *Othello*, and other colour-aware early modern texts, in post-colonial India. 'More students probably read *Othello* in the University of Delhi every year than in all British universities combined', she writes; 'A large proportion of them are women' (Loomba 1989: 10). Such students may well register the play's engagements with race, class, caste and sexuality in particularly intense, and perhaps troubling, ways:

> The violent and volatile nature of Indian sexual politics; the heterogeneous nature of Indian society; the acceleration of social and political fissures in recent years as well as the consolidation of the bourgeois state at another level; the revealed contingency of law and its manipulation by political and religious authority; – these all provide a material basis from which to approach the diverse constituents of Renaissance sexual politics.
>
> (Loomba 1989: 3)

Desdemona, read in this context, 'comes uncomfortably close to the battered wives that now crowd the Indian (especially urban) scene' (Loomba 1989: 40).

Shakespeare's, and *Othello*'s, capacity to generate discomfort of various kinds has become a growing critical and, indeed, political problem in the criticism of the 1990s and the first decade of the twenty-first century. Focussing on 'the anxiety that attaches to the bed as the site of racial transgression – the anxiety on which depends so much of the play's continuing power to disturb' – and on the ways on which 'ideas of adultery and disproportionate desire are specifically linked to the question of race', Michael Neill argues that *Othello* 'engages its audience in a conspiracy to lay naked the scene of forbidden desire', thus taking us 'into territory we recognize but would rather not see' (1989: 412). Neill leaves open the question of whether *Othello*'s 'power to disturb' indicates an exposure or an exploitation of racist anxieties; for Michael Bristol, however, the cultural history of the play reveals all too clearly the profoundly misogynist and racist nature of a text that, in his account, seems beyond recuperation. Regarding it as 'a comedy of abjection that depends on a background of racial hatred and violence' (1996: 176), Bristol uncompromisingly characterises *Othello* as a work which employs the techniques of charivari in order to punish its central characters for engaging in a grotesque inter-racial marriage; dismissing the idea that its early audiences might, like ourselves, sympathise with Othello 'simply on the grounds that he was the victim of a racist society' (181), he defines the Moor as an abject clown, an object of mockery and derision, partnered with the equally preposterous and artificial figure of Desdemona. The tragedy thus becomes 'a comic spectacle of abjection rather than the grand opera of misdirected passion' (186).

Othellophilia

Bristol's conclusion that, given the slanting of the text, 'an honest production' of *Othello* would be 'intolerable' (1996: 176) has disturbing implications for its teaching and performance; and although his essay has been reprinted a number a times and is widely cited, few writers on the play have opted to follow these through. *Othello* and Othello have continued to act as a focus for critical discussion of the interplay of race, gender and sexuality in the Shakespeare canon; more recent examples include work authored and edited by Callaghan (2000a, 2000b), Orlin (2004), Vaughan (2005) and Thompson (2006). Reflecting upon the general preoccupation with the play that she herself shares, Celia Daileader has coined the term 'Othellophilia': 'the critical and cultural fixation on Shakespeare's tragedy of inter-racial marriage to the exclusion of broader definitions, and more positive visions, of inter-racial eroticism'. Attempting to break with the long-standing critical habit of 'struggling ... to prove that *Othello* is or is not racist, either is or is not "about race"', Daileader proposes a different set of questions: '*Why this play? Why Othello?*' (2005: 6).

The answer, Daileader suggests, lies in the fact that the dominant 'canonical narratives' of inter-racial eroticism 'have involved black men and white women, and not black women and white men' (2005: 7). Daileader's discussion considers 'Othellophilia' as a cultural history of production and reproduction that ranges well beyond the play as read or performed, taking in Gothic fiction, *Gone with the Wind* and the films of Spike Lee; in the early modern context, she argues, *Othello* needs to be seen in relation to its 'alternative' as 'a model of inter-racial eroticism': *Antony and Cleopatra* (Daileader 2005: 31). Comparing the demonic racism and misogyny of the one text with the guarded ambiguities of the other, Daileader concludes that Cleopatra, unlike Othello, 'is not demonised'; although she is engaged in a relationship that is 'adulterous and politically detrimental', this 'is not portrayed as damnable or unnatural, as it would be if [Cleopatra and Antony's] races were reversed' (2005: 29). As Daileader points out, Cleopatra differs from Othello in that critical and theatrical tradition has not, until recently, recognised her as a black woman; but although the markers of racial difference attributed to her by Shakespeare's text are indeterminate, there seems 'no doubt that her affair with Antony is inter-racial' (29).

Daileader's position is that of a number of recent critics working on the intersections between gender and race; her observation that Cleopatra's blackness has been rendered invisible, either by default or by design, since the late seventeenth century reflects a growing awareness that the discourses of racial and sexual difference manifest themselves within early modern culture in places where race is, at first sight, not obviously at issue. Thus for Loomba, 'the introduction of racial difference is useful beyond analysing the representation of blacks; it also allows for a more complex perspective on the nature of authority itself, even where colour differentiation appears to be, or actually is, absent' (1989: 4).

In *Things of Darkness* (1995), Kim F. Hall extends the analysis of racial evocation and representation to the 'broad discursive network in which the polarity of dark and light articulates ongoing cultural concerns over gender roles'; arguing that 'dark and light ... became in the early modern period the conduit through which the English began to formulate the notions of "self" and "other" so well known in Anglo-American racial discourses' (1995: 2). As well as entailing a repositioning of Cleopatra as the African queen ('the embodiment of an absolute correspondence between fears of racial and gender difference and the threat they pose to imperialism' [153–54]) of an Egypt in which, as on Prospero's island, 'the separations of dark and light, self and other, are momentarily broken down, and the anxieties over that collapse are displayed and explored' (160), this also involves consideration of the gendered schematics of light, darkness and fairness in a range of Shakespearean and non-Shakespearean texts and cultural artefacts which are seen to fashion and construct whiteness and femininity as complex correlates.

Within the larger frame of a trading system that included the traffic in slaves, global travel, imperial expansion, military adventurism and colonisation, race also operates as a means of classifying and differentiating within and between groups of men and women, the conquerors and the subjects of conquest, the owners and the owned, masters and mistresses. In forms as varied as the courtly lyric, the court masque, the stage play and the aristocratic portrait, imagery of blackness and whiteness, as well as representations of the black man and black woman, serves as ' tropes of disorder, racial otherness and unruly sexuality' which 'become the terms by which European expansion first appropriates the strange newness of the lands "discovered" in the Renaissance' (Hall 1995: 25).

In a brief study of the *Sonnets* Hall acknowledges that the subject of whiteness has to date 'generally not been part of early modern scholarship', which in part reflects the consideration that 'most work on whiteness in other areas has pointed out that the most salient quality of whiteness is that it tends to be rendered invisible' (1998: 64–65). If one of the tasks confronting recent early modern race studies has been precisely to bring into critical visibility this most ideologically naturalised of cultural phenomena, another, related, project has been to rethink the meaning(s) of 'race' itself as what Ania Loomba calls 'one of the most powerful and yet most fragile markers of social difference' (2000: 203). Loomba argues that whereas the criticism of the last two decades of the twentieth century emphasised the processes whereby the modern ideologies of race (and the structures of exploitation that both produced and were produced by them) came into being, and were sustained and promoted throughout early modern culture, it is also possible to envisage this moment 'as the last period in history where ethnic identities could be understood as fluid' (203).

This sense of fluidity, imagined in terms of alterity or exchange, needs to be seen as a 'complex articulation between skin colour, religion, ethnicity and nationality' in which the term 'articulation' is used 'to describe not a simple coexistence but a relationship between different categories which transforms all of them' (Loomba 2000: 206). The articulation of alterity is perhaps most strikingly epitomised in the figure of the convert: the Moor, Turk or Jew who turns Christian, the inhabitant of a 'perpetually unstable condition' that, as well as graphically demonstrating that 'emergent modernity or cultural change are inextricable from ideas of race and nation', irresistibly evokes 'The romance and terror of self-fashioning' (209, 212). Gender is crucially at issue. Rather than exhibiting the 'fearful alterity' of the male convert (who is usually, sooner or later, both the agent and subject of violence), the recurrent figure of the 'fair maid of an alien faith and ethnicity romanced by a European, married to him, and converted to Christianity', operating within 'a vocabulary of romance and marriage instead of whoredom', signals the possibility of a 'controlled exchange' that offers a salutary, and potentially affirmative, alternative to what Daileader defines as the Othellophiliac narrative (212–13).

Further reading

Alexander, Catharine M. S. and Stanley Wells (eds) (2000) *Shakespeare and Race*. Cambridge: Cambridge University Press.

Bartels, Emily C. (2008) *Speaking of the Moor: From Alcazar to Othello*. Philadelphia, PA: Pennsylvania University Press.

Bristol, Michael D. (1996) *Big-time Shakespeare*. London and New York: Routledge.

Daileader, Celia (2005) *Racism, Misogyny, and the Othello Myth: Inter-racial Couples from Shakespeare to Spike Lee*. Cambridge: Cambridge University Press.

Hall, Kim F. (1995) *Things of Darkness: Economies of Race and Gender in Early Modern England*. Ithaca, NY: Cornell University Press.

Loomba, Ania (1989) *Gender, Race, Renaissance Drama*. Manchester: Manchester University Press.

Neill, Michael (1989) 'Unproper Beds: Race, Adultery, and the Hideous in *Othello*', *Shakespeare Quarterly*, 40: 382–412.

Pechter, Edward (1999) *Othello and Interpretive Traditions*. Iowa, IA: University of Iowa Press.

Vaughan, Virginia Mason (1994) *Othello: A Contextual History*. Cambridge: Cambridge University Press.

Timon of Athens

Date, text and authorship

c.1605; F 1623. Co-authored with Thomas Middleton.

Sources and influences

Plutarch, *Lives of the Noble Grecians and Romans* (trans. Thomas North, 1579); Lucian, *Timon Misanthropus*; *Timon* (performed at Inns of Court c.1602)

On stage

Old Vic, 1951 (dir. Tyrone Guthrie); RSC, 1965 (dir. John Schlesinger; Timon: Paul Scofield); Théâtre des Bouffes du Nord, Paris, 1974 (dir. Peter Brook); RSC, 1980 (dir. Ron Daniels; Timon: Richard Pasco); Red Shift, UK, 1989 (dir. Jonathan Holloway); Schauspielhaus, Bochum, 1990 (dir. Frank Patrick Steckel); Young Vic, 1991 (dir. Trevor Nunn; Timon: David Suchet); RSC, 1999 (dir. Gregory Doran; Timon: Michael Pennington); Cardboard Citizens, UK, 2006 (dir. Adrian Jackson).

On screen

BBC Television Shakespeare, UK, 1981 (dir. Jonathan Miller; Timon: Jonathan Pryce; Apemantus: Norman Rodway; Alcibiades: John Shrapnel; Painter: John Fortune; Poet: John Bird).

More than twenty years ago, in 1989, I went to see a production of *Timon of Athens* by the small-scale touring company Red Shift. This was, on paper, something to look forward to; it was a rare opportunity to see the play (the last professional production in Britain had been in 1980, by the RSC at the Other Place); and Red Shift had an appealingly original, innovative and occasionally iconoclastic way with classic texts, and I was expecting a reworking of Shakespeare, of a kind then in vogue, in the interrogative tradition of Brecht, Edward Bond, Charles Marowitz and, in the same year (in his *Seven Lears* at the Royal Court), Howard Barker. The fact that Timon was, for the first time on record on the professional English stage, to be played by a woman perhaps suggested a feminist perspective on a text in which misogyny is rampant and in which the only women, amazons and prostitutes, are derisively marginal; perhaps the production would speak directly to the arid, money-obsessed culture of the Britain of the 1980s. In the event, the performance I saw left me feeling indignant and not a little cheated: the piece was presented as a montage of mannered tableaux in which chunks of the play were ponderously interwoven with extracts from contemporary feminist writings about self-image and self-esteem; the cross-casting of the title role a device that enabled the production to make laboured connections between Timon's pathology and the symtomology of *anorexia nervosa*.

This was, admittedly, not the first time this link had been diagnosed: the BBC Television Shakespeare version of 1981 (directed by the medically trained Dr Jonathan Miller) had seen Jonathan Pryce as Timon with a conspicuously empty plate while his banquet guests gorged themselves; indeed, the protagonist's volte-face from self-abnegating accommodation to violent rage, and his inability to think in anything other than polarised extremes, could be seen to fit the classic anorexic pattern rather well. As an example of misprised directorial ingenuity Red Shift's *Timon* was nothing exceptional, especially in its own time, when the Shakespearean avant-garde found itself in dialogue with the earnest remnants of the alternative political theatre. But what fuelled my indignation on this occasion was the sense that the far more radical, and dangerous, option would have been not to adapt the play but to stage it as written; that the line of interpretation actually blunted the challenges of the play by seeking to rationalise a text that seemingly defies rationality, and that, rather than encouraging its readers to extract a tidy moral from its tragic action, leaves them disturbed and disoriented, both repelled by and implicated in its protagonist's searing misanthropy.

The lineaments of the play are clear enough, suggesting at one level the schematic dimensions of a fable or parable. The story of Timon was well known to Shakespeare's contemporaries: the narrative features in Plutarch's *Lives of the Noble Grecians and Romans*, as rendered in Thomas North's translation, and was the subject of an anonymously authored play acted at the Inns of Court around 1602, *Timon*; both of these served as sources for *Timon of Athens*. The play charts a clear path for its protagonist from an illusory prosperity and capacity for unrestrained largesse founded entirely on debt, to utter abjection and solitary death, via what he regards as his shameful betrayal by the ungrateful beneficiaries of his generosity. Timon begins the play showering hospitality, dispensing gifts and extending patronage to all and sundry; the instant he exhausts the equity in his relentlessly over-mortgaged assets and becomes no longer creditworthy, he is abandoned by his associates. Exiling himself from the community which becomes the target of his hatred, Timon literally and metaphorically strips himself of the ties that precariously bind him to it, relocating to a cave at the edge of the sea, adopting the lifestyle of a crazed ascetic and giving vent to an indiscriminate, universalising misanthropy that is expressed in some of the most vicious invective Shakespeare ever coined:

> Slaves and fools,
> Pluck the grave wrinkled senate from the bench
> And minister in their steads! To general filths
> Convert o'th' instant, green virginity!

(4.1.4–7)

> Spare not the babe
> Whose dimpled smiles from fools exhaust their mercy.
> Think it a bastard whom the oracle
> Hath doubtfully pronounced thy throat shall cut,
> And mince it sans remorse.

(4.3.118–22)

The play's parable-like trajectory is announced in the opening scene, in the course of a dialogue exchange between a Poet and a Painter (stock figures rather than realistic characters, they typify a play that works emblematically, trades in types and functions):

> When Fortune in her shift and change of mood
> Spurns down her late belovèd, all his dependents,
> Which laboured after him to the mountain's top
> Even on their knees and hands, let him fall down,
> Not one accompanying his declining foot.

(1.1.85–89)

Put like this (and this is exactly how the action proceeds), Timon's story is a stark moral tale of a reversal of fortune, a reminder of the perennial venality of humankind; to this extent the play's register is satirical, its dramatis personae a deftly sketched gallery of sycophants, time-servers and opportunists, its structure a matter of brutal oppositions (the lavish banquet and entertainment offered to Timon's guests in 1.2 versus the tureens of water and stones with which he assaults them in 3.7; the city of Athens versus the extra-mural wilderness) and cumulative ironies (the biblically resonant three scenes in which Timon's servants solicit from his creditors funds which are denied).

In some respects, then, *Timon* displays the single-mindedness and explicitness of alle-gory or fable, as well as the vicious directness of satire. As an all-out assault on greed and materialism, the play has appeared particularly timely to modern audiences, but it is rooted within the money culture of early seventeenth-century England, and more specifically in the precarious economy of patronage, gift exchange, reckless debt and conspicuous expen-diture that centred on the Stuart court. Athens is very much like Shakespeare's London; Timon a recognisably contemporary type. Yet for all its blunt power, the play's satirical intent, if that is what drives it, is not easy to identify. The message that it is at least unwise and probably suicidally misjudged to rely on the goodwill of those whose friendship has been bought is clear enough, but Timon himself remains an enigma from the beginning to the end (even the manner of his death is ambiguous). Is he, according to his own self-assessment, one who has handed away his wealth 'Unwisely, not ignobly' (2.2.169), and thus a sympathetic if not heroic figure? Or is he as much the target of criticism and satire as the venal figures who exploit and then abandon him?

Timon has obvious affinities with other late-period Shakespearean misanthropes: Lear and Coriolanus especially, both of whom embrace exile and the wilderness; but whereas Lear earns a self-recognition that moves him to atone for his past misdeeds and Coriolanus reneges upon his vow to wreak destruction on his home city, Timon simply perseveres in vitriolic obduracy to the bitter end, apparently conceding, or learning, nothing. Unlike every other great tragic hero, Timon has no kindred relationships of any sort (and the play as a whole is strikingly bereft of women, the only female parts being the amazons who grace Timon's first banquet and the prostitute camp followers who accompany Alcibiades); the closest he approaches to an affective relationship is with Flavius, the loyal steward. 'The middle of humanity thou never knewest', the cynic Apemantus tells him, 'but the extremity of both ends' (4.3.300–01); but the middle of humanity is exactly what the play itself seems so conspicuously to eschew.

Commentators and theatre practitioners in recent decades have been rather more ready to regard as virtues those aspects of the play that were once regarded as profound flaws: after Brecht and Beckett, both the scathing critique of early capitalism and the drama of the alienated outsider have fallen on more receptive ears, whilst the play's fragmented, inde-terminate and contradictory qualities have recommended it for rather than disqualified it from serious critical consideration. But doubts persist about whether the play adds up. For a long time this was due to what many commentators regarded as its most crucial failing: the near-certainty that the play is a product of collaboration, very probably with Thomas Middleton. Recognising significant variations in tone, style and perspective between scenes, editors have divided the play between the older writer and his younger colleague, with Shakespeare being generally ascribed authorship of the searing rhetoric of the second half and Middleton assigned the grounded satire of the first three acts. If for previous genera-tions collaboration spelt contamination, recent commentators have been willing to consider Middleton's contribution to the play's distinctiveness in a more positive light. Shakespeare and Middleton opted not to repeat the experiment of co-authorship (though Middleton acted as reviser of *Measure for Measure* and *Macbeth* during the 1620s), but *Timon* was a play neither could have written alone.

The play that has come down to us via the 1623 Folio (in which it was originally a late substitution for *Troilus and Cressida* when the latter hit publication difficulties) is clearly unfinished. Entitled *The Life of Timon of Athens* by the Folio's compilers, it is positioned alongside the tragedies, but the identification seems generically equivocal, as if Heminges and Condell were themselves not entirely sure where to place it. Like life, *Timon* is characterised by loose ends, and by situations which never achieve resolution. Construction is frequently wayward and inconsistent: seemingly important characters and narrative strands are introduced and then apparently forgotten, contrary to theatrical economy, dramatic logic and expectation. Alcibiades is an obvious example: appearing as from nowhere in 3.6 to plead the case before the Athenian Senate of a comrade who is condemned to death for a strangely unspecified misdemeanour, he returns in force in the fourth act determined to destroy the city, yet relents at the end, ominously promising to 'use the olive with my sword,/ Make war breed peace, make peace stint war' (5.5.87–88). Though he rails against the 'usury/ That makes the senate ugly' (3.6.97–98), Alcibiades's connection with Timon seems tenuous at best.

Yet even in its unfinished state *Timon* can prove in performance and in reading a more powerful and unsettling play than most heavy-handed attempts to improve upon or rationalise it. Awkward to categorise or interpret because it refuses to conform to what we expect either of a mature Shakespearean tragedy or of Middletonian satire, it presents a vision of an existence stripped to the bone that is probably far bleaker and more unyielding than most audiences are prepared to tolerate, and a form of dramatic experience that, refusing the middle of humanity, knows only the extremity of both ends.

Further reading

Burke, Kenneth (2007 [1963]) '*Timon of Athens* and Misanthropic Gold', in *Kenneth Burke on Shakespeare*, ed. Scott L. Newstock. West Lafayette, IN: Parlor Press, 101–12.

Empson, William (1951) 'Timon's Dog', in *The Structure of Complex Words*. London: Chatto and Windus, 175–84.

Jackson, Ken (2001) '"One Wish" or the Possibility of the Impossible: Derrida, the Gift and God in *Timon of Athens*', *Shakespeare Quarterly*, 52: 34–66.

Nuttall, A. D. (1989) *Timon of Athens*. Boston: Twayne.

King Lear

Date, text and authorship

c.1605; performed at court 26 December 1606; Q1 1608; Q2 1619; F 1623. Solely Shakespearean.

Sources and influences

The True Chronicle History of King Leir and His Three Daughters (early 1590s); *The Mirror for Magistrates* (1574); Raphael Holinshed, *Chronicles of England, Scotland and Ireland* (1577; second edition 1587); Sir Philip Sidney, *The Countess of Pembroke's Arcadia* (1590); Samuel Harsnett, *A Declaration of Egregious Popish Impostures* (1603); Michel de Montaigne, *Essays* (1580–88; trans. John Florio, 1603).

On stage

SMT, 1936 (dir. Theodore Komisarjevsky; Lear: Randle Ayrton); UK touring, 1937–51 (Lear: Donald Wolfit); SMT, 1950 (dir. John Gielgud and Anthony Quayle; Lear: John Gielgud); RSC, 1962 (dir. Peter Brook; Lear: Paul Scofield); RSC, 1976 (dir. Trevor Nunn; Lear: Donald Sinden); RSC, 1982, (dir. Adrian Noble; Lear: Michael Gambon; Fool: Antony Sher); RSC, 1990 (dir. Nicholas Hytner; Lear: John Wood); NT, 1990 (dir. Deborah Warner; Lear: Brian Cox); RSC, 1993 (dir. Adrian Noble; Lear: Robert Stephens); NT, 1997 (dir. Richard Eyre; Lear: Ian Holm); Young Vic, 1997 (Lear: Kathryn Hunter); RSC, 1999 (dir. Yukio Ninagawa; Lear: Nigel Hawthorne); RSC Academy, 2002 (dir. Declan Donnellan; Lear: Nonso Anozie); RSC, 2004 (dir. Bill Alexander; Lear: Corin Redgrave); RSC, 2007 (dir. Trevor Nunn; Lear: Ian McKellen); RSC, 2010 (dir. David Farr; Lear: Greg Hicks).

On screen

UK, 1970 (dir. Peter Brook; Lear: Paul Scofield); USSR, 1971 (dir. Grigori Kozintsev; Lear: Yuri Savit); BBC Television Shakespeare, UK, 1983 (dir. Jonathan Miller; Lear: Michael Horden); Granada TV, UK, 1984 (dir. Michael Elliott; Lear: Laurence Olivier); BBC TV, UK, 1998 (dir. Richard Eyre; screen version of 1997 NT production); UK, 2008 (dir. Trevor Nunn and Chris Hunt; video record of 2007 RSC stage production).

Offshoots

Broken Lance, USA, 1954 (dir. Edward Dymtryk); Edward Bond, *Lear*, Royal Court, 1970; Ronald Harwood, *The Dresser*, Royal Exchange, Manchester, 1980 (film version dir. Peter Yates, UK, 1983); *Ran (Chaos)*, France/Japan, 1985 (dir. Akira Kurosawa); Howard Barker, *Seven Lears*, Royal Court/The Wrestling School, 1989; *The King is Alive*, Denmark/Namibia, 2000 (dir. Kristian Levring); Marina Carr, *The Cordelia Dream*, RSC, 2008.

Ye gods

On 27 May 1606 Parliament passed a piece of legislation that would significantly impact upon what could be said on stage from then on: the 'Acte to Restraine Abuses of Players', which ordered that those involved in the making of plays and performances could no longer 'jestingly or prophanely speake or use the holy Name of God or of Christ Jesus, or of the Holy Ghoste or of the Trinitie, which are not to be spoken but with feare and reverence' (Chambers 1923, 4: 339). In general, its impact on the drama was that oaths were tempered and toned down: whereas before the ban speakers could use terms such as 'swounds' (God's or Christ's wounds) and invoke the name of the deity with relative freedom, plays written after 1606 are more circumspect and circumlocutory, so that even in a play dealing with the profane habits of low life such as *Measure for Measure* the dialogue is markedly less lurid, scurrilous and potentially blasphemous than Shakespeare's representation of a very similar milieu in the two parts of *Henry IV*.

If Shakespeare's overall response to the new restrictions was to practise tact, one other possible consequence was his turning to narratives and settings in a pre- or non-Christian context, as in the Roman plays. In *King Lear*, which was entered in the Stationers' Register on 26 November 1607 and recorded there as having been performed at court on St Stephen's night the previous year, Shakespeare appears to have entertained a more radical option, which was to take the opportunity afforded by the prohibition to transpose the oath-making and pious pledging that is woven into the fabric of everyday Jacobean speech into an alien, slightly fantastic register. Based on an old tragicomedy, the *History of King Leir*, which had been in the King's Men's possession since the 1590s, Shakespeare's *King Lear* appropriated a story which, despite the action's nominally pagan setting in pre-Christian Britain, is piously providential throughout, and inscribed within it a fully fledged alternative theology, creating a pantheistic universe characterised at best by indifference and at worst by sadistic cruelty.

No other play by Shakespeare has so many characters appealing so ardently, so often and so pointlessly, to their gods. The very first scene shows Lear cursing Cordelia in the name of Hecate, invoking Apollo as he turns on Kent and swearing by Jupiter (1.1.110, 159, 179), who is also called upon when he finds the disguised Kent in the stocks ('By Jupiter, I swear no!'), farcically prompting his messenger to comically respond with the name of the king of the gods' quarrelsome spouse: 'By Juno, I swear, aye!' (2.4.20–21). Having earlier in the play demanded that 'Nature … dear goddess' render Goneril sterile (1.4.252), Lear darkly assures her later in this scene that he will not yet 'bid the Thunder-bearer shoot' (2.4.222) but as the storm, in spite of these words, begins to unleash itself as the scene ends, it seems that Lear's favourite god either is responding to his plea or is a projection of his own violent rage. Crying to the 'heavens' for patience and presenting himself to the gods as 'a poor old man' (2.2.266–67), Lear finds himself cast out of doors and onto the heath, into a realm of the thunder god imaged as a place of cataclysmic disorder, a world of 'rain, wind, thunder, fire' in which 'Man's nature cannot carry/ The affliction nor the fear' (3.2.14, 46–47), a world, Lear hopes, in a punitive pagan reworking of the *Dies Irae*, in which terrible judgement will be visited upon the wicked and the corrupt as the 'great gods … Find out their enemies' – the perjurer, the adulterer, the hypocrite, the wretch that 'hast within … undivulgèd crimes,/ Unwhipped of justice' (3.2.47–51).

Lear's vengeful understanding of his gods consorts with his misogyny: in the depths of madness, he imagines women as divided at the waist between the divine and the bestial, between the virtuous and the chaste and the venereal and satanic: 'But to the girdle do the gods inherit./ Beneath is all the fiends'; there's hell, there's darkness,/ There's the sulphurous pit' (4.6.123–25). At key points in the play, the invocation of the gods seems deliberately contrived to flout the speakers' faith in their benevolence: insultingly plucked by the beard by Regan, Gloucester, a man who subscribes seriously to the efficacy of horoscopes, believes that 'it is the stars' that govern individual conditions, summons the 'kind gods' (3.7.35) and looks forward to the moment when he 'shall see/ The wingèd vengeance overtake such children' (3.7.66–67), an utterance which serves only to goad Cornwall to indulge in the grimmest of retributive ironies by pinioning him and blinding him; yet after this, Gloucester clings to the 'kind' gods that will forgive him for his abuse of Edgar (3.7.95).

In the next scene, as he begins to plan his suicide, Gloucester voices a considerably less benign view of the deities, stating simply that humans are to them 'As flies to wanton boys': immature sadists, 'They kill us for their sport' (4.1.37–38); by the end of the play, having been cheated even of mastery over the staging of his own exit, and tricked by his disguised son, via a fall from a non-existent cliff, into reawakening his former credulity by making himself believe that 'the clearest gods, who make them honors/ Of men's impossibilities' (4.6.73–74), have preserved his life, Gloucester is left merely with the fatalistic recognition that 'Men must endure/ Their going hence, even as their coming hither;/ Ripeness is all' (5.2.9–11). But this seems unutterably complacent when seen in the light of the play's terminal moments, initiated by Lear's final entrance:

> ALBANY The gods defend her! Bear him hence awhile.
>   EDMUND *is borne off.*
>   *Re-enter* LEAR, *with* CORDELIA *dead in his arms ...*
>
> (5.3.255–56)

It is one of the bleakest moments, certainly in Shakespeare's work and possibly in the whole of world drama: the reconciliation between the father rescued from madness and his most loved daughter, which Shakespeare's audiences would have expected from the source play to have provided the longed-for happy ending, utterly and arbitrarily destroyed, the futility and fatuousness of Albany's prayer on Cordelia's behalf cruelly exposed by the image of the father bearing his daughter's corpse.

Relentlessly undermining the beliefs of its older-generation characters in a benevolent pagan providence, the play also gives voice to a perspective that subjects their pantheistic world picture to a corrosive scepticism pretty indistinguishable from naked derision, most obviously in the viewpoint articulated, and the behaviour practised, by Edmund. As Gloucester's illegitimate would-be heir, Edmund is, in a calculatedly loaded term, his 'natural' son: proclaiming in his first soliloquy his allegiance to 'nature', as his 'goddess', and inviting the gods to 'stand up for bastards' (1.2.1–2, 22), he embodies a spirit of free-thinking, materialist enquiry that is at first invigoratingly independent of deference and cant. In the early stages, where Edmund engages his audience in an Iago- or Richard-like serio-comic connivance in villainy as he lampoons his father's superstitions and man-oeuvres his brother into performing the role of a gull, his exposé of the shallow, super-stitious determinism of his elders, the 'excellent foppery of the world', whereby 'we make guilty of our disasters the sun, the moon, and the stars' (1.2.109–12), represents the voice of reason.

Shakespeare's awareness of the philosophical work of Machiavelli and Montaigne is evi-dent here: As the play rapidly descends into violence and madness, it becomes evident that Edmund's utter disregard for the religious, familial and political ties and obligations that nominally prevent his – and Shakespeare's – society from tearing itself to pieces embodies a threat whose potency is measured in, amongst other things, the adulterous lust that it incites in his partners in degeneracy, the king's own daughters. Even in what might pass for normal times, the world of *Lear* is a tyrannous patriarchy, sustained by the violent exercise of power, in which, as the Fool's topsy-turvy account of the king shamefully subjecting himself to his daughters, 'when thou gavest them the rod, and put'st down thine own breeches' (1.4.150–51), reminds us, beating and whipping (of children by parents, of servants by their masters, of beggars and madmen, of whores and especially of Fools) are everyday occurrences.

Monsters of the deep

Edmund's goddess, nature, supposedly the base of the true and the good, is a scene of pitiless deprivation and cruelty, where 'The hedge-sparrow fed the cuckoo so long/ That it had it head bit off by it young … and we were left darkling' (1.4.190–92). Characters appeal as much to nature as to the gods for some kind of explanation or solace (the crazed Lear calls for Regan's dissection to find if there is 'any cause in nature' [3.6.71] to account for her hardness of heart) but nature offers little comfort and no reassuring answers; 'Allow not nature more than nature needs', Lear pleads in defence of his retention of his retinue of knights and 'Man's life's as cheap as beast's' (2.4.261–62); left to the state of nature without the intervention of human or divine law, Albany fears, humanity 'must perforce prey on itself,/ Like monsters of the deep' (4.2.50–51). As has often been noted, the play recurrently, even obsessively, configures human depravity in animalistic terms, cataloguing a bestiary that includes horses, goats, bears, serpents, lions, wolves, foxes, asses, apes, monkeys, boars, hogs, sheep, cats, frogs, toads, rats, tadpoles, worms, eels, snails and oysters, and fantastic and fabulous creatures such as dragons, centaurs and sea-monsters, and in which categories multiply within categories: not only birds but wagtails, owls, cuckoos, hedge-sparrows and wild geese; not only dogs but curs, mongrels, bitches, hounds, spaniels, mastiffs, greyhounds and ditch-dogs.

If the immediate effect is to proffer animal correlatives for human evil, the imagery also articulates the play's searching interrogation of what, if anything, separates the human from the beast; and of what, indeed, constitutes the human itself. Seeking sanctuary from the elements in a hovel, slipping into derangement and yet recognising for the first time the condition of the starved and homeless 'Poor naked wretches … That bide the pelting of this pitiless storm' (3.4.29–30), Lear comes face to face with humanity at its most abject, in the form of the mortified and self-mutilated flesh of Edgar as Poor Tom: rhetorically wondering whether man is 'no more than this?', Lear finds that this is 'the thing itself'; bereft of the flimsy accoutrements of his barely civilised world, 'unaccommodated man is no more but such a poor, bare, forked animal' (3.4.95–100). It is a harsh lesson, and one that the play at best only tentatively attempts to mitigate.

As the 'poorest shape/ That ever penury, in contempt of man,/ Brought near to beast' (2.3.7–9), Poor Tom, the Bedlam beggar, is a fiction, a role adopted by the fugitive Edgar to evade apprehension by his father's hunters; and yet so elaborate and detailed is the masquerade that for the scenes in which Edgar sustains the persona he seems to have a real and independent existence of his own. As Shakespeare's most graphic depiction of the extremities of Jacobean poverty and wretchedness, Poor Tom may have been a figure of compelling and perhaps disturbing immediacy for the play's first audiences; equally, however, the scope that he affords to incite horror and compassion may have been compounded with other elements. For many of Shakespeare's contemporaries, if not for Shakespeare himself, visiting the lunatics at Bedlam (that is, the Bethlehem Hospital in Bishopsgate) was an amusing diversion, a spectator sport; Edgar, who according to Edmund has the aspect of 'the catastrophe of the old comedy' (1.2.123), presents a persona that for some might have had its own comic potential.

One of Poor Tom's more impressive talents is his familiarity not only with the massed legions of the animal kingdom but with the parallel ranks of an elaborate compendium of devils and demons, the confederates of the 'foul fiend', Flibbertigibbet, Smulkin, Modo, Mahu and Frateretto. Poor Tom's demonic 'voices' are taken from what is generally regarded as one of Shakespeare's immediate sources, the pamphlet *A Declaration of Egregious Popish Impostures*, written by the Bishop of London's chaplain, Samuel Harsnett, and published in 1603; the tract is an exposé of bogus exorcism rituals conducted in secret by Catholic clergymen, whom Harsnett describes as being able 'so cunningly to act, & feigne the passions, and agonies of the deuil' (Muir 1957: 159). Edgar's account of the lengths to which he will go to immerse himself in character derive directly from Harsnett's narrative; and if Poor Tom's pedantic demonology is at one level a necessary subterfuge in order to sustain the veracity of his disguise, it might have also conferred upon him something of the (as the play shows it, bizarre and ludicrous) aura of a renegade Catholic missionary.

Every inch a king

Among those members of the audience at the play's first performance at Whitehall on St Stephen's night 1606, the one whose reaction presumably mattered most was the man occupying the most privileged seat in the great chamber. As a play dealing with the mythical prehistoric geopolitical entity of Britain, and which enacted the division of a kingdom (or, according to the quarto text, kingdoms) beneath the gaze of a monarch who hoped to effect its unification, the drama was clearly of potential interest to King James; he might have also noticed that the dukedoms of Regan and Goneril's husbands were those that had recently been created for two of his sons, Henry (1595–1612) and Charles (1600–49). Though some in the play's audience might have registered a connection in 1606 between the character who presides over the ending of the quarto text with the declaration that 'we that are young/ Shall never see so much, nor live so long' (5.3.324–25) and his six-year-old ducal namesake, few could have appreciated the historical irony whereby the real Duke of Albany, and from 1625 James's successor as king, would himself live only so long as to end his days on the executioner's block.

This moment of insurrection and regicide lay a quarter of a century in the future; but, for a tragedy presented as a Christmas entertainment before the monarch, *King Lear* entertains dramatic possibilities that daringly prefigure the political and intellectual revolution that eventually led, amongst other things, to the silencing of the King's Men themselves. We have already considered its critical engagement with materialist and pragmatist writings of Machiavelli and Montaigne, and its use of a pagan setting in order to conduct the thought-experiment of a non-providentialist universe; these philosophical and theological preoccupations are further linked to an exploration of civil unrest, political disorder, and of the interrogation of authority. In certain respects, particularly with regard to its gender politics, the play seems conventional to the point of being deeply conservative: the evil that Regan and Goneril represent is directly and luridly figured in terms of their identity as disorderly women, whose crimes involve a monstrous abrogation of patriarchal authority (in Goneril's case, of the husband as well as of the father); and Cordelia's restoration of her father's fortunes is a self-abnegating act of loyal daughterhood. However admirable it has appeared to subsequent generations of spectators, her refusal to play Lear's game in the opening scene may have seemed outrageous to the play's original audience.

Even though the traditional authority that trusts in the claims of custom, kinship and, ultimately, divine sanction is shown in the course of the play to be based on a set of fragile illusions, the action powerfully demonstrates the dire consequences of dividing, challenging or weakening it: the alternative to despotism is neither freedom nor democracy (a concept unthinkable in Jacobean England), but chaos. King James, the theorist of Absolutism, and increasingly autocratic antagonist of his English Parliament, would have agreed. Nonetheless, the play contains within it the recognition that the abuse of power is endemic in a system whose chain of command extends from the pettiest local official to the monarch himself: taking advantage of the privileges afforded by the Fool's lexicon of 'matter and impertinency mixed', or 'reason in madness' (4.6.168–69), Lear's insanity enables him to become the mouthpiece of a devastating social satire, wherein a farmer's dog barking at a beggar is held up as 'the great image of authority'; picturing the parish beadle preparing to scourge a prostitute even as he secretly 'lusts to use her in that kind' for which he whips her, and the successful moneylender persecuting the petty criminal, Lear acknowledges that there is one law for the rich and powerful, and another for the poor, weak and powerless: 'Plate sin with gold,/ And the strong lance of justice hurtless breaks;/ Arm it in rags, a pigmy's straw does pierce it' (4.6.150–61).

Given the time-honoured propensity of those in power to deflect, absorb or neutralise even the most direct and savage criticism, or simply not to recognise that it applies to them, James's Court may have heard these words with perfect equanimity, but the responses they might have elicited when spoken on the stage of the Globe may have been more mixed. The play's auspices may well have played a part in determining its scope for licensed social criticism: according to English and European tradition, the feast of St Stephen was the day that the parish poor boxes were broken open and their contents distributed (hence its subsequent renaming as Boxing Day), as well as a time for the rich and powerful to honour their charitable obligations to the needy, and for householders to show hospitality to the 'houseless heads' (3.4.31) of the destitute. When Lear urges pomp to 'take physic', to empathise with the poor and to 'shake the superflux to them,/ And show the heavens more just' (3.4.36–37), he is in line with what the Court would have understood to be the feast day's patrician spirit: he calls not for a programme of radical redistribution but for a corrective rebalancing of a system whose inequalities are assumed, in principle, to be just and divinely allocated. In folklore (as more recently commemorated in the Victorian carol 'Good King Wenceslas'), St Stephen's day was also known as the occasion of an encounter between the figure of a good king and a beggar which enables the former to exercise Christian generosity towards the latter; in Shakespeare's play, this narrative multiples into a meeting of kings, clowns, beggars and madmen.

Seen in this light, the performance of this play during the heart of one of the key Christian festivals suggests the complexity of its engagement with the religious culture of early modern England. While it is possible to interpret its conspicuous paganism as a reflection of Shakespeare's disbelief, there are also strong traces in the play of the basic Christian values of his time. In what seems an almost gratuitous aside, when she hears from Gloucester of his son's alleged treachery, Regan remembers that Edgar is Lear's godson (2.1.92); Lear's recognition of the plight of the 'poor naked wretches' is the moment where 'the pagan king for a moment grasps the nature of Christian *caritas*' (Shuger 1996: 53), and the whole speech exemplary of 'Protestant teaching about the value of adversity' (Foakes 1997: 273); the play is threaded through with echoes of the text of the Geneva Bible, culminating in Kent's anguished cry, as Lear bends over the body of Cordelia, that this is 'the promised end' (5.3.262), that is, Doomsday, the Apocalypse or Last Judgement, as figured in the Gospels of Matthew, Mark and Luke.

Whether these Christian traces are robust enough to survive for very long in the play's world may be open to doubt, but what matters is less the validity of Christian belief than the efficacy of the practices it is seen to instigate. Whether they are motivated by the imperatives of Christian charity or, more secularly, simple human decency, the play repeatedly ameliorates its scheme of desolation with representations of acts of kindness, fellow-feeling and selflessness: by Cordelia towards the father who has ordered her banishment and by Edgar towards the father who has been duped to seek his death, by Lear himself in the storm, whose discovery of 'houseless poverty' prompts him, after a lifetime of putting himself first, to invite his Fool to take shelter before him (3.4.27), and even by Edmund on the verge of death, whose unexpected confession that 'Some good I mean to do,/ Despite of mine own nature' (5.3.242–43), for all that it raises false hopes that will shortly be dashed, suggests a capacity for empathy in even the hardest of hearts (Goneril and Regan, however, are afforded no such last-moment redemption). If it is actions, rather than beliefs, that count for most in this world (which is actually a profoundly traditional Christian position), we might also remember that the injustice and pitiless cruelty of the *Lear* universe do not, of themselves, make it a godless one. The death of Cordelia is shockingly unfair, but anyone, Christian or not, who thinks that fairness, happiness or even survival is the message of the Gospels has not been reading them very attentively.

The terrors of the earth

In what is one of the play's most challenging incidents of this kind, the reassertion of basic, shared moral values takes the form of an act of striking insubordination. We have already considered the scene of the blinding of Gloucester in the context of its treatment of his apparently futile appeal to the 'kind' gods; here we may note that it is precisely when human physical cruelty is at its most extreme (and gratuitous, for Cornwall has already extracted from his victim the information he needs) that the possibility of radical action becomes not only a reality but an overriding moral imperative. Cornwall may by now have forfeited his right to any kind of authority, but the intervention of the unnamed servant who bids him to desist still creates a moment which, like Cordelia's 'nothing' in the first scene, may well have provoked gasps from its first witnesses: for a servant to 'stand up thus' (3.7.83) is not only an act of rebellion but a theatrical coup comparable to a piece of scenery coming to life to berate the actors.

The dangerous implications of the servant's challenge are rapidly contained as he swiftly pays the price of his action with his life, but it at least has the happy consequence of securing Cornwall's fatal exit; and it is followed by a further display of decency on the part of the servants who remain; while one declares that 'I'll never care what wickedness I do,/ If this man come to good' (103–04), the other promises to fetch 'flax and whites of eggs' (110), treatments for Gloucester's wounds, before turning him loose in company with the disguised Edgar. Cornwall and Regan may well continue to display boundless contempt towards their social inferiors (one of his last lines is an order to 'throw this slave/ Upon the dunghill' [100–01]), but they ignore their capacity for resistance at their peril. As the Russian film director Grigori Kosintsev brilliantly rendered it in his 1970 film of the play (a version haunted by the mass-scale crimes of Stalinism), the common people of the play are not only its true tragic protagonist but also their oppressors' nemesis.

In what came to be regarded as one of the legendary, as well as more controversial, productions of the play in the latter part of the twentieth century, Peter Brook's for the Royal Shakespeare Company in 1962, these ten lines of dialogue were cut (as was Edmund's parting attempt to 'do some good'); moreover, in keeping with the director's uncompromisingly bleak reading, the conclusion of the scene was rendered even more brutal both by the servants' callous indifference to Gloucester's plight and by the production's attempt to implicate the audience by suddenly bringing up the house lights for the interval while he was still blundering clumsily about the stage. As well as referencing the Epic theatre of Bertolt Brecht, Brook's production was strongly informed by an essay by the Polish theatre critic and director Jan Kott, which polemically links the action and existential vision of the play with the absurdist drama of Samuel Beckett and Eugène Ionesco, arguing that *King Lear* was, 'above all others, the Shakespearean play of our time' (1965: 162). Kott's reading, which forms one of the showcase arguments of his hugely influential – and much criticised – *Shakespeare Our Contemporary* was the culmination of a modernist postwar twentieth-century critical tradition that, acting in the shadow of Auschwitz and the Gulags, after Hiroshima and under the spell of the Cold War, understood itself to be uniquely privileged in its understanding of the play's horrors.

Regarded for much of the nineteenth century as unperformable, the play had been adapted by Nahum Tate in 1681 to incorporate a happy ending, a love interest between Edgar and Cordelia, Cordelia rescued and Lear restored to the throne; with Shakespeare's text itself restored at the beginning of the twentieth century, it increasingly came to be seen as a play dealing not with mythological ancient history but with the most urgent dilemmas and conflicts of modernity, in the process eclipsing the play that had held sway in cultural consciousness during the nineteenth, *Hamlet* (Foakes 1993). We cannot even begin here to do justice to the vast and multiform critical, theatrical and cinematic legacy that the play has generated, which has included performances in the title role by Garrick, Irving, Benson, Wolfit, Gielgud, Scofield, Olivier, Gambon, Cox and McKellen; and adaptations and creative responses from film-makers, novelists and dramatists and other creative artists that range from what must be one of the slightest and most tenuous Shakespearean allusions in the whole of popular music, Stephen Patrick Morrissey's two-minute pop song 'King Leer' (1990) to Aribert Reimann's opera *Lear* (1978), and from the 1954 Western *Broken Lance* to Howard Barker's *Seven Lears* (1989), an imaginative explanation of why Lear's wife is almost never, 'even in the depths of rage and pity', mentioned. Equally, I can only allude to the considerable body of the literature that these, and the play, have generated, and to refer the reader to these (see, for example, Elton 1966; Mack 1966; and Rosenberg 1971).

The division of the kingdom(s)

One aspect of the play's critical and performance history that does demand some brief attention here, however, is the fact that, in common with a number of Shakespeare's plays, it exists in two distinct versions: the quarto of 1608, and the Folio of 1623. Respectively entitled the *True Chronicle Historie of the life and death of King Lear and his three daughters* and *The Tragedie of King Lear*, these contain many differences, both major and minor, and with respect both to individual lines and passages and to entire scenes: among them the omission of the mock trial scene (3.6) and of the reports of the French invasion (3.1.) from the Folio, the later text's substantial revisions to the role of the Fool, and a host of verbal changes, cuts and additions, and reattributed speeches, including the shifting of the play's final lines from Albany in the quarto to the Folio's Edgar. For much of the play's afterlife, the texts have been treated by editors as variants, drafts or versions of the play from different stages in its theatrical or literary life which can legitimately be combined to produce a conflated text; this is the path taken by many important modern editions of the play, including the first, second and third series Arden, the New Cambridge; the Norton, in addition to printing the quarto and Folio versions, includes the conflated text which is the source of citations in the current volume.

In the early 1980s, however, a school of editorial thought emerged that challenged the long-standing practice of conflation, arguing that it resulted in the production of a hybrid, conjectural text that misleadingly conjoined distinct versions of a play that Shakespeare deliberately and sometimes drastically revised in the period between its first performance and whatever moment he abandoned work on the text, or texts, that his colleagues saw fit to publish in the Folio (Taylor and Warren 1983). One effect of the revisions, it has been argued, was to produce a more theatrically concise play; another was to make what was already a challengingly bleak experience even harsher. Thus, for example, the servants who offer assistance to Gloucester at the end of 3.7 in the quarto are absent from the Folio, an omission which, while it may be due to considerations of actor economy, removes what we have seen to be one of the play's potentially ameliorative moments (in this respect, Brook's cut in the 1962 production and 1970 film version at least had a textual mandate).

The idea that editors and readers should respect the discrete identities of quarto and Folio versions of the play (a line of thinking which has extended to the editorial treatment of *Hamlet*) was practically realised in the 1988 Oxford edition of the play, which included separately edited versions of both; the Norton edition, for which this provides the master-text, includes these on facing pages but also a conflated version. This is the version from which I quote, in part for the practical reason that any attempt to even begin to deal adequately with the differences between the two texts would have resulted in a doubling in length of this section (or even two versions of it …), but also, more importantly, in deference to the Norton editors' desire to offer their readers the opportunity to 'encounter the tragedy in the form that it assumed in most editions from the eighteenth century until very recently' (Greenblatt *et al.* 1997: 2315).

This, it seems to me, is an important point whose significance should not be under-estimated: even if the conflated *King Lear* is an editorial fabrication of doubtful legitimacy, it is one with a very real cultural and theatrical history, weight and presence; and if one of our challenges as readers, critics and theatregoers is to continue the conversation between ourselves and the past, present and future generations of those who have also, in Keats's words, found themselves compelled to 'burn through' this 'fierce dispute/ Betwixt damnation and impassioned clay', then the bastard offspring of editorial tradition must be not only acknowledged but warmly embraced. One recent editor, R. A. Foakes for the Arden third series, finds a creative way of combining the singularity of the individual texts with the plurality of conflation by clearly signalling the provenance of quarto- or Folio-only passages in the text, with the aim of offering 'an edition that seeks to give an idea of the work, while making the major differences between the versions easily recognizable', thus making it 'the decision of readers, actors and directors whether to prefer Q to F, F to Q, or to take readings from both' (Foakes 1997: 119). In the era of online editions and hypertext, these possibilities can only multiply.

Further reading

Elton, W. R. (1966) *King Lear and the Gods*. San Marino, CA: Huntington Library.

Foakes, R. A. (1993) *Hamlet versus Lear: Cultural Politics and Shakespeare's Art*. Cambridge: Cambridge University Press.

Greenblatt, Stephen J. (1988) 'Shakespeare and the Exorcists', in *Shakespearean Negotiations*. Berkeley, CA: University of California Press, 94–128.

Kozintsev, Grigori (1973) *King Lear: The Space of Tragedy*. Berkeley and Los Angeles, CA: University of California Press.

Kronenfeld, Judy (1998) *King Lear and the Naked Truth: Rethinking the Language of Religion and Resistance*. Durham, NC and London: Duke University Press.

Mack, Maynard (1966) *King Lear in Our Time*. Berkeley, CA: University of California Press.

Taylor, Gary and Michael Warren (eds) (1983) *The Division of the Kingdoms: Shakespeare's Two Versions of King Lear*. Oxford: Clarendon Press.

Macbeth

Date, text and authorship

c.1606; performed at the Globe April 1611; F 1623. Shakespeare's text adapted in early 1620s by Thomas Middleton.

Sources and influences

Raphael Holinshed, *Chronicles of England, Scotland and Ireland* (1587); George Buchanan, *Rerum Scoticarum Historia* (1583); Matthew Gwinne, *Tres Sibyllae* (1605).

On stage

Court Theatre, London, 1928 (dir. Barry Jackson); WPA Negro Theatre Project, New York, 1936 (dir. Orson Welles; Macbeth: Jack Carter); Piccadilly, 1942 (Macbeth: John Gielgud: Lady: Gwen Ffrangcon-Davies); SMT, 1955 (dir. Glen Byam Shaw; Macbeth: Laurence Olivier; Lady: Vivien Leigh); RSC, 1962 (dir. Donald McWhinnie; Macbeth: Eric Porter; Lady: Irene Worth); Royal Court, 1966 (dir. William Gaskill; Macbeth: Alec Guinness; Lady: Simone Signoret); RSC, 1967 (dir. Peter Hall; Macbeth: Paul Scofield: Lady: Vivien Merchant); RSC, 1976 (dir. Trevor Nunn; Macbeth: Ian McKellen; Lady: Judi Dench); Ninagawa Company, Tokyo, 1985 (dir. Yukio Ninagawa); RSC, 1986 (dir. Adrian Noble; Macbeth: Jonathan Pryce; Lady: Sinead Cusack); RSC, 1996 (dir. Tim Albery; Macbeth: Roger Allam; Lady: Brid Brennan); RSC, 1999 (dir. Gregory Doran; Macbeth: Antony Sher; Lady: Harriet Walter); Out of Joint, 2004 (dir. Max Stafford-Clark); Shakespeare's Globe, 2010 (dir. Lucy Bailey; Macbeth: Elliot Cowan; Lady: Laura Rogers).

On screen

USA, 1948 (dir. Orson Welles; Macbeth: Orson Welles; Lady: Jeanette Nolan); USA, 1971 (dir. Roman Polanski; Macbeth: Jon Finch; Lady: Francesca Annis); Thames TV, UK, 1978 (dir. Mike Hall; Macbeth: Ian McKellen; Lady: Judi Dench): BBC Television Shakespeare, UK, 1985 (dir. Jack Gold; Macbeth: Nicol Williamson; Lady: Jane Lapotaire); RSC, 2001 (dir. Gregory Doran; screen version of 1999 RSC production); Australia, 2007 (dir. Geoffrey Wright).

Offshoots

Joe Macbeth, UK, 1955 (dir. Ken Hughes); *Kumonosu-jô* (*Castle of the Spider's Web*, a.k.a. *Throne of Blood*), Japan, 1957 (dir. Akira Kurosawa); Welcome Msomi, *uMabatha; The Zulu Macbeth*, Natal, 1972; Tom Stoppard, *Cahoot's Macbeth*, 1979; *Ran* (*Chaos*), France/Japan, 1985 (dir. Akira Kurosawa); *Men of Respect*, USA, 1991 (dir. William Reilly); *Shakespeare: The Animated Tales: Macbeth*, UK/Russia, 1992 (dir. Nikolai Serebirakov); *Macbeth on the Estate,* BBCTV, UK, 1997 (dir. Penny Woolcock); *Scotland, PA*, USA, 2002 (dir. Billy Morrissette); *Shakespeare Retold: Macbeth*, BBC TV, UK, 2005 (adapt. Peter Moffat); David Greig, *Dunsinane*, RSC, 2010.

If *King Lear* is a work in which the proliferation of narratives, character trajectories and textual variants seems to embody the centrifugal energies of a society, a world and perhaps a universe in turmoil, *Macbeth* is characterised by contrast by its singularity, intensity and depth of focus. One of the few plays in the canon to be regularly performed in the theatre interval free, it is, at just over two thousand lines, half as long as *Hamlet* and two-thirds of the length of *King Lear* and *Othello*. In terms of narrative, it is clear, concise and single minded. Drawing highly selectively upon Holinshed's account of the eleventh-century Scottish ruler in order to compress the events of a reign that in historical fact lasted seventeen years into the space of what seems like months, Shakespeare reworks his source as a study of assassination and recrimination, and the regicide's rapid decline and removal. Written in the aftermath of the 1605 Gunpowder Plot, witnessed by Simon Forman at the Globe in 1611 and revised by Thomas Middleton some five years later, the play has been seen as an extended compliment by the monarch's own company to the Scottish King whose ancestors it references, and one of whose interests – witchcraft – it closely engages; yet the power of the play far exceeds its efficacy as an act of highly localised sycophancy.

Its grip is relentless. It opens with a crash of thunder and lightning flash, and the driving, drumbeat pulse of the witches' incantations, from which erupt the first of the play's multiple prophesies, oxymoronic pairings ('When the battle's lost and won' [1.1.4]), inversions ('Fair is foul, and foul is fair' [10]), and triangulations ('we three'; thunder, lightning and rain [1–2]); in swift succession there follows an entrance that, in the shape of a possibly mortally wounded soldier, stages in human form the imagery of blood that runs insistently throughout the play. It ends with the agent of the usurper's usurper bearing onstage the protagonist's severed head, a double blast of trumpets, and Scotland's new ruler sententiously proclaiming the defeat of 'this dead butcher and his fiend-like queen' and inviting, or rather ordering, his battle-hardened colleagues, 'each and every one', 'to see us crowned at Scone' (5.11.35, 40–41). In the interim the action is powered by atrocities narrated, imagined and enacted, in an imaginative universe where there is no middle ground but only the starkest and most violent, and most perverse, of antitheses and oppositions, a world plunged into darkness and lit by fire, in which loyalty and treachery are soaked equally in blood, in which dream, visions and apparitions are as real as reality itself, and in which both the performance and the consequences of violence are rendered with hallucinatory vividness.

It is also a work that takes its readers and spectators deep into the consciousness of a killer, exploring by means of a series of agonisingly self-searching soliloquies the protagonist's laceratingly vivid awareness of the consequences of his actions, as well as the motives of ambition, the limits of responsibility and the nature of guilt. Both brutal pragmatist and soaring metaphysician, Macbeth begins the play as Scotland's chief agent of state violence: faced with the rebel Macdonald, he is reported (in an exquisite braiding of the play's imageries of tailoring and butchery) as having efficiently 'unseamed him from the nave to th'chops' (1.2.22). He ends in isolation and defeat, voicing the desolate nihilism of a man whose life has been emptied of meaning:

> It is a tale
> Told by an idiot, full of sound and fury,
> Signifying nothing.

> (5.5.25–27)

Echoing the phrasing of Psalm 90, as used in the early modern burial service (which speaks of how the faithful 'bring our years to an end, as it were a tale to be told'), Macbeth's perversion of the liturgy serves to mark him as a soul in despair. Yet at the end, the victory of his opponents seems little more than the outcome of metaphysical trickery; having been assured that 'none of woman born/ Shall harm Macbeth', and that he would never taste defeat 'until/ Great Birnam Wood to high Dunsinane Hill/ Shall come against him'

(4.1.96–97, 108–09), it turns out that his nemesis is accomplished by phenomena as materially mundane as greenery deployed as camouflage and a combatant, in the form of Macduff, who happened to have been delivered by Caesarean section.

Here the victim of a bad cosmic practical joke, Macbeth is still a figure who, in his own imagination at least, operates on a titanic scale, and sees his own actions under the auspices of eternity, nowhere more so than when he anticipates the reverberations of his intended murder of Duncan:

> Besides, this Duncan
> Hath borne his faculties so meek, hath been
> So clear in his great office, that his virtues
> Will plead like angels, trumpet-tongued against
> The deep damnation of his taking-off,
> And pity, like a naked new-born babe,
> Striding the blast, or heaven's cherubin, horsed
> Upon the sightless couriers of the air,
> Shall blow the horrid deed in every eye
> That tears shall drown the wind.
>
> (1.7.16–25)

It is hardly surprising that this soliloquy, the most linguistically densely packed passage in the entire play, has been much discussed and scrutinised, for how one interprets it – and in particular how one interprets its metaphysics – is usually central to any reading of the play. As was emphasised by the critical tradition that considered it to be 'a discovery or anatomy of evil' (Hunter 1967: 7), or 'the greatest of morality plays ... the sublime story of a human soul on the way to damnation' (Muir 1971: lxv), the speech illuminates what in the play (if not in the worldview of the critic) may be taken as a secure moral and theological framework and context for Macbeth's actions. Duncan's kingship is, as Macbeth freely concedes, not only legitimate but also, the Christian iconography suggests, divinely sanctioned; so that the act of regicide is a blow struck against a political community bound by ties of kinship, against nature and against the divine order itself.

No one is more aware than Macbeth that to proceed 'further in this business' (1.7.31) is to irrevocably acquiesce in his own damnation, in this world and in the next; and, indeed, it appears that his prediction that the irresistible force of pity (imaged as the infancy that the Macbeths are determined to eradicate) will prevail is borne out by subsequent events, in which Macbeth's downfall is effected by a combination of the self-defeating escalating destructiveness of his own deeds and the forces of God and Nature mobilising themselves against tyranny and criminality. Read in this way, the moral of *Macbeth* is as clear cut as it is politically conservative: to regard its protagonist's crimes as a violation of natural and metaphysical order is to accept his enemy's valuation of him, and them. Perhaps this is how the play wishes us to react; but for critics of a more historicist and rationalist inclination, the forces of divine retribution that Macbeth envisages as witnesses of his 'horrid deed' are phantasms whose imagined operations are those of the ideology of a Jacobean absolutism that, depending upon how one takes it, Shakespeare's play either uncritically endorses or subversively undermines. From this perspective, what is offered in this speech is not the supernatural apparatus within which Macbeth should be judged, but a demonstration, or exposure, of the extent to which he has internalised the state's most powerful mechanism of self-regulation.

As the pioneering New Critic Cleanth Brooks observed in 1947 (Brooks's work is commented upon elsewhere in this volume; see 'Criticism', p. 347), the passage has also attracted a great deal of notice because of the counter-intuitive peculiarity of its signature image, the 'naked new-born babe' that presides over its closing movement. Observing that the equation of pity with a neonate is 'odd, to say the least' (Brooks 2004: 33), Brooks proceeds to resolve the conundrum of its oddness by elaborating the intricate interconnections between images of childhood and vulnerability, manliness, masking and concealment, blood, daggers and clothing that, he argues, both afford the play its poetic richness and coherence and define its moral and metaphysical landscape. As a brilliant, exemplary demonstration of close reading, Brooks's essay is one of the landmarks of a tradition of critical practice that has been particularly attentive to this play (and which is represented, in different ways, by the work of G. Wilson Knight, L. C. Knights and William Empson); it is also one which is dependent upon an understanding of the play-poem as a spatial rather than temporal experience, whose components are understood to exist in a condition of simultaneity rather than theatrical sequence.

In this respect, Brooks's mode of reading is not dissimilar to that of some of the post-structuralist interpretations of the play, which have paid equally close attention to the play's language whilst developing in radically different directions Brooks's sense of the oxymoronic and contradictory qualities of its discourse. For Malcolm Evans, who takes Macbeth's designation of the Witches as 'imperfect speakers' (1.3.68) as his keynote, the divisions, flaws and relentlessly multiplying semantic possibilities of and within the play's languages generate a conflict between the speech which attempts 'unequivocal identification of the ideology of divine right with nature' and that which 'is evident ... wherever "imperfect speaking" cuts into the first mode and restores to it a discordant element of linguistic materiality and heterogeneity' (Evans 1986: 120). Apply Brooks's and Evans's perceptions to the 'If it were done ... ' monologue and we hear a speaker who is, at least, double-tongued: at once helpless and Herculean, an image of raw human vulnerability and invincible spiritual power, the baby is equivocated in and out of discourse, and of existence, as Macbeth grapples with the intractable evasions, deferrals and contradictions, both of his dilemma in the here/but here-and-now, and of the play's metaphysics.

The milk of human kindness

Macbeth's babe is a sibling of a kind to the other significant infant that is mentioned later in the same scene: the child whom Lady Macbeth deploys as an example in the course of her assertion of her murderous determination:

> I have given suck, and know
> How tender 'tis to love the babe that milks me.
> I would, while it was smiling in my face,
> Have plucked my nipple from his boneless gums
> And dashed the brains out, had I so sworn
> As you have done to this.

(1.7.54–58)

The passage has notoriously provoked speculation about the Macbeths' back story (and has been mined by actors for motivation and clues to their relationship); what concerns us here, however, is its significance as a marker of the gender values of a play in which interpenetrations of masculinity, power, violence and sexuality are insistent. In the context of a world in which to be a man is to be a killer, in which extreme violence is deemed perfectly acceptable as long as it is sanctioned by the state, and in which advancement and advantage routinely secured the violation of one's own and others' bodily and moral integrity, 'it is hard to see why ... bloodthirsty talk of dashing out babies' brains is any more "unnatural" than skewering an enemy soldier's guts' (Eagleton 1986: 6).

Nonetheless, perhaps for the author of this scene, and certainly for many of its commentators, the Lady's subjunctive commitment to infanticide epitomises the unnaturalness of a character who on her first appearance calls upon the spirit world to 'unsex' her (1.5.39) in order to ready her for murder, and who, as a steely secularist who scornfully dismisses 'the eye of childhood/ That fears a painted devil' (2.2.52–53), successfully overrides the scruples of her conscience-stricken spouse to complete the act of slaughter in Duncan's bedchamber. Such behaviour is 'unnatural' because, according to the patriarchal script that the play in some respects appears to follow, it is unwomanly: traditionally associated with the production, preservation and nurturing of life rather than its destruction, women are simply not meant to murder (least of all to murder men who resemble their fathers).

To say that *Macbeth* is schematic in its representation of women is to put it mildly: on the one side, there is Lady Macduff, appearing in one scene only as an exemplar of good motherhood; on the other, Macbeth's Lady and the witches, opponents all of patriarchal order and authority, and all associated with the demonic and with uncontrolled, deviant sexuality. Just as the power of the witches resides in part in their morbid eroticism ('I'll drain him dry as hay', threatens the First Witch; 'Sleep shall neither night nor day/ Hang upon his penthouse lid' [1.3.17–19]), so too does the Lady's dominion over her husband stem from her capacity for sexual manipulation ('Art thou afeard/ To be the same in thine own act and valour/ As thou art in desire?' [1.7.39–41]). When it comes, the Lady's disintegration is, according to the play's system of poetic justice, correspondingly as total as is her previous command of herself, her husband and the scenes of murder and banqueting that she orchestrates with such finesse. The Lady ends the play trapped forever within a perpetual loop of guilt-induced hallucination, fixated reminiscence and the ritual expiation that, in literature's first and perhaps greatest depiction of the psychopathology of obsessive-compulsive disorder, inevitably manifests itself in the desperate housewife's choice of endless washing, endless cleaning and endless washing again.

Despite the best efforts of, on the one hand, those who would seek to return the play to the narrow envelope of early Jacobean royalist politics and, on the other, those who would detach it from the materiality of performance and history altogether, *Macbeth* has maintained a continuous presence in the theatre from the Restoration onwards, as a work that is recognised not only to speak with some urgency and immediacy to current considerations of power and political violence, but also, because it has the appearance of a universal fable, to provide a means of framing these concerns within the larger picture of what we understand of Shakespeare's cultural afterlife. The *Macbeth* of the modern stage, however, presents challenges that, amidst Shakespeare's tragic oeuvre, are possibly unique to this play. Not the least of these is its pervasive and insistent supernaturalism: for performers and audiences with no belief in ghosts, gods or witches, or in the agency of the abstractions labelled as good and evil, making the play happen is a process increasingly dependent upon systematic and ingenious transcoding, whereby what the Shakespearean text appears to stipulate is reworked to conform with the predominantly secular and realist strictures of late modern theatre practice. Banquo's ghost is an obvious case in point. The Folio is unambiguously specific about its appearance:

Enter the Ghost of Banquo, and sits in Macbeth's place.

(3.4.36.s.d.)

Enter Ghost.

(3.4.87.s.d)

In most modern productions, Banquo's ghost does not appear; in a move textually corroborated by both the Lady's and the attendant lords' failure to register the spectre seen by Macbeth alone, the incident is psychologised as projection or hallucination, so that the ghost is afforded an ontological status equivalent to that of the 'dagger of the mind' glimpsed by Macbeth at 2.1.33–47. The implication, at least for the duration of this scene, is that Macbeth is mentally unbalanced, and isolated within his guilt not only from his onstage companions but from the audiences who previously had been invited, and privileged, to share his point of view.

Contemporary practitioners' caution over the use of stage ghosts, bearing in mind the potential *Scooby-Doo* risibility of the convention, is entirely understandable; the problem it illuminates is that as soon as one begins to edit out those aspects of the received text that are perceived as awkward, embarrassing or difficult, it becomes increasingly difficult to know where to draw the line. If the Ghost of Banquo is a challenge, the witches present an even bigger headache: although most modern productions humanise them (often by presenting them as derelicts, social marginals or outcasts), the text makes it clear that, regardless of whether they exert any sway over Macbeth, they are at the very least gifted with powers of prophecy that, for example, allow them to reveal to him the parade of apparitions that traces the line of descent to James I. This can be, and has been, rationalised as more hallucination (as in the 1977 RSC production directed by Trevor Nunn, which made the apparitions the cast of Macbeth's bad trip, brought on by the brew the witches gave him to drink), but to do so is to defer rather than resolve the problems of credibility that this sequence, and these personae, generate. If we no longer believe in ghosts and witches, prophesies and the divine right of kings, components which are not incidental but profoundly integral to the play, why do or should we persist in believing in *Macbeth*? The theatre will doubtless continue to provide its answers.

Further reading

Bradley, A. C. (2007 [1904]) *Shakespearean Tragedy*. Fourth edition. Basingstoke: Palgrave.

Brooks, Cleanth (2004 [1947]) 'The Naked Babe and the Cloak of Manliness', in *Shakespeare: An Anthology of Criticism and Theory 1945–2000*, ed. Russ McDonald. Oxford: Blackwell, 19–34.

Brown, John Russell (ed.) (1982) *Focus on Macbeth*. London: Routledge and Kegan Paul.

Eagleton, Terry (1986) *William Shakespeare*. Oxford: Blackwell.

Kinney, Arthur F. (2001) *Lies Like Truth: Macbeth and the Cultural Moment*. Detroit, MI: Wayne State University Press.

Maley, Willy and Andrew Murphy (eds) (2004) *Shakespeare and Scotland*. Manchester: Manchester University Press.

Mullaney, Steven (1988) 'Lying Like Truth: Riddle, Representation, and Treason', in *The Place of the Stage: License, Play, and Power in Renaissance England*. Chiacgo, IL: University of Chicago Press, 116–34.

Coriolanus *and* Antony and Cleopatra

Coriolanus

Date, text and authorship

c.1609; F 1623. Solely Shakespearean.

Sources and influences

Plutarch, *Lives of the Most Noble Grecians and Romans* (trans. Thomas North, 1579).

On stage

Old Vic, 1938 (Coriolanus: Laurence Olivier); Old Vic, 1954 (Coriolanus: Richard Burton); Teatro Piccolo, Milan, 1956 (dir. Giorgio Strehler); SMT, 1959 (dir. Peter Hall; Coriolanus: Laurence Olivier); Berliner Ensemble, Berlin, 1963 (dir. Manfred Wekworth; Coriolanus: Ekkehard Schall; Volumnia: Helene Weigel); RSC, 1977 (dir. Terry Hands; Coriolanus: Alan Howard); *Coriolan et le monstre aux mille têtes*, Théâtre Repère, Québec, 1983 (dir. Robert Lepage); NT, 1984 (dir. Peter Hall; Coriolanus: Ian McKellen); Kick Theatre Company, UK, 1986 (dir. Deborah Warner); Chichester Festival Theatre, 1992 (dir. Tim Supple; Coriolanus: Kenneth Branagh; Volumnia: Judi Dench); RSC, 1994 (dir. David Thacker; Coriolanus: Toby Stephens); Almeida, London, 2000 (dir. Jonathan Kent; Coriolanus: Ralph Fiennes); Tobacco Factory, Bristol, 2001 (dir. Andrew Milton); RSC, 2007 (dir. Gregory Doran; Coriolanus: William Houston).

On screen

The Spread of the Eagle, BBC TV, UK, 1963 (dir. Peter Dews; Coriolanus: Robert Hardy); BBC Television Shakespeare, UK, 1984 (dir. Elijah Moshinsky; Coriolanus: Alan Howard; Aufidius: Mike Gwilym; Volumnia: Irene Worth).

Offshoots

Günter Grass, *Die Plebejer proben den Aufstand* (*The Plebeians Rehearse the Uprising*), Berlin, 1966.

Antony and Cleopatra

Date, text and authorship

c.1606; entered SR 20 May 1608; F 1623. Solely Shakespearean.

Sources and influences

Plutarch, *Lives of the Most Noble Grecians and Romans* (trans. Thomas North, 1579); Samuel Daniel, *Cleopatra* (1594).

On stage

St James's, London, 1951 (dir. Michael Benthall; Antony: Laurence Olivier; Cleopatra: Vivien Leigh); SMT, 1953 (dir. Glen Byam Shaw; Antony: Michael Redgrave; Cleopatra: Peggy Ashcroft); RSC, 1972 (dir. Trevor Nunn; Antony: Richard Johnson; Cleopatra: Janet Suzman); RSC, 1978 (dir. Peter Brook; Antony: Alan Howard; Cleopatra: Glenda Jackson); RSC, 1982 (dir. Adrian Noble; Antony: Michael Gambon; Cleopatra: Helen Mirren); NT, 1987 (dir. Peter Hall; Antony: Anthony Hopkins; Cleopatra: Judi Dench); Talawa, UK, 1991 (dir. Yvonne Brewster; Antony:

Jeffery Kissoon; Cleopatra: Dona Croll); NT, 1998 (dir. Sean Mathias; Antony: Alan Rickman; Cleopatra: Helen Mirren); Shakespeare's Globe, 1999 (dir. Giles Block; Antony: Paul Shelley; Cleopatra: Mark Rylance); RSC, 2006 (dir. Greg Doran; Antony: Patrick Stewart; Cleopatra: Harriet Walter); RSC, 2010 (dir. Michael Boyd; Antony: Darrell D'Silva; Cleopatra: Kathryn Hunter).

On screen

The Spread of the Eagle, BBC TV, UK, 1963 (dir. Peter Dews; Antony: Keith Mitchell; Cleopatra: Mary Morris); Spain/Switzerland, 1972 (dir. Charlton Heston; Antony; Charlton Heston; Cleopatra: Hildegarde Neil); ATV, UK, 1974 (dir. Jon Scoffield; Antony: Richard Johnson; Cleopatra: Janet Suzman); BBC Television Shakespeare, UK, 1981 (dir. Jonathan Miller; Antony: Colin Blakely; Cleopatra: Jane Lapotaire).

Offshoots

Carry on Cleo, UK, 1964 (dir. Gerald Thomas; Antony: Sid James; Cleopatra: Amanda Barrie).

O me alone

The Tragedy of Coriolanus is a play in which public political events are central. Probably written around the time of the start of the King's Men's residency of the Blackfriars playhouse in 1608, alluding directly to recent upheavals in the English Midlands (see 'Life and contexts', pp. 64–5) and dramatising the legend of the fifth-century BC Roman military hero whose anti-democratic instincts ultimately drove him into the arms of its enemies, leading to a doomed attempt to conquer his own home city, only two of the play's twenty-nine scenes are identifiably located in relatively private, rather than public, space: its action takes place in the Roman forum and capitol, on battlefields and in the streets. Like Shakespeare's other Roman dramas, it has reference points in both ancient history and its present: Rome's class system combines plebeians, citizens, patricians and English-style 'gentry' (3.1.0.s.d.; the Folio speech-headings and stage directions vary between Roman and English designations), and its partly toga-clad inhabitants sport beards and observe the etiquette of early modern hat-wearing.

It opens with the threat of insurrection, with starving, armed and mutinous Roman plebeians taking to the streets to protest against the hoarding of corn by their patrician superiors, and it ends with its titular protagonist ingloriously losing his life at the hands of the Volscian commoners. At its centre is a protagonist whose name as the action begins, Caius Martius (unusually and tellingly, he bears no cognomen, or family name), indicates how utterly constitutive military activity is of his being; having secured the support of the plebeians in his victorious campaign against the Volscians, his distinction is marked by the acquisition of a further honorific name, Coriolanus, that commemorates his heroism within the walls of the enemy town of Corioles. A consummate man of war, epitome of the Roman cult of manly fortitude, or *virtus*, Caius Martius Coriolanus has no time, and still less sympathy, for the arts of peace, and in particular for the crafts of negotiation, compromise and tactical dissimulation that are necessary to sustain Rome's survival through means other than sheer force.

The action unfolds by means of a series of confrontations founded upon brutally stark oppositions, reflecting the pervasively antithetical (and dialectical) orchestration of the play. In the first scene, the plebeians, driven, according to one of their leading spokesmen, 'in hunger for bread, not in thirst for revenge' (1.1.19–20), are faced down first by the conciliatory figure of the patrician Menenius Agrippa, who attempts to persuade his listeners not only of the folly of striking against the divinely sanctioned authority of the Roman state (grain shortages being acts of the gods, not men) but also of the organic inevitability of systematic inequity, by means of a fable of 'a time when all the body's members/ Rebelled against the belly', the moral of which is that by consuming the lion's share of the city's scarce resources its senatorial elite are actually acting selflessly for the common good, distributing sustenance

> through the rivers of your blood
> Even to the court, the heart, to th' seat o'th' brain;
> And through the cranks and offices of man
> The strongest nerves and small inferior veins
> From me receive that natural competency
> Whereby they live.

                                                                    (1.1.124–29)

Menenius's transparently ideological attempt to defuse a dangerously insurrectionary situation is succeeded by its antithesis in the shape of the rather less diplomatic efforts of Caius Martius himself, whose words of greeting to the plebeians on entry are poisonous insults, as he hails them as 'dissentient rogues' and 'scabs' (1.1.153–55).

Throughout the play, he is constitutionally incapable of addressing the Commons other than in anger and contempt (his catchphrase is 'hang 'em'; even a passing reference to 'the common file' on the battlefield at Corioles unleashes a Tourette's-style outburst: 'a plague – tribunes for them?' [1.7.43]). Having conceded representation in the Senate to the plebeians in the form of two tribunes, the patricians offer the victorious Coriolanus the role of consul, for which he is required by custom to publically present himself in a gown of humility before the people; when he proves incapable of adhering to the spirit of the ceremony and, further, unable to suppress his fury at 'the rabble' (3.1.139), thus provoking the citizens to riot, he is banished for the city's sake. In confrontation after confrontation, neither side can envisage the other in anything but the most polarised terms: for Coriolanus, the most modest gesture of democratic representation is the 'cockle of rebellion, insolence, sedition' (3.1.74); from the tribunes' point of view, his pride leads him to 'speak o'th' people as if you were a god/ To punish, not a man of their infirmity' (3.1.85–86).

It is not just that Coriolanus disowns any relationship between himself and the citizens that he despises as his inferiors; he also entertains fantasies of a kind of absolute autonomy that would allow him to act 'As if a man were author of himself/ And knew no other kin' (5.3.36–37). Coriolanus's hatred of the 'popular' is disproportionate, even in the eyes of the fellow members of his patrician class, but it appears all the more so because it seems more like a muscular reflex than a considered position: although the play, which has often been described as exemplary in its political balance, does not present his suspicion of the Commons as entirely without foundation (the tribunes especially lend themselves to portrayal as devious, manipulative and venal, and the view expressed by one of the citizens that 'if all our wits were to issue out of one skull, they would fly east, west, north, south' [2.3.18–20] seems likely to have found favour with the play's original audiences), it is the rigidity and inflexibility of his thinking, and his inability to register ambivalence, nuance and complexity, that ultimately determine his destiny. Coriolanus's status as the exemplar of *virtus* is that which also renders him the supreme embodiment of the aristocratic warrior code's contradictions: it is precisely those qualities that make him such an effective fighting machine that also make him, ultimately, so dangerously self-destructive. The Rome that he acts in defence of is an ideal, an abstraction: whereas the tribune Sicinius poses, with some justice, the question 'What is the city but the people?' (3.1.199), Coriolanus, contrarily, regards the mass of its inhabitants as a pestilential menace; yet it is to unheroic labours of these 'base slaves' (1.6.7) that he and Rome owe the victory at Corioles.

There is, then, a robotic, but also psychological and poetic, logic in Coriolanus's decision, once driven from the city he formerly pledged his life to defend to the death, to defect to his antagonists. Coriolanus needs enemies in order to function, even to exist, and if there is one man in the play he has any respect for, it is the one whom he regards as his sole equal, and deadliest rival, the Volscian general Tullus Aufidius. When they first meet on the field at Corioles, both men declare their mutual hatred, but the antipathy is that of mirror-images: 'We hate alike', declares Aufidius (1.9.2), while the Caius Martius of the first scene revealingly concedes, in what is for him a unique moment of imaginative projection, that 'were I anything but what I am,/ I would wish me only he' (1.222). In this light, his apparently perverse and potentially suicidal act of treachery in offering himself to the Volscians – and to Aufidius in particular – lays bare what, from the perspective of psychoanalytic criticism, might be regarded as its unconscious motivation: Coriolanus's symmetrical enmity towards Aufidius is in actuality an expression of his simultaneous, contradictory identification with him; his hatred and urge to annihilate an articulation of profound, unownable desire.

That there might be a homoerotic element to the relationship between Coriolanus and Aufidius is clearly signalled by the latter's exclamation, on the former's defection, that

> But that I see thee here,
> Thou noble thing, more dances my rapt heart
> Than when I first my wedded mistress saw
> Bestride my threshold.

(4.5.114–17)

This is not the first time in the play that male bonding is figured as heterosexual coupling: Martius himself, on the field of Corioles, demands to embrace his comrade Cominius 'In arms as sound as when I wooed, in heart/ As merry as when our nuptial day was done,/ And tapers burnt to bedward' (1.7.30–32). As far as the later tryst is concerned, the Roman and Volscian generals' mutual passion conjoins aggression and desire in a way that eventuates in Coriolanus's destruction, an act precipitated by what Aufidius represents as the shamefully childish and effeminate betrayal performed by the man he impugns in the final scene as a 'boy of tears' (5.6.103), when he reneges on his mission to 'Plough Rome and harrow Italy' (5.3.34). It is Martius's mother, Volumnia, who achieves what Rome's military defenders cannot, appealing to filial, marital and paternal loyalties that even he, in the end, is unable to deny, and which ultimately (and, as he recognises, fatally) prevail against the imperatives of the martial code which he has abided by all his life. Confronted with the spectacle of his kneeling mother, wife and son, and assailed by the vision of himself, as Volumnia imagines it, 'bravely' shedding their blood and trampling upon his mother's womb (5.3.118–25), Martius is, finally and literally, lost for words: as the stage direction, unique of its kind in the Shakespearean canon, dictates, his response to over fifty lines of impassioned persuasion is that '*[He] holds her by the hand, silent*' (5.3.183.s.d.).

Martius's capitulation to his mother is the climactic moment in a scene in which the art of verbal persuasion is counterpointed by a series of emblematic gestures of entreaty and submission, as Martius, Volumnia, Virgilia and Martius's young son successively curtsy, bow, kneel, sit and stand, in a sequence of assertions and interrogations of the competing,

and it seems contradictory, claims of patriarchal and maternal authority: kneeling according to convention before his mother in reflection of a 'deep duty' far beyond 'that of
common sons' (5.3.51–52), Martius is appalled and affronted when she ironically mirrors
the action, characterising it as an offence against propriety and the natural order, likened to
'the mutinous winds' striking 'the proud cedars 'gainst the fiery sun/ Murd'ring impossibility' (5.3.60–61); and in Volumina's 'unnatural' inversion of the child–parent relationship
is figured one of the central paradoxes explored in the play. The martial identity of a
Coriolanus is inextricable from a particularly Roman version of indissoluble, violent and
inviolable masculinity, wherein manhood is conceived as the defining prerogative of the
warrior elite, and weakness as provenance of the feminine and the effeminate; yet the play
makes it abundantly clear that it is the nurturing practices of the mothers that are
responsible for fashioning the sons into the men who they become.

This is vividly portrayed in a scene which, plotwise, has the status of an interlude but
which is essential to establishing the familial and cultural context from which Martius has
emerged. When, at the beginning of the play's third scene, Volumnia and Virgilia enter
and, as the stage direction stipulates in unusually precise detail, '*set them down on two low
stools and sew*' (1.3.0.s.d.), the stage seems to be set for women's work and domestic intimacy; but the ensuing dialogue pointedly flouts this expectation with a celebration both of
masculine violence and of the system of child-rearing that fosters it, in which protective
maternal instincts are powerfully subordinated to the demands of military service. Rather
than fearing for the prospects of her son sent to battle, Volumnia advises Virgilia, she
encourages him to 'seek danger where he was like to find fame', and revels in his victories:
'I sprang not more in joy at first hearing he was a man-child than now in first seeing he
had proved himself a man' (1.3.11–15).

If for a moment Virgilia conforms more closely to feminine stereotype by registering a
certain squeamishness at the thought of Martius's 'bloody brow/ With his mailed hand
then wiping' (1.3.31–32), Volumnia is scornfully dismissive: not only is it the case that
blood 'more becomes a man/ Than gilt his trophy', but

> The breasts of Hecuba
> When she did suckle Hector looked not lovelier
> Than Hector's forehead when it spit forth blood
> At Grecian sword, contemning.

> (1.3.37–40)

The collision of bloodshed and lactation is the extreme epitome of a perverse co-dependency
that runs through the play, and which paradoxically threatens to undermine the very
structures that it is intended to reinforce.

Martius's state of being, like that of the Roman state itself, is premised on the rigorous
exclusion and expulsion of elements accounted effeminate, weak and degenerate, but the
text's deconstructive knack of breaching the boundaries between apparent antitheses (here,
life-giving and death-dealing) reveals these efforts to be finally futile: it is a strange validation
of Hector's heroic masculinity for him to become imaged as his breastfeeding mother. A
parallel irony informs the account of the antics of Martius's son, as presented moments later
by the virtuous lady Valeria, who instances the boy's relentless pursuit of a 'gilded butterfly'
(1.3.57) and his tearing of it to pieces with his teeth, as an illustration of his nobility.
Observing that this replicates 'One on's father's moods' (1.3.62), Volumnia confirms that we
are seeing the parenting skills that produced the father also applied to the son, but also offers

a (for her unintended) perspective upon Martius's obduracy, since the shredding of a butterfly is less the act of a hero than of a psychopath. Again, incidentally, we might notice some slippage of gender roles and identities in Virgilia's rather understated response to the anecdote; invited to comment on Valeria's exclamation that ' 'tis a noble child', she refers to him as 'A crack' (1.3.63–64): routinely glossed by editors as 'lively lad', it conceivably also invokes the bawdy sense of vagina – though to what effect is open to question.

Body politics

A play much preoccupied with bodies and body parts, *Coriolanus* is one of Shakespeare's most comprehensive explorations of the relationships between the individual body, the iconic body and the body politic, concerns that are initiated in Menenius's parable of the belly in the first scene. The play's varied bodies are far from contented or, often, even complete entities. From the patrician perspective, common bodies are vile, odorous and treacherously corrupted: the First Citizen, the 'great toe' of the assembly of mutineers, is for Menenius its 'lowest, basest, poorest' member (1.1.144–46); the common mass, according to Martius, contemptibly harbours affections and loyalties akin to 'A sick man's appetite, who desires most that/ Which would increase his evil' (1.1.167–68). Later, when the tribunes and patricians debate his expulsion from Rome, the arguments hinge upon his relative dispensability as an organ of the state: 'He's a disease that must be cut away', declares Sicinius; Menenius counters, 'he's a limb that has but a disease'; Sicinius insists, 'The service of the foot,/ Being once gangrened, is not then respected for what it was' (3.1.296–309). For Menenius, who supplements his parable of the belly with a self-characterisation that reinforces the link between carefree carnality and elite privilege by confessing himself to be 'one that converses more with the buttock of the night than with the forehead of the morning' (2.1.46–48), the tribunes' lack of credibility as holders of judicial and political office is epitomised by their incontinent subservience to their own bodily functions: even when hearing cases, he alleges, 'if you chance to be pinched with the colic, you make faces like mummers, set up the bloody flag against all patience, and in roaring for a chamber-pot, dismiss the controversy bleeding' (2.1.66–69).

For himself, 'What I think, I utter, and spend my malice in my breath' (2.1.48–49): and whereas Menenius probably envisages his ventilations as benevolently fragrant, there is throughout the play a contrarily emphatic close identification of bad breath, the mouth, the voice and the common franchise. Martius, especially, repeatedly defines the fickle will of the people in terms of their 'voices' (a word used forty-eight times in the play, of which thirty occurrences take place in one scene [2.3]); the hated tribunes for him are 'the tongues o'th' common mouth' (3.1.23); when presented with the task of offering to display his wounds to the plebeians, his riposte is: 'As if I had received them for the hire/ Of their breath only!' (2.2.146–47). Against this, Martius's own claims to authority reside in the dumb articulacy of his own flesh, in the physical prowess of hand-to-hand combat and in the violent writing that warfare itself performs upon the martial body in the form of those wounds: for the hero who enters from battlefields of Corioles, an emblem of destruction 'from face to foot … a thing of blood' (2.2.104–05), to be wounded is to be most alive and energised, and to be enhanced rather than diminished: 'the blood I drop is rather physical/ Than dangerous' (1.6.18–19).

Martius's scars are already the vehicles of a narrative that seem to exceed their bearer, as Volumnia and Menenius elaborate ('Every gash was an enemy's grave' [2.1.141–42]), but to be called upon to give account of them, as is commanded and refused in the scene in the marketplace, is a provocation to anger and even shame, for it entails a kind of surrendering of that which truly constitutes Martius into common ownership: 'if he show us his wounds and tell us his deeds', the Third Citizen ruminates, echoing the doubter Thomas who demanded a similar testimony of Christ, 'we are to put our tongues into those wounds and speak for them' (2.3.5–8). For Martius such an intimate articulation is a prospect too demeaning to contemplate; bearing in mind that he is draped in a gown of humility he himself describes (2.3.105) as a 'womanish toge' (at least according to the Oxford and Norton editors; other editions follow the Folio's 'wolvish' but emend its sequent noun 'tongue'), and that, as Janet Adelman observes, the 'persistent identification of wound and mouth' reminds us that 'he is a feminized and dependent creature' (1992: 155), the bawdy association of wounds with the vagina suggests that what he truly fears is the comprehensive, humiliating effeminisation of being transformed into the passive recipient of the gaze, as well as the quasi-sexual attentions, of the crowd.

The wide arch

Coriolanus is preoccupied with the Roman body politic, with bodies disfigured, diseased and in pain; *Antony and Cleopatra*, a play which dates from around the same period, deals also with bodies in, and of, pleasure, in the process revelling in the practices, values and modes of being in opposition to which imperial Rome defines itself. The pleasures engaged in the play are manifold: feasting and drinking, music and dance, fishing, game-playing, sleep, time-wasting, powerful narcotics and, above all, sex. From the outset to its conclusion, the play's register is one of sensual excess ('this dotage of our General's/ O'erflows the measure' [1.1.1–2]), its preoccupations the expansive, the ecstatic and the transcendent, its recurrent concern the breaking and dissolution of borders, barriers and boundaries:

> Let Rome in Tiber melt, and the wide arch
> Of the ranged empire fall.
>
> (1.1.35–36)

> Eternity was in our lips and eyes,
> Bliss in our brow's bent, none our parts so poor
> But was a race of heaven.
>
> (1.3.35–37)

> For her own person,
> It beggared all description.
>
> (2.2.203–04)

> O see, my women,
> The crown o'th' earth doth melt.
>
> (4.16.64–65)

> I have
> Immortal longings in me.
>
> (5.2.271–72)

Extending the range of its action across the Mediterranean and over a period of ten years, *Antony and Cleopatra* bears witness to the end of the Roman republic; sharing a number of characters with *Julius Caesar*, to which it is a historical sequel, it is, like *Coriolanus*, a play of polarities, strong antitheses and stark choices: most obviously, between its twin settings, Rome and Egypt.

Within the play's imaginative geography, Rome is, or understands itself to be, the embodiment of orderliness, virtue, rationality and activity; Egypt, conversely, is a zone of licence, hedonistic indulgence, mysticism and limitless fecundity: the division is between a culture of masculinity governed by one of the most calmly efficient of Shakespeare's rulers and a matriarchy within which men are either actually or metaphorically castrated (eunuchs are in attendance from Antony and Cleopatra's first entrance). Unlike the densely imagined cities of *Julius Caesar* and *Coriolanus*, the Rome of this play seems more a cold abstraction than an inhabited place; Egypt, however, is rendered in seductive detail, a place of sybaritic luxury where 'The beds i'th' East are soft' (2.6.50), where one of Cleopatra's waiting-women, Charmian, is told when she wonders how many children she might bear, 'If every of your wishes had a womb,/ And fertile every wish, a million' (1.2.33–34), and where Cleopatra anachronistically solicits her women to play billiards and to cut the lace on her bodice (1.3.71); at its heart lies the Nile Delta, symptomatically a place between sea and earth, slippery, volatile and uncertainly constituted by both land and water.

As Antony informs Octavius Caesar, the Egyptians calibrate both diurnal and seasonal rhythms by the Nile's ebb and flow, 'By certain scales i'th' pyramid':

> They know
> By th' height, the lowness, or the mean, if dearth
> Or foison follow. The higher Nilus swells
> The more it promises; as it ebbs, the seedsman
> Upon the slime and ooze scatters his grain,
> And shortly comes to harvest.
>
> (2.7.16–22)

Himself a semi-rusticated 'seedsman' who by the time the play begins has more than matched Julius Caesar's breeding record with the Egyptian queen ('He ploughed her, and she cropped' [2.2.234], reports Agrippa, referring to Caesar's son who Octavius would subsequently have executed), Antony fully recognises the force of nature that can be neither contained nor controlled, and that has in it the capacity to engulf and the power to overwhelm, submerge and annihilate.

Such is precisely the privilege of Cleopatra herself, the 'serpent of old Nile' (1.5.25) who, recurrently defined as Egypt it- (or her-) self, is identified with both the life-giving and death-dealing river and the fabulous creatures that inhabit it, among them the crocodile, a beast that, like the serpent, is 'bred now of your mud by the operation of the sun' (2.7.25–26):

> ANTONY It is shaped, sir, like itself, and it is as broad as it hath breadth. It is just so high as it is, and moves with it own organs. It lives by that which nourisheth it, and the elements once out of it, it transmigrates.
> LEPIDUS What colour is it of?
> ANTONY Of it own colour too.
> LEPIDUS 'Tis a strange serpent.
> ANTONY 'Tis so, and the tears of it are wet.
>
> (2.7.39–46)

At one level, Antony is merely making a gentle mockery of his listener's desire for exotica, for a taste of the land of 'strange serpents' (2.7.23): deflecting and deflating the conventions of a travel narrative that would seek both to evoke the strangeness and to subject it to an explorer's taxonomies, he offers the crocodile as definition of self-evidence, as flatly, blankly tautological: it is what it is. At another, as a fabulous creature that eludes its narrators' efforts to capture it in words, the crocodile is in some ways kin to Cleopatra, whose 'own person', according to an Enobarbus engaged, in the play's most celebrated descriptive set-piece, in a parallel instance of exotic travelogue, 'beggared all description' (2.2.203–04); as an animal that 'transmigrates' (according to the Pythagorean theory of the passage of the soul from one entity to another), it is a shape-shifter; its tears may be wet, but they may also be false.

Like the crocodile, Cleopatra endlessly compels and eludes definition, in the play and beyond, usually in the process revealing the fantasies, the desires, and the failures and limits of comprehension, of those that make them. Even Enobarbus's account of the first encounter between Cleopatra and Antony ultimately can only render the female subject that 'did lie/ In her pavilion' (2.2.204–05) circumstantially, via the barge, the water, the movement of the oars, the 'strange invisible perfume' and the air itself, which 'but for vacancy/ Had gone to gaze on Cleopatra too,/ And made a gap in nature' (215, 222–24). Ostensibly the object of a universal gaze that includes Enobarbus's own attempts to ensnare her essence in verse, Cleopatra resists its entanglements by remaining in excess of its determinations; beyond representation, hers is the seductive power of an 'imagined, pro-mised, deferred presence' (Belsey 1996: 43), and, as the passenger of a barge that never quite arrives at its destination, she is uniquely placed to incite endless and insatiable desire: 'she makes hungry/ Where most she satisfies' (242–43).

It is in this conjunction of the sacred and the profane that Cleopatra's desire and desire for Cleopatra reside:

> For vilest things
> Become themselves in her, that the holy priests
> Bless her when she is riggish.
>
> (2.2.243–45)

The polarities are established in the very first scene: associated with darkness and deviance, and labelled as the bearer of a 'tawny front', a 'gipsy' and 'strumpet' (1.1.6, 10, 13), and thus as racially and sexually threatening, inferior and other, by Antony's censorious com-rade Philo, she is for Antony himself both a 'wrangling queen' (and the hint of the term's near-homophone 'quean', or whore, is possibly in play here and elsewhere) and a woman of flawless nobility in her 'infinite variety':

> Whom everything becomes – to chide, to laugh,
> To weep; how every passion fully strives
> To make itself, in thee, fair and admired!
>
> (1.1.51–53)

'She is cunning past men's thought', worries Antony; Enobarbus retorts that 'Her passions are made of nothing but the finest part of pure love' (1.2.132–34); furiously denounced by Scarus as 'Yon riband-red nag of Egypt' (3.10.10) for prompting Antony's retreat from the sea-fight with Caesar, she nonetheless remains for her lover the one whose 'beck might from the bidding of the gods/ Command me' (3.11.60–61).

Yet when Antony catches her apparently toying with Caesar's messenger he is swift in his invective:

Have I my pillow left unpressed in Rome,
Forborne the getting of a lawful race,
And by a gem of women, to be abused
By one that looks on feeders?

(3.13.106–09)

Labelled as a 'boggler' (111), that is, not only as an equivocator but also as one who has made liberal use of her 'bogle', or vagina (Bate and Rasmussen 2007: 2210), Cleopatra is at this moment for Antony no more than leftover meat, 'a morsel cold upon/ Dead Caesar's trencher' (3.13.117–18), incapable of regulating her own promiscuousness; yet by the end of the scene his rage has passed, as he assures his 'queen' that 'There's sap in't yet' (3.13.193–94). The benign view of Cleopatra is sustained in the succeeding scenes: 'my queen's a squire', he tells his now-constant companion, the pointedly named Eros (who, as the onstage personification of the play's linkage of sex and death, becomes the instrument of Antony's botched suicide), 'The armourer of my heart' (4.4.14, 7); believing that he scents victory, and hailing her as a 'great fairy', he addresses her as 'thou day o' th' world' and 'nightingale' (4.9.12–18), a bearer of light, good fortune and sweet music. It is the last time he or anyone else speaks of her in such terms; the next time they meet, following his defeat at Caesar's hands as a result of his engaging him by sea rather than on land, she is again the 'foul Egyptian', 'witch', 'Triple-turned whore' and 'greatest spot/ Of all thy sex' (4.13.10–47).

Past the size of dreaming

The vacillation between idealisation and vilification can in part be seen as character driven, an index of Antony's violently shifting perceptions of a lover that he perceives has placed him in a tragically contradictory position, torn between infatuated desire and his duties as a soldier, Roman and husband; in part, what prompts his outbursts of misogyny is that he knows only too well his erotic enthralment is the source both of his self-destruction and his shame. But the antitheses of goddess and whore (which, it hardly needs pointing out, far from being contradictory, have traditionally been mutually constitutive components of certain kinds of male thinking about women) are also the limit points of reference for the play's representation of a heroine who exists in the Roman imaginary as 'non-Roman, nonwoman, black woman, witch, slut, serpent, bitch, Egyptian, African' (Little 2000: 145).

Embodying the play's oppositions in her own words and actions, Cleopatra is by turns (and her 'turn' is that of an accomplished performer in both the theatrical and sexual sense) dominant, vulnerable, teasing, wounded and ferocious, and lethally witty; a figure of both frivolous contrariety ('If you find him sad,/ Say I am dancing; if in mirth, report/ That I am sudden sick' [1.3.3–5]) and sublime grandeur ('Husband, I come./ Now to that name my courage prove my title' [5.2.278–79]); a being of earth and water ultimately transfigured to 'fire and air' (5.2.279). Repeatedly flouting norms of gendered behaviour pertaining within early modern and imagined Roman culture, Cleopatra has so far subjugated Antony to her will that, in the eyes of some beholders, she has absorbed his very essence: 'Here comes Antony', observes Enobarbus, as she makes her entrance (1.2.69); though corrected by Charmian, he, and we, knows what he means well enough. She is no stranger to threatened or actual violence, coolly warning the messenger who tells her of Antony's initial reconciliation with Caesar that if he prove to be the bearer of bad news 'The gold I give thee will I melt and pour/ Down thy ill-uttering throat' (2.5.33–34), dragging him by his hair across the stage and drawing a knife on him; yet almost as precipitately she regains sufficient composure to remind herself that 'These hands do lack nobility that they strike/ A meaner than myself, since I myself/ Have give myself the cause' (2.5.82–84).

It is often said that Cleopatra is a consummate performer (and it is often said by those who tend to equate female sexuality with duplicity), and there is a sense in which, with Cleopatra, as with Antony, it is all theatre. In not one scene are the couple alone together, in private (unlike, for example, Brutus and Portia, Macbeth and his Lady, and Othello and Desdemona): within the frame of a play in which the domestic, the interpersonal, the public and the political are inextricable, their love is not just played out in front of witnesses but, perhaps, self-dramatisingly performed for others' as well as their own benefit. Antony and Cleopatra are intensely aware of themselves as legendary, mythological or monumental figures, a point of view that the play at times endorses and at other times qualifies or interrogates. For the prologue-like Philo, Antony begins, like an immense hunk of masonry, as the 'triple pillar of the world' (1.1.12); on the eve of his defeat, the scale of what is to come is registered in the scene of magical strangeness where soldiers, placed at every corner of the stage – for this moment also the four corners of the earth – hear the '*Music of the hautboys ... under the stage*' (4.3.9.s.d.), which signifies his abandonment by the god Hercules. Hercules was also, conjecturally, the Globe playhouse's own mascot deity; though the use of oboes, together with the intricate scoring that also includes the boy singer who accompanies the Bacchanalian revels on Pompey's galley (2.7), indicates the Blackfriars as a more likely performance venue.

Cleopatra's post-mortem panegyric to Antony is the strongest articulation of his Herculean myth:

> His legs bestrid the ocean; his reared arm
> Crested the world ...
> ... Realms and islands were
> As plates dropped from his pocket.
>
> (5.2.81–91)

Yet when she seeks confirmation from Dolabella whether 'there was, or might be, such a man/ As this I dreamt of', the answer is simply, flatly realist: 'Gentle madam, no' (5.2.92–94). This is not the answer she wants, but by insisting upon the validity of her vision of an Antony 'past the size of dreaming' (5.2.96) she not only offers a glimpse of a kind of lovers' truth that is beyond the prosaic real, and beyond history, but also prepares the ground for her own departure. Cleopatra's ascription of a global maritime command to Antony is ironic in view of the fact that it was opting to trust his fate to the sea that brought him to his end, but it serves to solidify and to elevate the man and the myth.

Antony's demise is a messy process of misprision (he orders Eros to kill him in the belief that Cleopatra is dead), mishap and disintegration: the warrior who at the start of the play imaged the rapture of dissolution by calling for Rome to melt into the waters of the Tiber finds himself towards its end unable to 'hold this visible shape' as Antony; likening himself to 'a cloud that's dragonish' (4.15.14, 2), he is a figure drawn from the bestiary of the fabulous composed of nothing more than water vapour and air. Cheated by Eros, robbed of the dignity of the Roman suicide in which he seeks to evade the implicitly sodomitical 'penetrative shame' (4.15.75) of subjugation to Caesar, Antony suffers yet further humiliation in a death scene that treads a fine line between high tragedy, bawdiness and slapstick. Brought to the monument for a final encounter with Cleopatra, his fate is to be hauled aloft to the monument which she cannot leave, in a scene which sustains to the end the play's interpretation of sex and death, in a series of double entendres that would bring a blush to the cheeks of the makers of the most irreverent of the play's spin-offs, *Carry on Cleo* (UK, 1964) – 'come, come, Antony … We must draw thee up'; 'O quick, or I am gone!'; 'How heavy weighs my lord!'; 'The soldier's pole is fall'n' (4.16.30–31, 32–33, 67).

Immortal longings

'I am dying, Egypt, dying' (4.16.19, 43): however Antony's ascent is managed, whether as a clumsy business of ropes and pulleys or heavy manual lifting, or as a soaring, final escape from earthbound kingdoms of clay, he, and the play, continues to adhere to the terms of address that have throughout purported to magnify the lovers beyond the quotidian and the individual, Never more than at this moment, Cleopatra is never less than queen of Egypt, or Egypt herself. It is a legend that the final act shows her fully determined to protect and preserve, and her death is expertly stage-managed. Like Antony, she imagines with dread her humiliation in defeat; and just as he saw himself paraded in Rome alongside Caesar's chariot, a degraded, branded object of display, so she envisages herself caricatured and diminished by 'quick comedians' who 'Extemporally will stage us, and present/ Our Alexandrian revels' (5.2.212–14):

> Antony
> Shall be brought drunken forth, and I shall see
> Some squeaking Cleopatra boy my greatness
> I'th' posture of a whore.

> (5.2.214–17)

It is an extraordinarily risky self-reflexive moment, foregrounding Cleopatra as performer at a moment when most modern spectators would expect to be most intensely engaged with her character; and one that perhaps betokens considerable confidence in the talents of the unknown youth that boyed Cleopatra's greatness at the Blackfriars around about the end of 1606, but that also introduces, at exactly the point when the imperatives of tragedy would seem least to demand it, a vision of Antony and Cleopatra glimpsed through the lenses of satire, comedy and burlesque. If it is a sign of Shakespeare's command of his medium that he was willing to take the risk, it also serves as a final reminder that, in the double perspective of a play staged by his own 'quick comedians', Cleopatra's greatness and the 'posture of a whore' co-exist, that Antony the ocean-straddling Colossus has been 'brought drunken forth', and that both, and neither, represent the truth of the myth that its action seeks to encompass.

As at Antony's death, the epic, the tragic and the comic continue to co-exist: even as she summons the robes, jewels and crown (having licensed Charmian to 'play till doomsday' [5.2.228]) that will complete her transformation into an icon of 'immortal longings', Cleopatra admits entry to the rustic clown that brings the instrument of her death, the 'pretty worm/ Of Nilus there, that kills and pains not' (239): the worm that, in the clown's bawdy lexicon, caused a 'very honest woman' to have 'died of the biting of it' (247), and of which, as a source of macabre, terminal pleasure, he wishes her joy. He is right to do so:

As sweet as balm, as soft as air, as gentle.
O Antony!
[*She puts another aspic to her arm*]
   Nay, I will take thee too.
What should I stay – [*She*] *dies*

(5.2.302–04)

There are verbal echoes of *Lear* in Charmian's urging of her mistress towards death ('O, break! O, break!' [301]; compare Kent's 'Break, heart; I prithee, break!' [5.3.311]), but this time the moment of death is one not of agonised extinction but of rapturous consummation, and of the new life, and peace, imaged in the 'baby' at Cleopatra's breast, 'That sucks the nurse asleep' (301–02). It is this that will define Cleopatra's legacy, rather than Caesar's plainly inadequate formal valediction to 'A pair so famous' (5.2.350), but the personal is also political; one of the things that frames the two deaths, and that makes them both fitting, and in the end necessary, is the gathering sense that Antony and Cleopatra have become history. The cult of *virtus* no longer serves the needs of the new order, the 'time of universal peace' (4.6.4), anticipated by Octavius Caesar (and, not coincidentally, coinciding with the birth of the Christian era), that posterity would come to know as the *pax Romana*; the inevitability of Cleopatra's defeat and the subsequent annexation of Egypt finally dissolve the distinctions that have defined Cleopatran autonomy and Roman imperial dominance.

Further reading

Adelman, Janet (1992) *Suffocating Mothers: Fantasies of Maternal Origin in Shakespeare's Plays, Hamlet to The Tempest*. New York: Routledge.

Dollimore, Jonathan (2004) *Radical Tragedy: Religion, Ideology and Power in the Drama of Shakespeare and his Contemporaries*. Third Edition. Hemel Hempstead: Harvester Wheatsheaf.

Fernie, Ewan (2002) *Shame in Shakespeare*. London: Routledge.

Hamer, Mary (1993) *Signs of Cleopatra: History, Politics, Representation*. London: Routledge.

Kahn, Coppélia (1997) *Roman Shakespeare: Warriors, Wounds, and Women*. London and New York: Routledge.

Parker, Barbara L. (2004) *Plato's Republic and Shakespeare's Rome: A Political Study of the Roman Works*. Cranbury, DE: Associated University Presses.

Patterson, Annabel (1989) *Shakespeare and the Popular Voice*. Oxford: Blackwell.

Rutter, Carol Chillington (2001) *Enter the Body: Women and Representation on Shakespeare's Stage*. London and New York: Routledge.

Wells, Robin Headlam (2000) *Shakespeare on Masculinity*. Cambridge: Cambridge University Press.

Wood, Nigel (ed.) (1996) *Antony and Cleopatra*. Theory in Practice. Buckingham: Open University Press.

The Tempest

Date, text and authorship

c.1610; performed at court 1 November 1611, and in 1612–13; F 1623. Solely Shakespearean.

Sources and influences

Robert Eden, *History of Travel* (1577); Michel de Montaigne, *Essays* (trans. John Florio, 1603); William Strachey, *A True repertory of the wreck and redemption of Sir Thomas Gates, Knight, upon and from the islands of the Bermudas* (1610).

On stage

SMT, 1957 (dir. Peter Brook; Prospero: John Gielgud); Roundhouse, 1968 (dir. Peter Brook and Jean-Louis Barrault); Mermaid, 1970 (dir. Jonathan Miller); NT, 1974 (dir. Peter Hall; Prospero: John Gielgud); Piccolo Teatro di Milano, 1978 (dir. Giorgio Strehler; Prospero: Tino Carraro); RSC, 1988 (dir. Nicholas Hytner; Prospero: John Wood); NT, 1988 (dir. Peter Hall; Prospero: Michael Bryant); Ninagawa Company, Tokyo, 1988 (dir. Yukio Ninagawa; Prospero: Hira Mikijirô); Cheek by Jowl, 1988 (dir. Declan Donnellan); Théâtre des Bouffes du Nord, Paris, 1990 (dir. Peter Brook); Théâtre Repère, Québec, 1992 (dir. Robert Lepage); RSC, 1993 (dir. Sam Mendes; Prospero: Alec McCowen; Ariel: Simon Russell Beale); RSC/Baxter Theatre, Cape Town, 2009 (dir. Janice Honeyman; Prospero: Antony Sher; Caliban: John Kani).

On screen

UK, 1979 (dir. Derek Jarman; Prospero: Heathcote Williams); BBC Television Shakespeare, UK, 1980 (dir. John Gorrie; Prospero: Michael Horden).

Offshoots

Forbidden Planet, USA, 1956 (dir. Fred McLeod Wilcox); *Tempest*, USA, 1982 (dir. Paul Mazursky); *Prospero's Books*, Netherlands/France/Italy/UK, 1991 (dir. Peter Greenaway; Prospero: John Gielgud); *Shakespeare: The Animated Tales: The Tempest*, UK/Russia, 1992 (dir. Stanislav Sokolov).

This island's mine

The historical context of England's emergence as a colonial and imperial nation is central to the determination of the meanings of blackness and whiteness, and of representations of cultural, ethnic, racial and gender difference. In this sense, much of the work conducted on the issue of Shakespeare and race has operated within the broader remit of postcolonial critical theory and practice, an approach which has been concerned, as key theorist Homi K. Bhabha summarises, with 'bear[ing] witness to the unequal and uneven forces of cultural representation involved in the contest for political and social authority within the modern world order'; which emerges from 'the colonial testimony of Third World countries and the discourses of "minorities" within the geopolitical divisions of East and West, North and South'; and which involves intervening 'in those ideological discourses of modernity that attempt to give a hegemonic "normality" to the uneven development and the differential, often disadvantaged, histories of nations, races, communities, peoples' (Bhabha 1994: 171).

The Shakespearean text which has long been recognised as offering more direct engagement with the preoccupations and conflicts of colonialism, and which in recent decades became a testing-ground for postcolonial criticism, is *The Tempest* – although this recognition, significantly, was first strongly articulated not by English or American critics but by writers and artists positioned geographically and culturally within the legacies of British (and French) colonial history: for example in the works of the French philosopher and psychoanalyst Dominique-Octave Mannoni (*Psychologie de la colonisation*, 1950; translated into English as *Prospero and Caliban: The Psychology of Colonization*, 1956), the Barbadan novelist, poet and critic George Lamming (*The Pleasures of Exile*, 1960; and *Water with Berries*, 1970), the Martinique-born poet and political activist Aimé Césaire (*Une Tempête*, 1969) and the Kenyan writer Ngugi Wa Thiong'o (*A Grain of Wheat*, 1967). By focussing on the Prospero–Caliban relationship, Thomas Cartelli writes, these authors 'regenerate out of their own first-hand experience of colonization a conception of Shakespeare as a formative producer and purveyor of a paternalistic ideology that is basic to the material aims of western imperialism' (1987: 10). The recent critical history of *The Tempest* has reflected the implications of this shift of perspective by rendering its investments in the colonial enterprise the central topic of discussion.

Two influential essays published in 1985 provide a point of departure. For Francis Barker and Peter Hulme, *The Tempest*'s significance(s) as a text within history and ideology stems from an 'imbrication' within the 'ensemble of fictional and lived practices' that constitute English colonialism whose 'nodal point' is 'the figure of usurpation': simultaneously riven with divisions and conflicts and determined to contain them, the play begins with a scene of insubordination in the 'boatswain's peremptory dismissal of the nobles to their cabins', then 'proceeds to recount or display a series of actual or attempted usurpations of authority'. The sequence of 'rebellions, treacheries, mutinies and conspiracies' that constitute the action of the play are 'embedded' within it as 'figural traces of the text's anxiety concerning the very matters of domination and resistance' (Barker and Hulme 1985: 198). Taking issue with the critical tradition that has tended to side with (and often idealise) Prospero (amply represented, for example, by D. J. Palmer's 1968 anthology of critical essays, which frames the relationship between Prospero and his subjects as that of 'the higher values of a life ordered by reason and order' to 'the baser instincts of untutored nature' [1968: 15]), and hence to identity with the coloniser, not the colonised, Barker and Hulme point out that 'Prospero's play and *The Tempest* are not the same thing': the narrative that Prospero presents of his acquisition of the island 'erases … all trace of the moment of his reduction of Caliban to slavery', while the accusation of attempted rape that he levels at his slave reiterates the need for colonial power to 'tell its own story, inevitably one of native violence' (Barker and Hulme 1968: 200–01).

The play struggles somewhat to keep both that story and 'Prospero's play' on track, most obviously when Prospero, remembering the 'foul conspiracy' (4.1.139) of Caliban and his associates, disrupts the masque he has himself orchestrated with a seemingly excessive display of anger, and thereby unwittingly exposes 'an unconscious anxiety concerning the grounding of his legitimacy, both as producer of his play and, *a fortiori*, as governor of the island' (Barker and Hulme 1968: 202). Even so, the crisis is rapidly and magically suppressed, and the violent challenge that is latent within Caliban's act of insurrection is neutralised by the generic positioning of the sub-plot: 'Caliban's attempt to put his political claims into practice' is discredited by it association with 'clownish vulgarity', and the conspiracy is 'framed in a grotesquerie that ends with the dubiously amusing sight of the conspirators being hunted by dogs' (203). As the authors remark, this was 'a fate, incidentally, not unknown to natives of the New World'; and although here and, inter-mittently, elsewhere the 'text's anxiety about the threat posed to its decorum by its New World materials' (203) is referred to specific practices of colonial exploitation and violence in the Americas, Barker and Hulme's primary interest, in this essay, is in a discourse of colonialism that operated irrespective of Shakespeare's own 'putative knowledge' of the 'congruent texts' that shaped and were shaped by that history (196).

Barker and Hulme suggest that *The Tempest* both entertains the contradictions of colonialism and colludes in their attempted suppression; Paul Brown, similarly, proposes that the play 'is not simply a reflection of colonialist practices but an intervention in an ambivalent and even contradictory discourse', in the form of a narrative which 'seeks at once to harmonise disjunction, to transcend irreconcilable contradictions and to mystify the political conditions which demand colonialist discourse' (1994: 48). It is a project which, formally and historically, is destined for failure: Brown concludes that *The Tempest* is 'a limit text in which the characteristic operations of colonialist discourse may be dis-cerned – as an instrument of exploitation, a register of beleaguerment and a site of radical ambivalence' (68). Whereas Barker and Hulme, and a significant number of succeeding commentators, emphasise the American aspect of English colonialism, Brown locates the play within the broader geography of 'the various domains of British world influence, which may be discerned roughly ... as the "core", "semiperiphery" and "periphery"', an imagined territory which extends outwards from England and Wales, via Ireland, to the New World; the mapping acknowledges the 'enormous scope of contemporary colonialist discourse', as well as enabling Brown to forge connections between the 'others' of legitimate rule that are found both at the limits of the British empire and within its heartland (51–52).

The bridge between the Old and New World dimensions of *The Tempest*, in this scheme, is Ireland, which, as an unevenly subjugated semiperipheral territory that was treated as '*both* a feudal fief under British lordship ... *and* also a colony', inhabited by subjects who were 'both truant civilians and savages', provides the analogue for Prospero's island, 'ambiguously placed between American and European discourse' (55, 57). Rather than trying to enfold *The Tempest* within the distinct history of Irish colonialism, Brown posits the locations of both as the site of what Barker and Hulme call 'Prospero's play', seen here as 'a reality principle, ordering and correcting the inhabitants of the island, subordinating their discourse to his own' (66). As for Barker and Hulme, Prospero does not and cannot have it all his own way: even though the threats of insurrection posed, in different ways, by Caliban, Ariel, Antonio and Sebastian are readily thwarted, Prospero 'requires a struggle with the forces of the other in order to show his power ... It is *he* who largely produces the ineffectual challenge as a dire threat' (68). The argument is clearly indebted to the 'sub-version–containment' model articulated by Stephen Greenblatt and then current within new historicism, as is Brown's desolate reading of Caliban's heartbreaking, momentary acquisition of a transcendent lyricism as he recalls his dream (' ... the isle is full of noises ... ' [138–46]), which is 'not the *antithesis* but the *apotheosis* of colonialist dis-course ... here at last is an eloquent spokesman who is powerless; here such eloquence represents not a desire to control and rule but a fervent wish for release, a desire to escape reality and return to dream' (Brown 1994: 66).

By making the exercise of power the subject of the play, Barker and Hulme, and Brown, indicate the parameters within which much subsequent discussion of the colonial and postcolonial *Tempest* has been conducted. Greenblatt had initiated the subversion–containment debate in an exploration of the relationship between colonial ideology, the early American experience and the *Henry IV* plays; in an essay published in 1988, he turned to *The Tempest* whilst only tangentially alluding either to the dynamics of master and slave or to the settlers and the indigenous inhabitants of the colonies. Reading the Bermudan and Virginian pamphlets that have widely been identified as a source for Shakespeare's play, Greenblatt follows William Strachey's narrative of the storm-induced shipwreck of an English fleet en route to the Virginia Company colony of Jamestown and the subsequent institution of 'the first martial law code in America' (1988: 154). The potential for insubordination, in this instance, lies not with the native Calibans, but in the settlers themselves: as the Virginia Company shareholders appeared to believe that 'only with a set of powerful inward restraints could the colonists be kept from rebelling at the first sign of the slippage or relaxation of authority' (150), the consequence was 'an exceptionally draconian code' which ensured that 'The group that had been shipwrecked in Bermuda passed from dreams of absolute freedom to the imposition of absolute control' (154). Appropriated and transformed for Shakespeare's ends, the materials of the Strachey narrative provide 'a violent tempest, a providential shipwreck on a strange island, a crisis in authority provoked by both danger and excess, a fear of lower-class disorder and upper-class ambition, a triumphant affirmation of absolute control linked to the manipulation of anxiety and to a departure from the island'; the difference being that *The Tempest* drives towards not the endorsement of totalitarianism but a forgiveness which is, nonetheless, 'the manifestation of supreme power', whose emblem is 'marriage rather than punishment' (154). In this reading, Caliban is only really of interest in relation to Prospero's 'famously enigmatic' confession to ownership of 'this thing of darkness' (5.1.278), which perhaps signals 'some deeper recognition of affinity, some half-conscious acknowledgment of guilt' (Greenblatt 1988: 157).

Thing of darkness

For Ania Loomba, conversely, whose interest lies in the intersections between colonial subjection, race, gender and sexuality, Caliban's ambiguous and contested status as an enslaved black subject is a central question, particularly with regard to the play's deeply problematic 'representation of black male sexuality' (1989: 148). Reflecting upon Prospero's accusation that Caliban attempted to rape Miranda, and its apparent corroboration by Caliban himself, Loomba emphasises the play's involvement with the cultural stereotype of the black rapist, which it upholds by perpetuating the idea that black men are 'aware of the damage they can do by making sexual advances towards white women' (150). There is, Loomba points out, a third party implicitly present in the confrontation between rapacious black male and the besieged and desexualised white womanhood represented by Miranda: Caliban's mother, Sycorax, whose 'licentious black feminity' offsets the 'passive purity' of Prospero's daughter (151). Having successfully eradicated Sycorax's and Caliban's territorial claim to the island by torturing and imprisoning the son while demonising the mother, Prospero thus 'consolidates power which is specifically white and male, and constructs Sycorax as a black, wayward and wicked witch in order to legitimise it' (152).

Loomba's analysis of the colonial contexts (or, as Barker and Hulme prefer, con-texts) of Shakespeare's works in their own time is grounded in an awareness of their ongoing histories of renegotiation within recent and contemporary postcolonial histories: noting the irony of the fact that 'one of the oldest of Delhi's colleges for women should have been called "Miranda House"' (Loomba 1989: 153), she also refers to a theatre production of *The Tempest* in the same city which, drawing upon the 'Aryan myth', was designed to appeal to Indian audiences prone to 'perceiving themselves as somehow less black than Africans', and hence 'closer to noble, white Prospero than monstrous, black Caliban'; this is but one instance of a complex cultural history which 'alerts us against reading the encounter of Third World readers with the white text as a uniform one' (146). The diversity of such encounters with *The Tempest*, as well as of those staged in the so-called First World, has been well explored in a number of critical works from the 1980s onwards. Trevor Griffiths traces the representation of Caliban in the British theatre from the late nineteenth century to the 1970s, a period bracketed by the rise of 'Social Darwinian ideas and Imperialistic doctrines' at one end and 'the retreat from Empire' at the other (1983: 159).

Alden T. Vaughan and Virginia Mason Vaughan's *Shakespeare's Caliban* ranges further, presenting a cultural history of an 'incredibly flexible' image that has ranged from 'an aquatic beast to a noble savage'; and that has seen Caliban transformed from the 'pure monster' of the late seventeenth century, via the nineteenth-century portrayal of the 'missing link – part beast, part human, and wholly Darwinian', to the more recent figure of 'the exploited native – of whatever continent and whatever color – who struggles for freedom, dignity, and self-determination from European and American Prosperos' (1991: ix, xxii). Christine Dymkowski's stage history for the 'Shakespeare in Production' series engages the play's colonial afterlife by extensively surveying the casting of Caliban as a black man, and concludes that, 'whatever the race of the actor playing the part, its overall interpretation continues to serve as an accurate index of which groups in society are presently alienated, disadvantaged and vulnerable, and, for that reason, threatening to and threatened by those in power' (2000: 71); Cartelli's *Repositioning Shakespeare* deals with the 'West Indian postcolonial', a phenomenon defined by 'hybridity as a social and cultural characteristic' and by 'appropriation as its primary medium of cultural exchange', and which has played 'a leading role in reshaping the plot (and repositioning the politics) of *The Tempest*, a play that has for so long spoken in its name' (1999: 13).

At stake here also are the institutional and cultural politics of Shakespearean criticism itself: readings of *The Tempest* operate within the larger remit of postcolonial criticism of the Shakespearean cultural and critical projects. For, as Orkin and Loomba argue in their introduction to the 1998 collection *Post-Colonial Shakespeares*, the task is not so much the production of more and more postcolonial readings either from the mainstream or from the margins, as the development of critical and theoretical perspectives that enable the Eurocentricity of both the dominant and would-be radical traditions to be challenged; a task which they define as 'provincializing Europe' (Loomba and Orkin 1998: 18). One thing that Orkin stresses is the importance of local knowledge: and in his *Local Shakespeares* he develops a mode of reading the plays in contexts outside of Europe and the United States (for example the South African 'Tswana models of conflict dispute' [Orkin 2005: 10]).

Plantation of this isle

The tendency to regard the originating history of *The Tempest*, as of allied texts of colonialism, through the lens of its histories of appropriation and counter-reading reveals a range of critical, ethical and political inclinations that, as discussed on pp. 339–41, might be defined 'presentist'. It has also provoked some commentators to suggest that the preoccupation with New World colonialism is, variously, a historical over-simplification, a retrospective and anachronistic imposition, and a distortion and diminishment of Shakespeare's play.

Taking issue with Paul Brown, discussed above, Deborah Willis argues that, despite his emphasis on the text's ambivalent relation to the colonial project, his reading

ensures that 'the play becomes wholly engulfed by colonial discourse, retaining little separate identity of its own', producing the implication that 'Shakespeare has done little more
than repeat ambivalences already present in the materials he is working with' (Willis 1989:
278). Disentangling Brown's concatenation of the colonial core, semiperiphery and periphery, Willis locates the play's concerns within the first of these, regarding it as 'an
extremely successful endorsement of the core's political order' that also 'registers anxiety
about the legitimacy of peripheral colonial ventures' (280). One important consequence of
this shift of emphasis is that, instead of attending primarily to Caliban (who is not 'an
embodiment of threat' but 'by turns sympathetic and ridiculous ... comically grotesque
rather than demonic'), we should take account of the 'far more sinister' figure whom Brown
largely ignores, Antonio, who reflects early modern anxieties 'about factious and rebellious
aristocrats, about the exclusion of younger brothers from power by primogeniture, and about
aggression unmodulated by a sense of familial or communal bonds' (286).

Jonathan Bate, in the course of a discussion focussing on Carribean counter-appropria-
tions of the play, queries the New Historicist approach, describing it as 'an exemplary
humanist text' because it is 'set on an island that is its own place ... a place in which one
could reflect upon the ideal society in the manner of More's *Utopia*' (2000: 176), and suggesting that reading *The Tempest* 'only in terms of cultural confrontation ... seems to
encourage talk of hostile exchange between culture and culture' (172–73). As an alternative,
by considering 'an improvisation on the voice of Ariel' (173), Bate directs us towards an
ecologically inflected re-reading of the nature–culture relationship in the play: observing
(apropos Prospero's lines at 1.2.292–94) that 'to harness the power of Ariel, you must split
open a pine', he concludes that 'The price of art is the destruction of a living tree. You can't
have music without dead wood; you can't have poetry without paper. Prospero makes gape
a pine and threatens to rend an oak in order to display his power' (174–75). And if Prospero is 'anti-nature', the best hope for the island that he vacates is that it be left as 'an
ecosystem which man must be content to leave alone' (175–76).

In a less utopian vein, and by way of initiating a more global dispute with postcolonial
readings, and with new historicism in particular, Richard Wilson contends that 'this last
comedy has been Americanized on campuses as a tragedy of colonialism in the New
World', and that the 'New Historicist success in relocating *The Tempest* in Virginia has
transported it too far from Virgil, and the Old World of Aeneas where its action is
set, between Tunis and Naples' (1997: 333). Anchoring the play very specifically within
the maritime economy of the sixteenth-century Mediterranean, Wilson emphasises the
centrality of the slave trade and piracy to both, so that 'Prospero's exacting negotiations to
free Ariel, Caliban, Ferdinand, and his aristocratic hostages' belong to a system of 'lucrative
turnover of capture and ransom' that depended 'not on the enslavement of Africans, who
were employed as "more potent ministers" or guards, but the bondage of Europeans' (336).
Rather more audaciously, Wilson proposes as a key player in this pirate narrative a possible
historical prototype for Prospero in the shape of Sir Robert Dudley, the Catholic son of the
Earl of Leicester, celebrated seafarer, trader and slave trafficker, and heir to Warwickshire's
Kenilworth Castle, or, as Wilson characterises him, 'Duke Roberto Dudley: pirate,
redemptor, and renegade Lord of Shakespeare's Stratford' (349).

Wilson's insistence upon the European and Mediterranean aspect (though not his
identification of Prospero with Dudley), is echoed by Jerry Brotton, who sees it as 'a politically
and geographically bifurcated play' which registers the ambivalence surrounding 'English
maritime encounters with territories over which it could exercise little political control' and
calls into question the 'awareness and confidence in New World issues' that New

Historicists have ascribed to 'texts that were only just beginning to come to terms with the colonial possibilities to the west of Europe' (Brotton 1998: 24, 26, 37). David Kastan asserts that '[t]he play is much more obviously a play about European dynastic concerns than European colonial activities' (1999a: 188). Robin Headlam Wells agrees: 'colonial exploitation was not part of Shakespeare's original play. Whatever it may have come to mean for later ages, *the Tempest* of 1611 is not about the founding of a new civilisation through subjugation of indigenous peoples: it is about the patching up of an old one by peaceful means' (2000: 252). The questioning seems set to continue: surveying the recent critical history of *The Tempest* in his Cambridge edition of the play, David Lindley noted that, just as the New World dimension had, for a time, seemed to provide the definitive context for the play, so too 'efforts to make the North African dimension of the play yield more than passing resonances struggle as yet to be fully convincing' (2002: 45). For Lindley, what has been seen as 'a play about power' might now 'rather be regarded as a play about the illusion of freedom' (81).

Further reading

Barker, Francis and Peter Hulme (1985) '"Nymphs and Reapers Heavily Vanish": The Discursive Con-texts of *The Tempest*', in *Alternative Shakespeares*, ed. John Drakakis. London: Routledge, 206–27.

Felperin, Howard (1972) *Shakespearean Romance*. Princeton, NJ: Princeton University Press.

Gillies, John (1994) *Shakespeare and the Geography of Difference*. Cambridge: Cambridge University Press.

Greenblatt, Stephen (1988) 'Martial Law in the Land of Cockaigne', in *Shakespearean Negotiations*. Berkeley, CA: University of California Press, 129–63.

Hulme, Peter and William H. Sherman (eds) (2000) *The Tempest and Its Travels*. London: Reaktion.

Orgel, Stephen (1975) *The Illusion of Power: Political Theatre in the English Renaisssance*. Berkeley, CA: University of California Press.

Ryan, Kiernan (2002) *Shakespeare*, third edition. Basingstoke: Palgrave.

Vaughan, Alden T. and Virginia Vaughan (1991) *Shakespeare's Caliban: A Cultural History*. Cambridge: Cambridge University Press.

The Winter's Tale

Date, text and authorship

Performed at the Globe May 1611 and at Court November 1611 and 1613; F 1623. Solely Shakespearean.

Sources and influences

Robert Greene, *Pandosto: The Triumph of Time* (1588); Ovid, *Metamorphoses* (trans. Arthur Golding, 1567).

On stage

Phoenix, London, 1951 (dir. Peter Brook; Leontes: John Gielgud; Hermione: Diana Wynyard); RSC, 1960 (dir. Peter Wood); RSC, 1969 (dir. Tevor Nunn; Leontes: Barrie Ingham; Hermione: Judi Dench); RSC, 1981 (dir. Ronald Eyre; Leontes: Patrick Stewart; Hermione: Gemma Jones); RSC, 1986 (dir. Terry Hands; Leontes: Jeremy Irons; Hermione: Penny Downie); NT, 1988 (dir. Peter Hall; Leontes: Tim Piggott-Smith; Hermione: Sally Dexter); Complicite, UK, 1992 (dir. Annabel Arden; Leontes: Simon McBurney; Hermione: Gabrielle Reidy; Mamillus/Paulina/Time/Old Shepherd: Kathryn Hunter); RSC, 1992 (dir. Adrian Noble); Royal Dramatic Theatre of Stockholm, 1994 (dir. Ingmar Bergmann); RSC, 1998 (dir. Gregory Doran; Leontes: Antony Sher; Hermione: Alexandra Gilbreath); Maly, St Petersburg, 1999 (dir. Declan Donnellan); NT, 2001 (dir. Nicholas Hytner; Leontes: Alex Jennings; Hermione: Claire Skinner); RSC, 2002 (dir. Matthew Warchus; Leontes: Douglas Hodge; Hermione: Anastasia Hille); RSC, 2006 (dir. Dominic Cooke; Leontes: Anton Lesser; Hermione: Kate Fleetwood); RSC, 2009 (dir. David Farr; Leontes: Greg Hicks; Hermione: Kelly Hunter).

On screen

BBC Television Shakespeare, UK, 1981 (dir. Jane Howell; Leontes: Jeremy Kemp; Hermione: Anna Calder-Marshall; Polixenes: Robert Stephens); RSC, 1998 (dir. Robin Lough and Gregory Doran; film record of 1998 RSC production).

Offshoots

Shakespeare: The Animated Tales: The Winter's Tale, UK/Russia, 1996 (dir. Stanislav Sokolov).

Things dying

A characteristic of Shakespeare's last plays is their habit of returning to narrative materials that he had previously used as the basis for tragedy and reworking them so as to conclude with resolution and reconciliation rather than catastrophe. In *Pericles* and *Cymbeline* the primary resource is *King Lear*; in *The Winter's Tale*, the template is provided by a tragedy, *Othello*, and a comedy, *Much Ado*, both of which centre upon false accusations of infidelity and both of which are maliciously engineered by the plays' respective villains: Iago and Don John. In both plays, moreover, the mechanisms by which jealous rage is instigated in the imagined cuckolds are clearly disclosed; in *Much Ado*, through the plot contrivance that brings Claudio beneath Hero's window in order to witness, as he thinks, his bride-to-be committing her betrayal, and in *Othello* through the deft placement of a couple of strategically placed questions whose seeming innocuousness ensnares their target within a trap of his own devising: 'Honest, my lord?'; 'Honest? Ay honest'; 'My lord, for aught I know'; 'What dost thou think'; 'Think, my lord?'; '"Think, my lord?" By heaven, thou echo'st me/ As if there were some monster in thy thought/ Too hideous to be shown!' (3.3.106–12). 'Honest' Iago's particular genius, and a large element of his diabolic charm, lies in his ability to claim to be doing one thing whilst engaged in its diametrical opposite, in this instance enflaming Othello's suspicions of Cassio (and Desdemona) by repeatedly asserting their honesty; one of the effects of Iago's horrible plausibility is to anchor the tragedy within the realms of the known and the credible.

Engaging a similar scenario (and progressing it, as in *Much Ado*, into a narrative of a wronged woman apparently taken for dead, taken into hiding and finally reunited with her contrite partner), *The Winter's Tale* affords at least one crucial difference: there is no external agent or catalyst to account for the protagonist's extreme and sudden swing from loving husband to imagined cuckold. The play opens with Leontes, the king of Sicilia, strenuously attempting to persuade Polixenes, his neighbour monarch and the man he regards as his closest friend, to extend an already prolonged sojourn at his court, which involves actively encouraging his queen, Hermione, to intervene to persuade him however she can. All is cordial, calm, courtly, with no hint of anything untoward between Polixenes and Hermione, and no sign that the king and queen's marriage is anything but affectionate, trusting and companionable; yet within barely a hundred lines Leontes explosively confesses to raging doubts about his wife's fidelity ('Too hot, too hot' [1.2.110]) and his young son's paternity ('Art thou my calf?' [1.2.129]).

Unlike Othello's, Leontes's jealousy is impossible to fathom; from the moment it first manifests itself it is fully fledged, rampaging, paranoid, obdurate and utterly isolated and isolating, a passion that works out its relentless force over the course of the play's first three acts until, equally precipitately, it dissipates with the announcement of Hermione's death. The fear and loathing in Leontes is in no small measure prompted by a sense of derangement:

> Yet they say we are
> Almost as like as eggs. Women say so,
> That will say anything. But were they false
> As o'er-dyed blacks, as wind, as waters, false
> As dice are to be wished by one that fixes
> No bourn 'twixt his and mine, yet it were true
> To say this boy were like me.

(1.2.131–37)

With its vertiginously rapid changes of tack, switches between subject and object, and between introspection and outward-facing address (to Leontes's son, Mamillus), its oscillations between misogynist invective, desperate assertion and anguished vulnerability, and its stockpiling of claims and counter-claims that each contain within them their own corrosive antitheses, the passage is an index of a disordered consciousness. It also typifies Shakespeare's late style: simultaneously intense, compacted and metrically varied and flexible, it eschews the end-stopped line in favour of enjambment (that is, organising units of utterance so that the breaks are placed in the middle of the verse line rather than at the end). The effect here, however, is not that of naturalistic speech but of the hallucinatory vividness of a bad dream.

That Leontes's fantasies about Hermione and Polixenes, the product of what the loyal Camillo courageously describes to his king's face as 'diseased opinion' (1.2.298), are utterly without foundation is never in doubt; indeed, Leontes himself, without being aware of the significance of what he is saying, provides a compelling and extraordinarily concise account of the corrupted imagination's capacity to pervert and to destroy:

> There may be in the cup
> A spider steeped, and one may drink, depart,
> And yet partake no venom, for his knowledge
> Is not infected; but if one present
> Th'abhorred ingredient to his eye, make known
> How he hath drunk, he cracks his gorge, his sides,
> With violent hefts. I have drunk, and seen the spider.
>
> (2.1.41–47)

The passage refers to the early modern assumption that the spider's contaminating presence would only register if brought to the attention of the drinker; in this instance, both Leontes's listeners and the play's audience know that there is no arachnid other than that which he has created for himself.

In one sense, then, the clear-cut distinctions that are enforced between Leontes's delusions and the reality of a situation that we know to be otherwise define the secure ground upon which the play's fiction stands. In another, and almost in spite of itself, the play works to undermine and interrogate such reassurances. Leontes's anguished visions of Hermione's lubriciousness may be objectively unreal, but they are rendered with such tactile immediacy that they at least partly implicate the play's audience within his own imaginings. In the most overt instance of this, Leontes addresses himself directly to his offstage listeners:

> There have been,
> Or I am much deceived, cuckolds ere now,
> And many a man there is, even at this present,
> Now, while I speak this, holds his wife by th'arm,
> That little thinks she has been sluiced in's absence,
> And his pond fished by his next neighbour, by
> Sir Smile, his neighbour.
>
> (1.2.191–97)

The pornographic frankness of the anatomical and body-fluid imagery (which incidentally envisages the wife's body, reduced to its sex organs – 'his pond' – as no more than a territorial constituent of the husband's estate, liable to the smiling predations of poacher-neighbours) is, in itself, disconcerting enough; its additional force derives from its rupturing of the fabric of the play's fiction to exploit the darkest fears of the men in its audience 'even at this present', some of whom, perhaps, are sitting beside and alongside the very wives and neighbours that they are solicited to distrust. Seen in this context, the terror of cuckoldry that manifests itself in Leontes's destructive behaviour is actually endemic within the condition of early modern manhood, for whom no woman, no offspring, can ever be truly known to be one's own, to be true.

For its first three acts, *The Winter's Tale* follows the pattern of a domestic tragedy, which culminates, at the moment that Leontes, in his ultimate act of hubris, defies the pronouncement of Apollo's oracle, in the death of Mamillus and the apparent death of Hermione, and thus in the king's immediate and absolute remorse. As a tragic micro-narrative that is compressed to the point of seeming blatantly schematic, this constitutes the first movement of the play. It is worth considering at this point what the play's audiences are given to expect, with regard not only to what might happen next, but to what kind of play it actually is.

An early clue is given in the first scene, when Hermione invites Mamillus to 'tell's a tale':

> MAMILLUS Merry or sad shall't be?
> HERMIONE As merry as you will.
> MAMILLUS A sad tale's best for winter. I have one
> Of sprites and goblins.
> HERMIONE Let's have that, good sir.
> Come on, sit down, come on, and do your best
> To fright me with your sprites. You're powerful at it.
>
> (2.1.25–30)

The exchange is, of course, metadramatic: announcing a 'sad' tale of winter that is emebedded within a drama calling itself a 'winter's tale', Mamillus begins the story of 'sprites and goblins', and of a man who 'Dwelt by a churchyard' (32) at the very moment that his father enters. Anyone who has spent time listening to children telling stories will recognise here the relaxed attitudes towards the fantastic, the macabre and the morbid that are the stock-in-trade of the juvenile raconteur; there is also an obvious connection to be made between the protagonist of the tale that Mamillus preserves for his mother's ears alone and the man who will spend the next sixteen years haunting a mausoleum, and who will at the end be persuaded to believe that something like his dead wife's funerary monument has come back to life. The play, it is inferred, is of the same order: a scary story to be told by the fireside, in which danger and death will be encountered, but in which all will finally be well.

At this point in the play, though, those who were familiar with Shakespeare's primary source might well have mapped a different trajectory. *The Winter's Tale* is based on the prose narrative *Pandosto: The Triumph of Time*, by Robert Greene, a work first published in 1588 and popular enough to be reprinted four times up until 1614, and more than a dozen times subsequently. Set, like Shakespeare's play, in Sicilia and Bohemia, Greene's story has Pandosto, the king of Bohemia, as the jealous husband of Bellaria, and the Sicilian king, Egistus, as his innocent rival, and follows a similar pattern of movement from court to country and back again. In addition to his reversal of the settings so that the traditionally Arcadian environment of Sicilia is transposed to a landlocked Bohemia that nonetheless features a sea-coast (perhaps a way of stressing the tale's manifest fictionality), Shakespeare made two crucial alterations to Greene's narrative.

In *Pandosto*, Bellaria's trial ends in her death; and when Pandosto's daughter Fawnia, the figure who corresponds to Perdita in Shakespeare's play, is brought to her father the meeting provokes him to an incestuous desire that drives him to suicide. The preservation of Hermione and her miraculous resurrection are Shakespeare's innovation, as are the addition of the chief architect of her survival and Leontes's nemesis, Paulina, a plum role for the King's Men's intellectual clown, Robert Armin, in Autolycus; the whole sheep-shearing festival scene that comprises the bulk of the fourth act; and the intervention of Time as Chorus at 4.1 (who thus eases the play across a sixteen-year gap 'since it is in my

power/ To o'erthrow law, and in one self-born hour/ To plant and o'erwhelm custom'
[4.1.7–9]). For the play's first audiences, at least, the first half of Shakespeare's play might
have created expectations of a tragic outcome. It is worth noting here that the testimony of
the play's sole early modern eyewitness, Simon Forman, who reported seeing it at the
Globe on 11 May 1611, makes no mention of the statue scene; indeed, he seemed most
impressed with the portrayal of 'the Rog that cam in all tottered like coll pixei' (Autolycus,
guised as one of Mamillus's 'sprites'), who enabled him to ponder the moral 'Beware of
trustinge feined beggars or fawninge fellouss'.

Forman either did not notice, or chose not to document, the moment when the play
turns from tragic to comic mode, from darkness to light, and from winter to summer,
which occurs at the climax of the third act, and which is suitably marked by one of the
most inspiring stage directions in the dramatic canon:

> *Exit, pursued by a bear.*
>
> (3.3.57.s.d.)

The hapless agent of an exit that sees the incredible in full pursuit of the imminently edible
is Antigonus, bearer of the infant Perdita, who is under Leontes's orders to dispose of the
child, and who has only just recounted a dream-vision of Hermione that contains an
anticipation of his demise. Modern productions have found differing ways of staging the
bear, ranging from actors in skins to large-scale scenic convulsions that turn the beast into
an atavistic force of nature; on Shakespeare's stage, the presence of ursine neighbours in the
entertainment district may have had a bearing upon its depiction in this play (bears feature
in the King's Men's play *Mucedorus*, which was performed at court in February 1610).
Whether or not a real tame bear was led onto the Globe platform at this point, it is
tempting to interpret Antigonus's terminal encounter with the fauna of Bohemia's impossible seashore as not only a little local difficulty but the enraged natural order's reaction to
Leontes's assault upon it (and perhaps also as the vengeance of the tethered and tormented
beasts of Henslowe's nearby baiting arenas). If Antigonus's naming carries echoes of the
Sophoclean tragic heroine Antigone, whose tragedy is the consequence of her opposition to
tyranny (a stance adopted in this play by his wife), his grisly fate at the bear's teeth and
claws invokes tragedy's roots in the drama of blood sacrifice.

Things new-born

It is immediately followed by one of the most audacious tonal shifts in the entire canon,
marked by the successive entries, first, of the Old Shepherd, the man who is to act as
the infant princess's foster-father for the next sixteen years, and, second, of the Clown.
Mistaking the child as an abandoned illegitimate ('This has been some stair-work, some
trunk-work, some behind-door-work' [3.3.70–71]), the Shepherd pledges to 'take it up for
pity' (72–73), in an act of simple, unaffected charity that is sharply contrasted with the
heartless comedy of the Clown's description of the terrible deaths of Antigonus and the
mariners:

> how the poor souls roared, and the sea mocked them, and how the poor gentleman
> roared, and the bear mocked him, both roaring louder than the sea or weather … The men
> are not yet cold under water, nor the bear half dined on the gentleman. He's at it now.
>
> (3.3.92–98)

The Clown's callous indifference towards those whose fates he describes so blithely is, in the context of tragedy, shocking, but it is the means of effecting the transition to the comedy and to romance. Straddling a shoreline that hosts both catastrophic violence and new life, the characters in this scene stand between two worlds: 'Thou metst with things dying', says the Shepherd to the Clown, 'I with things new-born' (3.3.104–05). It is a line whose antithetical poise encapsulates the double movement of the play.

The pastoral world of Bohemia that provides the setting for the play's fourth act, with its homely swains, disguising and gullings, and with its occasionally leisurely and digressive construction (Autolycus, like Touchstone, is an exquisite time-waster and agent of distraction), is similar to that of the earlier comedies, especially *As You Like It*; it also is strongly counterpoised against the patriarchal wilderness of the first half of the play as a zone in which female power, and in particular the power of fertility, of reproduction and of nurturing, reigns supreme. At its centre is the tiny survivor of Leontes's wrath, Perdita, the crowned Queen of the Feast, distributor of floral gifts and champion of nature over art (rehearsing the perennial Renaissance debate about the relative merits of these supposedly antithetical conceptions, Perdita and Polixenes position themselves on either side of the arguments for and against genetic engineering, a discussion rendered ironic in the dramatic context, since Perdita, the critic of 'art which in their piedness shares/ With great creating nature' [4.4.87–88], is herself confirmed as what she is through the exercise of 'art').

A space of recuperation, but also of tricksterdom and, for a while, potential tragedy (Polixines's opposition to his son Florizel's plan to marry a woman he thinks a Shepherd's daughter threatens to re-run the familial conflicts of the play's first movement), Bohemia is the ground on which the reconciliations of the play's final movement are built. Shakespeare's source was subtitled *The Triumph of Time*; his own treatment might well have been *The Triumph Over Time*, in that its rare promise is that the seemingly irreversible can, after all, be reversed; the irretrievable retrieved; the lost can be found and the dead restored to life. It is, the play well knows, the promise not of nature but of art; and one which, as the note of self-reflexivity that shadows the Gentlemen's recapitulations in the penultimate scene signals, tests the credulity of its watchers and listeners to the limit:

> Such a deal of wonder is broken out within this hour, that ballad-makers cannot be able to express it.
>
> (5.2.21–22)

> SECOND GENTLEMAN What, pray you, became of Antigonus, that carried hence the child?
> THIRD GENTLEMAN Like an old tale still, which will have matter to rehearse though credit be asleep and not an ear open.
>
> (5.2.53–56)

It may be only a yarn, but the effect is surely to intensify rather than undermine our emotional engagement. 'Were it but told you', Paulina advises Leontes, commenting on the miracle of Hermione's restoration but also, implicitly, on the narrative in which she moves and breathes, it 'should be hooted at/ Like an old tale' (5.3.117–18), but, as she and Shakespeare well know, the oldest – and the most fantastic – tales are more often than not those with the deepest power to move. All that is 'required', as Paulina simply puts it, is that 'You do awake your faith' (5.3.95). In its extraordinary final scene, *The Winter's Tale* makes this requirement of Leontes, his court and his surviving family – and of us.

Further reading

Belsey, Catherine (1999) *Shakespeare and the Loss of Eden: The Construction of Family Values in Early Modern Culture*. Basingstoke: Palgrave.

Bristol, Mchael D. (1996) *Big-time Shakespeare*. London and New York: Routledge.

Cavell, Stanley (1987) *Disowning Knowledge in Six Plays of Shakespeare*. Cambridge: Cambridge University Press.

Frye, Northrop (1965) *A Natural Perspective: The Development of Shakespearean Comedy and Romance*. New York: Columbia University Press.

McDonald, Russ (2006) *Shakespeare's Late Style*. Cambridge: Cambridge University Press.

Palfrey, Simon (1997) *Late Shakespeare: A New World of Words*. Oxford: Clarendon Press.

Paster, Gail Kern (1993) *The Body Embarrassed: Drama and the Disciplines of Shame in Early Modern Europe*. Ithaca, NY: Cornell University Press.

Pericles, Cymbeline *and* The Two Noble Kinsmen

Pericles, Prince of Tyre

Date, text and authorship

1608; entered SR 1608; Q1 1609; Q2 1611; Q3 1619; not in F 1623; F3 1664. Co-authored by Shakespeare and George Wilkins.

Sources and influences

John Gower, *Confessio Amantis* (1390); George Wilkins, *The Pattern of Painful Adventures of Pericles, Prince of Tyre* (c.1576).

On stage

SMT, 1958 (dir. Tony Richardson); RSC, 1969 (dir. Terry Hands); RSC, 1979 (dir. Ron Daniels); Cheek by Jowl, 1984 (dir. Declan Donnellan); RSC, 1989 (dir. David Thacker); RSC, 2002 (dir. Adrian Noble); Ninagawa Company, Tokyo, 2003 (dir. Yukio Ninagawa); RSC, 2006 (dir. Dominic Cooke).

On screen

BBC Television Shakespeare, UK, 1984 (dir. David Jones; Pericles: Mike Gwilym: Boult: Trevor Peacock).

Cymbeline

Date, text and authorship

1610; performed at the Globe April 1611; F 1623. Solely Shakespearean.

Sources and influences

Raphael Holinshed, *Chronicles of England, Scotland and Ireland* (1587); Giovanni Boccaccio, *Decameron* (trans. William Painter, 1566); Francis Beamont and John Fletcher, *Philaster* (1608–10); *Rare Triumphs of Love and Fortune* (1582).

On stage

SMT, 1957 (dir. Peter Hall; Innogen: Peggy Ashcroft); RSC, 1962 (dir. William Gaskill; Innogen: Vanessa Redgrave); RSC, 1987 (dir. Bill Alexander; Innogen: Harriet Walter); NT, 1988 (dir. Peter Hall; Innogen: Geraldine James); New York Shakespeare Festival, 1989 (dir. JoAnne Akalaitis); RSC, 1997 (dir. Adrian Noble); Shakespeare's Globe, 2001 (dir. Mike Alfreds; Posthumus/Cloten: Mark Rylance); RSC, 2003 (dir. Dominic Cooke); Kneehigh Theatre/RSC, 2006 (dir. Emma Rice).

On screen

BBC Television Shakespeare, UK, 1983 (dir. Elijah Moshinsky; Cymbeline: Richard Johnson; Queen; Claire Bloom; Innogen: Helen Mirren; Posthumus: Michael Pennington; Iachimo: Robert Lindsay; Cloten: Paul Jesson).

Offshoots

Theatre of Blood, UK, 1973 (dir. Michael Hickox).

The Two Noble Kinsmen

Date, text and authorship

c.1613; Q1 1634; not in F 1623; F3 1664. Co-authored by Shakespeare and John Fletcher.

Sources and influences

Geoffrey Chaucer, *The Knight's Tale* (c.1392–95); Richard Edwards, *Palaemon and Arcyte* (performed 1566).

On stage

RSC, 1986 (dir. Barry Kyle; Palamon: Gerard Murphy; Arcite: Hugh Quarshie; Jailer's Daughter: Imogen Stubbs); Shakespeare's Globe, 2000 (dir. Tim Carroll); RSC, 2006 (dir. William Oldroyd).

To sing a song that old was sung …

Thus, in the consciously archaic, rolling octosyllables of medieval balladry, and of the mystery and miracle plays still seen on platform stages in the England of Shakespeare's youth, begins *Pericles*, a 'mouldy tale', in Ben Jonson's words, of peripatetics, parenting and perversion that leads its eponymous protagonist on an epic tour of the Mediterranean that taking him from youth to middle age, that sees him flee a king's assassins after he has tactlessly solved the riddle that betrays the secret of royal incest, marry the daughter of a virtuous king, lose his wife during a storm at sea and surrender his daughter to unknown care in a foreign land, and become a recluse refusing either to shave or to cut his hair, all before finally being reunited with both the wife and daughter he thought dead; and that also sees the wife, Thaisa, retrieved from apparent death by drowning, and the daughter, Marina, kidnapped by pirates and delivered into the hands of a brothel-keeper, whose trade she succeeds in sabotaging by virtue of her determined preservation of her chastity.

Cheerfully disregarding the unities of time, place and action favoured by Shakespeare's neoclassical contemporaries (Jonson, notably, among them), but threaded through by the ballad-style commentary of the narrator, the fourteenth-century poet John Gower, the play spans decades and continents and proliferates plotlines, incidents and characters, introducing (and successively discarding) assassins, scheming queens and murderous daughters, loyal counsellors, wise sailors and honest fishermen, jousting knights, pirates, the goddess Diana, and whoremongers and their clients. If the play's opening prologue draws attention to the familiarity of a folktale that had 'been sung at festivals,/ On ember-eves and holy-ales' (1.5–6), its concluding lines insist upon the conventional moral to be drawn from it, as well as attempting the seemingly impossible task of tying together at least some of its loose ends:

> In Antiochus and his daughter you have heard
> Of monstrous lust the due and just reward;
> In Pericles, his queen and daughter seen,
> Although assailed with fortune fierce and keen,
> Virtue preserved from fell destruction's blast,
> Led on by heav'n, and crowned with joy at last.

> (22.108–13)

At last, indeed.

It will, perhaps, already be evident why *Pericles* has not been rated particularly highly by commentators and why, until recently, it has been staged relatively rarely (there is only one screen version generally available: the unexceptional BBC Television Shakespeare version of 1984). With (so we are told) its trite moralising, credibility-defying narrative, sing-song versification and two-dimensional or incomprehensible characterisation, as well as its unsettling combination of fairy-tale grotesquery (kicking off with a display of severed heads in the first scene), deviant sexuality (father–daughter incest) and sordid realism (the brothel scenes in Mytilene being an all-too vivid evocation of the stews of early modern London), and its curiously passive title character, *Pericles* breaks most of the recognized rules of Shakespearean good taste: a text, like the other late plays, preoccupied with the relations between parent and child, and especially between father and daughter, it is probably not suitable for children, but possibly not entirely suitable for adults either.

The play's deficiencies, in the eyes of its detractors, are compounded by the likelihood that it is a collaboration between Shakespeare and the minor dramatist George Wilkins, and that, moreover, its only authoritative text is that of the quarto of 1609 (for reasons unknown, the compilers of the Folio did not include it in the canon, though it had been demonstrably successful as a King's Men play), an edition regarded as corrupt and ridden with errors. A number of editions (most radically the Oxford, which is also used by the Norton edition cited by this book) have attempted to clarify and supplement the quarto by grafting onto it text taken from the prose version of the story, *The Painful Adventures of Pericles, Prince of Tyre*, published under Wilkins's name in 1608, thus reinforcing that author's claims to the work.

It is generally agreed that Wilkins wrote most of the play up to the end of what in Oxford and Norton is identified as Scene 10 (or Act 2, Scene 5 in most other editions), and that Shakespeare takes the helm at the beginning of Scene 11, with Pericles '*a-shipboard*' (11.1.s.d.), Lear, as it were, in reverse gear, soliciting 'The god of this great vast' to subdue the power of an angry sea that threatens to overwhelm the vessel upon which his wife is about to give birth:

> rebuke these surges
> Which wash both heav'n and hell; and thou that hast
> Upon the winds command, bind them in brass,
> Having called them from the deep. O still
> Thy deaf'ning dreadful thunders, gently quench
> Thy nimble sulph'rous flashes.

(11.1–6)

If Pericles conspicuously both evokes and rewrites Shakespeare's earlier stormbound monarch here, he is also Lear-like in his loss (but more in resignation than in anger) of a beloved daughter and in his part in their subsequent, redemptive recovery and reconciliation, here staged in a scene which powerfully echoes *King Lear*, 4.7:

> Give me a gash, put me to present pain,
> Lest this great sea of joys rushing upon me
> O'erbear the shores of my mortality
> And drown me with their sweetness! [*To* MARINA] O, come hither,
> [MARINA *stands*]
> Thou that begett'st him that did thee beget,

> Thou that wast born at sea, buried at Tarsus,
> And found at sea again!

(21.178–84)

Conjoining ecstasy and annihilation, the figure of the sea, as both the dealer of death and the source of life, conveys the mythical and elemental force of the reunion; as incarnated in Marina, whose naming aligns her with the play's narrative and metaphorical heart, the force, and grace, of the 'great vast' is redemptive in ways that resonate well beyond the encounter between father and child.

There is much in the play that is legendary and archetypal; it also accommodates a powerful strand of dirty realism in the brothel scenes (16–19), wherein the degraded state of the sex trade in Mytilene is deftly sketched in the opening exchange between a pair of its senior managers and their henchman:

> PANDER Search the market narrowly. Myteline is full of gallants. We lose too much money this mart by being wenchless.
>
> BAWD We were never so much out of creatures. We have but poor three, and they can do no more than they can do, and they with continual action are even as good as rotten.
>
> PANDER Therefore let's have fresh ones, whate'er we pay for them …
>
> … The poor Transylvanian is dead that lay with the little baggage.
>
> BOULT Ay, she pooped him, she made him roast meat for worms. But I'll go search the market.

(16.3–21)

Rife with death-dealing venereal infections, populated by abused and exhausted prostitutes, their handlers and a pathetic gallery of clients who between them exhibit the worst aspects of predatory and exploitative male sexuality, and characterised as an economy in which virginity is openly touted as a commodity, the Mytelinean underworld is, if anything, an even worse place than *Measure for Measure*'s Vienna.

It is into this environment that the abducted Marina is introduced, and in which, in the way of romance, she proceeds not only to preserve her own chastity but also, by harnessing the arts of performance to preach divinity in the whorehouse, to convert its pox-ridden libertines into apostles of virtue, propelling them 'out of the road of rutting for ever' (19.8–9). It is in such confrontations between the materials of romance and the resources of realism that the distinctive character of the play resides. And it is when the play in performance has revelled in its fantasticality and embraced its unevenness, rather than attempted to reconcile its dissonances, that it has revealed itself as delightful, engaging and deeply moving.

Dreams and visions

In the preface to his *Dream Play*, the playwright August Strindberg wrote in 1901:

> Everything can happen, everything is possible and probable. Time and place do not exist; on an insignificant basis of reality, the imagination spin, weaving new patterns; a mixture of memories, experiences, free fancies, incongruities and improvisations. The characters split, double, multiply, evaporate, condense, disperse, assemble … just as a

dream is more often painful than happy, so an undertone of melancholy and of pity for
all mortal beings accompanies this flickering tale.

(Strindberg 1982: 175)

Obliquely confirming Shakespeare's uncanny capacity to pre-empt his dramatic legacy, this
description of a work which stands as a vital link between high naturalism and the modern
avant-garde might equally well be applied to *Cymbeline*, a play which contains a succession
of incidences of, and references to, sleep, dreams and visions, and of sleepers awaking to
find themselves in incomprehensible situations, and which is pervaded by a sense of the
strange, the arbitrary, the hallucinatory and the unreal. Its male lead, if that is what he is,
Posthumus Leonatus, is so named because he was born after his father's death; but the
name is apt for a man who is even from the beginning a dead man walking, exiled from
Cymbeline's Court, duped into believing that his wife has been unfaithful to him, mistaken
for the headless corpse of his clownish rival by his wife, and imprisoned both by the
invading Romans and his own countrymen before he is finally restored to favour.

Its heroine, if that is what she is, Innogen, is visited in her sleep by a man who emerges
from a trunk full of treasures, drugged into a deathlike coma from which she awakes,
doubting reality, to encounter a decapitated body, and who remains in the guise of a male
page until the end of the play. The nominal protagonist, Cymbeline, is a reactive, flatly
characterless figure, dominated for most of the action by his wicked Queen (a nameless
force straight from fairy tale), whose primary role in the final scene is to react with bewilderment and incredulity to the increasingly fantastic revelations as they successively unfold
('Does the world go round?' [5.6.232]). Anachronism is no stranger to Shakespeare's
drama, but in this play the cultural and temporal juxtapositions are even sharper and odder
than usual: envisaging the presence of the Romans in a Britain which evokes both the
legendary kingdom of antiquity and the provisional geopolitical entity that was the king of
Scotland and England's own Jacobean dream, the foreign invaders are also seventeenth-
century Italians; when Posthumus (an Englishman with a Latin name) travels to Rome he
finds himself in the company of Frenchmen, Dutchmen and Spaniards.

The play is haunted by ghosts and echoes of Shakespeare's own works. *Cymbeline* was
seen by Simon Forman, probably at the Globe in 1611, and published as the last of the
tragedies in the Folio, although since the early nineteenth century it has been categorised as
a romance. This placement of the play, which, in terms of the number and complexity of
the reconciliations and resolutions that effect its finale, has technically the happiest ending
in the canon, has struck some as anomalous, though possibly explicable in terms of its
semi-legendary historical setting and its relation to the Jacobean genre of tragicomedy.
Viewed as a text which, along with the first of the Folio comedies, *The Tempest*, bookends
the Shakespearean corpus, *Cymbeline* is a play which offers a retrospection upon the entire
canon by performing upon it the work of condensation, displacement, juxtaposition and
transposition that Strindberg, after Freud, sees as characteristic of dreamwork, combining
genres, situations and motifs from earlier works, resurrecting characters and plotlines,
entwining Roman and English history, and reworking tragedy as comedy, comedy as near-
tragedy. Leonatus and Innogen take their names from the governor and his wife in *Much Ado*
(the latter, aptly, a 'ghost' character who never appears in the play); they find themselves
implicated within an infidelity scenario scripted by one Iachimo (modernised as Giacomo
in the Norton edition), a near homophonic kinsman of Iago; though their nemesis lacks
both the ensign's lethally persuasive charm and the steely consistency that ensures that he
neither repents nor explains at the end of his play: Giacomo does both, at length.

When Giacomo slides from the trunk in Innogen's bedchamber, he imagines himself as the rapist Tarquin (who 'thus/ Did softly press the rushes ere he wakened/ The chastity he wounded' [2.2.12–14]), whose story had been told by Shakespeare in *Lucrece* (whose publisher, Richard Field, is, in a weird Shakespearean in-joke, perhaps alluded to in the pseudonym that Innogen selects for the man she believes to be her dead husband – 'Richard du Champ' [4.3.379]). Like the heroines of the earlier romantic comedies, Innogen adopts male disguise and heads into the wilds of Wales (affording the matchless line 'Accessible is none but Milford way' [3.2.82]); unlike them, she is not liberated by the transformation but progressively disempowered by it: becoming more and more indistinct as the play proceeds, her fate is to be designated 'a piece of tender air' (5.6.437–38). She adopts the submissive role of 'cavekeeper,/ And cook' (4.2.300–01) for her incognito brothers in rural exile, and offers herself for service in the Roman army; when she does present herself, still attired as a page, to her husband, he fails to recognise her, and knocks her to the ground in fury: 'Shall 's have a play of this? Thou scornful page,/ There lie thy part' (5.6.227–28).

Posthumus and Innogen are reconciled, but at the expense of her meekly accepting second place to her brothers, the restored true heirs to the throne. Sons of another Lear redux, the princes are themselves partly dramatic descendants of the lords-in-exile of *As You Like It*; despising courtly and mainstream social values (offered money by Innogen-as-Fidele, Arviragus rejects it as 'dirt' [3.6.53]), and also casually capable of extreme violence: Guiderius hacks off the hapless Cloten's head, brings it on stage, and exits to 'throw't into the creek/ Behind our rock, and let it to the sea' (4.2.152–53). Here, as elsewhere, the tone of the play is troubling and ambiguous: as in the nightmarish scene of Innogen's awakening alongside Cloten's body, which can be played both for its full-blooded horror (as in the 1983 BBC Television Shakespeare version, in which the corpse is presented with nauseating grisliness) and for its macabre potential for grotesque farce, a range of reactions are possible to Guiderius's blithe brutality. Whether Cloten's fate is poetically just is hard to determine: although he is clearly a villain, sadistically intent on raping Innogen in her husband's clothing, his actual behaviour is almost invariably characterised by incompetence and failure, so that it is hard to imagine him executing his intentions had he had the opportunity to put them into practice; more Dogberry than Don John, and less Iago than Roderigo, an Oswald rather than an Edmund, Cloten is, as his name ('clot') signifies, not the machiavel he fancies himself to be but a stooge, a fall-guy, a joke.

Yet that is not all: Cloten's determination to occupy Posthumus's place, the ease with which he dons his clothes ('How fit his garments serve me!' [4.1.2]) and Innogen's misprision suggest that he is not just Posthumus's antagonist but also his perverse double, even duplicate (an idea that has been fruitfully exploited in productions which cast the same actor in both roles). At the outset, the opposition between high-born knave and fool and noble commoner, good guy and bad guy, is clear enough; but what becomes disconcertingly apparent as Giacomo's deception plot unfolds is that the sexual violence that Cloten aims to inflict upon Innogen replicates the aggression inherent in Posthumus's own misogyny. Voicing the fear of universal cuckoldry that afflicts early modern manhood at its most anxious, Posthumus's reaction to Innogen's alleged infidelity is to declare that 'We are bastards all' and to launch a bitter onslaught against women in general:

> there's no motion
> That tends to vice in man but I affirm
> It is the woman's part; be it lying, note it,
> The woman's; flattering, hers; deceiving, hers;

Lust and rank thoughts, hers, hers; revenges, hers;
Ambitions, covetings, change of prides; disdain,
Nice longing, slanders, mutability,
All faults that man can name, nay, that hell knows,
Why, hers in part or all ...

(2.5.20–28)

The play does not endorse Posthumus's position (he is, we know, quite wrong about Innogen, whose chastity is not at all in doubt, and who remains consistently faithful, loyal and true throughout), although the portrayal of the Queen, the only other significant female 'part' (the term is sexually and metatheatrically loaded) in the play, who is cast in the role of regal dominatrix, allows sufficient scope for stereotypes of female duplicity and wanton destructiveness. And though the more virulent strains of misogyny in the play are deviant, patriarchal power, less ineptly exercised, is normative: one among the many consolations of the romance denouement is the apparent power shift between Innogen and Posthumus, wherein the latter appears to have acquired the upper hand.

Echoes of other plays and dramatic registers are heard in the play's intermixture of Roman and English – or here, pointedly, British – history: when Cymbeline's court faces the delegation led by Augustus Caesar's envoy, the Queen gives voice to the robust, insular patriotism, harbouring imperial aspirations ('Britain's a world/ By itself'), of *Richard II*, *King John* and *Henry V*:

Remember, sir, my liege,
The kings your ancestors, together with
The natural bravery of your isle, which stands
As Neptune's park, ribbed and paled in
With banks unscalable ...

(3.1.12–20)

Unmistakeably evoking John of Gaunt's 'sceptred isle' and the heroic 'remembrance of those valiant dead' urged upon Henry V (1.2.115), the Queen's panegyric summons to memory a legendary Britain that lies in the play's own future; when at the end Cymbeline seals the *pax Romana* with agreement of a truce between Rome and the nascent British empire, the gesture instantaneously encompasses past, present and what is to come.

Its preoccupation with British national identity was shared by the King's Men's patron: *Cymbeline* is a peculiarly topical play, though the nature of its investments in James's political project is not straightforward. A key presence in the play is the Roman deity Jupiter, who is repeatedly evoked in the dialogue and who makes a literal appearance, on the back of an eagle, in 5.5, in the most portentous and fully realised spectacular of the play's dream-visions. The most fabulous of the play's fictions, Jupiter was a god very dear to James's own heart; as well as tracing his continuity to the Roman emperors, he fancied his own Jove-like propensity to descend upon his Parliament raining metaphorical thunderbolts upon its recalcitrant members (Marcus 1988). Whether the play can or should be read as a deferential homage to James's concerns is, however, questionable: at the very least, its nominal protagonist can hardly be construed as a flattering portrayal of a strong ruler. Even though the conflict with Rome presents a threat to British sovereignty, there are no great political principles at stake: indeed, it appears that the dispute stems from tax evasion on the part of the British Crown, which has neglected to maintain its payments to its Roman overlords. A play which, in common with Shakespeare's other romances, recurrently stages self-reflexive doubts about its own credibility, it draws attention to its artifice and freely combines Jacobean *Realpolitik* and the fantastic, refusing to allow itself to be forced into the mould of allegory.

Two cousins and a daughter

When the Royal Shakespeare Company opened its third auditorium in Stratford-upon-Avon in 1986, it did so with *The Two Noble Kinsmen*, a play that had not been staged in the town since 1959, when it was given an amateur performance in a temporary open-air theatre on the banks of the River Avon; prior to this, the play had been professionally performed only a handful of times, and not at all between the late seventeenth and early twentieth centuries. The unusual choice of play reflected the Swan's brief as a venue for, as its director Barry Kyle put it, 'the plays that influenced Shakespeare and the plays that Shakespeare influenced' (Kyle 1987): dedicated at least in its first seasons to what might be termed the Shakespearean penumbra, and presenting itself as a souped-up reconstruction of an approximately Jacobean-style private playhouse, the Swan appeared to offer Shakespeare's late collaboration with John Fletcher an opportunity to prove its worth as an unjustly marginalised work. To add to the novelty (and to dispel any impression that the Swan was intended as an antiquarian venture), the director and designer opted to set the production in Japanese-style medieval Samurai costumes, drawing upon the vocabularies of Noh and Kabuki (whose platform stage the Swan resembles) to provide a frame of reference for the play's formal and ceremonial aspects.

Overall, the production and the new theatre that it showcased were reasonably reviewed, with most critics recognising that both served the play well, in that they brought out the theatrical artifice, schematic patterning and antithetical structure of a drama (derived from Chaucer's *Knight's Tale*) in which the cousins Palamon and Arcite (the 'noble kinsmen' of the title) vie for the affections of Emilia, the sister of Theseus (who with his bride Hippolyta is afforded an excursus from *A Midsummer Night's Dream*), after the ruler has jailed them, a rivalry that culminates in mortal combat in which Palamon is narrowly defeated, and which is followed by Arcite's death as a result of a riding accident; throughout, the fortunes of Emilia, who is for the most part the passive focus of the kinsmen's competing affections, are paralleled with those of the unnamed daughter of their jailor, whose sudden, irrational and unrequited passion for Palamon mirrors that of the male leads for Emilia whilst providing the antithesis of her demure inactivity.

The play's character groupings of twos (the kinsmen, the young women, Venus and Mars) and threes (Palamon, Arcite and Emilia, the three queens who face Theseus, Hippolyta and Emilia in ritual entreaty in 1.1; the three knights apiece that accompany the kinsmen) define one aspect of its formal design; another is suggested by its use of set-pieces, emblems and tableaux. The first act opens with a masque-like sequence in which Hymen, Greek god of marriage, enters accompanied by a singing juvenile (one of the many indications that this was a play written for the Blackfriars playhouse) and garlanded nymphs; the act concludes with the three mourning queens in a funeral procession; Emilia presents an offering at the altar of Diana; Theseus and Hipplolyta are treated to the spectacle of a morris dance. As well as providing a formalised, exotic setting for these and other elements of the play's artifice, the Samurai setting of the 1986 production suggested a world ruled by a warrior code of conduct analogous to the medieval chivalric values which predominate in the play, and which drive both the kinsmen's almost arbitrary desire for Emilia and their competitive destructiveness. Regarded as a tragicomedy, the play concludes on a disconcertingly queasy note, with Theseus sententiously struggling to square the messiness of its conclusion with a sense of divine or poetic justice ('Never fortune/ Did play a subtler game ... Yet in the passage/ The gods have been most equal' [5.6.112–15]), before ultimately abandoning the search for justice and meaning in the capricious workings of fate:

> Let us be thankful
> For that which is, and with you leave dispute
> That are above our question.
>
> (5.6.134–36)

The mixture of equivocation and baffled fatalism that characterises this ending is perhaps one of the factors that has caused it to be viewed as markedly different in tone and spirit from Shakespeare's other late plays.

The other consideration is that, like *Henry VIII*, *Kinsmen* is the product of a collaboration between Shakespeare and the younger dramatist John Fletcher. Shakespeare is generally assigned the authorship of the first and most of the fifth act as well as the first two scenes of the third, which credits him with most of the plot material relating to the noble protagonists; as primary author of the remainder, Fletcher is responsible for what its patchy performance history has revealed to be the more interesting and actable aspects of the play, notably the story of the Jailer's Daughter, who goes from smitten to besotted to insane as a consequence of a misconceived and, given the difference in their social rank, impossible passion for Palamon (Imogen Stubbs, making her stage debut in the role, was widely agreed to be the star of Kyle's production). Compared to the pallid and largely indistinguishable titular figures, the Daughter is a vital, vivid and varied role: in a play full of echoes and refractions of Shakespeare's other works (*The Two Gentlemen of Verona*, *A Midsummer Night's Dream*, *Troilus and Cressida*, *Venus and Adonis*), she evokes both the witty heroines of the romantic comedies and their audience-intimate clowns (she takes the part of the 'She-Fool' in the morris dance), but also, once she descends into madness, emphatically and repeatedly, Ophelia.

At one point, Fletcher, or Shakespeare (or both), engineers a narrative account that appears pointedly contrived to recall Gertrude's report of Ophelia's death by drowning as well as Ophelia's own floral remembrancing:

> As I late was angling
> In the great lake that lies behind the palace,
> From the far shore, thick set with reeds and sedges,
> As patiently I was attending sport,
> I heard a voice ...
> ... I laid me down
> And listened to the words she sung, for then,
> Through a small glade cut by the fishermen,
> I saw it was your daughter ...
> ... Then she talked of you, sir –
> That you must lose your head tomorrow morning,
> And she must gather flowers to bury you ...
>
> (4.1.52–78)

The difference, here, is that the Daughter's drowning is prevented; and, moreover, that her madness, unlike Ophelia's, is liable to cure – although the form of that cure is one that has disquieted many modern commentators on the play.

The reporter here, who is the agent of the Daughter's salvation both at the scene of her threatened death by water and at the end of the play, is the similarly anonymous Wooer, his auditor her father, the Jailer; in consultation with the Doctor, who advises that the cure for her erotomania is sex ('Please her appetite,/ And do it home – it cures her, *ipso facto,/* The melancholy humour that infects her' [5.4.35–37]), the pair embark upon the course of persuading the deranged Daughter that the Wooer is Palamon, a deception that culminates in the consummation that is just what the Doctor ordered. In the heartlessly abstract, it sounds cruel, probably misogynist: in practice, the Daughter is both a tough and a touchingly vulnerable figure, whose predicament is presented with a directness and emotional immediacy that is a world apart from that of courtly romance. Nowhere is this better realised than in the Daughter and Wooer's final lines in the play:

Come, sweet, we'll go to dinner,
And then we'll play at cards.
JAILER'S DAUGHTER   And shall we kiss too?
WOOER A hundred times.
JAILER'S DAUGHTER   And twenty.
WOOER   Ay, and twenty.
JAILER'S DAUGHTER And then we'll sleep together.
DOCTOR [*to the* WOOER]   Take her offer.
WOOER [*to the* JAILER'S DAUGHTER]
      Yes, marry, will we.
JAILER'S DAUGHTER But you shall not hurt me.
WOOER I will not, sweet.
JAILER'S DAUGHTER   If you do, love, I'll cry.

(5.4.107–12)

As *Shakespeare Quarterly*'s reviewer recorded, the final line in the 1986 RSC production 'drew tears from the Wooer – and from many in the audience too' (Warren 1987: 83). That is unsurprising: it is when the play is at its simplest and most direct that it is most poignant.

Further reading

Knight, G. Wilson (1947) *The Crown of Life: Essays in Interpretation of Shakespeare's Final Plays.* London: Oxford University Press.

McMullan, Gordon and Jonathan Hope (eds) (1992) *The Politics of Tragicomedy: Shakespeare and After.* London: Routledge.

Marcus, Leah (1988) *Puzzling Shakespeare: Local Reading and Its Discontents.* Berkeley, CA: University of California Press.

Mullaney, Steven (1988) '"All That Monarchs Do": The Obscured Stages of Authority in *Pericles*', in *The Place of the Stage: License, Play, and Power in Renaissance England.* Ann Arbor, MI: University of Michigan Press, 135–52.

Ryan, Kiernan (2002) *Shakespeare.* Third edition. Basingstoke: Palgrave.

Sinfield, Alan (2006) 'Intertextuality and the Limits of Queer Reading in *A Midsummer Night's Dream* and *The Two Noble Kinsmen*', in *Shakespeare, Authority, Sexuality: Unfinished Business in Cultural Materialism.* London and New York: Routledge.

Wickham, Glynne (1980) '*The Two Noble Kinsmen* or *A Midsummer Night's Dream, Part II*?', in *The Elizabethan Theatre*, VII, ed. G. R. Hibbard. Hamden, CT: Archon Books, 167–96.

Wilson, Richard (1993) *Will Power: Essays on Shakespearean Authority.* Hemel Hempstead: Harvester Wheatsheaf.

Henry VIII, or All Is True

Date, text and authorship

c.1613; performed at the Globe 29 June 1613; F 1623. Co-authored by Shakespeare and John Fletcher.

Sources and influences

Edward Halle, *Union of the Noble and Illustre Famelies of Lancastre and York* (1548, second edition 1550); Raphael Holinshed, *Chronicles of England, Scotland and Ireland* (1577, second edition 1587); John Foxe, *Book of Martyrs* (1563); Samuel Rowley, *If You See Me, You Know Me* (1603–05).

On stage

His Majesty's, 1910–12 (dir. Herbert Beerbohm Tree); Festival Theatre, Cambridge, 1931 (dir. Terence Gray); SMT, 1949, 1950, Old Vic, 1953 (dir. Tyrone Guthrie); RSC, 1969 (dir. Trevor Nunn); RSC, 1983 (dir. Howard Davies); Chichester Festival Theatre, 1991 (dir. Ian Judge); RSC, 1996 (dir. Gregory Doran); Shakespeare's Globe, 2010 (dir. Mark Rosenblatt).

On screen

BBC Television Shakespeare, 1979 (dir. Kevin Billington; Henry: John Stride; Wolsey: Timothy West; Cranmer: Ronald Pickup; Katherine: Claire Bloom).

With the exception of the early performance in 1613 that resulted in the destruction of the first Globe playhouse (see 'Life and contexts', pp. 66–8), *Henry VIII* is not nowadays generally regarded as a play likely to set the house on fire. It was noteworthy enough to occasion one of the few reasonably detailed eyewitness accounts that survive of Shakespeare performed in its own time, in the form of Sir Henry Wotton's letter to Sir Edmund Bacon describing the events of 29 June 1613. It was revived frequently from the Restoration through to the start of the twentieth century, in lavish style that responded to the opportunities that the play affords for set-piece spectacle, pageantry and historical tableaux, and to the star parts offered by the roles of the Duke of Buckingham, Cardinal Wolsey and Queen Katharine; but after the First World War, which saw the apotheosis of the tradition in the final performances of Herbert Beerbohm Tree's 1910 production, the popularity of the play went into decline.

The special place that the death-dealing, six-wived Tudor monarch who is the play's title role occupies in popular historiography (represented by such screen treatments as *The Private Life of Henry VIII* [1933], *A Man for All Seasons* [1966], *Carry on Henry* [1971] and BBC TV's *The Tudors* [2007–08]) has rendered the play uniquely immune to the tactics of modernisation that have served to reinvigorate the other history plays, so that its infrequent twentieth- and twenty-first-century productions have tended either to perpetuate slimmed-down and economised versions of the Victorian spectacular tradition or to parody or critique it; there has been only one full-length filmed attempt at the play, the BBC Television Shakespeare production of 1979 (extracts of Tree's production were filmed in 1910).

Although the play has recently attracted increasingly positive critical interest (notably in the Arden third series edition, edited by Gordon McMullan, whose near-two-hundred-page introduction leads to the conclusion that it is 'a much more subtle, complex and valuable textual experience' than the critical tradition would have us believe [McMullan 2000: 199]), it was for a long time disregarded or considered an anomaly, particularly generically. Though grouped with the histories in the Folio (its first publication), it is, like *King John*, out of time in relation to the other plays in the sequence, dramatising events taking place between 1520 and 1533.

Lacking the social range and varied action of both of the earlier tetralogies, its political world is that of the courtroom and council chamber, but not the battlefield; its most prominent street scenes are those of the coronation procession of Queen Anne and of the parading of the newly christened Princess Elizabeth, both rendered in, for Shakespeare, unprecedented detail:

THE ORDER OF THE CORONATION
1. *[First, enter]* trumpet*[ers, who play]* a lively flourish.
2. Then, *[enter]* two judges.
3. *[Then, enter the]* LORD CHANCELLOR, with *[both the]*
   purse *[containing the great seal]* and *[the]* mace *[borne]*
   before him.
4. *[Then, enter]* choristers singing; *[with them,]*
   music*[ians playing.]* ...

(4.1.36.s.d.)

Enter trumpet[er]s, sounding. Then [enter] two aldermen, [the] Lord Mayor [of London], GARTER *[King-of-Arms],* CRANMER *[the Archbishop of Canterbury, the] Duke of* NORFOLK *with his marshal's staff, [the] Duke of* SUFFOLK, *two noblemen bearing great standard bowls for the christening gifts; then [enter] four noblemen bearing a canopy, under which [is] the Duchess of Norfolk, godmother, bearing the child [Elizabeth] richly habited in a mantle, [whose] train [is] borne by a lady.*

(5.4.0.s.d.)

Seemingly the antithesis of the theatrical idiom that in *Henry V* had solicited its audiences to 'Piece out our imperfections with your thoughts' (Prologue 23), the play's events are presented with such a wealth of ceremonial and naturalistic detail that Wotton was moved to write that it was 'sufficient in truth within a while to make greatness very familiar, if not ridiculous' (Pearsall Smith 1907: 2, 32).

For later respondents, the play has seemed ridiculous, even distasteful, less for its excess of truth than for its evasion of it. It has not escaped the notice of even the most credulous of the play's spectators that the hands that in the final scene cradle the infant princess and future queen of England would, shortly after the play's action ends, be stained with the blood of her mother, one among the many sent by Henry to the executioner's block; the play also treats the English Reformation as tangential to its central action. Perceived at worst as a static succession of masque-like tableaux punctuated by valedictory scenes (the Duke of Buckingham, en route to his execution, pausing to offer a self-vindicating scaffold speech addressed to the crowds [2.1]; the disgraced Cardinal Wolsey, bidding 'Farewell, a long farewell, to all my greatness' [3.2.352]; Queen Katharine, who is afforded a strong trial scene [3.1.], bowing out with a dream-vision of spirits that heralds her imminent death

[4.2]), the play selectively addresses the reign of a monarch whose legitimacy, unlike that of his Shakespearean predecessors, is never once in doubt. Closer to Prospero than to the earlier Richards and Henries, Henry Tudor is a curious blank at the play's centre, both an impassive observer of the manoeuvrings that surround him and their ultimate manipulator and beneficiary. Though this offers a detailed exposition of the politics of the Tudor succession, it makes for less than compelling drama.

Like the late romances, also, *Henry VIII* makes use of quasi-emblematic methods reminiscent of the Morality drama, providing Henry's divorced and dying first wife, Katharine, with an attendant named Patience, and staging her dream-vision in the manner of a masque, in which masked and robed spirits deliver garlands to the former queen in her sleep, provoking her, '*as it were by inspiration*', to make '*signs of rejoicing, and holdeth her hands up to heaven*' (4.2.82.s.d.). Nonetheless, this was a play in which, as its original title at the Globe performance declared, 'All is True'; a claim which was reinforced by a Prologue which, reprising the cajolery of the first Chorus to *Henry V*, emphasised the facticity of the events to be revealed:

> Such as give
> Their money out of hope they may believe,
> May here find truth, too ...
> Think ye see
> The very persons of our noble story
> As they were living ...
>
> (Prologue 7–9, 25–27)

At the end, as in *Henry V*, the play invokes the double perspective of actual and theatrical histories, in Archbishop Cranmer's overlong, overwrought eulogy to the infant Elizabeth and her successor: the awareness remains that its wondrous future lies in its audience's rather less glorious present and immediate past, that its fabled queen-to-be had been dust for a decade.

'Let none think flattery', says Cranmer of the words he utters, 'for they'll find 'em truth' (5.4.16), before going on to picture Elizabeth's England in terms which even the most credulous of his auditors might have recognised as historical fantasy, as a happy land where

> every man shall eat in safety
> Under his own vine what he plants, and sing
> The merry songs of peace to all his neighbours.
> God shall be truly known, and those about her
> From her shall read the perfect ways of honour,
> And by those claim their greatness, not by blood.
>
> (5.4.33–38)

Is this, in a play which tells us that 'all is true' and invests the words *truth, truly* and *true* with almost talismanic force, 'truth'? The play leaves its audiences with no certain answers: though Henry's reply to Cranmer is that he has 'made me now a man' (5.4.64), confirming the political gravity of the moment and perhaps intimating that the rule of patriarchy is now finally secure, the Epilogue that follows admits that ' 'Tis ten to one this play can never please', that some of its spectators probably slept through the show, whilst others had turned up in the hope of some topical satire, and that in any case the men in the audience would be well advised to defer to their wives and female companions, and to follow their lead by putting their hands together one final time, 'for 'tis ill hap/ If they hold when their ladies bid 'em clap' (Epilogue, 13–14).

Further reading

Cogswell, Thomas and Peter Lake (2009) 'Buckingham Does the Globe: *Henry VIII* and the Politics of Popularity in the 1620s', *Shakespeare Quarterly*, 60: 253–78.

Kermode, Frank (1965) 'What Is Shakespeare's *Henry VIII* About?', in *Shakespeare: The Histories*, ed. Eugene M. Waith. Englewood Cliffs, NJ: Prentice Hall, 168–79.

Richards, Jennifer and James Knowles (eds) (1999) *Shakespeare's Late Plays: New Readings*. Edinburgh: Edinburgh University Press.

Slights, Camille Wells (1999) 'The Politics of Conscience in *All Is True* (or *Henry VIII*)', *Shakespeare Survey*, 43: 59–68.

Tennenhouse, Leonard (2005 [1986]) *Power on Display: The Politics of Shakespeare's Genres*. London and New York: Routledge.

Part III
Criticism

Prologue

A critical century

Although critical interpretation, appreciation and analysis of Shakespeare's plays and poems have been around as long as the works themselves – beginning as early as 1598, with Francis Meres's thumbnail reviews in *Palladis Tamia: Wit's Treasury* – the modern era to which this guide confines its attentions effectively began in 1904, with the publication of A. C. Bradley's *Shakespearean Tragedy*. As a work simultaneously addressed to a specialist, student and lay readership, Bradley's systematic exposition and analysis of the workings of the 'big four' tragedies not only proved to be hugely influential in the scope of its arguments and its critical method; it was also instrumental, along with Sir Henry Newbolt's report on the teaching of English, published in 1921, in the development of literary studies itself as a profession and higher-level study.

With its interest in the drama of character (and its conviction, elaborated by Newbolt and others, that the study of literature could both act as a form of philosophical investigation and be morally beneficial), Bradley's work established terms of readerly (and theatrical) engagement with Shakespeare's works that would last for half a century, if not more, and that are today still persistently considered as the 'commonsense' way of thinking about them: treated as play-poems inhabited by men and women whose actions and motivations are recognisably real, comprehensible and amenable to analysis and judgement, Shakespeare's texts continue to speak directly to us by virtue of their unrivalled access to an unchanging, trans-historical human nature. The appeal of Hamlet down the ages, according to this way of looking at it, is that, at least in some respects, he is just like you and me; the corollary of this position being the conviction that some things never change.

Bradley's position is by no means as unreflective or reactionary as it has sometimes been made to appear (certainly when one compares his efforts to bring the plays to life with the Victorian philological scholarship which preceded him, his determination to make them accessible by whatever means available becomes entirely understandable), and he was in an important sense a progenitor of one of the major strands in twentieth-century criticism, inspiring work that was, variously, imitative and innovative, work that has misguidedly psychologised and biographised Shakespeare's dramatis personae (as well as Shakespeare himself, either directly or by inference), and work that has recognised the enduring power and value of emotional realism, and of the investments that actors, spectators and readers continue to make in marks on paper, however anachronistic and theoretically naïve these may be. Nonetheless, the Bradleian paradigm was already under some pressure by the 1920s on a number of different fronts.

The first was what came to be known as the New Bibliography, a movement initiated in the first decade of the century by the textual scholars W. W. Greg and A. W. Pollard, who began by drawing distinctions between authorial and non-authorial (or 'good' and 'bad') quarto texts that would hold sway for nearly a century, and who went on, joined by R. B. McKerrow, to establish the foundations upon which much subsequent editorial practice was built. Through a meticulous study of the material properties of early modern books, and of the practices of the publishing industry, the New Bibliographers traced the routes and patterns of transmission of texts from manuscript to playhouse script to printing house, using the evidence of orthography and typography to determine the relationship between what Shakespeare was deemed to have written, or revised, and the printed versions.

If all this threatened to leave Bradley's earnest deliberativeness looking unscientific and old-fashioned, so too did the arrival of an equally long-lived 'new' critical paradigm, the 'New Criticism' that rose to prominence in the 1930s and that retained its command over much of the scholarly profession until the 1970s. Initially associated with a group of universities in the American Deep South and with Cambridge University in the UK (where, as developed by I. A. Richards, L. C. Knights, Williams Empson and F. R. Leavis, it termed itself 'practical criticism' or 'close reading'), New Criticism's predominance after the Second World War was one of the factors that led to a shifting of the Shakespeare studies industry's centre of gravity across the Atlantic. As a form of critical practice (widely disseminated and institutionalised in the anthologies, edited by its founding fathers Cleanth Brooks and Robert B. Heilman, *Understanding Poetry*, 1938 [Brooks 1958], and *Understanding Drama*, 1945 [Brooks and Heilman 1947]) that emphasised close and disciplined attention to the words on the page, and that treated Shakespeare's plays as lyric poems untainted by the exigencies of character, history and live theatre, New Criticism was perfectly geared to the needs and priorities of an expanding but geographically dispersed college professoriate located a long way from research libraries, archives and major theatres with a classical repertoire.

The immediately postwar years also saw the emergence of the other dominant critical dispensation during the period, the historicism associated with figures such as Lily B. Campbell in the United States and E. M. W. Tillyard in Britain. Setting itself against both the universalising character analysis of the Bradley school and the ahistorical formalism of close reading, this approach sought to locate Shakespeare's works firmly within the political and religious values and beliefs of its age, which it held to be orderly, profoundly conservative and orthodox. Representing the twin poles of Shakespearean criticism, both New Criticism and 'old' historicism had by the mid-1970s long since exhausted their capacity for innovation, and for a time it appeared that a force that could claim a genealogy extending back to the 1920s, performance criticism (or stage-centred criticism), offered a way out of the impasse in which research and teaching now found themselves.

Energised by the establishment of the Royal Shakespeare Company in the 1960s, an operation that seemingly institutionalised the alliance between scholarship and theatrical practice of which previous generations of critics could only dream, stage-centred criticism characterised itself as revolutionary force for renewal, situating past and present performance at the centre of critical debate and insisting upon not only its legitimacy but also its authority. Its arguments were carried, decisively, and continue to be felt: if there is anything that can be described as a near-universal consensus within Shakespearean scholarship, criticism, editing, teaching and performance today, it is the notion that if the plays belong anywhere it is in the medium for which they were devised.

The end of the decade that was dominated by the ascendancy of stage-centred criticism and the decline of the critical movements that had lasted for more than thirty years was marked, in 1980, by two works: Stephen Greenblatt's landmark new historicist study

Renaissance Self-Fashioning and the first collection of feminist essays on Shakespeare, *The Woman's Part*, edited by Carolyn Lenz, Gayle Greene and Carol Neely. As these and the various new political and historicist criticisms that followed in their wake are the subject of the pages that follow, it is sufficient to note here that their publication coincided with, and contributed to, the inauguration of a period of critical history which has now lasted longer than the ages of Bradley, Tillyard and Cleanth Brooks, and in which we are still living and working.

Since 1980, under the broad auspices of new historicism, feminism and gender studies, and cultural materialism, Shakespeare studies has been enlivened and enriched by the cross-disciplinary fertilisation that has brought, to name but a few, the insights of social, cultural and economic history, of philosophy and of anthropology to bear on our understanding of literary texts and performances, and by the pluralisation and specialisation that have fostered, again to nominate some among many, post-structuralist Shakespeares, queer Shakespeares, postcolonial Shakespeares, neo-historicist Shakespeares, eco-Shakespeares, cognitive Shakespeares, presentist Shakespeares and cyber-Shakespeares. Whether one interprets this seemingly unstoppable productivity and variety as the sign of a discipline in rude health or in possibly terminal crisis is a matter of temperament and ideological positioning; and whether it represents the state of criticism as it is likely to be for some time to come, or conceals the imminence of still further transformations that with hindsight will come to be seen as both as inevitable and as unexpected as those that have preceded it, history alone will reveal. It is time now for these criticisms to speak for themselves.

1 Histories

Ruling ideas

Towards the end of the second of the Induction scenes that frame the main action of *The Taming of the Shrew*, the drunken tinker Christopher Sly is told that he is about to be entertained by a troupe of travelling players. Informed that they will present the 'pleasant comedy' (Ind. 2.126) that is the story of Katharina and Petruccio, Sly asks whether this is a comonty,/ A Christmas gambol, or a tumbling trick' (133–34); the reply, offered by the boy page who has disguised himself as his 'wife', is that it is 'more pleasing stuff ... It is a kind of history' (135–36). For modern readers and hearers, this might sound a little odd, at least with regard to the drama that it introduces: dealing with events that are domestic and contemporary, and not only purely fictitious but farcically improbable, *Shrew* could hardly be more removed from 'history' in general and from the genre of historical drama in particular. In this instance, the term retains what was at the time of the play's composition its common usage. If, since the seventeenth century, history has commanded authority by being nominally attached to matters of fact, rather than fiction, myth or fable, early modern writers and readers would have applied the term more flexibly, on the understanding that the stories that were increasingly being fashioned about England's past and present were themselves assembled from a range of sources, reflected diverse and conflicting interests, and were arranged in patterns that assumed the didactic or exemplary significance of the events that they purported to narrate and explain.

Written at the moment when a new historical consciousness was also informing the output of the popular stage, in the form of the chronicle plays and historical dramas that included Shakespeare's *Henry VI* plays (published 1594–95) and *Richard III* (published 1597), Marlowe's *Edward II* (1592), Greene's *Friar Bacon and Friar Bungay* (1589) and the anonymous *The Famous Victories of Henry V* (c.1588), *Shrew* incidentally preserves some of the more equivocal senses of 'history' as it was apprehended by Shakespeare and his contemporaries: history as story or narrative, from which (as Sly finds out) lessons could and should be drawn, though these need not necessarily be taken at face value. In the chronicle plays themselves, at least before Shakespeare intervened in the genre in order to pioneer a less heterogeneous, more analytic and altogether more secular method of historical dramatisation, England's rulers mix freely with the personae of myth and folklore: in *Famous Victories*, the legendary Henry V is both carnivalesque Robin Hood and military warlord, 'the mirror of Christendom' in Tudor chronicler Edward Halle's phrase; in *Friar Bacon and Friar Bungay* the magical exploits of the thirteenth-century Franciscan Friar Bacon lead, amongst other things, to an encounter with King Henry III.

In Shakespeare's hands, historical drama assumed a more stable, generically consistent form as, in one of the English theatre's most ambitious projects ever attempted, he set himself to the task of dramatising the course of English history from 1398 (Henry Boling-broke's challenge to Thomas Mowbray, which precipitates the events that will lead to the deposition of Richard II) to 1485, which saw the accession of Henry VII and the inauguration of the reign of the Tudors. Supplementing the eight plays that comprise the so-called first and second tetralogies, Shakespeare also wrote about two monarchs whose reigns fell outside the chronological range of these sequences: one, *The Life and Death of King John* (c.1596), dealing with the king who ruled from 1199 to 1216; the other, *The Famous History of the Life of King Henry the Eighth* (1613), with the last of the Tudor kings, whose reign began in 1509 and ended with his death in 1547, and who is last seen in the play holding the infant princess who will become Elizabeth I. For the compilers of the 1623 First Folio (which was the occasion of the first publication of *Henry VI, Part 1, King John* and *Henry VIII*), the plays formed a coherent generic group, and they organised them chronologically; in terms of their circumstances of initial publication and performance, the plays appeared out of sequence, with the *Henry VI* plays appearing before *Richard II*, the two parts of *Henry IV* and *Henry V*.

The events which lie in the historical future of the second tetralogy are already part of its theatrical memory, creating a sense of double time which is specifically invoked in the closing Chorus of *Henry V*:

> Henry the Sixth, in infant bands crowned king
> Of France and England, did this king succeed,
> Whose state so many had the managing
> That they lost France and made poor England bleed,
> Which oft our stage hath shown ...
>
> (V. Epilogue 9–13)

At the very moment when the English nation appears to be at its most triumphant, united under the rule of its greatest king, victorious over its traditional enemy, Shakespeare's historical drama looks both forward and backward, reminding its Globe audiences of the transience of the moment, and of the chronicles that Shakespeare had co-authored with Nashe, Greene and Peele for Henslowe's Rose a decade earlier. In the Folio, the plays' titles 'focus attention on the monarch as the organising principle of historical narrative' (Smith 2007: 145); the plays that were first published in octavo and quarto were advertised in more generically indeterminate terms which suggest other narrative emphases, and other kinds of appeal. *Henry VI, Part 2* appeared in 1594 as *The First Part of the Contention of the two Famous Houses of York and Lancaster with the Death of the Good Duke Humphrey. Henry IV, Part 1* was printed in 1598 as *The History of Henrie the Fourth; With the battell at Shrewsburie betweene the King and Lord Henry Percy, surnamed Henrie Hotspur of the North, With the humorous conceits of Sir John Falstaffe*. The play billed at the Globe in 1613 as *All Is True* became, in the Folio, *The Life of Henry VIII*. The diverse sources of interest that were signalled in the quartos' titles suggest the centrifugal tendencies of a body of plays that repeatedly depart from the plan imposed by the linear, king-centred chronology of the Folio: the monarchs whose plays these are supposed to be act alongside clowns and commoners, the alleged facts of history share the stage with the stuff of folklore, legend and myth, and the action moves effortlessly from the battlefields of fifteenth-century England and France to the taverns of early modern London.

We begin this chapter, which examines the changing significances that have been attributed to the historical contexts and conditions of production of Shakespeare's work, with an overview of the histories because it was primarily this group of plays that prompt-ted twentieth-century scholars to investigate this relationship in the first place. The point of departure is the emergence of historicist criticism during the 1940s, the period which saw the first systematic and sustained attempts to rethink the implications of Ben Jonson's prefatory slogan in the First Folio, that Shakespeare was 'not of an age, but for all time' by positioning Shakespeare and his works within a system of beliefs quite removed from and alien to modern thinking, a system that profoundly shaped the patterning, structure and style of the plays, and the ethical, political and cosmological implications of the actions they dramatise. I shall reserve for consideration in a later chapter the developing body of research into the conditions and conventions of Shakespeare's stage, which was in the first instance conducted quite separately from the kinds of cultural, intellectual and political contextualis-ing that we shall be concerned with here – although more recently, as we shall see, these approaches have tended to converge.

Shakespeare's embeddedness within his own age was the theme of two works by Amer-ican scholars published in the 1940s, namely Theodore Spencer's *Shakespeare and the Nature of Man* (1942) and Lily B. Campbell's *Shakespeare's 'Histories': Mirrors of Eliza-bethan Policy* (1947). Spencer does not address the history plays at length (his main focus is upon the tragedies), but his model of the relationship between art, politics and Eliza-bethan culture prefigured the work of those that did, in that it was defined by the 'com-bined elements of Aristotelianism, Platonism, Neo-Platonism, Stoicism, and Christianity ... almost indistinguishably woven in a pattern which was universally agreed upon, and which, in its main outlines, was the same as that of the Middle Ages'. Furthermore, Elizabethans 'did not question the existence of kingship, though they might be violently anxious about *who* should be king. There was an eternal law, a general order – in the universe, in the ranks of created beings, in the institution of government' (Spencer 1966: 1). This 'order' was cosmic, natural and political, and organised hierarchically, although thanks to the influence of such thinkers as Copernicus, Montaigne and Machiavelli, who between them interrogated the cosmological, natural and political order, it was increasingly being called into doubt: Shakespeare wrote at the intersection between these contending views of the world, his art registering the 'violation' of 'the whole inherited picture of man in the system of the universe, of Nature, and of the state', seeing 'individual experience in relation to the all-inclusive conflict produced by this violation' (Spencer 1966: 50).

Campbell, as her subtitle indicated, was more concerned to argue that Shakespeare's perspective was fundamentally conservative and securely religious: 'in the history plays there is a dominant political pattern characteristic of the political philosophy of his age' (1964: 6), and the plays acted as 'mirrors' in which Elizabethan spectators 'could see their own national problems being acted out on the stage before them, and in which they could witness the eternal justice of God in the affairs of the body politic' (255). The first third of Campbell's book is devoted to the task of tracing the roots of Shakespeare's dramatic his-toriography within Renaissance practices of historical writing and thinking; thereafter she discusses individual plays as components within a larger design which reflects the Eliza-bethan perception that the 'cycles of history' were 'mapped out ... in moral terms as recurring patterns of sin and punishment': 'the understanding of the moral significance of this pattern is basic to the understanding of the Shakespeare history sequences' (121, 124). Shakespeare's purpose was explicitly didactic, in that he 'used history to teach politics to the present' (125), and implicitly topical: the general moral is that 'rebellion against a king is rebellion against the King of kings ... and will surely call forth God's vengeance' (156); the specific lesson of *Richard II*, for example, is that the story of his deposition clarifies 'the political ethics of the Tudors in regard to the rights and duties of a king', which 'might equally well have served as a warning to Elizabeth and to any one who desired to usurp her throne' (212).

If there is something a touch chilling about the theocratic authoritarianism which Campbell ascribes to Shakespeare, it is partly explicable as a product of the historical moment of the book's composition and completion; like Spencer's work, *Shakespeare's 'Histories'* reflects the conservative cultural climate of wartime America. If Spencer was relatively forthright in identifying the secular trends of Shakespeare's age as an awful harbinger of his own time ('Machiavelli has helped to produce what may be only the first of a series of Hitlers' [Spencer 1966: 221]), Campbell was more circumspect, leaving the reader to draw her own conclusions as to the relevance of the Shakespearean example to the present. In her preface, she registered the impact of the war in terms of its capacity to interfere with the pursuit of scholarship, recording how the pressures of wartime economies deprived her of access to photostats and document transcriptions, and how the 'round-the-calendar teaching schedule' almost caused the research to be 'terminated'; more seriously, she also records her 'sincere regret' that 'the difficulties of wartime transportation' had denied her access to E. M. W. Tillyard's recently published *Shakespeare's History Plays* (1944). Here she refers to the scholar who subsequently became virtually synonymous with the school of thought that dominated historicist criticism from the 1940s to the 1960s, and which during that period constituted the New Criticism's only serious competitor. Tillyard's *Shakespeare's History Plays*, together with *The Elizabethan World Picture* (1943), dictated the terms of engagement not only for those who concurred with his position, but also for those who emphatically did not.

In all line of order: E. M. W. Tillyard's historicism

Tillyard's central thesis is that, despite the apparent evidence of the drama to the contrary, Elizabethans firmly believed in order, degree and hierarchy: the 'civil war and disorder' depicted in the history plays were meaningless 'apart from a background of order to judge them by'. This 'order' was political, natural and metaphysical (or, to use Tillyard's preferred term, 'cosmic') and 'was one of the genuine ruling ideas of the age', and it was articulated in terms of imagery of 'a chain, as set of correspondences, and a dance' (Tillyard 1963: 7). The world picture, Tillyard asserted, was less humanist and secular than medieval and 'solidly theocentric' (12).

The touchstone text is Ulysses's peroration upon degree in *Troilus and Cressida*, 1.3.74–137:

> The heavens themselves, the planets, and this centre
> Observe degree, priority, and place,
> Infixture, course, proportion, season, form,
> Office and custom, in all line of order ...

> (1.3.85–88)

As an example of an 'explicitly didactic' passage (which Tillyard aligns with similar statements in political and religious tracts such as Thomas Elyot's *The Book of the Governor*, the Church Homily *Of Obedience* and Hooker's *Laws of Ecclesiastical Polity*), this speech outlines a 'general conception of order' that is 'taken for granted' (Tillyard 1963: 17). Taking Ulysses's rhetoric at face value, Tillyard derives from it a broad cultural network of correspondences whereby 'the sun, the king, primogeniture hang together; the war of the planets is echoed by the war of the elements and by civil war on earth'; this is a world 'constantly threatened with dissolution, and yet preserved from it by a superior unifying power' (17).

Ulysses's conception of 'degree' (which Tillyard equates with Shakespeare's, and with that of 'the ordinary educated Elizabethan' [7]), the 'ladder to all high designs' (1.3.102), refers to the chain of being, which extended 'from the foot of God's throne to the meanest of inanimate objects' (Tillyard 1963: 33), which accounted for the divisions within and between the human, natural and spiritual worlds and which, for Shakespeare, placed man 'between beast and angel' (42). There are correspondences between man, the body politic and the macrocosm ('the idea of man summing up the universe in himself had a strong hold' [99]), which reflect the characteristically Elizabethan habit of mind, capable of 'the agile transition from abstract to concrete, from ideal to real, from sacred to profane' (114).

The 'larger cosmic order' expounded in *The Elizabethan World Picture* was offered by Tillyard as an expansion of the first chapter of *Shakespeare's History Plays*, in which he attempted to contextualise those works within the frame of the 'Elizabethan political order … the Golden Age brought in by the Tudors', which was 'nothing apart from the cosmic order of which it is a part'. Thus when Shakespeare dramatises 'the concrete facts of English history', he does so mindful of 'the principle of order behind all the terrible manifestations of disorder' (Tillyard 1962: 25), manifestations that included the civil wars, rebellions, riots and regicides that are so tellingly realised in both history play sequences. Indeed, the notion that Shakespeare's histories constitute a consciously composed sequential narrative is one of the major innovations inaugurated by Tillyard's study (see 'Works', pp. 152–6). Commenting on the ordering of the plays in the Folio, he states that 'the two tetralogies make a single unit', in that, throughout, Shakespeare 'links the present happenings with the past' (Tillyard 1962: 153). For Spencer, the 'general plan' of the history plays realises the trope of 'violation' schematically: 'an existing order is violated, the consequent conflict and turmoil are portrayed, and order is restored by the destruction of the force or forces that originally violated it' (1966: 73); in his construction of the histories an as epic interconnected sequence, Tillyard extended this pattern to encompass the entire span of plays. Shakespeare's aim, for Tillyard, was to arrange 'the most exciting and significant stretch of English history into a pattern; a pattern of such magnitude that it needed the space of eight plays and about ten years in the execution' (Tillyard 1962: 155).

If this furnished evidence of Shakespeare's artistic superiority over his colleague playwrights, and of his ability to refashion an episodic, opportunistic dramatic format that had previously been satisfied merely to 'provide a repertory of recreational anecdote, serve as memorial of great men, and to convey separate moral lessons' (Tillyard 1962: 106), it was also symptomatic of his more sophisticated political understanding; as 'practical playwrights writing for a popular audience', the authors of chronicle plays would have been aware of 'the theory of degree and the hierarchical conception of the universe', but seemed 'little interested in them' (110). Shakespeare, however, had more thoroughly absorbed, and more intelligently reflected upon, the varied lessons of the Tudor historiographers, of the compendium of exemplary biographies, *The Mirror for Magistrates*, and of the Church Homilies, all of which, in Tillyard's reading, highlighted the wickedness of rebellion and promoted the virtues of obedience, stable rule and orderly succession.

One of the opportunities afforded by this perspective is that it allows Tillyard to take the *Henry VI* plays considerably more seriously than previous critics had (and to credit Shakespeare with their sole authorship, which he considered a compliment); Tillyard discerns a 'masterly inclusiveness' that 'raises to greatness a series of plays which in the execution are sometimes immature and ineffective' (1962: 156). Unifying the disparate strands of the first tetralogy is their 'insistence on cause and effect' (160) and their reiteration of a simple, powerful lesson: 'that the present time must take warning from the past and utterly renounce all civil dissension' (161). The second tetralogy, also 'conceived ... as one great unit' (240), achieves 'a great symphonic theme' (243) and is seen to be strongly influenced by Samuel Daniel's epic poem *The First Four Books of the Civil Wars* (1595), which help-fully supplies the explicit political rationale that Shakespeare unaccountably failed to pro-vide; quoting Daniel's statement that his work aims to show 'the deformities of civil dissension, and the miserable events of rebellions, conspiracies, and bloody revengements', Tillyard asserts that 'Daniel's intention in the *Civil Wars* is precisely Shakespeare's in his History Plays' (245).

In *Richard II*, which shows the initial violation of order, theme is allied to style, as the play 'makes more solemn and elaborates the inherited notions of cosmic correspondences and chivalric procedure' (Tillyard 1962: 261). In *Henry IV* (treated as 'a single play' [269]), the Morality-play structure dramatises the testing of Prince Hal, who is 'Shakespeare's studied picture of the kingly type': 'a man of large powers, Olympian loftiness, and high sophistication' (275). Falstaff, who in more senses than one possesses the greatest capacity to unsettle Tillyard's presiding scheme of order, is written of with some warmth: as the figure who 'enlarges the play ... into the ageless, the archetypal' (290), he is the 'symbol of the ribald in man', standing for 'sheer vitality, for the spirit of youth ready for any adven-ture', an amalgamation of Dr Johnson and Mr Pickwick, 'not only Schweik but Volpone, not only Brer Rabbit but the *Miles Gloriosus*' (291).

If Tillyard here seems to be not just acknowledging the force of Falstaffian licence and misrule but almost revelling in it, he swiftly moves to stifle its subversive implications, for the 'harmlessly comic Vice' ultimately proves 'the epitome of the Deadly Sins at war with law and order' (Tillyard 1962: 292). Any regret occasioned by Henry's rejection of Falstaff is a product of Victorian sentimentality, attributable to 'the sense of security created ... by the predominance of the British navy', which 'induced men to rate this very security too cheaply and to exalt the instinct of rebellion above its legitimate station' (296). 'Schooled by recent events', writes Tillyard, in a book planned, written and published during the course of his country's war with Hitler's Germany, 'we should have no difficulty now in taking Falstaff as the Elizabethans took him' (296). It is at such moments that another, more covert agenda to Tillyard's historicism becomes evident: just as the dream of 'order' which he ascribes to the Elizabethans is all too obviously a projection of contemporary anxieties, so too the timeless 'England' that lay at the heart of Tillyard's histories can be seen as nos-talgic patriotic fantasy, particularly desired and valued because under threat.

A little unexpectedly, in the context, *Henry V* emerges rather less well: it is a work in which Shakespeare 'conscientiously ... fulfilled his double obligation: to the chroniclers and to his public' (Tillyard 1962: 314), but which has as its hero a king 'who could at best stand for Elizabethan political principle' but 'could only fail when great weight was put on him' (310), and who, as 'the man who knew exactly what he wanted and went for it with utter singleness of heart' was 'the very reverse of what Shakespeare was truly growing interested in' (318). Perhaps because *Henry V* provides a less than satisfactory conclusion to the cycle, as Tillyard conceived it, *Shakespeare's History Plays* concludes with a discus-sion of a play in which the mechanisms of providence can more convincingly be made to seem visible: *Macbeth*, in which Tillyard's familiar 'pervading cosmic theme of disorder seeking to upset the divine order of nature', though 'more important than the actual poli-tical theme', nonetheless contrives to make this 'the finest of all mirrors for magistrates' (319–20).

Tillyard was not unique in his approach to Shakespeare, the histories and history in his own time: in addition to the work of Campbell, a number of like-minded scholars produced studies which shared many of his assumptions, methods and conclusions, among them J. Dover Wilson's *The Fortunes of Falstaff* (1943), which emerged out of his editorial work on the New Cambridge editions of *Henry IV*, and which was composed as an extended rebuttal of A. C. Bradley's liberal treatment of Falstaff in an essay included in his *Oxford Lectures on Poetry* (1909), and which answered Bradley's disquiet over the rejection of Falstaff with the conclusion that Shakespeare's contemporaries would have found it 'fine and appropriate' (Wilson 1943: 122). Wilson's critical work is now little read; what is remarkable about Tillyard's criticism is its longevity. In terms of its general circulation, use and consumption, as well as its influence and peer response, it continues to enjoy considerable literary, if not academic, currency: for generations of readers, Tillyard's worldviews have apparently remained instructive, perhaps even appealing, in a period in which they have fallen into academic disrepute. Intended 'to help the ordinary reader to understand and enjoy the great writers of the age' (Tillyard 1963: 8), and experiencing numerous reprints in hardback during the 1940s and 1950s, both *Shakespeare's History Plays* and *The Elizabethan World Picture* were reissued in the early 1960s by Penguin Books and subsequently reissued and reprinted in paperback many times; the most recent reprint of the former being in 1991, and of the latter in 1998.

Other, more anecdotal, kinds of evidence suggest that, despite the concerted efforts of critics after Tillyard to the contrary, these works remain stubbornly in use: my own university library houses multiple copies of both books, which, the record of the date stamps

J[ohn]. Dover Wilson (1881–1969)

Editor and literary critic

In the midst of a successful and demanding career as an educationist, Wilson experienced (as he described it in his memoir, *Milestones on the Dover Road*, 1969) a Damascene conversion to the cause of Shakespeare, brought on by reading an essay by W. W. Greg questioning the veracity of the Ghost's testimony in *Hamlet*. Devoting much of his energy over the course of the next two decades to the purpose of proving Greg wrong, an enterprise which resulted in the critical study *What Happens in Hamlet* (1935) and a critical edition of the play in 1936, which took the at the time radical step of basing itself on the Second Quarto rather than the Folio, Wilson also seized the opportunity, in 1919, to assume joint editorship of the Cambridge (or New) Shakespeare alongside Sir Arthur Quiller-Couch. From 1921 to 1966 he oversaw the development of the entire series, acting as sole editor of many plays, and then entrusting the task of later, and lesser, entrants to the canon to a number of collaborators. Wilson's insistence upon the theatrical provenance of Shakespeare's scripts shaped the course of textual editing during the twentieth century, though he was notoriously prone to interpolating descriptive (and overly directive and judgemental) stage directions: his *Hamlet* edition, for example, sets the scene for *The Murder of Gonzago* with '*The hall of the castle, with seats set to both sides as for a spectacle; at the back a dais with curtains, concealing an inner stage*', and describes Claudius's reaction thus: '*the King, very pale, totters to his feet … he rushes from the hall*'. Wilson's output was prodigious, but, as Stanley Wells records, he had another side to him: according to legend, 'Wilson's wife would lock him in his study to encourage him to get on with his work, whereupon he would escape out of the window to play golf' (Wells 2002: 363). It will strike a chord with anyone who has ever faced a writing deadline; which includes, perhaps, the readers – and certainly the writer – of this book.

A[ndrew]. C[ecil]. Bradley (1851–1935)

Literary critic

Both acclaimed and denounced as one of the most important Shakespearean critics of the twentieth century, Bradley is primarily known for his landmark work *Shakespearean Tragedy*, first published in 1904 and never out of print since. A philosopher by training prior to becoming a literary scholar, Bradley held that 'what imagination loved as poetry reason might love as philosophy, and that in the end these are two ways of saying the same thing' (1965: 394); *Shakespearean Tragedy*, accordingly, is an attempt not only to subject the quartet of major tragedies to the minutest of dramatically oriented close readings, but also to develop through literary analysis a new form of secular ethics. Often accused of circumstantial elaboration and speculation that suggests that Shakespeare's characters have ulterior lives offstage and beyond the text, as well as of ignoring the plays' poetic provenance (neither charge really stands up when set against the evidence of Bradley's own words), Bradley, whose work has outlived that of his detractors, is a critic whose method has been likened by the theatre director Harley Granville Barker to that of 'a very great actor's conception of the parts' (Granville Barker 1923: 20). Though aspects of *Shakespearean Tragedy* strike many modern readers as irrelevant (his lengthy animadversions upon 'The Subject of Shakespearean Tragedy'), offensive (his racial difficulties over Othello), misguided (concerns about credibility and consistency that properly belong to the domain of realist drama) or horribly sentimental (his account of Cordelia), its continuing strength lies in the expansiveness as well as the density of its imaginative and critical engagement with Shakespeare's work.

reveals, are borrowed on average two to three times a month. To begin to account for the persistence of Tillyard's appeal, we need to acknowledge the attractions of his method as well as its deficiencies. As Jonathan Dollimore and Alan Sinfield concede, in the context of a searching critique of Tillyard and Campbell, 'if we look again at what Tillyard was opposing, his historicism seems less objectionable' (1985: 206); as Graham Holderness adds, Tillyard 'positioned the plays firmly within a context in which the terms history, historical evidence, historiography, must be regarded as indispensable theoretical factors in the activity of interpretation' (1992: 6). More recently, and perhaps surprisingly, Tillyard's work has been identified as containing the seedlings of ecocriticism: as Gabriel Egan suggests, from 'the new perspectives provided by holograms, fractals, and genetics, Tillyard's version of an alleged Elizabethan concern for macrocosmic/microcosmic correspondences looks considerably less naïve than critics have given him (and, indeed, the Elizabethans) credit for'. Thinking such correspondences within the terms of modern science provides the basis for 'sophisticated analogical thinking that we must not dismiss out of hand' (Egan 2006: 26).

Tillyard's legacy

In lieu of an anachronistic, loosely construed universalism, Tillyard was determined to situate Shakespeare's work culturally and historically, within habits of thought and belief that were, as he expresses it, 'quite taken for granted', and hence 'the least disputed and the least paraded in the creative literature of the time' (1963: 7). Shakespeare, for Tillyard, was of his time but not reducible to it, and it was this very historicity that accounted for his universality; he was 'the voice of his own age first and only through being that, the voice of humanity' (1962: 243). If Tillyard's efforts to refer Shakespeare's drama to other forms of writing, with the aim of identifying a common metaphysical and political agenda, laid the foundations upon which later critics would build, his tactics of reading the texts as encrypted allegories of order indicated the potential of a historicised close reading that was more congenial to the New Critical enterprise than it might initially have appeared, although his fashioning of those works into a literature devoid of contradiction, irony and ambiguity would have been less so.

Tillyard's hermeneutic method is consistent with his larger critical agenda. If his version of historicism encourages us to read Shakespeare's texts as transparent articulations of the 'ruling ideas' of his age, it not only presumes a stable and ordered relationship between literary language, theatrical representation and orthodox thought, but also, in keeping with his theme, tames the texts' incipient unruliness and multiplicity. Sermons, political tracts, epic poetry and drama all speak with the same voice, and, according to a radically instrumentalist view of the efficacy of language, work upon their readers and auditors in the same ways; literature and drama precisely map belief. By disclosing the master code that governed the works of Shakespeare and his contemporaries, Tillyard's account promised to resolve its inconsistencies, its paradoxes and its lacunae. It is not difficult to see the appeal of this to the sort of reader who is interested not in ambivalence, indeterminacy, and multiple and shifting meanings, but in clear and firm answers.

The decade after the first publication of these two works, during which they would have found a receptive readership in Churchill, Eden and Macmillan's Britain and Eisenhower's America, witnessed both the inauguration of a school of historicist criticism modelled upon and influenced by Tillyard's vision of order and the first stirrings of dissent against it. In *Shakespeare from Richard II to Henry V* (1957), D. A. Traversi echoed the broad terms of Tillyard's providentialist scheme, repeating the claim that 'royal office is assumed to be divinely instituted, the necessary guarantee of order in a state nationally and patriotically conceived', and that the cycle only reaches a resolution 'after the consequences of the original crime have worked themselves out through the body politic in disintegration and bloodshed' (2), but placed more emphasis upon the personal costs of political action, as well as offering a more dialectical account of their figuration of order and disorder: 'the Prince and Falstaff represent contrasted poles, upon whose clash and subsistent interrelation the conception which animates these plays finally turns' (9).

Tillyard's presence was registered in the critical apparatus of the major editions of the histories published in the 1950s and 1960s, including the Arden Shakespeare second series. A. S. Cairncross's Arden editions of the three parts of *Henry VI*, for example, were published between 1957 and 1964. In his introduction to *Henry VI, Part 2* Cairncross endorses Tillyard's claim that the histories 'present or imply a comprehensive world picture, and a systematic development of one theme explicitly stated in Edward Hall's Chronicle' (Cairncross 1962: xxxix); describing *Henry VI, Part 3* as 'a study in anarchy', he harnesses a Tillyardian citation of correspondences ('anarchy in the state, in the family, in the mind of the individual') to the conclusion that 'the weakness of the king, who should control and maintain the bonds of society' brings about his own demise, which he characterises as 'the supreme outrage against the political order, and the divine order on which it rested' (Cairncross 1964: liii). During the same period, in a genuinely new development in the relationship between the theatrical and scholarly communities, Tillyard's work also provided the critical frame of reference for several landmark theatre productions, notably Anthony Quayle and Michael Redgrave's staging of the second tetralogy at the Shakespeare Memorial Theatre, Stratford-upon-Avon, in 1951, Sir Barry Jackson's Birmingham Rep *Henry VI* in 1953 (which, Tillyard reported, 'greatly confirmed' his view of the plays [1954:39]) and, in a more complex and ambivalent fashion, the Royal Shakespeare Company's productions of both tetralogies between 1963 and 1964.

Questioning authority: the 1960s

At the same time, critics began to take issue with Tillyard, pointing out the narrowly selective and partial nature of his reading of Shakespeare's sources and influences, and questioning the wisdom of attributing an obsolete medieval worldview to the Elizabethans. In *The English History Play in the Age of Shakespeare*, Irving Ribner conceded that 'what Tillyard says of Shakespeare is largely true' but questioned the close connection with Halle, arguing that this 'compresses the wide range of Elizabethan historical drama into entirely too narrow a compass'. Observing that Halle's providentialism 'represents a tradition which, when Shakespeare was writing, was already in decline', Ribner pictures Shakespeare's period as 'one of flux and uncertainty, with new and heretical notions competing in men's minds against old established ideas which could no longer be accepted without doubt and questioning' (1965: 10). Tudor history plays were both the products of and active contributions to this culture of conflict and interrogation; noting that 'there is room for Marlowe as well as Shakespeare' (10), and extending the remit of his investigation to the non-Shakespearean work that Tillyard either disregarded or denigrated, Ribner demonstrates that sceptical and secular modes of dramatic historiography ran alongside (sometimes counter to) its more didactic forms.

Shakespeare, in this context, occupies a position somewhere between the 'absolute orthodoxy' of Thomas Heywood and the 'open challenging' of Marlowe, reflecting his 'more critical, but nevertheless orthodox, acceptance of Tudor doctrine' (Ribner 1965: 29). The idea of critical orthodoxy fashions a space for Shakespeare the creative artist and independent thinker: because he 'never limits his attention to the mere political roles of his characters', the plays cannot be 'political propaganda' but 'the expression of a profoundly moral view of human relations' (158). Nonetheless, the scheme of the second tetralogy is not that different to that proposed by Tillyard, in that it traces 'the tragedy of initial downfall, the education process, and then the victorious emergence of the ideal king' (Ribner 1965: 193).

In his 1957 British Academy Shakespeare Lecture, L.C. Knights posited a more sharply divergent view, suggesting that the Tillyardian preoccupation with 'what was peculiar to an age' was actually a barrier to true understanding, not a means of facilitating it: 'May it not be that what was most nourishing of creative achievement in the past was what, in the tradition of the time, is – or should be – most available for us now?' (Knights 1957: 116). Not one of Shakespeare's 'greater' plays, Knights stated, 'can be adequately "explained" by anything outside itself' (124); his 'political' plays had to be seen as 'creative explorations of conceptions such as power, authority, honour, order, and freedom … Their real meaning is only revealed when political life is seen, as Shakespeare makes us see it, in terms of the realities of human life and human relationships' (129). Such a Shakespeare could not be confined or limited to the 'ideas of his time', although this understanding did imply a model of the relationship between the personal and the political that reflected aspects of the Leavisite ideal of the 'organic society' that Knights, as a founding member of the infuential journal *Scrutiny*, had done a great deal to cultivate. This emphasis was taken up by M. M. Reese, who in *The Cease of Majesty* (1961), acknowledging Knights as an 'inspiration' (ix), aligns Shakespeare with the 'religious, poetical and romantic' historiography of Raleigh, whereby 'two conceptions of history, as following God's inexorable pattern and as offering a storehouse of practical lessons to guide man's independent choice, were complementary and not mutually exclusive' (18–19).

The culmination of this critical reaction against Tillyard was Robert Ornstein's *A Kingdom for a Stage* (1972), the first chapter of which ('The Artist as Historian') clearly identifies the aesthetic as the crucial ground of argument. Firmly rejecting the Tillyardian inference that Shakespeare could have been content to 'follow the lead of the plodding didacticists who supposedly created the genre of the History Play, and like them dedicate his art to moralistic and propagandist purposes', Ornstein repeated Knights's charge that the overly narrow and antiquarian historicism which insists on Shakespeare's orthodoxy is dangerously reductive, in that it 'turn[s] living works of theater into dramatic fossils or repositories of quaint and dusty ideas' (Ornstein 1972: 2).

In a key passage, Ornstein locates the 'heart of the matter' in

> an implicit refusal by historical scholarship to grant that the ultimate standard for the interpretation of art is aesthetic. Insisting on the primacy of Shakespeare's didactic intention, scholarship would have us believe that the interpretation of the History plays does not depend on sensitivity to nuances of language and characterization or awareness of Shakespeare's poetic and dramatic methods; it depends instead on the appropriate annotation of the doctrine of the plays.
>
> (Ornstein 1972: 8)

The important distinction here, it seems, is between 'interpretation' and 'scholarship': the one is associated with sensitivity, receptiveness and creativity, the other is the activity of a cold-hearted, reactionary bureaucrat; this is polemical and schematic, perhaps, but indicative of the emotional and political stakes that underpin the debates around Shakespeare's history. What Ornstein is not advocating, however, is a rejection of historicism per se: his own reading of the historical contexts of Shakespeare's drama, and of the historical understanding displayed in them, places significant weight upon the 'diversity, contradictions, shadings, and facets' of Elizabethan belief (Orstein 1972: 10), which are manifested in the contradictions within and between the chronicles, in their readiness to set providentialist didacticism against a more pragmatic accommodation with the realities of history and human action, and, in the drama and poetry, in 'the variousness of their approaches to the past' (21).

Ornstein here echoes the more detailed account given by Henry A. Kelly, whose *Divine Providence in the England of Shakespeare's Histories* (1970), in the course of an exhaustive examination of the chronicles, demonstrated that, far from there being a Tudor Myth, there were contending York and Lancaster Myths, and, since 'God is always assumed to support the cause of justice', the political allegiances of the chronicler condition 'attitudes toward the supernatural impetus behind the visible cause of events' (viii). Shakespeare, in his turn, 'eliminated all the purportedly objective providential judgments made by the histories', as well as 'simplistic evaluations of complex moral situations' (305). Like Kelly, Ornstein is as sceptical of the idea that either the love of order or the fear of disorder would have driven Shakespeare to write 'play after play to persuade his audiences of the need for order and disobedience' (1972: 25), as he is of the conclusion that such attempts at persuasion, whether by the theatres or by the state, would have been effective anyway: 'Since a century of Tudor and Stuart dogmatizing about the holy duty of obedience did not save Charles I from his God-fearing enemies, we can assume that had there been compelling political reasons or had Elizabeth been as tactless and inept as Charles in dealing with her opposition, she too might have been dethroned and perhaps executed' (Ornstein 1972: 27). The Shakespeare that is constructed by Ornstein is a freethinking artist, not an ideologue; and it is this independence of mind and spirit that ranks the achievement of the histories alongside that of the canon as a whole: 'To see in the tetralogies the same openness of mind and breadth of humanity that we find in the comedies and tragedies is to know that in writing the History Plays Shakespeare surrendered nothing to the dictates of orthodoxy' (Ornstein 1972: 31).

Shakespeare their contemporary

Ornstein's determination to wrest the histories from the grasp of an antiquarian historicism and to return them to the grounds of the aesthetic is underpinned by the suspicion that they have been subjected to a form of generic discrimination: reduced to the history and orthodox thought of their own time because it was possible for historicist critics to get away with it. Alluding in passing to 'those who would have us read Shakespeare's tragedies "through Elizabethan eyes"' (1972: 3), Ornstein also draws attention to a trend towards historicisation that did not limit its remit to the histories: Tillyard himself dealt with the problem comedies (1950; reprinted 1965) and the romances (1951). The 1960s also saw the publication of a range of studies which tended to characterise Shakespeare's relation to his own age in ambivalent and dynamic terms. A. P. Rossiter's *Angel with Horns* (1961) took strong issue with the Tillyard postion, arguing that the 'dialectic' of the histories was 'ambivalence': although Shakespeare accepted the Tudor Myth as a 'frame', his critical intelligence compelled him to 'undermine it, to qualify it with equivocations: to vex its applications with sly or subtle ambiguities: to cast doubts on its ultimate human validity' (Rossiter 1989: 59).

The instabilities that Rossiter supposed that Shakespeare detected within the Elizabethan world picture had wider ramifications: thus *Troilus and Cressida*, far from epitomising the doctrine of Order, dramatised its collapse (see 'Works', pp. 204–9). Confronted with, as he perceives it, Cressida's betrayal of him with Diomed, Troilus invokes 'rule in unity itself' only to recognise that 'This is and is not Cressid' (5.2.144, 149). As Rossiter reads it, this passage radically negates Ulysses's vision of order (which Tillyard had regarded as exemplary): 'the universe *ought* to be an integral whole, in which everything has its proper status in a divinely-ordained hierarchical order', but instead, it is suggested, 'there *is* no "rule in unity itself", no principle of integrity' (Rossiter 1989: 135). This questioning is symptomatic of the play's historicity, in that it is specifically 'Jacobean' in its interrogation of traditional values and its embrace of 'the perplexities (rather than the triumphs) of Renaissance individualism' (148); but it is also the source of its modernity, in that Troilus's anguished witnessing 'is a thoroughly Existentialist performance' (135).

Rossiter's concern with the dialectical qualities of Shakespearean drama, as well as his interest in the nature of the relationship between its historic origins and its contemporary relevance, found echoes in a more specifically Marxist inflection in the pioneering collection of essays *Shakespeare in a Changing World* (1964), edited by Arnold Kettle. The 'changing world' of the title is, Kettle suggests, 'neither Shakespeare's nor ours' but also 'both Shakespeare's and ours'; what vitally connects the twentieth century to the seventeenth is 'the rate and density of change', which is so 'exceptionally powerful' that 'whatever conclusions they may draw from the changes, men are unusually conscious of change and its necessities' (Kettle 1964: 9–10). The historically minded critic, the editor and contributors to this collection recognise that 'we are all, Shakespeare and ourselves, characters in history'; fortunately, 'no other literature can help us more than Shakespeare's plays to see ourselves as we are' (9). As Robert Weimann puts it in his contribution to the volume, the relationship between then and now is defined by 'the necessary tension between the work of art as a historical phenomenon and as a living force in our present day culture' (Kettle 1964: 18).

Although the notion of Shakespeare's 'changing world' invites some rather schematic periodising ('Elizabethan drama grew in a no-man's land between the two historical epochs that we call the feudal and the capitalist', writes V. G. Kiernan [Kettle 1964: 43]), it also encourages the contributors to lay particular stress upon his works' orientation towards the future as well as the past, and to depict Shakespeare as a champion of liberal, progressive and, in places, even radical values. The author of the histories is no mouthpiece for orthodoxy but one keenly aware of the contradictions underpinning the apparent triumph of Henry V, himself 'the new *national* king, the herald of the Tudor monarchy' (101). *Macbeth*, considered as a critical exploration of bourgeois individualism, reveals its protagonist's 'affiliations with the early "heroic" days of capitalism' (122); *Othello* investigates 'the situation of the alien (including the class alien) in a hierarchical, predatory and therefore not yet fully human society' (126), whilst insisting that 'human dignity … is indivisible' (145). The optimistic, activist spirit of the collection is epitomised by the closing statement of its final essay, which, suggesting that if Shakespeare is to continue to act as a 'living presence' criticism 'should not lend his name to work which celebrates nothingness', cites the pivotal moment in *King Lear* (3.5) where Cornwall's servant, raising his sword against his master in an attempt to stop the blinding of Gloucester, 'stands up for tortured humanity', and 'through the pleasure, knowledge and hope it brings into life, we know the freedom to be won as the domination of man by man is defeated' (Kettle 1964: 265–66).

Referring to critical work which 'celebrates nothingness', the author of this essay, Alick West, has in his sights the Polish theatre director and scholar Jan Kott, whose *Shakespeare Our Contemporary*, first published in English translation in 1965, had asserted the continuity between Shakespeare and the nihilism of the modern Theatre of the Absurd, especially the plays of Samuel Beckett, which are, West claims, characterised by their 'denial of history' (Kettle 1964: 260). Such a charge could equally well be levelled at Kott himself; just as we should not try to 'pretend that we are members of the audience of the old Globe theatre', Kettle warns, so too 'to try to read a Shakespeare play as though he were our contemporary is to ask for trouble' (9). This, of course, is precisely what Kott was attempting to do; as an impassioned reaction against both the conservative historicism of the Tillyard school and its more liberal and progressive alternatives, *Shakespeare Our Contemporary* provoked strong responses from the proponents of both, and wielded considerable influence upon Shakespearean theatrical production worldwide for over three decades.

Starting from the premise that, with Shakespeare, every age 'finds in him what it is looking for and what it wants to see', Kott claimed that the twentieth-century spectator, steeped in the knowledge (or direct experience) of the horrors of Nazi and Soviet totalitarianism, the police state, the death camps, the Gulags and Hiroshima, was no longer 'terrified – or rather, not amazed – at Shakespeare's cruelty' (1965: 5). Kott reads the histories in terms of 'the image of the Grand Mechanism' (9), whose 'cog-wheels are both great lords and hired assassins', which 'forces people to violence, cruelty and treason', and 'according to whose laws the road to power is at the same time the way to death' (32). Shakespeare's history is a brutally indifferent machine devoid of purpose or teleology, 'the King is no Lord's Anointed, and politics is only an art aimed at capturing and securing power' (40). Kott's technique of reading, like the main conclusions he arrives at about the plays' ruling values, is the absolute antithesis of Tillyard's, and sharply distinguished from the contextualising interpretative practice and cautious allegorising characteristic of the majority of historicisms that we have considered thus far: the plays are systematically ransacked for contemporary resonances which are no mere 'parallels' but desperately immediate truths: thus in Richard of Gloucester's subjugation of Lady Anne (*Richard III*, 1.2) we 'must find … the night of Nazi occupation, concentration camps, mass-murders … the cruel time when all moral standards have been broken, when the victim becomes the executioner, and vice versa' (Kott 1965: 37). This was, in its time, fresh and provocative, and its appeal to theatre and film directors (including Peter Hall and Peter Brook) as a template for a modernising practice is undeniable, but it should also be recognised that Kott's apparent repudiation of the Tillyardian world picture is couched in terms which uncannily replicate some of its signature imagery: both the Grand Mechanism and the Staircase of Power, even if their operations are anything but benign, are secular analogues of the Chain of Being and the Cosmic Dance. If in Tillyard's hands the ruling order tended towards the imposition of obedience, Kott's version of the same enforced a lesson that, in the end, is not that dissimilar: the system, no matter how vicious, arbitrary and absurd, is always the ultimate victor.

Kott's anti-historicism merits consideration in the current context in part because its reference points in current theatre and history posit an accessible and seemingly radical (if radically nihilist) alternative to the more measured pronouncements of the forms of historicism that were dominant in the 1950s and 1960s. Returning to Ornstein's work for a moment, however, we can also discern here, as in Kettle's collection, the outlines of a different and more politically engaged way of thinking about the situatedness of Shakespeare, and of the critic, within contemporary history; one that anticipates the tenor of the historicist scholarship of a decade later; it is worth noting that Ornstein was posthumously honoured with a *Festschrift* in which a number of key contributors to that movement registered their indebtedness to his work (Gajowski 2004). *A Kingdom for a Stage* was written in the mid-1960s and published in 1972; thus falling under the shadow of the civil rights movement and the ongoing war in Vietnam. Noting that scholars seemed to positively relish the orthodoxy of Shakespeare's political thought, Ornstein writes that this approach 'has some of the characteristics of a security investigation and clearance', and identifies a 'left and right wing in the criticism of Shakespeare', the one 'libertarian (or Falstaffian) in sympathies', the other 'conservative and mindful of the need for authority and discipline' (1972: 3–4). Elsewhere, he connects the 'stresses of social and economic change' with the cultural paranoia and repressive policing of 'England in the 1590's and America in the 1950's', remarking that 'the hunting down of subversives had its psychological and political uses in both eras' (25).

Behind such sentiments lies a model of the relationships between academic discourse and practice, citizenship, teaching and political conviction that is subtly different to the diplomatically disengaged scholarship of the past: engaging the works with current history is not only the right but the duty of the critical thinker. In *The Tragedy of State* (1971), J. W. Lever was even more forthright: 'the needling word "relevance"', he declared, was the critic's first priority, and 'if he doesn't ask himself, his students will certainly ask him, in no deferential tone' (1971: 1). As a work not primarily concerned with Shakespeare, but with his contemporaries, the book licenses itself to be more adventurous in its assessment of the politics of the drama. Advancing the by now familiar charges against 'that hotch-potch of antiquated science, fancy, and folklore dignified by some modern scholars as the Elizabethan World Order' ('the so-called "chain of being" was in an advanced condition of rust by the end of the sixteenth century') (5), Lever offered a series of strongly contemporary readings of statecraft in Jacobean tragedy that regarded their setting as 'the set-up, the system, the establishment, the *status quo*', afflicted by a 'sense of impermanence and flux' (6). Stressing conflict and contradiction, the social causes and implications of the tragic action, and 'the effects of power upon the human heart and mind' (93), Lever sketched the clear outlines of the concerns that, within a decade, would come to dominate the study of Shakespeare in, and as, history.

Refashioning the Renaissance

The turning point in the twentieth-century history of historical criticism, it is generally acknowledged, was in 1980, the year in which the relatively liberal political legacy of the 1960s finally ran out, leading, in the United States, to a resurgence of neo-conservatism that was epitomised by the election of President Ronald Reagan; the previous year, in the United Kingdom, the equally fundamentalist right-winger Margaret Thatcher had assumed office promising to break with the postwar consensus around industrial relations and the welfare state. In the critical arena, the factors that converged to effect what can genuinely be accounted a paradigm shift in the discipline of historicist scholarship had been taking shape since the mid-1970s, but 1980 seemed decisive, and was marked by two events: a series of lectures delivered by the French philosopher Michel Foucault at the University of California, Berkeley, and the publication of Stephen Greenblatt's landmark study *Renaissance Self-Fashioning: From More to Shakespeare*. In the lectures, which Greenblatt subsequently cited as instrumental in the formation of what soon came to be known as New Historicism, Foucault offered a summation of the project that, along with a number of other prominent theorists allied to post-structuralism, he had been developing since the 1960s, in works such as *Madness and Civilisation* (1967), *The Order of Things* (1970), *The Birth of the Clinic* (1973), *Discipline and Punish* (1977) and *The History of Sexuality* (1981). Foucault's account of power is allied to that of another French post-structuralist working more squarely within the Marxist tradition, Louis Althusser, another of the formative influences on the New Historicism.

The theoretical and analytic models furnished by the work of Foucault and Althusser were partnered, at first in the work of Greenblatt but subsequently more widely, with the

Michel Foucault (1926–84)

French philosopher and historian

In a series of interdisciplinary investigations whose remit encompasses philosophy, literary theory, historiography, sociology, and the histories of science, medicine and law, Foucault proposed a radical, anti-humanist critique of the intellectual inheritance of the Enlightenment and, in particular, of the abstraction with which it has been most preoccupied (or which, as Foucault contends, it has contrived to construct): 'man'. For Foucault, 'man' is a chimera, an ideological fiction. The self that, in Enlightenment thought, serves as the source of agency and freedom is no more than a product of the various discourses that produce human beings as subjects: defined by sexual, commercial, legal, educational and religious mechanisms that are intricately invested with power, the subject's very being is a consequence of the internalised practices of discipline, surveillance and desire that administer it. By its very nature, power is not exercised by the state, or by its rulers or administrators, but is inherent in its very structure: as Foucault remarks, 'this machine is one in which everyone is caught, those who exercise this power as well as those who are subjected to it' (1980: 156). It is a view of power, and of politics, which renders distinctions between oppressive and more open, liberal or democratic regimes redundant. Viewed historically, the epistemic shift has been from the blatant exercise of power as physical force or as outright repression to more covert forms of manipulation, superficially more benign but in actuality, for Foucault, more insidious, and more irresistible. Thus, to take but one influential example, the historic shift away from the grisly spectacle of public execution to the ostensibly more liberal regime of the prison represents, for Foucault, less the application of humanitarian principles than the elaboration of increasingly sophisticated systems of manipulation, surveillance and control.

Louis Althusser (1918–90)

French philosopher

Althusser's much-cited essay 'Ideology and Ideological State Apparatuses' (1971b) offered to reformulate the account of ideology that had been proposed by Karl Marx and Friedrich Engels in *The German Ideology* (1845): whereas Marx and Engels had argued that the dominant ideas in any social system reflected the perspectives and served the interests of its ruling class, and as such could be scientifically exposed and refuted as 'false consciousness', Althusser contends that ideology works in far more subtle, pervasive and deeply rooted ways, reflecting 'not the system of the real relations which govern the existence of individuals, but the imaginary relation of those individuals to the real relations in which they live' (1971: 155). Ideology manifests itself not just as philosophical, political or religious truths or myths, but also, more insidiously and more persuasively, as 'common sense', in the 'obviousnesses which we cannot fail to recognise and before which we have the inevitable and natural reaction of crying out (aloud, or in the "still, small voice of conscience"): "That's obvious! That's right! That's true!"' Thus the 'elementary ideological effect' (161) is to construct human subjects as apparently free individuals; work which is sustained by the cultural apparatuses of the state – which extend from its educational systems to its family structures, and include its works of art and literature, its conventions of representation, mimesis, performance.

mode of the cultural analysis developed by the anthropologist Clifford Geertz, a practice which Geertz termed 'thick description'. In Geertz's influential *The Interpretation of Cultures* (1973), a work which covers such topics as religious practices in Java and cockfighting in Bali, this is defined as a 'semiotic' conception of culture, whereby anthropological research is 'not an experimental science in search of law but an interpretative one in search of meaning'; thus 'the object of ethnography' is 'a stratified hierarchy of meaningful structures in terms of which twitches, winks, fake-winks, parodies, rehearsals of parodies are produced, perceived, and interpreted, and without which they would not … in fact exist' (Geertz 1993: 5, 7).

If the idea of social behaviour as cultural performance is appealing, so too is the direct comparison of thick description with the work of the 'literary critic': one of the axioms of the method being that there is no 'objective' position for the analyst 'outside' the domain of her investigation: 'what we call our data are really our own constructions of other people's constructions of what they and their compatriots are up to' (Geertz 1993: 9). For Greenblatt, the implication of this perspective for the study of literature and drama is that it is possible neither to 'assume the literary as a stable ground' nor to 'take for granted the existence of an autonomous aesthetic realm': literature's boundaries are 'contested, endlessly renegotiated, permeable', and these 'contests and negotiations' are 'all social; they do not occur in a private chamber of the artist's imagination, for that imagination, in its materials and resources and aspirations, is already a social construct' (Greenblatt 1988: vii).

The new historicisms of the early 1980s promised a more thoroughgoing immersion of Shakespeare's texts in cultural history than had yet been envisaged, as well as a radical departure from the notions of creative autonomy and independence, and of the timelessness and universality of great works of literature, that had underpinned both conservative historicism and its counter-arguments. By the time these words were published, they reflected the consensus of a recognisable school or movement with a variety of adherents; in 1980, both the interdisciplinarity of this approach and its radical interrogation of the very idea of human selfhood had the power to surprise, unsettle and provoke.

In *Renaissance Self-Fashioning*, Greenblatt characteristically accounts for the trajectory of the new critical practice in quasi-anecdotal, autobiographical terms:

> When I first conceived this book several years ago, I intended to explore the ways in which major English writers of the sixteenth century created their own performances, to analyze the choices they made in representing themselves and in fashioning characters, to understand the role of human autonomy in the construction of identity. ... But as my work progressed, I perceived that fashioning oneself and being fashioned by cultural institutions – family, religion, state – were inseparably intertwined. In all my texts and documents, there were, so far as I could tell, no moments of pure, unfettered subjectivity; indeed, the human subject itself began to seem remarkably unfree, the ideological product of the relations of power in a particular society.
>
> (Greenblatt 1980: 256)

Here, in a nutshell, are the central principles of post-Foucault, post-Althusser, post-Geertz post-structuralism as they impact upon the study of early modern texts and histories, as well as an outline of the boundaries within which subsequent arguments within the discipline – particularly with regard to the extent and limits of the subject's (un)freedom – would be conducted.

These concerns are pursued across the course of the sixteenth century via an examination of six key figures: the humanist scholar and politician Thomas More, William Tyndale, the architect of the vernacular Bible, the courtier-poets Sir Thomas Wyatt and Sir Philip Sidney, and Christopher Marlowe and Shakespeare. The fashioning of identity, for Greenblatt, is a 'resolutely dialectical' affair, whereby every proposition that is made about the period is required to entertain its antithesis:

> If we say that there is a new stress on the executive power of the will, we must say that there is the most sustained and relentless assault upon the will; if we say that there is a new social mobility, we must say that there is a new assertion of power by both family and state ... if we say that there is a heightened awareness of the existence of alternative modes of social, theological, and psychological organization, we must say that there is a new dedication to the imposition of control upon those modes.
>
> (Greenblatt 1980: 1–2)

The patterns of domination and submission, assertion and subservience, and conformity and heterodoxy that are played out in the literary works under discussion are also evident, to a greater or lesser extent, in the biographies of their authors, in that self-fashioning operates 'without regard for a sharp distinction between literature and social life' (Greenblatt 1980: 3), literary texts can be viewed as the focus of 'converging lines of force in sixteenth century culture; their significance for us is not that we may see *through* them to underlying and prior historical principles but rather that we may interpret the interplay of their symbolic structures with those perceivable in the careers of their authors and in the larger social world' (5–6).

The historicist method employed by Greenblatt here, which seeks to triangulate texts, authors, and their contexts and conditions of intelligibility, is an attempt to produce what he terms 'a *poetics of culture*' (1980: 4–5); the phrase is revealing in its emphasis, in that it suggests an aesthetic orientation that subsequent commentators would question (why 'poetics' rather than 'politics'? And does the term suggest culture can or should be 'read', new-critical-style, as if were itself a kind of 'text'?). Also potentially contentious is Greenblatt's intense and intricate conjunction of textual exegesis and literary and other forms of biography, which is most comprehensively and successfully realised in the lengthy first chapter on Thomas More, which reads the author of *Utopia*, and the work itself, within the frame of a theological vision of the world as absurd theatre, in which the 'consequence of life lived as histrionic improvisation is that the category of the real merges with the fictive': 'To make a part of one's own, to live one's life as a character thrust into a play, constantly renewing oneself extemporaneously and forever aware of one's own unreality – such was More's condition, such, one might say, his project' (31). More's condition, Greenblattt suggests, is culturally representative; his insight into that condition absolutely unique.

Here, as throughout, Greenblatt's 'poetics of culture', by attaching itself to 'arresting figures who seem to contain within themselves much of what we need, who both reward intense, individual attention and promise access to larger cultural patterns' (1980: 6), seems delicately poised between a theory of literary genius that is reminiscent of the humanist critical tradition and the less individualised sociology of art favoured by the Marxist one (this is also a way of negotiating the problematic of agency and subjection summarised on pp. 328–30). More, and, in different ways, Tyndale, Wyatt and Spenser, are liable to bear this weight of scrutiny because their high public profiles and extensively documented biographies render the relations between lives and texts particularly suggestive; with the more enigmatic figures of Marlowe and Shakespeare, the approach is necessarily more circumspect, and possibly more inconclusive.

With regard to the latter, Greenblatt's reading of the 'improvisation of power' in *Othello* leads to the tentative conclusion that Shakespeare possessed an Iago-like 'limitless talent for entering into the consciousness of another, perceiving its deepest structures as a manipulable fiction'; unlike Marlowe, Shakespeare seemed to be his culture's 'dutiful servant, content to improvise a part of his own within its orthodoxy', although 'any reductive generalization about Shakespeare's relation to his culture seems dubious' because 'his plays offer no single timeless affirmation or denial of legitimate authority and no central, unwavering authorial presence' (Greenblatt 1980: 252–54). In a book as carefully crafted as this, Shakespeare's elusiveness provides the deferred culmination of a complex system of dialectical counterpointing of texts and writers that sets More against his antagonist Tyndale, and conformist Spenser against rebel Marlowe: 'Shakespeare does not resolve the aesthetic and moral conflict' between them, 'though his theater is enigmatically engaged in both positions' (8).

One of the particularly engaging, and methodologically and stylistically influential, aspects of *Renaissance Self-Fashioning*, and one for which Greenblatt's writing is justly acclaimed, is its richness as storytelling: the More chapter, in particular, derives some of its narrative drive and cumulative force from an elaborate recursive structure which repeatedly returns the reader to the vivid image which provides its inception, of More seated 'at the table of the great' during one of Cardinal Wolsey's agonising dinner parties. Even more characteristic of a technique for which new historicist criticism would become notorious are the opening pages of the chapter dealing with Marlowe, which consist of a detailed account of the destruction of an African village by a crew of British merchant venturers in 1586. Just as the reader begins to wonder where this is leading, Greenblatt furnishes a clue: 'If, on returning to England in 1587, the merchant and his associates had gone to see the Lord Admiral's Men perform a new play, *Tamburlaine the Great*, they would have seen an extraordinary meditation on the roots of their own behaviour' (1980: 194). There is, as Touchstone would have it, much virtue in 'if' (*As You Like It*, 5.4.92): what links text, theatrical event and historical anecdote is more than a cheerfully audacious coincidence of dates; at stake in all is a common cultural logic of aggressive mercantile imperialism. Both the text and the single, almost arbitrarily selected, event are understood as instances of cultural practice which epitomise the operations of power in sixteenth-century England, although neither is simply reducible to it. Of all of the mannerisms that new historicists inherited from Greenblatt, the strategic deployment of the apparently fortuitous but ultimately telling anecdote was the most characteristic, as well, as, for some, the most irksome.

If the history of which he writes is, as Greenblatt contends, resolutely dialectical, in the sense that its scrutiny yields an intense awareness of the opposition between innovation and its (often internal) resistances, Greenblatt's own writing registers its awareness of its own place in critical history by self-consciously dramatising this process as both disciplinary transformation and personal journey. What we may notice is that Greenblatt's own frequent critical and authorial acts of self-fashioning themselves uncannily double the sixteenth-century practices with which the book is preoccupied; unsurprisingly, of course, for as Greenblatt admits, 'it is everywhere evident ... that the questions I ask of my material and indeed the very nature of this material are shaped by the questions I ask of myself' (1980: 5).

The passage quoted at the beginning of this discussion of Greenblatt's work (see p. 316) itself transcribes the transition from one paradigm to another in explicitly autobiographical terms, sketching the reinvention of a slightly naïve critical interest in selves like himself (as Greenblatt memorably put it at the beginning of his next sole-authored book, *Shakespearean Negotiations*, 'I began with the desire to speak with the dead' [1988: 1]) to a, perhaps more poignant, figure, disabused of the illusions of 'pure, unfettered subjectivity' (though it's hard to imagine anyone who would seriously entertain such a fantasy) and tragically cognisant of the illusory quality of his own freedoms. Even so, 'to let go of one's stubborn hold upon selfhood, even selfhood conceived as a fiction, is to die ... I want to bear witness at the close to my overwhelming need to sustain the illusion that I am the principal maker of my own identity' (257).

The impact of *Renaissance Self-Fashioning* was substantial and immediate, and although it was not a work produced in isolation, it provided the template for the work attached to the critical movement that variously defined itself as cultural poetics, the new historicism and New Historicism. One of the shifts of perspective engineered, or at least attempted, by *Renaissance Self-Fashioning* is a partial decentring of Shakespeare: both the overall balance of material and the logic of its model of textual (and self-)authorship should imply a Shakespeare who is less distinct from his contemporaries and predecessors, and less unique, and less creatively and intellectually autonomous, than previous modes of historicism had sought to argue. And yet this displacement is, after all, only partial: despite the carefully wrought positioning of exceptional creativity within a dense cultural matrix of enablement and restraint, Shakespeare (by virtue of his capacity to 'improvise') retains a creative and intellectual autonomy not afforded to his contemporaries and predecessors. Greenblatt's seminal work was contemporaneous with a body of criticism that, sharing its concern with the construction of subjectivities, the politics of literary forms, the mechanisms of state power and the scope for resistance to their operation, and literature and the theatre's implication therein, consciously went further in its efforts to divest Shakespeare of the status of isolated individual genius by positioning the (no longer 'his' in the familiar sense) texts within a broader historical and cultural field (see, for example. Barker *et al.* 1981; Sinfield 1983; Goldberg 1983; Cohen 1985). Also emergent at this moment, at the intersection between the concerns of post-structuralist theory, postmodern historiography and the identity politics of the new British and American left, are forms of historicism specifically geared towards the investigation of constructions of gender and sexuality, and, subsequently, ethnicity and race.

Subversion and containment

The 1980s heralded not only a rapid diversification of critical approaches under the aegis of the new historicisms (and of cultural materialism, of which more on pp. 325–8) but also an exponential expansion of publishing activity in the field; and while (if we are to avoid a mere reiteration of names and titles) this enforces a certain selectivity upon an account such as this, it is also the case that the perspective that is afforded by historical distance diminishes the closer one moves to the present, and this selectivity must itself recognise its own partial and provisional status. However, there is a further factor – and one which, aptly enough, pertains to the material cultures of scholarship, publishing and pedagogy within which critical ideas circulate – which is of relevance here.

As well as witnessing significant growth in student numbers in higher education, the 1980s also saw the beginnings of an important shift in the practices of an academic publishing industry which saw itself increasingly geared towards the needs of an expanding constituency of student consumers inspired, encouraged or required to engage with the new critical dispensation: besides (and, increasingly, in the place of) the traditional scholarly monograph, the period saw the emergence of guides (and the current volume bears testimony to this long-term trend), readers and anthologies as the primary vehicles for the broader dissemination of new critical ideas, and in which, as often as not, scholarship published prior to around 1980 tended not to feature. The new historicism, along with other critical schools influenced by post-structuralism, benefited from this change, particularly so in the case of a number of repeatedly anthologised essays and extracts which, if frequency of citation and reproduction is any index of impact and influence, very swiftly established themselves as canonical instances of its practice.

Consider three much-cited and much-reprinted essays, first published in the early 1980s, which have widely been acknowledged as exemplary of the new historicism. The first of these, Greenblatt's 'Invisible Bullets: Renaissance Authority and Its Subversion, *Henry IV* and *Henry V*', was originally published in the final issue (before it mutated into the still-extant house journal of new historicism, *Representations*, a year later) of the deconstructively inclined journal *Glyph* in 1981; it was reworked for Jonathan Dollimore and Alan Sinfield's collection *Political Shakespeare* (1985; second edition 1994), and for Peter Erickson and Coppélia Kahn's *Shakespeare's 'Rough Magic': Renaissance Essays in Honor of C. L. Barber* (1985), and included in Greenblatt's *Shakespearean Negotiations* (1988); it has been anthologised in Richard Wilson and Richard Dutton's *New Historicism and Renaissance Drama* (1992) and in Russ McDonald's *Shakespeare: An Anthology of Theory and Criticism, 1945–2000* (2004), and in *The Greenblatt Reader* (Payne 2005). Praised as 'the most important, and surely the most influential essay of the past decade' (Kinney 1990: 1) and denounced as a piece whose 'grave defects' generate serious doubts 'about the value or validity of this whole school of criticism' (Vickers 1993: 267), 'Invisible Bullets' has been widely seen as the epitome of the new historicist practice: 'Any attempt to characterize New Historicism and evaluate its contribution to our understanding of Renaissance literature', wrote Tom McAlindon (in a profoundly hostile article intended to expose Greenblatt's, and New Historicism's, shortcomings), could 'legitimately confine itself' to Greenblatt's essay (McAlindon 1995: 411).

As in the case studies elaborated in *Renaissance Self-Fashioning*, Greenblatt does not start with a Shakespeare play but, on this occasion, with three sets of textual evidence: the accusation of atheism levelled at Christopher Marlowe by the Elizabethan spy Richard Baines, Machiavelli's writings on religion in *The Prince* and the *Discourses*, and a pamphlet authored by the mathematician and astronomer Thomas Harriot, *A Briefe and True Report of the New Found Land of Virginia* (1588), a work that arose from a visit to the New World in the company of Sir Walter Raleigh. The initial interest lies in the various ways in which these texts, by paying attention to the expediency rather than the theologically sanctioned principle of statecraft, entertain heterodox opinion within a discourse of ostensible political religious orthodoxy; in Harriot's text, in particular, we have a testing of 'the Machiavellian hypothesis of the origin of princely power in force and fraud', as well as 'a sense of religion as a set of beliefs manipulated by the subtlety of the priests to help ensure social order and cohesion' (Greenblatt 1994: 20–21). Harriot's means of investigating these potentially deeply subversive speculations is an exercise in what might be called comparative anthropology: conceived as a record of the first English colony in Virginia and of its encounters with the indigenous inhabitants, the *Briefe and True Report* documents the everyday and ritual practices and religious beliefs of the Algonkian Indians, as well as the impact of the European settlers' attempts to impose their own culture upon them.

Viewing Algonkian religious belief from the standpoint of 'true' Christian religion, Harriot 'objectively' registers it as 'false'; ironically, however, the logic underlying the colonists' determined discrediting of the Indians' worldview implicitly calls Christianity into question also, paradoxically creating the situation whereby 'Harriot tests and seems to confirm the most radically subversive hypothesis in his culture about the origin and function of religion by imposing his religion … upon others' (Greenblatt 1994: 23). This instance of what Greenblatt, in a key formulation, terms 'subversion and its containment' (25) finds confirmation in the specific incident which afford the essay its title: recording the epidemic effect of the settlers' contacts with an indigenous population lacking resistance to the diseases they had imported with them, Harriot records 'the Indians' own anxious speculations about the unintended but lethal biological warfare that was destroying them', in particular the theory that the English were 'shooting invisible bullets into them' (26).

The point, for Greenblatt, is not that Harriot was being intentionally or subconsciously subversive, mischievously ironic or self-deluding in his unwitting exposure of the contradictions within his culture's own political theology, but that the subversive implications of his account – and this is the crux of this essay, as it is of the mode of new historicism that it inaugurates – are actually *produced* by the power mechanisms in whose service he writes and acts. Simultaneously coercive and heterodox, caught within the dynamics of containment and subversion, Harriot's text is symptomatic of early modern textual culture, which in turn reproduces (albeit not in straightforward ways) the operations of power within the early modern state. Turning to Shakespeare's plays, Greenblatt finds that these are 'centrally and repeatedly concerned with the production and containment of subversion and disorder, and the three modes … in Harriot's text – testing, recording, and explaining – all have their recurrent theatrical equivalents' (Greenblatt 1994: 29). In the *Henry IV* plays and *Henry V*, we witness the construction of the ideal ruler, in the person of Prince, then King, Henry, through 'the constant production of its own radical subversion and the powerful containment of that subversion' (30). Immersing himself in the plebeian and criminal subcultures of Eastcheap, Hal has 'sounded the very bass-string of humility' (2.5.5–6) so as 'to know how to play all the chords and hence to master the instrument' (32); given to role-playing and theatrical improvisation, he embodies the principle that 'Theatricality ... is not set against power but is one of power's essential modes' (33).

Viewed as a whole, the sequence offers a full account of the subversion–containment model: in the first part of *Henry IV*, the audience is, 'like Harriot, surveying a complex new world, testing upon it dark thoughts without damaging the order that those thoughts would seem to threaten'; in the second, it is, 'more like the Indians, compelled to pay homage to a system of beliefs whose fraudulence somehow only confirms their power'; in *Henry V*, we find that 'we have all along been both coloniser and colonised, king and subject' (Greenblatt 1994: 42). Read thus, the ironies and ambiguities that have been evident to later twentieth-century critics of this play 'serve paradoxically to intensify the power of the king and his war ... the very doubts that Shakespeare raises serve not to rob the king of his charisma but to heighten it' (43). State power is all-pervasive and inescapable, 'subversion' only ever a potentiality. And those elements which we think subversive in Renaissance texts are only so because they are, for us, non-threatening: paraphrasing a reported remark of Kafka's on the possibility of hope, Greenblatt concludes that 'There is subversion, no end of subversion, only not for us' (45).

Dreams of power

The case for containment is even more strongly argued by Leonard Tennenhouse in another much-cited essay, 'Strategies of State and Political Plays: *A Midsummer Night's Dream, Henry IV, Henry V, Henry VIII*' (1985): believing that Shakespeare 'uses his drama to authorise political authority' (Tennenhouse 1994: 111), and broadening the scope of his analysis to account for the politics of works that had previously not been accounted as political, Tennenhouse suggested that 'the histories written under Elizabeth represented political problems and resolved them in terms resembling the romantic comedies and the Petrarchan lyrics of the same period', often by temporarily licensing and authorising forms of inversion that were ultimately harnessed to the interests of state power; in particular, 'figures of carnival ... play a particularly instrumental role in the idealising process that proves so crucial in legitimising the state' (109, 121). In like manner, *A Midsummer Night's Dream* ('a play surely characteristic of Shakespeare's romantic comedies' [111]) sanctions transgression (in this case, the rebellious actions of the lovers) in order to enable power to adapt; in the end, 'the introduction of disorder into the play ultimately authorises political authority' (112). This dimension of *Dream* was also the theme of an influential essay by Louis Montrose, '"Shaping Fantasies": Figurations of Gender and Power in Elizabethan Culture', which was published in *Representations* in 1983 and revised for *The Purpose of Playing* (1996), and reprinted in various anthologies in 1988, 1992, 1996, 1998, 1999 (twice) and 2004. Montrose's interest lies in the 'dialectical character of cultural representations', that is, in the text's capacity not only to reflect and embody the cultural milieu in which it operates, but to actively work upon it also: 'the fantasies by which the text of *A Midsummer Night's Dream* has been shaped are also those to which it gives shape' (Montrose 2004: 481).

At the heart of the play is the fantasy figure of Queen Elizabeth herself, whose 'pervasive *cultural presence* was a condition of the play's imaginative possibility'; the goal of the essay is to explore 'how Shakespeare's play and other Elizabethan texts figure the Elizabethan sex/gender system and the queen's place within it' (Montrose 2004: 482). Weaving together materials which include the royal astrologer Simon Forman's account of an erotic dream about his ruler, a French ambassador's description of the queen's display of her body during an audience, travellers' narrative encounters with African and South American

Amazons, and Elizabethan theories of heredity, Montrose situates *Dream* within an intricate social network of dreams and fantasies in which 'Sexual and family experience were invariably politicized; economic and political experience were invariably eroticized', and where 'the social and psychological force of Elizabethan symbolic forms depended upon a thorough conflation of these domains' (503). For Montrose, the ideological inclination of the play is towards containment, in that its 'festive conclusion' rests on 'a process by which the female pride and power manifested in misanthropic warriors, possessive mothers, unruly wives, and willful daughters are brought under the control of lords and husbands' (501), but in a sophisticated and self-aware way: metadramatically, it is 'a representation of fantasies about the shaping of the family, the polity, and the theater' (503).

Connections, locations, intersections

The essays by Greenblatt, Tennenhouse and Montrose, published within a few years of each other, exemplify an approach which for a while defined the parameters of new historicist enquiry, particularly in the United States. This model of Renaissance culture (and, indeed, of history in the larger sense), in which, as Graham Holderness describes it, 'dissent is always already suppressed, subversion always previously contained, and opposition always strategically anticipated, controlled and defeated' (1992: 13), suggests a particularly fatalistic application of Foucault's repressive hypothesis, although as an account of early seventeenth-century England it is a little at a loss to explain how and why, in the 1640s, authority experienced a crisis so intense and extensive as to bring about the deposition and execution of Charles I. For the next decade, the subversion–containment debate informed key works in the field in various ways. In *Power on Display* (1986) Tennenhouse extended the remit of the essay discussed on the previous page to examine the 'politics of Shakespeare's genres' in the sonnets and the comedies.

Greenblatt's *Shakespearean Negotiations* (1988) attempted a further refinement of his own initial formulations of the nature of Renaissance power by envisaging the conditions of creation of Shakespeare's works as 'a sublime confrontation between a total artist and a totalizing society'; the latter defined (in reference back to the world picture) as 'one that posits an occult network linking all human, natural, and cosmic powers and that claims on behalf of its ruling elite a privileged place in this network'. It is the very density of this historical overdetermination that accounts for the singular greatness of Shakespeare as maker of 'a set of unique, inexhaustible, and supremely powerful works of art' (Greenblatt 1988: 2). Greenblatt advances the idea that Shakespeare's works are particularly invested with what he calls 'social energy', a conception which is 'manifested in the capacity of certain verbal, aural, and visual traces to produce, shape, and organize collective physical and mental experiences' (6).

The task of cultural poetics, then, is to trace how this 'energy', as Greenblatt's subtitle has it, circulates both within early modern culture and, by extension, our own; mimetic activity is always a matter of borrowing, purchase, acquisition, appropriation and exchange; and the early modern playhouse is a relatively privileged site of adventurous artistic investigation, capable of representing 'the sacred as well as the profane, contemporary as well as ancient times', allowing 'the most solemn formulas of the church and state' to 'mingle with the language of the marketplace', and engaging the energies of 'Power, charisma, sexual excitement, collective dreams, wonder, desire, anxiety, religious awe, free-floating intensities of experience' (Greenblatt 1988: 19). These concerns are explored in four chapters which address Shakespeare's work genre by major genre: 'in the histories, a theatrical acquisition of charisma through the subversion of charisma' ('Invisible Bullets' again); 'in the comedies, an acquisition of sexual excitement through the staging of transvestite friction' (*Twelfth Night* in the light of Renaissance theories of hermaphroditism); 'in the tragedies, an acquisition of religious power through the evacuation of a religious ritual' (*King Lear* read alongside Samuel Harsnett's exposure of the bogus theatre of Catholic exorcism, *A Declaration of Egregious Popish Impostures*); and 'in the romances, an acquisition of salutary anxiety through the experience of a threatening plenitude' (strategies of manipulation and control in *The Tempest*). Beginning with 'the desire to speak with the dead', Greenblatt concludes by confirming both the persistence of this desire and its necessary qualification: 'if I wanted to hear the voice of the other, I had to hear my own voice. The speech of the dead, like my own speech, is not private property' (20).

In the same year as *Shakespearean Negotiations* there appeared two works which sought to localise new historicist preoccupations through a particular attentiveness to the highly specific shaping significances of place, space and performative context. In *The Place of the Stage* (1988), Steven Mullaney sought to unearth the implications of the early modern playhouses' location within the geographically and socially marginal, and culturally ambiguous, zone of the 'Liberties' that surrounded the boundary walls of the city of London: this positioning, Mullaney argued, inscribed within the drama and performance 'a liberty that was at once moral, ideological, and topological – a freedom to experiment with a wide range of available ideological perspectives and to realize, in dramatic form, the cultural contradictions of the age' (1988: ix–x). Leah Marcus's *Puzzling Shakespeare: Local Reading and Its Discontents* (1988) also addressed the problematics of location and localisation, detailing the contemporary resonances of *Henry IV, Part 1*, *Measure for Measure*, *Cymbeline* and *King Lear* – in the latter instance, with particular reference to its performance before King James at court on St Stephen's Night, 26 December, 1606 (see 'Life and contexts', pp. 60–1; 'Works', pp. 242–3). This event Marcus argues, is traceable in the quarto version of the play: readable as 'an extended political exemplum promoting charity toward the Scots', and, by virtue of the liturgical significance of the date, transmitting an unmistakeable 'moral message about hospitality toward the poor and castoff', the context of this single court performance can be seen to 'frame the play itself, "solve" and disentangle some of interpretative cruxes' (1988: 154–55).

Though this seems a little reminiscent of the long-dormant practice of microscopically topical reading that previous generations of critics had notoriously applied to such texts as *Twelfth Night* (Hotson 1954) and *Macbeth* (Paul 1950), Marcus acknowledges the limits (the 'Discontents' of her subtitle) of the approach when applied to Shakespearean drama (as compared to that of his more time-bound contemporaries); 'there is a point at which the method's power to "explain" a text must yield to intransigent textual elements which disrupt the explanation … What we call Shakespeare is somehow mysteriously different, impervious to history at the level of specific factual data, the day-to-day chronicling of events' (Marcus 1988: xi). Mining a similar vein, but from a declaredly more conservative position, Alvin Kernan's *Shakespeare, the King's Playwright* attempted to retrieve a more tangible impression of the contextual positioning of the court performance of Shakespeare's plays, seeking 'interpretations that have a chance of coming fairly close to what ordinary attendants at court would have seen and heard in the Great Hall of the palace' (1995: xxi). Observing that the material evidence of court performances is considerably more abundant and available than that pertaining to playhouse practice, Kernan argues that to see this as one of the key settings of Shakespeare's works is to understand them as the output of a 'patronage dramatist', who can be characterised as 'a helpful royal servant, a propagandist for the monarchy, a radical conservative' (xv, xxii). This view is in direct opposition to the (allegedly) new historicist account of Shakespeare as 'a crypto-revolutionary', since, in this context, 'where the players quite obviously had to please their patron and dramatize acceptable political and social values', it is 'obvious … that Shakespeare could not have been a rebellious romantic artist' (183–84).

Elsewhere, critics willing to work within or alongside the new historicist paradigm engaged in an ongoing debate about its enabling assumptions and working methods. In *Carnival and Theater* (1985), Michael Bristol took issue with the subversion–containment model from a perspective theoretically influenced by Mikhail Bakhtin, Emile Durkheim and the *Annales* school of historiography. Criticising the tendency of existing new historicist scholarship to disengage early modern drama from its social context of articulation within popular forms and practices of festivity, Bristol stresses the centrality of the relationship between theatre and Carnival, seen as 'a concrete social reality in the context of early modern Europe' which has '*both* a social and an antisocial tendency', and which needs to be understood in terms of its 'unselfconscious, ritual character' and 'its utility as a durable strategy for maintaining social cohesion, as well as its selfconsciously pragmatic character as an instrument for altering the status quo' (Bristol 1985: 25). Annabel Patterson (*Shakespeare and the Popular Voice*, 1989) reiterated this emphasis on the resistant and oppositional potential of the cultures of performance within which Shakespeare's works participated, and, disputing the 'impersonality of the Foucauldian model' promulgated by Greenblatt and others, urged a return to

> a less totalitarian account of how Shakespeare's theater probably functioned, in a network not of power in the abstract and in nobody's hands, but rather of local ordinances, unwritten and unstable policies, fads, fashions, pretexts, improvisations, human impulses, and the occasional application of discipline and punishment both to texts and to persons.
>
> (Patterson 1989: 24–25)

Mullaney's already highly influential formulation of the interaction between licence, marginality and the cultural geography of London was questioned by Douglas Bruster (*Drama and the Market in the Age of Shakespeare*) in a study which centralised the civic culture of the marketplace as the determinate environment of early modern drama: rather than inhabiting the potentially subversive space of the city's margins, the playhouses 'were both responsive and responsible to the desires of their playgoing publics, and were potentially no more marginal a part of London than their publics demanded' (Bruster 1992: 10). Shaped by economic forces rather than the abstract, totalising mechanisms of power, Renaissance plays were 'dramatic commodities' designed 'to answer the various manifestations of social desire'; addressing the 'often mystifying nature of the city's relationship with the market', dramatists 'link[ed] the sexual and the economic, the urban and the rural, and the ancient with the modern … to explore and define the character of the socioeconomic changes affecting London' (3, xii–xiii). Jean Howard's *The Stage and Social Struggle in Early Modern England* (1994) is more heavily weighted towards Shakespeare, and its attention to the 'complicated and often contradictory' (153) operations of the theatres of the period reads them as the site of 'the social struggles generated by the dual facts of massive social change and equally massive resistance to its acknowledgement' (10).

New historicism was characterised from the outset by a high degree of autocritical self-awareness, and by the 1990s its proponents and its interrogators were extensively given to reflect upon the movement as itself a situated, historically and culturally contingent phenomenon. Introducing the 1992 anthology *New Historicism and Renaissance Drama*, Richard Wilson questioned both its version of history and its politics, observing that, as a product of 'the last days of the Cold War', American scholarship tended to 'equate the transactions of language with those of capitalism'; citing Greenblatt's *Shakespearean Negotiations*, Wilson claimed that 'Written at the climax of the speculative boom fuelled by junk bonds, this subsumption of language into the techniques of the dealing room chimed with Reaganomics and its campaign to universalise market competition as human nature' (Wilson and Dutton 1992: 6, 9). In *Will Power* (1993), Wilson attacks new historicism even more vigorously, turning Foucault, sardonically characterised as a 'Gaullist technocrat' (14), against his American appropriators: 'With its mystification of the market as the Word of God, American New Historicism merely perpetuated the conflation of language and history which the Shakespearean drama began, and proved what Foucault early recognised: that the post-modern theory that "There is nothing outside the text" was the apotheosis, rather than the nemesis, of capitalist authorship' (9).

Repudiating the new historicist tactic of 'extending the principles of textual analysis to every social and material reality, from gender to slavery to Cardinal Wolsey's hat' (1993: 9), Wilson proposes that the 'localist history' that emerged in the 1980s, and the model of local reading initiated by Leah Marcus, offers a means of 'opening the Shakespearean texts up to their historical contingency and even provinciality'; such a *'newer* historicism' would 'respond to Foucault's partition of universal history into local *histories*, without being seduced by the post-modern fashion of ultra-relativism', thereby producing 'studies of specific plays in (local) places' (16–17). For Wilson, this is to read *As You Like It* alongside the anti-enclosure riots of the early 1590s, Shakespeare's comedies as 'one of the earliest discourses to measure the state by the sexual fertility of its subjects' (130) and Shakespeare's own last will and testament as 'a blueprint for the transfer of common wealth and benefits into private property and capital', and hence as 'an instance of a historic movement which preoccupies his plays' (187).

Wilson's charge was that the practitioners of 'cultural poetics' were more complicit with the dominant ideologies of their own time than they cared to recognise or admit, a point that might seem to have been borne out by the evident marketability of their work. Reflecting the circumstances of academic production that I have already referred to, the consolidation of the movement was seen in the various collections and anthologies that appeared at this time, among them Greenblatt's *Representing the Renaissance* (1989), H. Aram Veeser's *The New Historicism* (1989), David Kastan and Peter Stallybrass's *Staging the Renaissance* (1991), Ivo Kamps's *Shakespeare Left and Right* (1991) and *Materialist Shakespeare: A History* (1995), and the Macmillan 'New Casebooks' series, launched in 1992 with volumes on *Hamlet*, *Macbeth* and the histories. If it is not quite appropriate to define new historicism as a settled orthodoxy by this time, it can certainly be regarded as a dominant force within the field.

Cultural materialism

Taking stock of the state of the discipline in 1996, Steven Mullaney summarised the achievement of the new historicism as its 'effort to redraw the boundaries of literary studies, to reconceive, in terms of a mutually constitutive and open-ended dialectic, the relationship between literary and other cultural discourses', whilst also noting that it continued to be subject to attack on various fronts: as a 'politically evasive, essentially liberal movement complicit in the structures of power and domination it purports to analyse', on the one hand, and as 'part of a pernicious conspiracy, allied with feminism and ethnic studies, bent on perverting immortal literature and timeless, universal values' on the other (Mullaney 1996: 18–20). For Mullaney, the future of new historicism lay in the further development of a 'productive, polyvocal, far from harmonious but necessary dialogue with materialist feminism, cultural materialism and other participants in the broader field of cultural studies' (34), thus registering the significance of some of the more considered criticisms that had been made of the practice from the outset.

Mullaney's review was conducted in the context of a contribution to Terence Hawkes's collection *Alternative Shakespeares Volume 2* (1996), the sequel to the ground-breaking *Alternative Shakespeares* (edited by John Drakakis): as a whole, Hawkes's volume registers the diversification of the various historicisms that had arisen since the publication of its predecessor volume in 1985. This survey has up to this point – somewhat artificially – focussed upon scholarly work produced under the aegis of new historicism (or cultural poetics) in the United States; here we turn to the largely British-based critical school that emerged during the same period: cultural materialism. For Hawkes, new historicism and cultural materialism inhabit a common field of investigation, which is 'to locate all of a culture's signifying practices squarely and accurately in the context of the larger material social process' (1996: 7). Such is the broad project of the essays in Hawkes's collection, which, less oriented towards the header forms of post-structuralism that had been found in *Alternative Shakespeares* (see pp. 351–3), deal with bodies, questions of race and cultural difference, technologies of print and the dynamics of spectatorship. For Hawkes, 'Getting Shakespeare and early modern culture "right" is not its aim. Getting to grips with what our inherited notions of "right" conceal from us is' (1996: 15).

In this respect at least, the second instalment of *Alternative Shakespeares* signalled its continuity with the first. However, as John Drakakis observes in the collection's afterword, the championing of 'a burgeoning radical pluralism' was now due for reconsideration: 'in the original volume there were important and, as it turns out, proleptic, tensions available to the discerning reader' (1996: 239). Not the least of these is a tension which has been (perhaps too formulaically) characterised as a transatlantic professional divide, between, as Drakakis puts it, 'British cultural materialism, with its ardent politics', and 'the more professionally urbane, politically reticent American new historicism' (239–40). In 1996, this was not a new charge: indeed, the suspicion that there were cultural, theoretical and political differences between new historicism as practised, predominantly, in the United States and British cultural materialism had been around for at least a decade. The term 'cultural materialism' was first suggested by Raymond Williams (1977: 5) as invoking the principle and praxis of dialectical materialism, a specifically Marxist mode of engagement with literature and culture; and the work produced under its auspices was shaped, both theoretically and methodologically, by some of the key influences upon American new historicism and post-structuralism (Foucault, Althusser, Lacan, Derrida), as well as by the interdisciplinary work of Williams himself, by the developing field of cultural studies, by radical historians such as E. P. Thompson and Christopher Hill, and by thinkers within the tradition of Continental Marxism, including Walter Benjamin and Antonio Gramsci.

British cultural materialism differentiated itself from new historicism in its professions of political urgency, and by its insistence upon the contemporary context and significance of its readings of early modern literature and culture; Shakespeare, in particular, was regarded as an ideological force to be reckoned with in the present as well as in his own time. In their preface to the flagship collection *Political Shakespeare* (1985; second edition 1994), Jonathan Dollimore and Alan Sinfield defined the approach succinctly:

Historical context undermines the transcendent significance traditionally accorded to the literary text and allows us to recover its histories; theoretical method detaches the text from immanent criticism which seeks only to reproduce it in its own terms; socialist and feminist commitment confronts the conservative categories in which most criticism has hitherto been conducted; textual analysis locates the critique of traditional approaches where it cannot be ignored. We call this 'cultural materialism'.

(Dollimore and Sinfield 1994: vii)

There is, quite intentionally, plenty here to rile proponents of 'traditional' criticism, but the explicit proclamation of 'socialist and feminist commitment' is especially unmannerly, perhaps even to new historicists. The difference of tone between the cultural materialists and the new historicists is partly a matter of historical and cultural context. Whereas the leftist inclinations of American scholarship can be traced back to the campus radicalism of the 1960s, operating largely independently of class-based politics, the commitments of the postwar British left were forged by its conflicted relation to a mainstream political system able to accommodate a parliamentary Labour Party nominally defined as socialist, as well as by a more acute sense of the need to relate analysis to activism.

In the politically polarised culture of 1980s Britain, intellectual resistance to the dominance of what seemed to many to be a viciously retrograde form of free-market conservatism operated in the absence of any viable practical opposition to it. Cultural materialism also distinguished itself from new historicism from the beginning by its more extensive and inclusive definition of 'culture'. As Dollimore and Sinfield put it (echoing the concerns explored within the field of British cultural studies from the 1970s onwards), rather than confining their attention to the conventionally designated artefacts of 'high' culture, cultural materialists should be interested in 'the cultures of subordinate and marginalised groups like schoolchildren and skinheads, and … forms like television and popular music and fiction'; the consequence is that '"high culture" is taken as one set of signifying practices among others' (1994: viii).

Combining essays exemplary of new historicism (Greenblatt's 'Invisible Bullets', Tennenhouse's 'Strategies of State'), interventions informed by recent developments in the study of gender and sexuality, and case studies of Shakespeare in action in contemporary culture, including education, theatre and film, *Political Shakespeare* displayed a pioneering eclecticism that provided a point of departure for subsequent work in the field; as Dollimore's introduction took pains to emphasise, it also laid out the key differences within and between American and British approaches to the politics of Renaissance culture. Referring to the subversion–containment model, Dollimore proposed a third term – consolidation – and argued that we should 'speak not of a monolithic power structure producing its effects but of one made up of different, often competing elements, and these not merely producing culture but producing it through appropriations' (1994: 12).

To be fair, few (if any) new historicists have ever proposed such a 'monolithic' account of early modern power (least of all Greenblatt, who later complained of how readers of 'Invisible Bullets' habitually, and misleadingly, 'refer to a supposed argument that any resistance is impossible' [1990b: 75]), but the distinction serves to highlight the importance that Dollimore, in common with the majority of British cultural materialists, attaches to the possibilities of progressive – even radical – social change. Thus whilst acknowledging 'the effectiveness and complexity of the ideological process of containment', it is nonetheless crucial to maintain that 'the very desire to disclose that process is itself oppositional and motivated by the knowledge that, formidable though it be, it is a process which is historically contingent and partial – never necessary or total' (Dollimore 1994: 15). Herein lies one of the important stated differences of perspective between new historicism and cultural materialism (although even in 1985 the difference was more rhetorical than real).

Tragically radical, radically tragic

The self-consciously oppositional stance set out in Dollimore's introduction is elaborated in greater detail in his *Radical Tragedy* (1984; second edition 1989; third edition 2004), a book which merits direct comparison with Greenblatt's *Renaissance Self-Fashioning* (1980) in terms both of its immediate impact upon Renaissance scholarship and of its enduring significance and influence: in his preface to the third edition, Terry Eagleton wrote that whereas 'Some critical studies are full of insight' not many 'are *necessary*', and that *Radical Tragedy* 'ranks among the necessary critical interventions of our time' (2004: xiii). Dollimore's thesis, briefly stated, is that 'a significant sequence of Jacobean tragedies, including the majority of Shakespeare's, were more radical than has hitherto been allowed'; and that this radicalism contributed to the subsequent undermining of the institutions of church and state in 'a theatre in which they and their ideological legitimation were subjected to sceptical, interrogative and subversive representations' (2004: 4–5).

Dramaturgically, Elizabethan and Jacobean plays are akin to the various avant-gardes represented by Bertolt Brecht, Antoinin Artaud and Jean Genet; intellectually, these works are informed by the scepticism, heterodoxy and pragmatism of thinkers such as Montaigne, Machiavelli and Francis Bacon. These writers in turn are seen to anticipate major tenets of materialist and post-structuralist and materialist theory, especially in the works of Althusser, Derrida and Marx, by delivering a radical critique of what Dollimore takes to be the period's twin dominant ideologies, the providentialist account of history and governance, and 'the essentialist conception of man' (2004: 155).

Thus the writings of Machiavelli and Montaigne enact 'a process of demystification whose basis is a radical relativism' (Dollimore 2004: 15), while the dramas of Shakespeare, Marlowe, Marston, Webster, Middleton, Jonson and Chapman collectively participate in the Jacobean theatre's 'interrogation of providentialism':

> hitherto man had been understood in terms of his privileged position at the centre (actual and metaphysical) of the cosmic plan; to repudiate that plan was, inevitably, also to decentre man (actually and ideologically). More specifically, in subverting the purposive and teleologically integrated universe envisioned by providentialists, these playwrights necessarily subverted its corollary: the unitary subject integrated internally as a consequence of being integrated into the cosmic design.
>
> (Dollimore 2004: 19)

A comparison with Greenblatt is instructive here: by heavily accenting the subversive potentiality of the drama and by focussing on its radicalism, Dollimore clearly begs to differ both from the more guarded and qualified formulations of *Renaissance Self-Fashioning* and from the (alleged) containment thesis of 'Invisible Bullets'.

Radical Tragedy eschews the syntactical and analytic even-handedness that is characteristic of Greenblatt's work for a resolutely partial, combative and often wilfully tendentious method of argument: in place of Greenblatt's lengthily elaborated, elegantly self-referential networks of intertextualised cultural, textual and personal history, Dollimore develops his case through a series of concise readings designed to unlock the mechanisms of subversion

Bertolt Brecht (1896–1956)

German playwright, poet and theatre director

Second perhaps only to Stanislavsky as one of the key influences on twentieth-century theatre, Brecht and his extended – and often unacknowledged – team of collaborators were responsible for a body of theory and practice that extended well beyond the bounds of the political theatre movement. Employing a battery of anti-illusionist devices and techniques designed to render the ordinary extraordinary, discourage uncritical empathy, stimulate thought, appeal to reason and transform the spectator from passive consumer to active agent, the project of Epic (as opposed to Dramatic, or Aristotelian) theatre, as Brecht saw it, was to demonstrate that social reality was historically contingent, dialectical and open to intervention and change, to show how things were but also how they might be different. Brecht repeatedly turned to early modern theatre practices and to the plays of Shakespeare, Marlowe and others as a model for his own dramaturgy: one of his last productions before moving to Weimar Berlin was a version of *Edward II* (1924), and in 1936 he reworked *Measure for Measure* as the anti-Nazi satire *Round Heads and Pointed Heads*. His adaptation of John Webster's *The Duchess of Malfi*, written while in exile in Hollywood, remained unproduced; on his return to what was now the German Democratic Republic in the late 1940s he began work on an adaptation of Shakespeare's *Coriolanus*, which attempted to rewrite the play for the circumstances of post-Nazi Germany, to demonstrate the triumph of the popular will over demagoguery, and to show that no hero should think himself indispensable. Unfinished at Brecht's death, the adaptation was staged by the company he founded, the Berliner Ensemble, in 1964. The influence of Brecht upon the Shakespearean theatre worldwide has been considerable, though more often at the level of visual style than of politics. His theoretical writing also played a part in the development of cultural materialist criticism, particularly in the United Kingdom, during the 1980s.

in the texts; thus *Troilus and Cressida*, 'more strategically than nihilistically', is seen to exploit 'disjunction and "chaos" to promote critical awareness of both the mystifying language of the absolute and the social reality which it occludes' (Dollimore 2004: 44); and in *King Lear* 'man is decentred not through misanthropy but in order to make visible social process and its forms of ideological misrecognition' (191). Why Shakespeare, or anyone else, would choose the profession of dramatist rather than, say, that of political philosopher (or even literary critic) to pursue these speculations is a question that Dollimore does not seek to address. Still, he is alert to the drama's playfulness, and its tonal affinities with the theatrical modernisms of Genet and Artaud; thus *The Revenger's Tragedy* is celebrated for its gleeful deployment of a 'subversive black camp' which is 'at once mannered and chameleon': it 'celebrates the artificial and the delinquent, it delights in a play full of innuendo, perversity and subversion'; and 'through parody it declares itself radically sceptical of ideological policing' (149).

Throughout, Dollimore champions the radicalism of Jacobean tragedy, its questioning of received beliefs and values, its potentially devastating implications for its makers' and its audiences' sense of self, as a source of liberation and a matter for celebration; here, as in other respects, his position departs from that of Greenblatt. Considering the implications of anti-essentialist critique for our ways of not just theorising but experiencing subjectivity, Dollimore cites the anxious reflections upon the illusory nature of autonomous selfhood that frame the conclusion of *Renaissance Self-Fashioning* (discussed on pp. 314–19), that are encapsulated in Greenblatt's plea that 'to let go of one's stubborn hold upon self-hood, even self-hood conceived as a fiction, is to die' (1980: 257). *Radical Tragedy* posits this challenge in a direct form. For what it is worth, I vividly recall my own first reading of it, as a neophyte and fairly impressionable graduate student (in one sitting, and as it happens, on a train journey to London, and to the production of *Mother Courage* that caused me to lose my faith in Brecht): the experience exhilarated and unsettled me in a way that few, if any, academic reading encounters have done since. Dollimore addresses Greenblatt's (and – though he would hardly have known or perhaps cared about it – my own) desire to sustain the illusion of subjectivity with the contention that 'perhaps the opposite is true': 'by abandoning the fiction we may embrace freedom in and through [quoting Derrida 1978: 292] "*affirmation*" which "*determines the noncentre otherwise than as loss of the centre*"' (Dollimore 2004: 181). Whereas the Greenblatt of 1980 (and, in different ways, the Greenblatt of subsequent decades) admits himself not yet ready to surrender the critical and, indeed, ontological frameworks within which he had fashioned his own self, Dollimore positively embraces the implications of anti-essentialism that for Greenblatt are a source of anxiety; reiterating the Derrida quotation at the end of his book, he daringly extrapolates from it a 'radical' political programme for the present, centred on 'not essence but potential, not the human condition but cultural difference, not destiny but collectively identified goals' (Dollimore 2004: 271).

Shakespeare is not significantly privileged over his contemporaries: at fifteen pages, *King Lear* is afforded only slightly more space than Fulke Greville's obscure and tedious tragedy *Mustapha*, and rather less than Webster's *The White Devil*. This dispassionate levelling of the early modern playing field serves to locate Shakespeare's works within a broader discursive context of radical philosophical scepticism, but it also tends to attribute to very diverse writers, thinkers and forms of writing a paradoxical uniformity of subversive opinion. There are some surprising parallels with Tillyard here; although he notes that the selective and partial methods of his critical predecessor had been conclusively 'discredited' (2004: 90), Dollimore occasionally employs a not dissimilar tactic of mapping intellectual ideas onto literary texts, this time identifying subversion rather than 'order' as their motivating agenda. Dollimore critics were not slow to point this out, registering that the historicism of *Radical Tragedy* was in some ways a reversion to the 'ideas of the time' method that had been operative during the 1960s; for some new historicists, more seriously, even as he gestured hyperbolically from the Jacobean stage towards the English 'revolution' of 1642, Dollimore seemed to prioritise the relatively autonomous circulation of radical thought over the social contexts and practices of early modern literature and theatre situates the drama within the history of ideas rather than history itself.

True enough; but such criticisms perhaps underestimate the importance of one the central objectives of the book, which was its assault on what Dollimore regarded as the prevailing, and dominant, literary critical tradition; it will already be evident that the radicalism that Dollimore ascribes to Jacobean drama is in some senses a strategic and consciously anachronistic back-projection, polemically crafted as part of an argument with the critical philosophies and practices of the present, rather than an 'objective' exercise in historicism, whether of the new or old variety. Preoccupied, as Dollimore characterises it, with 'aesthetic and ideological conceptions of order, integration, equilibrium and so on', humanist criticism is ill equipped to deal with a drama which deliberately 'transgresses or challenges the Elizabethan equivalent of the modern obsession with a *telos* of harmonic integration' (2004: 5).

According to this account, critics of Jacobean tragedy have taken their bearings from A. C. Bradley and T. S. Eliot, who between them contrived the 'two dominant positions' on the nature and function of the drama: either 'aesthetic form was seen to create an ideal unity, a fictive alternative to the chaotic real', or 'it was seen to represent or invoke an order of truth beyond the flux and chaos of history' (Dollimore 2004: 69). In opposition to both positions, Dollimore invokes Brecht's theory and practice as 'the crucial link between Jacobean drama and the contemporary materialist criticism', both as an adaptor of the works and as someone who 'anticipated most of the important issues in materialistic critical theory' (53). In Dollimore's Brecht, then, we find a theorist who 'completely rejected the *telos* of harmonic integration' (63), and who instead emphasised dialectical conflict and contradiction, utilising forms of theatre that solicited judgement rather than empathic identification, and that sought to make the everyday strange and unfamiliar rather than falsely 'natural' or obvious; Walter Benjamin's dictum that in Brecht's theatre the 'untragic hero' is 'like an empty stage on which the contradictions of our society are acted out' (1977: 17) is cited as 'true also of protagonists in Jacobean theatre' (Dollimore 2004: 153).

Dollimore is perhaps more interested in Brecht as a theoretician who discovered some aspects of early modern drama a prototype for his own Epic theatre, and whose development of a Marxist aesthetics prefigures the advent of theory, than as a dramatist, dramaturg or maker; other critics writing around the same time attempted to engage more directly with the implications of Brecht's legacy for modern theatre practice. The final essay in the first edition of *Political Shakespeare*, by Margot Heinemann (1994), examines 'How Brecht Read Shakespeare'; in the same volume, Graham Holderness writes of the 'Brechtian' strategies apparent in the productions of the *Henry VI* plays that Jane Howell directed for the BBC/Time Life Television Shakespeare series in 1983, which, he suggests, 'recreate some of the radical potentialities of the Elizabethan theatre' (1994: 222). Holderness also draws upon Brecht to discuss Howell's productions, as well as Elizabethan theatre practice more generally, in his *Shakespeare's History* (1985), a work which (focussing on the first tetralogy) attempts to display the full investigative range of the cultural materialist project in one volume by engaging with theatre, film and television performances, the history of criticism (notably the historicisms practised by Tillyard, Dover Wilson and G. Wilson Knight) and, in the lengthiest section ('Chronicles of Feudalism'), Shakespeare's own achievement as an imaginative historiographer. The history plays, Holderness contends, 'embody a conscious understanding of feudal society as a peculiar historical formation, revealing unique cultural characteristics, codes of value, conventions of manners, based on particular structures of political organisation and social relationship', and Shakespeare recognised that this society was 'visibly different in fundamental ways from the society of the late sixteenth century' (1985: 31–32).

Shakespeare's 'history' is hereby multiply historicised: the plays are both exercises in historical imagination and the subject of a subsequent history of reinscription in which they have been appropriated for both radical and reactionary ends. In *Richard II*, 'both the providential and the pragmatic views of history are strategically manipulated within the framework of a theory conscious of the relativity of both', whereas the *Henry IV* plays embody Shakespeare's 'dissatisfaction with the tragic determinism of the literary chronicle-drama' in 'a comic mode of historical drama which challenges deterministic historiography with the utopian purity of an inflexible and unqualified demand for freedom' (Holderness 1985: 38–39); in *Henry V*, 'Shakespeare's dramaturgy … is like that of Brecht', seizing upon 'a particularly contradictory character in a particularly complex historical situation' and finding there 'the appropriate analogy for the contradictory revelations of his historiography' (140, 144). As these quotations suggest, contradiction, in the dialectical sense in which it is understood within Marxist cultural criticism, is a key term in Holderness's critical lexicon: the conflict between antithetical forces, class interests and ideologies, rather than being framed in terms of either subversion or containment, is the engine of historical change.

Eminent Shakespeareans

The mid-1980s saw the publication of a number of other key works operating under the auspices of cultural materialism, whose specific emphases (for example on the historical construction and deconstruction of the subject, on language, and on sexuality and gender) situate them elsewhere in this volume; examples include Francis Barker's *The Tremulous Private Body* (1984), Catherine Belsey's *The Subject of Tragedy* (1985a), Malcolm Evans's *Signifying Nothing* (1986) and the feminist scholarship that was inaugurated by the publication of *The Woman's Part*, edited by Carolyn R. Lenz and others in 1980. If a key feature of much of the work that we have been considering in this chapter has been its critical attention to the institutional histories and ideological orientations of Shakespearean scholarship itself, this interest was articulated in particularly inventive ways in the work of Terence Hawkes, who, as general editor of Routledge's ground-breaking 'New Accents' series from the mid-1970s onwards, had been instrumental in introducing the Anglo-American literary-critical profession to European post-structuralist and political criticism.

Working in a vein which Hawkes has made distinctively his own, *That Shakespeherian Rag* comprises a series of case studies of the 'eminent Shakespearians' (1986: ix) A. C. Bradley, Sir Walter Raleigh, T. S. Eliot and J. Dover Wilson; deftly interweaving biography, disciplinary and cultural history, and a historicised post-structuralist reading of Shakespeare's texts (and of Bradley and company's readings of them), Hawkes explores ' the ways in which those works of art have been processed, generated, presented, worked upon ... as part of the struggle for cultural meaning' (123). His materials include the intricate connections between Bradley's tortuous speculations upon the various 'silences' that he finds in *Hamlet* and the intimations of the unspoken (and perhaps the unspeakable) in Bradley's own poetry; Raleigh's self-identification as Prospero as part of his mission to promulgate English literature as a pacifying and civilising force; and, in his account of the genesis of J. Dover Wilson's *What Happens in Hamlet* (1935), a cautionary tale about the long-term implications of reading radical criticism on trains (in this instance, an article on *Hamlet* by W. W. Greg). Asserting that 'Our "Shakespeare" is our invention: to write him is to read him' (1996: 124), Hawkes suggests that the art of the critic should aspire to that of the jazz musician, whose role 'is not limited to the service, or the revelation, or the celebration of the author's/composer's art'; its task, therefore, should be one of 'Responding to, improvising on, "playing" with, re-creating, synthesizing and interpreting "given" structures of all kinds, political, social, aesthetic' (118).

Hawkes continues in this vein of sharply politicised playfulness in *Meaning by Shakespeare* (1992), where we find Nedar, the absent mother of *A Midsummer Night's Dream*'s Helena, haunting Harley Granville Barker's 1914 production of the play, itself shadowed by the suffragette protests in which that show's Helena, Lillah McCarthy, participated; Lear's call for a map (1.1.37) addressed both to Barker's 1940 Old Vic production of the play and to the points of difference between new historicism and cultural materialism; and the role of a Stratford production of *Coriolanus* in the 1926 General Strike. The final chapter is a reprint of a review article originally published in the *London Review of*

Books, which surveyed recent new historicist and cultural materialist work. Prominent among this is a work whose author would probably not at that time have defined himself as a new historicist or cultural materialist: Gary Taylor's *Reinventing Shakespeare*, offered as a 'cultural history' of bardolatry (or, as he christened it, though the term failed to catch on, 'Shakesperotics') from the Restoration to the present, addressing 'everything that a society does in the name – variously spelled – of Shakespeare' (1990: 6). Taylor's charges are direct: by venerating Shakespeare, isolating him from his contemporaries and attempting to reconstruct him as 'ours', critics, readers and theatre practitioners grotesquely inflate his 'importance and uniqueness', according him an inordinate cultural power which 'disfigures and corrupts' (407, 411). Taylor's book is hailed by Hawkes as 'a genuine contribution to our knowledge of how [our] culture works', although weakened by an 'under-theorized ... commitment to a "real" (albeit unremarkable) Shakespeare lying beneath all the "reinventions"' (Hawkes 1992: 150).

Many readers of the *London Review of Books* thought otherwise; and for eighteen months its letters page gave voice to the outrage of those who considered that Taylor and Hawkes represented the forces of cultural vandalism. Nonetheless, *Reinventing Shakespeare* was only one of many works that, over the course of a decade, scrutinised the academic and popular institutional histories of Shakespeare, often in polemical and combative terms. *The Shakespeare Myth*, edited by Graham Holderness, sought to demonstrate how Shakespeare 'functions in contemporary culture as an ideological framework for containing consensus and for sustaining myths of unity, integration and harmony in the cultural superstructures of a divided and fractured society' (Holderness 1988b: xiii); Michael Bristol's *Shakespeare's America/America's Shakespeare*, focussing more closely upon the evolution of the scholarly industry in the United States, regarded 'the interpretation of

Harley Granville Barker (1877–1946)

Theatre director, playwright and literary critic

Described by John Gielgud as 'a young genius' who 'wore sandals and ate nuts', Barker began a precocious professional career as an actor at the age of fourteen, had his first play produced three years later, and in 1903, together with the critic William Archer, drafted *Schemes and Estimates for a National Theatre*, a comprehensive, fully costed manifesto and blueprint for a venture that would take over half a century to achieve realisation. He followed his plays *The Voysey Inheritance* (1905) and, in 1907, *Waste* (which had the distinction of being banned by the Lord Chamberlain) with the direction and management of three seasons at the adventurous Court Theatre, of recent European and British drama to the commercial stage. In 1912 he directed two ground-breaking Shakespeares at the Savoy theatre: *The Winter's Tale* and *Twelfth Night*, which with their rapid pacing, mostly uncut texts, and non-realist décor inaugurated a new era in Shakespearean production. *A Midsummer Night's Dream* followed in 1914: dispensing with the Victorian conventions that had festooned the play with gauzes, Mendelssohn's Wedding March and flower fairies, it confronted audiences with a male Oberon, an English folk music score and fairies that looked like orientalised statues. By 1918 this young man in a hurry, having had the good fortune to acquire a wealthy American second wife, had had enough of the professional theatre and, at the age of forty, retired. Though he returned infrequently to direct work, including a production of *King Lear* at the Old Vic in 1950 starring John Gielgud, his major output thereafter was the multi-volume *Prefaces to Shakespeare* (1923–47), a series of performance-oriented close readings that have retained their currency amongst theatre professionals.

Shakespeare and the interpretation of American political culture as mutually determining practices' (1990: 3). Hugh Grady's *The Modernist Shakespeare*, an incisive survey of twentieth-century criticism which, making use of 'the unique qualities of Shakespearean criticism in order to investigate and clarify the institutions and cultural forms which produce it', registers the 'complex interaction' of the 'aesthetic paradigm' of Modernism and the historical paradigm of modernisation to tell 'a sobering story of interest disguised as disinterest, of critical ingenuity passed off as an objective property of iconic texts, of the presumptuous arrogance of professional literary critics, and of desperate symbolic attempts to save meaning, truth, and beauty in the increasingly hostile modern age' (Grady 1991: 1, 5).

Richard Halpern's *Shakespeare among the Moderns* extended its remit to theatre and film as well as criticism, in order to 'investigate the ways in which canonical modernism – principally Anglo-American modernism – set the tone for the twentieth century's reception of Shakespeare', and to argue the claim that postmodernity 'represents a mutation, rather than a cessation, of the modernist paradigm' (1997: 1–2). Earlier histories of productions and reception were also addressed: Margreta de Grazia's *Shakespeare Verbatim* is a Foucauldian investigation of the history of Shakespearean editing, and in particular of the pivotal moment marked by Edmond Malone's break with the tradition of prior-itising the text 'closest to the editor rather than that closest to the author; the text that had undergone the most rather than the least mediation' (1991: 52). Jonathan Bate's *Shakespearean Constitutions* (1989) documents the various interactions between Shakespeare, public life, and political discourse that, throughout the eighteenth century, led to the formation of the national bard; Michael Dobson, in *The Making of the National Poet* (1992), considers the same period in terms of the national and cultural politics of its stage adaptations.

By the mid-1990s, the idea that literature, theatre and criticism alike are the products of history, and that all are irretrievably political activities, had become routine, although significant arguments were still to be had about the kinds of history, and politics, that cultural materialism ought to concern itself with. Revisiting the subversion–containment debate in 1992, Alan Sinfield wrote that the concerns which had been central to the study of Renaissance drama for a decade and a half 'seem to have arrived at a point of statement', and, proposing a new emphasis on 'the scope for dissident reading and culture', suggested that 'the term *dissidence* is ... preferable to *transgression* or *subversion*' as a way of cir-cumventing the new historicist 'entrapment model', and as activity which can be taken 'to imply refusal of an aspect of the dominant, without prejudging an outcome' (Sinfield 1992: x, 49).

Moving between texts, histories and cultures, past and present, Sinfield's interest is in 'faultline stories', defining the task of political criticism as 'to observe how stories negotiate the faultlines that distress the prevailing conditions of plausibility' (1992: 47). *Faultlines* moderates some of the stronger claims of earlier cultural materialist work, for example the post-structuralist argument that, with regard to early modern texts, 'character' is 'an altogether inappropriate category of analysis': Sinfield points out that the contrivance of 'character effects', whilst not amounting to 'a modern conception of character', nonetheless suggests 'not just an intermittent, gestural, and problematic subjectivity, but a continuous or developing interiority or consciousness' (58–62). Historical difference is vital, but not absolute: 'These people were very different from us, but not totally different' (62). An important component of the critique of entrapment and the advocacy of dissidence, moreover, is disciplinary: anatomising the ways in which the new historicist narrative of the containment of subversion mirrors the institutional and professional co-option of historicism's own radical intent, Sinfield argues that the dissident critic

> should seek ways to break out of the professional subculture and work intellectually (not just live personally) in dissident subcultures ... we should cultivate ways of writing and speaking, and opportunities to do them, that might be appropriate for nonacademic subcultures where we can reasonably claim an affiliation.
>
> (Sinfield 1992: 294)

The method entails paying close attention to the *petit récits* that postmodern commentators (among them Foucault and Lyotard) have preferred to advocate against the 'grand narratives' of history. In various ways, this points towards the preoccupations of the criticism of the last decade.

After theory: history bites back

The publication of a new edition of the complete works, *The Norton Shakespeare*, in 1997 was one sign of the institutional dominance of American new historicism as the century drew to a close: co-edited by Greenblatt, Walter Cohen, Jean E. Howard and Katharine Eisaman Maus, the volume comprehensively demonstrates a double vision of Shakespeare's works as, according to Greenblatt in his 'General Introduction', both 'the product of peculiar historical circumstances and specific conventions, four centuries distant from our own', and entities whose 'fantastic diffusion and long life' owe to their 'extraordinary malleability, their protean capacity to elude definition and escape secure possession' (Greenblatt *et al.* 1997: 1). If, in the same year, John Drakakis could reiterate the familiar cultural materialist premise that 'Shakespearian texts, like all texts ... either can be the objects of mastery or alternatively can be recognised as sites of struggle' (1997: 332), the argument of Jonathan Bate's *The Genius of Shakespeare*, an account of Shakespearean cultural history by a critic whose previous work had shown some degree of affiliation with materialist criticism, appeared to point in a rather different direction: 'Like the fittest organism in the natural world', writes Bate, Shakespeare's work 'survives' as 'a triumph of evolution'; if there is an equivalent in the universe of literature to the one constant in relativity theory, it is the eponymous 'genius of Shakespeare' (Bate 1997: 316).

The last decades of critical history have seen these and other historicist positions repeated, elaborated and interrogated in a variety of ways. The title of David Kastan's *Shakespeare after Theory* (1999a) signalled what its author hoped was a new understanding of the state of the discipline: proposing that the scholars and students were now inhabiting a post-theoretical critical landscape. Now that the lessons of new historicism and cultural materialism had been thoroughly learned, and its principles and procedures assimilated into the mainstream of critical practice, Kastan argued, it was time to revive a more straightforward, less self-interrogative and more empirically driven form of historical materialism, and to work to

> restore Shakespeare's artistry to the earliest conditions of its realization and intelligibility: to the collaborations of the theater in which the plays were acted, to the practices of the book trade in which they were published, to the unstable political world of late Tudor and early Stuart England in which the plays were engaged by their various publics.
>
> (Kastan 1999a: 16)

Addressing a wider readership, Kastan's introduction to his monumental edited collection *A Companion to Shakespeare* (1999b), published in the same year, reiterated the point that to value Shakespeare we should 'begin with the recognition of his distance from us rather than with an assumption of his essential contemporaneity'; otherwise 'we listen less to his concerns than to his anticipations of our own' (Kastan 1999b: 4). To this end, the *Companion* divides its twenty-eight essays into seven sections, accounting with 'Shakespeare the Man', 'Living', 'Reading', 'Writing', 'Playing', 'Printing' and, in a brief sequel dealing with the cultural afterlife, 'The Myth'; the aim is to 'make visible the sustaining collaborations of [Shakespeare's] art' and to construct 'a detailed and arresting mosaic of Shakespeare's artistic environment, of the cultural and material mediations that permitted the plays to be written, performed, printed, and read' (5). For Kastan, the historical information contained in the essays is 'what (or at least some of what) we ideally should know as we read or see Shakespeare' (6); the task falls to Michael D. Bristol, in a final essay running to some dozen pages, to attempt to explain how the desire for Shakespeare that has outlived his, or their, original material circumstances might be reconciled to such forms of knowledge: 'The idea of a great vernacular poetry endowed with the power to shape our dreams represents a deferred or unrealized hope for the possibility of expressive unity and completeness' (Bristol 1999: 501).

The claim that Shakespeare studies was now 'after' theory and that historically informed scholarship could now stop worrying about its own contemporary commitments and investments found both supporters and opponents (indeed, *Shakespeare after Theory* repeatedly stages arguments with itself over this issue). Kastan's position is representative of a more general sense, which operates across a wide spectrum of political opinion and critical method, that the historicisms that reached a condition of dominance within Shakespeare studies by the end of the twentieth century had exhausted their capacity for innovation, challenge and surprise. For commentators who had been hostile to political criticism from the outset, this was no occasion for regret: Tom McAlindon, for example, one of its long-standing opponents, writes in his study of the *Henry IV* plays that 'the interpretive model of class and colonialist domination in common use today' is 'irrelevant' to the histories, and that when Shakespeare created them 'he was not only speaking of his own brief time but making repeatable, permanently valid statements' (McAlindon 2001: 24).

This position is elaborated at greater length in *Shakespeare Minus 'Theory'* (McAlindon 2004; the sarcastic scare quotes are indicative of McAlindon's position). Boldly announcing that his aim is 'to concentrate on what I judge to be the play's intended meanings; to take due account of the entire text in the process of interpretation; to attend where profitable to aspects of historical context other than the political; to enhance appreciation of the dramatist's conscious art; and to encourage readers to empathise with his perspectives on character, action, and life' (1), McAlindon denounces political criticism as 'joyless and constricting, a denial of the right to that imaginative entry into the author's vision which is the chief reason for becoming a student of literature in the first place' (20). There follow extended rebuttals of Greenblatt and Dollimore, plus determinedly against-the-grain readings of *Coriolanus* as 'an Essentialist Tragedy' (McAlindon 2001: 123), *The Tempest* as a play deeply preoccupied with prayer, and *Doctor Faustus* as a work that ultimately confirms the Renaissance humanist conviction that 'the body may be torn, but the self remains with the soul' (166). McAlindon's polemic, and scorn for cant, is invigorating, though the tendency to agglomerate often very disparate radical critics and criticisms into a unified movement is not always convincing.

A more measured reaction to new historicism and cultural materialism is offered by the editors and contributors to the collection *Neo-Historicism: Studies in Renaissance Literature, History and Politics* (Wells *et al.* 2000), in which it is pointed out that the metacritical interrogation that proponents of these approaches have laid claim to has been intrinsic within historicist scholarship since at least the 1940s, and asserted that 'texts give expressive and significant form to actions, feelings, and ideas which remain interesting to us by virtue of our common human nature' (25). Again, unfashionably, 'Art is a universal human practice and the literary works of art that remain interesting to us are likely to be those which put into play problems and conflicts of value which can still be called universal to the extent that we, as human beings, are still involved with versions of them' (26). Though many might argue with this, it is difficult to take issue with what is offered as the cardinal rule of 'neo-historicism', which is:

> that there is an historical dimension to all valid acts of textual interpretation: that there is no unifying principle ... that will explain the course of history; that there will be multiple histories of any age, reflecting the complexity of the past ... that while the questions we ask about the past are inevitably driven by present needs and concerns, a sense of historical perspective is best achieved, not by recruiting past thinkers as precursive spokesmen and women of modern values, but by recognising the otherness of the past.
>
> (Wells *et al.* 2000: xi)

The impression given by advocates of neo-historicism that they are against a settled (and in its own way rather conservative) orthodoxy is reinforced by the suspicion that one sign of the consolidation of the new historicism and of cultural materialism has been their dissemination in forms that have become available to, and in theory usable by, a broader constituency of consumers than the professional cadre that is the primary readership for their kinds of scholarly monograph and essay.

In addition to the steady stream of anthologies, casebooks, guides and readers that have already been mentioned, one of the most visible, pervasive and, in the long run, practically significant recent manifestations of new historicist and cultural materialist scholarship has been its assimilation into the new editions of the plays themselves that have appeared during the past decade. *The Norton Shakespeare* is a prominent example; the third series of the Arden Shakespeare (one of whose General Editors, Ann Thompson, was already established as a leading feminist critic) includes volumes whose critical and editorial apparatuses work within its broad remit, and some of which are major works of historicist scholarship in their own right – for example Gordon McMullan's *Henry VIII* (2000). The most widely remarked, as well as the most provocative, refashioning and mainstreaming of American new historicism in recent years is Stephen Greenblatt's best-selling biography *Will in the World* (2004). Subtitled *How Shakespeare Became Shakespeare*, and thus invoking a man, a writer and a cultural phenomenon, this is a brazenly, and rewardingly, speculative imaginative account of the life and works (its key phrases are: possibly, perhaps, let us imagine) that finds in Falstaff a portrait of both Shakespeare's (or Will's, as he is disarmingly nominated throughout) own alcoholic father and the doomed bohemian Robert Greene, and in his conjectured attendance at the public execution of the queen's physician Roderigo Lopez the source for Shylock. Equally well received was James Shapiro's *1599: A Year in the Life of William Shakespeare* (2005), a work which hit upon the expedient of narrating the cultural, theatrical and political events of what is seen as a key moment in the writer's and his company's professional careers.

Materialities

Since the 1990s, there has been an extension and diversification and specialisation within the fields of early modern historical enquiry. A growing area of interest has been the materiality of early modern culture; this is represented by two collections of essays: *Subject and Object in Renaissance Culture*, edited by Margreta de Grazia, Maureen Quilligan and Peter Stallybrass (1996), and *Staged Properties in Early Modern English Drama*, edited by Jonathan Gil Harris and Natasha Korda (2002). In the first collection, many of the luminaries of new historicism and cultural materialism (among them Greenblatt, Montrose, Orgel, Dollimore and Garber) reconvene to consider, 'in the period that has from its inception been identified with the emergence of the subject', the question of '*where is the object?*' (de Grazia *et al.* 1996: 2). Land, tools, weapons and clothing, printed books and images, crowns, communion bread and human skulls, the craft of joinery and the property relations inherent in the practices of slavery: these are some of examples of the Renaissance world of objects, object-relations and objectifications that the collection exhumes in order to illuminate 'the way material things ... might constitute subjects who in turn own, use and transform them' (5). Urging 'an exploration of the intricacies of subject/object relations', the declared aim is 'to undo the narrative we have been telling ourselves over and over again: the rise of subjectivity, the complexity of subjectivity, the instability of subjectivity' (11).

Harris and Korda's collection applies this perspective to the material objects furnishing the early modern stage, both socially located ('regarded as *properties*, they may no longer seem to be so trifling: as objects owned by acting companies, impresarios, and players, as objects belonging to – proper to – the institutions of the theatre, stage properties encode networks of material relations that are the stuff of drama and society alike' [Harris and Korda 2002: 1]) and implicated within the construction of dramatic subjectivities: 'early modern conceptions of identity always required external things', although 'the objects of the early modern English public stage were not merely indispensable adjuncts to or determinants of Hamlet's legendary interiority' (15). So their contributors turn their attention to such things as costumes, beards, beds and tables, Innogen's ring and Othello's handkerchief, and to questions such as the relationship between Philip Henslowe's prop catalogue and the early modern household inventory, and the participation of women within the emerging theatre economy.

One particular area that has been opened up by the new attention to 'household stuff' has been a new interest in the drama's connections with the domestic sphere, and in the intersections it reveals between family structures, everyday life and the home environments which are also places of work. The outstanding work in this field is Wendy Wall's *Staging Domesticity* (2002), which delves into the domestic guides and manuals, cookbooks, medical and child-rearing textbooks of the period in order to trace the representation of household work and domestic life in its drama; viewed in this light, the early modern stage was uncannily akin to the sixteenth-century kitchen, 'a slaughterhouse strewn liberally with blood and carcasses', domain of 'the housewife, who so evidently had her finger on the pulse of life and death', and whose pleasure in her work, like that of a player and his audiences, 'might involve the fantasy of taming, displaying, barbing, and spitting bodies' (Wall 2002: 3–5). At stake is a questioning of the totalising model of the operations of power, particularly in relation to the formation of English national identity, that has been ascribed to new historicism, and also of feminist accounts of the domestic and familial arena as a space of patriarchal mastery.

Thus Wall investigates how the drama registers 'the paradoxical ways domesticity signified in the cultural imagination and how it helped to structure social, sexual, gendered and national identifications' (2002: 6); paradoxical because the family unit and the household might serve as a microcosmic model of state and nation whilst simultaneously a space distinct from, and even at odds with, their interests; and because the women, or housewives, who ruled these spaces, whilst theoretically under the jurisdiction of their husbands, could also legitimately consider their lords and masters as subject to their culinary and medical control. The result, as when Wall slyly invites us to incorporate into our imaginings of early modern domesticity 'the image of Lady Macbeth consulting a Renaissance cookbook as she whipped up a narcotic for Duncan's guards' (17), is that the works of Shakespeare and his contemporaries spring to outrageous life:

> A prince trembles with uncontrollable passion at the sight of a milkmaid with her hands buried deep in milk; a householder hysterically sorts through a basket of soiled laundry to find traces of his sexual humiliation; a journeyman dreams of piping hot pancakes and live food marching in the London streets; a servant gleefully narrates the phantasmagoric tale of people butchered and eaten at the dinner table; a fieldworker panics that a lost needle might sodomize him; a housewife rapaciously medicates boy actors in sexually provocative ways.
>
> (Wall 2002: 1)

As a conspectus of the early modern drama, this vividly evokes its capacity to make 'banal or unremarkable situations appear weighty, fantastic suddenly odd' (Wall 2002: 1); what it also points towards (as when fairies invade the households of *The Merry Wives of Windsor* and *A Midsummer Night's Dream*) is 'the potential uncanniness of domesticity, the fantastical quality of everydayness that made submission to household tasks a precarious but formative activity' (126).

Presentism

Wall's propensity to discover the fantastic within the everyday, and to articulate the drama's local habitation within the formations of private and national fantasy, offers a recipe for a new form of historicist scholarship that is not prepared to rest content with the reheated dialectics of subversion and containment, of texts and contexts, of representations and material practices, and of subjects and objects, no matter how suggestive and productive these frames of reference have been in the past. In one respect, though, Wall's historicism invokes the epistemological tradition that predates new historicism but, as we have seen, animates the work of Kastan: interrogating the post-1970s feminist tendency to read early modern gender relations through the prism of the 'inequalities of the modern family', she describes as 'presentist' the view that the Renaissance household is 'a place of privacy, unremunerated labor, and a recognizable gender oppression' (Wall 2002: 158–59). By so doing, she cites one of the key terms of debate within and between contemporary historicisms and the legacies of cultural materialism. In Wall's view, presentism, whether embraced wittingly or not, interferes with proper scholarly objectivity and prevents genuine historical understanding and an awareness of the *difference* of the past; we overcome this by 'highlighting precisely those features … that have become alien to later observers' (7).

For some recent critics, however, presentism is not a default position to be wary of, nor an anachronistic confusion of the critic's own situation and priorities with those of the past, but a stance and a perspective that are consciously and strategically adopted for both methodological and political ends. The idea that our understanding of Shakespeare's works in their own time is profoundly shaped by our experiences of them in the here and now has, of course, been fundamental to the various forms of scholarship that are considered throughout this book: in performance and film studies, in particular, but also, for more clearly political reasons, in criticism that attends to questions of gender, sexuality and race. The increasing attention that has been paid to the presence of Shakespeare within popular culture has also had an implicitly presentist emphasis, in that the investigation of the ongoing histories of Shakespearean, semi-Shakespearean or quasi-Shakespearean appropriations, adaptations, quotations and allusions can proceed unimpeded by considerations of the works' point of origin as an arbiter of meaning.

If in such work the meanings and effects of pop-cultural Shakespeares in the present or recent past displace or even dismiss questions of their textual and historical foundations, so that the criticism of presentism that Wall poses is not really relevant, a number of writers have made a more sustained effort to theorise a presentist criticism that is capable of historicising Shakespeare whilst being quite frank about its emphasis on his (or its) anticipation of contemporary preoccupations. One of these is Hugh Grady, who in *Shakespeare, Machiavelli, and Montaigne* (2002) identifies his method (previously utilised in his *Shakespeare's Universal Wolf* [1996]) as presentist 'in the sense of using theory from our cultural present to help understand and reinterpret works from the past' and also 'historicist' in its 'investigation into those qualities of the Jacobean *mentalité* analogous enough to suppositions of our own cultural present to allow for an interpretative "translation" into a late twentieth-century idiom' (Grady 2002: 2).

The claim is that the self-confessed presentist is only professing openly what new historicists, and to a lesser extent cultural materialists, had practised covertly or unconsciously. This is not altogether new; after all it was Greenblatt who, right at the outset, admitted that 'the questions I ask of my material and indeed the very nature of this material are shaped by the questions I ask of myself' (1980: 5); what is new is the determination to follow through the implications of this recognition, whilst also being aware that its ramifications are by no means straightforward. This is perhaps reflected in a certain caution in Grady's phrasing: evident in the qualified 'analogous enough', and in the scare quotes that suspend 'translation' as an inexact synonym (or perhaps analogy) for what the critical practice may be doing. In *Shakespeare in the Present*, Terence Hawkes is more forthright: asserting that 'none of us can step outside time', he points out that the critic's 'situatedness' effectively 'constitutes the only means by which it's possible to see the past and perhaps comprehend it'; history, he contends, 'is far too important to be left to scholars who believe themselves able to make contact with a past unshaped by their own concerns' (Hawkes 2002: 3). This involves the reversal and inversion of existing critical assumptions and priorities. Echoing a remark of Terry Eagleton's published sixteen years previously, that 'it is difficult to read Shakespeare without feeling that he was almost certainly familiar with the writings of Hegel, Marx, Nietzsche, Freud, Wittgenstein and Derrida' (Eagleton 1986: ix–x), Hawkes notes that the presentist critic 'will always feel entitled to ask how the influence of Shakespeare on Marx or Freud matches up to the influence of Marx or Freud on Shakespeare' (Hawkes 2002: 4). To consider the past through the eyes of the present is the best, perhaps the only, means of facing the future; as Kiernan Ryan puts it, 'To discover that Shakespeare's drama had all along been "dreaming on things to come" would be to reclaim a rich legacy: the prospect of a critical practice through which the world as it was and the world as it is could engage in a dialogue –

a genuine, unpredictable dialogue – about the world as it might one day be' (Ryan 2002: 176).

Spiritualities

Hawkes's *Shakespeare in the Present* was published in the 'Accents on Shakespeare' series, of which he is General Editor, and one of whose principles is that each book 'promises a Shakespeare inflected in terms of a specific urgency'. While this remit, which can be extended beyond this particular series to a significant proportion of recent scholarship, has encompassed work which can fairly straightforwardly attribute its lineage to the established axes of new historicism and, more closely, cultural materialism (examples being Desmet and Sawyer's *Shakespeare and Appropriation* [1999]; Dympna Callaghan's *Shakespeare without Women* [2000a]; Jean E. Howard and Scott Cutler Shershow's *Marxist Shakespeares* [2000]; and Alan Sinfield's *Shakespeare, Authority, Sexuality* [2006]), it has also begun to foster forms of criticism whose presentist orientation has afforded a 'specific urgency' to concerns which these dispensations have, arguably, afforded insufficient attention. Among these are ecopolitics (Egan 2006), philosophy, aesthetics, and religion and spirituality. Introducing the collection *Philosophical Shakespeares* (2000), John J. Joughin emphasises the value to materialist criticism of regarding Shakespeare's works as 'philosophical dramas' in the sense that 'they retain an ethical dimension without transcending those social, historical and linguistic limitations, which simultaneously remain in need of redress, and actually conjure an ethical situation into being' (10).

The recent philosophical turn, stimulated in part by the growing influence of thinkers such as Emmanuel Levinas and Slavoj Žižek, is closely tied to the renewed interest in the aesthetic singularity of Shakespeare. Ewan Fernie has recently argued for a presentist criticism that acknowledges the 'strangeness' of the literary text as 'the difference beyond historical difference': 'On the one hand, the literary text absorbs history into itself and constitutes an experience of historicity. On the other, it confounds history as the manifestation of what is historically unprecedented within history'. The result: Shakespeare's work '*retains* the power to draw our minds beyond what is thinkable – to lead thought beyond complacent presentism to a place where the future might be conceived' (Fernie 2005a: 181).

In Fernie's criticism, the presentist aesthetic operates within the framework of the kinds of postmodern spirituality that are explored by Levinas, Žižek, Alain Badiou and in the late writings of Derrida; a position, which as his introduction to the collection *Spiritual Shakespeares* has it, is concerned with how the 'spiritual intensities' in Shakespeare's works contribute to 'ideas of emancipation and an alternative world' (Fernie 2005b: 8). In an earlier work, Fernie focuses the question of spirituality on the phenomenon of shame, which he treats as a 'constant preoccupation, even an obsession', in Shakespeare's work, as an 'ethical wake-up call' and as a 'spiritual opportunity' (2002: 1, 6, 21). For Fernie and others, the 'spiritual' is not necessarily identifiable with, or reducible to, the religious; nonetheless, the avant-garde thinking evident in this recent work can be seen in the context of a more general revival of interest in early modern religious practice and belief within historicist scholarship (it has also prompted lively counter-reactions, as, for example, in Eric S. Malin's *Godless Shakespeare* [2007]).

Introducing the third and presumably final volume in the *Alternative Shakespeares* franchise, Diana Henderson marks one of its areas of difference from its predecessors by noting that in several of its essays 'religion is considered not as an independent variable or a glib label … but as a set of cultural texts and practices that is and was thoroughly enmeshed with sociopolitical and ethical assumptions' (Henderson 2008: 7). The pervasive presence of the English Bible within Shakespeare's work has, of course, long been recognised; Steven Marx's *Shakespeare and the Bible* argues that Shakespeare 'read the Bible with a very wide range of interpretative responses to its vast plenitude of meanings', and points out, first, that 'understanding the plays' references requires a thorough familiarity with the Scriptures' and, second, that 'these references generate … "strong" readings – that is, they illuminate fresh and surprising meaning in the biblical text' (Marx 2000: 8, 13). Here, as well as Shakespeare reading the Bible, we find the Bible reading Shakespeare.

Elsewhere, scholars have breathed new life into the long-standing debate around Shakespeare's own relations to Catholicism. Greenblatt's *Hamlet in Purgatory* (2001) is a work in which its author candidly, and movingly, acknowledges an autobiographical dimension: recalling his own experience of mourning the death of his father and of finding himself impelled to take the responsibility of saying kaddish, he writes of how 'this practice … which with a lightly ironic piety I, who scarcely knew how to pray, undertook for my own father, is the personal starting point for what follows' (Greenblatt 2001: 9). What follows is an intricate investigation of early modern beliefs about the afterlife, remembrance and ghosts, in which the play of *Hamlet* is poised in the indeterminate place between Catholic ritual and Protestantism, and where the realm of Purgatory is ultimately transfigured into the liminal space of the stage, home of a 'cult of the dead that I and the readers of this book have been serving' (257). A conference on the topic of 'Lancastrian Shakespeare', hosted by one of that county's universities in 1999, focussed the issue of Shakespeare and Catholicism regionally as well as biographically; its outcome was two volumes of essays (*Region, Religion and Patronage* [Dutton *et al.* 2003a] and *Theatre and Religion* [Dutton *et al.* 2003b]) in which, in the course of over five hundred pages and twenty-seven papers, contributors explore the multiple ramifications of a relationship which remains tantalisingly ambiguous.

That it should be so, as Gary Taylor observes in the final essay in one of the volumes, is both salutatory and astonishing:

> If we are to believe the moving stories told elsewhere in this volume, the emotional sources of *Hamlet* and *King Lear* are the tragedies of Elizabethan Catholic martyrs. But what is surely the most salient fact about those plays … is that any Catholic meanings they may have had were encrypted, simultaneously buried and made cryptic … Shakespeare transformed all that real grief, real pain, real loss, real sacrifice, all that individual and collective religious trauma, into an apparently secular affective commodity.
>
> (Taylor 2003: 255)

That questions of religion should now present themselves as the most pressing, as well as, quite possibly, the most intractable historical issues to be faced by twenty-first-century scholarship will come as no surprise: as Richard Wilson notes, 'Only now, with the return of a religious fundamentalism driven by the belief that martyrs dying in a *jihad* attain paradise, while their enemies go to eternal damnation, has it become possible, perhaps, to take seriously evidence of sectarian warfare in this author's background' (Wilson 2003: 31).

But 'Lancastrian Shakespeare' is, by these lights, also potentially an oppositional Shakespeare, a figure envisaged as something other than the Stratford-based Protestant English nationalist and as a focus of resistance to an Elizabethan state steeped in its own methods of terror: 'For though the startling idea that he was born and brought up not "in love" but *in hate* for Elizabeth and her empire remains only a hypothesis, there can be few theories with a greater potential for transforming the way we see and study Shakespeare' (Wilson 2003: 32). In *Secret Shakespeare*, Wilson's elaboration of 'what Shakespeare did not write', that is, his silence about contemporary religious conflicts and controversies and its associated 'sectarian violence', points towards a Shakespeare aligned with 'those moderate Catholics who reacted against the suicidal violence of the fanatics with a project of freedom of conscience and mutual toleration' (2004: 1, ix). And the resonances for the present are, once again, quite explicit: 'We know so much more about religious violence than critics before 11 September 2001. For as I write this, on the site of Shakespeare's Gatehouse, the "Ring of Steel" around Blackfriars and the City, first erected to counter the Catholic IRA, is being reinforced, to seal the precinct even more securely from a world elsewhere' (7).

Whether or not this should be described as a presentist position is perhaps less important than the forcefulness of, to use Hawkes's terminology, the 'specific urgency' that it invokes. As a project whose development and dissemination significantly predate the watershed moment of 9/11 (earlier versions of parts of the book were published as far back as 1997), *Secret Shakespeare* in itself is not a 'response' to a new political and cultural order defined by religious fundamentalism, terrorist action and potentiality, and state terror. But as an intervention that speaks to its time by discovering within Shakespeare's texts and histories a non-sectarian, anti-fundamentalist ethic of moderation, tolerance, and free-thinking enquiry, it offers at least some hope for the futures both of Shakespeare and of criticism. Understanding Shakespeare historically, that is, as a phenomenon reciprocally shaped by the conflicts and emergencies of his time and our own, has never been more necessary.

2   Languages

Close reading

Whether considered from the perspective of political, economic, cultural, theatrical or critical history, 1933 was undoubtedly a momentous year. In Germany, the year began with the election of Adolf Hitler as Chancellor, an event followed a month later by the burning of the parliament building, the Reichstag, and a week after that by the election of Hitler's National Socialist Party on nearly 50 per cent of the popular vote. At the start of March, Franklin D. Roosevelt assumed office as the thirty-second President of the United States, and immediately committed his administration to the implementation of the New Deal. In the United Kingdom, books published included George Orwell's *Down and Out in Paris and London* and H. G. Wells's *The Shape of Things to Come*. Among the films on release were *King Kong*, *Duck Soup*, *The Private Life of Henry VIII* and *Sons of the Desert*. On the London stage, John Gielgud triumphed in the lead role in Gordon Daviot's *Richard of Bordeaux* at the New Theatre and Charles Laughton played in *Henry VIII* and *Measure for Measure* at the Old Vic. And a twenty-seven-year-old lecturer in English Literature at Manchester University, L. C. Knights, published a paper that he had delivered to the Shakespeare Association the previous year, in which he rhetorically posed the question: 'How Many Children Had Lady Macbeth?'

Knights's intention in this essay, as he defined it, was to issue a fundamental challenge to the prevailing critical orthodoxy, evident in academic scholarship, popular commentary and theatrical practice, which was based on the assumption that 'Shakespeare was pre-eminently a great "creator of characters"', a view which Knights dismissed as 'the most fruitful of irrelevancies' (1946: 13). Identifying this view with the A. C. Bradley-influenced school of criticism that had been dominant within the Shakespeare industry since the publication of his *Shakespearean Tragedy* in 1904 (the essay's title satirises Bradley's notorious speculative endnotes), Knights argued that we should instead regard 'character' as 'merely an abstraction from the total response in the mind of the reader or spectator, brought into being by written or spoken words'; more controversially, he went on to assert that 'the Shakespeare play is a dramatic poem', using 'action, gesture, formal grouping and symbols', relying upon 'the general conventions governing Elizabethan plays' and aiming to 'communicate a rich and controlled experience by means of words'. Thus 'to stress in the conventional way character or plot, or any of the other abstractions that can be made, is to impoverish the total response' (Knights 1946: 16).

None of this necessarily implied a defensive critical retreat either from the theatre or from history, and Knights's later work showed him to be far more concerned with the drama's relation to the latter than this manifesto statement suggests (and the cultural and historical circumstances in which Knights's polemic was composed might indicate why this might have seemed like an attractive option). But it was by and large the principle which defined the critical agenda for what would become known in the United Kingdom as practical criticism and in the United States as the New Criticism, both of which would become maturely professionalised critical practices, dominant within the academy and beyond from the 1930s through to the 1960s. Knights defined his principles for reading Shakespeare succinctly:

> We have to elucidate the meaning ... and to unravel ambiguities; we have to estimate the kind and quality of the imagery and determine the precise degree of evocation of particular figures; we have to allow full weight to each word, exploring its 'tentacular roots', and to determine how it controls and is controlled by the rhythmic movement of the passage in which it occurs.
>
> (Knights 1946: 28)

With its rational, analytic tone and quasi-scientific vocabulary, its emphasis upon 'precision and particularity' (Knights 1946: 28), and its rhetoric of measurement, calibration and dissection, Knights's exposition of critical method announced the inception of several decades of scholarly activity geared towards the production of 'readings' of Shakespeare's poems and plays.

The advocacy of 'close reading' did not, of course, spring from nowhere. Its principles and procedures had been established with some precision in 1929, in what can be seen as the close reading industry's technical manual, I. A. Richards's *Practical Criticism*, a work which drew upon its author's observations of the responses of his Cambridge undergraduate students to anonymised poems, presented as text cases, 'to provide a new technique for those who wish to discover for themselves what they think and feel about poetry' and to 'prepare the way for educational methods more efficient than those we use now in developing discrimination and the power to understand what we hear and read' (Richards 1929: 3). William Empson's more playful *Seven Types of Ambiguity* (1930) supplied another marker against which Knights's approach could define itself: concerned with literary ambiguity which is understood 'in an extended sense' to include 'any verbal nuance, however slight, which gives rise to alternative reactions to the same piece of language', Empson's study seeks 'to consider a series of definite and detachable ambiguities, in which several large and crude meanings can be separated out, and to arrange them in order of increasing distance from simple statement and logical exposition' (1961: 1–3). Because practical criticism of this kind was particularly attuned to the analysis of poetry (and, even more particularly, to the work of the rediscovered 'metaphysical' poets and to contemporary modernist lyric poetry, as exemplified in the work of T. S. Eliot – also important as a critical theorist at this moment – and Ezra Pound), Knights's designation of Shakespeare's plays as poems, rather than as plays, was inevitable.

Knights also acknowledged his 'indebtedness' to the 'highly personal method' (1946: 11) of his near-namesake G. Wilson Knight, a figure whose personal and intellectual eccentricities have, as Hugh Grady points out, tended to overshadow his formative role as 'the earliest significant critic attempting to reinterpret Shakespeare's plays as Modernist artworks' (Grady 1991: 89). In a series of highly idiosyncratic books which began, in 1930, with *The Wheel of Fire* (followed by *The Imperial Theme* in 1931 and *The Crown of Life* in 1947), Knight pursued the path of 'interpretation', an activity explicitly differentiated from 'criticism', which to him suggested 'a certain process of deliberately objectifying the work under consideration; the comparison of it with other similar works in order especially to show in what respects it surpasses, or falls short of, those works; the dividing its "good" from its "bad"; and, finally, a formal judgement as to its lasting validity'. Interpretation, conversely, 'tends to merge into the work it analyses', offering a 'reconstruction of vision' rather than a judgement of it; mirroring the experience of the rapt, 'child-like' theatre spectator, interpretation stages a 'translation from one order of consciousness to another ... uncritically, and passively, it receives the whole of the poet's vision; it then proceeds to re-express this experience in its own terms' (Knight 1960: 1–3).

What followed from this were enthusiastic, impressionistic and often dazzling meditations on the plays. *The Wheel of Fire* deals with the quartet of major tragedies (as well as *Troilus and Cressida*, *Measure for Measure* and *Timon of Athens*). It begins with a mischievously counter-intuitive reading of *Hamlet*, which, thematising the play in terms of 'the contest between (i) human life, and (ii) the principle of negation' (Knight 1960: 43), turns upon the nineteenth-century sentimentalisation of the 'sweet prince' by describing its hero as 'inhuman' and 'evil': 'the poison of his mental existence spreads outwards among things of flesh and blood, like acid eating into metal', and his presence in the play is as 'the only discordant element, the only hindrance to happiness, health, and prosperity; a living death in the midst of life' (38–40).

In an essay on 'The *Othello* music', Knight pushes his 'interpretative method' still further: conceding at the outset that in this play 'we are faced with the vividly particular rather than the vague and universal', he nonetheless opts 'to regard Othello, Desdemona and Iago as suggestive symbols rather than human beings' in order to extricate the 'clear relation existing between *Othello* and other plays of the hate-theme' (Knight 1960: 97). *Macbeth* is 'a vision of evil'; evil that is seen working 'in terms not of "character", or any ethical code, but of the abysmal deeps of a spirit-world untuned to human reality' (140, 158). *King Lear*, 'the perfect fusion of psychological realism with the daring flights of a fantastic imagination', Knight interprets as a tragedy rooted in 'fantastic comedy' (161) and 'cosmic mockery' (175), a comedy of the grotesque which reaches its apotheosis in Gloucester's fall: 'the grotesque merged into the ridiculous reaches a consummation in this bathos of tragedy: it is the furthest, most exaggerated, reach of the poet's towering fantasticality' (171).

As these examples indicate, Knight is not a writer given to understatement; viewing the plays hyperbolically, his prose careers from the lyrical to the preposterous, vying to embody the titanic struggles played out in the dramas themselves, and his method is generally to assert rather than to argue, to convey something of the lurid form which they have assumed in the theatre of his own dreams. *The Imperial Theme* and *The Crown of Life* are calmer works; in the first of these, Knight offered to balance the dark imaginings of his first book with essays on 'Life-themes' in *Hamlet* and *Macbeth*, as well as in the Roman tragedies, 'positive values' conveyed through 'images suggestive of brightness and joy'; but neither these values nor their associated imagery 'can be appreciated whilst we confine our attention to logical analysis of plot and subtle psychologies of "character"' (Knight 1951: 1). 'Character', in particular, is regarded by Knight as a impediment to genuine imaginative engagement: 'the "character" cannot be abstracted from those imaginative effects of poetry and poetic-drama of which he is composed ... the Shakespearian play is a drama of action: but the contestants are imaginative, not purely personal, forces' (19, 28). By the time of *The Crown of Life*, which deals with the last plays, these imaginative forces had assumed a mystical character of their own, 'that spiritual quality which alone causes great work to endure through the centuries', which 'should be the primary object of our attention' and which in late Shakespeare is manifest as 'order, reason, and necessity' (Knight 1948: 9–10).

Words and images

Mindful that 'a preoccupation with imagery and symbols … can lead to abstractions almost as dangerous as does a preoccupation with character' (1946: 11), Knights effectively reined in the romantic excesses of Knight's approach, in the instance of his essay through what he calls an 'elucidation' of *Macbeth* as 'a statement of evil' (29); this was a play which 'has greater affinity with *The Waste Land* than *The Doll's House*' (30). Wielding a term, already favoured by Knight (who applies it indiscriminately to abstractions, patterns of imagery and persons), that became central to the lexicon of Shakespearean close reading, Knights identifies the play's 'themes' ('the reversal of values and of unnatural disorder' [29]), and then proceeds to elaborate the ways in which the text both sustains and exercises variations upon these themes, producing 'the system of values that gives emotional coherence to the play' (47–48). This sense of 'emotional coherence' articulated one of the key critical principles of the New Criticism: that the Shakespeare-play-as-poem needed to be approached, and critically expounded upon, as an integrated and unified work of art, imaged in the resonant phrase that provided the title to Cleanth Brooks's key contribution to the movement, as a 'well-wrought urn'.

In an essay first published in 1947 (and frequently anthologised since), in a classic example of the New Critical method applied to Shakespeare, Brooks turned his attention to *Macbeth*, rescuing its babies from the fate that, were L. C. Knights to have his way, would await the contaminated bathwater of character criticism by exhaustively elucidating the multifarious ways in which the imagery of infancy, coupled with that of murderous violence, defines the pattern and structure of the play but also, invoking an opposition between pitiable vulnerability and inhuman evil, seems to epitomise the totality of the human condition.

As Brooks, writing under the shadow of Belsen and Hiroshima, eloquently summarises:

> The clothed daggers and the naked babe – mechanism and life – instrument and end – death and birth – that which should be left bare and clean and that which should be clothed and warmed – these are facets of two of the great symbols which run through the play … between them – the naked babe, essential humanity, humanity stripped down to the naked thing itself, and yet as various as the future – and the various garbs which humanity assumes, the robes of honor, the hypocrite's disguise, the inhuman 'manliness' with which Macbeth endeavors to cover up his essential humanity – between them, they furnish Shakespeare with his most subtle and ironically telling instruments.
>
> (Brooks 2004: 34)

One of Brooks's critical reference points is the work of Caroline Spurgeon, whose *Shakespeare's Imagery and What It Tells Us* (1935), though it is invoked in rather slighting terms by Brooks ('her interest in classifying and cataloguing the imagery of the plays has obscured for her some of the larger and more important relationships' [Brooks 2004: 25]), was a key text for Shakespearean New Criticism. Spurgeon's book is certainly nothing if not systematic in its attempts to record and categorise the types of imagery, and their patterns of association and organisation, in Shakespeare's work; its first editions included coloured charts demonstrating the 'range and subjects of images' in five representative plays, classified in terms of Nature, Animals, Domestic, Body, Daily Life, Learning, Arts, and Imaginative, and subsequently subdivided (for Nature, into Growing Things [Trees, Plants,

Flowers, Fruit], Weather, Sea [Ships, Sea], Cel[estial] Bodies [Stars, Sun], Gardening, Seasons, Farming and Elements [Water, Air, Earth]) and rendered at a scale of thirty images to the inch.

Chapter by chapter, Spurgeon takes the reader through, to take only a small sample, 'The Song of Birds' (1935: 73), 'Sewing and Mending' (125), 'Weeds in Gardens and Evil in Men' (167), 'Linked Ideas: Dog, Licking, Candy' (195) and 'Macbeth's Ill-Fitting Garments' (325), with all occurrences and variations throughout the canon scrupulously documented. Spurgeon's taxonomies enable her to distinguish the distinctive patterns and deployments of imagery within individual plays, as well as to register variations between genres and periods; but what will strike contemporary readers as questionable, misguided or even bizarre about her statistically oriented approach is her determination to read Shakespeare's imagery through the lens of biography. For Spurgeon, image-study unquestionably 'enables us to get nearer to Shakespeare himself, to his mind, his tastes, his experiences, and his deeper thought than does any other single way ... of studying him' (x). Thus in the chapter entitled 'Shakespeare's Senses' images of sunrise and sunset reveal how the 'spectacle of the rising sun seems ever to inspire and delight Shakespeare', while 'the sight of the setting sun, on the other hand, depresses him' (63); images of hearing indicate 'the sensitiveness of Shakespeare's ear' and 'his real musical knowledge, both theoretical and technical' (69); and food imagery conveys 'the loathsomeness of greasy, dirty, ill-cooked or ill-served food, and the intense feeling of repulsion which it arouses in him' (85). This looks now like a late flowering of the Victorian combination of philology and sentimental bardolatry, and was criticised by subsequent new-critically inclined Shakespeareans, but Spurgeon's desire to render the Shakespearean canon as a holistic totality, implicitly expressive of a life well lived, is only a more pronounced version of the general critical obsession with unity.

Spurgeon's work was taken up and developed into a more durable form by the German scholar Wolfgang Clemen, whose *The Development of Shakespeare's Imagery* (1951) ran to ten editions by 1977. In this work, Clemen dissociates the evolutionary patterns and trajectory of Shakespeare's uses of figurative language from its author's imagined biography, employing an 'organic' method of analysis which proceeds from the recognition that 'an image often points beyond the scene in which it stands to preceding or following acts; it almost always has reference to the whole of the play. It appears as a cell in the organism of the play, linked with it in many ways' (Clemen 1951: 3). Clemen's recourse to the terminology of bioscience, though a traditional enough nod towards Shakespeare's long-standing status as a 'poet of nature', was unusually prescient. Two years after his book appeared in English, James Watson and Francis Crick published in the scientific journal *Nature* the paper which identified the structure of DNA, the genetic basis of cellular life; Clemen's vision of the relationship of image to text as akin to that of cell to organism similarly promised to revolutionise the understanding of how the language of Shakespeare's plays works.

In particular, Clemen argues that imagery has to be treated as part of the imaginative and dramaturgical totality of the play, and warns against the New Critical habit of extracting passages in order to examine them as lyric poetry; stressing the importance of 'the sequence of time, the process of the successive exposition' (5), he points out that imagery is dynamic rather than static, and its effects sequential, cumulative and contextual:

> just as every detail has its proper place in that dramatic structure, and is only to be
> understood when this has been examined, so, too, each image, each metaphor, forms a

link in the complicated chain of the drama. This progress of dramatic action must, therefore, be understood in order to appreciate the function of the image.

(Clemen 1951: 7)

Modestly describing his own work as 'a first tentative endeavour to indicate some of the ways in which the examination of the development of Shakespeare's art against the background of the growth of his dramatic art may be pursued', and inveighing against the kind of quasi-technocratic specialisation that involved 'concentrating all the attention and all available resources of research on one element only', Clemen urged critics to investigate 'the interdependence of style, diction, imagery, plot, technique of characterization and all the other constituent elements of the drama' (1951: 231).

The watchword was, as ever, unity (with cognates such as integrity, synthesis and design in close attendance). However, the approach taken by M. M. Mahood in *Shakespeare's Wordplay* (1957) provides an indication of one of the subsequent directions that language-centred study would take. More prepared than her immediate critical predecessors to register the full implications of the theatrical provenance of the plays, Mahood sought an accommodation between a Bradleyan understanding of 'the characters in action' that are the language's 'theatrical embodiment' and the Shakespearean pun, whose function is 'to connect subject and object, inner force with outer form' (Mahood 1957: 41). Starting from Samuel Johnson's designation of the verbal quibble as 'the fatal Cleopatra for which he lost the world and was content to lose it' (9) and reading *Romeo and Juliet*, *Richard II*, the *Sonnets*, *Hamlet*, *Macbeth* and *The Winter's Tale*, Mahood isolates the study of Shakespearean wordplay as something which 'can take us to the central experience of each play as surely as can our interest in its imagery' (55). It is, Mahood contends, 'the prerogative of poetry to give effect and value to incompatible meanings' (72), and her running theme is the pun's propensity to articulate conflict, paradox and contradiction, whether personal (in the *Sonnets*, wordplay is the 'means whereby Shakespeare makes explicit both his conflict of feelings and his resolution of the conflict' [91–92]), political (in *Richard II*, 'to doubt the real relationship between name and nominee, between a word and the thing it signified, was to shake the whole structure of Elizabethan thought and society' [73]) or at the critical intersection between them, as in *Hamlet*, in which it 'contributes to the dramatic realisation of a psychological conflict between the demands of an accepted ethical code and Hamlet's particular vision of evil' (113).

The word's capacity for play is not limited to the apparent prescriptions of the text; Empsonian ambiguity can be elaborated into an indeterminacy which is an effect both of the text and of its conditions of articulation and reception. In a gesture which anticipates the practices that would later operate under the aegis of reader-response criticism, Mahood concedes that, for a modern readership 'that relishes *Finnegans Wake*', the potential to discern wordplay that is conspicuously in excess of the text's conscious designs is considerable:

the prosperity of a pun ... lies in the ear of him that hears it; and however faithful to Shakespeare's intentions we try to remain by excluding certain meanings not current in his day, our acceptance or rejection of certain meanings, and the precedence we give one meaning over another, are bound to be matters of personal and subjective choice.

(Mahood 1957: 11–12)

Although Shakespeare's plays, in Mahood's account, tend towards a resolution of the conflicts that their incessant verbal quibbling embodies, they nonetheless suggest that the texts' inherent capacity for shifting and multiple meanings points towards the arbitrariness and instability of language itself: because 'Shakespeare's experience with words has shown him that the existence of a name did not necessitate the existence of the thing named' (Mahood 1957: 175), his work dramatises 'his own dilemma between linguistic scepticism and faith in the power of words' (179).

Post-structuralism

Without referring directly to the theory of language which was first elaborated by the Swiss linguist Ferdinand de Saussure in his posthumous *Course in General Linguistics* (1915), Mahood identifies an Elizabethan, and Shakespearean, conception of the relationship between concepts, words and things, which bears what Terry Eagleton calls 'the hallmark of the "linguistic revolution" of the twentieth century', that is, 'the recognition that meaning is not simply something "expressed" or "reflected" in language: it is actually *produced* by it' (Eagleton 1983: 60). Saussure's key contribution to this revolution was to insist that the relationship between word and referent (or, to use the terminology that he bequeathed to structuralist analysis, signifier and signified) was conventional and arbitrary rather than meaningful in itself. The implications of this recognition are registered in Mahood's responsiveness to Shakespearean indeterminacy, although her final words find in *The Tempest*, which celebrates 'the truth of poetry, the validity of the conceptual life in words', the strategies of recuperation which ultimately pull the works back from the abyss of non-meaning:

> the world of words had once seemed to Shakespeare tragically incompatible with the world of things. Now he finds in the world built from Prospero's words of magic the truth of what we are. Belief in words is foremost among the lost things which are found again in Shakespeare's final comedies.
>
> (Mahood 1957: 188)

The emphasis on balance, resolution and synthesis returns Mahood's work to the dominant Anglo-American critical tradition, whereby the activities of linguistic 'play' can be squared with the aesthetics of textual unity; subsequent criticism in the post-structuralist tradition has emphasised the capacity of textual 'play' to disrupt and unsettle, to undermine from within the apparent unity and coherence of the text.

The theoretical foundations of this critical approach were laid in an essay first published just less than a decade after Mahood's book appeared. In 'Structure, Sign and Play in the Discourse of the Human Sciences' (1966) Jacques Derrida interrogated Saussurean linguistics, and its derivatives, on the grounds that the radical implications of the structuralist account of language had been 'neutralized or reduced' by its need to assign the structure 'a center ... referring it to a point of presence, a fixed origin', a tendency which inherently 'limit[s] what we might call the *play* of the structure' (Derrida 1978: 278). Instead, Derrida proposes, it is necessary

> to begin thinking that there was no center, that the center should not be thought in the form of a present-being, that the center had no natural site, that it was not a fixed locus but a function, a sort of nonlocus in which an infinite number of sign-substitutions came into play. This was the moment when language invaded the universal problematic, the moment when, in the absence of a center or origin, everything became discourse – provided we can agree on this word – that it is say, a system in which the central

signified, the original or transcendental signified, is never absolutely present outside a system of differences.

(Derrida 1978: 280)

In short, 'the absence of the transcendental signified extends the domain and the play of signification infinitely' (280).

Derrida's initial subject of critique in this essay is the structural anthropology of Claude Lévi-Strauss (which itself exercised some influence on the myth-based Shakespearean criticism led by Northrop Frye during the 1960s; see Sandler 1986), but the implications for literary criticism soon became manifest in the emergence of deconstruction during the 1970s. Far from being a relatively straightforward matter of correspondence between words and things, signifiers and signifieds, according to Derrida, the production of meaning is inherently provisional, contingent and unstable. Words are not tied to things but to other words, and it is their difference from each other that defines them as meaningful, and yet because significance can only be grasped with reference to other signifiers, other networks of significance, its condition is one of perpetual deferral, while every utterance is disrupted, interrupted and haunted by the traces of that which it is not. The western philosophical tradition, which Derrida characterises as 'metaphysical', is given to organising meaning through implicitly hierarchal binary oppositions – God and man, nature and culture, speech and writing, man and woman, and so on – which it is the business of deconstruction to identify and interrogate, and to demonstrating how aspects of one half of the pairing are, often covertly, inherent within its partner. The project for literary criticism, then, is not to demonstrate how the work, and, in the context we are considering, the Shakespearean text, achieves, or least strives for, unity; instead, it seeks out the points where it can be seen to differ from itself, to undermine its own logic, coherence and impression of integrity, and where it is most conducive to 'play'.

Deconstruction's influence was largely registered, at least in the American academy as represented by the 'Yale School' led by Paul de Man, J. Hillis Miller and Geoffrey Hartmann, in critical work that primarily addressed nineteenth- and twentieth-century poetry and prose fiction; in Shakespearean scholarship, its defining moment is evidenced by the work included in two collections of essays, edited, respectively, by Patricia Parker and Geoffrey Hartmann and by John Drakakis: *Shakespeare and the Question of Theory* and *Alternative Shakespeares*, both of which appeared in 1985. In both collections, post-structuralism is one of a range of theoretical approaches that includes Marxism, feminism, structural anthropology, new historicism and post-Lacanian psychoanalysis, brought to bear both upon Shakespeare's texts and upon their histories of reception and appropriation. Parker and Hartmann's volume brackets under the rubric 'Language, rhetoric, deconstruction' essays in which 'analyses of language and figure, deconstructive strategies of reading' lead to a broader engagement with 'the "rope-tricks" of rhetoric to which modern theory has been so influential in returning critical attention' (Parker and Hartmann 1985: vii–viii). The overall aim is to 'raise for debate' issues that apply not only to Shakespeare but to 'the larger field of thinking and theorizing about literature itself – from its formal and linguistic structures to its relations with power, politics, gender, and history' (xi) (Parker's *Shakespeare from the Margins* [1996] is a brilliant elaboration of Shakespeare's language resources, in particular wordplay, which pays particular attention to the apparently marginal or incidental aspects of the works).

The second most frequently cited author in *Alternative Shakespeares* (after Shakespeare) is Derrida; most prominently in the essays by Christopher Norris and Malcolm Evans, and as exemplary instances of post-structuralist close reading these deserve a little close reading of their own. Norris, an authority in deconstruction and literary theory rather than a career Shakespearean, contributes an essay entitled 'Post-structuralist Shakespeare: Text and Ideology'. In truth, the piece deals almost exclusively with the second term of the subtitle, in relation to Shakespeare, rather than the first, citing Derrida's notorious maxim 'there is no "outside" to the text' (Derrida 1976: 73; Norris 1985: 47) in order to investigate the politicised textuality of 'literary criticism at large, and more specifically the history of Shakespeare studies as inscribed within the national culture', where 'the question of the text and its "juridical" limits is nowhere posed with more insistent (and problematic) force' (49). Moving swiftly from the Shakespearean criticism of Dr Johnson to that of F. R. Leavis, Norris posits a scope for Derridean play in Shakespeare's texts that critics have been forced to acknowledge as 'the *exorbitant* character of Shakespeare's English, its resistance to rational or common-sense accounting':

> On the one hand the plays are held up, by critics from Coleridge to Leavis, as the central and definitive achievement of literary language at full stretch ... But there remains, on the other hand, a persistent problem in accommodating Shakespeare's language to any kind of moral or prescriptive norm.
>
> (Norris 1985: 57–58)

Pursuing his interest in the institutional processing of literature within the frameworks of history and ideology, Norris then presents a reading of Leavis's reading of Bradley's reading of *Othello*, which is described as 'a primer for criticism, a test-case of what responsive reading ought to be when measured against the vital complexity of Shakespeare's language' (Norris 1985: 58); what emerge, contrary to the expressly polemical intent of Leavis's essay, are 'curious patterns of compulsive repetition which take rise from their resolutely *partial* understanding of the text' (60), prompting Leavis to play his 'tough-minded' Iago to Bradley's 'feebly romanticizing' Othello, and eventuating in a bizarre critical *pièce-à-clef*, 'a scene of displaced re-enactment where critics have no choice but to occupy positions already taken up by characters in the play' (62). Nowhere does Norris attempt a post-structuralist reading of *Othello* as a means of countering or superseding Leavis's and Bradley's; partly because to do so would run the risk of ensnaring himself in the same game, but also because the production of such 'alternative' readings, by themselves, is neither the essay's nor the collection's point: the value of post-structuralism is that it affords 'an understanding of the ideological compulsions at work in this persistent allegory of errors', and thus a critique of the project of claiming Shakespeare 'in the name of autonomous subjectivity and universal human experience' (56).

Here the baton passes to Malcolm Evans, who in 'Deconstructing Shakespeare's Comedies' gives a bravura demonstration of how post-structuralism can work upon Shakespeare's texts. Commencing, in classic deconstructionist fashion, by latching onto a seemingly incidental aspect of a marginal Shakespeare play – Launce's routines with his staff, his shoe and his dog in *The Two Gentlemen of Verona* (2.3 and 4.2), which represents 'mimicry in crisis' (Evans 1985: 68) – Evans elaborates a densely allusive, wide-ranging and punningly adventurous account of the manifold ways in which the comedies unsettle their own claims to coherence, setting word against action, and textuality against theatre:

> the figures who speak and gesticulate on stage in the Comedies are much more than imaginary people. They are literally and ostentatiously "characters" – hieroglyphs, letters,

elements in a signifying system which flaunts its own abstractions against the claims of a *mimesis* which strives for the unmediated *presence* of its represented world.

(Evans 1985: 72)

Citing Derrida's notion of the supplement, Evans observes that the recurrent conditionals of Shakespearean comedy ('If I were a woman'; 'If truth holds true contents'; and so on) involve a 'provisional reversal of polarities – in which the supplement takes priority and hierarchical or centred structures are undermined' which 'is its own undoing' (1985: 73–74). Evans, like Norris, is also concerned with the institutional processing of Shakespeare's comedies (and of 'Shakespeare' in culture more generally), remarking upon how established reading practices curtail, contain and suppress their potential for play by opting to focus upon 'the affirmation of metaphysical values (love, self-knowledge, "nature", atonement)' and by being preoccupied with 'purely formal or generic concerns' (85).

That this is a reductive caricature of 'traditional' criticism hardly needs pointing out (and it is reflective of the polemical mode of theoretical criticism at this time), but that is in part the point, as what Evans presents in this essay is a self-assured, virtuoso and fundamentally *comic* critical performance of Shakespearean deconstruction that has the great virtue of refusing to take itself too seriously and that is prepared to apply its fierce critical logic to the institutionalisation of deconstruction itself. Contemplating Bottom's addled exposition of his 'dream', Evans writes that 'it is as if "natural" language had taken an afternoon nap and woken to find that the bottom has fallen out of its world and the world out of its bottom' (1985: 75); noting the comedies' general lack of 'theoretical rigour', he remarks: 'If so, applying deconstruction's off-side law, blow the whistle and shout "Metaphysics!"' (84). As Kiernan Ryan observes, Evans's 'exemplary disintegration' concludes with a gesture marked by a 'kamikaze consistency' (Ryan 2002: 13), as it proceeds to interrogate post-structuralism's own claims to radicalism; having enacted to the full its possibilities, Evans concludes by registering its amenability to co-option within the academy as a depoliticised, de-historicised interpretative methodology, a 'souped-up, mildly hallucinogenic formalism' (Evans 1985: 77).

Truth's true contents

Evans followed this essay with a fuller investigation of 'truth's true contents' in *Signifying Nothing* (1986), for which this phrase forms part of the subtitle, a book defined as 'a study of Shakespeare based on contemporary theories of the subject, the sign and ideology' (1986: 8). It is an ambitious work; setting himself against 'an idealist criticism which always purports to recover (at last) some hitherto inadequately revealed aspect of the text "as it really is"', Evans declares that properly joining battle with this 'orthodoxy' would take 'four or five carefully interrelated volumes', dealing respectively with 'the history of the Bard as a cultural signifier', 'the semiotic processes that have accommodated at once the closures of each new interpretation or analysis of form, genre, and so on', 'the text's particular preoccupation with – and manifestation of crisis in – representation and the signifier', and 'the hybrid forms of Elizabethan drama, its divided acting space and contending theatrical modes' (8–9).

As 'none of these books, but a sketch for all of them' (9), *Signifying Nothing* develops readings of selected comedies and tragedies from the multiple perspectives and positions that these emphases afford, and the findings are arresting, original, and frequently provocative and disorienting. In another bravura display of the possibilities of deconstructive close reading, 'truth's true contents', an apparently relatively innocuous phrase used by the goddess Hymen when orchestrating the partnerings of the lovers in the final scene of *As You Like It* ('Here's eight that must take hands/ To join in Hymen's bands/ If truth holds true contents' [5.4.126–28]), is here revealed to be amenable to (at least) 168 variant interpretations, a multiplex 'truth' that 'burlesques the climactic moment of conventional plots by increasing the opacity of its constitutive materials and deferring further the presence of this final illumination to itself' (Evans 1986: 161). In *Hamlet* we find 'the very conditions of its representation as theatrical illusion … woven into the "doubleness" of the play's language … Before the ever-receding horizon of the real, the "natural" subjects and signs of everyday life as reconstituted in the text of *Hamlet* shimmer like mirages, or like actors who half pretend to be people whose conversation strays incessantly to the problem of acting' (132–33).

This comment is extremely germane to the book's own highly developed critical self-reflexivity, and in particular to its crafty use of unreliable narrative. Employing a method of investigative critical biography that has been applied by Terence Hawkes to A. C. Bradley, John Dover Wilson and others (1986, 1992, 2002), Evans frames a reading of *The Tempest* as a colonial text by positioning it within its history of appropriation in the context of twentieth-century British educational imperialism and its discontents, as relayed through the unpublished journal of a British teacher of 'Shakespeare appreciation' (Evans 1986: 13), Edward Harrison, who was apparently based in British Honduras between 1929 and 1930, and who may have been one of the unnamed Cambridge undergraduates quoted in Richards's *Practical Criticism*. 'Everything he writes', Evans records, 'is, unconsciously, an elaborate circumstantial reading of *The Tempest*' (20), a work which sits alongside travel books and essays on Marx as part of this would-be radical's cultural arsenal, intended for 'arming Caliban, 300 years later, against Prospero' (20, 28).

Evans's account of Harrison's abortive literary insurrection might be accounted one of the more intriguing episodes in the history of appropriation, and one that casts a fresh light on the institutional processing of Shakespeare within English studies – were it not for the fact that both Harrison and his journal are part of an elaborate spoof. That Harrison, last heard of mysteriously disappearing 'in the course of an eccentric scheme to carry ice, by dory, from Punta Gorda up the Sarstoon River to the Indians and *chicleros* of the Peten rainforests' (Evans 1986: 108) is a creation worthy of Jorge Luis Borges or Thomas Pynchon (whose *Gravity's Rainbow* supplies one of the book's epigrams: 'If they can get you asking the wrong questions, they don't have to worry about the answers') seemed to have been missed by many of the book's first reviewers, although the hoax is signalled through footnotes; in true deconstructive fashion, the joke is at the expense of the 'authority' of both critical discourse and history itself.

However, the end of the book posits a more direct and presumably more serious, challenge to the literary-critical industry when it advocates the abolition of the category of 'literature' itself, and the instigation of 'a broader concern with language, discourse and culture' (Evans 1986: 250) which would entail studying Shakespeare alongside, say, the Ranter pamphlets of Abiezer Coppe (whose *Selected Writings* were published in 1987 by none other than the Aporia Press), thereby to discover 'a rhetoric which is, in Foucault's terms, "*only* literarature", a language turned in on itself, capable of producing its imaginary transcendences, distances and redoublings only within an ideology which masters it and always draws it back into the finite processes of hegemony and class struggle' (261).

At this point, a suspicious reader might begin to wonder whether *Signifying Nothing* is itself engaged in a kind of slyly self-deconstructive game, in that it is both the apotheosis of post-structuralist Shakespearean criticism and, given deconstruction's determination to dismantle binary oppositions, a wickedly ingenious parody of it. The combination of theoretical sophistication, political earnestness and self-referential irony bears some affinities with the approach adopted by Terry Eagleton in *William Shakespeare*, his contribution to the 'Rereading Literature' series, which was published in the same year, and which in just over one hundred pages develops 'a particular case about Shakespearian drama, one centred on the interrelations of language, desire, law, money and the body' (Eagleton 1986: ix); succinctly put, the case is that: 'his plays value social order and stability, and ... they are written with an extraordinary eloquence, one metaphor breeding another in an apparently unstaunchable flow of what modern theorists might call "textual productivity". The problem is that these two aspects of Shakespeare are in potential conflict with one another' (1).

It is a position with which the Evans of *Signifying Nothing* would probably be in agreement, but, as it happened, that book turned out to be Evans's last word on the subject of Shakespeare. Having called for an end to English studies as it was conventionally understood, Evans did not stick around to implement the dispiriting scenario that he proposed in its place, but engineered an exit worthy of a character in a David Lodge campus novel, or of Edward Harrison himself, by quitting the academic profession to work in marketing, first as a consultant for Semiotic Solutions, and then as co-founder of Space Doctors, where, according to the company's website, he has 'played a key role in applying academic semiotics to marketing needs, developing accessible tools that deliver actionable insight and competitive advantage for brands', designing and implementing 'semiotic projects for a wide range of clients including Unilever, BT, Mercedes (Maybach), Campbell's, Glaxo, Ford, Egg, Coca Cola, American Express, Tesco, Vodafone, Procter & Gamble and Guinness UDV' (Space Doctors 2007). Reader, take heart: even in the place beyond academia that some like to call the 'real world', there is life after literary theory.

Language in history

In spite of, sometimes consciously in opposition to, post-structuralism, Shakespeare's language continued to serve as a focus for critical work that proceeds from significantly different theoretical and political bases. George T. Wright's *Shakespeare's Metrical Art* (1988) is primarily concerned with an aspect of Shakespeare's language that has tended to elude both image-based and deconstructive critics: its metre. Locating Shakespeare's innovations in verse form within a historical narrative that extends from Chaucer to Milton, Wright presents a detailed exposition of the 'vast range of metrical resources English poets of this period found and nurtured in the iambic pentameter line' (1988: xii), resources that are harnessed in Shakespeare to 'an aesthetic and an ethic of mutual dependence and obligation' (258); what this builds towards, in terms of dramatic vocabulary, is a kind of heightened realism and, in terms of dramatic philosophy, pragmatism and inclusiveness:

> In effect, two forces contend in Shakespeare's verse: the force of life and the force of pattern. From one point of view, pattern *is* life; order and design are fulfilling, satisfying, even redemptive, while human passion is clumsy, destructive and blind. But pattern may also be neat and trivial, merely pretty, merely decorative; and from it the vigorous and insistent human force rebels and flinches, asserts its individuality in exceptional action and verse ... The drama of Shakespeare is played out not only through a dialogue of characters but also through a dialogue of differently formed and framed verse

lines, which speak to each other and to us of the variety, grace and plenitude of human speech and trouble.

(Wright 1988: 282)

It will be evident that the seemingly unproblematic conception of 'character', the regard for 'order' and the implication that Shakespeare's texts communicate an apparently trans-historical humanity are at odds with the post-structuralist account of the relationship between subject and discourse. Wright's study is a key work for the student of metrics, not least because its scrupulous attention to the syllabic, syntactic and rhythmic structures of Shakespeare's verse provides a model of close engagement that has come to complement, rather than substitute for or oppose, theoretically and historically based investigation.

Differences with post-structuralism have been more forcefully expressed. The arguments that were rehearsed against 'theory' in the wake of its emergence are recounted elsewhere in this volume; here we may simply note that the robust celebration of Shakespeare's lit-erary supremacy has continued to serve as an imagined bulwark against the deconstructive and historicist tide. In *Shakespeare's Language* (2000), Frank Kermode polemically enlisted Shakespeare's words in the struggle against the cultural relativism that

maintains that the reputation of Shakespeare is fraudulent, the result of an eighteenth-century nationalist or imperialist plot', as well as against the 'related notion, almost equally presumptuous ... that to make sense of Shakespeare we need first to see the plays as involved in the political discourse of his day to a degree that has only now become intelligible.

(Kermode 2000: viii)

Kermode follows a biographical trajectory that takes Shakespeare from the textbook rhet-orician of the early plays to the accomplished practitioner of a literary craft that 'does not lose all contact with the eloquence of the earlier work, but moves deliberately in the direction of a kind of reticence that might ... be thought close to silence', operating 'in a context more complex and ambiguous' (Kermode 2000: 13). The critical phase in Shake-speare's artistic development occurred around 1599, when the Lord Chamberlain's Men moved into the Globe Playhouse, and this provides the structural division in Kermode's study between the exploratory and developmental earlier work and the mature canon; alert both to obscurity and Empsonian ambiguity, Kermode proffers a sequence of close readings of representative or symptomatic moments in virtually all of the plays whose function and relative weight are determined by their position within this evolutionary chronology.

One particularly original language-centred response to, amongst other things, the pro-vocations of post-structuralism is Simon Palfrey's highly original and richly imaginative *Late Shakespeare: A New World of Words*, which, focussing primarily but not exclusively on the last plays, extends the new historicism's interest in their engagement with the poli-tics of the courtly, colonialism and gender into an investigation of 'the travel of words, texts, ideas ... the plays' fascination with the genetics of speech and writing, and with the political mutations of each' (Palfrey 1997: vii). In Shakespearean romance, Palfrey argues, we encounter 'a kinetic dialectic, unresolved and combative, between co-existing yet anti-nomic ideologies', and the 'only way' to make sense of it 'is to attend, as much as possible without prejudice, to all the play's voices with an equal will to listen' (4). Acknowledging that a key principle of the new historicism of the 1980s and 1990s had been its recognition that 'literary and "non-literary" texts, and their tropes, circulate inseparably within cultural exchange systems', Palfrey points out that the emphasis upon 'the impossibility of textual autonomy' has 'precluded a close and sustained attention either to a text's language or to the priority of its sources and analogies'; when overdetermined by 'a rather immobile concept of a panoptically manipulative state', this critical practice has worked to 'rob both self and language of suppleness, surprise, and liberty' (8–9).

In its place, Palfrey elaborates a model of literary engagement that seeks to address the 'critical challenge' of

> how best to reconstruct renaissance discourse, engaged as it is with recovering, revamping, and at times challenging ancient models ... Shakespeare's intellectual world is kinetic, disjunctive, swiftly alive to contradictory possibilities. Above all, it is this fact of a world in process, unfinished, clamorous and turbulent, which must be respected and, through rigorous attention to the plays' mnemonic and metaphoric multiplicity, retrieved.
>
> (Palfrey 1997: 13–14)

The 'multiplicity' that Palfrey has in his sights includes the double tradition of 'romance' that Shakespeare inherited, comprising both the aristocratic milieu of Spenser and Sidney, 'highly-wrought, esoteric imitatios of classical, medieval, and continental epic-pastoral', and the products of the 'popular media': 'gauche, episodic bastardizings of archetypal heroic exemplars' (Palfrey 1997: 36); the potential for the genre to voice 'social and political criticism', and, as 'a mode with roots in idealism and transformation', 'to include or lead to projections both constructive and, at times, utopian' (47); and, importantly, 'the genetic links between language and the body' which 'enjoy an almost Ovidian capacity for partition, division, accretion, transmutation; for wickedly punning literalisms where an airy wish or word takes on physical form; and for the half-laughing denial of "common sense" as much as neoplatonic certitudes' (81). Shakespeare's scripting of this 'unstable choreography' envisages 'the promiscuous body of carnival' (81–82), the populist, grotesque corporeality of which is conjoined with a conception of 'characters ... built out of metaphoric patterns', and of consciousness as 'a seat of stimulus, response, organization, complementarily crowded and individual, single- and multi-tracked, centrifugal and centripetal' (viii).

I cannot do justice here to the range and diversity of Palfrey's readings of the Romances, which variously address their relation to Renaissance humanism, their representation of heroism, the use of body metaphors and their treatment of gender, but his close reading of Stephano's first encounter with the paired Trinculo and Caliban beneath the gaberdine in *The Tempest* 2.2 exemplifies its capacity to balance the most abstruse and esoteric of aesthetic and mimetic speculations with an awareness of the context of popular performance, and of the earthy, the profane and the scatological. Probing Stephano's exclamations over his discovery of the 'confutacious' voices which emerge from either end of the stage monster, Palfrey remarks that 'the moment might oddly evoke an impresario's discovery of tragic-comic pastoral, the ugly generic mule ready to be dusted off and sold to a half-mocking public', a recognition which 'further suggests the antinomic medium upon which he has stumbled and in which he partakes' (1997: 26).

More, these 'foul' and 'backward' voices (*Tempest*, 2.2.91) 'evoke the activity of cacology, of carnivalesque inversion and faeces', as Shakespeare 'sustains the excremental metaphors, as though enveloping the whole scene of burlesque recapitulation and rebirth within a symphony of farts' (Palfrey 1997: 26). And it doesn't stop there: 'the "forward" and "backward" voices cohere and engage despite the absence, or dispersal, or chimerical quality, of the speaking body: the hybrid is never "real", and it quickly breaks up into its constituent parts, a jester and a moon-calf' (27). The scene in turn models the mimetic and metaphoric action of the play, and of Shakespearean romance, as a whole: 'When Trinculo and Caliban become ... one body, they exemplify the way metaphorical dialogue in these plays undresses and reorganizes the assumptions, indeed the very assumption, of both conventional place and verisimilitudinous character'. Thus Caliban's 'nameless, perfectly meta-dramatic elusiveness' provides the figure for 'romance' itself (27). It is with Caliban, positioned as an icon of the plays' ambivalent positioning within history, that the book closes:

> an archetype of the subject, as much as of subjection. Waxing and waning with violence, memory and desire, Caliban projects as much as he bears ... Monstrously anachronistic, littered uncomprehendingly from a world long ago or far ahead, Caliban is riddled with the pain, and the bewilderment, of both posthumousness and precipitousness.
>
> (Palfrey 1997: 264)

Like his author, he faces, 'Janus-minded', both past and future, looking forward and backward, 'a figure whose symbiotic nostalgia and radicalism render him an unstable analogy of both history and romance' (Palfrey 1997: 264).

Rhetorics, metrics, linguistics

The critical texts that have been issued to accompany the issue of the Arden Shakespeare third series are representative of the ways in which language-centred scholarship continues to operate in a variety of modes, ranging from the study of early modern rhetoric and versification, and in the more technically specialised fields of grammatology, sociolingistics and discourse analysis. The collection *Reading Shakespeare's Dramatic Language: A Guide* (2001), edited by Sylvia Adamson, Lynette Hunter, Lynne Magnusson, Ann Thompson and Katie Wales, includes essays on, for example, 'Style, Rhetoric and Decorum', 'Puns and Parody', 'Narrative' and 'Language and the Body'. The aim, the editors state, is to consider Shakespeare's language from both 'literary' and 'linguistic' perspectives, 'offering strategies from practical criticism, from an understanding of rhetoric, and from contemporary English studies and the theatre', as well as delving into 'Shakespeare's verbal toolbox, describing the sounds, words and grammar of Elizabethan English, as well as the rich repertoire of regional and social varieties that Shakespeare heard around him and that we can still hear today in the voices of his characters' (Adamson *et al.* 2001: xii).

In 1994, Arden series advisor Jonathan Hope published *The Authorship of Shakespeare's Plays*, a work that aimed, through a deployment of the statistical methods of sociolinguistics, to settle questions of attribution on objectively quantitative terms, and which paid particular dividends with respect to allocating the collaborative authorial contributions to *Timon of Athens*, *The Two Noble Kinsmen* and *Henry VIII*; in *Shakespeare's Grammar*, published for Arden in 2003, Hope produced 'a systematic descriptive grammar of Shakespeare' intended for use both by textual editors and by teachers and students, which presents 'Shakespeare's idiolect (that is, his particular version of early modern English) within a coherent linguistic structure, so that readers could get a sense of the interrelatedness of many of the features of Early Modern English' (Hope 2003: 2–3). Two further Arden volumes, respectively expanding upon the theatrical and the cross-cultural contexts of language, are *Shakespeare, Language and the Stage* (2005), edited by Lynette Hunter and Peter Lichtenfels, and

Shakespeare and the Language of Translation (2004), edited by Ton Hoenselaars, which, exploring a field which has, as its editor puts it, 'retained the status of *terra incognita* for many anglophone students and scholars of Shakespeare' (1), examines the linguistic and other implications of rendering Shakespeare's English into French, German, Portuguese, Spanish, Bulgarian, Japanese, Mandarin Chinese, British Sign Language and Scots.

Russ McDonald's *Shakespeare and the Arts of Language* provides a concise and lucid overview. McDonald is particularly interested in 'the importance of pleasure in the study of early modern theatre', and hence in

> the power of words to beguile by means of their sounds; of their weight, both semantic and aural; their connotative colours and nuances; the effects of sounds and colours when combined with others like them, or different from them; the pleasures and affective possibilities of patterned language; the effect of sound when it 'seem[s] an echo to the sense' (Alexander Pope), and also when it does not; the music of ideas, harmonious or dissonant, that derives from arresting semantic combinations.
>
> (McDonald 2001: 3)

McDonald's exposition of the sources and strategies of verbal pleasure in Shakespeare includes a historical account of the development of the vernacular as a medium of literary expression, in the light of the English language's 'new-found respectability and prominence, its dynamic instability, and its potential for eloquence' (2001: 10); as well as an outline of the rhetorical traditions that Shakespeare and his contemporaries inherited, as evident in 'his acquaintance with the rhetoricians' arguments and his application of many of their specific formulae', and as revealed in 'Shakespeare's joy in verbal patterning and poetic artifice' (37).

A key point here is that the significance of Shakespeare's 'rhetorical training' was 'not only verbal but also philosophical', in that 'learning to promote opposing positions in equally convincing terms appears to have generated … a kind of perspectival understanding of the world, a consciousness of the provisional nature of all philosophical positions'. Shakespeare is even-handed, in that he 'encourages in his audience a receptiveness to multiple points of view, a refusal of absolutes, an awareness of the competing claims of incompatible interpretations' (McDonald 2001: 49). This is, implicitly, a cultural and political positioning of Shakespeare, as well as an ethical and aesthetic one; similarly, in his discussion of figurative language, imagery and metaphor, McDonald directs attention to 'the cultural contexts of Shakespeare's figurative vocabulary' (88), a lexicon which 'must have been enriched by the audience's familiarity with the local geography, civic controversies, and other such pages from what we call the social text' (87).

Like Mahood, McDonald concludes by reflecting upon 'Shakespeare's attitude towards his own medium', which he discerns in terms of an antithesis, 'combining enthusiasm with anxiety, optimism about its benefits with suspicion of its dangers' (McDonald 2001: 164). It is an antithesis which finds a resolution of sorts in the tragicomic fantasy vision of the last plays, which 'reward the audience by temporarily granting wishes that the conditions of mortality normally forbid … Language permits these impossible joys a momentary reality' (192). The linguistic particularities of Shakespeare's final plays are also the subject of McDonald's *Shakespeare's Late Style* (2006), a work which resists the tradition of sentimentality that has gathered around the works of this period by focussing upon a stylistic idiom and technique that, represented by, for example, Buckingham's speeches in *Henry VIII*, 1.1, described as a 'showcase for the late Shakespearean style', amounts to 'a kind of jagged music, but music nonetheless' (138) (the idea of 'late writing' as a cultural construct is considered by Gordon McMullan in *Shakespeare and the Idea of Late Writing* [2007]).

Observing that the preoccupation with 'the unreliability and inadequacy of language' has prompted some recent critics to turn 'the Renaissance playwright into a proto-modernist' (2001: 180), McDonald registers his own scepticism about the post-structuralist criticism that had been surveyed earlier in this chapter: 'we should not allow such ahistorical errors to go unchallenged' (181). McDonald's sensitivity to the historicity of Shakespeare's language is representative of the general accommodation that recent criticism has reached between theory, history and formal analysis; recent and contemporary approaches to Shakespeare's language tend now to be culturally sensitive and historicised, working across and between literature, linguistics and performance, and registering a concern with the discursive and political contexts and effects of the written and spoken word as much as with its formal patterning.

McDonald also pays close attention to metre. Noting that Shakespeare's employment of the basic component of early modern stage speech, the ten-syllable blank verse line, or iambic pentameter, 'develops over the course his career from regular to irregular, from smooth to rough, from rhythmically simple to rhythmically various' (2001: 89), McDonald stresses that this process of evolution 'does not merely parallel his thematic evolution; it helps to produce it' (95). Thus the regularity and symmetry of the verse in the early plays was suited to their manifest formality and often schematic employment of opposition and antithesis; as Shakespeare's verse developed, a more varied and flexible approach to the relationships between sounds, sense, metre and sentence structure reflected the works' 'dismantling of antithetical categories', its 'breaking down of simple oppositions combined with more intense scrutiny of its parts' (96). By the time we reach the last plays, we encounter a 'forceful challenge to the metrical foundation, which effectively diminishes the regularity and lineal equivalence heard in the earlier plays'; paradoxically, 'the speech rhythms have become more nearly "natural" or conversational, and yet the plays themselves … have become more artificial' (106). Throughout his career, Shakespeare's treatment of metre and meaning is informed by his 'perspectival understanding', in that 'the rhythms of verse physically embody the theme of mutuality and moderation to which Shakespeare seems unfailingly committed' (8).

Speaking the speech

Questions of metre and rhythm, insofar as they have a crucial bearing upon how the text is to be spoken, are particularly pressing in the context of theatrical practice, and if academic studies have tended to overlook this fundamental constituent of the text, it has been addressed in detail by the numerous Shakespearean manuals and handbooks designed for the use of actors, and often written by theatre practitioners, that have appeared during the past two decades, and it is appropriate to say a brief word about these before leaving the subject. These include the former Royal Shakespeare Company director John Barton's *Playing Shakespeare* (published in 1984 and still in print), *The Actor and the Text* (1993, subsequently reprinted many times), by the same company's voice director, Cicely Berry, and various works by Patsy Rodenburg (Head of Voice at the National Theatre and the London Guildhall School of Music and Drama), from *The Need for Words* (1993) to *Speaking Shakespeare* (2005). The fact that these works tend to enjoy a considerably more extended shelf-life than most academic works attests to their popularity with theatre practitioners, but they should be handled with care, not least because their orientation towards the needs of a profession whose prime site of employment is soap opera rather than

Shakespeare can lead to claims about the nature and purpose of the Shakespearean text that many scholars would find questionable, if not alarming.

Barton confidently asserts that blank verse 'is basically the alternation of light and strong stresses', that this rhythm 'approximates more closely than any other to our natural everyday speech' and that Shakespeare 'often uses it as a vehicle for *naturalistic speech*' (1984: 26–27), a view that is reiterated by Berry, who states that because 'the rhythm of the iambic pentameter is very like ordinary speech rhythms, a lot of the time we observe the metre instinctively – or accidentally – and it easily falls into a naturalistic speech pattern' (2000: 52–53); for Rodenburg, the iambic is the 'life-giving beat' that is 'the first and last we hear – that of our heart', which 'charts the heartbeat … of the character' and which continues 'throughout the play, as throughout life, never stopping' (2005: 97, 108). The appeal of such reassurances to actors and readers anxious to normalise, and render playable, a discourse which can seem alien and incomprehensible is obvious, but potentially misleading. The claim that iambic pentameter is fundamentally a matter of alternate stresses in a ten-syllable line is a drastic simplification, and the unproblematised notion that the verse prioritises the construction of 'character' through 'natural'-sounding speech foists a modern conception of selfhood, and of its articulation through the spoken word, onto texts that originated within a theatrical and cultural milieu that played by radically different rules, and in which these conceptions would have been barely imaginable.

The anachronistically naturalistic inclinations of the Shakespearean acting manuals (and of the semi-autobiographical writings of the actors themselves) have been the subject of some discussion within performance criticism (Worthen 1997: 95–150; Werner 2001: 19–49). Here, the recognition that existing dominant approaches to the task of speaking the speech are tendentiously ahistorical and theoretically unsophisticated also prompts reflection upon how a more genuinely historicised practice, one that registers and creatively engages both the proximity *and* the distance between early modern speech and our own, might be fostered (assuming that this is a viable or even desirable prospect). In *Pronouncing Shakespeare* (2005), a book which was the consequence of an experiment in 'original pronunciation' in a production of *Romeo and Juliet* at Shakespeare's Globe in 2004, the linguist David Crystal indicated one way of answering this challenge, and although both the enterprise itself and the lessons that are derived from it (inevitably overdetermined by

---

John Barton (b. 1928)

Theatre director

Recruited to the Royal Shakespeare Company in 1960 by Peter Hall from King's College, Cambridge, Barton was one of the shaping forces of the company in its early years. A renowned teacher of the principles of verse delivery that are expounded in the television series, and accompanying book, *Playing Shakespeare* (1984), Barton established an approach to text whose impact has been felt both within the RSC and beyond. With Peter Hall, he co-directed one of the RSC's biggest, company-defining, early successes, *The Wars of the Roses*, in 1963; singly or in collaboration he has directed more than fifty productions, notably including three of *Troilus and Cressida* (1960, 1968 and 1976), an acclaimed *Richard II* (1973), in which Ian Richardson and Richard Pasco alternated the parts of Richard and Bolingbroke, and the ten-part *The Greeks* (1980), his own adaptation of the Oresteian legend from the works of Homer, Aeschylus, Sophocles and others.

the Globe's mandate of attempted 'authenticity') are open to question, it seems a fitting way to conclude this section.

Invited to act as an academic advisor to the project, Crystal produced a phonetic transcription of the play rendered into Elizabethan dialect (in response to the inevitable question, 'But how do you know?' [2005: 45], Crystal provides fifty pages of text-based evidence) to serve as the script for three special performances during the production's run. In itself, this produced a curious estrangement of the text: Crystal's transcription of the prologue, for example, begins 'Two 'hə. ... ', where 'ə' is 'goh-oo', rather than, as in standard English Received Pronunciation, 'ow', 'ɛ' is 'fair' rather than 'fair' and so on. Crystal documents the process through which the actors, once they overcame their initial resistance to the Original Pronunciation (OP) script (said one, 'Well, *I'm* just going to do *this*, and if they don't like it, they can **** themselves' [102: Crystal's asterisks]), found that the liberation from RP (received pronunciation) not only seemed to make the language more tactile, dynamic, somatically grounded and 'earthy' but also fissured settled relationships between characterisation, ethnicity and social class that are embedded within the standard forms of Shakespearean stage speech.

Occupying, as Crystal puts it, 'a unique dialect space, resonating with several modern accents and yet at a distance from all of them' (2005: 149), the OP variously evoked 'West Country, Irish, Scottish, Northern' whilst also sounding 'close ... to Caribbean' (92) In particular, in a production where Juliet was played by Kananu Kirimi, a Scots actor with a Kenyan background, Romeo by Tom Burke and Mercutio by James Garnon, self-described as 'a public school boy from Leicestershire' (122), OP, inflected with the traces of regional and ethnic dialect that RP works so assiduously to erase, seemed to register and acknowledge the cultural and ethnic diversity of the cast; as Joel Trill, who played Escalus, and 'whose family background is West Indies', observed, 'As someone playing a high-ranking character, the option of using an accent other than RP was immensely liberating' (92).

This seemed to resonate with the production's audiences too:

> I made the point of asking some of the youngsters the next day, during the interval, how they were finding it ... 'Cool.' 'Wicked.' Why? One fifteen-year-old lad, in a strong south London accent, piped up. 'Well, they're talking like us.' They weren't, of course. None of the actors had anything like a Cockney accent. But I knew what he meant. The actors were talking in a way that they could identify with. Had they been to other theatre shows before? Yes. And what did they think of the voices then? 'Actors always sound posh,' said one. There was a chorus of assent. 'But not here,' chipped in another. RP nil, OP one.
>
> (Crystal 2005: 137–38)

In some ways, we are on familiar ground here, in that OP is imagined to act as a means of overcoming historical and cultural distance and difference, as yet another tactic for transmitting a bland, reassuring and inclusive Shakespearean universality that can even extend to the social constituencies that the theatre has traditionally ignored or excluded (here, working class London schoolchildren).

Nonetheless, it is worthwhile acknowledging that, as inhabitants of a metropolis that entertains over three hundred languages, these school students might have been particularly well placed to appreciate the resonances of linguistic diversity. As a historian of language, Crystal is able to account for OP's uncanny capacity to engage a wide range of sensibilities, and to seemingly invite 'everyone' to feel 'at home with it': it is simply, because 'we are talking about an accent (more precisely, a group of accents) which is the ancestor of the accents we hear in English today' (Crystal 2005: 93). Viewed idealistically, OP functions on these terms as a kind of resurrected Anglophone Esperanto, capable, when harnessed to Shakespeare, of accommodating the multiplicity of globalised English(es) and perhaps even potentially capable of reconciling the divisions within and between them. The overwhelmingly positive professional, scholarly and audience response to the OP experiment was couched in terms which suggested that its primary achievement was to physicalise Shakespearean speech as a mysterious yet palpable interiority, enabling the actors to get 'more in touch with their bodies' as, in the reported words of Cicely Berry, the words seemed to emerge 'from within the actors'; for the actors, as the OP 'pulled the emotions forward' it generated a sense of 'simple sincerity', 'brought vitality and removed pomposity' (Crystal 2005: 156–57). This was a different kind of Shakespeare, in some ways, but ultimately still one that was, however strangely, real and true.

Predictable as many of these endorsements may be, they do not necessarily exhaust the larger implications of the experimental project, which need not be limited to the complacent reassertion of Shakespearean timelessness. Crystal writes that it is his firm belief that accent is a 'deep-rooted feature of human identity', and that 'there is no more powerful means of expressing who we are and where we are from' (Crystal 2005: 148); this conviction was confirmed by the experiment but also, in rather unsettling and revelatory ways, tested by it, for what it returns us to is the post-structuralist dictum that identity is not *expressed* through language but *constructed* by it. Crystal's remark was prompted by the comments of James Garnon, who found that the OP created a perilous disjuncture between the historicity of the text, the 'authenticity' of its mode of delivery, and the imperatives of the moment and context of performance; recalling the Queen Mab speech (*Romeo and Juliet*, 1.4.55–95), he noticed that what in RP 'always feels like poetry' here 'suddenly felt real': 'I didn't feel I was conjuring Mab out of nothing but that she could be as real as all the other bugs.' Yet when he 'suddenly looks into the audience', and stands face to face with the modern stand-ins for 'Lovers, Courtiers, Lawyers, Soldiers, Parsons', the accent seems misplaced and fake: 'the rural sounds suited a rural idyll but jarred against the modern people I was looking at … the audience and I weren't speaking the same language' (Crystal 2005: 147–48). The contradictions between being 'authentic' and being 'real', and between the demands of the sixteenth-century text and those of twenty-first-century performance, expose the dilemma of the modern Shakespearean performer in an especially acute form; it is a dilemma that the OP accentuates rather than resolves. As Crystal entirely fittingly concludes, 'I am beginning to realize that this experiment may never be over' (171).

3 Subjectivities

Character building

In 2004 Imogen Stubbs played Gertrude in Trevor Nunn's production of *Hamlet* at the Old Vic. Hers was a novel piece of casting in a variety of ways, not least because Stubbs was, at the age of forty-three, 'the youngest-looking Gertrude in living memory' (Rees 2006), described as 'unusually glamorous' (Gross 2004) and 'intriguingly both a besotted wife and doting mother' (Johns 2004). For the majority of reviewers, Stubbs succeeded in creating and sustaining a plausibly rounded and consistent characterisation; however, in an essay detailing her preparation for and performance of the role published two years later, Stubbs identified one of the key challenges of playing Gertrude as 'how little dialogue Gertrude is given, even in the scenes in which she appears', prompting her and her director to wonder, 'Why is she silent, when she is silent?' The answer that Stubbs and Nunn found to this question is firmly rooted in character: 'increasingly she dares not articulate what is going on inside her head, and after a certain point there is an element of knowing, but not knowing, about what Claudius is doing and is planning to do' (Stubbs 2006: 37).

As an instance of a performer appearing to compensate for the limitations of her text by elaborating its subtext, thereby enhancing the spoken by the unspoken, this intervention is

Trevor Nunn (b. 1940)

Theatre, television and film director

Following a brief stint at the Belgrade Theatre, Coventry, Nunn joined the Royal Shakespeare Company in 1966, and became its Artistic Director in 1968. As well as directing numerous main-stage productions that included the epic *The Romans* cycle in 1972 and award-winning musical version of *The Comedy of Errors* in 1976 (later televised), he directed Ian McKellen and Judi Dench in the leads in a studio-scale *Macbeth*, also in 1976, at the Other Place, in what remains one of the most intense and compelling stagings of the play. Following the success of *The Life and Adventures of Nicholas Nickleby* (1980), Nunn was instrumental in steering the embattled RSC of the early 1980s into the arms of the commercial theatre sector, directing *Les Misérables* for the company in 1985, which swiftly transferred to the West End and beyond, where it has remained ever since, as well as a string of mega-musical hits that began with *Cats* (1981). Appointed as Artistic Director of the National Theatre in 1997, he directed a large-scale *Troilus and Cressida* in the Olivier auditorium in 1999, as well as a naturalistic *Merchant of Venice* in the Cottesloe in the same year. Like *Macbeth* and his 2008 RSC *King Lear*, *Merchant* was subsequently filmed; in 1996, he directed a feature film of *Twelfth Night*.

not that exceptional; indeed, it seems a representative example of the strategies employed within the mainstream acting tradition to produce the partial and contradictory figures of Shakespeare's texts as sophisticated, interesting, recognisable and sympathetic characters. As Michael Dobson points out in the introduction to the volume in which Stubbs's essay features, she 'understood her function as an actress to be the plausible enactment of Gertrude's personal story as it might appear in an immediately recognizable present-day context', a mission which was for the most part convincingly accomplished, although not completely so, especially with regard to aspects of the play 'which do not lend themselves to this form of intimate psychological and social realism': thus Stubbs's account of 'her struggles to find an adequate motivation' for the passage that commences with 'There is a willow grows aslant a brook … ' (*Hamlet*, 4.7.137) is 'an object lesson in the potential mismatch between Shakespeare and Stanislavsky' (Dobson 2006: 4).

This mismatch has long been acknowledged by academic critics; as far back as 1935 M. C. Bradbrook refuted the idea that Elizabethan and Jacobean playtexts might be well-served by the disciplines of realism by declaring that '*Othello* wants not Eugene O'Neill to support it' (1969: 3); two years previously, as we saw on pp. 344–5, L. C. Knights had (in an essay entitled 'How Many Children Had Lady Mabeth?') no less polemically dismissed character-based interpretation as 'the most fruitful of irrelevancies' (1946: 13). Yet the published discourse of Shakespearean theatre practitioners has remained one of the strongest redoubts of a kind of closely read practical character analysis whose classic phase was inaugurated at the turn of the twentieth century in the critical, theoretical and theatrical work of three figures, who, in very different manners, initiated ways of thinking about, and approaching the construction of, Shakespearean personae both on and off stage. Although the perspective adopted by this chapter is to address these concerns by means of more recent interrogations of subjectivity, gender and sexuality, they merit consideration not only as a prior context for these debates but as models of critical thought and theatrical practice that are not likely to go away any time soon. The key figure here is Konstantin Stanislavsky himself, as a number of commentators have documented (Worthen 1997; Holmes 2004). Various attempts to record and to rationalise the application of the Stanislavskian preparatory process can be found in successive volumes of the 'Players of Shakespeare' series (1985–2007), to which Dobson's collection is successor, and in actors' memoirs such as Antony Sher's *Year of the King* (1985) and Brian Cox's *The Lear Diaries* (1992).

Bradley and Freud

The second key influence (and one which is regarded by many modern commentators as monumentally malign, although he has recently enjoyed a minor rehabilitation) is the implicit target of L. C. Knights's derision, A. C. Bradley, notorious not only for the speculative footnotes that Knights's title sought to parody but also for his alleged treatment of Shakespeare's plays as if they were nineteenth-century realist novels. *Shakespearean Tragedy* was published in 1904 (the year of the premiere of Stanislavsky's production of Chekhov's *The Cherry Orchard* at the Moscow Art Theatre), and almost immediately effected a profound impact on the discipline of Shakespearean scholarship as well as on the study and teaching of English literature more generally. The product of a scholar who had turned from philosophy to literature, the work was an attempt to put into practice his belief that 'what imagination loved as poetry reason might love as philosophy … in the end these are two ways of saying the same thing' (Bradley 1965: 394).

Konstantin Stanislavsky (1863–1938)

Actor and theatre director

Co-founder of the Moscow Art Theatre in 1897, Stanislavsky instigated a system of actor training rooted in physical expressiveness, creative identification and psychological verisimilitude that has remained in use in acting schools worldwide to the present day. Known in translation in the Anglophone world in the semi-fictionalised texts *An Actor Prepares* (1937), *Building a Character* (1950) and *Creating a Role* (1961), as well as in the autobiographical *My Life in Art* (1952), Stanislavsky's techniques, which were initially evolved to address the demands of the plays of Anton Chekhov and other naturalist dramatists (though Shakespeare was an important part of the Moscow Art Theatre repertoire, and *Othello* provides the central, extended case study of *Creating a Role*), have prompted performers of Shakespeare to dig for buried or complex motives, to aim for consistency and coherence of characterisation, and to find ways of empathising and identifying with their roles, often and perhaps especially where the text seems to discourage their efforts to do so. As an actor, Stanislavsky played Benedick in *Much Ado*, Othello (both 1896) and Brutus in *Julius Caesar* (1903). It would be wrong to label Stanislavsky as a doctrinaire realist, however (though the American domestication of the system as the Method of the 1950s has tended to encourage this). His 1911–12 *Hamlet*, a collaboration with the scene designer Edward Gordon Craig, which served to position the Moscow Art Theatre firmly on the international map, was a remarkable example of a conflicted convergence between two visionary aesthetics rooted in very different forms of theatrical idealism; between Craig's abstractionism, on the one hand, and Stanislavsky's attentiveness both to individual psychology and to the allegorical possibilities of the play.

Focussing on the quartet of 'major' tragedies (*Hamlet, Othello, King Lear, Macbeth*), *Shakespearean Tragedy* is an exploration of the ramifications of the proposition that Shakespeare's 'main interest' in these works 'may be said with equal truth to lie in action issuing from character, or in character issuing in action' (Bradley 2007: 6). The dialectical shape of the formula is important: the equal weighting afforded to 'action' and 'character' reflects the counterpoised philosophical and psychological components of Bradley's account of what he calls the 'substance' of Shakespeare's tragedies. This is further suggested in his summation of Shakespearean characterisation:

> His tragic characters are made of the stuff we find within ourselves and within the persons who surround them. But, by an intensification of the life which they share with others, they are raised above them; and the greatest are raised so far that, if we fully realize all that it is implied in their words and actions, we become conscious that in real life we have known scarcely any one resembling them. Some, like Hamlet and Cleopatra, have genius. Others, like Othello, Lear, Macbeth, Coriolanus, are built on the grand scale; and desire, passion, or will attains in them a terrible force. In almost all we observe a marked one-sidedness, a predisposition in some particular direction; a total incapacity, in certain circumstances, of resisting the force which draws in this direction … It is a fatal gift, but it carries with it a touch of greatness; and when there is joined to it nobility of mind, or genius, or immense force, we realize the full power and reach of the soul.
>
> (Bradley 2007: 12)

Presenting Shakespearean characters as beings like and unlike the 'ourselves' of his (presumed) male contemporaries, Bradley encourages the reader to identify and empathise with them but also to admire them as elevated by art beyond the ordinary, into the realms of genius and greatness; their 'one-sidedness', a modernisation and secularisation both of the Greek concept of *hamartia* and of the early modern humoral conception of personality organisation.

Conceived by Aristotle and Hegel as an imitation of an action in which abstract or impersonal forces or ethical principles are placed in contention, tragedy, for Bradley, works towards the catastrophic conclusion that 'follow[s] inevitably from the deeds of men ... the main source of these deeds is character' (2007: 7). The substance of *Shakespearean Tragedy*, then, is its restless, provisional and often elaborately circumstantial investigation of the relations between the actions that the men and women of the tragedies perform and the hypothesised reasons why they do so, between motivation, execution and avoidance, between speech and silence, and between thoughts, imaginings, words and deeds.

Although Bradley's method has often been described as a novelistic method of inter-pretation (in the 1930s, F. R. Leavis crudely caricatured the Bradleian account of *Othello* as 'a psychological novel written in dramatic form and draped in poetry' [1962: 136]), it has affinities with the customary procedures of the modern actor, particularly after Stanislavsky, in preparing a role: as that exemplary man of the theatre Harley Granville Barker com-mented in the 1920s, Bradley's readings were 'like a very great actor's conception of the parts' (1923: 20). The same could not always be said for the considerable body of character criticism that followed in his wake, which ranges from Barker's own *Prefaces to Shakespeare*, published between 1923 and 1947, to the recent notorious example of Harold Bloom's *Shakespeare and the Invention of the Human*, in which Bloom, presumptuously presenting himself as Bradley's heir, announces that 'Personality, in our sense, is a Shakespearean invention, and is not only Shakespeare's greatest originality but also the authentic cause of his perpetual pervasiveness', and, in the course of a volume that runs to nearly seven hundred and fifty pages, concludes that 'when we are wholly human, and know ourselves, we become most like either Hamlet or Falstaff' (Bloom 1999: 4, 745).

Bradley is not entirely to blame for the excesses of the critical tradition that he instigated (least of all for the pedagogic triangulation of 'character' with 'plot' and 'themes'), but his decisive contribution both to the institutional mission of English literary criticism and to the fostering of reading and critical practices content to believe, as Terence Hawkes puts it, that 'the words on the page transparently express character, and that a vital consistency exists between these elements' (1986: 36) has been subjected to serious and searching cri-tiques by cultural materialist critics. These include John Drakakis, whose assessment of Bradley's ideological influence upon modern criticism identifies a privileging of the integ-rity and independence of character that subsequent writers have explicitly or implicitly reiterated: 'The demands of family and state ... are placed in an anterior relation to the autonomous consciousness of the tragic protagonist', and the idea that these demands 'might conceivably *determine* character, or that the notion of character so produced may be anything but unified, is well beyond the problematic that Bradley fashions from Hegel' (Drakakis 1985: 7).

Drakakis's interrogation of Bradley's position is informed by the theoretical decentring of the subject of 'man', derived from the work of Michel Foucault, Jacques Derrida, Louis Althusser and others, which, as surveyed in previous chapters (see pp. 314–15, pp. 350–51), was central to the projects of new historicism and cultural materialism. This section is concerned with critical work which has emphasised the importance of sexuality and gender identity in the construction of subjectivities, and it is appropriate here to mention a third key contributor to the formation and development of character-based criticism: Sigmund

Freud. Contemporaneous with Bradley and Stanislavsky (*The Psychopathology of Everyday Life* was published in 1904), Freud made extensive use of Shakespeare not only in his writings on art and literature and on the psychic life of the artist but also as a means of expounding the central precepts of psychoanalytic theory, in particular the Oedipus complex, for which *Hamlet* (even more than its ostensible main reference point, Sophocles' *Oedipus*) stands as the supreme dramatic exemplar. For Freud, Shakespeare's plays operate as do all literary works, encoding unconscious desires by participating in the operations of dreamwork: condensation, decomposition, displacement, projection and so on; thus, for example, in an essay published in 1913, he wrote that Cordelia's positioning as the mute third of a female trio marks her (according to Freud's diagnosis of the folklore and fairy-tale motif) as the Mother and Death.

The reading strategies here incline towards the allegorical and symbolic; but as well as being structurally and thematically symptomatic in themselves, Shakespeare's works also supplied him with narratives that played out the classic Freudian scenarios of rivalry and desire between parents, children and siblings, as well as characters illustrative of real-life psychopathological types. Thus, still with regard to *King Lear*, he later speculated that 'the secret meaning of the tragedy' was to be found in the king's 'repressed incestuous claims on the daughter's love' (Holland 1964: 65). The self-defined status of psychoanalysis as a discipline which aimed to map the universal mechanisms of the human psyche invited Freud to treat Shakespeare's characters as if they were timeless, contemporary and real; as if their neuroses, expressed and repressed desires, drives and conflicts were those of all human beings throughout history, and most immediately those confessed or unearthed on his Viennese consultation couch.

By providing the key to unlock the mysteries of the soul, psychoanalysis afforded an explanation of the most enduring of literary enigmas, Hamlet's prevarication: as Freud put it, 'it was not until the material of the tragedy had been traced back by psychoanalysis to the Oedipus theme that the mystery of its effect was at last explained' (1985: 254–55). Freud's scattered reflections on *Hamlet* were marshalled into a sustained argument by his disciple Ernest Jones, in an essay first published in 1910 and reprinted in 1923, and extended to book length in *Hamlet and Oedipus* (1949), which attributes Hamlet's delay to 'intellectual cowardice, that reluctance to dare the exploration of his inmost soul' (Jones 1949: 91), a reluctance that stems from his repressed murderous aggression towards his father and desire for his mother. The impact of Jones's thesis can be gauged not only from the scope for argument and development that it opened up in the commentaries on the play that followed, but also from the fact that it provides a rare example of a critical reading impacting directly and immediately upon performance. For theatre director Tyrone Guthrie and actor Laurence Olivier, Jones's initial essay served as an inspiration for their 1937 production of *Hamlet* at the Old Vic, and although the Oedipal aspect went unnoticed at the time, it assumed a much more graphic form in Olivier's 1948 film version; and subsequent stage productions and films have echoed Olivier's emphasis.

The psychoanalytic method pioneered by Freud and Jones and exemplified by the latter's interpretation of *Hamlet* has been significant for character criticism and performance in its extension of textual, and subtextual, ambiguity and multiplicity to take account of unconscious motivation, repression and conflict, as well as providing a model of the family romance which has been applied in diverse ways across the Shakespearean canon: both applications are comprehensively surveyed in Norman N. Holland's *Psychoanalysis and Shakespeare* (1964) and Murray M. Schwartz and Coppélia Kahn's collection *Representing Shakespeare* (1980). Commenting on the latter volume, Philip Armstrong argues that it demonstrates the more problematic aspects of the universalising and literalist dimensions of the Freudian inheritance, whereby 'the modern Western nuclear family is taken as the norm, and masculinity as the model for self-identity, using Eriksonian developmental models applied without regard for historical differences, non-hetero sexualities, or non-Oedipal relationships' (2001: 168). Armstrong's observation occurs in a sharp account of what he describes as 'the current state of both Shakespearean criticism and psychoanalytic theory, each of which owes more to the other than is generally admitted', because 'Shakespeare has been in *psychoanalysis* for as long as psychoanalysis itself has been around, and in two senses: that is, Shakespeare has been both subject *to* psychoanalysis and a constitutive presence *in* psychoanalysis at least since Freud's inaugural formulation of the Oedipus complex' (1, 5).

But if in this sense Shakespeare and psychoanalysis have historically been mutually self-reinforcing, the psychoanalytic tools that have served to strengthen the project of character construction and criticism have also the very considerable potential to dismantle it, in that the most unsettling of Freud's discoveries, that of the unconscious, entails the dethronement of the rational, self-motivating and self-aware humanist self that it is the business of that project to affirm. If the Id is in charge rather than the Ego, the meaningfulness, capacity for ethical choice and agency that Bradley and successors have sought to locate in character in action are dispersed and subordinated, the integrity of the self an illusion. As Armstrong points out, Ernest Jones's discussion of *Hamlet* represents the workings of the unconscious as 'the enslavement of human agency to forces which remain obscure and illegible', thereby mounting 'a sustained and radical attack on humanism' (Armstrong 2001: 27); the post-structuralist reworking of Freud developed by Jacques Lacan progresses the attack several stages further. Acknowledging that Freud had ensured that 'the very centre of the human being was no longer to be found at the place assigned to it by a whole humanist tradition', Lacan repudiated the co-option of psychoanalysis to the therapeutic cause of ego psychology; far from acting as a 'talking cure', a return to the fundamental principles of psychoanalysis restored the practice's capacity to expose 'the self's radical ex-centricity to itself' (1977: 114, 171).

Like Althusser, who incorporated Lacan's theory of identity-formation into his model of ideological interpellation, Lacan designated selfhood as *subjectivity*: one is, or rather becomes, a subject within language (I, *je*, *ich*); and, since language is the modus operandi of power as well as desire, one undergoes subjection by virtue of this positioning. Because subjectivity, for Lacan, is an effect of signification, produced by the play of linguistic differences, it is inherently divided and incomplete, marked by lack and absence; identity is a phantasm enacted within the realms of the imaginary, 'the scene of a desperate delusional attempt to be and to remain "what one is" by gathering to oneself ever more instances of sameness, resemblance, and self-replication; it is the birthplace of the narcissistic "ideal ego"' (Bowie 1991: 92).

Lacan's account of subjectivity, which also emphasises the significance of the phallus in the ordering of signification and hence of the production of gender identity and sexual difference, is among those that have acted as a provocation and a stimulus to cultural materialist and, in particular, feminist scholarship, which is surveyed in the pages that follow (though his formulations have also been vigorously contested): as Valerie Traub observes in the context of her study of eroticism in Shakespearean drama, the double appeal of Lacanian psychoanalysis is that it offers 'a reading of the simultaneous construction of gender and sexuality that problematizes even as it upholds patriarchal prerogatives', whilst also presenting 'a theory of the radical contingency of a speaking subject always constructed through social practices' (Traub 1991: 95). It has also been vigorously contested, both within feminism and beyond, as well as from positions which have sought to reinstate forms of character criticism, and of allied concepts of selfhood, akin to those which cultural materialism has apparently displaced.

Women's parts

One feature of Imogen Stubbs's efforts to fashion a 'non-matronly' Gertrude defined against 'staid, queenly stereotype' (Stubbs 2006: 35) is that it is implicitly, but pervasively, underpinned by a particular kind of feminist (or perhaps post-feminist) theatrical tradition and sensibility: one that sees the task of the female performer as that of reclaiming Shakespeare's women from reductive and misogynist stereotyping, and of attempting to ensure that, as performer Juliet Stevenson put it in the collection of interviews that had introduced the topic to the Shakespearean critical community two decades previously, women's roles would be 'as complex in performance as men's', restoring them 'to their flawed and rounded complexity' (quoted in Rutter 1988: xxvii).

From the standpoint of contemporary feminist criticism and gender theory, such a position may seem, at the very least, a little naïve, and at worst a recipe for unwitting collusion with the textual prescriptions and value-systems of a canon of work whose irredeemably patriarchal and heterosexist nature three decades of feminist criticism have only served to confirm. Writing in 2000 in an essay entitled 'Misogyny Is Everywhere', Phyllis Rackin suggests that Kathleen McLuskie's contention (first expressed in 1985, with regard to *Measure for Measure*) that 'the narrative and the sexuality under discussion are constructed in entirely male terms', thereby forcing feminist criticism into the unrewarding role of merely 'exposing its own exclusion from the text' (McLuskie 1994: 97), now seems 'increasingly applicable to the entire Shakespearean canon' (Rackin 2000: 47).

In its cultural moment, the alignment (or lack thereof) between Stubbs's currently not untypical take on one of Shakespeare's traditional problem women (and in particular on her age and her silences) and the concerns of recent criticism can be discerned from the perspective adopted towards these topics in two scholarly productions also published in the year that Stubbs's essay appeared. Ann Thompson and Neil Taylor's Arden third series edition of *Hamlet*, in common with an increasing proportion of its companion volumes, is edited in the light of the recognition that '[a] feminist editor must interrogate the assumptions made about gender in the text itself and in the previous transmission and elucidation of the texts, drawing on feminist studies of the ways in which Shakespeare has been reproduced and appropriated by patriarchal cultures' (Thompson 1997: 91). With respect to this play, it registers that 'feminist critics have expressed difficulties with the play, deploring both the stereotypes of women depicted in it and the readiness of earlier critics to accept Hamlet's view of the Queen and Ophelia' (Thompson and Taylor 2006: 35).

At the level of textual commentary, this awareness prompts the editors to question the traditional reaction to Hamlet's declaration to his mother that 'You cannot call it love, for at your age/ The heyday in the blood is tame' (3.4.66–67): 'Hamlet's assumption, in all three texts, that his mother is too old to experience sexual desire has been regularly endorsed by (male) editors, who also feel that she must be too old to excite it' (Thompson and Taylor 2006: 341). Viewed in this light, it is an open question whether Nunn's casting of Stubbs as a youthfully attractive and sexually active Gertrude is a subversion of male assumptions about women's sexuality or a subtle reinforcement of them. Alan Sinfield, meanwhile, is more forthright in voicing his suspicion of the play's representation of Gertrude, noting that 'she illustrates a subtle male bias – in what she does not say'; listing a succession of moments where we might expect from Gertrude a comment, a reply or a response that is not supplied (the moments Stubbs chose to play by imagining Gertrude 'dar[ing] not to articulate' the interiority that she as a performer needed to inhabit), he concludes that the 'scandal of Gertrude' is that 'the Shakespearean text is interested in what she is thinking and feeling only when she is in dialogue with Hamlet. Her interiority – the state of her sex life and her eternal soul – is significant only when it intersects with the concerns of the male lead' (Sinfield 2006: 25–26).

The distance between Stubbs and Sinfield seems to mark a particularly stark polarisation of the positions of the practitioner and the scholar, and one to which we shall return later. In the early stages of feminist Shakespearean criticism, however, the prospect of a broad convergence of interests and priorities between scholarship and more mainstream, as well as radical, feminist activism and theatrical practice seemed for a time rather more viable. The starting-point for modern feminist criticism is generally ascribed to the mid-1970s, a period which (in the wake of the second wave feminism articulated in works such as Germaine Greer's *The Female Eunuch* [1970]) saw the publication of Juliet Dusinberre's *Shakespeare and the Nature of Women* (1975; second edition 1996; third edition 2003). Concerned with early modern beliefs about chastity, male authority, property rights, religion and education, Dusinberre's project is historicist, and takes particular account of, it is argued, the emancipatory and egalitarian implications of the rise of Puritanism for the social and familial position of women; drawing upon the historians Lawrence Stone and Christopher Hill for their respective accounts of the 'crisis' in the sixteenth-century English aristocracy and of the socially radical dimensions of Puritanism (Stone 1965; Hill 1958, 1964), Dusinberre contends that, 'at its most exciting during Shakespeare's lifetime', Calvinist Protestantism, by 'replacing the legal union of the arranged marriage with a union born of the spirit', acted as a progressive middle class social force that provoked 'agitation for women's rights and for changed attitudes to women' (2003: 104, 2, 5).

The drama of Shakespeare and his contemporaries not only enthusiastically embraced the 'challenge … to explore assumptions about women in their plays' (Dusinberre 2003: 8) but is explicitly identified as 'feminist in sympathy' (5); the 'spirit' of Shakespeare's own plays is 'profoundly democratic in that he sees men and women, from the milkmaid to the Empress, the fool to the wise man, the Prince to the gravedigger, as equal' (82). Shakespeare's feminist sympathies are thus evident in his depiction of 'Ophelia, chained into femininity by Polonius, and Helena in *All's Well that Ends Well*, determined to escape those chains' (306); of Cleopatra, afforded 'her own moral law that in being always an artist she was in fact true to her own nature' (69); of the Doll Tearsheet who 'cocks a snook at a society which rewards virtue in women with subjection' (122); and of Kate in the *Shrew*, who 'inhabits a world too sophisticated to stomach the … theology of subjection with which her forbear, the Kate of the anonymous *The Taming of a Shrew*, regales her hearers' (78), whose final speech 'should not be taken at face value' (105) and whose 'submission', paradoxically, 'gives her power over Petruchio' (108).

Central to Dusinberre's readings is the conjunction of the Puritan feminism which animates the texts and the dramatists' interest in and commitment to an emergent realism; referring to the dramaturgy's 'secular and naturalistic setting and … evocation of individual character' (Dusinberre 2003: 185), the stress throughout is upon Shakespeare's female characters as real and psychologically complex individuals, rather than stereotypes, to the extent that even the fact that the roles were played by boys meant that their presence 'in the secular drama of character and personal relations spurred the dramatists to look beyond a femininity susceptible of imitation, to ways of representing women which would be less superficial' (11). In effect, what is presented here is a form of revisionist, historicised character criticism, an attempt to reclaim Shakespeare's women from the margins to which patriarchal tradition had assigned them.

Dusinberre's overly positive account of the emancipatory impact of reforming Renaissance Puritanism was qualified and contested in the feminist scholarship that immediately followed, as was her blatant gesturing towards contemporary relevance, as demonstrated by her comment that 'Moll Cutpurse is the Germaine Greer of the Elizabethan stage' (Dusinberre 2003: 98) and Luciana 'Shakespeare's Evelyn Home' (as she was called in the first edition; in subsequent editions, this dated allusion to the conservative *doyenne* of the women's magazine advice pages of the 1950s and 1960s became 'Shakespeare's Agony Aunt'). In the prefaces to the second and third reissues of the work she essayed partial answers to the objections it had provoked, as represented, for example, by Lisa Jardine, who counters the claim that the religious reforms of the Renaissance 'gave women a freedom and a voice they had hitherto never had' by expressing puzzlement as to 'why feminist social historians and critics are so eager to see emerging emancipation in the seventeenth century, and especially to read liberation into concessions which they would readily recognise as trivial in their own day' (Jardine 1983: 38, 63). For Dusinberre, however, the point, and the context, of her first book was its immersion in its cultural and political moment: writing in 1996, she points out that in the 1970s 'feminism was inseparable from anger', and that it was this that fuelled her 'determination to build a bridge between Shakespeare's world and my own', as 'a patriarchal world under pressure to change' (Dusinberre 2003: xxxv, xxxix).

Within this frame of reference, Shakespeare needed to be seen, strategically, as an opponent of patriarchy, not the epitome of it, the force of his cultural authority harnessed and appropriated rather than contested; to return to the question of the relation between critical and theatrical practice with which we began this section, we should note that the realist-oriented mode of feminist engagement that drives Dusinberre's book was not only simultaneously evident in a number of key Shakespeare productions of the late 1970s but has proved equally enduring. Dusinberre herself cites the instances of *Troilus and Cressida*, 5.2, which now 'forces the audience to encounter its own horror at the passing from hand to hand of a young and defenceless woman' and of Gertrude as 'a woman pursuing her own desires in a world which denies her the right to do so' (2003: xlviii) as indicative of feminism's impact and influence, and as, implicitly, a way of putting its claims to the test of public legitimacy.

As its successive reissues attest, *Shakespeare and the Nature of Women* taps into an optimistic, liberal-feminist sensibility whose mainstream popularity is in marked contrast to its compatibility with many of the feminist criticisms that have come after (and, especially, to its capacity to serve as material for target practice for work that immediately followed it). In 1980, *The Woman's Part: Feminist Criticism of Shakespeare* appeared; edited by Carolyn Ruth Swift Lenz, Gayle Greene and Carol Thomas Neely, its seventeen essays attempted to 'liberate Shakespeare's women from the stereotypes to which they have been confined', to 'examine women's relations to each other', to 'analyze the nature and effect of patriarchal structures' and to 'explore the influence of genre on the portrayal of women'; as in Dusinberre's work, the contributors shared the conviction that 'like the male characters the women are complex and flawed, like them capable of passion and pain, growth and decay' (Lenz *et al.* 1980: 4–5). The idea that Shakespeare was a writer capable of intimate insight and generally in favour of positive female role modelling is reflected, for example, in Carole McKewin's piece on the private conversations between Shakespeare's women, which, it is suggested, 'provide opportunities for self-expression, adjustment to social codes, release, relief, rebellion and transformation', and which, in the 'sororal atmosphere of feminism', are well worth eavesdropping upon (1980: 129). Elsewhere, Shakespeare is seen as the originator of an essentialist vision of womanhood that seems to reaffirm general-isations about femininity rather than interrogate them: thus Paula S. Berggren writes that, for Shakespeare, 'only the women, sometimes witch, sometimes saint, sometimes mother, command the innate energy that renews and revives' (1980: 31); and the collection concludes with an essay on the late plays that muses lyrically, sentimentally and somewhat bafflingly upon Shakespeare's understanding of 'the spirit of the maiden phoenix that flut-ters up periodically in women, if not in men as well', and of 'the intricacies of that endless dance where daughters escape and follow, reject and recreate, their once and future fathers' (Frey 1980: 312).

Conceding 'a substantial debt to New Criticism' (Lenz *et al.* 1980: 10), the editors also point to the 'close alliance with psychoanalytic critics' (9) fostered by a number of con-tributors, notably Coppélia Kahn, whose *Man's Estate: Masculine Identity in Shakespeare*, which appeared the following year, announces that 'Shakespeare and Freud deal with the same subject: the expressed and hidden feelings in the human heart', and whilst Shake-speare had 'no formal theory of the unconscious' he nonetheless 'possessed extraordinary and sophisticated insight into it' (1981: 1). Surveying the entire range of the canon, and tracing the successive 'ages of man' from adolescence to fatherhood, Kahn explores both the mechanisms of male identity-formation in the works and the forces which seek to undermine them, emphasising the protagonists' simultaneous domination of and depen-dency upon the women who surround them: although Shakespeare 'accepts conventional arguments for patriarchy' he 'objects to the extreme polarization of sex roles', and his works 'reflect and voice a masculine anxiety about the uses of patriarchal power over women, specifically about men's control over women's sexuality' (12).

A later important psychoanalytic study, Janet Adelman's *Suffocating Mothers* (1992), presents a series of close readings of the mature and late comedies and the tragedies, pur-suing the theme of the relations between masculine identity-formation and the figure of the maternal body, wherein selfhood is 'grounded in paternal absence and in the fantasy of overwhelming contamination at the point of origin' (1992: 10). In Adelman's reading, Shakespeare's maternal body 'is always already sexual, corrupted by definition'; it also 'brings death into the world because her body itself is death: in the traditional alignment of spirit and matter, the mother gives us the stuff – the female matter – of our bodies and thus our mortality' (27).

From *Hamlet* onwards, Adelman argues, the plays' structure 'is marked by the struggle to escape from this condition, to free the masculine identity of both father and son from its origin in the contaminated maternal body' (1992: 17), while 'all sexual relationships will be tinged by the threat of the mother, all masculine identity problematically formed in rela-tionship to her' (35). The progress of Shakespeare's dramaturgy is thus accorded a strong developmental line, each play contributing towards a larger pattern of exploration unified by a powerful psychic master-narrative. The so-called problem plays

> focus on the dangerous return home to the maternal body through the representation of sexual union, as though explicating Hamlet's failed relationship with Ophelia: *Troilus* and *Othello* play out the deeply ambivalent desire for erotic return to that body and the recoil from desire: *All's Well* and *Measure* play out the extraordinary contortions and con-trivances through which the return might provisionally be made safe.
>
> (Adelman 1992: 36–37)

The later tragedies return to maternity's most negative incarnations: '*Lear* records the horrific discovery of the suffocating mother at the center of masculine authority and the terrible vengeance taken on her; *Macbeth* and *Coriolanus* record the attempt to create an autonomous masculinity in the face of this discovery' (Adelman 1992: 37). Whether the plays, and perhaps their author, are complicit with or critical of these fantasies is also an issue; but 'Despite Shakespeare's sometimes astonishing moments of sympathetic engagement with his female characters', they generally tend to be 'more significant as screens for male fantasy than as independent characters making their own claim to dramatic reality ... their sexual bodies will always be dangerous, the sign of the fall and original sin' (35–36).

The patriarchal Bard

Fully fledged feminist psychoanalytic readings of Shakespeare, as have psychoanalytic readings more generally, have fallen out of fashion since the 1990s, in part because the universalising tendencies of the method have been called into question, and also because Freud's own heteronormative and patriarchal inclinations have been increasingly called to account. As early as the mid-1980s, however, the limitations of Freud's prescriptions were already apparent, as indicated in different ways by the assessments of the state of the field offered by Lisa Jardine and Kathleen McLuskie. A work marked by its combative approach to contemporary feminist criticism, Jardine's *Still Harping on Daughters: Women and Drama in the Age of Shakespeare* (1983) sets out to counter what she regards as the parallel critical tendencies either to sentimentalise or to demonise Shakespeare's treatment of women; the former view is represented by Dusinberre, the latter by Kahn, who is charged with the belief that 'the tools of psychoanalysis applied to male/female relationships in the plays will lay bare a timeless conflict between male and female sexuality' (Jardine 1983: 6). Rejecting both approaches as both partisan and anachronistic, Jardine proffers an investigation of an archive of 'contexts in which male and female members of the Elizabethan audience brought to the theatre a set of expectations, attitudes and beliefs about significant femaleness (and significant maleness)' which, she avers, 'the reader is unlikely to have encountered before' (7).

To this end, Jardine places the dramatic explorations of clothing and costume that are found in *Shrew* and *The Roaring Girl* alongside Philip Stubbes's moralising reflections upon Elizabethan sumptuary codes and anti-women tracts such as *Hic Mulier*; the 1562 'Homily on matrimony' against the exploration of marital relations in *The Comedy of Errors*; and the anti-theatrical polemics of John Rainoldes and the homoerotic poems of Thomas Randolph in conjunction with the phenomenon of the cross-dressed boy player. Here, as throughout, Jardine determines to overturn the more optimistic and idealistic projections of feminist criticism (and, in this particular instance, performance), arguing that, far from the gamine, 'healthily asexual heroines in Royal Shakespeare Company productions' (1983: 29), this figure is of erotic interest for being *male*, the object of the fascinated gaze of the sodomite and the pederast. The emphasis is not upon the possibilities of identification, but upon historical difference, and Jardine repeatedly warns us against retrospectively interpreting as positives behaviour and character attributes which early modern audiences would have viewed in a very different light.

For Kathleen McLuskie, however, Jardine's 'summary dismissal of feminist criticism in favour of historical criticism' risks asserting a 'spurious notion of objectivity' that 'draws the criticism back into the institutionalised competition over "readings"' (McLuskie 1994: 107, 91–92). This point is made in McLuskie's much-cited contribution to Jonathan Dollimore and Alan Sinfield's collection *Political Shakespeare* (1985; second edition 1994), which provided a reckoning of feminist work in the field to date and attempted to differentiate between the competing and complementary claims of the responsibilities of historicism, contemporary ethical and political priorities, and the pleasures and sometimes painful challenges of the texts. Arguing that the task of feminist critical practice is to assert 'the specificity of a feminist response' (1994: 92), McLuskie examines *Measure for Measure* and *King Lear* as texts in which, respectively, sexuality and the family serve as the focus of feminist critique.

Recognising that 'the texts are often contradictory' and that 'the gap between textual meaning and social meaning can never be completely filled for meaning is constructed every time the text is reproduced in the changing ideological dynamic between text and audience', McLuskie nonetheless contends that *Measure for Measure*, a play in which each woman is 'defined theatrically by the men around her for the men in the audience' (1994: 96), is deeply problematic insofar as its narrative and representational strategies 'resist feminist manipulation by denying an autonomous position for the female viewer', and that to attempt to occupy that position would involve 'refusing the pleasures of the drama and the text, which imply a coherent maleness in the point of view' (95, 97). Feminist reading and spectating involve neither straightforward identification nor repudiation, but are a matter of struggle and the negotiation of contradictions – not least, the contradiction between critical principles and pleasure.

The problem is particularly acute in Shakespearean tragedy, where 'the human nature implied ... is most often explicitly male'; in the case of *King Lear*, McLuskie argues, the narrative's 'connection between sexual insubordination and anarchy' has an 'explicitly misogynist emphasis' (1994: 98). McLuskie proceeds to expose the misogyny of a play 'in which patriarchy, the institution of male power in the family and the State, is seen as the only form of social organisation strong enough to hold chaos at bay' (99), but, in an important move, acknowledges that 'any dispassionate analysis of the mystification of real socio-sexual relations in *King Lear* is the antithesis of our response to the tragedy in the theatre' (100). We might know what we ought to say about this play, McLuskie suggests, but to articulate the contradictions of what we feel about it may be more difficult; and the real challenge for feminists is to attempt to mediate the oppositions and convergences to which the differences produced in and by history give rise. As she memorably writes of the death of Cordelia, even 'the most stony-hearted feminist could not withhold her pity even though it is called forth at the expense of her resistance to the patriarchal relations which it endorses' (102). The solution to the dilemma lies in attending more fully not only to the plays' originating historical moment, as advocated by Jardine (who in subsequent works such as *Reading Shakespeare Historically* [1996] pursued an historicist path that confirmed the essentially critical relation of *Still Harping* to feminism), but also to 'the process of the text's reproduction', on the understanding that, despite its 'misogynist meaning', the text itself 'contains possibilities for subverting these meanings and the potential for reconstructing them in feminist terms' (103). In this sense, then, can feminist criticism – and performance – 'assert the power of resistance, subverting rather than co-opting the domination of the patriarchal Bard' (106).

Changing the subject

McLuskie's essay appeared at a propitious moment for feminist criticism in the Anglo-American academy: in addition to the works already mentioned, it belongs to a period that also includes Linda Woodbridge's *Women and the English Renaissance* (1984), Carol

Thomas Neely's *Broken Nuptials in Shakespeare's Plays* (1985), Peter Erickson's *Patriarchal Structures in Shakespeare's Drama* (1985), Margaret W. Ferguson, Maureen Quilligan and Nancy K. Vickers's *Rewriting the Renaissance* (1986) and a number of important essays (including, for example, Karen Newman's reading of femininity and monstrosity in *Othello*, Elaine Showalter's cultural history of Ophelia and Joel Fineman's feminist-post-structuralist reading of *The Taming of the Shrew*, all 1985; and Peter Stallybrass's influential investigation of the silence, chastity, enclosure and the grotesque female body [1986]). Catherine Belsey's *The Subject of Tragedy* (1985a; reprinted in 1991), which combines the project of feminism with that of cultural materialism, made a particular impact.

Belsey's 'subject', in a double sense, is early modern tragedy but also the figure that the drama predates and radically problematises, 'the liberal-humanist subject', man, whose 'essence is *freedom*' and who is imagined in post-Renaissance philosophy, political and legal discourse, and fiction and drama as the 'unconstrained author of meaning and action'; focussing on a critical juncture within literary and social history, Belsey aims to demonstrate how this ideological mirage 'was constructed in conflict and contradiction – with conflicting and contradictory consequences' (1985a: 8–9). The book is divided into what post-structuralists would immediately recognise as the most fundamental of cultural (not natural) binaries, with sections headed 'Man' and 'Woman'. The first part traces the far-from-smooth transition from the medieval drama, characterised by emblematic, non-realist conventions of personification in which 'the representative human being has no unifying essence', to the post-Restoration scenic theatre, which 'addressed a unified and unifying spectacle to a series of unified spectator-subjects who, as guardians of the liberties of the people of England, each possessed a degree of sovereignty in the new regime'; between these two periods stands an early modern stage that 'brought into conjunction and indeed collision the emblematic mode and an emergent illusionism' (18, 26).

Theatrical techniques and technologies are a means through which dramatic and spectatorial subjectivities are manufactured, and the clash between the residues of a theologically inflected medieval tradition, the staging practices of the Elizabethan playhouse, and an emergent realism, produces dramatis personae who, as Lacanian subjects, are divided and discontinuous, rendering it extremely difficult 'to read these plays simply as humanist texts, endorsing the unified human subject or affirming a continuous and inviolable interiority as the essence of each person' (Belsey 1985a: 40). But this, Belsey argues, is exactly what criticism operative within the liberal humanist paradigm, character criticism especially, attempts to do; nowhere more so than with regard to its exemplary text, *Hamlet*. Counter to this, Belsey posits a Prince of Denmark who is 'the most discontinuous of Shakespeare's heroes ... traversed by the voices of a succession of morality fragments, wrath and reason, patience and resolution' (41–42). The traditional search for Hamlet's true soul is no more than a work of critical mourning, a 'choric elegy for lost presence' (53).

Belsey cites Francis Barker's reading of the play, which, if anything, is even more hardcore in its Foucauldian anti-humanism: evoking the world of the play as 'one of relentless surfaces, without depth or mystery', in which 'there is little that remains ultimately opaque', he proposes that Hamlet's insistence upon his own unique claim to 'modern depth' is, literally, a hollow gesture: 'at the centre of Hamlet, in the interior of his mystery, there is, in short, nothing' (Barker 1984: 27–28, 35–36). For both Barker and Belsey, the point of evacuating Hamlet of his interiority is in part polemical: for the former, 'To construct the story of this past is to pay some of the price that continues to be exacted for what was done to us in the seventeenth century' (Barker 1984: 68) (Barker's sense of grievance is nothing if not long term), and for the latter, re-reading the play, amongst others, in this way 'is to offer a contribution to that rearrangement of our knowledge which signals the end of the reign of man' (Belsey 1985a: 33).

The boy actress

The last phrase works in two ways. Most immediately, it evokes Foucault's prophesy, at the close of *The Order of Things*, that post-structuralism would eventually ensure that the humanist icon, man, 'would be erased, like a face drawn in sand at the edge of sea' (1970: 14). It also signifies the specifically feminist inflection of this project that is developed at length in the second half of the book, 'Woman', which explores the implications of the 'inequality of freedom' between men and women, which in the sixteenth and seventeenth centuries meant that 'Woman was produced in contradistinction to man, and in terms of the relations of power in the family' (Belsey 1985a: 9). In general terms, although Belsey insists that the operation of patriarchal power during the period was by no means monolithic or uncontested, her readings of the various ways in which early modern tragedies, alongside other texts, enforced women to silence and subservience tend to emphasise the ruling order's strategies of containment, oppression and misogynist violence.

Belsey presents a more positive account of the possibilities of resistance in an influential essay published in the same year as *The Subject of Tragedy*, 'Disrupting Sexual Difference', a contribution to John Drakakis's collection *Alternative Shakespeares* (1985), which significantly shifts the focus from tragedy to comedy, and which explores a topic which had been of interest to feminist scholars from Dusinberre onwards: the practice of cross-dressing on Shakespeare's stage. Dusinberre considered her chapter on the boy actor 'the most original in the book', claimed that 'Disguise freed the dramatist to explore … the natures of women untrammelled by the customs of femininity' and, oddly, concluded that '[t]he apparently artificial stage convention of boys playing women leads to a portrait of the individual woman which courts naturalism' (2003: xlix, 271); Jardine, as we have noted, narrowed the scope of the convention's appeal to the homoerotic.

Belsey's concern, conversely, is with the plurality rather than the alleged singularity of the meanings to which the presence and spectacle of the transvestite boy (and, especially, the boy playing a woman playing a boy) might give rise. Starting from the post-structuralist premises that meaning is 'an effect of difference' and hence 'unfixed, always in process, always plural', and that 'subjectivity is not a single, unified presence but the point of intersection of a range of discourses', and, historically, from the proposition that 'The contest for the meaning of the family which took place in the sixteenth and seventeenth centuries disrupted sexual difference', Belsey draws our attention to a range of 'shapes, phantasms perhaps, that unsettle the opposition defining the feminine as that which is not masculine' (1985b: 166, 188, 178): the roaring girl, the Amazon, the boy player and the woman playing the man.

Considering the figures of Rosalind-as-Ganymede, Julia-as-Sebastian and Viola-as-Caesario as examples of such phantasmic subversives, Belsey argues that they speak 'from a position which is not that of a full, unified, gendered subject', provocatively posing, 'at certain critical moments', the 'unexpected question, "Who is speaking?"' (1985b: 180). The implications of this unsettling of meaning, Belsey argues, extend well beyond their significance for Shakespeare's plays and stage: what they call into question are the organising categories of sexual identity itself, positing in their stead 'a plurality of places, of possible beings, for each person in the margins of sexual difference, those margins which a metaphysical sexual polarity obliterates' (189).

The point is not to redeem Shakespearean comedy for post-structuralism and feminism by imputing to it (or to its author) a radicalism that transcends its moment and context, nor to overestimate the opportunities for female liberation during the period (Belsey concludes that 'It is not obvious from a feminist point of view that, in so far as they seem finally to re-affirm sexual polarity, Shakespeare's comedies have happy endings. It is certain from the same point of view that the contest for the meaning of the family in the sixteenth and seventeenth centuries did not' [1985b: 190]); it is rather to create a critical space in which the play of difference can generate resonances in the present. As for McLuskie, Shakespeare's texts are troublesome and contradictory: both documents of patriarchy and sources of subversive pleasure.

Belsey's essay performs the arguments between past and contemporary meanings that are directly engaged by McLuskie; and as a critical intervention conceived within the framework of British cultural materialism, its orientation as much (if not more) towards the present – and future – is a willed political tactic. And, as such, it serves as a point of departure for a consideration of the considerable body of literature on the topic of male, and female, cross-dressing that followed. Some critics, particularly from the 1980s through to the early 1990s, have echoed and extended Belsey's emphasis upon the transgressive potential of the practice; other have disputed it. For Jonathon Dollimore, the exciting, but also daunting, question is: 'Which, or how many, of the several gender identities embodied in any one figure are in play at any one time?' (1986: 65); surveying a series of plays deploying cross-dressed heroines, Phyllis Rackin positions Shakespeare's treatment of gender identity in the 'ambiguous middle ground' between Lyly's depiction of it as 'arbitrary, unreal, and reversible' and Jonson's as 'an ineluctable reality': at the end, Shakespeare 'marries his unlike lovers, joining male and female characters on his stage just as he joins masculine and feminine qualities in the androgynous figures of his boy heroines' (Rackin 1987: 31, 37).

Jean E. Howard has sought to place the discussion on an empirical footing by attempting to locate the issue within the wider context of non-theatrical cross-dressing during the period, returning to Stubbes's pronouncements in the *Anatomie of Abuses* and other polemics as well as mining contemporary court records for evidence of the treatment of women apprehended in men's clothing: she concludes that whilst there is evidence that transvestism generated considerable anxiety within 'a sex-gender system under pressure', and 'threatened a normative social order based upon strict principles of hierarchy and subordination, of which women's subordination to man was a chief instance', nonetheless 'the subversive or transgressive potential of this practice could be and was recuperated in a number of ways' (Howard 1988: 418). More significant than the absence of women onstage, Howard argues, was their actual and substantial presence in playhouse audiences; theatregoing, she concludes, placed women 'at the crossroads of change and cultural contradiction', thereby 'calling into question the "place" of women, perhaps more radically than did Shakespeare's fictions of crossdressing' (440).

McLuskie seeks to bring the debate back down to earth in a different way when she observes that 'the fictions of Elizabethan drama would have been rendered nonsensical if at every appearance of a female character – say Ursula the pig woman or the Duchess of Malfi – their gender was called into question'; even so, 'in the world of the commercial theatre the meaning of boys playing women had to be negotiated in every case' (McLuskie 1989: 102). Her view of the cross-dressing of Shakespeare's comic heroines is that, far from evoking androgyny, it was 'a means of asserting their true femininity' (104), a point also made by Woodbridge, who concludes that 'transvestite disguise in Shakespeare does not blur the distinction between the sexes but heightens it' (1984: 154).

Stephen Greenblatt offers a rather different perspective, drawing upon Renaissance theories of physiology (which understood female genitalia to be 'an inverted version of the male genitals' [1988: 80]) to claim that early modern culture's 'conception of gender as teleologically male ... finds its supreme literary expression in a transvestite theater' (88). He concludes:

> If a crucial step in male individuation is separation from the female, this separation is enacted inversely in the rites of cross-dressing; characters like Rosalind and Viola pass through the state of being men in order to become women. Shakespearean women are in this sense the representation of Shakespearean men, the projected mirror images of masculine self-differentiation.
>
> (Greenblatt 1988: 92)

In an essay published in 1989, Stephen Orgel argues that women were (anomalously, in the context of early modern European theatre) kept off the English professional stage because the prospect of female sexuality was far more disconcerting than male homoeroticism; he subsequently extended the arguments of this essay to book length in his *Impersonations*, which, amongst other provocations, suggests that 'Everyone in this culture was in some respects a woman' (Orgel 1996: 124). Like Jardine, Orgel identifies the pleasure that early modern spectators took in 'taking' boys for women as primarily homoerotic; but he also considers this homoeroticism to be culturally sanctioned rather than scandalous, and not necessarily misogynist.

Jardine takes a characteristically robust line in an essay which attempts to resolve the contradictory textual and historical evidence into 'a single, coherent version of the erotic possibilities contained under a kind of rubric of transvestism in the early modern period', rendered, via a consideration of the homologies between women, servants and boys within the household service economy, as 'a consistent positioning of dominant to dependent member of the early modern community' (Jardine 1992: 28). The essay is a contribution to the collection *Erotic Politics*; as outlined by editor Susan Zimmerman in an introduction which extensively cites Lacan and Freud alongside Althusser and Marx, the 'inescapable and distinctive erotic element' of transvestite acting positions it as a central component in the production of, as the collection's subtitle has it, 'Desire on the Renaissance Stage' (Zimmerman 1992: 6). Cross-dressing features substantially in seven of the anthology's ten essays; in Zimmerman's own contribution, notably, as the catalyst for 'the symbolic deconstruction of the symbolic androgyne and the concomitant release of repressed sexual energies'; thus, in its 'blurring of oppositional categories, the reaching back towards indeterminacy, it empowered its audience to explore, in some measure, the polymorphous disposition that underlies all sexuality' (47).

At this point, one begins to wonder whether there isn't a certain amount of erotic and political over-investment here, and more generally, in what is, after all, only an adolescent boy in a posh frock. As Michael Shapiro remarks in a judicious, even-handed and wide-ranging full-length study of the topic, it is 'our own fascination with sexual identity and gender roles' that has stimulated 'considerable attention to various forms of cross-dressing in other historical periods' (1994: 1); the forms that this fascination has taken indicate that the alterity of the boy player is almost as much the object of the desire of modern critics as it is that of early modern spectators. Perhaps one of the reasons why the boy actress has so seized the critical imagination is that he appears to offer a position where it seems possible for feminist criticism *not* to find itself restricted, as McLuskie and Rackin have it, to having to rehearse 'its own exclusion from the text'; occupying the liminal space between sexual differences, the boy also operates in the realms between inside and outside, text and performance, and the known and the conjectural.

Orgel is franker than most about what is at stake in all of this: prefacing *Impersonations* with an autobiographical reminiscence about his own experience of transvestite performance at school, he recalls how, towards the end of the 1940s, he suddenly found himself playing opposite girls for the first time; when he calls up his former teacher to ask why this happened, he is told that it was because of the worry that cross-dressing was 'turning the boys into pansies'. This was, Orgel admits, the answer that he 'had been waiting to hear', and though deciding 'not to reveal to my old teacher that his fears had been realized in me', he identifies this as the moment that 'writing this book became irresistible' (1996: xiv). 'Nobody's Perfect', the main title of Orgel's 1989 paper, is of course the sublime final line of Billy Wilder's classic 1959 transvestite film comedy *Some Like It Hot*, uttered by an infatuated male admirer in response to the revelation by 'Daphne' (Jack Lemmon in drag) that 'I'm a man'; Orgel emphasises that cross-dressing continues to fascinate not as a contested and very live issue but as a source of pleasure and, sometimes, outrage.

By the end of the 1990s, the subject of the boy player seemed to have run its course, in part because the discussion seemed in danger of becoming increasingly circular and repetitive, but also because the more utopian aspects of the preoccupation with diversity and polymorphous sexuality seemed a little overstated when considered in the context of the increasingly close consideration of the interrelations between gender and sexuality and the construction of race (symptomatically, Dympna Callaghan's *A Feminist Companion to Shakespeare* [2000b] contains only six indexical entries for 'cross-dressing', as compared to fifteen for 'colonialism' and thirty-four for 'race'). Ironically, it was at the very point that transvestism appeared to slip out of academic fashion that it acquired a fresh lease of life on the catwalk of popular performance and media culture. The Shakespearean film comedy hit of the decade, *Shakespeare in Love* (1996), wittily traded upon the erotics of a gender reversal; in 1995 the National Theatre courted critical controversy by casting Fiona Shaw in the title role in Deborah Warner's production of *Richard II* (see Rutter 1997); and in 1997 the reconstructed Shakespeare's Globe opened on Bankside, operating according to a loosely historicist mandate that, claiming cross-casting as an authentic 'original practice', has accommodated a succession of cross-dressed and cross-cast productions, both all-male (notably *Antony and Cleopatra*, 1999, and *Twelfth Night*, 2002) and all-female (*Richard III* and *Shrew*, 2003, *Much Ado*, 2004).

James C. Bulman concludes an upbeat assessment of the Globe's all-male productions with the suggestion that they have 'allowed us to turn our gaze on our own spectatorship and find there a willingness to entertain culturally transgressive notions of gender and sexuality that, rightly or wrongly, scholars have presumed to find among spectators 400 years ago' (2005: 585), but, reflecting on the 2003 *Shrew*, G. B. Shand is less sanguine, finding merely a 'benign, genial, ultimately toothless' form of cross-gender impersonation that begs the question: '[w]hen the dominant culture goes away unconcernedly amused, has battle even been joined?' (2005: 559–60). The transvestites that have graced the contemporary Globe stage may be rather more prosaic figures than the fabulous androgynes of critical fantasy, but, contrary to the claims of some its proponents, the Globe cannot answer the most intractable questions about the kinds of performance experiences that were engaged in its historical antecedent, and the nature of the boy player, and the early modern spectator's interest in him, is likely to remain as enigmatic as ever.

Broadening the field

One of the characteristics, and indeed guiding political principles, of feminist criticism from its outset has been its pluralism; in a methodological, disciplinary and political sense, but also with regard to the objects of its enquiry. The project of feminist Shakespearean criticism was initially defined by the related tasks of anatomising misogyny, and its alternatives, in the texts (and histories) of the early modern period and in their subsequent reproductions, and of fashioning spaces in which female critics, readers and spectators might be able to formulate productive responses to these. As it developed, however, feminist criticism widened the scope of its investigations to take into consideration not only the copious textual and historical evidence of misogyny and women's oppression, but also such opportunities as existed for transgression and resistance; at the same time, it broadened its primary focus on instances of where the representation of women, femininity and female sexuality are directly at issue to take account of works (and genres) where actual women appear to play a marginal role. Surveying the state of the critical field in 1988, Ann Thompson expressed regret that feminist criticism to date had tended to observe traditional canonical hierarchies, and to neglect 'the earliest plays (apart from the inevitable promotion of *The Taming of the Shrew*) and the history plays' (1988: 85). Jean E. Howard and Phyllis Rackin's *Engendering a Nation* (subtitled *A Feminist Account of Shakespeare's Histories*) answered this challenge, in an investigation of the 'interconnections between Englishness, aggressive masculinity, and closeted womanhood' (1997: 10).

Howard and Rackin's volume was one of the first in a series of 'Feminist Readings of Shakespeare' edited by Thompson, which, she stressed, sought to 'demonstrate the full range of possibilities offered by feminist criticism and to challenge the standard over-simplifications voiced by hostile critics'; its key questions would be: 'How does Shakespeare construct masculinity and femininity' and 'How has theatrical and critical tradition represented and re-read these texts in relation to the issue of gender difference?' (Howard and Rackin 1997: xv). Two further volumes indicated a similar concern with extending the boundaries of feminist enquiry. In *Roman Shakespeare*, Coppélia Kahn proceeds from the recognition that 'the degree to which ... Romanness is virtually identical with an ideology of masculinity has gone unnoticed, and it has been generally assumed that Shakespeare didn't notice it either', to argue that, 'on the contrary, he dramatized precisely this linkage and, in doing so, demystified its power' (1997: 2). Philippa Berry's concerns in *Shakespeare's Feminine Endings* are those of a feminist epistemology and ontology, addressed through the major tragedies, whose 'exploration of death through a series of feminine, or what might best be described as *feminized* figures (since they invariably problematize the boundaries of both gender and desire)' exploits 'contemporary uncertainty as to death's meaning what was felt by many at this liminal moment of religious and intellectual crisis' (Berry 1997: 7). The aim is to demonstrate 'how the tragedies' oblique reordering of human knowing implies an amplification and differing, not only of conventional Christian views of death, but also of the emergent "modern" model of knowledge and identity' (9).

As one of the array of disciplinary positions, theoretical perspectives and methodologies that contributed to the formation of new historicism and cultural materialism, feminism has from the outset engaged in an active but also critical dialogue with other modes of historical enquiry: in an essay published in 1986, Jean E. Howard interrogated new historicist claims to be above partisanship, emphasising the overtly situated and committed status of feminist critical practice, and urging that 'there is no transcendent space from which one can perceive the past "objectively"' (1986: 22) (not that Greenblatt, or others, ever said that there was). One of the first major outputs of the increasing rapprochement between new historicism and what was increasingly coming to be termed gender (rather than feminist) criticism is Valerie Wayne's collection *The Matter of Difference* (1991). Acknowledging that, to date (and especially in the United States), it had been 'psycho-analytic feminism associated with Freud' that had commanded the largest share of critical attention, Wayne calls for a 'materialist feminism' that 'offers a potentially radical alternative to the depoliticising tendencies of some new historicist practice and to the idealised or essentialised effects of some feminist criticism' (1991: 11).

With theoretical roots in the Althusserian reframing of Marxism, particularly with regard to its understanding of ideology, materialist feminism is interpreted in this collection in terms of a focus not 'on gender or on the ideological' but on 'money and women's work, rape in English law and drama, prosecutions for sexual crimes and slander, on the circulation of homoerotic desire, the disarticulation between oppressions of class and gender, changes brought about by the material conventions of theatre attendance, and rhetorical practices in this profession' (Wayne 1991: 12). In an afterword which considers the future of feminist criticism, Catherine Belsey confirms this concern with 'experience as the location of cultural meanings' and with 'meaning as material practice' (260), but also introduces another element: as a 'product of its own present', materialist feminism needs to be seen as the 'ally' of postmodernism, in that they 'share a scepticism which is both epistemological and political' and their common commitment to plurality 'discredits supremacism on the part of any single group'; postmodernism, like feminism, 'celebrates difference of all kinds, but divorces difference from power' (261–62).

The anthology *Shakespeare and Gender* (1995), edited by Deborah E. Barker and Ivo Kamps, offers an overview of the field in the shape of reprints of key essays dating from the mid-1970s through to the early 1990s and an assessment of the then current state of play, concluding that despite the 'rapidly increasing volume, scope, and vehemence of antagonistic approaches to gender scholarship' it had now 'left the critical margins and justly taken a position at the very centre of academic discourse' (Barker and Kamps 1995: 17). In a sense, the centrality of gender scholarship is indicated less by the continued production of critical work self-identified as feminist than by the incorporation of its paradigms and methodologies into virtually every aspect of academic practice. Gender studies has been particularly important to the development of critical work addressing Shakespeare's histories of popular cultural reproduction, in performance and on screen.

Feminist critics, and critics sympathetic to and influenced by feminism, have regarded the consideration of gender identity and sexuality as instrumental to a more thorough and far-reaching transformation of our understanding of history and culture. 'Because it commands a view from the margins', Dympna Callaghan writes in her *Feminist Companion*, feminist scholarship 'is especially well placed to access the eccentric categories of Renaissance knowledge – those aspects of thought in the period ranging from female circumcision to early modern ideas about the blood – that sit uneasily with our own but are nonetheless central to the period's core concerns – in this instance, religion and national identity' (2000b: xv). In the anthology of essays which this remark introduces, this marginal perspective affords feminist readings of, for example, *The Tempest* in relation to early modern ideas about cliteridectomy (Sachdev 2000) and *Romeo and Juliet* to the temporality of Roman Catholic ritual (Berry 2000); the collection as a whole evinces a particular interest in the interplay between constructions of gender and sexuality, and those of race and ethnicity, in the context of early modern colonialism.

In that racial depictions are implicated in the related work of the production of marginality, otherness and subordination, this is an area which has proved particularly amenable to feminist analysis. As Callaghan argues in *Shakespeare without Women*, racial and gender (and class) representations are not simply parallel or complementary; they are interdependent, though not homologous; 'One has only to think of Cleopatra, who serves simultaneously as a symbol of woman, of female sovereignty, or racial difference, and of subjected nationhood, in order to recognize that race is not an ancillary representational category' (Callaghan 2000a: 7). For Callaghan, the fact of woman's absence from the early modern stage provides a point of departure for an investigation of how its means of representing gendered and racial 'others' are founded upon systematic exclusion: in 'all the long critical history of Othello and of whether or not he is a veritable Negro or just off-white, there has been very little attention paid to the bald fact that both black Othello and Desdemona were played by white males' (24).

What becomes a man

Callaghan's study proceeds from the recognition that male subjectivity and masculinity are to be treated not as givens but as categories as constructed as any of the others under consideration, but, as Bruce R. Smith notes in his *Shakespeare and Masculinity*, 'Only recently has masculinity been subjected to the same critical scrutiny as femininity' (2000: 2). Defining Shakespearean masculinity as always 'a matter of contingency, of circumstances, of performance' (4), Smith considers early modern men from a series of vantage points: as 'persons' ('gender is a performance ... carried out by what Shakespeare and his contemporaries understood as "persons"'; social role-play 'attest[s] that masculinity is also a function of persons as *agents*' [37]); and in terms of 'ideals' of maleness (the 'models of action and eloquence that a man might want to imitate' [41]), 'passages' ('man's existence as a series of life-*stages*, in every sense of the word' [69]) and 'others' (the '[w]omen, foreigners, social inferiors, sodomites' who 'help to define masculinity' [126]).

Smith provides a compact account of a topic that has attracted increasing interest in the last decade, as represented by works such as Robin Headlam Wells's *Shakespeare on Masculinity* (2000) and Tom MacFaul's *Male Friendship in Shakespeare and His Contemporaries* (2007). Wells identifies a gap in gender criticism by pointing out that 'masculine honour was a political issue throughout the period when Shakespeare was writing his tragedies and tragic-comedies' (2000: 5), offering a study of the heroic ideal in the major tragedies, evaluating 'Shakespeare's heroes: their folly and their greatness, their cruelty and their tenderness, their destructiveness and their charm', whilst wryly registering their contradictions: '"He was great of heart", says Cassio of the man who, in the name of honour, has just murdered his wife; "He has my dying voice", says Hamlet of the Viking marauder who has no inhibitions about finding quarrel in a straw when honour is at the stake. Both speak for the masculine principle of honour in a society under threat from barbaric forces' (206).

MacFaul positions his investigation as at odds with what has become a strong critical emphasis since the early 1990s, by downplaying the homoerotic component of early modern male relationships. In this respect, his study takes issue with a body of work which, influenced by the thinking of Foucault and the research of gay historians such as Alan Bray, sought to uncover the dynamics of same-sex desire – with particular attention to men – in the works of Shakespeare and his contemporaries, whilst reiterating Foucault's contention that the modern category of the 'homosexual', as an *identity*, is, as Bray puts it, 'an anachronism and ruinously misleading' when applied to early modern subjects (1982: 16).

Bruce R. Smith's magisterial study *Homosexual Desire in Shakespeare's England* (1991), which proceeds from the recognition that, in the early modern period, 'sexuality was not, as it is for us, the starting place for anyone's self-definition' (10–11), develops a 'cultural poetics' of its subject that acutely registers the complexities and contradictions of a cultural system that on the one hand 'could consume popular prints of Apollo embracing Hyacinth' and on the other 'order hanging for men who acted on the very feelings that inspire that embrace' (14). As Smith points out, sodomy, the word most immediately deployed to define and categorise same-sex acts, genital activity and desires, is within early modern English culture a flexible and wide-ranging term, equally applicable to immoral or 'unnatural' (that is, non-reproductive) heterosexual acts, and understood to be on a par with similarly deviant or transgressive behaviours and practices such as witchcraft, treason and murder. Lacking a conception of the homosexual as a distinct sexual identity, Renaissance culture considered homosexual acts as temptations to which all men were liable, generating what Smith describes as the 'startling ambiguity' of 'the disparity that separates the extreme punishments prescribed by law and the apparent tolerance, even positive valuation, of homoerotic desire in the visual arts, in literature, and ... in the political power structure' (13–14).

Attending to what he calls the 'scripts of sexual desire', Smith argues that 'Moral, legal, and medical discourse are concerned with sexual *acts*; only poetic discourse can address homosexual *desire*' (1991: 16–17), and it is this focussing of interest that differentiates cultural poetics from social history. Thus the concern is with 'the "imaginative vocabulary" that sixteenth- and seventeenth-century writers possessed for talking about homosexual desire – the repertory of character types, plot motifs, images, and themes that offered ways of conceptualizing homosexual experience and playing it out in the imagination' (19); drawing extensively upon the heritage of classical literature and mythology, these writers tended to return to the key tropes and narrative structures that provide the organisation of Smith's analysis: combatants and comrades, the passionate shepherd, the shipwrecked youth, knights in shifts, master and minion, and the secret sharer. For Smith, the body of work produced in this period is also characterised by a progression from the 'licit to illicit, from socially inclusive to socially elite, from public to private' (24), as marked by the differences between the public pronouncements of Marlowe's stage figures and the coded utterances of the personae of Shakespeare's sonnets. If Marlowe 'introduces us to the possibility of a homosexual subjectivity' (223), the sonnets 'address the connection between male bonding and male homosexuality with a candor that most readers, most male readers at least, have not been willing to countenance' (270).

Queer reading

Smith's reading is presented to a certain extent against the grain of a critical tradition that had preferred to keep even the sonnets as straight as it can manage (though Norman Holland had claimed on behalf of psychoanalysis a quarter of a century previously that 'Probably no other psychoanalytic angle on Shakespeare has provoked such an angry response from professional Shakespeareans as the notion that the *Sonnets* are homosexual' [1964: 85]); and he is candid about the 'political purpose' of the work: it is 'an attempt to consolidate gay identity in the last decade of the twentieth century, to help men whose sexual desire is turned toward other men realize that they have not only a present community but a past history' (Smith 1991: 27). These are also, broadly, the terms of reference of Jonathan Goldberg's more polemical *Sodometries*, published the following year, whose subtitle announces a conjunction of 'Renaissance texts' and 'modern sexualities', and whose opening pages commence not in the early modern period but with reflections upon contemporary American racism and homophobia in the context of the lead-up to the (first) Gulf War, and of the 1986 United States Supreme Court ruling (in the case of *Bowers v. Hardwick*) that the Constitution 'recognizes no fundamental right of privacy for consensual acts of what the court termed homosexual sodomy' (1991: 6).

For Goldberg, who states that 'In all that I've written, I hope that the pressure of the Supreme Court decision ... can be felt' (1991: 25), sodomy is – then and now – an 'utterly confused category' (1–26) that 'named sexual acts only in particularly stigmatizing contexts' (19); his is a search for 'the sites of sexual possibilities, the syntax of desires not readily named', in order to understand 'how relations between men (or between women or between men and women) in the period provide the sites upon which later sexual orders and later sexual identities could batten' (22). The material for this investigation includes the sixteenth-century culture of high literariness, as fashioned by Edmund Spenser and Mary Sidney Herbert, the Countess of Pembroke, transvestism and inversion in the works of Marlowe, and the desirability of Prince Hal.

The ruling of the Supreme Court in *Bowers v. Hardwick* appears again in Goldberg's edited collection *Queering the Renaissance*, in a contribution by Janet E. Halley: described as a 'historiography of sodomy' in which 'sodomy is always and everywhere the same, always and everywhere opprobriated, always and everywhere joined in a purportedly stable equation with homosexual identity', it offers an 'important contemporary context' for the collection as a whole (Halley 1994: 15). An interdisciplinary collection addressed to the non-canonical as well as the canonical, *Queering the Renaissance* touches upon Shakespeare relatively infrequently, but notably so in Goldberg's own contribution on *Romeo and Juliet*, which, via an examination of the anal eroticism that circulates around Rosaline/Mercutio's 'open arse' (2.1.38) here yields the suggestion that 'the sexual field in which desire operates in the play is the forbidden desire named sodomy' (Goldberg 1994: 228).

Goldberg's queering of a text he describes as 'fundamental for the heterosexual imaginary' (1994: 2) is consciously and conspicuously interventionist, and as such it signals the politics as well as the methodology of queer reading, which, as Sinfield describes it, extends the scope of its 'purposefully dissident' scrutiny from instances where 'explicit same-gender awareness' (2006: 20, 29) is highly visible to the places where heteronormative tradition would least expect to find it. Sinfield provides examples of this: in an essay which demonstrates 'How to Read *The Merchant of Venice* Without Being Heterosexist', he argues that this play reveals 'same-gender passion' as 'compatible with marriage' (67); imagining a production of *Twelfth Night* which ended with Olivia, Sebastian and Antonio as a *ménage à trois*, Sinfield suggests that rather than ending up as a 'defeated and melancholy outsider', Antonio might thus be 'delighted with his boyfriend's lucky break' (66). Conversely, contrasting the 'intensity of same-gender bonding' (76) that he finds in *The Two Noble Kinsmen* with the compulsory heterosexuality promoted in *A Midsummer Night's Dream*, Sinfield speculates that 'To get what I regard as a happy ending I would show the boys and girls successfully resisting the effects of Oberon's drugs, and producing some more interesting interpersonal combinations', whilst conceding that 'the more effective move would be to disclose the tragedy in the conventional ending': which could consist of presenting the lovers as 'manifestly brainwashed and infantilized by Puck's manipulations of their minds and bodies into cross-gender pairings' (82).

Overall, Shakespeare's texts may be conservative in their sexual politics, but they may nonetheless 'speak with distinct force to gay men and lesbians, simply because he didn't have to sort out sexuality in modern terms' (Sinfield 2006: 67). Sinfield's work is, at the time of writing, only the latest instance of a critical literature that includes not only the work already cited but also, notably, that of Dollimore and Mario DiGangi. Dollimore's *Sexual Dissidence*, which ranges widely from the medieval to the contemporary, focuses on the notion of transgression that is 'performed in the name of inversion, perversion, and rein-scription' (1991: 285) whilst interrogating the Foucauldian consensus that in the early modern period 'sexual deviance was conceptualized only as a form of behaviour' (239). In *The Homoerotics of Early Modern Drama*, DiGangi qualified the sodometrical model out-lined by Goldberg by arguing for 'the pervasiveness of nonsodomitical or nonsubversive relations in early modern England' (1997: 9). Homoeroticism is posed as an alternative to sodomy, and the drama demonstrates the thesis that 'No more intrinsically orderly or dis-orderly than heteroerotic relations, homoerotic relations could sustain one ideology (the master–servant hierarchy) while challenging another (companionate marriage)' (18–19).

Queer reading does not confine itself to the content of the early modern text and to the dynamics of performance, but also, as demonstrated by Jeffrey Masten in his study of authorial collaboration, *Textual Intercourse*, extends to the mechanisms of its composition and production. Masten charts 'the correspondences between, on the one hand, models and rhetorics of sexual relations, intercourse, and reproduction and, on the other, notions of textual production and property' (1997: 4), and, through an examination of a range of authorial relationships and practices that includes works by Shakespeare, Shakespeare and Fletcher, and Beaumont and Fletcher, traces a shift from a collaborative and the homoerotic model of authorship to a patriarchal, quasi-absolutist and solitary one.

Queer sexualities, and others, in performance are the subject of Stanley Wells's *Looking for Sex in Shakespeare*, which surveys 'homosexual interpretations on page and stage', and which also tracks the history of changing attitudes to the sonnets, noting that whilst per-vious generations of critics 'tended homophobically to resist' the idea that the sequence might be homoerotic, 'recent readers may have swung too far in the opposite direction in their efforts to present a liberated Shakespeare' (2004: 8–9). Wells concludes that 'As human beings develop their ideas about human sexuality', the plays 'go on yielding new depths of meaning, demonstrating relationships which hold the mirror up to more and more aspects of humanity' (96); however, attractive as it may be to imagine that Shake-speare's work is sufficiently inclusive to be able to address the full spectrum of human sexual activities and desires, it appears that there are some varieties of eroticism beyond even its imaginative compass.

DiGangi claims that his 'reading of less familiar city comedies and tragicomedies has turned up unexpected instances of female homoeroticism' (1997: 27), but for Smith, if in the early modern period 'female sexuality in general has only a peripheral place', then 'lesbianism seems almost beyond notice' (1991: 28), and this view has been echoed, as well as modified, by a number of writers, among them Valerie Traub, whose contribution to Goldberg's *Queering the Renaissance* highlights the difficulties inherent in the issue by defining her topic as 'The (In) Significance of "Lesbian" Desire in Early Modern England'; as she puts it, '"lesbian desire" is a deliberate come-on … enticing as it may sound, it doesn't exist' (1994: 62); or not, at any rate, in the form that modern readers might immediately recognise. Female homoeroticism is discernible, for example, in *As You Like It*, *Twelfth Night* and *A Midsummer Night's Dream*, but the plays' ultimate project is to negate it, render it insignificant: 'an originary, prior homoerotic desire is crossed, abandoned, betrayed; correlatively, a heterosexual desire is produced and inserted into the narrative in order to create a formal, "natural" mechanism of closure' (73).

Also considering the subject of female eroticism in early modern drama, Theodora A. Jankowski (who elsewhere ingeniously argues for early modern virginity to be designated a queer sexuality [Jankowski 2000a]) similarly cautions against the anachronistic use of the modern terminology of lesbianism, positing in its place a 'lesbian void', figured in terms of 'two different "spaces", each a kind of "female realm", where erotic relationships between women could occur: within the newly created private spaces of the early modern aristocratic home and within the mistress–servant relationship' (Jankowski 2000b: 301). Hypothetically positioned within these spaces, it becomes possible to disclose the hitherto hidden homo-eroticism of the relationships of Hermione and Paulina, Portia and Nerissa, and Hero and Margaret. The larger aim is 'to try to "see" the previously invisible, to consider where "lesbians" have been hidden and how we might draw them out of the – consciously or unconsciously constructed – early modern "closet" into which they have been relegated' (314–15).

The sexual politics of this mode of reading are plain enough, but both as a mode of historical recovery and as a method of retrieving marginalised experience or aspects of character it is not only riskily, if necessarily, highly speculative, but speculative in a fashion that implies a rather unexpected reversion to one of Bradley's most criticised habits: to attempt to fix the whereabouts of Hermione and Paulina during the interval between the Queen's exit and her final reappearance is to recall his narrative elaborations of events prior to the beginning of *Hamlet*, of the location of Hamlet at the time of his father's death, of when and where the murder of Duncan was first plotted, and even of the significance of Macduff's 'He has no children' (*Macbeth*, 4.3.249).

Characters reunited

If what we are witnessing here is a return to the original scene of character criticism, perhaps we should not find it that surprising; still less should we regard it as illegitimate: another way of framing this interpretative practice is to call upon Michael Bristol's propo-sition that, despite the determined efforts of the New Criticism, cultural materialism and post-structuralism to eradicate character from literary-critical discourse, it continues to command fascination because it enables readers and spectators to 'reflect about ethical choices and ethical consequences' on the basis of observation of 'motives, intentions, atti-tudes' as well as actions (Bristol 2000: 95). Of course, the post-structuralist, Foucauldian and Lacanian version of the early modern subject hardly went unchallenged: by critics intent on reinstating a commonsense conception of character that was no less ideological than those employed by criticism they denigrated as politically motivated (Vickers 1993; Bradshaw 1993; Bloom 1999; Lee 2002), but also by scholars seeking to develop a historically situated model of Renaissance selves that allowed scope for forms of interiority and self-consciousness that are not anachronistically conflated with modern or postmodern definitions of subjectivity.

Katherine Eisaman Maus proposed an alternative emphasis upon a 'rhetoric of inward-ness' in place of post-structuralism's concern with subjectivity, contending that 'Hamlet's boast of "that within" ... deals eloquently but almost truistically in matters that would have been commonplace for his original audience' (Maus 1995: 3); while Elizabeth Hanson has found in Hamlet's gestures towards interiority traces of an individuated form of dissidence: 'when Hamlet rails that Guildenstern ... "would pluck the heart out of my mystery" ... he assumes a position, as the resistant object of another man's scrutiny, within a scenario that recurs insistently in the discourses of Renaissance England'. Connecting this moment to the theatrical regime of the seventeenth-century scaffold, she observes that the imagery 'links his situation both to the actual culmination of many discovering operations of the Eliza- bethan state, the extraction and display of the traitor's heart at execution, and to moments of resistance to such operations' (Hanson 1998: 1). *Hamlet* is also the subject of the first of two works published in 1992 which aim to rehabilitate the unfashionable term: Bert O. States's *Hamlet and the Concept of Character*, which deploys early modern humoral theory to develop an account of character, 'the qualitative and intentional face of human action' (States 1992: 143), dynamically poised between agency and determinism, which in Hamlet's case takes the form of 'the tension and conflict of the sanguine and melancholy principles' (82). In *Reading Shakespeare's Characters*, Christy Desmet accepts the force of the post- structuralist account of the construction of subjectivity in discourse, whilst advocating and practising a contemporary form of ethically oriented character criticism whose antecedents predate even Bradley.

Since the 1990s, the high tide of theory, which Foucault hoped would eventually wash away the image of man, has ebbed, and the critical terminology of character has recovered some of the legitimacy it was believed by some to have surrendered forever, a shift that is evidenced in the collection *Shakespeare and Character*, edited by Paul Yachnin and Jessica Slights, whose keynote essay, by Michael Bristol, polemically confronts current theoretical wisdom:

> Whenever I teach a Shakespeare play, or discuss one with a friend, or attend a perfor-
> mance, I find myself relating to the characters just as I do with real people. We don't
> need any specialized historical knowledge to understand Constance or Shylock or Lady
> Macduff if we are really alive to our own feelings and capable of empathy with other
> people – the real ones, I mean. Our response to these dramatic moments is under-
> written by the shared complexity of our human nature. Engagement with a character has
> a moral dimension; it corresponds to the imperative of respect for our human vulner-
> ability to loss and grief. We learn about our own complex human nature by thinking
> about and coming to respect Shakespeare's characters.
>
> (Bristol 2008: 21, 38)

As Simon Palfrey puts it in his *Doing Shakespeare*, although post-structuralism was right to critique the tendency to 'project our own presupposed idea of selfhood – our intuitive trust in a self-present "I" – onto dramatic personae', it had perhaps fallen prey to 'the alternative danger', which was to 'deflect the emotional power of these plays' and to 'ignore the fun- damental centring of political and ethical effect in the experience – in *our* experience – of characters' (Palfrey 2005: 174). Palfrey's definition nimbly summarises the current terms of discussion of character: Shakespeare character is 'always in process, being formed out of all sorts of textual and theatrical effects', constructed out of 'both the society and relationships represented in the play; and the techniques and structures and playwright and playhouse', whose 'inwardness is invariably inferred from external phenomena' and whose experience is 'represented through shared or conflated bodies'; the total effect of which is 'to raise questions about the limits of self-responsibility or the security of self-identity' (190).

Children too

Gender criticism's interest, from the outset, in the developmental dynamics, politics and erotics of the family has rendered it particularly well placed to investigate what has until relatively recently been regarded as a marginal category of experience, and subject of representation, within early modern culture: childhood. Seeking to 'historicize and thus denaturalize family values', Belsey's *Shakespeare and the Loss of Eden* sets out 'to trace representations of the emergence of the loving family in three linked fields: Shakespeare's plays, English visual culture of the sixteenth and seventeenth centuries, and interpretations of the Book of Genesis in the period'; between them, these texts and images tell a 'story of the nuclear family' that is 'both idealistic and sceptical' (Belsey 1999: xiv–xv). The story is told through *Love's Labour's Lost*, *As You Like It*, *Hamlet* and, in particular, 'Shakespeare's only full-length dramatization of relationships within the loving family', *The Winter's Tale*, a play in which 'affection unaccountably gives way to murderous violence' (24). Reading the play's figuration of parent–child relationships against the iconographies of seventeenth-century funerary monuments, Belsey discerns in them the emergence of the 'newly affective family' (98) but also the anxious perception that this entity is 'extraordinarily fragile, and the fragility is related to the high expectations that the ideal elicits' (100). In *The Winter's Tale*, this tension is reflected in the fact that 'the murderous passion of Leontes springs from within the loving family itself, wells up at a moment of supreme harmony between the couple and shared courtesy towards their guest, at a time when the meaning of the family as parenthood is most clearly evident in Hermione's pregnancy' (102); its tragic consequence is that 'the most helpless victims of parental love-turned-to-hate are the children … Mamillius, allowed to charm the audience at the beginning of the play, is not restored to life at the end' (127).

Belsey is among the contributors to one of the two books dedicated to the subject of children published in 2007. The first of these, *Shakespeare and Childhood* (edited by Chedgzoy, Greenhalgh and Shaughnessy), addresses 'the agency of Shakespeare's children, and of the children who have continued to engage Shakespeare in performance, in reading and conversation, and through the arts of the imagination' (Chedgzoy *et al.* 2007: 10), whilst also recognising 'the fundamental difficulty of making sense both of children as subjects, and of childhood as a cultural concept and social formation' (17). The collection is divided into two sections. The first part assembles essays dealing with representations of children and childhood in the early modern period, locating the works of Shakespeare and his contemporaries in the context of, for example, gender difference in father–child relationships, discourses of dynastic continuity and royal authority, mourning and sonnet-writing, education and the professional activities of the boys' companies (a topic covered at greater length by this essay's author, Lucy Munro, in *Children of the Queen's Revels* [2005]). The second part charts the post-seventeenth-century history of 'how concepts of childhood, as well as of Shakespeare, are intrinsically bound up with questions of ideology, especially with issues of class, and economic and cultural privilege', as well as how that history 'reveals the democratization of both these cultural formations over time' (Chedgzoy *et al.* 2007: 118), and includes examinations of adaptations of Shakespeare for children, the role of Victorian children's periodicals, theatrical memoirs, children's fictions featuring Shakespeare, *A Midsummer Night's Dream* on film and Shakespearean references in popular teen culture; the volume concludes with a comprehensive annotated checklist of children in Shakespeare's plays.

Carol Chillington Rutter's *Shakespeare and Child's Play* is likewise concerned with the dialogue between the early modern origins and contexts of children in Shakespeare and their contemporary reincarnations, with a particular emphasis upon stage and screen performance, and with an eye upon their articulations of gender, sexuality, race and class. Taking issue with the critical preconception that children are 'trivial' in Shakespeare's writing, Rutter positions them as 'central, constitutive of adult projects'; at once 'the embodiment of the future the adult plans but knows that he will not live to see and the nostalgic recollection of the adults' innocent past'; they are 'stubbornly material, getting in the adult's way. But they are also ghosts, hauntings' (Rutter 2007: xiv). Declaring that she is 'looking at boys', Rutter evokes 'children remembered, storied, imagined, fantasised', all of them 'telling stories that reframe the stories that we tell about ourselves' (xii). The key plays are *Titus Andronicus*, *The Winter's Tale* and *Macbeth*; the material under scrutiny includes Penny Woolcock's *Macbeth on the Estate* and Julie Taymor's *Titus*, and productions by the Royal Shakespeare Company, the National Theatre, Kneehigh and others; throughout, the concern is to determine how 'we (actors, directors, designers, film-makers, spectators, cultural makers and consumers) position the child to perform cultural work, to play out preoccupations, anxieties, fears, aspirations, dreams and desires' (xvi). In this sense Rutter's study (like the contributions to *Shakespeare and Childhood*) is the progeny of the critical practices that have been the subject of this chapter; but towards the end of her final section, she also offers a fresh perspective upon the tensions between critical and performance practice that were highlighted at its start, illustrated in that instance by Imogen Stubbs's entirely representative desire to deepen and enrich her characterisation of Gertrude by attributing to her a complexity and autonomy that the text explicitly denies.

In a reading of *Macbeth* on the English stage and screen during the 1980s and 1990s, Rutter revisits L. C. Knights's denunciation of both the character criticism that allegedly descended from A. C. Bradley and the actor's need to substantiate character through the elaboration of back stories (see pp. 344–7). Observing that whereas for Knights the question ('How many children?') is self-evidently fatuous and not even worth the semblance of an attempt at an answer, Rutter points out that for many women and men in the roles it has, conversely, been '*the* question actors wanted answered'; and, indeed, in the key productions of the last decades of the twentieth century 'locating the "missing child" has become the crucial performance trope defining the Macbeths' partnership' (Rutter 2007: 171). Although it is tempting to register these preoccupations as no more than a continuation and intensification of a Stanislavsky-dominated psychologically realist tradition, Rutter argues that – whether the actors are aware of it or not – there is something more at stake, politically: that, in a climate of ongoing cultural crisis around children and childhood, the 'missing child' is also 'a site where the nation would search its deep anxieties about relatedness and separation, about authority and autonomy, about locating the child in contemporary culture, about valuing the child's life' (172).

What Rutter offers here is a potential rapprochement between a theorised, historicised, performance-centred gender criticism and the terms of reference which animate both the actor's understanding of her craft and the pioneering works of feminist criticism to which it remains allied. What she also offers, in the figure of the child who is both present and absent, familiar and other, deviant and conformist, absolutely central and disconcertingly liminal, is a compelling focus for further investigation of the sexual, gender and political identities and positionalities that have been the concern of the criticisms addressed in this chapter, whose running theme, to borrow Rutter's phrasing (2007: 204), has been how 'we are "knowen" to ourselves "in playe"'.

Part IV
Screen and stage

1 Film

Stage, page and screen

The history of Shakespeare on film begins in 1899, with the attempts of the Victorian actor-manager Herbert Beerbohm Tree to document his celebrated stage production of *King John* (of which all that survives is a seventy-five-second fragment depicting Tree as the king in his death throes). It continues through the three decades that preceded the arrival of sound in the form of hundreds of now-lost silent shorts, ranging from solemn records of stage productions and the 'quality' or 'prestige' pictures of companies such as Vitagraph (beginning with *Macbeth* in 1908) to more frivolous entries, such as the quirky 1907 George Méliès-directed fantasy, *Shakespeare Writing 'Julius Caesar'*, which depicts the author overcoming his writer's block by dreaming the play into existence.

Until the late 1980s, however, many academic commentators on Shakespeare in the cinema considered that the significant instances of the artform belonged to the epoch of sound (whose beginning was marked by the 1929 *The Taming of the Shrew*, starring Mary Pickford and Douglas Fairbanks, which was legendarily credited as 'by William Shakespeare, with additional dialogue by Samuel Taylor'): Max Reinhardt and William Dieterle's *A Midsummer Night's Dream* (1935); Laurence Olivier's *Henry V* (1944), *Hamlet* (1948) and *Richard III* (1955); Orson Welles's *Macbeth* (1948), *Othello* (1952) and *Chimes at Midnight* (1966); Franco Zeffirelli's *Taming of the Shrew* (1966) and *Romeo and Juliet* (1968); as well as the Russian Grigori Kozintsev's *Hamlet* (1964) and *King Lear* (1970); and Japanese Akira Kurosawa's versions of *Macbeth*, *Kumonoso jô* (1957; also known as *Throne of Blood*), and *King Lear* (*Ran*, 1985).

In 1989, Kenneth Branagh's *Henry V* inaugurated a second wave of mainstream Shakespearean film-making, defined in part by his own films (*Much Ado about Nothing* [1993], *Hamlet* [1996], *In the Bleak Midwinter* [1995] and *Love's Labour's Lost* [2000]), by arthouse works such as Peter Greenaway's *Prospero's Books* (1991), but also by a determined reaction to the 'heritage' traditions of the genre, pre-eminently in Baz Luhrmann's hugely influential popular hit *William Shakespeare's Romeo + Juliet* (1996), in Richard Lonraine's *Richard III* (1995), Al Pacino's *Looking for Richard* (1996), Julie Taymor's *Titus* (1999) and Michael Almereyda's *Hamlet* (2000), and in derivatives and spin-offs such as *Shakespeare in Love* (1998), *10 Things I Hate about You* (1999), *O* (2001), *Scotland, PA* (2001), *Stage Beauty* (2004) and *She's the Man* (2006). The first decade of the twenty-first century has seen the release of further Shakespearean films in the period costume tradition, such as Michael Hoffman's *A Midsummer Night's Dream* (1999), Michael Radford's *The Merchant of Venice* (2004) and Branagh's *As You Like It* (2006).

On the edges of the mainstream, and following in a counter-cinematic tradition that includes such works as Derek Jarman's *The Tempest* (1979) and Jean-Luc Godard's *King*

Lear (1987), are films as various as Troma Entertainment's gross-out cult comedy *Tromeo and Juliet* (1996) and Kristian Levring's *The King is Alive* (2000). Beyond the local context of the American and European cinemas, Shakespeare continues to provide material for what Michel Garneau terms 'tradaptation' (cited in Hodgdon 2002: v), as evidenced, for example, by Farhan Akhtar's *Dil Chahta Hai* (2001) and Vishal Bhardwaj's *MaqBool* (2003), Bollywood reworkings of *Much Ado* and *Macbeth* respectively. The relation between Shakespeare and the moving image has been diverse from the very outset, and the possibilities continue to multiply as the digitalisation of culture encourages these to move between and across media and formats, and films migrate from celluloid and video to DVD and the hard drive, and from there to the clipped, file-sharing culture of the internet, through which more screened Shakespeare is available for viewing, sharing, commentary, tagging, re-editing and creative manipulation than ever before.

For many consumers of Shakespeare today, film and television versions (often encountered in bite-sized chunks on a phone or computer screen rather than swallowed whole) provide a first point of entry into the works, while Shakespearean media scholarship is now confidently established as an important subdiscipline; but, especially when viewed in relation to the longevity of the Shakespearean cinema itself, it is a relatively youthful one. For most of the twentieth century, the general response of Shakespeare scholars to Shakespeare in the cinema (and, in the postwar period, on television) was, at best, to ignore it or, more typically, to condemn it out of hand. As Charles Eckert wrote in 1972, introducing an anthology of reviews from the 1930s to the 1960s, there seemed little point in including the responses of academics who fastidiously 'wince at every cut line, at every omitted character, and at every simplification of Shakespeare's thought', and whose 'discussions … are too often recitals of the specific passages omitted, of the superiority of one or another stage performance' (1972: 2).

Supporters of Shakespearean film have cited the early modern stage as its prototype, as a conjunction of high art and low medium. Shakespeare's dramaturgy has been claimed as a prototype of montage technique, as in Peter Brook's comparison of avant-garde film to the 'non-localised stage' in which 'every single thing under the sun is possible, not only quick changes of location: a man can change into twins, change sex, be his past, his present, his future, be a comic version of himself and a tragic version of himself, and be none of them, *all at the same time*'; in short, a film made in this mode might approximate to 'the free theatre-free cinema that the original Elizabethan Shakespeare must have been' (quoted in Eckert 1972: 38–39).

The theatrical, the realist and the filmic

In the first full-length critical work in the field, *Shakespeare on Film* (1977), Jack J. Jorgens is more cautious. Conscious of the need not only to demonstrate the aesthetic worth of the films under consideration but also to establish the legitimacy of his critical project, Jorgens begins by outlining an interdisciplinary approach which, drawing upon 'the combined resources of literary, theatrical, and cinematic criticism' (1977: 250), is concerned with the '*possibilities*' of Shakespearean film rather than its '*problems*' (ix). Transposing to the cinema a literary-critical terminology inherited from the New Criticism, and a method of cinematic analysis derived from *auteur* theory, he pays close attention to film's capacity to provide visual and aural analogies for Shakespeare's patterns of verbal imagery and to forge a style capable of achieving 'the integration of all expressive effects' (34); he observes that 'stylistic truth and unity come from the overall vision of the actors and the film artist' (35).

Peter Brook (b. 1925)

Theatre and film director

The most admired most influential as well as most imitated practitioner in the modern theatre, Brook began his career with the rarely staged *King John* at the Birmingham Rep in 1945, followed by *Love's Labour's Lost* at the Shakespeare Memorial Theatre a year later. Initially attracted to the more recalcitrant elements of the canon (*Measure for Measure*, a play considered 'difficult' at the time, in 1950; *Titus Andronicus*, in the first-ever production at the SMT in 1955), as well as to the mainstream (*Hamlet* in a West End season of 1955; *The Tempest* at Stratford in 1957), Brook was at once both unmistakeably the star of his own productions and a director whose work was, and remains, impossible to categorise. For *King Lear* in 1962 he turned to the work of Samuel Beckett and the nihilist critical perspective of Jan Kott, in a production (which became the basis for his 1970 film) conspicuously influenced by the Theatre of the Absurd; his celebrated *A Midsummer Night's Dream* in 1970 raided Meyerhold, Chinese acrobatics and the circus in order to turn the received image of the play inside out. *Dream* put into action the manifesto announced in Brook's *The Empty Space* (1968), a work which influentially advocated a theatre of spontaneity, direct encounter and celebration. Moving to Paris to found the Centre International de Recherche Théâtrale (Centre for International Theatre Research), and based from 1974 in the dilapidated Bouffes du Nord, Brook assembled a multi-ethnic company whose task, as he saw it, was to attempt to devise a truly global performance language. The 1974 *Timon of Athens*, referencing the storytelling conventions of African and Asian theatre, established a marker for the work that followed, which included *The Tempest* (1990) and *Hamlet* (2000; Brook directed a film version of this production in 2002). Beyond Shakespeare, Brook devised and directed a version of the Sanskrit epic *The Mahabharata* (1989), a production which attracted both acclaim and fierce criticism.

For Jorgens, there are three operative modes in Shakespearean film: the theatrical, the realist and the filmic.

The 'theatrical' mode, in Jorgens's scheme, is found in both the filmed theatre performance and in films which adopt as a matter of style 'the look and feel of a performance worked out for a static theatrical space and a live audience', conveyed through 'lengthy takes in medium or long shot ... the frame acting as a kind of portable proscenium arch', in which 'meaning is generated largely through the words and gestures of the actors' (Jorgens 1977: 7). The realistic mode, which Jorgens characterises as the dominant mainstream form, caters for audiences' taste for 'the spectacle of historical recreations', accommodating 'duels, battles, shipwrecks, tortures, assassinations, storms, coronations, trials, suicides, feasts, and funerals' (8), and replaces the theatrical film's interest in actors with 'actors-in-a-setting' (10).

Finally, there is the filmic mode, the method of 'the film poet, whose works bear the same relation to the surfaces of reality that poems do to ordinary conversation', that is, marked by an 'emphasis on the *artifice* of film, on the expressive possibilities of distorting the surfaces of reality' (Jorgens 1977: 10). This is clearly Jorgens's preferred style ('the filmic mode is truest to the effect of Shakespeare's verse' [12]), and clearly bears a direct relation to Brook's vision of the avant-garde Shakespearean film; in practice, however, 'good Shakespearean films' tend to adopt a more synthetic approach, in that they 'often move fluidly between modes and styles, merge several simultaneously' (15).

As well as offering a useful initial taxonomy of film types and vocabularies which informs the discussion of a canon of 'classic' Shakespearean films which the book both defines and legitimates, Jorgens's tripartite scheme indirectly suggests a strategy for managing the antagonisms between literary, theatre and film studies as disciplinary domains. In offering the filmic mode as 'truest' to Shakespeare, Jorgens wants to claim textual authority for the elements of Shakespearean cinema which conspicuously signal their autonomy from theatrical and literary models; more indirectly, he also wishes to answer the charge levelled at the Shakespearean cinema from the other side of the divide that very few, if any, of its achievements are particularly innovative or significant within the wider film canon (the films of Kurosawa and Welles possibly excepted): *Shakespeare on Film* concludes with the plea for film critics to 'consider the ways in which Shakespeare's intricate dramatic structures, rich characterizations, and poetry, often in a figurative sense more "cinematic" than any film, might enrich the cinema' (Jorgens 1977: 251).

If this was an invitation which went largely unheeded, Shakespearean film scholarship was nonetheless encouraged in the late 1970s and 1980s by the development of video technology, which transformed both the viewing experience and the scope for critical re-viewing. In 1976, the year in which the Sony Corporation launched the VHS format, the quarterly *Shakespeare on Film Newsletter* began publication, which also offered coverage of the increasing numbers of television productions (dominated, notably, by the very mixed achievement of the BBC Television Shakespeare, which ran from 1978 to 1985). In 1988 Anthony Davies's *Filming Shakespeare's Plays* consolidated and extended the work of canon-formation initiated by Jorgens in a series of intricate close readings of the films of Olivier, Welles, Brook and Kurosawa. Like Jorgens, Davies begins by considering the relationship between theatre and cinema, proposing (in an argument that is consciously indebted to the film theorist André Bazin) that the 'essential distinctions' between the media lie in 'the complex field of spatial relationships' (1988: 5). Whereas in the theatre 'experience amounts to a reciprocal action between the presenters ... of a dramatic work and the audience', in that 'the theatre audience is "playing the game of theatre" which is in the first place a spatial game, for the spectator has to invest a specific and defined area with special significance' (5–6), the cinema 'aims at spatial realism', creating an 'illusion of horizontal and vertical mobility' and 'moving the action from the confines of theatrical enclosure and creating new relationships between the actor and the décor, between space and time and between the dramatic presentation and the audience' (7–9).

This perspective allows Davies to take a more nuanced view of the realist aspect of Shakespearean film than Jorgens's reference to 'actors-in-a-setting', since 'an implicit yearning for spatial expanse' in the plays themselves prompts, and partly legitimates, 'geo-historical realism' (Davies 1988: 13); it also allows a more detailed diagnosis of the problems of the 'theatrical' mode (represented here by Stuart Burge's 1965 film of the 1964 National Theatre production of *Othello*). 'The function of stage décor is to give theatrical resonance to dialogue, to facilitate the centripetal concentration of power in the actor', Davies writes, while 'the screen ... reflects a dramatic image which is centrifugal, but which retains its power through the dynamic reciprocity between actor and spatial detail'; Burge's film is an 'aesthetic collision' because it fails 'to reconcile these oppositions of spatial nature' (13). The solution, however, is not to abandon theatricality (this would be 'disastrous in the cinematic adaptation of a stage play' [15]) but to reconcile the 'centripetal' orientation of theatre with the 'centrifugal' energies of film, a synthesis which is most convincingly achieved in the films of Welles and Olivier, which 'accommodate essential theatricality within a dramatic framework which is filmic' (25). Unlike Jorgens, and, as we shall see, some more recent commentators, Davies characterises the classic Shakespearean film's affiliation to the theatre in positive terms: 'a Shakespearean film cannot satisfactorily remain confined to the theatre stage. Neither can it abandon that intrinsic theatricality which beats in the heart of Shakespearean drama' (184).

Having defined the project of Shakespearean film-making in terms of this dynamic opposition, Davies offers a sequence of formalistic analyses of eight key films, placing a premium upon conceptual and stylistic coherence, structural balance and symmetry, patterns of iterative imagery. Olivier's *Henry V* earns praise because, despite 'the diversity of its constituent elements', it achieves an 'organic structuring of space and time' (Davies 1988: 39); the same director's *Hamlet* is, similarly, 'organically integrated' (64). Davies's essentially appreciative rather than deconstructive approach was been adopted in a number of studies which followed. Lorne Buchman's *Still in Movement*, which appeared in 1991, pursued a spatial analysis similar to Davies's: tracing 'how the plays are operating as products of cinematic technique' (1991: 5), Buchman investigates the 'spatial multiplicity' of Shakespearean films, as well as 'how the spectator works with that spatial field according to an interplay of identification and alienation' (31); the films he views are seen to create a dialectic between subjective experience and the social world.

Returning in particular to the films of Kosintsev and Welles, Buchman explores the ways in which 'film provides a new space for Shakespeare's poetry', how the technique of the close-up 'becomes the field that can articulate the social *gest* of the performance moment' and how Shakespeare's 'theatrical self-consciousness' can be matched by the 'filmic self-consciousness' of movie directors (1991: 148). Buchman is not just enthusiastic about the film medium's potential to illuminate, expand and transform our sense of Shakespeare's performance possibilities; he also indicates that there is, in a cinema-dominated age, no going back either, as 'cinematic adaptation guides us to ask different questions about the drama, to explore the plays in a distinctive way because they appear to us in a new context' (148).

Buchman's perception not only that film posed new challenges to thinking about Shakespeare's dramaturgy but that it might also provide a route towards a reinvigorated, democratic and popular pedagogy appeared to be shared by Samuel Crowl, whose 1992 study *Shakespeare Observed* is fuelled by the conviction that 'film gave us our liberty in thinking and writing about Shakespeare, and that led us and our students back to the theatre' (1992: 4); Crowl combines film and performance criticism in the attempt to 'articulate ways of recovering those pleasures we have shared in several modern film and stage productions of Shakespeare' (18). Moving readily between theatre and the cinema, Crowl steers a course through the work of Polanski, Peter Hall, Welles and Branagh in terms which are avowedly 'more personal and less theoretical' than much then current performance criticism, mapping 'a developing dialogue between and among film and stage productions themselves' (11), and arriving at clear, unambiguously positive verdicts on, for instance, Polanski's *Macbeth*, Welles's *Chimes at Midnight* and Hall's *Midsummer Night's Dream* ('the finest realization we have of a Shakespearean comedy on film' [75]).

The evaluative, generally supportive approach to Shakespearean film that is adopted by Davies, Buchman and Crowl is also characterised by its inclusiveness, and informed by a more widespread perception that the field Shakespearean film studies, like that of performance studies, is a relatively tolerant broad church, capable of accommodating very different critical methodologies and theoretical positions without the rancour that, particularly during the theory wars of the 1980s, marked debates in other areas of the discipline. The liberal eclecticism of the field has been confirmed by numerous anthologies of critical writing that have appeared since the 1980s, beginning with James C. Bulman and H. R. Coursen's *Shakespeare on Television* (1988); and running from Anthony Davies and Stanley Wells's *Shakespeare and the Moving Image* in 1992 (which mainly recycled articles from

Shakespeare Survey 39 [1987], the topic of which was Shakespeare on film and television; the theme of *Shakespeare Survey 61* [2008] was 'Sound and Screen') to Russell Jackson's *Cambridge Companion to Shakespeare on Film* (2000), in which questions of adaptation and intermediality sit alongside genre analysis (both Shakespearean and cinematic), auteur studies and 'critical issues' (representations of race, gender and sexuality; the matter of 'offshoots').

Differences in view

One feature of Jackson's collection lacking in much previous writing in the field is the practical perspective supplied by the editor's experience as a text advisor to Kenneth Branagh and to John Madden for *Shakespeare in Love*; and this perhaps inflects the wry pragmatism of Jackson's account of the tendency of some 1980s and 1990s critics to engage in 'the interrogation of the cultural functions of the plays themselves and their interpretation', which had resulted in 'some directors being taken to task for harnessing one hegemony (Shakespeare as a figurehead of conservative anglocentric culture) to another (international big business)' (Jackson 2000: 8). Jackson refers here to a body of film scholarship which, emerging at the same time as the writing summarised in the previous paragraph, directly challenged many of the key principles and methods of a critical consensus which barely had time to settle.

A point of departure was provided in 1985 by Graham Holderness, whose contribution to Jonathon Dollmore and Alan Sinfield's agenda-setting collection *Political Shakespeare* challenged the Shakespearean film and television canon on explicitly ideological grounds. Stating that 'the primary function of cinema as a cultural industry in a bourgeois economy is to reproduce and naturalise dominant ideologies' (1994: 206), Holderness identifies the task of materialist film scholarship as tracing how that function is exercised both institutionally and through individual films. Taking issue with an earlier essay by Catherine Belsey (1983; reprinted 1998), which argued that, as 'the final realisation of the project of perspective staging', mainstream cinema is an inherently reactionary medium, in that it 'inevitably narrows the plurality of an Elizabethan text' (1998: 65–66), Holderness proposes that the distinction between 'naturalistic, illusionistic cinema and its opposite' enables us to identify not only those films which 'operate simply as vehicles for the transmissions of ideology' and those which 'block, deflect or otherwise "work on" ideology in order partially to disclose its mechanisms' (210).

The difference between realist and filmic Shakespeares is thus political as well as formal: whereas the former encourages the film camera to 'efface itself in a privileging of its object, constituting reality as objective in the illusionistic manner of naturalism', the latter, by 'violating those naturalist conventions', and by 'emphasising and exploiting its mobility', calls 'the spectator's attention to the mechanisms of its own perception' and thus releases the viewer from 'the tyranny of the empathetic illusion to a freer consideration of reality and of the artifice which produces it' (Holderness 1994: 210). The terms of reference and the terminology are, significantly, as much theatrical as cinematic: the concern with empathy and alienation drawing upon Brecht's theory and practice of Epic theatre as filtered through Jean-Luc Godard's Marxist counter-cinema; in effect, Holderness constructs an alliance between two of Jorgens's modes in order to see off the third. Moreover, the more one looks at the classic Shakespeare films, the more one finds them in sympathy with this project, whether this be in the 'grainy black-and-white photography, stylised acting, direct addresses to camera, lightning changes of focus, rapid superimpositions, violations of screen direction ... the Brechtian titles, the absence of music, the distorted images, zoom-fades, blurred visions, surreal apparitions' of Brook's *King Lear* (Holderness 1994: 209), the 'deliberate disruption of naturalist film convention' in Hall's *Midsummer Night's Dream* that takes the form of hand-held camerawork and direct address, 'offering the spectator an open awareness of the medium as a conjuring and simulating power' (212), or in the 'epic detachment' of Kurosawa's *Kumonosu jô*, which employs the 'choreographed artifice of Noh drama' and displays an understanding of the tragedy as 'social rather than psychological or supernatural' that 'has meaning only within the historical world of the film' (213–15).

In *Shakespeare, Cinema and Society* (1989), John Collick extended this line of argument, claiming that while 'orthodox film criticism' had tended to operate 'within a very narrow area' by concentrating 'on those movies that support traditional assumptions about the nature of literature' and, in the process, 'selectively edit[ing] out those elements that appear disruptive or challenging' (1989: 9–10). Against this he poses a critical approach to film which 'recognises that its form, content and cultural position is determined by the economic and political forces that condition its production' (8), and which seeks to set key works of the British, American, Russian and Japanese Shakespearean cinemas in their generic, historical, economic and cultural contexts.

Tracing the continuities between the methods of the Victorian spectacular theatre, in particular its taste for the *tableau vivant* as a means of animating a mythologised national history, and the strategies adopted by the early silent films, Collick reassesses their much-derided 'theatricality' as a conscious attempt to harness the 'elitism of a highly developed aesthetic tradition': 'for a film to be successfully associated with the reproduction of Shakespeare in respectable middle-class culture, it had to imitate the theatre experience' (Collick 1989: 40–41). The subsequent history of Shakespeare on screen, Collick demonstrates, reveals the medium's attempts to accommodate diverse, competing and often contradictory agendas. Rather than exhibiting the 'organic structuring' praised by Anthony Davies, Olivier's *Henry V* combines 'the decline of the Victorian spectacular Shakespeare tradition', 'the nascent theories of Expressionist stagecraft and cinematic montage' and a soundtrack on which 'speeches are delivered with the precise and measured enunciation of a BBC radio broadcast'; the result is 'a jumble of different structures' (49–50).

The Reinhardt–Dieterle *Midsummer Night's Dream*, by contrast, 'produced as a conscious exercise in prestige building' (Collick 1989: 83), amalgamates Expressionist and Symbolist stagecraft, surrealist film, the Hollywood musical, cartoon comedy, period epic and screwball comedy, creating an 'overwhelming dream-fantasy atmosphere' that 'ensures that the different styles merge without any significant disruption' (89). The most distinctive sections of Collick's study, however, are those which locate Grigori Kozintsev's and Akira Kurosawa's Shakespeare films in the respective contexts of Soviet and Japanese cinema, history and society. Kosintsev, an associate of Meyerhold and Eisenstein, whose films are also informed by his experience of the 'anarchic comedies and morality plays, circuses with acrobats and clowns' staged by the agitprop group FEKS (Factory of the Eccentric Actor) during the revolutionary period, by 'factory art and pre-Stalinist cinema', by the Noh theatre and by Bakhtin's theory of the 'positive grotesque', which aims at 'the inversion of the rational, authoritative world picture' (123–24), 'comes closest' in his films *Hamlet* and *Korol Ler*, 'to realising a radical reproduction of Shakespeare in the cinema', derived from 'a vital, populist culture that combined the carnivalesque of folklore with the violent and absurdist forms of Futurism' (147).

Kurosawa, inheriting a 'national cinematic idiom' (Collick 1989: 170) which predates the global dominance of Hollywood realism, and whose theatrical predecessors are the Noh drama and Bunraku puppet theatre rather than the proscenium-based theatre of spectacle, produces in *Kumonosu jô* a version of *Macbeth* which 'employs the strictly demarcated boundaries of the Noh to entrap characters and eliminate any single, coherent point of reference' (179); differing from Holderness in his assessment of the film's politics, Collick concludes that the film 'represents an impasse in the liberal view of politics in Japan during the late 1950s' (181). *Ran*, however, is more optimistic: 'far less experimental in its approach to Shakespeare' (185), it is 'an open-ended film that acknowledges the potential for change – if only by suggesting that engagement with reality is preferable to spiritual escapism' (186).

The work of Holderness and Collick marks a significant shift from more formalistic treatments of Shakespearean cinema not only in terms of its angle of approach to the classic films but also because (reflecting the larger concerns of cultural materialist criticism) it raises questions about the process of canon formation itself. This enables Collick to positively value the work of cinematic practitioners who occupy a marginal, dissident or alternative position in relation to the mainstream, notably Derek Jarman, whose 1979 *The Tempest* juxtaposes queer, arthouse, occult and punk sensibilities with the iconographies of Renaissance alchemy and the Elizabethan masque, producing a dreamlike 'celebration of transgression' (Collick 1989: 98) which, 'through conscious references to the artifice of film and drama', transforms the play into a 'positive affirmation of underground culture' (102).

In a similar vein, in an essay published in 1993, Holderness reviewed the critical history of Shakespearean film, described the canon of 'great films of great plays by great directors' as a 'cultural apparatus' (2002: 69, 71) whose dominance was ripe for challenge. Seeking a 'filmed Shakespeare' which might answer to 'contemporary definitions of Shakespearean textuality' as 'remarkably unstable, self-contradictory, fissured, labile, permeated by a radical undecideability' (73–74), he posits Jarman's *Tempest*, Celestino Coronado's *Hamlet* (1979) and Cambridge Experimental Theatre's 1987 video exploration of the same play as alternatives to the canon whose deconstructive techniques provisionally 'offer some degree of filmic equivalent to the modern theoretically activated Shakespearean text' (88).

Textualities and sexualities

A better-known example of filmic deconstruction, not mentioned by Holderness, is Jean-Luc Godard's 1987 *King Lear*, a film comprehensively panned by the critics, when first released, as a shambles and a travesty: subtitled 'A picture shot in the back', this is 'a modernized, fragmented, constantly self-interrupting work, only part of which – a fraction of the dialogue and the sub-plot involving "Don Learo", a retired mafia chief, and his daughter, Cordelia – derives from Shakespeare's text' (Donaldson 1990: 189). Thus Peter S. Donaldson in his *Shakespearean Films/Shakespearean Directors* (1990) goes on to chronicle the doings of Norman Mailer (who departs in the first reel to be replaced by Burgess Meredith), the theatre director Peter Sellars as William Shakespeare Jr, the Fifth, Woody Allen as the Fool, Mr Alien (seen at the end with Sellars editing film footage 'using a travel-size sewing kit and safety pins to make splices' [Donaldson 1990: 218]) and Godard himself as Professor Pluggy, a 'high-tech' shaman sporting 'mock-Rastafarian dreadlocks fashioned from RCA cords, dogtags, and Christmas ornaments' (207).

Godard, Donaldson writes, 'burlesques, interrupts, and disconnects Shakespeare's text', but also 'acknowledges Shakespeare as a decisive precursor in these very techniques'

(1990: 218); and in this respect Godard's *King Lear* is offered as a perversely exemplary instance of 'the process of appropriation by which the conventions and practices of the Elizabethan stage are refashioned in the contemporary medium of film, and by which the work of individual film artists is nourished and challenged by the task of adapting Shakespeare' (xi–xii). The key to Godard's film, in Donaldson's account, lies in its treatment of gender politics: as 'the locus ... of the self-critique of patriarchy and of the totalizing aesthetic and psychological assumptions that support it', *King Lear* offers a 'deconstruction of "the father" as source, authority, and hegemonic center', as well as an 'unruly interplay of selves and texts'; Godard responds to 'the exclusion, objectification, and commodification of women, sharing the male roles of the play with female voices, infiltrating Shakespeare's text with words by women writers [Virginia Woolf's *The Waves*], foregrounding the process by which the propagation of male culture entails the subordination of female bodies and female images' (218–19).

Godard's *King Lear* provides an end-point to the first book-length study of sexuality in Shakespearean film: drawing upon psychoanalytic and feminist film scholarship, Donaldson proposes a series of readings of both canonical and less familiar works, as he summarises:

> Olivier's *Henry V* is read in relation to its translation of the convention of the 'boy actress' into cinematic terms. Olivier's *Hamlet* is seen as a tragedy of narcissistic self-enclosure and as the artistic reprise of a childhood sexual trauma suffered by the director ... Orson Welles's *Othello* is approached through analogies between the film screen as mirror and the fantasies of maternal insufficiency that haunt its protagonist. Franco Zeffirelli's *Romeo and Juliet* is presented as an antipatriarchal, homoerotic reading of Shakespeare's play.
>
> (Donaldson 1990: xii–xiii)

Donaldson's use of biographical materials ('psychological issues arising in childhood, even at times specific images associated with early fears or traumas', which are 'revived in the work of adaptation' [1990: xii]) is distinctive, and occasionally provocative. Olivier's *Henry V*, for example, calls up its director's adolescent experience of transvestite acting, playing female Shakespearean roles en route to 'a troubled and painful but successful growth toward an adult male heterosexual identity' (23); the film's final image, 'a marriage of male lead and boy actor, evokes the specific terms of Laurence Olivier's assumption of an adult male identity' (25).

But the 'overdetermined relation' (Donaldson 1990: 25) of the film to Olivier's biography is only part of its more general tactic of 'claiming from the female' in order to validate its cinematic, historiographical and propagandist project: 'the shift from "playhouse" to cinematic space is prominently marked by the replacement of boys by women ... Like "real" battles, "real" women serve to mark or index the superseding of the bare platform stage by the representational plenitude of epic filmmaking' (6); by the end, 'the various ways in which women, the images of women, or qualities thought to be proper to women are transposed into male forms' cohere in 'the restoration of bonds of love and solidarity between the men' (18–19). Male bonding assumes a homoerotic form in Donaldson's discussion of Zeffirelli's *Romeo and Juliet*, as realised in 'moments of tenderness between Romeo and Mercutio' and in 'the powerful undercurrent of *macho* denial of feeling between men in the text which Zeffirelli has conditioned us to read as disavowal' (169–70); in this instance, the spectator's own desires are implicated:

> Making use of heterosexual film conventions governing the deployment of the male gaze, as well as on [sic] his own contrary or complementary presentation of men as *objects* of an admiring gaze, Zeffirelli creates a spectatorial position neither simply male or female nor simply identificatory or detached.
>
> (Donaldson 1990: 170)

Donaldson's emphasis upon the Shakespearean cinema's manipulation of the spectatorial gaze reflects a preoccupation within film theory (and in particular within feminist film scholarship) which has subsequently informed much of the work that has been done on the films' strategies of gender representation and their construction of sexuality.

In her contribution to the *Cambridge Companion to Shakespeare on Film* (2000), Carol Chillington Rutter defines the agenda of this critical project by itemising the variety of ways in which women feature – often in excess of the texts in which they appear – on the Shakespearean screen:

> Film returns again and again to certain motifs: women running, women framed (in doorways, windows, wimples, hats …); dressing up and dressing down; women seeing themselves in mirrors, both literal and figurative; women confined: put into corseted costumes and claustrophobic rooms, walled gardens, curtained beds, narrow labyrinths; women released into open landscapes. Film's historic interest in female bodies … constantly exceeds the specifications of Shakespeare's texts: on film, female bodies proliferate, women's roles multiply, filling the *mise-en-scène* with supplementary extra-texts that are there to be read with – or against – the dominant narrative.
>
> (Rutter 2000: 243)

Women in Shakespearean film, Rutter contends, do considerably more than the texts instruct, imply or authorise: 'not only are there more women in Shakespeare's films than playtexts but they have much more to perform' (2000: 243). The disparity between what's in the script and what's on the screen arises because 'in the movies … meanings are going to reside in the extra-textual narratives the camera constructs by its looking' (242); examples range from Loncraine's *Richard III*, which reads its women's roles 'off contemporary culture, finding an immediately decipherable visual language for the 1990s to reproduce something like the potency women project in the original script, *circa* 1590' (248), to Trevor Nunn's *Twelfth Night*, whose 'photographic strategies work to suggest for everybody a shadow twin of the opposite sex, opposite, but somehow attached' (250).

In tragedy, Rutter proposes, Shakespeare 'habitually uses the woman's body to proxy the crisis of masculine self-representation that is the play's narrative focus'; she goes on to point out that 'eleven major films of these four plays [*Hamlet, King Lear, Othello, Macbeth*] … have produced significant reassessments of the parts women play in tragedy' (Rutter 2000: 251). Rutter's *Enter the Body* pursues this concern at length, mediating between texts, contemporary performances and films in the pursuit of 'the work bodies do on Shakespeare's stage, both with and beyond his words' (2001: xiii). This includes, for example, the work undertaken by the women who perform as corpses: Ophelia, variously represented by Jean Simmons in Olivier's film (with her 'impossibly symmetrical eyebrows scored in black', which turn her into 'Rebecca of Sunnybrook Farm trying to vamp herself up as Jean Harlow' [31]); Helena Bonham-Carter in Zeffirelli's, who 'personalizes Elsinore's contradictions, has them written on her gawky body' (33) and, most chillingly of all, by Kate Winslet in Branagh's, whose punishment for being sexually active is death, who is depicted as a stand-in 'vampire bride' who in the funeral scene brings the Prince 'to a place where his Hamlet can, using the corpse as proxy, symbolically lay to rest his fantasies about Gertrude's erratic sexuality' (51).

While Rutter trains the lens of gender critique primarily upon the problematic visual pleasures of the tragic cinema, Barbara Hodgdon turns our gaze towards comedy, and in particular to the sado-masochistic delights of the films of *The Taming of the Shrew*. Observing that the text's games of domination and submission are framed by 'models of looking … voyeurism, fantasy, and consumerism – [that] are all metaphors for film and television viewing' (1998: 9), Hodgdon investigates the variety of ways in which successive screen *Shrew*s 'interpellate a woman spectator in a play so relentlessly directed toward affirming patriarchal prerogatives', exploring 'how viewers, men as well as women, can become bound up in and by *Shrew*'s gender economy, by the pleasurable array of subject positions it puts on offer' (xiii).

The proliferation of criticism addressed to Shakespeare, film and television at the end of the 1980s was afforded a further impetus by a new wave of Shakespearean films themselves, inaugurated by Kenneth Branagh's well-received *Henry V* in 1989. As a director who comprehended the idea of the truly 'filmic' Shakespearean film in terms of neither Jorgens's avant-garde 'film poetry' nor the materialist's cinema of alienation, but of its potential to harness the energies of popular film genres, Branagh initiated a 1990s mini-boom in Shakespeare films which reflected the medium's tendency to confuse distinctions between high art and popular entertainment, between reactionary, liberal and progressive textual politics, and between genres, modes and styles. In the case of *Henry V*, a postmodern sense of the film's relationship with film history was advertised through the conspicuous intertextualising of Olivier's version (which has been well documented), and through its referencing of, amongst other things, the Western, the Vietnam movie and war reportage; subsequent Branagh movies would attempt to occupy the territory of romantic comedy (*Much Ado*), period epic (*Hamlet*), Ealing Comedy (*In the Bleak Midwinter*) and, in a spectacularly misguided attempt at retro-chic, golden-age Hollywood musical (*Love's Labour's Lost*). Increasingly, through the 1990s, Shakespearean film critics prioritised current films, and were encouraged in this by the new cinema's manifest self-awareness, its postmodern habit of allusiveness and pastiche, and its knowing manipulation of convention and mixing of styles, which seemed to hit a contemporary nerve.

During the same period, the consensus about what could be legitimately included in the field of study expanded to incorporate all manner of cinematic spin-offs, spoofs, parodies, travesties and loose adaptations that responsible scholarship had hitherto ignored; indeed, the films themselves blurred the oppositions so the differences between adaptation, version and derivative were no longer easily definable or important. Thus Robert F. Willson, Jr's *Shakespeare in Hollywood, 1929–1956* (2000), presenting a brisk and enthusiastic survey of Shakespeare during the 'Golden Age', combines accounts of what were, relatively speaking, Shakespearean blockbusters (the 1929 *Shrew*, 1935 *Dream*, 1936 *Romeo and Juliet* and 1953 *Julius Caesar*), discussed in relation to their industry origins (United Artists, Warners', MGM), low-budget auteurist experiment (Welles's *Macbeth*) and 'offshoots', including Ernst Lubitsch's sublime black comedy *To Be or Not to Be* (1942), *Forbidden Planet* (1956) and the 1954 Western *Broken Lance*. As Willson concedes, these films 'have not been hailed as exceptional, innovative renditions of Shakespeare's plays', and, Welles excepted, 'they are studio-driven, not the products of recognized, respected auteurs'; their value is that they constitute 'a uniquely American and popular body of Shakespearean films' (2000: 14–15).

World pictures

Lynda E. Boose and Richard Burt's 1997 collection *Shakespeare, the Movie: Popularizing the Plays on Film, TV, and Video* both signalled a determination to pull Shakespearean cinema out of the arthouse and onto the terrain of popular culture, and reflected the multi-media contexts in which the production and consumption of screen Shakespeares was now taking place. Describing the collection as 'a generic potlatch' (Boose and Burt 1997: 1), the editors suggest that the diversity of the material considered (ranging from the 1920 silent *Hamlet* featuring Asta Nielsen's cross-dressed prince to Shakespeare references in *Porky's 2* and *Dead Poets Society*) provokes wide-ranging questions about 'Shakespeare's status as legitimating author-function, about the relation between original and adaptation, about youth culture and pedagogy, and finally, about the relation between the popular as hip and the popular as politically radical' (2). In particular, the question of popularisation needs to be addressed 'not only through the media and institutions in which Shakespeare is now reproduced – mass culture, Hollywood, celebrity, tabloid – but above all, youth culture' (17).

In a world in which youth culture is no longer the exclusive provenance of the young, but rather provides the template for consumer culture in general, Shakespearean films, and Shakespeare-related films, have drawn upon the iconographies, generic reference points, and visual and musical idioms of increasingly diverse performance media, a trend which was definitively marked by Baz Luhrmann's *William Shakespeare's Romeo + Juliet* (1996), which appropriated the discourse of pop music video not only through its contemporary urban setting, hyper-volatile camerawork and breathless pace but also in its gleefully promiscuous referencing of everything from Wagnerian opera to 1970s disco, *Rebel Without a Cause* to the Spaghetti Western.

Romeo + Juliet also demonstrated that it was possible to turn Shakespeare into a popular hit by treating the spoken text as a malleable, indeed largely dispensable, adjunct to the visuals: the film's relation to the play is defined through the workings of mythology and cultural memory rather than 'realisation'. Luhrmann's film, which perhaps most fully embodied the zeitgeist identified in *Shakespeare, the Movie*, appeared too late to be addressed in detail there, but this was rectified in the collection's sequel (or remake), *Shakespeare, the Movie, II* (2003), which responded to the post-Luhrmann wave by consolidating the contemporary focus of its predecessor volume, dropping the essays which had dealt with canonical pre-1980s material to make space for Luhrmann, Almereyda, Hoffman, Edzard and Dogme 95, as well as for more loosely 'Shakespearean' films, including the hardcore porn version of *Macbeth*, *In the Flesh* (1998), the Singaporean *Romeo and Juliet* spin-off *Chicken Rice War* (2000) and the Bollywood *Much Ado*, *Dil Chahta Hai* (2001).

As Burt points out, the diversity of the collection is a reaction to rapidly changing patterns of consumption and production, and to technological advances, as viewing takes place 'in media that are both old and new … and that are both increasingly integrated – such as the computer as home theater – and dispersed – such as cell phones and portable DVD players' (Burt and Boose 2003: 4); in this respect, the revised subtitle (*Popularizing the Plays on Film, TV, Video and DVD*) does more than acknowledge new technologies: it also recognises that the digital format invites us to consider 'DVD extras such as menu trailers, deleted scenes, audio commentaries, interviews, "making of" documentaries, music videos, video games', and to acknowledge that screen Shakespeare circulates 'not only in cinematographic and televisual contexts but, more broadly, in other mass media such as comics, novelizations, advertising, video games' (1–2).

Within a globalised economy, Shakespeare can no longer be located with any degree of assurance or stability within traditional national cultures. *Shakespeare, the Movie* both attested to the long-standing dominance of (theatrically rooted) British and European definitions of 'classic' Shakespearean film, and traced the thoroughgoing Americanisation of Shakespearean cinema during the 1990s, thereby 'playing out one more version of the way that America, through the aesthetic medium that is as peculiarly American as the stage is English, tries to come to terms with its own, unregenerate fascination with the Bard of Avon' (Boose and Burt 1997: 19). *Shakespeare, the Movie, II* seeks to progress the argument several stages further: acknowledging that, 'since the first edition', 'Shakespeare's popularisation has been transformed ... by globalization and the emergence of transnational cinema' (Burt and Boose 2003: 5), Burt contends that 'Shakespeare's cinematic migrations and mobility across the globe', reflecting his 'postcanonical status' and taking the form of 'the full range of citations and spin-offs from the hermeneutic to the post-hermeneutic', function 'as a type of currency without any particular meaning, location, traceable source of value, but as nevertheless somehow signs of that which can be exchanged' (268–69).

Burt's willingness to attend to the 'post-hermeneutic' citation of Shakespeare on film reflects the interests of an increasingly visible strand within Shakespearean screen scholarship, which, shaped more by film and cultural studies than by literary or performance criticism, engages with movies which, contrary to the classics of the Shakespearean film canon, make few (if any) claims to seriousness or artistic value. This approach is taken to the point of no return in Burt's *Unspeakable ShaXXXspeares: Queer Theory and American Kiddie Culture* (1998), which offers 'a study of Shakespeare as a symptom of the American national unconscious' via 'a series of replays of Shakespeare that are often so far from their "originals" they no longer count as interpretations of the plays at all' (Burt 1998: xiv–xv). Burt's survey covers cartoons, sitcoms, blockbusters, gross-out comedies and – provocatively – the fairly specialist subgenre of Shakespearean hardcore pornography, which has yielded such classics as *A Midsummer Night's Cream* (2000) and *Taming of the Screw* (1997), and which provides a limit case for cultural criticism in the sense that it is rooted in paradox: 'the more Shakespeare's plays are made pornographic ... the further one moves away from the text' (84). Whatever tenuous purchase porn treatments of Shakespeare might have had upon the plays and the more mainstream performance traditions to which they refer, the imperatives of the form not only render them incapable of connecting in any meaningful way with their source material but, in the process, also comically expose the fatuity of attempting to address such texts within a Shakespeare studies framework: 'the cultural critic may imagine that every piece of cultural trash ... can be recycled, but the instance of Shakespeare porn suggests otherwise' (125).

James R. Keller and Leslie Stratyner's volume *Almost Shakespeare* (2004) operates in a similar vein: a collection to be devoted entirely to cinematic derivatives and offshoots, it not only deals with works already familiar to Shakespearean cinephiles (*Prospero's Books, My Own Private Idaho, 10 Things I Hate About You*) but also finds Shakespeare in places where few had previously thought to look for him, including *CSI: Miami, Sex, Lies, and Videotape* and *The West Wing*. Describing this as 'the creation of extended conceits' in terms of 'cramming Shakespeare into new and improbable contexts', the editors attribute the pleasure of this kind of appropriation to its 'startling improbability' and the intrigue in attempting to 'match the Shakespearean pieces to the fragments of contemporary culture' (Keller and Stratyner 2004: 2–3). Keller and Stratyner joke about a Shakespeare who is 'suffering from a multiple personality disorder' (1), but the real point is not that such excursions can be laughed off as peripheral to the real business of teaching and criticism; it is that popular culture is the ground on which the majority of pedagogic transactions take place, and it may even have the upper hand. Courtney Lehmann and Lisa Starks make the point directly in their introduction to the collection *Spectacular Shakespeare*: 'to teach Shakespeare today, we must teach today's Shakespeare – as refigured through the distorting lens of the movie camera' (2002: 9).

A cinema for a new century

As the title of Mark Thornton Burnett and Ramona Wray's 2000 collection *Shakespeare, Film, Fin de Siècle* indicates, Shakespearean scholarship which concentrates upon contemporary film tends to be self-conscious about its own historical location: in this instance marked by the connection between Beerbohm Tree's *fin-de-siècle* progenitor of Shakespearean cinema, *King John*, 'a poeticized version of the past ... romantically recasting a history of Victorian social reform', and the tendency of the films of 'the end of the twentieth century' to 'survey and represent a host of previous moments in which [Shakespeare's] transmission and circulation are implicated', including the 1930s neo-fascist retro-chic of Loncraine's *Richard III*, the 1890s milieu of Branagh's *Hamlet* and Noble's *Dream*, the 1590s of *Shakespeare in Love*, and the timeless mid-century Ealing Comedy world of *In the Bleak Midwinter* (Burnett and Wray 2000: 3–4). Assessing a cinema, that, like Kenneth Branagh's Hamlet gazing at his own reflecton in the image that adorns the volume's cover, simultaneously looks forward and backwards, Burnett and Wray, and their contributors, contemplate 'Shakespeare films of the last decade' which 'have used a constructed "now" to negotiate what is to come' (4), as well as looking forward to a 'present generation of Shakespeare on film' which, following the logic of popular cinema, promises 'to bring the karate kids, the morphing monsters and the space bugs to the dramatists, and vice versa' (8).

Branagh is also central to Samuel Crowl's *Shakespeare at the Cineplex: The Kenneth Branagh Era* (2003), which regards the 'long decade' of 1989–2001 as operating under his commercial and artistic shadow. This is very much a homage to and celebration of this director, seen as the figure most committed to 'eras[ing] the fault lines separating popular and elite forms of entertainment' (Crowl 2003: 13). This has been achieved, however, by carefully targeted and differentiated niche marketing: Crowl locates the 1990s boom in relatively small-scale, low-budget, independent Shakespeare films within the cultural economy of the suburban cineplex itself, symbolised by a new cinematic architecture, wherein 'the venue no longer was one large auditorium with a single screen but multiple small screening rooms', which, 'like the proliferation of cable television channels, demand more product, which has paradoxically created a market for what has come to be termed the independent film – the category that encompasses most of the Shakespeare films released in the long decade' (2–3).

Reiterating Jackson's characterisation of the independent movie as marked by 'attention to theme, character relationship and social relevance, and targeted at a market somewhere between the art-house and the mainstream' (2000: 5), Crowl cites Jorgens's account of the 'realist' mode in order to emphasise that it is this (rather than the 'film poetry' of Olivier, Welles and Kurosawa) that was dominant during the 1990s. Not that realism is unselfconscious about its own sources and conventions: assessing the fifteen major films released during this period, Crowl's study discovers a 'willingness not only to take the Hollywood film as a model, but to delight in quoting from Hollywood genres and specific films as well' (2003: 11); the survey concludes with four examples from the end of the period which 'signal interesting new directions for the genre':

Each of the four, in differing fashions, radically extends (*Love's Labour's Lost*), stylistically complicates (*Titus* and *Hamlet*), or humorously revises (*Children's Midsummer Night's Dream*) the realistic and naturalistic model forged by Zeffirelli and updated and revised by Branagh in his first three Shakespeare films.

(Crowl 2003: 19)

Crowl also finds a kind of answer to Jorgens's hope that Shakespearean film might 'enrich' the cinema (Jorgens 1977: 251), in that he is able to show some of the ways in which the 1990s corpus of Shakespearean films has influenced the mainstream: thus Branagh's *Henry V* is seen to have 'helped to inspire the return of the genre of the good war film' (Crowl 2003: 223), epitomised by Stephen Spielberg's *Saving Private Ryan* (1998) and the television series *Band of Brothers* (2000).

So successful has cineplex Shakespeare been in dominating both the educational market and recent film criticism that the historical significance, international traditions and enduring value of its antecedents may be in danger of being marginalised, if not forgotten. Kenneth S. Rothwell's *A History of Shakespeare on Screen* (1999; second edition 2004) redresses the balance: both an authoritative critical overview and an essential reference work, it addresses an encyclopaedic range of film and television versions, histories, as well as their contexts of production and reception. Rothwell's methods of organising and categorising this vast and diverse corpus are pragmatically varied: chapters on silent film and Hollywood's 'four seasons' of Shakespeare are succeeded by auteur-centred studies of Olivier and Welles; Shakespeare's fortunes on television and in digital media sit alongside sections on directors in thrall, respectively, to 'spectacle and song' (Castellani and Zefferelli) and 'the age of angst' (Richardson, Hall, Brook).

For Rothwell, 'the history of Shakespeare in the movies' is 'the search for the best available means to replace the verbal with the visual imagination' (2004: 5), as well as a matter of progressively 'liberating the Shakespeare movie from theatrical and textual dependency and moving towards the filmic' (25); it is also a narrative of the struggle the film artist (exemplified by Welles) and industry pressures (personified, in a phrase taken from *King John*, 2.1.574, as 'tickling commodity'). One of the strengths of the book is its attentiveness to the changing circumstances of viewing and critical evaluation, as revealed by the evidence of contemporary reactions of films which have subsequently been re-viewed in very different terms.

The second edition of this volume also registers that a significant cultural shift had taken place since the publication of the first, prompting a rethinking of its critical categories: 'nowadays Shakespeareans defer to filmmakers. Subservience has yielded to subversion', a change which 'has toppled the sovereignty of text over performance to the point that the term "transgressive" … as a label for bizarre adaptation, has become meaningless' (Rothwell 2004: xi). Stephen Buhler's *Shakespeare in the Cinema: Ocular Proof* (2002) is equally wide-ranging, and themed in terms of 'shared patterns of adaptation' (3) which extend and challenge some of the established ways that Shakespeare films have been grouped and characterised. Buhler's examination of three films of *Othello* considers how the play tests 'cinema's status as representational medium' (3); a chapter on documentary rethinks Jorgens's notion of the 'theatrical' film to include not only Tree's *King John* alongside Pacino's *Looking for Richard* but also a 1936 MGM speculative biographical sketch, *Master Will Shakespeare*, and a later chapter similarly redefines the 'filmic' mode via a series of versions which 'assert themselves as films as distinct from theater: that is, they exploit – and often advertise – the medium's illusionistic powers or its radical plasticity' (4); 'Shakespeare and the Screen Idol' considers 'who it is that most benefits from the conjunction of Shakespeare, the star system, and ... the bottom line' (52).

Set alongside this is a consideration of how Shakespeare has elicited cinematic 'trans-gression', whether generic ('rather than conform to the dictates of genre, [film-makers] may choose to mix them; Shakespeare's plays, with their insistence on complicating the generic boundaries they have helped to construct ... almost demand it' [Buhler 2002: 126]), sexual (transvestism in Sarah Bernhardt's 1900 and Asta Nielsen's 1920 films of *Hamlet*) or poli-tical (Mankiewicz's 1953 *Julius Caesar*, read as an allegory of McCarthyism). Buhler con-cludes with a discussion of Julie Taymor's *Titus*; like Rothwell, he finds in this film evidence to counter the claim of a quarter-century of Shakespearean film criticism that cinema is best when furthest from the theatre: the work of a director who works 'cinema-tically in the theatre and ... theatrically in the cinema' (quoted in Rothwell 2004: 269), *Titus* thrives upon 'her personal negotiations between stage and film', suggesting that 'most of the successful adaptations of Shakespeare for the screen have served as interventions in cinema's ongoing relationship with the literary, the dramatic, and other visual arts' (Buhler 2002: 192–93).

Jump cuts

The study of Shakespeare and the screen media has been a settled component of teaching and research for some time; any new Shakespeare film will now routinely be subjected to detailed scholarly scrutiny within months of release, and it has been clear for some time that film and television incarnations of the plays have, for many viewers, effectively supplanted theatrical production as the primary domain in which Shakespeare is seen in 'performance'. The fact that Shakespearean film scholarship is now firmly underpinned by the disciplinary base of media, film and cultural studies accounts both for the relaxation of concerns which were once far more intense (about fidelity to the text, about typologies of adaptation) and for the openness of its field of enquiry. Recent scholarship has built upon previous investigations of filmic treatments of gender and sexuality, power, ideology and national identity by beginning to consider how these interact in Shakespearean films with constructions of race and ethnicity, and with the mechanisms of cultural exchange.

Examples include Diana E. Henderson's *Collaborations with the Past*, which gives 'special attention to the remediated representation of gender and nationhood' (2006a: 15), and her edited collection *A Concise Companion to Shakespeare on Screen*, in which the recognition that, in a world of twenty-four-hour global media, where 'cameras have become crucial in creating political change, social action, and communal responsibility ... Never has it been so urgent and important ... that we as students, consumers, and producers of screen images comprehend and convey the skills needed to analyze and interpret them well' (2006b:2); a perspective shared by Mark Thornton Burnett's *Filming Shakespeare in the Global Marketplace* (2007) and his and Ramona Wray's *Screening Shakespeare in the Twenty-First Century* (2006); Sarah Hatchuel's Branagh-oriented *Shakespeare, from Stage to Screen* (2004); Judith Buchanan's *Shakespeare on Film* (2005); Carolyn Jess-Cooke's *Shakespeare on Film: Such Things as Dreams Are Made Of* (2007); Maurice Hindle's *Studying Shake-speare on Film* (2007); and Thomas Cartelli and Katherine Rowe's *New Wave Shakeseare on Screen* (2007).

Perhaps the most intriguing area for future development within the field, however, lies in the potential for film theory and criticism to intersect with other, possibly unexpected, practices of scholarship. The most obvious point of contact is with performance studies, especially now that this generally no longer confines its remit to live theatre. Crossover has been a feature of the discipline from the beginning, but so too has the sense that the formal and ontological distinctions between media remain as critical problems. An example of this can be seen in W. B. Worthen's deployment of the most 'post-theatrical' of Shakespeare films, Almereyda's *Hamlet*, to define and contextualise the 'performativity' of Shakespeare's Globe (and, in particular, the 2000 production of *Hamlet* that coincided with the film's release):

> Cutting the text, modernizing the performance, transforming the medium: nothing could be farther from the Globe's reconstructed liveness than Almereyda's deeply citational *Hamlet*. Yet the film clarifies a crucial question about *Hamlet* at the Globe, and perhaps about the Globe itself. Almereyda's film appears to produce the metatheatrical inquiry of Shakespeare's play … in the most widespread and vital idiom of contemporary performance in western technological culture, an idiom (as Hawke's *Hamlet* demonstrates) that is accessible to us, that many of us see, use, and perform, and perhaps more often than we go to the theatre. Shakespeare's play, on the sterile promontory of the reconstructed Globe, still recalls its original theatrical discourse, the power of the theatre, of *this* theatre to infect the name of action. But as Almereyda's film implies, theatre is no longer … our master trope for interrogating acting, action, performance.
>
> (Worthen 2003: 113)

If Worthen's assessment (perhaps rather pessimistically) registers that the cultural dominance of film demands that we reconsider the formerly privileged position of the Shakespearean live theatre, the theoretical prominence of film studies also indicates adventurous new ways of thinking about early modern texts and performances at their point of historical origin.

Barbara Freedman's *Staging the Gaze* (1991) provides a compelling example of this. Proceeding from the recognition that Shakespeare's comedies 'play upon the lure of a spectator consciousness; they no sooner tantalise us with a stable position of mastery than they mock this stance by staging audience, character, plot, and theme as sites of misrecognition' (Freedman 1991: 2), Freedman splices together film theory, psychoanalysis, Renaissance optics and theories of perspective, and the early modern trope of 'learned ignorance' less to '"apply" psychoanalysis to Shakespeare's comedies' than to 'explore, from multiple perspectives, the myth of mastery and the play of denial as performed in their reception', placing 'Renaissance theater, psychoanalysis, and critical theory in a dramatic interplay of reciprocally reflecting gazes' (5). Courtney Lehmann's *Shakespeare Remains* (2002), is, on the face of it, a study of Shakespeare and (mostly postmodern) film in the generally recognised sense, in that it contains chapters on Almereyda's *Hamlet*, Branagh's *Henry V* and *Shakespeare in Love*, but it breaks important new ground by deploying film texts, and film theory, to read Shakespeare's work in its own time as well as ours. Thus *Hamlet* is treated as 'a locus of early cinematic thinking' (Lehmann 2002: 20), which 'articulates a nascent cultural preoccupation with the idea of "passing show" as that which *surpasses* theater, generating … "the desire called cinema"' (90). Luhrmann's *Romeo + Juliet*, widely recognised as a hyperbolically postmodern, post-historical, even post-cinematic, film, becomes an intricate negotiation with the problems of adaptation and cultural inheritance, in a discussion which focusses in particular upon Shakespeare's own use of his source, Arthur Brooke's *Tragicall Historye of Romeus and Juliet* and the film's uncanny habit of 'reproducing Arthur Brooke's *imagery* "to the letter"' (146), thereby engaging a cultural legend of the star-crossed lovers that predates even Shakespeare's versioning of it.

The conclusion is that the film asks us to 'rethink … authorship in the age of adaptation' (Lehmann 2002: 160); likewise, drawing upon theories of montage and auteurship, Lehmann discerns an affinity between postmodern and early modern conceptions and practices of authorship: 'we should rethink Shakespeare in relation to Hitchcock', which means recognising Shakespeare as 'a montage of historically charged collisions between bodies and texts that cannot be reduced to the work either of a solitary "author" or an ever-metamorphosing dramatic and textual "apparatus"' (18–19); the project, as Lehmann defines it, being to initiate 'a long-overdue process of *theoretical* adaptation that replaces the burning of historical bridges between the early modern and the postmodern, Romanticism and poststructuralism, theater and cinema with the timely creation of montage effects' (24). By proposing to build such bridges between the modern cinema, the texts it has staged, adapted and transformed, and the historical conditions of their formation, Lehmann points to one future for Shakespearean film criticism by provocatively extending the domain of film to incorporate its own pre-history. Having found Shakespeare in the cinema, we can now look for the cinema in Shakespeare.

2 Performance

The complete Shakespeare

Between April 2006 and June 2007, those possessed of sufficient determination, free time and disposable income to live in or visit Stratford-upon-Avon would have had a unique opportunity to witness every one of Shakespeare's works in performance. Beginning at the Royal Shakespeare Theatre with *Romeo and Juliet* and ending with *King Lear* at the same theatre just over a year later, the marathon season featured thirteen Royal Shakespeare Company productions, among them the *Henry VI* plays, which also formed the start of a complete Histories Cycle, and a Christmastime *Merry Wives – The Musical*; the RSC also played host to productions by national and international companies that included the British-based Cardboard Citizens, Kneehigh Theatre and Forkbeard Fantasy, and others from Germany, Italy, Russia, the United States, Brazil, Saudi Arabia, South Africa, China and Japan.

Performed in the Royal Shakespeare Theatre, in its temporary replacement the Courtyard Theatre, which opened in 2006 prior to the Royal Shakespeare Theatre's closure the following year for major refurbishment, and in a range of venues around Stratford, the productions were as varied as the companies that presented them: the two parts of *Henry IV* from the Chicago Shakespeare Theater, *Titus Andronicus* in Japanese, directed by Yukio Ninagawa, an all-male *Twelfth Night* in Russian from Moscow's Chekhov International Theatre Festival (directed by Declan Donnellan, founder of Cheek by Jowl), *Othello* from South Africa's Baxter Theatre Centre, and the same play violently reworked in obscenely colloquial German and directed by Luk Perceval of the Münchner Kammerspiele, the Little Angel Theatre enacting *Venus and Adonis* with puppets and the Tiny Ninja Theatre of New York presenting *Hamlet* with a cast of miniature plastic figurines, and *A Midsummer Night's Dream*, directed by Tim Supple, which drew its cast, and its seven languages, from across the Indian subcontinent and Sri Lanka.

Critical opinion was divided as to the merits and the achievements of the Festival. Early on, the *Shakespeare Survey* reviewer Michael Dobson wondered whether it was all merely 'a desperate gambit for energizing Stratford' (2007: 285), though the RSC's artistic director Michael Boyd was quoted as hoping that, as a consequence of the exposure of the work of the Festival, 'Stratford-upon-Avon will never be the same again' (Higgins 2006), and as many reviewers were irked by the more adventurous interventions as were intrigued or excited by them. Perceval's *Othello* provoked particularly strong reactions: the *Times* reviewer spoke for many when he described it as 'screamingly pretentious' and 'deadly' (Marlowe 2006). As is often the case with foreign productions of Shakespeare seen on British soil, the very idea of performing in languages other than English tends to generate scepticism and sometimes open hostility; commenting on an earlier and smaller-scale international Shakespeare Festival hosted by the Barbican Centre in London in 1994, Peter Holland pointed to the prevalence of 'parochialism' and 'xenophobic suspicion at the sheer unEnglishness of the work' in the season's reviews (Holland 1997: 255). On the other hand, reviewers and audiences also showed themselves to be generously receptive towards the 'unEnglish' work showcased in Stratford from 2006 to 2007: Supple's wonderful *Dream*, especially, enraptured its audiences (myself among them), and was aptly described by one critic as 'magical, mysterious, unforgettably sexy' (Spencer 2007). Overall, it seems fair to concur with Jonathan Bate's conclusion that the Festival that could be described as 'a celebration of collaboration, innovation and internationalism' (2007: 188).

Five decades of performance criticism

Bate's perspective on the event bears the authority of an especially privileged insider. The later period of the Complete Works Festival was also the year of publication of a new edition, also operating under the auspices of the RSC. Edited by Bate and Eric Rasmussen, and featuring a foreword by Michael Boyd, the RSC Shakespeare *Complete Works* carried the blessing of a company whose work has itself been the subject of close academic scrutiny from its inception, and which has had a tradition of strongly signalling its own scholarly responsibilities and alignments. For Boyd, Bate, as 'one of the foremost Shakespeare scholars of his generation', is also 'a valued presence in the RSC rehearsal room' (Boyd 2007: lxv); Bate and Rasmussen's edition, and even more so the single-play volumes that have followed it, in return draw extensively upon the database of RSC production history to vividly render the image of the text in modern performance.

The RSC *Complete Works* is the culmination of a dialogue between the theatre and academic criticism that began in earnest in the early 1960s, when the company was formed under the leadership of its new artistic director Peter Hall, whose task at the end of the 1950s had been to transform the ailing annual Shakespeare festival seasons at the Shakespeare Memorial Theatre into a vital force within British, and world, theatre. Hall instituted a permanent ensemble company that offered its members two-year contracts and the prospect of a season in Stratford followed by one at its newly acquired London base, the Aldwych Theatre; he forged links between Shakespeare, contemporary drama and the theatrical avant-garde by enlisting director Peter Brook as a colleague and by committing the RSC to the commissioning of new plays, requiring his actors to perform in both modern and classical works; and, with the aid of ex-Cambridge University academic John Barton, he established a systematic programme of performer training, focussing, in particular, on the fundamentals of verse speaking. In key productions of the period, the RSC announced its receptiveness to contemporary scholarship, notably in Peter Brook's 1962 *King Lear*, whose theatrical and philosophical frame of reference conspicuously matched the absurdist, Beckettian vision articulated in Jan Kott's essay '*King Lear*, or Endgame' (in *Shakespeare Our Contemporary*, 1965), and in the Hall–Barton collaboration *The Wars of the Roses* (1963), an adaptation of the *Henry VI* plays that included large swathes of pastiche early Shakespearean verse written by Barton himself.

This was not the first time that Shakespearean theatre practice and critical writing had operated in alliance with each other, of course. The beginnings of the dialogue lay in the work of the would-be reformer and revivalist William Poel, who in a succession of predominantly amateur experimental productions between 1881 and 1931, and in books, articles and pamphlets, both demonstrated and argued for the abandonment of pictorial

Peter Hall (b. 1930)

Theatre and film director

Before making his Stratford-upon-Avon debut in 1956 with *Love's Labours Lost*, Hall had already established himself as a comprehensively all-round directorial star of the London stage, conversant both with the outer limits of the contemporary avant-garde (the London premiere of Samuel Beckett's *Waiting for Godot*, which he directed at the Arts Theatre in 1955) and with the commercial West End (the musical *Gigi*, at the New Theatre the following year). In 1960 he succeeded Glen Byam Shaw as Artistic Director of the Shakespeare Memorial Theatre and immediately instituted the reforms that transformed the ailing annual festival into what would become the world's leading classical repertory company. Securing a royal charter and, subsequently, substantial Arts Council funding, creating a permanent ensemble, renaming the theatre (as the Royal Shakespeare Theatre), and establishing a base in London at the Aldwych Theatre, Hall believed that Shakespeare, performed alongside and seen in the context of modern playwrights, should be staged in ways that were both classically rigorous and urgently contemporary. His key productions defined the RSC's identity and house style, including *The Wars of the Roses*, co-directed with John Barton in 1963–64, *Hamlet* in 1965 (starring a startlingly young and provocatively unromantic Prince in the gangly shape of David Warner), as well as Pinter's *The Homecoming* in the same year. Hall left the RSC in 1968 and became Artistic Director of the National Theatre in 1973, a post he held until 1988. Steering the National through the most fraught period in its history, Hall directed *Coriolanus* in 1984 and a season of late plays in the Cottesloe during his final season. On leaving the National he founded the Peter Hall Company, directing, amongst others, *The Merchant of Venice* with Dustin Hoffman as Shylock (1989), *Hamlet* (1994) and *As You Like It* in 2003, starring his daughter Rebecca Hall as Rosalind. A self-confessed 'fundamentalist' on the matter of verse-speaking (for Hall, the scoring of Shakespeare's verse is as precise as that of Mozart's or Pinter's, and demands equal punctiliousness), Hall was one of the major backers of the Rose Theatre in Kingston, a performance space loosely based on Henslowe's Rose. In that venue, in 2010, he directed the seventy-five-year-old Judi Dench as Titania in *A Midsummer Night's Dream*.

staging and a return to Elizabethan-style methods (see especially *Shakespeare in the Theatre* [1913]). Poel's own efforts were mostly dismissed or derided but his principles found more general acceptance when mediated through the work and writings of his immediate successor, Harley Granville Barker, whose multi-volume *Prefaces to Shakespeare* (1923–47) adumbrate a performance-oriented approach to the plays that continues to command a fairly substantial readership (they were reprinted as recently as 2006; in a foreword to the 1993 reprint, theatre director Richard Eyre tendentiously hailed Granville Barker as 'a man who, alone amongst Shakespearean commentators before Jan Kott, believed in the power of Shakespeare on stage' [Eyre 1993: iv]).

Barker's advocacy of scenic economy and rapid pace was informed by his professional experience at the Savoy Theatre; a more idiosyncratic perspective was offered during the same period by a very different practitioner-critic, G. Wilson Knight, whose *Principles of Shakespearian Production*, appearing in successively revised and expanded versions between 1936 and 1963, sought to ally his own practical forays into Shakespearean staging with his highly impressionistic method of image-centred interpretation: defining the Shakespearean text in quintessentially modernist terms as 'an aural time-sequence with rhythmic modulations' which 'creates in the mind a result that may be imaged as spatial, solid, and rich in sense-suggestion', he insists that its producer needs to be alert to 'the play's metaphysical core … its wholeness' and embrace its resonance as universal metaphor rather than the literalism of its action (Knight 2002: 41–42).

Professionally informed performance criticism was also offered by the theatre director Tyrone Guthrie, whose energies as an advocate of the open-stage movement in the 1950s and 1960s were matched by a critical output represented by books such as the essay collection *In Various Directions* (1965) and the polemical autobiography *A Life in the Theatre* (1959), which drew upon the lessons of a long career in the commercial and non-commercial theatres, and in particular his experience of constructing the arena stage of the Stratford Festival in Ontario, to call time on the still-dominant picture frame stage, to proclaim the death of realism and to advocate a new form of 'ritual' performance. For Guthrie, the 'real magic' of theatre lies in the fact that it is 'charming, interesting and exciting not the nearer it approach[es] "reality", but the farther it retreat[s] into its own artifice' (1959: 180). Elsewhere during the 1950s the work of Shakespearean theatres and festivals began to be documented in detail, usually in celebratory rather than critically reflective forms: both the Old Vic and the Shakespeare Memorial Theatre published pictorial records of their work on a roughly annual basis from the 1940s onwards; and the first three seasons at the Stratford Festival were commemorated in a series of volumes co-edited by Tyrone Guthrie and Robertson Davies and others (1953, 1954 and 1955).

To these may be added theatrically rooted memoirs, retrospectives and surveys and histories of performance (for example Farjeon 1949; Sprague 1953; Webster 1957), works of production history (the first instalment of Marvin Rosenberg's monumental quartet detailing the major tragedies on stage line by line, *The Masks of Othello*, appeared in 1961; it was followed by volumes on *King Lear* in 1971, *Macbeth* in 1978 and *Hamlet* in 1993) and critical and reflective articles and reviews in the journals *Shakespeare Quarterly* and *Shakespeare Survey* (for example Kemp 1954; David 1959). The first of the eleven volumes of the indispensable reference work *The London Stage*, covering 1660 to 1800, was published in 1960; to be supplemented from 1973 onwards by Highfill, Burnim and Langhans's *Biographical Dictionary* of performers and stage personnel during the same period and, from 1976, by J. P. Wearing's *The London Stage*, covering the period between 1890 and 1959.

None of this yet amounted to a recognisable critical movement or school within Shakespearean scholarship as a whole, which during the 1950s and early 1960s was still largely under the double sway of Tillyardian historicism and New Criticism. In this context, then, Richard David's call (in 1959) for dialogue between actors and scholars, whilst merely reiterating a summons that had been previously issued by Poel, Granville Barker, Guthrie and others, heralded the beginning of a rapprochement that, under the auspices of the RSC itself, would before long become considerably more substantial and meaningful than had ever previously been attempted or envisaged. As mentioned earlier, the productions that were instrumental in defining its early sense of direction and identity conspicuously flaunted their affiliations with the contemporary critical avant-garde; and the impression of intellectual substance, and scholarly seriousness and commitment, was strengthened by the company's fostering of forms of documentation that not only put the work on an altogether more self-critical footing than had previously been attempted in the professional Shakespearean theatre, but also increasingly invited serious and sustained scholarly scrutiny.

In 1963, the RSC published a pamphlet, *Crucial Years of the RSC*, which outlined the vicissitudes of the first three seasons but also provided a platform for Hall, Brook and others to theorise and polemicise about the current state of Shakespearean performance, as well as to launch a kind of manifesto for its future: for Hall, contemporary urgency was the key, manifested in his conviction that the RSC could find 'Samuel Becket [sic] in *Lear*' and 'the Cuban crisis in *Troilus*' (1963: 14). This was followed in 1964 by a volume covering the first three years of its work, *Royal Shakespeare Company, 1960–63* (Goodwin 1964), which, in addition to comprehensive production documentation, included an essay by Peter Hall, 'Shakespeare and the Modern Director', in which he defined his task as 'by diligent scholarship and hard work, to express Shakespeare's intentions in terms that modern audiences can understand' (Hall 1964: 41). Foremost among the first postwar generation of university-educated English theatre directors, Hall had studied English Literature at Cambridge University under F. R. Leavis; Shakespeare's intentions, as he at this time understood them, could be retrieved by recourse to a potent (and contradictory) amalgamation of the historicism of Tillyard and the modernism of Jan Kott, and were realised through scrupulous attention to the text that explicitly invoked his mentor's practice of close reading.

The exemplary RSC

Addressing an academic readership as well as the theatregoing public, Hall issued criticism with a challenge and an invitation, to which criticism was immediately eager to respond. In 1966 John Russell Brown (subsequently to play a formative role in the development of performance-based criticism) published *Shakespeare's Plays in Performance*, in which he urged 'a decisive movement away from literary criticism towards theatrical study', and which suggested that contemporary stage practice had begun to assume the imperatives and the habits of scholarship; in addition to the business of mounting a play, theatre directors answered 'the need to make Shakespeare "come alive"' through their own forms of research and pedagogy: in that they 'search, debate, justify and try to learn' (Brown 1969: 15, 209). The work of the RSC itself provided Brown with ample empirical evidence for his own investigation, and his interest was shared by others, in that the company's work quickly became the primary, and often the sole, focus of performance criticism's attention.

Apart from the consideration that the RSC's institutional status commanded attention if not always unqualified approval, there were obvious and sound practical reasons for this: the company was unique among Shakespeare-producing organisations, nationally and internationally, for the longevity of its runs, with productions remaining in repertory for up to two years (in Stratford and in London) and sometimes even longer, as well as being taken on national and worldwide tours, enabling critics to engage with them in hitherto unprecedented depth and detail by means of repeated visits (Richard David's *Shakespeare in the Theatre* [1978] is a prime instance of this, being a record of work, mostly at Stratford, during the 1970s whose primary aim is to effect 'the precise recording of supreme or characteristic moments in this most fleeting and insubstantial of all the arts' [David 1978: xiii]). The company's efforts to create a record of its own achievement, not only in its souvenir volumes and yearbooks but also in published scripts (*The Wars of the Roses* in 1970, *Henry V* in 1975, *The Plantagenets* in 1989), have from the outset operated alongside the archiving activities of the Shakespeare Centre Library at the Shakespeare Birthplace Trust, which houses comprehensive records of all Stratford productions from 1879 onwards.

The first full-length account of the RSC, David Addenbrooke's *The Royal Shakespeare Company: The Peter Hall Years* (which carries a foreword by Hall and an afterword by his successor, Trevor Nunn) was published in 1974. It was followed by numerous works in which the RSC's output is the primary or substantial focus of attention. Chronologically, these are: Stanley Wells, *Royal Shakespeare* (1977), an account of four key productions between 1959 and 1973; David's *Shakespeare in the Theatre* (1978); Colin Chambers, *Other Spaces* (1980), a concise history of the RSC's work at the Other Place and the Warehouse during the 1970s; Sally Beaumann's gossipy *The Royal Shakespeare Company: A History of Ten Decades* (1982); Gary Taylor's *Moment by Moment by Shakespeare* (1985); Michael L. Greenwald, *Directions by Indirections* (1986), a study of John Barton's work with the company; J. R. Mulryne and Margaret Shewring, *The Golden Round* (1989), covering the first years of the Swan; Barbara Hodgdon, *The End Crowns All* (1992), a reading of the histories in performance that focusses particularly on their endings and their attempts, or not, to secure closure; Robert Shaughnessy, *Representing Shakespeare* (1994), which also considers the histories in their ideological and cultural contexts; Peter Holland, *English Shakespeares* (1997), covering the RSC during the 1990s: Michael Adler, *Rough Magic* (2001), a behind-the-scenes account; Colin Chambers, *Inside the Royal Shakespeare Company* (2004); and Alycia Smith-Howard, *Studio Shakespeare* (2006), on the Other Place. Since the 1980s, the RSC's work has featured prominently centrally in a range of series detailing the stage and screen histories of individual plays: Macmillan's 'Text and Performance' (launched in 1983 with volumes on *A Midsummer Night's Dream* and *Hamlet*), Manchester University Press's 'Shakespeare in Performance' (from 1991, with *Henry IV, Part 1*, *King Lear* and *Merchant*), Cambridge University Press's 'Shakespeare in Production' (from 1996: *Dream*), and the Arden Shakespeare's 'Shakespeare at Stratford' (from 2002: *Richard II*, *Merchant* and *The Winter's Tale*).

Individual RSC productions have also attracted extensive academic attention, notably Hall and Barton's *Wars of the Roses*, Barton's 1973 *Richard II*, Terry Hands's 1975 *Henry V*, Trevor Nunn's 1976 *Macbeth* and, above all, Peter Brook's acclaimed 1970 *Dream*, which wrenched the play out of its traditional woodland setting to locate it in a featureless white box (invoking the ideal realm of Brook's key treatise on theatre, *The Empty Space*, which begins with the statement that 'I can take any empty space and call it a bare stage' and urges us to 'open our empty hands and show that really there is nothing up our sleeves' (Brook 1968: 11, 109), and which substituted actors costumed as Chinese acrobats for fairies, and circus skills and gymnastic virtuosity for magic, in which Bottom's ass's head was represented by a clown's red nose and a pair of Mickey Mouse ears, and which introduced the now-routine doubling of Oberon and Titania with Theseus and Hippolyta. A touchstone for subsequent Shakespearean production, for stage histories of the play and for critical reflections on the play in performance (see Warren 1983; Halio 2003; Griffiths 1996; Hodgdon 1998), and for general histories of twentieth-century Shakespearean theatre (Kennedy 1993; Bate and Jackson 1996), the production is comprehensively documented in Glenn Loney's *Peter Brook's Production of* A Midsummer Night's Dream *for the Royal Shakespeare Company* (1974) and, more controversially, David Selbourne's *The Making of* A Midsummer Night's Dream (1982), an eyewitness account of rehearsals pointedly dedicated to the show's cast (but not its director) that was subsequently disowned by Brook as profoundly misrepresentative.

Revolution and after

Although it is now seen as a defining moment within late twentieth-century theatre, Brook's production divided critical opinion: hailed by some reviewers as, in the words of the *Times* reviewer, 'a masterpiece' (Wardle 1970), it was received by others more coolly:

described by Benedict Nightingale of the *New Statesman* as 'Shakespeare as he might be conceived by a science fiction addict, or, indeed, performed by enthusiastic vegans', this was 'a hectic, abrupt journey from the Hayward Gallery to Disneyland, from Billy Smart's Circus to International Wrestling on ITV, from August Bank Holiday, Isle of Wight, to the grind and clank of the industrial Midlands' (Nightingale 1970). For John Russell Brown (as for Selbourne), the revelatory quality of Brook's production was more apparent than real, in that in his orchestration of the setting and performance idiom of the show, the director 'was forcing his actors to discover what he had been looking for, instead of encouraging them to draw on their own, freely given creativity' (Brown 1974: 42–43).

Brown's observation is offered in the context of a vigorous interrogation and critique of contemporary Shakespearean theatre and scholarship, both of which, he contends, are mired in their 'conceptual basis', which turns Shakespeare's texts into 'plays of ideas: they are considered as arguments, and they are produced so that they reflect, at all points, and by every means, a unifying, relevant and individually perceived theme' (Brown 1974: 17). Arguing against this stultifying and reductive practice, Brown offers 'an alternative way of performing the plays, one that goes against almost all accepted conditions of performance' (3), that seeks to recover the essence and spirit of the early modern stage by adopting an actor-led, director-free ethos of the ensemble, through which, though 'unfixed by detailed rehearsal and direction, the drama would be held together by the structure of its action' (85).

Brown's advocacy of, as his title has it, a 'free Shakespeare' (the first term is both adjective and verbal imperative) represents performance criticism at its most polemical; and he has continued to argue for an approach which is 'exploratory and experiential, involving imagination and sensation as well as observation, analysis, and critical judgement' (2002: 230), in works such as *Shakespeare and the Theatrical Event* and *Shakespeare Dancing*, which concludes that 'the most potent effects of performance are felt rather than understood: they are received by the senses and never wholly dependent on an intellectual recognition that can be verbalized' (2005a: 204). Brown is also the general editor of the 'Shakespeare Handbooks' series (launched in 2005 with volumes on *Macbeth*, *Twelfth Night*, *The Merchant of Venice* and *As You Like It*), whose aim is 'to help readers to envisage for themselves how the play can come alive in their minds, as on a stage' (Brown 2005b: vii).

In Brown's criticism, Shakespearean performance is a matter of potentiality and imaginative possibility rather than documented theatre history, which has been tried and found wanting. Others have been more sanguine about the possibilities and realised achievements of actual performance, and equally ready to mobilise these to polemical effect. The key figure here is J. L. Styan, whose *The Shakespeare Revolution* (1977) announced the ascendancy of 'stage-centred' criticism, figured in terms of a dynamic rapprochement between scholarship and the theatre, whereby 'Actors and scholars will teach each other, not what Shakespeare "means", but what his possibilities are beyond logic ... The scholar will modify the actor's illumination, the actor will modify the scholar's, a process of infinite adjustment' (Styan 1977: 237). Styan's optimistic scenario proceeds from the premise that the 'first and last values of drama are revealed in the response of an audience in a theatre, and all else must be secondary and speculative' (3), and that the task of the modern theatre should be to recapture the essentials of the 'flexible Elizabethan mode of performance, playing to the house, stepping in and out of character, generating a stage action allegorical and symbolic, making no pretence at the trappings of realism', which 'encouraged a verbally acute, sensory and participatory, multi-levelled and fully aware mode of experience for an audience' (5).

As a version of early modern performance, this is, of course, very much 'speculative'; as a template for Shakespeare in the present it is a fusion of the widely divergent practices of the directors Styan considers (Poel, Granville Barker, Nigel Playfair, Barry Jackson, Guthrie and Brook) and of twentieth-century popular and avant-garde theatre forms, from Brecht, cabaret and the music hall to the encounter-based, environmental and experiential vocabularies of the 1960s and 1970s.

For Styan, the narrative of both criticism and performance in the twentieth century is a progressive (even 'revolutionary') one, a story of experimentation, discovery and revelation that culminates in the triumph of Brook's *Dream*, and of a contemporary Shake-scene represented by the work of John Barton in Stratford and Joseph Papp in New York, where 'past traditions of realistic presentation are being stripped away', and where 'the spirit of Elizabethan ritual and role-playing' reminds the spectator 'of Shakespeare's essential theatricality in a way that Brecht would fully have endorsed' (Styan 1977: 234). We might pause here to note that an endorsement from Brecht of a trans-historical notion of 'essential theatricality' seems unlikely: although he described the Elizabethan stage as one 'full of A-effects' (Brecht 1965: 58), hailed it as 'earthly, profane and lacking in magic' (59), and urged that one should 'stage the plays in a spirit of experiment' (60), he insisted that the principle should be to 'play these old works historically, which means setting them in powerful contrast to our own time' (63–64). But for Styan twentieth-century performance's rediscovery of a non-illusionist Shakespeare eradicates the historical distance, and difference, between then and now, as well as between the very different theatrical modernisms he cites: 'Had they but known', he writes, 'the students of Elizabethan dramatic convention might eventually have found themselves marching in step with such scandalous avant-gardists as Pirandello, Cocteau, Brecht, Genet and others who have returned its former elasticity to the stage' (Styan 1977: 4–5).

It is partly by postulating such alliances as these, however improbable (as W. B. Worthen remarks, '*Brecht?* Marching *in step?* [1997: 159]), that Styan succeeds in rendering Shakespeare in performance vital, contemporary and strangely familiar, and the optimism that animates *The Shakespeare Revolution* is reflected in the performance criticism during the late 1970s and early 1980s, as reflected, for example in Philip C. McGuire and David A. Samuelson's collection *Shakespeare: The Theatrical Dimension* (1979), Ann Pasternak Slater's *Shakespeare the Director* (1982), McGuire's *Speechless Dialect* (1985), Jay L. Halio's *Understanding Shakespeare's Plays in Performance* (1988), Marvin and Ruth Thompson's *Shakespeare and the Sense of Performance* (1989) and Samuel Crowl's *Shakespeare Observed* (1992). More recent contributions include Lois Potter and Arthur F. Kinney (eds) *Shakespeare, Text, and Theater* (1999) and Grace Ioppolo (ed.) *Shakespeare Performed* (2000). In these works, performance criticism is a reading strategy conducted in relation to both the historical conditions of Shakespeare's theatre and stagecraft and the practicalities and achievements of contemporary production, twin phenomena which are assumed, at their best, to be mutually complementary and reciprocally illuminating. During the 1970s, the synergy between the academy and the professional theatre also appeared to be reflected in a shared interest in the hot topic of Shakespearean metadrama, that is, in the self-reflexive dimensions of the plays themselves and in theatre that was about theatre: books such as James L. Calderwood's *Shakespearean Metadrama* (1971) and *Metadrama in Shakespeare's Henriad* (1979) found their practical counterparts in Brook's *Dream*, Hands's *Henry VI*, and Barton's *Richard II* and *Hamlet* (1980). Anne Righter had established the last two productions' intellectual foundations in *Shakespeare and the Idea of the Play* in 1962.

There were, however, dissenting voices: in *Imaginary Audition,* Harry S. Berger, Jr interrogates what he sees as the unduly uncritical slant of much performance criticism, which, he says, produces an unfeasible opposition between the 'Slit-eyed Analyst' and 'Wide-eyed Playgoer', and argues for 'decelerated reading' characterised by 'slowness' that 'derives in part from the complex and multidirectional acts of attention that characterise ... imaginary audition' (Berger 1989: 45). Not all performance-centred critics accepted the proposition that the specifically early modern aspects of Shakespeare's theatricality are transferable to the modern stage. One important voice qualifying the developing consensus is that of Alan C. Dessen, who has argued for the sometimes radical incommensurability of the two: it is by attending closely to the choices that are made by contemporary productions, he argues, that one can become aware of 'a revealing gap between modern psychological cultural reasoning and the interpretive logic of Shakespeare and his audience' (1987: 221). In *Elizabethan Stage Conventions and Modern Interpreters,* Dessen defines the critical and theatrical challenge in terms of the rupture between the pre-realist Elizabethan stage and the sensibilities of late twentieth-century playgoers and performers (regardless of Brecht and the rest) 'conditioned by the logic of naturalism' (1984: 3).

The problem is not just that the representational conventions of early modern texts may sometimes seem bizarre or incomprehensible (or 'odd, illogical, or intrusive' [Dessen 1984: 11]), but that we can 'never be sure when we are talking the same language, when we are sharing the same assumptions' (9). Sharing Styan's distrust of realism, Dessen is more insistently historicist in his scepticism as to whether the 'real' Shakespearean theatricality that it has served to obscure is so readily recoverable. In *Rescripting Shakespeare* (2002), Dessen employs the historical provenance of the text to assess modern productions with regard to what he terms their 'price tags' and 'trade-offs', recognising that as Shakespeare's scripts are adjusted to the exigencies of company resources, actors' capabilities and audiences' tastes, there will be both gains and losses: 'my recurring questions will be: what is the cost or price exacted for these gains? What do such choices exclude or preclude? Wherein lie the trade-offs?' (Dessen 2002: 5). *Recovering Shakespeare's Theatrical Vocabulary* (1995) emphasizes that Shakespeare's scripts were designed 'for players, playgoers, and playhouses that no longer exist', and that 'in reading one of the early printed texts of a Shakespeare play, we enter into the middle of a conversation – a discourse in a language we only partly understand – between a dramatist and his actor-colleagues, a halfway stage that was completed in a performance now lost to us' (Dessen 1995: 4–5).

Staging history

Dessen is the co-editor, with Leslie Thomson, of *A Dictionary of Stage Directions in English Drama, 1580–1642* (1999), a volume which tabulates the more than 22,000 stage directions found in the texts of over five hundred plays produced between 1580 and the early 1640s to identify 'the only substantive clues to the language shared by ... theatrical professionals' (Dessen and Thomson 1999: ix). Dessen and Thomson's *Dictionary* is a formidable contribution to the body of historical scholarship of the sixteenth- and seventeenth-century stage whose foundations were laid in the 1920s with the publication of E. K. Chambers's four-volume compendium of primary documents pertaining to the companies, staging, playhouses, play publication, censorship and city and government regulation, *The Elizabethan Stage* (1923) (G. E. Bentley's seven-volume *The Jacobean and Caroline Stage* appeared between 1941 and 1968). Following the pioneering research of scholars such as J. C. Adams (1961), M. C. Bradbrook (1962), Bernard Beckerman (1962) and R. A. Foakes (Foakes and Rickert 1961), the publication in 1970 of Andrew Gurr's *The Shakespearean Stage, 1574–1642* (third edition 1992) marked the beginning of a phase in theatre scholarship whose contours have been partly defined by Gurr's own output as one of its foremost authorities. In subsequent studies which, in their successive editions, have become standard reference works, Gurr has addressed the Shakespearean theatre from the perspective of its companies (*The Shakespearian Playing Companies*, 1996) and audiences (*Playgoing in Shakespeare's London*, 1987, 1996 and 2004).

The Shakespearean Stage opens with a tantalising snippet of theatre history ('Hamlet, like any other Shakespearean nobleman, wore his hat indoors' [Gurr 1992: 1]) to initiate a series of speculations about the social and cultural ramifications of the by-play with hats in Hamlet's exchange with Osric. This serves as prologue to a work which, like its successors, is remarkable for the vividness with which it locates early modern plays and performances within professional practice, the customs of theatregoing and the everyday life of the city. *The Shakespearian Playing Companies* is an account of the early modern theatre industry that surveys a spectrum of professional activities and organisations ranging from the 'strikingly democratic' Lord Chamberlain's/King's Men, which operated the sharer system, to 'impresario-led companies' such as the King's and Queen's Revels Children, described by Gurr as subject to 'an autocratic form of rule imposed on a profession which had grown into being by means of a long tradition of collaborative and democratic practices' (1996: 8–9).

As Gurr sees it, the 'prime paradox' of the period is the model of democratic and egalitarian organisation that was advanced by the sharer system, and the threat to good order that was perceived to inhere in the business of playing itself co-existed with the fact that 'the survival and growing prosperity of such companies, the King's Men above all, was due almost entirely to the support and consistent protection given them by the highest authority in the land' (Gurr 1996: 9). Gurr defines the project of *Playgoing in Shakespeare's London* in terms which encompass both material circumstances ('the shape and design of the auditorium, the numbers in an audience, and the consequent behaviour patterns characteristic of Shakespearean playgoing') and, more speculatively, the habits of mind and frames of reference of the playgoers themselves: 'the education, the routine prejudices, the playhouse traditions, and everything the playgoer expected from the playgoing experience' (Gurr 2004a: 7).

For Gurr, the factor that clearly and profoundly differentiates the early modern playhouse from practically all performance spaces that have been operational since the re-opening of the theatres in England after the Restoration in 1660, and especially those we are familiar with today, is that it is primarily a place of audition rather than vision: Shakespeare and his contemporaries, he affirms, generally refer to *hearing* rather than *seeing* a play (this position is echoed elsewhere – see Orrell 1983; Smith 1999; Gurr and Ichikawa 2000 – though the evidence for this has been contested by Gabriel Egan [2001], whose searches of linguistic databases lead him to conclude that the opposite is the case). The disparity between the expectations and experience of the early modern playgoer and her modern counterpart, accustomed to prioritise the needs of the spectator over those of the listener, has particularly pressing implications, Gurr contends, for modern attempts to replicate or reconstruct the early modern playhouse, one of the most fundamental being that 'modern spectators, trained for viewing, automatically position themselves at the "front", and modern actors therefore automatically play to them in two dimensions instead of the original three' (2004a: 1–2).

The reinvention of Shakespeare's Globe

Gurr affords a critical perspective upon the enterprise with which, as a principal academic advisor, he was closely associated from the moment in the early 1980s that it began to become a practicable proposition: Shakespeare's Globe on London's Bankside. The Globe project, which had been the dream of the American actor and director Sam Wanamaker since the 1940s, initially secured the approval of the academic community in the form of a motion of support passed at the first World Shakespeare Congress in 1971, the year in which Gurr's *Shakespearean Stage* was published. Ten years later, Gurr failed to persuade the third World Shakespeare Congress to confirm its backing, but, having nonetheless solicited several hundred scholarly signatures to a letter of support, he joined forces with fellow theatre historian John Orrell, the architects Theo Crosby and Jon Greenfield, and archaeologists from the Museum of London to embark on a venture that, financed entirely by private donations, finally received its official opening in 1997. Wanamaker's Globe was not the first attempt at a reconstruction of an Elizabethan playhouse: in 1912, the Earl's Court show included a miniature Globe replica as part of its 'Shakespeare's England' exhibition, in which were staged play excerpts (see O'Connor 1987); the Folger Shakespeare Library in Washington, DC opened its own scaled-down version in the 1970s; and there are (very approximate) Globe replicas in Odessa, Texas, in Cedar City, Utah, in Tokyo, and in Rome. What distinguished the Bankside project was the unprecedented levels of scholarly, financial and, as became increasingly clear, emotional and ideological investment that it has attracted.

The history of the enterprise is well documented. The publication of Orrell's *The Quest for Shakespeare's Globe* (1983) coincided with the initiation of the serious architectural planning stage; it was followed by Orrell and Gurr's *Rebuilding Shakespeare's Globe* in 1989, the year in which the foundations of the Rose and original Globe playhouses were uncovered near to the building site upon which the reconstruction was taking shape. Barry Day's breezy inside story, *This Wooden 'O': Shakespeare's Globe Reborn*, published in association with the Shakespeare Globe Trust, came out in time for the Prologue season of 1996; J. R. Mulryne and Margaret Shewring's collection *Shakespeare's Globe Rebuilt*, which includes specialist contributions on the historical and archaeological aspects of the project, and on décor, iconography and Tudor carpentry techniques, as well as an essay by the new Artistic Director and leading Globe actor Mark Rylance, was published for the opening in 1997.

Since then there has been a volume of *Shakespeare Survey* (1999) themed 'Shakespeare and the Globe', in which the Bankside project features prominently, and three further books: Pauline Kiernan's *Staging Shakespeare at the New Globe*, which enthusiastically chronicles the first seasons in the belief that the theatre 'offers an opportunity to recover something of the dynamic which existed in the theatrical space for which Shakespeare and his contemporaries wrote many of their plays so that it can invigorate live theatre today' (1999: xi); Rob Conkie's *The Globe Theatre Project* (2006), which, though still critically sympathetic to the more forward-looking aspects of the Globe's activities, registers their contradictory positioning and offers a theoretically aware perspective upon them, in particular with respect to its pursuit of 'authenticity' (subsequently modified to 'original practices'); and Christie Carson and Farah Karim-Cooper's *Shakespeare's Globe: A Theatrical Experiment* (2008).

Like Kiernan's book, the last of these features contributions from Globe practitioners and staff as well as theatre scholars. The readiness to incorporate the theatre maker's voice into

Globe performance scholarship, which has been an aspiration of the performance criticism movement since its inception (and manifested, for example, in the Cambridge University Press 'Players of Shakespeare' series, Michael Pennington's 'User's Guides' [1997, 2000, 2005], Jonathan Holmes's *Merely Players?* [2004] and Michael Dobson's collection *Performing Shakespeare's Tragedies Today* [2006]), is a strong feature of new Globe critical discourse, which, like the theatre it attends to, tends towards the hybrid and the dialogical, as well as displaying a marked degree of self-consciousness. As a space which, while privileging the live encounter within an especially hallowed place and space, is operationally a child of the digital age – although Sam Wanamaker could hardly have envisaged it as such – the Globe has been even more adept at self-documentation than the RSC has been, not only in its comprehensive video archiving of its production work but also in the online materials which are but one element of its status as a globally networked educational and research resource.

Even before it opened (indeed, even before building started) the Bankside Globe was the subject of controversy and sometimes bitter dispute. The complex and protracted negotiations between the scholars, designers, builders and local authority planners and regulators are well documented in the works already cited; what also should be recognised is that one of the major, unexpected outcomes of the prologue seasons of 1995 and 1996 was that quite a few of the actors charged with the task of actually working in the prototype Globe found it to be not the ideal platform for Shakespeare that its enthusiasts had so long dreamed of and wished for, but actually a fairly problematic space. Performers' discontent with the Globe's stage focussed in particular on the location of the pillars supporting its overhanging canopy: positioned, according to the scholars' reading of the architectural evidence, much further forward than the actors would have preferred, these were felt to interfere with sightlines and disrupt the actors' efforts to build a rapport with audiences.

A compromise was eventually worked out, but it is apparent that there was more at stake in the debate than the pragmatics of stage placement and audience address. With the debate polarised as 'Orrell and Gurr v. the actors' (Day 1996: 305), the conflicts that surfaced were between the Wanamaker (and academic) mantra of authenticity and the imperatives of expediency and practicality, and they made uncomfortably evident the competing and potentially contradictory agendas underpinning the Globe's multiple functioning as educational and research resource, would-be experimental laboratory, working commercial theatre, theme park and tourist attraction.

My own awareness of these conflicts was brought sharply into focus by the experience of what was advertised as a practitioner-led workshop session at an academic conference hosted by the Globe in the autumn of 1996. Framed as an exploratory investigation of the 'balcony' scene of *Romeo and Juliet* enacted upon the Globe stage, Mark Rylance's workshop was an artful exercise in goading his academic audience-participants into making fools of themselves. Proceeding from an initial event that saw Rylance and his colleagues delivering the text standing in a line and in a monotone, and then satirically inviting us to theatrically animate it – '*you* tell us what to do' – the session degenerated into the low farce with a hive of scholars issuing contradictory, tendentious and frequently risibly impractical performance briefs. Although this is an impression that had been encouraged by the wilfully confrontational nature of the exercise, the lesson that emerged was that the actor and the scholar could not be further apart. And for me, what lent this incident an unforgettable poignancy and force was the presence of the conference's star speaker, Andrew Gurr, who sat silently in the galleries throughout the whole event, a broad-brimmed hat shading his eyes from the low afternoon sun that glared from behind the tiring house.

Enter theory

The Shakespearian Playing Companies significantly begins with a number of major caveats: warning that the writing of theatre history ('a field game played in fog by untested rules') is, variously, like assembling an incomplete jigsaw composed of fuzzy-edged pieces, attempting to picture a perpetually moving and indistinct target from different angles, and skimming over the bedrock of fact 'on a downdraft of "possibly"s, "probably"s, and "most likely"s', Gurr introduces a work which is 'like a hovercraft pretending to be a camera, made of soft-edged jigsaw pieces' (1996: 3). Bizarre as it sounds, the image also seems strangely appropriate to the Globe itself, an equally conjectural, multi-identitied hybrid fabricated from partial and ambiguous fragments of evidence, an enterprise which solidifies Gurr's gaseous conditionals in the seemingly convincing form of timber, plaster and thatch but which remains a highly speculative work of fiction.

Seen in retrospect, it is telling that the period of the Globe's construction coincided with the rise of the new historicism and cultural materialism, whose theoretical positions and critical practices, as charted on pp. 314–32, threatened to undermine the project's intellectual foundations on an even more fundamental level. From the perspective of the latter, the problem with Shakespeare's Globe is less a matter of its historical accuracy or practical utility than of its ideologically driven cultural mission. The early modern playhouses analysed in Gurr were, to say the least, considerably more complex formations than either the 'cockney picture palace' (as Richard Wilson acidly terms it) visualised in Laurence Olivier's 1944 film of *Henry V* ('the trailer for D-Day') (Wilson 1993: 23) or the theatrical melting pot that provided the final destination of the water-crossing huddled masses of Alfred Harbage's *Shakespeare's Audience* (1941), but for John Drakakis, mounting a frontal assault that was published nearly a decade before the theatre actually opened, the spirit of the latter study was unmistakeably at work in the Globe project.

Citing Philip Brockbank's comment (made in an unpublished conference paper delivered in 1984) that part of the Globe's importance lay in its potential for its neighbourhood to 'recover some of the importance as a centre for popular civilization that it had in Shakespeare's time', Drakakis aligns this with 'the curiously distorted, but so far unrefuted, view of Elizabethan audiences propounded by Alfred Harbage': the belief that the original Globe accommodated a playgoing version of a harmonious, organic community (Drakakis 1988: 29). Quoting Gurr's observation that 'Shakespeare's London more than most conurbations had a many-headed public divided against itself' (Gurr 1992: 141), Drakakis advances an account of the original Globe that emphasises fracture, antagonism and contradiction, in order to counter the impression fostered by the reconstruction that its predecessor was 'an institution whose values and practices accord directly with a universal democratic instinct which the inhabitants of Southwark are now required to re-learn' (Drakakis 1988: 31).

Drakakis's essay contributes to a collection of essays and interviews, *The Shakespeare Myth*, in which contemporary performance is interrogated from a cultural materialist perspective; elsewhere in the volume, Alan Sinfield surveys the appropriation of Shakespeare in recent British drama, and Christopher McCullough reads the work of the RSC in terms of its affiliations to the 'Cambridge English' methodology of close reading. McCullough's essay picks up the critique of the RSC presented by Sinfield in one of his contributions to *Political Shakespeare*, which argues that it is the company's invention of the winning formula of 'Shakespeare-plus-relevance', characterised as 'the combination of traditional authority and urgent contemporaneity' (Sinfield 1994: 183), that has both sustained its critical and theatrical hegemony and defined the dominant paradigm of modern Shakespearean production.

Laurence Olivier (1907–89)

Actor and theatre director

Olivier was ten years into his career as a professional actor, having made a series of impetuous and often misjudged forays onto the commercial stage and into the movie business, before he essayed his first major Shakespearean role. This was in John Gielgud's 1935 London production, in which he and the director, the established leading actor of the English classical stage, alternated the parts of Romeo and Mercutio; from then on, he never looked back, moving swiftly to the Old Vic and in the space of two years, from 1937 to 1938, from Hamlet and Henry V to Sir Toby Belch, Coriolanus and Macbeth, all under the direction of Tyrone Guthrie. In 1936 he appeared in his first Shakespeare film, as Orlando in Paul Czinner's *As You Like It*; and in 1944 directed his first Shakespearean feature, *Henry V*. Conceived as a patriotic contribution to the war effort (it is dedicated to the troops of the D-Day landings), it was also a dazzling meditation on the relationship between Shakespeare's text, his theatre and the cinematic medium. Olivier's portrayal of Henry was partly derived from his performance for Guthrie, as was his performance in his film version of *Hamlet* (1948), which committed to celluloid the Oedipal interpretation that Guthrie had somewhat surreptitiously introduced to the stage of the Old Vic in 1937, and which has since become common theatrical and critical currency. *Richard III* followed in 1955, memorialising a malign-comic portrayal that spawned a thousand imitations and parodies (including, unforgettably, Peter Sellers in 1965, covering the Beatles' 'A Hard Day's Night' in 'Sir's' characteristic style). In the interim, Olivier acted at the Old Vic, playing, amongst others, Hotspur and Justice Shallow, as well as Lear (1946), and at the Shakespeare Memorial Theatre, in 1955 playing Malvolio, Macbeth and the lead in Peter Brook's revelatory production of *Titus Andronicus*. After a powerful, athletic Coriolanus in Peter Hall's production at the SMT in 1959, he went on to act as founding Artistic Director of the National Theatre at the Old Vic, playing Othello in 1964 and Shylock in 1970. Both performances were filmed (though the blackface excesses of the former have not survived the test of time), as was his Lear in 1983. Often placed in opposition to John Gielgud in temperament and style, Olivier regarded himself as a muscular, earthy counterpoint to his friend's delicacy and ethereality. Honoured with a peerage, he was afforded the equivalent of a state funeral in an event broadcast live across the world from Westminster Abbey.

Other essays in *Political Shakespeare* are illustrative of the new historicist positioning of the early modern stage at the heart of social and ideological contestation, epitomised by Stephen Greenblatt's assertion that 'theatricality … is one of power's essential modes' (1994: 33). The first decade of historicist and cultural materialist approaches to early modern theatre and performance, as represented, for example, by the work of Holderness (1985), Mullaney (1988), Patterson (1989), Bruster (1992) and Howard (1994), has been considered in an earlier chapter; here we will also note that the movements' general preoccupation with the power relations invested in theatrical performance, and with the (potentially subversive) marginality and liminality of the stage, has an important antecedent in the work of Robert Weimann's *Shakespeare and the Popular Tradition in the Theater* (published in German in 1967, and in English translation in 1978). Weimann distanced his study from 'the older sociologically oriented criticism' offered by both orthodox Marxism and conventional historicism, which, he suggests, assumed that 'the theater *reflected* contemporary society and that the social composition and dramatic taste of its audience determined or "explained" the nature of the plays'; proposing instead to 'understand verbal artistry as an element in the total function of the Shakespearean stage', and to consider 'dramatic speech' as 'a process between actors and audiences and as a vision of society, as an integral part of the history of the nation that Shakespeare's theater both reflected and helped to create' (Weimann 1978: xii).

Tracing the drama's roots in popular festivities, clowning and the folk play, Weimann emphasises the transitional nature of an Elizabethan stage defined by the dynamic, dialectical interplay between *platea* and *locus*; that is, between the representational and the non-representational, between the conventions of direct performer–audience interaction and those of an embryonic realism, between located action and the anachronistic and placeless space of the platform stage, 'between ritual and *mimesis*' (Weimann 1978: 245), and between play and game. Thus Shakespeare's art is 'a dramaturgy of kings and clowns, of "mongrell Tragicomedie," a theater in which the localized throne was nonetheless functionally connected with the more downstage *platea* position', the latter being occupied not only by 'Apemantus, Thersites, Falstaff, Launce, the gravediggers, the simple countrymen, the nurse, the clowns, and fools' (244), but also by Hamlet.

In *Author's Pen and Actor's Voice*, Weimann sets two contending sources of authority, the text and the common player, in dialectical opposition, arguing that on Shakespeare's stage the 'recurring tension' between them 'constituted a source of strength through concomitant theatrical practices marked by doubleness and contrariety' (2000: 3). Weimann and Douglas Bruster's *Prologues to Shakespeare's Theatre* considers the vital but previously overlooked role played by prologues, which, 'as theatrical beginnings', assert 'intentions and decisions', indicate 'relations of privilege, governance and legitimacy', and 'sort out potential continuities and discontinuities among diverging claims and expectations on the part of authors, performers, and spectators'. Prologues, in short, 'authorize the theatre to produce and perform plays as well as the right of the audience to evaluate these practices' (Bruster and Weimann 2004: ix).

Weimann's work is characterised by its concern with what in *Shakespeare and the Popular Tradition* he terms the relationship between 'the past significance and the present meaning of Shakespeare's theater' (1978: xiii); in his most recent work, this is figured in the largely implicit context of contemporary performance, 'against which some of the most peculiar and peculiarly telling discourses of the Elizabethan theatre can be read in fresh perspective', a landscape defined by the oeuvres of 'Beckett, Müller, Handke, not to mention Robert Wilson, Richard Foreman and others' (Bruster and Weimann 2004: x). The alignment of early modern dramaturgy with the contemporary avant-garde may be partly reminiscent of what we have already encountered of Styan's notoriously eclectic citation of the variety of theatrical modernisms, but Weimann's insistence that 'it seems impossible to relegate the pastness of Shakespeare's theater to the "pure" historian and its contemporaneousness to the "pure" critic or modern producer' (1978: xiii) presented a methodological challenge that the criticisms that followed attempted, with varying degrees of success, to accommodate. New historicists and cultural materialists alike acknowledged the interdependence of past and present and the centrality of performance to this relationship, but few critics in the early stages were inclined to regard the theatre in a positive light.

Within new historicism, strong claims could be made on behalf of early modern players and playhouses as figures and spaces cast in a subversive or scandalous relation to authority; ultimately, however, the stage's entanglement in the coercive mechanisms of power meant that the final word went to containment: as Greenblatt put it at the close of the much-cited essay 'Invisible Bullets', 'There is subversion, no end of subversion, only not for us' (1994: 45). Cultural materialists, meanwhile, found in modern theatre practice (particularly that located in the mainstream institutions) further manifestations of a discredited liberal humanism, variously articulated in reactionary fantasies of the resur-rected early modern stage, in reified literariness and in the bankrupt ideology of realist character. According to Sinfield, modern performance is characterised by its habit of 'sub-merging the range of historical and future possibilities into a permanent human wisdom author-ised, allegedly, by Shakespeare' (1994: 203); for Drakakis, the 'naïve and extravagant claims to historical authenticity' embedded within the Globe project merely represent yet another 'misguided attempt to reclaim a once vibrant and deeply contradictory art … for an age of mechanical reproduction' (1988: 29).

As a reaction against a tradition of appreciative and documentary criticism that tends to eradicate historical difference and to locate performance in a political vacuum, cultural materialist scepticism about the modern Shakespearean theatre is legitimate enough. Such analyses persuasively dissect the motivations of theatre practitioners as expressed in their documented opinions and statements of intent: Sinfield's case against the RSC is built almost entirely on the evidence of directorial statements and of materials such as the pub-lished script of *The Wars of the Roses*; the means and ends of actual productions and production strategies play a fairly minor role in the argument. But they also reinforce the suspicion that there is little on the contemporary theatre scene to like, and still less to trust. Some solace and a prototype for an alternative, oppositional Shakespeare could be found in the theory and practice of Brecht; in particular in the application of his dictum that the old works ought to be played historically, 'in powerful contrast to our own time', though what this might mean in terms of actual production choices was not obvious.

As Graham Holderness saw it, the early modern stage could be readily annexed (as in Brecht's own description in the *Messingkauf*) to the Epic theatre as a place where 'the audience would always sustain an awareness of the constructed artifice of the proceedings, would never be seduced into the oblivion of empathetic illusion' (1985: 212), but instances of such Brechtian good practice in the modern theatre were considerably harder to come by. In an essay published in 1988, Holderness compared two RSC productions seen during the summer of the previous year, Jonathan Miller's *Shrew* in the Royal Shakespeare Theatre and Deborah Warner's *Titus* in the Swan, as, respectively, examples of reactionary and radical production. Whereas the former was directed so as to align Miller's 'conception of Renaissance gender politics' with 'his modern psychologistic notions of character' (and was, as a consequence, 'abhorrent'), Warner's production is endorsed as producing the play 'very much, as Brecht advised, *historically* … The bare platform of the Swan forces the play back on to its intrinsic and original structure, leaving no opportunity for pic-torial or naturalistic or psychological attempts to explain, elucidate or complete the strange, contradictory, unsettling structure of the Elizabethan play' (Holderness 1988b: 154, 155–56).

This was a more constructive stance towards at least some aspects of actual con-temporary practice, but the credibility of the claim that as 'genuinely new and radical creative work' (Holderness 1988b: 158) Warner's production, performed according to the laws of Epic theatre, shared political ground with cultural materialism is somewhat strained, especially when we consider that other reviewers of the show, writing from a decisively non-cultural materialist standpoint, found it equally impressive for very different reasons: Stanley Wells, for example, who praised its rehabilitation of a play 'profoundly concerned with both the personal and the social consequences of violence' (1989: 181), and Alan Dessen, who described the production as 'stunning' (1989: 65). Michael Pennington and Michael Bogdanov's English Shakespeare Company, founded in 1986 as an alternative to the national companies, gained kudos in some quarters for its irreverent, anti-establishment stance, and Bogdanov praised *Political Shakespeare* for what he saw as its analysis of 'the underlying radical political subversion contained in Shakespeare's work' (Pennington and Bogdanov 1990: 27). Responding to the English Shakespeare Company's (ESC) staging of the histories, Isobel Armstrong presented another pairing of the theatrically radical with the retrograde, in this instance by contrasting Bogdanov's work with the National Theatre's 1986 *King Lear*. Witheringly dismissing *Lear* as characterised by 'intellectual and political coherence', and taking it to task for having 'missed, or fudged, the opportunity to explore an increasingly devastating critique in the least conservative of Shakespeare's plays' (as though a flagship production starring Anthony Hopkins and mounted in the Olivier auditorium were likely to do anything else), Armstrong finds that Bogdanov's production of the histories 'pushes the plays towards radical critique by foregrounding their deconstructive moments' (Armstrong 1989: 7, 8, 12).

From theory to practice

Just as it was difficult to argue the eclecticism and aggressive sloganeering of the ESC's productions was much more than a particularly lively variation on Sinfield's 'Shakespeare-plus-relevance' formula, it was also becoming clear that attempting to evaluate contemporary production in terms of its adherence to contemporary scholarly standards of radical aspiration, theoretical coherence and historical rigour, and its potential for 'critique', might not be the most appropriate way of addressing the complex and multiple challenges of performance analysis. The starting point, accordingly, for James C. Bulman's ground-breaking essay collection *Shakespeare, Theory and Performance* is 'the radical contingency of performance – the unpredictable, often playful intersection of history, material conditions, social contexts, and reception that destabilizes Shakespeare and makes theatrical meaning a participatory act' (1996: 1). This offered both an overview of the historical development and the then current disciplinary configuration of performance criticism and a series of new perspectives on performance which attend to the interplay between gender, race and class, and between texts, bodies, spaces and technologies.

In addition to essays which historicise the work of Styan and Dessen and of the 'Shakespeare revolution' as a whole, the volume features contributions which address, for example, Shakespearean voice training and verse-speaking (which produce 'the conflation of self-knowledge, universal truth, and Shakespeare, all "found" in and "expressed" through the transcendent body and voice' [Knowles 1996: 106]), and the corporeality of the Shakespearean actor's presence, 'whereby the spectator participates the present body of the actor, sometimes in a displaced but nonetheless deeply engaged and meaningful way' (Dawson 1996: 43). The collection's concerns find their richest articulation in Barbara Hodgdon's essay 'Looking for Mr. Shakespeare after "The Revolution": Robert Lepage's Intercultural *Dream* machine', which not only earns first prize for portmanteau title but also provides a winning combination of investigative projects. It offers a close analysis of Robert Lepage's controversial, ostensibly intercultural, mud-and-water *Dream* at the National Theatre in 1992, and a diagnostic reading of the xenophobic and frequently racist critical response that the production provoked. It contextualises the production both within Lepage's own oeuvre and in relation to the history of the play within English culture (and in particular to Brook's production), And it re-reads the moment of Styan's 'Shakespeare Revolution', meditates on the *Dream* and psychoanalysis, concluding with more general reflections on the future direction of Shakespearean performance criticism in the context of the global stage:

In seeking to negotiate further that distinctly multicultured as well as intercultural terrain, future studies need to take place not at the locus of examining director-auteurs and the ideotexts of their mise en scènes or the theatrical apparatus itself, but at the point of historical reception, where 'theatre' collides with spectators who may transform it into 'a strange eventful history'.

(Hodgdon 1996: 86)

Hodgdon's essay is included in her *The Shakespeare Trade* (1998), a work exemplary of an interdisciplinary Shakespearean performance criticism that moves between theatre, film, media and cultural studies, presenting a set of case studies that document how Shakespeare's 'cultural capital, his chief stock-in-trade, and that of the Elizabethan age, circulate in and have been appropriated and exploited by recent cultural practices'; like Dessen, Hodgdon is interested in 'trade-offs', but rather than seeing these primarily as transactions between performance and the text, she is concerned with 'the trade-offs such practices enact between high and low culture, between theatre and cinema, between "Shakespearean" bodies and "popular" bodies, between national and local histories' (Hodgdon 1998: xi). It is, Hodgdon declares, a 'collector's history', and her attention ranges from cinematic and theatrical reworkings of *Shrew, Othello, Antony and Cleopatra* and *Dream* to the cultural legacy of Elizabeth I and the Stratford-upon-Avon tourist economy.

Importantly, Hodgdon stresses, though her work accepts (and develops) the cultural materialist case that 'performance is an ideological practice ... situated in power relations', it is centrally concerned with 'pleasures offered, rejected, and taken' (which include making 'argument itself a source of pleasure, one subject of writing') (Hodgdon 1998: xi–xii), whilst also registering the awareness that this double perspective may well bring pleasure and ideology into conflict as well as collaboration. Thus, for example, Hodgdon's compelling evocation of the 'stunning oneiric images' of Lepage's *Dream*, which deployed Shakespeare's text 'as a machine for performing the body erotic', enacted on 'the mud and the bed, the primordial ooze and the site of sex and dreams', is woven into the recognition that the production seeks 'to mystify and naturalize culture', picturing the unconscious as 'a Jungian catchall for a world-soul or a transcultural humanity' (178, 189). In performances of *Shrew*, Hodgdon discerns that 'something like a new characterology is in process, taking place through and being shaped by the bodies of performers ... who insist on their own unruliness, trouble their textually gendered markings, refuse to stay in place'. Yet in the case of this play, for the female spectator especially, a more troubling question remains: 'What does this play, this performance, make me that I no longer want to be?' (38).

The relationship between regulation and unruliness is also a key concern in the work of W. B. Worthen, whose *Shakespeare and the Authority of Performance* starts from the proposition that 'to think of performance as conveying authorized meanings of any kind, especially meanings authenticated in and by the text, is finally to tame the unruly ways of the stage' (1997: 3). Considering the ways in which critics and performers habitually seek recourse to Shakespearean authority in order to validate their own practices, Worthen examines its operations in the work of the director, the actor and the stage-centred critic, whilst acknowledging that his argument 'runs counter to the claims of contemporary performance criticism', in that he regards the stage 'not as the natural venue where Shakespeare's imagined meanings become realized, but as one site among many where "Shakespearean" meanings are produced' (38). Observing that 'the work of directing ... is to stage an ongoing dialogue with authority' (69), Worthen compares the contrasting directorial approaches of Charles Marowitz and Jonathan Miller, the former iconoclastically seeking to subvert Shakespeare 'in order to value the director's creative collaboration' (71; see Marowitz 1991), the latter advancing a sophisticated notion of the play's afterlife (Miller 1986) which, Worthen argues, is 'a way to preserve the authority of the original in a mode of transmission – theatre – that now stands apart from the "literary" ontology of plays' (1997: 74).

Ostensibly divergent in the extreme, the positions of both directors nonetheless evince 'a theoretical crisis characteristic of the modern Anglo-North American theatre: how to legitimate the critical work of theatre, when theatre is understood ... as an essentially *r*eproductive art' (Worthen 1997: 74–75). Actor training, meanwhile, 'teaches performers how to represent the "subjects" of the drama, and subjects the performers themselves to a way of interpreting, inhabiting, and acting'; a way which is mapped in 'actor training texts and actors' accounts', which repeatedly link 'the propriety of performance to the right expression of Shakespearean authority' (98). Examining a range of actor training manuals as well as contributions to the 'Players of Shakespeare' series, Worthen concludes that 'Actorly reading is notably trained on questions of character, the integrated, self-present, internalized, psychologically motivated "character" of the dominant mode of modern theatrical representation, stage realism' (127). Finally, performance criticism 'has been sustained by a sense that its critical activity can recover authentically Shakespearean insights and meanings, meanings which reside in the essential stabilities of Shakespeare's text, and the privileged access that the stage has to them' (170).

Beyond Shakespeare

The fetish of Shakespearean authority, as Worthen sees it, allows, or compels, us to 'reify Shakespearean drama ... as sacred text, as silent hieroglyphics we can only scan, interpret, struggle to decode', and that far from enriching the performance experience, it diminishes and impoverishes 'the work of our own performances, and the work of the plays in our making of the world' (1997: 191). The allied problem with much of Shakespearean performance criticism, partly as a consequence of its attachment to this authority, is that it has tended to address the history and current practice of Shakespearean stage production in terms of internal traditions and interconnections: Shakespearean performances are compared to, and evaluated against, other Shakespearean performances, or discussed in relation to the text and original staging conditions. Rarely is Shakespearean stage production considered alongside that of other Elizabethan and Jacobean plays, whose performance histories are themselves seldom accorded even a fraction of comparable coverage, though exceptions include Richard Cave, Elizabeth Schafer and Brian Woolland's collection of essays and interviews *Ben Jonson and Theatre* (1999), Stevie Simkin's *A Preface to Marlowe* (2000), Martin White's *Renaissance Drama in Action* (1998) – which includes material on Webster, Kyd, Ford and Brome – Edward J. Esche's collection *Shakespeare and His Contemporaries in Performance* (2000) and Roberta Barker's *Early Modern Tragedy, Gender and Performance, 1984–2000* (2007).

The convergences and departures between Shakespeare and his contemporaries in performance are of less interest to Worthen than the more pressing and immediate issue of the relationship between Shakespeare and contemporary performance. Artaud, Brecht, Stanislavsky, Ibsen and David Mamet are reference points in Worthen's discussion of current stage practice, but he indicates that the performance context that he has in mind is more broad based, encompassing popular culture and the theatrical avant-garde (thus enabling him to read Peter Sellars's 1994 *Merchant* in relation to the 1995 film *Strange*

Days and to Anna Deavere Smith's verbatim work *Twilight: Los Angeles*, first staged in 1992) but also the wider arena of performative activities in which theatre itself has experienced a 'crisis of authority' (Worthen 1997: 93). Worthen's interrogation of Shakespearean authority is implicated within a disciplinary repositioning and reconfiguration, prompted by the much-debated edict issued by one of the founders of modern performance studies, Richard Schechner, that 'theatre as we have known and practiced it – the staging of written dramas – will be the string quartet of the 21st century: a beloved but extremely limited genre, a subdivision of performance' (1992: 8).

Whether this is a legitimate account of the current state of the artistic field has been disputed (and Schechner subsequently conceded that his announcement of the demise of scripted drama was premature [Schechner 2000]), but one thing it did do was define the priorities of performance studies as an emergent discipline, which proceeds from the basis that performance 'must be construed as a "broad spectrum" or "continuum" of human actions ranging from ritual, play, sports, popular entertainments, the performing arts (theatre, dance, music) and everyday life performances to the enactment of social, professional, gender, race, and class roles, and on to healing (from shamanism to surgery), the media, and the internet', and considered within an interdisciplinary frame which synthesises 'the social sciences, feminist studies, gender studies, history, psychoanalysis, queer theory, semiotics, ethology, cybernetics, area studies, media and popular culture theory, and cultural studies' (Schechner 2002: 2).

From this perspective, accustomed to the contemplation of performance at work in anything from the Mardi Gras parade to terrorist attacks, the traditional forms of discussion of Shakespeare in performance might appear narrow, reactionary and rather dull; the project of Worthen's criticism, and of a number of contributions to the field that have followed, is to redefine the place of Shakespearean performance within this expanded and transformed perception of the cultural and disciplinary contexts within which it is now located. Worthen begins *Shakespeare and the Force of Modern Performance* with the declaration that it is about 'a small slice of performance: the stage performance of scripted drama' (2003: 1), a slightly apologetic opening that acknowledges the ascendancy of the performance studies paradigm whilst also offering a rationale for the continuation of a selective focus on Shakespeare, whose plays, not perhaps uniquely but with particular clarity and intensity, 'enable us to consider an important but often misconceived aspect of dramatic performance: the function of writing, of the script, in the theatre' (3).

Drawing upon the speech-act theory of J. L. Austin, whose *How to Do Things with Words* (1962) disseminated the idea of the 'performative' utterance, and upon the critical re-readings of his theory developed by Jacques Derrida (1982), Elin Diamond (1996), Judith Butler (1990, 1997) and Andrew Parker and Eve Kosofsky Sedgwick (1995), which locate the performative within mechanisms of power and subjection, Worthen offers a definition of theatre as 'a citational practice' that is 'engaged not so much in citing texts as in reiterating its own regimes of performance', and that exerts a force which 'goes well beyond the force of mere speech, subjecting writing to the body, to labor, to the work of production' (2003: 9). In the case of Shakespeare, the key questions are:

> How does contemporary performance construct the force of the past? Does it ascribe that force to a governing text? Or is that 'pastness' inevitably an effect of the performative force of present modes of acting, an elaborate effect of contemporary Shakespearean performativity?
>
> (Worthen 2003: 39)

Seeking the answers to these questions, Worthen examines films as well as performances and performance venues: Branagh's *Henry V* and *Love's Labour's Lost*, Luhrmann's *Romeo + Juliet* and *Moulin Rouge!*, Taymor's *Titus*, Almereyda's *Hamlet* and *Hamlet*; at Shakespeare's Globe, described as a space 'informed by the audience's familiarity with cognate performance forms: living-history sites, battlefield reenactments, theme parks, and themed performance in general' (Worthen 2003: 84). The selection of case studies also incorporates the non-canonical, the marginal and the non-western, including the South African *Umbatha: The Zulu Macbeth* and the Brazilian company Grupo Galpão's *Romeu e Julieta*, hosted by the Globe in 1997 and 1998 respectively. Presented in the mode of Brazilian street theatre, *Romeu e Julieta* is an example of intercultural performance that demonstrates how 'the commodification of Shakespearean performance within the rhetoric of globalized commerce frames the force of Shakespearean drama' (122), in this instance by being 'constantly in negotiation between the global and the local, enabling different kinds of force at different sites of performance' (161).

The relationship that Worthen explores between performance and textuality has also been the concern of recent scholarship operating at the intersection between textual bibliography, performance and theatre history, a body of work whose inception was marked by the publication of Stanley Wells and Gary Taylor's Oxford Shakespeare *Complete Works* in 1988, which, based on the principle that '[t]he theatrical version' represents Shakespeare's finally realised intentions, opts 'to print the more theatrical version of each play' (Taylor and Wells 1988: xxxvi–xxxvii). This edition also broke with tradition by printing the quarto and Folio texts of *King Lear* as two distinct versions of the play (rather than, as previous editors had done, conflating them to produce a hybrid text); an innovation that was prefigured in the arguments rehearsed in Taylor and Michael Warren's collection *The Division of the Kingdoms* (1983). This was controversial; so too was the Oxford editors' decision to rename the Falstaff of *1 Henry IV* as Sir John Oldcastle, on the basis that the character originally 'bore the name of his historical counterpart, the Protestant martyr, Sir John Oldcastle', and that Shakespeare was forced to change the name under pressure from his descendents, the Cobham family, whose ranks included the Lord Chamberlain, William Brooke (Taylor and Wells 1988: 453).

Taylor subsequently moved on to act as general editor of the Oxford *Thomas Middleton: The Collected Works* (2007a), declaring that Shakespeare's reputation and popularity had peaked and it was now experiencing a slow and painful 'decline in cultural authority' that would lead to his eventual demise (Taylor 1999: 199). The edition includes *Timon of Athens*, *Measure for Measure* and *Macbeth* as instances of Middleton rewriting Shakespeare (arguments for which are rehearsed at some length in Taylor and John Jowett's *Shakespeare Reshaped, 1606–1623* [Jowett and Taylor 1993]); whereas this once might have been seen as a provocative gesture, it is a measure of the shift in editorial principles and practices that Taylor and Wells largely pioneered, as well as generally more open attitudes towards Shakespearean authorship, that it has been accepted without demur (Shakespeare's career as a collaborator is also the subject of Brian Vickers's *Shakespeare, Co-Author* [2002]). The convergence between bibliography and performance brokered by Wells and Taylor is evident in the stated principles of the Arden Shakespeare third series ('Both the introduction and the commentary are designed to present the plays as texts for performance' [Proudfoot *et al.* 1995]) and has generated work concerned with the mechanisms of construction of, and divisions and instabilities within, texts that exist in multiple versions. Writing from a perspective in which philology is mediated by post-structuralism and new historicism, Leah S. Marcus directs our attention to the 'literary artifact as reinvested with the enriching welter of historical circumstances that helped to determine its shape at inception, and with the shifting material forms in which it was made available to early and later readers' (1996: 24–25), and calls for the 'unediting' of early modern texts.

Building on her study of actors' parts and rehearsal practices in *Rehearsal from Shakespeare to Sheridan* (2000), Tiffany Stern's *Making Shakespeare: From Page to Stage* explores 'how the versions of plays we have are only written testaments to moments in the life of an unstable text', and in particular the implications of the fact that 'The unit of play that concerned the actor – even the moment before performance – was his separate part, not the full text' (2004: 2, 88). In their introduction to the collection *Textual Performances* (2004), Lukas Erne and M. J. Kidnie identify the current challenge for criticism as 'how best to engage editorially with evidence provided by historical research into the playhouse, author's study, and printing house, and into the complex relations among these spaces of early modern production', and its project as being 'to understand the range of pragmatic editorial methodologies that are emerging from the fray, how they respond to the surviving documentary evidence, and how they might speak (or fail to speak) to each other' (Erne and Kidnie 2004: 4–5). But the ascendancy of the performance-text has also been questioned, notably by Erne, whose *Shakespeare as Literary Dramatist* sets itself against the current critical consensus that pictures Shakespeare as a practical man of the theatre indifferent to seeing his works in print, and that treats his plays as scripts or scores rather than literary works; on the contrary, Erne argues, 'Shakespeare, "privileged playwright" that he was, could afford to write plays for the stage *and* the page' (2003: 20).

Erne's interrogation of the dominance of performance as the primary frame of reference within editorial and critical practice coincided with an increasing self-reflexivity within performance criticism more generally. In the 'Series Introduction' to the first of the five volumes in the 'Redefining British Theatre History' series, Peter Holland acknowledges that 'the theorizing of performance including its historical traces has grown immensely over the past fifteen years', but declares that 'previous assumptions need fundamental questioning' to establish 'a future for the field' that 'can be enunciated in modes as yet undervalued' (2003: xvi–xvii). This is the latest stage in the history of a subdiscipline that has gone from documentation and advocacy, through appreciation and contextualisation, to cultural critique and philosophical, ethical and political interrogation; the questions to be asked of Shakespearean performance are not only whether and how it works, but what it does, and what it is, and what it might be.

The narrative of performance criticism (aptly structured as a Shakespearean drama in five acts) is itself charted in the introduction to Hodgdon and Worthen's massive collection *A Companion to Shakespeare and Performance* (2005), which, at nearly seven hundred pages and with thirty-four essays ranging from the early modern period to the present, represents the state of the art of performance criticism at the beginning of the twenty-first century. Announcing that the volume assembles 'a group of critics who are in the process of reconfiguring the intricate instabilities and contingencies that emerge in conversations "about" and "between" Shakespeare and performance' (1), Hodgdon's introduction tracks the emergence of 'stage-centred' criticism during the 1970s, its subjection (and resistance) to theoretical self-reflexiveness during the 1980s, the impact of mass- and multi-mediatisation during the 1990s and, most recently, the challenges of performance studies; importantly, Hodgdon emphasises that the collection's title (Shakespeare *and* rather than *in* performance) marks its difference from the criticisms that have preceded it: 'the focus here is as much on how performance occurs "in between" these two terms as on how it might be located in one or the other' (6). In place of a performance *criticism* characterised by its 'essentializing orthodoxy', what is offered is 'the theoretical heterodoxy of Shakespeare performance studies' (7), one of whose traits is to refuse to respond to 'the loss or disappearance of performance by attempting to preserve it, by documenting, recording, and recoding it' (8).

Although not all of the essays in the collection subscribe to this last brief in particular, the statement is indicative of the radical challenges that the new disciplinary formation sets itself to face. It is also a response to the frequently cited and much-debated provocation issued by performance theorist Peggy Phelan a decade earlier:

> Performance's only life is in the present. Performance cannot be saved, recorded, documented, or otherwise participate in the circulation of representations *of* representations: once it does so, it becomes something other than performance. To the degree that performance attempts to enter the economy of reproduction it betrays and lessens the promise of its own ontology. Performance's being, like the ontology of subjectivity proposed here, becomes itself through disappearance.
>
> (Phelan 1993: 146)

Here is a riposte to the tradition of performance criticism that has prized the documentation and memorial preservation of the objects of its scrutiny above all else; appropriately, it is Phelan who contributes the keynote essay to Worthen and Hodgdon's collection, a meditation on the architecture of the new Globe, *King Lear*, and Freud's life and death drives, which come together to enable us to 'recognize our own aspiration towards self-erasure ... and our desire to resist getting lost, to be grounded within a space we might call home' (Phelan 2005: 33).

Phelan's concern with performance's ontological investment in disappearance, mourning and loss also provides one of two crucial points of orientation for Peter Holland's collection *Shakespeare, Memory and Performance* (2006), the other being Joseph Roach's 'Performance genealogies', which 'draw on the idea of expressive movements as mnemonic reserves, including patterned movements made and remembered by bodies, residual movements retained implicitly in images or words (or in the silences between them), and imaginary movements dreamed in minds' (Roach 1996: 26). In Holland's collection the genealogies of Shakespearean performance take the shapes of cinema's memories of theatre, the costume archive's traces of the bodies of actors who once animated its contents, the transformations wrought upon Desdemona's handkerchief, her 'first remembrance of the Moor' (*Othello*, 3.3.295), and the slips and tricks of memory that the theatre plays upon the most observant of its participants.

Like Phelan, Roach is a theatre historian and theorist rather than a Shakespeare scholar; and if it is symptomatic of the theoretical and methodological orientation of Holland's volume that he and she are its most frequently cited critical authorities, it is also indirect evidence that some of the most invigorating and original critical thinking about Shakespeare and performance to appear since the 1990s has not been confined to the (loosening) disciplinary boundaries of Shakespearean performance criticism. Phelan's *Mourning Sex*, which begins with a discussion of Caravaggio's 1601 painting *The Incredulity of St Thomas* and ends with the film *Silverlake Life* (1993), a video diary documenting life and death with AIDS, and which is structured as a taxonomy of traumatised body parts, has a chapter on the excavation, in 1989, of the remains of the Rose playhouse in Southwark and the ensuing campaigning and public debate in which 'the theatre remains became a body defined, graphically, as a hole', as both rectum and open grave (Phelan 1997: 19).

Roach's *Cities of the Dead*, a book whose scope encompasses burial rituals in New Orleans, the self-fashioning of Madonna, the career of Thomas Betterton and Buffalo Bill's Wild West show, amongst much more, and which explores 'social processes of memory and forgetting', includes material on Betterton's Hamlet and the London performance of Davenant's *Macbeth* for the visiting Iroquois ambassadors in 1710; throughout, Shakespearean performance history is part of the larger pattern of 'a variety of performance events, from stage plays to sacred sites, from carnivals to the invisible rituals of everyday life' (Roach 1996: xi). Two more books, both published in 2006, are also worth noting here: Nicholas Ridout's *Stage Fright, Animals, and Other Theatrical Problems*, which, in the course of an investigation of theatrical anomalies, disruptions and embarrassments, draws upon the experience of being directly addressed by Sam West in the RSC 2000 *Richard II* to investigate the potential for shame that is part of the predicament of the audience; and Simon Shepherd's *Theatre, Body and Pleasure*, which uses Shakespeare's drama and theatre as key reference points in a study of theatre as 'a place which exhibits what a human body is, what it does, what it is capable of', an exhibition that 'may amount to an affirmation of currently held views or … may be an unsettling challenge to assumptions' (Shepherd 2006: 1).

Beyond words

Shepherd's work arises from a context of close engagement with theatrical practice not only as a spectator but as a maker and performer, and as such it exemplifies a growing subsector of Shakespearean performance studies that reflects the insights and addresses the needs of the academic as practitioner, and that investigates the potentialities of performance in pedagogic as well as professional contexts: examples include Aers and Wheale (1991), Reynolds (1992), Riggio (1999) and Hartley (2005). A recurrent concern has been the interface between contemporary Shakespeare and contemporary dramaturgy, and, reflecting this, other recent studies have explored the potential synergies between Shakespearean production and the theatrical avant-garde (which, as noted earlier, offered a contemporary touchstone for Bruster and Weimann's historicist approach): examples include Andy Lavender's *Hamlet in Pieces* (2001), an account of three radical theatrical reworkings by Peter Brook, Robert Lepage and Robert Wilson; the case studies addressed by Bryan Reynolds and his collaborators in *Performing Transversally* (2003); Tony Howard's encyclopaedic stage history, *Women as Hamlet* (2007) and Graham Holderness's discussion of the work of the Arabic director Sulayman Al-Bassam (Holderness 2008).

Bridget Escolme's *Talking to the Audience* (2005) takes issue with the cultural materialist conjunction of Althusserian anti-essentialism with the theory and practice of Brecht, and proposes that 'the cracks and fissures' sought by cultural materialists 'are to be found at moments when the illusion of being face to face with fictional presences in the theatre is at its strongest', and that 'this illusion is produced "outwardly", in the encounter between performer and audience' (Escolme 2005: 11). Escolme examines a range of mainstream productions staged by the RSC, the National Theatre and Shakespeare's Globe between 1998 and 2003; however, the performance vocabulary that she finds most apposite to the production of early modern subjectivity-effects is not the dramaturgy of Epic theatre but the postdramatic antics of practitioners who have embraced 'the overtly, embarrassingly theatrical as both an aesthetic and a theme' (16): Forced Entertainment (whose own sole instance of Shakespearean experimentation, a five-day workshop on *King Lear* culminating in a shambolic one-off performance, is the final case study in my own *The Shakespeare*

Effect [Shaughnessy 2002]), the Pina Bausch Tanztheater and the Wooster Group (who finally caught up with Shakespeare in 2007, in the form of a live 'reconstruction' of the 1964 film of the Gielgud-directed, Richard Burton-starring *Hamlet* [Worthen 2008; Werner 2008]). Escolme's narrative ends, accordingly, with an account of two productions which enable this claim to be put to the test: the Italian company Societas Raffaello Sanzio's drastic reinventions of *Hamlet* and *Julius Caesar*, first performed in 1992 and 1997 respectively. At the start of *Giulio Cesare*, the performer playing the tribune 'inserts an endoscope into his throat. The resultant pictures of his vocal chords at their twitching, convulsive work are projected onto a screen'; Brutus and Cassius are played by anorexic women; other members of the cast include a live horse and a stuffed cat; it is a production which asks: 'What does it mean to be human in this play, and who gets to be – or perform – human?' (Escolme 2005: 130–31).

Amleto poses this question in an even more disconcerting form: conceived as a collage of scenes from the play performed by a cast of stuffed toys and Paulo Tonti, who, in a 'virtuoso piece of naturalistic acting' displays the symptomatology of profound autism, careering around 'a disused gymnasium that is covered in the Societas Raffaello Sanzio's dangerous-looking electrics, speaking only tiny fragments of Shakespeare's text, shooting blanks and speaking to a series of filthy children's toys' – and yet 'offer[ing] us *Hamlet* in a way that naturalistic stage convention does not' (Escolme 2005: 142).

Escolme opts to end with *Amleto* because the spectacle of the performance of autism seems to offer a compelling summation of the problematics of identity and communication that concern her book; as Petra Kuppers sees it (discussing the production in the context of performance and disability), the play *Hamlet* in this show 'is nothing but a vague memory, held without connection or emotion … reduced to defecate waste and words'; here 'autism becomes a master trope for both the theater and the formation (and unmaking) of self' (Kuppers 2003: 78–79). It also provides a fitting conclusion to this chapter, which began by referring to another instance of cross-cultural exchange in international Shakespearean performance, the RSC Complete Works Festival of 2006. But *Amleto*, a display of autism conducted in fragments of a language whose sense was conveyed to non-Italian audiences via surtitles and performed over the mangled wreckage of the greatest textual monument to verbal articulacy in human history, can be seen to resonate in other ways.

Autism as a condition is characterised by what the leading authority on the condition has termed 'mindblindness', that is, by the inability to 'read people's actions as directed at goals and as driven by desires', and hence to imagine the selfhood of the other and to empathise; the inability to differentiate between truth and fiction (or being and acting) because 'In order to pretend, one must understand how pretending is different from not pretending' (Baron-Cohen 1995: 59, 76). It is manifested verbally in repetitive and mechanistic speech patterns (echolalia) and typified by obsessive self-stimulation and highly routinised behaviour; as such the condition would seem to be at odds with the most fundamental principles of the communicative contract between performer and audience (I know not 'seems').

Amleto is thus also an extreme, unsettlingly strange instance, to propose a new twist to what Dennis Kennedy calls 'Shakespeare without his language', of a 'foreign' performance that is, and is not, Shakespeare. If the proper response to the strange is to 'as a stranger, give it welcome', then, as Kennedy points out, contemplating Shakespeare when he is 'deprived of his tongue' reminds us of how even in 'our own' language he is 'foreign' to us, and allows us to 'see more clearly how Shakespeare is alien, as well as what we continue to find indigenous or domestic about him' (Kennedy 1996: 146). I am irresistibly reminded of a much-reprinted short prose poem (with which parents or carers of autistic children will be familiar) by Emily Perl Kingsley, 'Welcome to Holland' (1987), which likens the experience of raising an autistic child to suddenly discovering, having planned the vacation of a lifetime in Italy, that you have been re-routed to Holland, that that is where you must stay, and that the pleasures and discoveries that you were confidently anticipating have been replaced by a very different set of challenges, involving frustration, disappointment and grief but also unexpected joys.

As the novelist Nick Hornby, recalling his own experience as a father of an autistic son, puts it, 'you learn to let go of the ambitions you once had for him very quickly (and you learn too that many of those ambitions were worthless anyway, beside the point, precious, silly, indulgent, intimidatingly restrictive)' (2003: 127). To recognise autism as difference as well as – or in preference to – disability is to acknowledge the challenge that it poses to one's sense of self but also to expand one's sense of what it is to be human. So, in a different but related way, I want to suggest, do our encounters with the Shakespeares, foreign, domestic, immediate and alien, performed on stage, on screen, in the reader's imagination, in popular culture and in the criticisms that have been surveyed in preceding pages. Hornby, writing of his son's love of music, confesses that it shows him 'why I love the relationship that anyone has with music: because there's something in us that is beyond the reach of words, something that eludes and defies our best attempts to spit it out' (2003: 127).

For Hornby, this is 'the best part of us', and, consciously or not in echo of *The Tempest*, 1.2.405, 'probably, the richest and strangest part' (Hornby 2003: 127). Four hundred years old, Shakespeare's works and words, for good or ill, continue to hold a unique place within world culture as an infinitely malleable resource and as the nearest thing available to a common repository of values and beliefs, but also, crucially, as phenomena that can never be fully articulated, and that can never, really, ever be encountered for the first time, that have been visited by ourselves and others many, many times before and that will be again, and that as a consequence are shadowed by what might have been and what might yet be, Holland *and* Italy, as well as what was, and what is.

Nothing lasts forever, certainly not Shakespearean criticism, even more certainly not Shakespearean performance; perhaps not even Shakespeare: regardless of Ben Jonson's pronouncement that his great rival was not of an age, but for all time, and of continued predictions both of his immortality and of his imminent demise, we cannot know whether we are close to the end of the Shakespearean adventure story or merely at its beginning. In the meantime, we can carry on reading, spectating, making and criticising Shakespeare, and we continue to ask ourselves what we want from, and mean by, these activities, what, to borrow Terence Hawkes's phrase, '*we* mean *by* Shakespeare' (1996: 3). And through it all, we carry on being alternately admiring, passionate, exasperated, worried and exhilarated by a body of work that retains its unrivalled capacity to provoke and to beguile, and to generate wonder and delight.

A Shakespearean chronology
1899–2008

1899	Arden Shakespeare first series is inaugurated with Edward Dowden's edition of *Hamlet*; the death scene from Beerbohm Tree's stage production of *King John* becomes the first example of Shakespeare on film.
1904	A. C. Bradley's *Shakespearean Tragedy* and Sigmund Freud's *The Pyschopathology of Everyday Life* published; Konstantin Stanislavsky directs Anton Chekhov's *The Cherry Orchard* at the Moscow Art Theatre.
1912	Harley Granville Barker directs *The Winter's Tale* and *Twelfth Night* at the Savoy Theatre.
1914	Barker directs *A Midsummer Night's Dream* at the Savoy; Lilian Baylis establishes a permanent Shakespeare ensemble at the Old Vic Theatre; outbreak of First World War.
1917	Bolshevik Revolution in Russia.
1918	Hostilities end with the Armistice; women in the UK acquire the vote.
1919	First World War formally ends with the Treaty of Versailles.
1920	Svend Gade's *Hamlet* released.
1921	First editions of New Shakespeare series and first volume of Granville Barker's *Prefaces to Shakespeare* published.
1922	Mahatma Gandhi leads a campaign of civil disobedience in British-occupied India.
1923	E. K. Chambers's *The Elizabethan Stage* published; Shakespeare Association of America founded.
1926	Shakespeare Memorial Theatre destroyed by fire; the General Strike.
1929	Sam Taylor's *The Taming of the Shrew*, the first full-length Shakespearean talking picture, released.
1932	Rebuilt Shakespeare Memorial Theatre opens in Stratford.
1933	Tyrone Guthrie becomes Artistic Director of the Old Vic; L. C. Knights's 'How Many Children Had Lady Macbeth?' published; Adolf Hitler becomes Chancellor of Germany.
1934	John Gielgud plays Hamlet in the West End.
1935	Max Reinhardt and William Dieterle's *A Midsummer Night's Dream* released; J. Dover Wilson's *What Happens in Hamlet* published.
1936	George Cukor's *Romeo and Juliet* and Paul Czinner's *As You Like It* released.
1937	Guthrie directs Laurence Olivier as Hamlet at the Old Vic.
1939	Outbreak of Second World War.
1943	E. M. W. Tillyard's *The Elizabethan World Picture* published.

1944	Tillyard's *Shakespeare's History Plays* published; Laurence Olivier's *Henry V* released.
1945	End of Second World War.
1947	Declaration of Indian independence.
1948	Olivier's *Hamlet* and Orson Welles's *Macbeth* released; State of Israel founded; *Shakespeare Survey* begins publication.
1949	Bertolt Brecht establishes the Berliner Ensemble.
1950	*Shakespeare Quarterly* begins publication.
1951	The Arden Shakespeare second series launched with Kenneth Muir's edition of *Macbeth*; the Festival of Britain; University of Birmingham's Shakespeare Institute founded.
1952	Welles's *Othello* released.
1953	Guthrie opens the Festival Theatre in Stratford, Ontario.
1955	Peter Brook directs Olivier in *Titus Andronicus* at the Shakespeare Memorial Theatre; Sergei Yutkevitch's *Othello* and Olivier's *Richard III* released.
1957	Jerome Robbins and Leonard Bernstein's *West Side Story* premieres in New York; Akira Kurosawa's *Kumonoso jô* released.
1960	The Royal Shakespeare Company formed under the direction of Peter Hall.
1962	Brook directs *King Lear* for the RSC.
1963	Hall and John Barton adapt the *Henry VI* plays as *The Wars of the Roses* for the RSC; the National Theatre, under the artistic directorship of Olivier, opens with *Hamlet* at the Old Vic.
1964	Jan Kott's *Shakespeare Our Contemporary* published in English translation; Grigori Kosintsev's *Hamlet* released; Olivier performs as Othello at the National Theatre.
1965	Hall directs David Warner in *Hamlet* for the RSC; Stuart Burge's *Othello* and Welles's *Chimes at Midnight* released; US military forces sent to Vietnam; abolition of the death penalty in the UK.
1967	Franco Zeffirelli's *The Taming of the Shrew* released.
1968	Trevor Nunn succeeds Hall as Artistic Director of the RSC; Zeffirelli's *Romeo and Juliet* and Hall's *A Midsummer Night's Dream* released; Brook's *The Empty Space* published; campus riots in Paris and in the United States.
1969	Tony Richardson's *Hamlet* and Kosintsev's *King Lear* released.
1970	Brook directs *A Midsummer Night's Dream* for the RSC.
1971	Brook's *King Lear* and Roman Polanski's *Macbeth* released.
1973	Hall succeeds Olivier as Artistic Director of the National Theatre; the RSC's studio theatre, the Other Place, opens.
1975	The new National Theatre complex on the South Bank opens with Hall's *Hamlet*; Buzz Goodbody directs *Hamlet* at the Other Place; the US ends military involvement in Vietnam.
1976	Nunn directs *Macbeth* at the Other Place.
1978	Terry Hands joins Nunn as joint Artistic Director of the RSC.
1979	The BBC/Time Life Television Shakespeare series begins broadcasting; election of Conservative government under UK's first woman prime minister, Margaret Thatcher.
1980	Stephen Greenblatt's *Renaissance Self-Fashioning* published; Derek Jarman's *The Tempest* released; election of Ronald Reagan as president of the USA.
1981	Declan Donnellan and Nick Ormerod found Cheek by Jowl.

1982	The Oxford Shakespeare begins publication.
1983	Jonathan Dollimore's *Radical Tragedy* published.
1984	First volumes in the New Cambridge Shakepeare series published; Bill Alexander directs Antony Sher as Richard III for the RSC.
1986	The RSC's third auditorium, the Swan, opens; Stanley Wells and Gary Taylor's *The Oxford Shakespeare: The Complete Works* published.
1987	Yukio Ninagawa's *Macbeth* performed in London.
1988	Richard Eyre succeeds Hall as Artistic Director of the National Theatre.
1989	Foundations of the Rose playhouse excavated; Kenneth Branagh's *Henry V* released; fall of the Berlin Wall.
1990	Zeffirelli's *Hamlet* released.
1991	Donnellan directs *As You Like It* for Cheek by Jowl; Adrian Noble succeeds Hands as Artistic Director of the RSC; Peter Greenaway's *Prospero's Books* released; First Gulf War; break-up of the Soviet Union.
1992	Christine Edzard's *As You Like It* released.
1993	Branagh's *Much Ado about Nothing* released.
1994	Barbican Centre, London, hosts Everybody's Shakespeare festival.
1995	Arden Shakespeare third series launched; Oliver Parker's *Othello*, Richard Loncraine's *Richard III* and Branagh's *In the Bleak Midwinter* released.
1996	Shakespeare's Globe opens on Bankside; Branagh's *Hamlet*, Nunn's *Twelfth Night*, Al Pacino's *Looking for Richard* and Baz Luhrmann's *William Shakespeare's Romeo + Juliet* released.
1997	Nunn becomes Artistic Director of the National Theatre; Stephen Greenblatt, Walter Cohen, Jean E. Howard and Katharine Eisaman Maus's *The Norton Shakespeare* published.
1998	John Madden's *Shakespeare in Love* released.
1999	Gregory Doran directs Sher as Macbeth for the RSC; Julie Taymor's *Titus*, Michael Hoffman's *A Midsummer Night's Dream* and Gil Junger's *10 Things I Hate About You* released.
2000	Michael Almereyda's *Hamlet*, Branagh's *Love's Labour's Lost* and Kristian Levring's *The King Is Alive* released.
2001	Nicholas Hytner succeeds Nunn as Artistic Director of the National Theatre; terrorists crash hijacked aeroplanes into the World Trade Center and the Pentagon (11 September); US leads invasion of Afghanistan.
2002	Michael Boyd becomes Artistic Director of the RSC.
2003	Second Gulf War: American-led forces participate in invasion of Iraq.
2005	Michael Radford's *The Merchant of Venice* released.
2006	The RSC hosts the Complete Works Festival in Stratford-upon-Avon.
2007	Jonathan Bate and Eric Rasmussen's *RSC Shakespeare: The Complete Works* published.
2008	Barack Obama elected President of the USA.

Bibliography

Ackroyd, Peter (2005) *Shakespeare: The Biography*. London: Chatto and Windus.

Adams, John Cranford (1961) *The Globe Playhouse: Its Design and Equipment*. Second edition. London: Constable.

Adamson, Sylvia, Lynette Hunter, Lynne Magnusson, Ann Thompson and Katie Wales (eds) (2001) *Reading Shakespeare's Dramatic Language: A Guide*. London: The Arden Shakespeare.

Addenbrooke, David (1974) *The Royal Shakespeare Company: The Peter Hall Years*. London: William Kimber.

Adelman, Janet (1992) *Suffocating Mothers: Fantasies of Maternal Origin in Shakespeare's Plays, Hamlet to The Tempest*. New York: Routledge.

Adler, Steven (2001) *Rough Magic: Making Theatre at the Royal Shakespeare Company*. Carbondale, IL: Southern Illinois University Press.

Aebischer, Pascale (2004) *Shakespeare's Violated Bodies: Stage and Screen Performance*. Cambridge: Cambridge University Press.

Aebischer, Pascale, Edward J. Esche and Nigel Wheale (eds) (2003) *Remaking Shakespeare: Performance across Media, Genres and Cultures*. Basingstoke: Palgrave.

Aers, Lesley and Nigel Wheale (eds) (1991) *Shakespeare in the Changing Curriculum*. London: Routledge.

Alexander, Catharine M. S. and Stanley Wells (eds) (2000) *Shakespeare and Race*. Cambridge: Cambridge University Press.

Althusser, Louis (1971) *Lenin and Philosophy*. New York: Monthly Review Press.

Armstrong, Isobel (1989) 'Thatcher's Shakespeare?', *Textual Practice*, 3: 1–14.

Armstrong, Philip (2001) *Shakespeare in Psychoanalysis*. London: Routledge.

Austin, J. L. (1962) *How to Do Things with Words*. Oxford: Clarendon Press.

Ayres, Philip J. (ed.) (1999) *Sejanus His Fall*. The Revels Plays. Manchester: Manchester University Press.

Bakewell, Michael (1970) 'The Television Production', in *The Wars of the Roses*, ed. John Barton and Peter Hall. London: BBC Books, 231–36.

Barber, C. L. (1959) *Shakespeare's Festive Comedy: A Study of Dramatic Form and Its Relation to Social Custom*. Princeton, NJ: Princeton University Press.

Barker, Deborah E. and Ivo Kamps (eds) (1995) *Shakespeare and Gender: A History*. London: Verso.

Barker, Francis (1984) *The Tremulous Private Body: Essays on Subjection*. London: Methuen.

——(1993) *The Culture of Violence: Essays on Tragedy and History*. Manchester: Manchester University Press.

Barker, Francis and Peter Hulme (1985) 'Nymphs and Reapers Heavily Vanish: The Discursive Contexts of *The Tempest*', in *Alternative Shakespeares*, ed. John Drakakis. First edition. London: Methuen, 191–205.

Barker, Francis, Jay Bernstein, John Coombes, Peter Hulme, Jennifer Stone and Jon Stratton (eds) (1981) *1642: Literature and Power in the Seventeenth Century*. Colchester: University of Essex.

Barker, Roberta (2007) *Early Modern Tragedy, Gender and Performance, 1984–2000: The Destined Livery*. Basingstoke: Palgrave.

Baron-Cohen, Simon (1995) *Mindblindness: An Essay on Autism and Theory of Mind*. London: MIT Press.

Barroll, Leeds (1991) *Politics, Plague and Shakespeare's Theater: The Stuart Years*. Ithaca, NY: Cornell University Press.

Bartels, Emily C. (2008) *Speaking of the Moor: From Alcazar to Othello*. Philadelphia, PA: Pennsylvania University Press.

Barthelemy, Anthony Gerard (1987) *Black Face, Maligned Race: The Representation of Blacks in English Drama from Shakespeare to Southerne*. Baton Rouge, LA: Louisiana State University Press.

Barton, Anne (1975) 'The King Disguised: Shakespeare's *Henry V* and the Comical History', in *The Triple Bond: Plays, Mainly Shakespearean, in Performance*, ed. Joseph Price. University Park, PA: Pennsylvania State University Press, 92–117.

Barton, John (1984) *Playing Shakespeare*. London: Methuen.

Barton, John and Peter Hall (1970) *The Wars of the Roses*. London: BBC Books.

Bate, Jonathan (1989) *Shakespearean Constitutions: Politics, Theatre, Criticism, 1730–1830*. Oxford: Clarendon Press.

——(1993) 'Sexual Perversity in *Venus and Adonis*', *Yearbook of English Studies*, 23: 80–92.

——(ed.) (1995) *Titus Andronicus*. The Arden Shakespeare, third series. London: Routledge.

——(1997) *The Genius of Shakespeare*. London: Picador.

——(2000) 'Caliban and Ariel Write Back', in *Shakespeare and Race*, ed. Catharine M. S. Alexander and Stanley Wells. Cambridge: Cambridge University Press, 165–76.

——(2007) 'The RSC Complete Works Festival: An Introduction and Retrospective', *Shakespeare*, 3: 83–88.

——(2008) *Soul of the Age: The Life, Mind and World of William Shakespeare*. London: Viking.

Bate, Jonathan and Russell Jackson (eds) (1996) *Shakespeare: An Illustrated Stage History*. Oxford: Oxford University Press.

Bate, Jonathan and Eric Rasmussen (eds) (2007) *William Shakespeare: Complete Works*. Basingstoke: Palgrave.

Beaumann, Sally (ed.) (1976) *The Royal Shakespeare Company's Centenary Production of 'Henry V'*. Oxford: Pergamon Press.

——(1982) *The Royal Shakespeare Company: A History of Ten Decades*. London: Oxford University Press.

Beckerman, Bernard (1962) *Shakespeare at the Globe 1599–1609*. New York: Macmillan.

Belsey, Catherine (1985a) *The Subject of Tragedy: Identity and Difference in Renaissance Drama*. London: Methuen.

——(1985b) 'Disrupting Sexual Difference: Meaning and Gender in the Comedies', in *Alternative Shakespeares*, ed. John Drakakis. First edition. London: Methuen, 166–90.

——(1996) 'Cleopatra's Seduction', in *Alternative Shakespeares, Volume 2*, ed. Terence Hawkes. London: Routledge, 38–62.

——(1998 [1983]) 'Shakespeare and Film: A Question of Perspective', *Literature/Film Quarterly*, 11; reprinted in *Shakespeare on Film: Contemporary Critical Essays*, ed. Robert Shaughnessy. New Casebooks. Basingstoke: Macmillan, 61–70.

——(1999) *Shakespeare and the Loss of Eden: The Construction of Family Values in Early Modern Culture*. Basingstoke: Macmillan.

Benjamin, Walter (1977) *Understanding Brecht*, trans. Anna Bostock. London: New Left Books.

Bennett, Susan (1996) *Performing Nostalgia: Shifting Shakespeare and the Contemporary Past*. London: Routledge.

Bentley, G. E. (1941–68) *The Jacobean and Caroline Stage*, 7 vols. Oxford: Clarendon Press.

——(1971) *The Profession of Dramatist in Shakespeare's Time, 1590-1642*. Princeton, NJ: Princeton University Press.

Bentley, G. R. (ed.) (1958) *Othello*. The Pelican Shakespeare. Baltimore, MD: Penguin.

Berger, Harry S., Jr (1989) *Imaginary Audition: Shakespeare on Page and Stage*. Berkeley, CA: University of California Press.

Berger, Thomas L. and Jesse M. Lander (1999) 'Shakespeare in Print, 1593–1640', in *A Companion to Shakespeare*, ed. David Scott Kastan. Oxford: Blackwell, 395–413.

Berggren, Paula S. (1980) 'The Woman's Part: Female Sexuality as Power in Shakespeare's Plays', in *The Woman's Part: Feminist Criticism of Shakespeare*, ed. Carolyn Ruth Swift Lenz, Gayle Greene and Carol Thomas Neely. Urbana, IL: University of Illinois Press, 17–34.

Berry, Cicely (1993) *The Actor and the Text*. London: Virgin.

Berry, Philippa (1992) 'Woman, Language, and History in *The Rape of Lucrece*', *Shakespeare Survey*, 44: 33–39.

——(1997) *Shakespeare's Feminine Endings: Disfiguring Death in the Tragedies*. London: Routledge.

——(2000) 'Between Idolatry and Astrology: Modes of Temporal Repetition in *Romeo and Juliet*' in *A Feminist Companion to Shakespeare*, ed. Dympna Callaghan. Oxford: Blackwell, 358–72.

Bhabha, Homi K. (1994) *The Location of Culture*. London: Routledge.

Billington, Michael (ed.) (1990) *Directors' Shakespeare: Approaches to Twelfth Night*. London: Nick Hern.

Bishop, T. G. (1996) *Shakespeare and the Theatre of Wonder*. Cambridge: Cambridge University Press.

Blakemore-Evans, G. (ed.) (2006) *The Sonnets*. New Cambridge Shakespeare. Cambridge: Cambridge University Press.

Bloom, Harold (1999) *Shakespeare and the Invention of the Human*. London: Fourth Estate.

Boose, Lynda E. and Richard Burt (eds) (1997) *Shakespeare, the Movie: Popularizing the Plays on Film, TV, and Video*. London: Routledge.

Booth, Stephen (ed.) (1977) *Shakespeare's Sonnets*. New Haven, CT: Yale University Press.

Bowie, Malcolm (1991) *Lacan*. Glasgow: Fontana.

Boyd, Michael (2007) 'Foreword', in *William Shakespeare: Complete Works*, ed. Jonathan Bate and Eric Rasmussen. Basingstoke: Palgrave, 64.

Bradbrook, M. C. (1962) *The Rise of the Common Player: A Study of Actor and Society in Shakespeare's England*. London: Chatto and Windus.

——(1969 [1935]) *Themes and Conventions of Elizabethan Tragedy*. Cambridge: Cambridge University Press.

Bradley, A. C. (1965 [1909]) *Oxford Lectures on Poetry*. London: Macmillan.

——(2007 [1904]) *Shakespearean Tragedy*. Fourth edition, with an introduction and notes by Robert Shaughnessy. Basingstoke: Palgrave.

Bradshaw, Graham (1993) *Misrepresentations: Shakespeare and the Materialists*. Ithaca, NY: Cornell University Press.

Bray, Alan (1982) *Homosexuality in Renaissance England*. London: Gay Men's Press.

Brecht, Bertolt (1965) *The Messingkauf Dialogues*, trans. John Willett. London: Methuen.

Bristol, Michael D. (1985) *Carnival and Theater: Plebeian Culture and the Structure of Authority in Renaissance England*. London: Methuen.

——(1990) *Shakespeare's America/America's Shakespeare*. New York: Routledge.

——(1996) *Big-Time Shakespeare*. London and New York: Routledge.

——(1999) 'Shakespeare: The Myth', in *A Companion to Shakespeare*, ed. David Scott Kastan. Oxford: Blackwell, 489–501.

——(2000) 'Vernacular Criticism and the Scenes Shakespeare Never Wrote', *Shakespeare Survey*, 53: 89–102.

——(2008) 'Confusing Shakespeare's Characters with Real People: Reflections on Reading in Four Questions', in *Shakespeare and Character: Theory, History, Performance and Theatrical Persons*, ed. Paul Yachnin and Jessica Slights. Basingstoke: Palgrave, 21–40.

Bristol, Michael D. and Kathleen McLuskie (eds), with Christopher Holmes (2001) *Shakespeare and Modern Theatre: The Performance of Modernity*. London: Routledge.

Brockbank, Philip (ed.) (1985) *Players of Shakespeare*. Cambridge: Cambridge University Press.

Brook, Peter (1968) *The Empty Space*. Harmondsworth: Penguin.

Brooks, Cleanth (1958) *Understanding Poetry*. Revised edition. New York: Henry Holt and Co.

——(2004 [1947]) 'The Naked Babe and the Cloak of Manliness'; reprinted in *Shakespeare: An Anthology of Criticism and Theory, 1945–2000*, ed. Russ McDonald. Oxford: Blackwell (2004), 19–34.

Brooks, Cleanth and Robert B. Heilman (1947) *Understanding Drama*. London: Harrap.

Brooks, Harold (ed.) (1979) *A Midsummer Night's Dream*. The Arden Shakespeare, second series. London: Methuen.

Brotton, Jerry (1998) '"This Tunis, Sir, Was Carthage": Contesting Colonialism in *The Tempest*', in *Postcolonial Shakespeares*, ed. Ania Loomba and Martin Orkin. London: Routledge, 23–42.

Brown, John Russell (1969) *Shakespeare's Plays in Performance*. Harmondsworth: Penguin.

——(1974) *Free Shakespeare*. London: Heinemann.

——(ed.) (1982) *Focus on Macbeth*. London: Routledge and Kegan Paul.

——(1999) *New Sites for Shakespeare: Theatre, the Audience and Asia*. London: Routledge.

——(2002) *Shakespeare and the Theatrical Event*. Basingstoke: Palgrave.

——(2005a) *Shakespeare Dancing: A Theatrical Study of the Plays*. Basingstoke: Palgrave.

——(2005b) *Macbeth*. The Shakespeare Handbooks. Basingstoke: Palgrave.

——(2007) *A. C. Bradley on Shakespeare's Tragedies: A Concise Edition and Reassessment*. Basingstoke: Palgrave.

——(2008) *The Routledge Companion to Directors' Shakespeare*. London: Routledge.

Brown, John Russell and Bernard Harris (eds) (1961) *Early Shakespeare*. London: Edward Arnold.

Brown, Paul (1994), '"This Thing of Darkness I Acknowledge Mine": *The Tempest* and the Discourse of Colonialism', in *Political Shakespeare: Essays in Cultural Materialism*, ed. Jonathan Dollimore and Alan Sinfield. Manchester: Manchester University Press, 48–71.

Bruster, Douglas (1992) *Drama and the Market in the Age of Shakespeare*. Cambridge: Cambridge University Press.

Bruster, Douglas and Robert Weimann (2004) *Prologues to Shakespeare's Theatre: Performance and Liminality in Early Modern Drama*. London: Routledge.

Brydon, Diana, and Irena R. Makaryk (eds) (2002) *Shakespeare in Canada: A World Elsewhere*. Toronto: University of Toronto Press.

Bryson, Bill (2007) *Shakespeare: The World as Stage*. London: HarperPress.

Buchanan, Judith (2005) *Shakespeare on Film*. Harlow: Pearson Longman.

Buchman, Lorne (1991) *Still in Movement: Shakespeare on Screen*. Oxford: Oxford University Press.

Buhler, Stephen M. (2002) *Shakespeare in the Cinema: Ocular Proof*. Albany, NY: State University of New York Press.

Bullough, G. R. (1957–75) *Narrative and Dramatic Sources of Shakespeare*, 8 vols. London: Routledge & Kegan Paul.

Bulman, James C. (ed.) (1996) *Shakespeare, Theory, and Performance*. London: Routledge.

——(2005) 'Queering the Audience: All-Male Casts in Recent Productions of Shakespeare', in *A Companion to Shakespeare and Performance*, ed. Barbara Hodgdon and W. B. Worthen. Oxford: Blackwell, 564–87.

Bulman, James C. and H. R. Coursen (eds) (1988) *Shakespeare on Television: An Anthology of Essays and Reviews*. Hanover, NH and London: University Press of New England.

Burke, Kenneth (2007) *Kenneth Burke on Shakespeare*, ed. Scott L. Newstock. West Lafayette, IN: Parlor Press.

Burkhardt, Sigurd (1968) *Shakespeare's Meanings*. Princeton, NJ: Princeton University Press.

Burnett, Mark Thornton (2007) *Filming Shakespeare in the Global Marketplace*. Basingstoke: Macmillan.

Burnett, Mark Thornton and Ramona Wray (eds) (2000) *Shakespeare, Film, Fin de Siècle*. Basingstoke: Macmillan.

——(2006) *Screening Shakespeare in the Twenty-First Century*. Edinburgh: Edinburgh University Press.

Burns, Edward (ed.) (2000) *Henry VI, Part 1*. The Arden Shakespeare, third series. London: Arden Shakespeare.

Burrow, Colin (ed.) (2002) *Complete Sonnets and Poems*. The Oxford Shakespeare. Oxford: Oxford University Press.

Burt, Richard (1998) *Unspeakable ShaXXXspeares: Queer Theory and American Kiddie Culture*. Basingstoke: Macmillan.

——(ed.) (2002) *Shakespeare after Mass Media*. Basingstoke: Macmillan.

——(2006) *Shakespeares after Shakespeare: An Encyclopedia of the Bard in Mass and Popular Culture*. Westport: CT: Greenwood Press.

Burt, Richard and Lynda Boose (eds) (2003) *Shakespeare, the Movie, II: Popularizing the Plays on Film, TV, Video and DVD*. London: Routledge.

Burton, Hal (ed.) (1967) *Great Acting*. London: BBC Books.

Butler, Judith (1990) *Gender Trouble: Feminism and the Subversion of Identity*. New York: Routledge.

——(1997) *Excitable Speech: A Politics of the Performative*. New York: Routledge.

Cairncross, A. S. (ed.) (1962) *Henry VI, Part 2*. The Arden Shakespeare, second series. London: Methuen.

——(1964) *Henry VI, Part 3*. The Arden Shakespeare, second series. London: Methuen.

Calderwood, James L. (1971) *Shakespearean Metadrama*. Minneapolis, MN: University of Minnesota Press.

——(1979) *Metadrama in Shakespeare's Henriad*. Berkeley, CA: University of California Press.

——(1992) *A Midsummer Night's Dream*. Harvester New Critical Introductions to Shakespeare. Hemel Hempstead: Harvester Wheatsheaf.

Callaghan, Dympna (2000a) *Shakespeare without Women*. London: Routledge.

——(ed.) (2000b) *A Feminist Companion to Shakespeare*. Oxford: Blackwell.

——(2007) *Shakespeare's Sonnets*. Oxford: Blackwell.

Callow, Simon (2002) *Henry IV*. London: Faber.

Campbell, Lily B. (1964 [1947]) *Shakespeare's 'Histories': Mirrors of Elizabethan Policy*. London: Methuen.

Carroll, William C. (1985) *The Metamorphoses of Shakespearean Comedy*. Princeton, NJ: Princeton University Press.

Carson, Christie and Farah Karim-Cooper (eds) (2008) *Shakespeare's Globe: A Theatrical Experiment*. Cambridge: Cambridge University Press.

Cartelli, Thomas (1987) 'Prospero in Africa: *The Tempest* as Colonial Text and Pretext', in *Shakespeare Reproduced: The Text in History and Ideology*, ed. Jean E. Howard and Marion O'Connor. London: Methuen, 99–115.

——(1999) *Repositioning Shakespeare: National Formations, Postcolonial Appropriations*. London and New York: Routledge.

Cartelli, Thomas and Katherine Rowe (2007) *New Wave Shakespeare on Screen*. Cambridge: Polity Press.

Cave, Richard, Elizabeth Schafer and Brian Woolland (eds) (1999) *Ben Jonson and Theatre: Performance, Practice and Theory*. London: Routledge.

Cavell, Stanley (1987) *Disowning Knowledge in Six Plays of Shakespeare*. Cambridge: Cambridge University Press.

Cerasano, S. P. and Marion Wynene-Davies (eds) (1992) *Gloriana's Face: Women, Public and Private, in the English Renaissance*. Detroit, MI: Wayne State University Press.

Césaire, Aimé (1969) *Une Tempête*. Paris: Seuil.

Chambers, Colin (1980) *Other Spaces: New Theatre and the RSC*. London: Methuen.

——(2004) *Inside the Royal Shakespeare Company: Creativity and the Institution*. London: Routledge.

Chambers, E. K. (1923) *The Elizabethan Stage*, 4 vols. Oxford: Clarendon Press.

——(1930) *William Shakespeare: A Study of Facts and Problems*, 2 vols. Oxford: Clarendon Press.

Charnes, Linda (1993) *Notorious Identity: Materializing the Subject in Shakespeare*. Cambridge, MA: Harvard University Press.

——(2006) *Hamlet's Heirs: Shakespeare and the Politics of a New Millenium*. London and New York: Routledge.

Chedgzoy, Kate (1995) *Shakespeare's Queer Children: Sexual Politics and Contemporary Culture*. Manchester: Manchester University Press.

Chedgzoy, Kate, Susanne Greenhalgh and Robert Shaughnessy (eds) (2007) *Shakespeare and Childhood*. Cambridge: Cambridge University Press.

Cheney, Patrick (2004) *Shakespeare, National Poet-Playwright*. Cambridge: Cambridge University Press.

Clayton, Tom, Susan Brock and Vicente Fores (eds) (2004) *Shakespeare and the Mediterranean: The Selected Proceedings of the International Shakespeare Association World Congress, Valencia 2001*. Newark, DE: University of Delaware Press.

Clemen, Wolfgang (1951) *The Development of Shakespeare's Imagery*. London: Methuen.

Cogswell, Thomas and Peter Lake (2009) 'Buckingham Does the Globe: *Henry VIII* and the Politics of Popularity in the 1620s', *Shakespeare Quarterly*, 60: 253–78.

Cohen, Walter (1985) *Drama of a Nation: Public Theater in Renaissance England and Spain*. Ithaca, NY and London: Cornell University Press.

Collick, John (1989) *Shakespeare, Cinema and Society*. Manchester: Manchester University Press.

Conkie, Rob (2006) *The Globe Theatre Project: Shakespeare and Authenticity*. Lewiston, NY: The Edwin Mellen Press.

Cox, Brian (1992) *The Lear Diaries*. London: Methuen.

Crowl, Samuel (1992) *Shakespeare Observed: Studies in Performance on Stage and Screen*. Athens, OH: Ohio University Press.

——(2003) *Shakespeare at the Cineplex: The Kenneth Branagh Era*. Athens, OH: Ohio University Press.

——(2006) 'Looking for Shylock: Stephen Greenblatt, Michel Radford and Al Pacino', in *Screening Shakespeare in the Twenty-First Century*, ed. Mark Thornton Burnett and Ramona Wray. Edinburgh: Edinburgh University Press, 113–26.

Crystal, David (2005) *Pronouncing Shakespeare: The Globe Experiment*. Cambridge: Cambridge University Press.

Daileader, Celia R. (2005) *Racism, Misogyny, and the Othello Myth: Inter-racial Couples from Shakespeare to Spike Lee*. Cambridge: Cambridge University Press.

David, Richard (1957) 'Drams of Eale', *Shakespeare Survey*, 10: 126–34.

——(1959) 'Actors and Scholars: A View of Shakespeare in the Modern Theatre', *Shakespeare Survey*, 12: 76–87.

——(1978) *Shakespeare in the Theatre*. Cambridge: Cambridge University Press.

Davies, Anthony (1988) *Filming Shakespeare's Plays*. Cambridge: Cambridge University Press.

Davies, Anthony and Stanley Wells (eds) (1992) *Shakespeare and the Moving Image: The Plays on Film and Television*. Cambridge: Cambridge University Press.

Davies, Robertson, Tyrone Guthrie, Boyd Neel and Tanya Moisewitsch (eds) (1955) *Thrice the Brinded Cat Hath Mew'd: A Record of the Stratford Shakespearean Festival, 1955*. Toronto: Clarke, Irwin & Co.

Dawson, Anthony B. (1996) 'Performance and Participation: Desdemona, Foucault, and the Actor's Body', in *Shakespeare, Theory, and Performance*, ed. James C. Bulman. London: Routledge, 29–45.

Day, Barry (1996) *This Wooden 'O': Shakespeare's Globe Reborn*. London: Oberon.

Day, Gillian (2002) *Richard III*. Shakespeare at Stratford. London: Arden Shakespeare.

de Grazia, Margreta (1991) *Shakespeare Verbatim: The Reproduction of Authenticity and the 1790 Apparatus*. Oxford: Clarendon Press.

——(1994) 'The Scandal of Shakespeare's Sonnets', *Shakespeare Survey*, 47: 35–49.

——(2007) '*Hamlet*' *without Hamlet*. Cambridge: Cambridge University Press.

de Grazia, Margreta, Maureen Quilligan and Peter Stallybrass (eds) (1996) *Subject and Object in Renaissance Culture*. Cambridge: Cambridge University Press.

Delgado, Maria M. (2006) 'Journeys of Cultural Transference: Calixto Bieito's Multilingual Shakespeares', *Modern Language Review*, 101: 106–50.

Derrida, Jacques (1976) *Of Grammatology*, trans. Gayatri Chakrovorty Spivak. Baltimore, MD: Johns Hopkins University Press.

——(1978) *Writing and Difference*, trans. Alan Bass. London: Routledge.

——(1982) *Margins of Philosophy*, trans. Alan Bass. Chicago, IL: University of Chicago Press.

Desens, Merliss C. (1994) *The Bed-Trick in English Renaissance Drama*. Newark, DE: University of Delaware Press.

Desmet, Christy (1992) *Reading Shakespeare's Characters: Rhetoric, Ethics, and Identity*. Amherst, MA: University of Massachusetts Press.

Desmet, Christy and Robert Sawyer (eds) (1999) *Shakespeare and Appropriation*. London: Routledge.

Dessen, Alan C. (1984) *Elizabethan Stage Conventions and Modern Interpreters*. Cambridge: Cambridge University Press.

——(1987) 'Modern Productions and the Elizabethan Scholar', *Renaissance Drama*, 18: 205–23.

——(1989) *Titus Andronicus*. Shakespeare in Performance. Manchester: Manchester University Press.

——(1995) *Recovering Shakespeare's Theatrical Vocabulary*. Cambridge: Cambridge University Press.

——(2002) *Rescripting Shakespeare: The Text, the Director and Modern Productions*. Cambridge: Cambridge University Press.

Dessen, Alan C. and Leslie Thomson (eds) (1999) *A Dictionary of Stage Directions in English Drama, 1580–1642*. Cambridge: Cambridge University Press.

Diamond, Elin (ed.) (1996) *Performance and Cultural Politics*. London: Routledge.

DiGangi, Mario (1997) *The Homoerotics of Early Modern Drama*. Cambridge: Cambridge University Press.

Dionne, Craig and Parmita Kapadia (eds) (2008) *Native Shakespeares: Indigenous Appropriations on a Global Stage*. Aldershot: Ashgate.

Dobson, Michael (1992) *The Making of the National Poet: Shakespeare, Adaptation and Authorship, 1660–1769*. Oxford: Clarendon Press.

——(ed.) (2006) *Performing Shakespeare's Tragedies Today: The Actor's Perspective*. Cambridge: Cambridge University Press.

——(2007) 'Shakespeare Performances in England, 2006', *Shakespeare Survey*, 60: 284–319.

Dollimore, Jonathan (1986) 'Subjectivity, Sexuality, and Transgression: The Jacobean Connection', *Renaissance Drama*, New Series, 17: 53–81.

——(1991) *Sexual Dissidence: Augustine to Wilde, Freud to Foucault*. Oxford: Oxford University Press.

——(1994) 'Introduction: Shakespeare, Cultural Materialism and the New Historicism', in *Political Shakespeare: Essays in Cultural Materialism*, ed. Jonathan Dollimore and Alan Sinfield. Manchester: Manchester University Press, 2–17.

——(2004) *Radical Tragedy: Religion, Ideology and Power in the Drama of Shakespeare and his Contemporaries*. Third edition. Hemel Hempstead: Harvester Wheatsheaf.

Dollimore, Jonathan and Alan Sinfield (1985) 'History and Ideology: The Instance of *Henry V*', in *Alternative Shakespeares*, ed. John Drakakis. First edition. London: Methuen, 206–27.

——(eds) (1994) *Political Shakespeare: Essays in Cultural Materialism*. Second edition. Manchester: Manchester University Press.

Donaldson, Peter S. (1990) *Shakespearean Films/Shakespearean Directors*. London: Unwin Hyman.

Drakakis, John (ed.) (1985) *Alternative Shakespeares*. First edition. London: Methuen.

——(1988) 'Theatre, Ideology and Institution: Shakespeare and the Roadsweepers', in *The Shakespeare Myth*, ed. Graham Holderness. Manchester: Manchester University Press, 24–41.

——(1992) '"Fashion It Thus": *Julius Caesar* and the Politics of Theatrical Representation', *Shakespeare Survey*, 44: 65–73.

——(1996) 'Afterword: The Next Generation', in *Alternative Shakespeares, Volume 2*, ed. Terence Hawkes. London: Routledge, 238–44.

——(1997) 'Afterword', in *Shakespeare and National Culture*, ed. John J. Joughlin. Manchester: Manchester University Press, 326–37.

Duncan-Jones, Katharine (ed.) (1997) *Shakespeare's Sonnets*. The Arden Shakespeare. London: Thomas Nelson.

——(2001) *Ungentle Shakespeare: Scenes from His Life*. London: Arden Shakespeare.

Duncan-Jones, Katharine and H. R. Woudhuysen (eds) (2007) *Shakespeare's Poems*. The Arden Shakespeare, third series. London: Arden Shakespeare.

Dusinberre, Juliet (2003) *Shakespeare and the Nature of Women*. Third edition. Basingstoke: Palgrave.

——(2006) *As You Like It*. The Arden Shakespeare, third series. London: Arden Shakespeare.

Dutton, Richard, Alison Findlay and Richard Wilson (eds) (2003a) *Region, Religion and Patronage: Lancastrian Shakespeare*. Manchester: Manchester University Press.

——(eds) (2003b) *Theatre and Religion: Lancastrian Shakespeare*. Manchester: Manchester University Press.

Dymkowski, Christine (ed.) (2000) *The Tempest*. Shakespeare in Production. Cambridge: Cambridge University Press.

Eagleton, Terry (1983) *Literary Theory: An Introduction*. Oxford: Blackwell.

——(1986) *William Shakespeare*. Rereading Literature. Oxford: Blackwell.

——(2004) ' Foreword', in Jonathan Dollimore, *Radical Tragedy: Religion, Ideology and Power in the Drama of Shakespeare and His Contemporaries*. Third edition. Basingstoke: Palgrave, x–xiii.

Eckert, Charles (ed.) (1972) *Focus on Shakespearean Films*. Englewood Cliffs, NJ: Prentice.

Edelman, Charles (ed.) (2002) *The Merchant of Venice*. Shakespeare in Production. Cambridge: Cambridge University Press.

Edmond, Mary (1991) 'It Was for Gentle Shakespeare Cut', *Shakespeare Quarterly*, 42: 339–44.

Edmondson, Paul and Stanley Wells (2004) *Shakespeare's Sonnets*. Oxford Shakespeare Topics. Oxford: Oxford University Press.

Edwards, Philip (ed.) (1985) *Hamlet*. New Cambridge Shakespeare. Cambridge: Cambridge University Press.

Egan, Gabriel (2001) 'Hearing or Seeing a Play? Evidence of Early Modern Terminology', *Ben Jonson Journal*, 8: 327–47.

——(2003) 'Shylock's Unpropped House and the Theatre in Shoreditch', *Notes and Queries*, 248: 37–39.

——(2006) *Green Shakespeare: From Ecopolitics to Ecocriticism*. London: Routledge.

Elam, Keir (1984) *Shakespeare's Universe of Discourse: Language-Games in the Comedies*. Cambridge: Cambridge University Press.

Eliot, T. S. (1932) 'Seneca in English Translation', in *Selected Essays 1917–1932*. London: Faber and Faber.

——(1951) *Selected Essays*. London: Faber and Faber.

Elton, W. R. (1966) *King Lear and the Gods*. San Marino, CA: Huntington Library.

Empson, William (1951) *The Structure of Complex Words*. London: Chatto and Windus.

——(1961 [1930]) *Seven Types of Ambiguity*. Harmondsworth: Penguin.

Engle, Lars (1993) *Shakespearean Pragmatism: Market of His Time*. Chicago, IL: University of Chicago Press.

Erickson, Peter (1985) *Patriarchal Structures in Shakespeare's Drama*. Berkeley, CA: University of California Press.

Erickson, Peter and Coppélia Kahn (eds) (1985) *Shakespeare's 'Rough Magic': Renaissance Essays in Honor of C. L. Barber*. Newark, DE: Delaware University Press.

Erne, Lukas (2003) *Shakespeare as Literary Dramatist*. Cambridge: Cambridge University Press.

Erne, Lukas and M. J. Kidnie (eds) (2004) *Textual Performances: The Modern Reproduction of Shakespeare's Drama*. Cambridge: Cambridge University Press.

Esche, Edward J. (ed.) (2000) *Shakespeare and His Contemporaries in Performance*. Aldershot: Ashgate.

Escolme, Bridget (2005) *Talking to the Audience: Shakespeare, Performance, Self*. London: Routledge.

Evans, Malcolm (1985) 'Deconstructing Shakespeare's Comedies', in *Alternative Shakespeares*, ed. John Drakakis. First edition. London: Methuen, 67–94.

——(1986) *Signifying Nothing: Truth's True Contents in Shakespeare's Text*. Brighton: Harvester.

Eyre, Richard (1993) 'Shakespeare Alive!', in *Granville Barker's Prefaces to Shakespeare*. London: Nick Hern/National Theatre.

Farjeon, Herbert (1949) *The Shakespearean Scene: Dramatic Criticisms*. London: Hutchinson.

Felperin, Howard (1972) *Shakespearean Romance*. Princeton, NJ: Princeton University Press.

Ferguson, Margaret W., Maureen Quilligan and Nancy Vickers (eds) (1986) *Rewriting the Renaissance: The Discourses of Sexual Difference in Early Modern Europe*. Chicago, IL: University of Chicago Press.

Fernie, Ewan (2002) *Shame in Shakespeare*. London: Routledge.

——(2005a) 'Shakespeare and the Prospect of Presentism', *Shakespeare Survey*, 58: 169–84.

——(ed.) (2005b) *Spiritual Shakespeares*. London: Routledge.

Fineman, Joel (1985) 'The Turn of the Shrew', in *Shakespeare and the Question of Theory*, ed. Patricia Parker and Geoffrey Hartmann. London: Methuen, 138–59.

——(1986) *Shakespeare's Perjured Eye: The Invention of Poetic Subjectivity in the Sonnets*. Berkeley, CA: University of California Press.

Foakes, R. A. (1993) *Hamlet Versus Lear: Cultural Politics and Shakespeare's Art*. Cambridge: Cambridge University Press.

——(ed.) (1997) *King Lear*. The Arden Shakespeare, third series. Walton-on-Thames: Nelson.

Foakes, R. A. and R. T. Rickert (eds) (1961) *Henslowe's Diary*. Cambridge: Cambridge University Press.

Fotheringham, Richard, Christa Jansohn and R. S. White (eds) (2008) *Shakespeare's World/World Shakespeares*. Newark, DE: University of Delaware Press.

Foucault, Michel (1967) *Madness and Civilisation: A History of Insanity in the Age of Reason*. London: Tavistock.

——(1970) *The Order of Things: An Archaeology of the Human Sciences*. London: Tavistock.

——(1973) *The Birth of the Clinic: An Archaeology of Medical Perception*, trans. Alan Sheridan. London: Tavistock.

——(1977) *Discipline and Punish: The Birth of the Prison*, trans. Alan Sheridan. London: Tavistock.

——(1980) *Power/Knowledge: Selected Interviews and Other Writings, 1972–1977*, ed. and trans. Colin Gordon. Brighton: Harvester.

——(1981) *The History of Sexuality, Volume 1: An Introduction*, trans. Robert Hurley. Harmondsworth: Penguin.

Fowler, Alastair (1970) *Silent Poetry: Essays in Numerological Analysis*. London: Routledge and Kegan Paul.

Freedman, Barbara (1991) *Staging the Gaze: Postmodernism, Pyschoanalysis, and Shakespearean Comedy*, Ithaca, NY: Cornell University Press.

French, Emma (2006) *Selling Shakespeare to Hollywood: The Marketing of Filmed Shakespeare Adaptations from 1989 into the New Millennium*. Hatfield: University of Hertfordshire Press.

Freud, Sigmund (1985 [1913]) 'The Theme of the Three Caskets', in *Art and Literature*, ed. Albert Dickson and James Strachey. The Penguin Freud Library, vol. 14. Harmondsworth: Penguin, 233–47.

——(1985) *Art and Literature*, ed. Albert Dickson and James Strachey. The Penguin Freud Library, vol. 14. Harmondsworth: Penguin.

Frey, Charles (1980) '"O Sacred, Shadowy, Cold and Constant Queen": Shakespeare's Imperiled and Chastening Daughters of Romance', in *The Woman's Part: Feminist Criticism of Shakespeare*, ed. Carolyn Ruth Swift Lenz, Gayle Greene and Carol Thomas Neely. Urbana, IL: University of Illinois Press, 295–313.

Frye, Northrop (1965) *A Natural Perspective: The Development of Shakespearean Comedy and Romance*. New York: Columbia University Press.

Furness, H. H. (ed.) (1877) *Hamlet*. New Variorum Shakespeare, 2 vols. Philadelphia, PA: J. B. Lippincott.

——(1904) *Love's Labour's Lost*. New Variorum Edition. Philadelphia, PA: J. B. Lippincott.

Gajowski, Evelyn (ed.) (2004) *Re-Visions of Shakespeare: Essays in Honor of Robert Ornstein*. Newark, DE: University of Delaware Press.

Garber, Marjorie (1987) *Shakespeare's Ghost Writers: Literature as Uncanny Causality*. London: Methuen.

——(1997 [1981]) *Coming of Age in Shakespeare*. London and New York: Routledge,

Geertz, Clifford (1993 [1973]) *The Interpretation of Cultures: Selected Essays*. Glasgow: Fontana.

Gillies, John (1994) *Shakespeare and the Geography of Difference*. Cambridge: Cambridge University Press.

——(2005) 'Stanislavski, *Othello*, and the Motives of Eloquence', in *A Companion to Shakespeare and Performance*, ed. Barbara Hodgdon and W. B. Worthen. Oxford: Blackwell, 267–84.

Girard, René (1991) *A Theatre of Envy: William Shakespeare*. Oxford: Oxford University Press.

Goldberg, Jonathan (1983) *James I and the Politics of Literature: Jonson, Shakespeare, Donne, and Their Contemporaries*. Baltimore, MD: Johns Hopkins University Press.

——(1992) *Sodometries: Renaissance Texts, Modern Sexualities*, Stanford, CA: Stanford University Press.

——(ed.) (1994) *Queering the Renaissance*. Durham, NC: Duke University Press.

Goodwin, John (ed.) (1964) *Royal Shakespeare Company 1960–63*. London: Max Reinhardt.

Grady, Hugh (1991) *The Modernist Shakespeare: Critical Texts in a Material World*. Oxford: Clarendon Press.

——(1996) *Shakespeare's Universal Wolf: Studies in Early Modern Reification*. Oxford: Clarendon Press.

——(ed.) (2000) *Shakespeare and Modernity*. London: Routledge.

——(2002) *Shakespeare, Machiavelli and Montaigne: Power and Subjectivity from Richard II to Hamlet*. Oxford: Oxford University Press.

Granville Barker, Harley (1923–47) *Prefaces to Shakespeare*. London: Sidgwick and Jackson.

——(1923) 'Some Tasks for Dramatic Scholarship', in *Essays by Divers Hands: Being the Transactions of the Royal Society of Literature of the United Kingdom*, ed. F. S. Boas. New series, vol. 3. London: Humphrey Milford, Oxford University Press: 17–38.

Green, Mary Anne Everett, ed. (1857) *Calander of State Papers Domestic: James I, 1603–1610*, London.

Greg, W. W. (ed.) (1914) *Gesta Grayorum*. London: Malone Society.

Greenblatt, Stephen J. (1980) *Renaissance Self-Fashioning: From More to Shakespeare*. Chicago, IL: University of Chicago Press.

——(ed.) (1988a) *Representing the English Renaissance*. Berkeley, CA: University of California Press.

——(1988b) *Shakespearean Negotiations: The Circulation of Social Energy in Renaissance England*. Berkeley, CA: University of California Press.

——(ed.) (1989) *Representing the English Renaissance*. Berkeley, CA: University of California Press.

——(1990a) *Learning to Curse: Essays in Early Modern Culture*. London: Routledge.

——(1990b) 'Resonance and Wonder', in *Literary Theory Today*, ed. Peter Collier and Helga Geyer-Ryan. Cambridge: Polity Press, 74–90.

——(1994) 'Invisible Bullets: Renaissance Authority and Its Subversion', in *Political Shakespeare: Essays in Cultural Materialism*, ed. Jonathan Dollimore and Alan Sinfield. Manchester: Manchester University Press, 18–47.

——(2001) *Hamlet in Purgatory*. Princeton, NJ: Princeton University Press.

——(2004) *Will in the World: How Shakespeare Became Shakespeare*. London: Pimlico.

Greenblatt, Stephen J., Walter Cohen, Jean E. Howard and Katharine Eisaman Maus (eds) (1997) *The Norton Shakespeare*. New York: W. W. Norton & Co.

Greenwald, Michael L. (1986) *Directions by Indirections: John Barton of the Royal Shakespeare Company*. Newark, DE: University of Delaware Press.

Greer, Germaine (2007) *Shakespeare's Wife*. London: Bloomsbury.

Griffiths, Trevor R. (1983) 'This Island's Mine: Caliban and Colonialism', *Yearbook of English Studies*, 13: 159–80.

——(ed.) (1996) *A Midsummer Night's Dream*. Shakespeare in Production. Cambridge: Cambridge University Press.

Gross, John (2004) 'Too Wet Behind the Ears Theatre', *Sunday Telegraph*, 2 May.

Gurr, Andrew (1971) 'Shakespeare's First Poem: Sonnet 145', *Essays in Criticism*, 21: 221–26.

——(1992) *The Shakespearean Stage, 1574–1642*. Third edition. Cambridge: Cambridge University Press.

——(1996) *The Shakespearian Playing Companies*. Oxford: Clarendon Press.

——(1999) 'Prologue: Who Is Lovewit? What Is He?', in *Ben Jonson and Theatre: Performance, Practice and Theory*, ed. Richard Cave, Elizabeth Schafer and Brian Woolland. London: Routledge, 5–19.

——(2004a) *Playgoing in Shakespeare's London*. Third edition. Cambridge: Cambridge University Press.

——(2004b) *The Shakespeare Company, 1594–1642*. Cambridge: Cambridge University Press.

Gurr, Andrew and Mariko Ichikawa (2000) *Staging in Shakespeare's Theatres*. Oxford: Oxford University Press.

Guthrie, Tyrone (1959) *A Life in the Theatre*. London: Hamish Hamilton.

——(1965) *In Various Directions: A View of Theatre*. London: Michael Joseph.

Guthrie, Tyrone, Robertson Davies and Grant McDonald (eds) (1953) *Renown at Stratford: A Record of the Shakespeare Festival in Canada, 1953*. Toronto: Clarke, Irwin & Co.

——(eds) (1954) *Twice Have the Trumpets Sounded: A Record of the Stratford Shakespearean Festival, 1954*. Toronto: Clarke, Irwin & Co.

Halio, Jay L. (1988) *Understanding Shakespeare's Plays in Performance*. Manchester: Manchester University Press.

——(ed.) (1995) *Shakespeare's Romeo and Juliet: Texts, Contexts, and Interpretation*. Newark, DE and London: Associated University Presses.

——(2003) *A Midsummer Night's Dream*. Second edition. Shakespeare in Performance. Manchester: Manchester University Press.

Hall, Kim F. (1995) *Things of Darkness: Economies of Race and Gender in Early Modern England*. Ithaca, NY: Cornell University Press.

——(1998) '"These Bastard Signs of Fair": Literary Whiteness in Shakespeare's Sonnets', in *Postcolonial Shakespeares*, ed. Ania Loomba and Martin Orkin. London: Routledge, 64–83.

Hall, Peter (1963) 'Avoiding a Method', in *Crucial Years of the RSC*. London: Max Reinhardt.

——(1964) 'Shakespeare and the Modern Director', in *Royal Shakespeare Company 1960–63*, ed. John Goodwin. London: Max Reinhardt, 41–48.

Hall-Smith, Sue (2006) 'Recent Stage, Film and Critical Interpretations', in *Titus Andronicus*, ed. Alan Hughes. New Cambridge Shakespeare, updated edition. Cambridge: Cambridge University Press, 45–60.

Halley, Janet E. (1994) '*Bowers v. Hardwick* in the Renaissance', in *Queering the Renaissance*, ed. Jonathan Goldberg. Durham, NC: Duke University Press, 15–39.

Halpern, Richard (1997) *Shakespeare among the Moderns*. Ithaca, NY: Cornell University Press.

Hamer, Mary (1993) *Signs of Cleopatra: History, Politics, Representation*. London: Routledge.

Hanson, Elizabeth (1998) *Discovering the Subject in Renaissance England*. Cambridge: Cambridge University Press.

Harbage, Alfred (1941) *Shakespeare's Audience*. New York: Columbia University Press.

Harris, Bernard (2000 [1958]) 'A Portrait of a Moor', *Shakespeare Survey*, 11: 89–99; reprinted in *Shakespeare and Race*, ed. Catharine M. S. Alexander and Stanley Wells. Cambridge: Cambridge University Press (2000), 23–36.

Harris, Jonathan Gil and Natasha Korda (eds) (2002) *Staged Properties in Early Modern English Drama*. Cambridge: Cambridge University Press.

Hartley, Andrew James (2005) *The Shakespearean Dramaturge: A Practical and Theoretical Guide*. New York: Palgrave Macmillan.

Hatchuel, Sarah (2004) *Shakespeare, from Stage to Screen*. Cambridge: Cambridge University Press.

Hating-Smith, Tori (1985) *From Farce to Metadrama: A Stage History of 'The Taming of the Shrew'*. Westport, CT: Greenwood Press.

Hattaway, Michael (1982) *Elizabethan Popular Theatre: Plays in Performance*. London: Routledge & Kegan Paul.

——(ed.) (1990) *The First Part of King Henry VI*. New Cambridge Shakespeare. Cambridge: Cambridge University Press.

Hawkes, Terence (ed.) (1974) *Coleridge on Shakespeare*. Harmondsworth: Penguin.

——(1986) *That Shakespeherian Rag: Essays on a Critical Process*. London: Methuen.

——(1992) *Meaning by Shakespeare*. London: Routledge.

——(ed.) (1996) *Alternative Shakespeares, Volume 2*. London: Routledge.

——(2002) *Shakespeare in the Present*. London: Routledge.

Hazlitt, William (1957 [1817]) *The Round Table and Characters of Shakespear's Plays*. London: Dent.

Heinemann, Margot (1994) 'How Brecht Read Shakespeare', in *Political Shakespeare: Essays in Cultural Materialism*, ed. Jonathan Dollimore and Alan Sinfield. Manchester: Manchester University Press, 226–54.

Henderson, Diana E. (2006a) *Collaborations with the Past: Reshaping Shakespeare across Time and Media*. Ithaca, NY: Cornell University Press.

——(ed.) (2006b) *A Concise Companion to Shakespeare on Screen*. Oxford: Blackwell.

——(ed.) (2008) *Alternative Shakespeares 3*. London: Routledge.

Hendricks, Margo (1996) '"Obscured by Dreams": Race, Empire, and Shakespeare's *A Midsummer Night's Dream*', *Shakespeare Quarterly*, 47: 37–60.

——(2000) 'Surveying "Race" in Shakespeare', in *Shakespeare and Race*, ed. Catharine M. S. Alexander and Stanley Wells. Cambridge: Cambridge University Press, 1–22.

Hendricks, Margo and Patricia Parker (eds) (1994) *Women, 'Race', and Writing in the Early Modern Period*. London and New York: Routledge.

Hendricks, Margo and Stanley Wells (eds) (2000) *Shakespeare and Race*. Cambridge: Cambridge University Press.

Heritage, Paul (2006) 'Parallel Power: Shakespeare, Gunfire and Silence', in *Performance and Place*, ed. Leslie Hill and Helen Paris. Basingstoke: Palgrave, 192–206.

Hibbard, G. R. (ed.) (1964) *Three Elizabethan Pamphlets*. London: Harrap.

Higgins, Charlotte (2006) 'My Kingdom for a Goat', *Guardian*, 14 February.

Highfill, Philip H., Jr, Kalman A. Burnim and Edward Langhans (eds) (1973–93) *A Biographical Dictionary of Actors, Actresses, Musicians, Dancers, Managers and Other Stage Personnel in London, 1660–1800*, 16 vs. Carbondale, IL: Southern Illinois University Press.

Hill, Christopher (1958) *Puritanism and Revolution*. London: Secker and Warburg.

——(1964) *Society and Puritanism in Pre-Revolutionary England*. London: Secker and Warburg.

Hill, Errol (1984) *Shakespeare in Sable: A History of Black Shakespearean Actors*. Amherst, MA: University of Massachusetts Press.

Hindle, Maurice (2007) *Studying Shakespeare on Film*. Basingstoke: Palgrave.

Hinman, Charlton (1963) *The Printing and Proof-Reading of the First Folio of Shakespeare*. Oxford: Clarendon Press.

Hodgdon, Barbara (1991) *The End Crowns All: Closure and Contradiction in Shakespeare's History*. Princeton, NJ: Princeton University Press.

——(1996) 'Looking for Mr Shakespeare after "The Revolution": Robert Lepage's Intercultural *Dream* Machine', in *Shakespeare, Theory, and Performance*, ed. James C. Bulman. London: Routledge, 68–91.

——(1998) *The Shakespeare Trade: Performances and Appropriations*. Philadelphia, PA: University of Pennsylvania Press.

——(2002) 'From the Editor', *Shakespeare Quarterly*, 53: iii–x.

Hodgdon, Barbara and W. B. Worthen (eds) (2005) *A Companion to Shakespeare and Performance*. Oxford: Blackwell.

Hoenselaars, Ton (ed.) (2004) *Shakespeare and the Language of Translation*. London: Arden.

Holden, Anthony (1999) *William Shakespeare: His Life and Work*. London: Little, Brown.

Holderness, Graham (1985), *Shakespeare's History*. Dublin: Gill and Macmillan.

——(ed.) (1988a) *The Shakespeare Myth*. Manchester: Manchester University Press.

——(1988b) 'The Albatross and the Swan: Two Productions at Stratford', *New Theatre Quarterly*, 3: 152–58.

——(ed.) (1992) *Shakespeare's History Plays*. New Casebooks. Basingstoke: Macmillan.

——(1994) 'Radical Potentiality and Institutional Closure: Shakespeare in Film and Television', in *Political Shakespeare: Essays in Cultural Materialism*, ed. Jonathan Dollimore and Alan Sinfield. Manchester: Manchester University Press, 206–25.

——(2002) *Visual Shakespeare: Essays in Film and Television*. Hatfield: University of Hertfordshire Press.

——(2008) '"Silence Bleeds": *Hamlet* across Borders: The Shakespearean Adaptations of Sulayman Al-Bassam', *European Journal of English Studies*, 12: 59–77.

Holinshed, Raphael (1965) *Holinshed's Chronicles*, ed. H. Ellis, 6 vols. New York: AMS Press.

Holland, Norman L. (1964) *Psychoanalysis and Shakespeare*. New York: McGraw-Hill.

Holland, Peter (ed.) (1994) *A Midsummer Night's Dream*. The Oxford Shakespeare. Oxford: Oxford University Press.

——(1997) *English Shakespeares: Shakespeare on the English Stage in the 1990s*. Cambridge: Cambridge University Press.

——(2003) 'Series Introduction: Redefining Theatre History', in *Theorizing Practice: Redefining Theatre History*, ed. W. B. Worthen and Peter Holland. Basingstoke: Palgrave Macmillan, xv–xvii.

——(2004) 'William Shakespeare', in *Oxford Dictionary of National Biography*, ed. H. C. G. Matthew and Brian Harrison. Oxford: Oxford University Press, vol. 49, 939–76.

——(ed.) (2006) *Shakespeare, Memory and Performance*. Cambridge: Cambridge University Press.

Holland, Peter and Michael Cordner (eds) (2007) *Players, Playwrights, Playhouses: Investigating Performance, 1660–1800*. Basingstoke: Palgrave Macmillan.

Holland, Peter and Stephen Orgel (eds) (2004) *From Script to Stage in Early Modern England*. Basingstoke: Palgrave Macmillan.

Holmer, Joan Ozark (1995) *The Merchant of Venice: Choice, Hazard and Consequence*. Basingstoke: Macmillan.

Holmes, Jonathan (2004) *Merely Players? Actors' Accounts of Performing Shakespeare*. London: Routledge.

Honan, Park (1999) *Shakespeare: A Life*. Oxford: Oxford University Press.

Honigmann, E. A. J. (1985) *Shakespeare: The 'Lost Years'*. Manchester: Manchester University Press.

——(ed.) (1997) *Othello*. The Arden Shakespeare, third series. London: Arden Shakespeare.

Hope, Jonathan (1994) *The Authorship of Shakespeare's Plays*. Cambridge: Cambridge University Press.

——(2003) *Shakespeare's Grammar*. London: Arden.

Hornby, Nick (2003) *31 Songs*. Harmondsworth: Penguin.

Hortman, Wilhelm (1998) *Shakespeare on the German Stage: The Twentieth Century*. Cambridge: Cambridge University Press.

Hotson, Leslie (1954) *The First Night of Twelfth Night*. London: Hart-Davis.

Howard, Jean E. (1986) 'The New Historicism in Renaissance Studies', *English Literary Renaissance*, 16: 13–43.

——(1988) 'Crossdressing, the Theatre, and Gender Struggle in Early Modern England', *Shakespeare Quarterly*, 39: 418–40.

——(1994) *The Stage and Social Struggle in Early Modern England*. New York: Routledge.

Howard, Jean E. and Marion O'Connor (eds) (1987) *Shakespeare Reproduced: The Text in History and Ideology*. London: Methuen.

Howard, Jean E. and Phyllis Rackin (1997) *Engendering a Nation: A Feminist Account of Shakespeare's Histories*. London: Routledge.

Howard, Jean E. and Scott Cutler Shershow (eds) (2000) *Marxist Shakespeares*. London: Routledge.

Howard, Tony (2007) *Women as Hamlet: Performance and Interpretation in Theatre, Film and Fiction*. Cambridge: Cambridge University Press.

Hughes, Alan (ed.) (2006) *Titus Andronicus*. New Cambridge Shakespeare, updated edition. Cambridge: Cambridge University Press.

Hulme, Peter and William H. Sherman (eds) (2000) *The Tempest and Its Travels*. London: Reaktion.

Hunter, G. K. (ed.) (1967) *Macbeth*. The New Penguin Shakespeare. Harmondsworth: Penguin.

——(2000 [1964]) 'Elizabethans and Foreigners', *Shakespeare Survey*, 17: 37–52; reprinted in *Shakespeare and Race*, ed. Margo Hendricks and Stanley Wells. Cambridge: Cambridge University Press, 37–63.

——(2004 [1967]) '*Othello* and Colour Prejudice', *Proceedings of the British Academy*, 53: 139–63; reprinted in *Othello: Authoritative Text, Sources and Contexts, Criticism*, ed. Edward Pechter. New York: W. W. Norton & Co. (2003), 248–62.

Hunter, Lynette and Peter Lichtenfels (eds) (2005) *Shakespeare, Language and the Stage*. London: The Arden Shakespeare.

Ioppolo, Grace (ed.) (2000) *Shakespeare Performed: Essays in Honor of R. A. Foakes*. Newark, DE: University of Delaware Press.

Jackson, Gabriele Bernhardt (1988) 'Topical Ideology; Witches, Amazons, and Shakespeare's Joan of Arc', *ELR*, 18: 40–65.

Jackson, Ken (2001) '"One Wish" or the Possibility of the Impossible: Derrida, the Gift and God in *Timon of Athens*', *Shakespeare Quarterly*, 52: 34–66.

Jackson, MacDonald P. (1965) *A Lover's Complaint: Its Date and Authenticity*. Auckland, New Zealand: University of Auckland.

——(2006) 'Shakespeare and the Quarrel Scene in *Arden of Faversham*', *Shakespeare Quarterly*, 57: 259–93.

Jackson, Russell (ed.) (2000) *The Cambridge Companion to Shakespeare on Film*. Cambridge: Cambridge University Press.

Jackson, William A. (ed.) (1957) *Records of the Court of the Stationers' Company, 1602 to 1640*. London: Bibliographical Society.

Jankowski, Theodora A. (2000a) *Pure Resistance: Queer Virginity in Early Modern English Drama*. Philadelphia, PA: University of Pennsylvania Press.

——(2000b) ' … in the Lesbian Void: Woman–Woman Eroticism in Shakespeare's Plays', in *A Feminist Companion to Shakespeare*, ed. Dympna Callaghan. London: Routledge, 299–319.

Jardine, Lisa (1983) *Still Harping on Daughters: Women and Drama in the Age of Shakespeare*. Brighton: Harvester.

——(1992) 'Twins and Travesties: Gender, Dependency and Sexual Availability in *Twelfth Night*', in *Erotic Politics: Desire on the Renaissance Stage*, ed. Susan Zimmerman. London: Routledge, 27–38.

——(1996) *Reading Shakespeare Historically*. London: Routledge.

Jess-Cooke, Carolyn (2007) *Shakespeare on Film: Such Things as Dreams Are Made Of*. London: Wallflower.

Johns, Ian (2004) 'Court between Two Generations', *The Times*, 29 April.

Jones, Eldred (1965) *Othello's Countrymen: The African in English Renaissance Drama*. Oxford: Oxford University Press.

Jones, Ernest (1949) *Hamlet and Oedipus*. London: Gollancz.

Jorgens, Jack J. (1977) *Shakespeare on Film*. Bloomington, IN: Indiana University Press.

Joughin, John J. (ed.) (1997) *Shakespeare and National Culture*. Manchester: Manchester University Press.

——(ed.) (2000) *Philosophical Shakespeares*. London: Routledge.

Jowett, John (ed.) (2000) *Richard III*. The Oxford Shakespeare. Oxford: Oxford University Press.

Jowett, John and Gary Taylor (1993) *Shakespeare Reshaped, 1606–1623*. Oxford: Clarendon Press.

Kahn, Coppélia (1981) *Man's Estate: Masculine Identity in Shakespeare*. Berkeley, CA: University of California Press.

——(1997) *Roman Shakespeare: Warriors, Wounds, and Women*. London: Routledge.

Kamps, Ivo (ed.) (1991) *Shakespeare Left and Right*. London: Routledge.

——(ed.) (1995) *Materialist Shakespeare: A History*. London: Verso.

Kastan, David Scott (1999a) *Shakespeare after Theory*. London: Routledge.

——(ed.) (1999b) *A Companion to Shakespeare*. Oxford: Blackwell.

Kastan, David Scott and Peter Stallybrass (eds) (1991) *Staging the Renaissance*. London: Routledge.

Keller, James R. and Leslie Stratyner (eds) (2004) *Almost Shakespeare: Reinventing His Works for Cinema and Television*. London: McFarland.

Kelly, Henry A. (1970) *Divine Providence in the England of Shakespeare's Histories*. Cambridge, MA: Harvard University Press.

Kemp, T. C. (1954) 'Acting Shakespeare: Modern Tendencies in Playing and Production', *Shakespeare Survey*, 7: 121–27.

Kennedy, Dennis (1993) *Looking at Shakespeare: A Visual History of Twentieth-Century Performance*. Cambridge: Cambridge University Press.

——(ed.) (1993) *Foreign Shakespeare: Contemporary Performance*. Cambridge: Cambridge University Press.

——(1996) 'Shakespeare without His Language', in *Shakespeare, Theory, and Performance*, ed. James C. Bulman. London: Routledge, 133–48.

Kermode, Frank (1965) 'What Is Shakespeare's *Henry VIII* About?', in *Shakespeare: The Histories*, ed. Eugene M. Waith. Englewood Cliffs, NJ: Prentice Hall, 168–79.

——(2000) *Shakespeare's Language*. Harmondsworth: Penguin.

Kernan, Alvin (1995) *Shakespeare, the King's Playwright: Theater in the Stuart Court, 1603–1613*. New Haven, CT: Yale University Press.

Kerrigan, John (ed.) (1991) *Motives of Woe: Shakespeare and 'Female Complaint'*. Oxford: Clarendon Press.

Kettle, Arnold (ed.) (1964) *Shakespeare in a Changing World*. London: Lawrence and Wishart.

Kiernan, Pauline (1999) *Staging Shakespeare at the New Globe*. Basingstoke: Macmillan.

Kinney, Arthur F. (1990) *Rogues, Vagabonds and Sturdy Beggars: A New Gallery of Tudor and Early Stuart Rogue Literature*. Amherst, MA: University of Massachusetts Press.

——(2001) *Lies Like Truth: Macbeth and the Cultural Moment*. Detroit, MI: Wayne State University Press.

Kishi, Tetsuo and Graham Bradshaw (2005) *Shakespeare in Japan*. London: Continuum.

Knafla, Louis A. (2004) 'Henry Stanley', in *Oxford Dictionary of National Biography*, ed. H. C. G. Matthew and Brian Harrison. Oxford: Oxford University Press, vol. 52, 211–13.

Knight, G. Wilson (1948 [1947]) *The Crown of Life: Essays in Interpretation of Shakespeare's Final Plays*. London: Methuen.

——(1951 [1931]) *The Imperial Theme: Further Interpretations of Shakespeare's Tragedies*. London: Methuen.

——(1960 [1930]) *The Wheel of Fire: Interpretations of Shakespearian Tragedy*. London: Methuen.

——(2002 [1963]) *Shakespearian Production; With Especial Reference to the Tragedies*. London: Routledge.

Knights, L. C. (1946) *Explorations*. London: Chatto and Windus.

——(1957) *Shakespeare's Politics*. London: British Academy.

Knowles, Richard Paul (1996) 'Shakespeare, Voice, and Ideology: Interrogating the Natural Voice', in *Shakespeare, Theory, and Performance*, ed. James C. Bulman. London: Routledge, 92–112.

Knowles, Ronald (ed.) (1998) *Shakespeare and Carnival: After Bakhtin*. Basingstoke: Macmillan.

——(2001) *Shakespeare's Arguments with History*. Basingstoke: Palgrave.

Knutson, Rosalyn L. (1995) 'Falconer to the Little Eyases: A New Date and Commercial Agenda for the "Little Eyases"', *Shakespeare Quarterly*, 46: 1–31.

——(1999) 'Shakespeare's Repertory', in *A Companion to Shakespeare*, ed. David Scott Kastan. Oxford: Blackwell, 346–61.

Kolin, Philip C. (ed.) (1997) *Venus and Adonis: Critical Essays*. New York: Garland.

Korda, Natasha (2002) *Shakespeare's Domestic Economies: Gender and Property in Early Modern England*. Philadelphia, PA: University of Pennsylvania Press.

Kott, Jan (1965) *Shakespeare Our Contemporary*, trans. Boleslaw Taborski. London: Methuen.

Kozintsev, Grigori (1973) *King Lear: The Space of Tragedy*. Berkeley and Los Angeles, CA: University of California Press.

Kronenfeld, Judy (1998) *King Lear and the Naked Truth: Rethinking the Language of Religion and Resistance*. Durham, NC and London: Duke University Press.

Kuppers, Petra (2003) *Disability and Contemporary Performance: Bodies on Edge*. London: Routledge.

Kyle, Barry (1987) 'Role of the Swan', *Plays International*, September.

Lacan, Jacques (1977) *Écrits: A Selection*, trans. Alan Sheridan. London: Tavistock.

Lake, Peter (1999) 'Religious Identities in Shakespeare's England', in *A Companion to Shakespeare*, ed. David Scott Kastan. Oxford: Blackwell, 57–84.

Lamming, George (1960) *The Pleasures of Exile*. London: Michael Joseph.

——(1970) *Water with Berries*. London: Longman.

Lanier, Douglas (2002) *Shakespeare and Modern Popular Culture*. Oxford: Oxford University Press.

Laroque, François (1991) *Shakespeare's Festive World*, trans. Janet Lloyd. Cambridge: Cambridge University Press.

Lavender, Andy (2001) *Hamlet in Pieces: Shakespeare Reworked: Peter Brook, Robert Lepage, Robert Wilson*. London: Nick Hern.

Leavis, F. R. (1962) *The Common Pursuit*. Harmondsworth: Penguin.

Lee, John (2002) *Shakespeare's Hamlet and the Controversies of Self*. Oxford: Oxford University Press.

Leggatt, Alexander (1991) *King Lear*. Shakespeare in Performance. Manchester: Manchester University Press.

Lehmann, Courtney (2002) *Shakespeare Remains: Theater to Film, Early Modern to Postmodern*. Ithaca, NY: Cornell University Press.

Lehmann, Courtney and Lisa S. Starks (eds) (2002) *Spectacular Shakespeare: Critical Theory and Popular Cinema*. Madison, NJ: Farleigh Dickinson University Press.

Leishman, J. B. (ed.) (1949) *The Three Parnassus Plays*. London: Nicholson and Watson.

Lenz, Carolyn Ruth Swift, Gayle Greene and Carol Thomas Neely (eds) (1980) *The Woman's Part: Feminist Criticism of Shakespeare*. Urbana, IL: University of Illinois Press.

Lerner, Laurence (2000) 'Wilhelm S and Shylock', in *Shakespeare and Race*, ed. Catharine M. S. Alexander and Stanley Wells. Cambridge: Cambridge University Press, 139–50.

Lever, J. W. (1971) *The Tragedy of State*. London: Methuen.

Lindley, David (ed.) (2002) *The Tempest*. The Cambridge Shakespeare. Cambridge: Cambridge University Press.

Little, Arthur J. (2000) *Shakespeare Jungle Fever: National-Imperial Re-Visions of Race, Rape, and Sacrifice*. Stanford, CA: Stanford University Press.

Loney, Glenn (ed.) (1974) *Peter Brook's Production of 'A Midsummer Night's Dream' for the Royal Shakespeare Company: The Complete and Authorized Acting Edition*. Chicago, IL: Dramatic Publishing Company.

Long, William B. (1999) '"Precious Few": English Manuscript Playbooks', in *A Companion to Shakespeare*. Oxford: Blackwell, ed. David Scott Kastan, 414–32.

Loomba, Ania (1989) *Gender, Race, Renaissance Drama*. Manchester: Manchester University Press.

——(2000) '"Delicious Traffic": Racial and Religious Difference on Early Modern Stages', in *Shakespeare and Race*, ed. Catharine M. S. Alexander and Stanley Wells. Cambridge: Cambridge University Press, 203–24.

——(2002) *Shakespeare, Race, and Colonialism*. Oxford: Oxford University Press.

Loomba, Ania and Martin Orkin (eds) (1998) *Postcolonial Shakespeares*. London: Routledge.

McAlindon, Tom (1995) 'Testing the New Historicism: "Invisible Bullets" Reconsidered', *Studies in Philology*, 92: 411–38.

——(2001) *Shakespeare's Tudor History: A Study of Henry IV, Parts 1 and 2*. Aldershot: Ashgate.

——(2004) *Shakespeare Minus 'Theory'*. Aldershot: Ashgate.

McCloud, Randall (Random Cloud) (1991). '"The Very Names of the Persons": Editing and the Invention of Dramatick Character', in *Staging the Renaissance*, ed. David Scott Kastan and Peter Stallybrass. London: Routledge, 88–96.

McCullough, Christopher (1988) 'The Cambridge Connection: Towards a Materialist Theatre Practice', in *The Shakespeare Myth*, ed. Graham Holderness. Manchester: Manchester University Press, 112–21.

——(2005) *The Merchant of Venice*. The Shakespeare Handbooks. Basingstoke: Palgrave.

McDonald, Russ (2001) *Shakespeare and the Arts of Language*. Oxford Shakespeare Topics. Oxford: Oxford University Press.

——(ed.) (2004) *Shakespeare: An Anthology of Criticism and Theory, 1945–2000*. Oxford: Blackwell.

——(2006) *Shakespeare's Late Style*. Cambridge: Cambridge University Press.

MacFaul, Tom (2007) *Male Friendship in Shakespeare and His Contemporaries*. Cambridge: Cambridge University Press.

McGuire, Philip C. (1985) *Speechless Dialect: Shakespeare's Open Silences*. Berkeley, CA: University of California Press.

McGuire, Philip C. and David A. Samuelson (eds) (1979) *Shakespeare: The Theatrical Dimension*. New York: AMS Press.

Mack, Maynard (1966) *King Lear in Our Time*. Berkeley, CA: University of California Press.

McKerrow, R. B. (ed.) (1958) *The Works of Thomas Nashe*, 4 vols. Oxford: Oxford University Press.

McKewin, Carole (1980) 'Counsels of Gall and Grace: Intimate Conversations between Women in Shakespeares's Plays', in *The Woman's Part: Feminist Criticism of Shakespeare*, ed. Carolyn Ruth Swift Lenz, Gayle Greene and Carol Thomas Neely. Urbana, IL: University of Illinois Press, 117–32.

MacLure, Millar (ed.) (1979) *Marlowe: The Critical Heritage, 1588–1896*. London: Routledge & Kegan Paul.

McLure Thomson, Elizabeth (ed.) (1965) *The Chamberlain Letters: A Selection of the Letters of John Chamberlain Concerning Life in England from 1597 to 1626*. London: John Murray.

McLuskie, Kathleen (1989) *Renaissance Dramatists*. Hemel Hempstead: Harvester Wheatsheaf.

——(1994) 'The Patriarchal Bard: Feminist Criticism and Shakespeare: *King Lear* and *Measure for Measure*', in *Political Shakespeare: Essays in Cultural Materialism*, ed. Jonathan Dollimore and Alan Sinfield. Manchester: Manchester University Press, 88–108.

McMillin, Scott (2004) 'The Sharer and His Boy: Rehearsing Shakespeare's Women', in *From Script to Stage in Early Modern England*, ed. Peter Holland and Stephen Orgel. Basingstoke: Palgrave Macmillan, 231–45.

McMullan, Gordon (ed.) (2000) *King Henry VIII*. The Arden Shakespeare, third series. London: Arden Shakespeare.

——(2007) *Shakespeare and the Idea of Late Writing: Authorship in the Proximity of Death*. Cambridge: Cambridge University Press.

McMullan, Gordon and Jonathan Hope (eds) (1992) *The Politics of Tragicomedy: Shakespeare and After*. London: Routledge.

Mahood, M. M. (1957) *Shakespeare's Wordplay*. London: Methuen.

Maley, Willy and Andrew Murphy (eds) (2004) *Shakespeare and Scotland*. Manchester: Manchester University Press.

Malin, Eric S. (2007) *Godless Shakespeare*. London: Continuum.

Marcus, Leah S. (1988) *Puzzling Shakespeare: Local Reading and its Discontents*. Berkeley, CA: University of California Press.

——(1992) 'The Shakespearean Editor as Shrew-Tamer', *ELR*, 22: 177–200.

——(1996) *Unediting the Renaissance: Shakespeare, Marlowe and Milton*. London: Routledge.

Marlowe, Sam (2006) 'Othello', *The Times*, 1 May.

Mannoni, Dominique-Octave (1964) *Prospero and Caliban*, trans. Pamela Powesland. New York: Praeger.

Marowitz, Charles (1991) *Recycling Shakespeare*. Basingstoke: Macmillan.

Marsden, Jean E. (ed.) (1991) *The Appropriation of Shakespeare: Post-Renaissance Reconstructions of the Works and the Myth*. New York: St Martin's Press.

Marx, Karl and Friedrich Engels (1970 [1845]) *The German Ideology*, ed. C. J. Arthur. London: Lawrence and Wishart.

Marx, Stephen (2000) *Shakespeare and the Bible*. Oxford: Oxford University Press.

Massai, Sonia (ed.) (2005) *World-Wide Shakespeares: Local Appropriations in Film and Performance*. London: Routledge.

Masten, Jeffrey (1997) *Textual Intercourse: Collaboration, Authorship, and Sexualities in Renaissance Drama*. Cambridge: Cambridge University Press.

Matthew, H. C. G. and Brian Harrison (eds) (2004) *Oxford Dictionary of National Biography*, 60 vols. Oxford: Oxford University Press.

Maus, Katherine Eisaman (1986) 'Taking Tropes Seriously: Language and Violence in Shakespeare's *Rape of Lucrece*', *Shakespeare Quarterly*, 37: 66–82.

——(1995) *Inwardness and Theater in the English Renaissance*. Chicago, IL: University of Chicago Press.

Maxwell, J. C. (ed.) (1953, 3rd edn 1961) *Titus Andronicus*. The Arden Shakespeare, second series. London: Methuen.

——(ed.) (1956) *Pericles*. The New Shakespeare. Cambridge: Cambridge University Press.

——(ed.) (1957) *Timon of Athens*. The New Shakespeare. Cambridge: Cambridge University Press.

——(ed.) (1962) *Henry VIII*. The New Shakespeare. Cambridge: Cambridge University Press.

Melchiori, Giorgio (ed.) (1989) *The Second Part of Henry IV*. New Cambridge Shakespeare. Cambridge: Cambridge University Press.

Meres, Francis (1973 [1598]) *Palladis Tamia; Wit's Treasury*. New York: Garland.

Miller, Jonathan (1986) *Subsequent Performances*. London: Faber.

Miola, Robert S. (1983) *Shakespeare's Rome*. Cambridge: Cambridge University Press.

——(1992) *Shakespeare and Classical Tragedy: The Influence of Seneca*. Oxford: Clarendon Press.

Montrose, Louis (1996) *The Purpose of Playing: Shakespeare and the Cultural Politics of the Elizabethan Theatre*. Chicago, IL and London: University of Chicago Press.

——(2004 [1983]) '"Shaping Fantasies": Figurations of Gender and Power in Elizabethan Culture', *Representations* 1; reprinted in *Shakespeare: An Anthology of Criticism and Theory, 1945–2000*, ed. Russ McDonald. Oxford: Blackwell, 481–510.

Muir, Kenneth (1957) *Shakespeare's Sources*. London: Methuen.

——(ed.) (1971) *Macbeth*. The Arden Shakespeare, second series. Tenth edition. London: Methuen.

Mullaney, Steven (1988) *The Place of the Stage: License, Play and Power in Renaissance England*. Chicago, IL: University of Chicago Press.

——(1996) 'After the New Historicism', in *Alternative Shakespeares, Volume 2*, ed. Terence Hawkes. London: Routledge, 17–37.

Mulryne, J. R. and Margaret Shewring (1989) *This Golden Round: The Royal Shakespeare Company at the Swan*. Stratford-upon-Avon: Mulryne and Shewring.

——(eds) (1997) *Shakespeare's Globe Rebuilt*. Cambridge: Cambridge University Press.

Munro, Lucy (2005) *Children of the Queen's Revels: A Jacobean Theatre Repertory*. Cambridge: Cambridge University Press.

——(2007) '*Coriolanus* and the Little Eyases: The Boyhood of Shakespeare's Hero', in *Shakespeare and Childhood*, ed. Kate Chedgzoy, Susanne Greenhalgh and Robert Shaughnessy. Cambridge: Cambridge University Press, 80–95.

Neely, Carol Thomas (1985) *Broken Nuptials in Shakespeare's Plays*. New Haven, CT: Yale University Press.

Neill, Michael (1989) 'Unproper Beds: Race, Adultery, and the Hideous in *Othello*', *Shakespeare Quarterly*, 40: 383–412.

——(1997) *Issue of Death: Mortality and Identity in English Renaissance Drama*. Oxford: Clarendon Press.

Newman, Karen (1987) '"And Wash the Ethiop White": Femininity and the Monstrous in *Othello*', in *Shakespeare Reproduced: The Text in History and Ideology*, ed. Jean E. Howard and Marion O'Connor. London: Methuen, 143–62.

Ngugi Wa Thiong'o (1967) *A Grain of Wheat*. London: Heinemann.

Nicholl, Charles (2007) *The Lodger: Shakespeare on Silver Street*. London: Allen Lane.

Nightingale, Benedict (1970) 'Dream 2001 AD', *New Statesman*, 4 September.

Norris, Christopher (1985) 'Post-structuralist Shakespeare: Text and Ideology', in *Alternative Shakespeares*, ed. John Drakakis. First edition. London: Methuen, 47–66.

Nungezer, Edwin (1968 [1929]) *A Dictionary of Actors and of Other Persons Associated with the Public Representation of Plays in England before 1642*. New Haven, CT: Yale University Press.

Nuttall, A. D. (1989) *Timon of Athens*. Boston: Twayne.

O'Connor, Marion F. (1987) 'Theatre of the Empire: "Shakespeare's England" at Earl's Court, 1912', in *Shakespeare Reproduced: The Text in History and Ideology*, ed. Jean E. Howard and Marion O'Connor. London: Methuen, 68–98.

Odell, George C. (1966 [1920]) *Shakespeare from Betterton to Irving*, 2 vols. New York: Dover Publications.

Olivier, Laurence (1986) *On Acting*. London: Weidenfeld and Nicholson.

Orgel, Stephen (1975) *The Illusion of Power: Political Theatre in the English Renaissance*. Berkeley, CA: University of California Press.

——(1989) 'Nobody's Perfect: Or Why Did the English Stage Take Boys for Women?', *South Atlantic Quarterly*, 88: 7–29.

——(1996) *Impersonations: The Performance of Gender in Shakespeare's England*. Cambridge: Cambridge University Press.

——(2002) *The Authentic Shakespeare*. London: Routledge.

Orgel, Stephen and Roy Strong (1973) *Inigo Jones: The Theatre of the Stuart Court*, 2 vols. Berkeley, CA: University of California Press.

Orkin, Martin (1987) '*Othello* and the "Plain Face" of Racism', *Shakespeare Quarterly*, 38: 166–88.

——(2005) *Local Shakespeares: Proximations and Power*. London: Routledge.

Orlin, Lena Cowen (ed.) (2004) *Othello: Contemporary Critical Essays*. New Casebooks. Basingstoke: Palgrave.

Ornstein, Robert (1972) *A Kingdom for a Stage: The Achievement of Shakespeare's History Plays*. Cambridge, MA: Harvard University Press.

Orrell, John (1983) *The Quest for Shakespeare's Globe*. Cambridge: Cambridge University Press.

Orrell, John and Andrew Gurr (1989) *Rebuilding Shakespeare's Globe*. London: Weidenfeld and Nicholson.

Palfrey, Simon (1997) *Late Shakespeare: A New World of Words*. Oxford: Clarendon Press.

——(2005) *Doing Shakespeare*. London: Arden Shakespeare.

Palmer, D. J. (ed.) (1968) *The Tempest: A Collection of Critical Essays*. London: Macmillan.

Parker, Andrew and Eve Kosofsky Sedgwick (eds) (1995) *Performativity and Performance*. New York: Routledge.

Parker, Patricia (1987) *Literary Fat Ladies: Rhetoric, Gender, Property*. London: Methuen.

——(1996) *Shakespeare from the Margins: Language, Culture, Context*. Chicago, IL: University of Chicago Press.

——(2008) 'Cutting Both Ways: Bloodletting, Castration/Circumcision and the "Lancelet" of *The Merchant of Venice*', in *Alternative Shakespeares 3*, ed. Diana E. Henderson. London: Routledge, 95–118.

Parker, Patricia and Geoffrey Hartmann (eds) (1985) *Shakespeare and the Question of Theory*. London: Methuen.

Parker, R. B. (1984) 'War and Sex in *All's Well that Ends Well*', *Shakespeare Survey*, 37: 99–113.

——(ed.) (1994) *Coriolanus*. The Oxford Shakespeare. Oxford: Oxford University Press.

Paster, Gail Kern (1993) *The Body Embarrassed: Drama and the Disciplines of Shame in Early Modern England*. Ithaca, NY: Cornell University Press.

Patterson, Annabel (1989) *Shakespeare and the Popular Voice*. Oxford: Blackwell.

Paul, Henry N. (1950) *The Royal Play of Macbeth*. New York: Macmillan.

Payne, Michael (ed.) (2005) *The Greenblatt Reader*. Oxford: Wiley-Blackwell.

Pearsall Smith, Logan (ed.) (1907) *The Life and Letters of Sir Henry Wotton*, 2 vols. Oxford: Clarendon Press.

Pechter, Edward (1999) *Othello and Interpretive Traditions*. Iowa City, IA: University of Iowa Press.

Pennington, Michael (1997) *Hamlet: A User's Guide*. London: Nick Hern Books.

——(2000) *Twelfth Night: A User's Guide*. London: Nick Hern Books.

——(2005) *A Midsummer Night's Dream: A User's Guide*. London: Nick Hern Books.

Pennington, Michael and Michael Bogdanov (1990) *The English Shakespeare Company: The Story of 'The Wars of the Roses' 1986–1989*. London: Nick Hern.

Pequigney, Joseph (1985) *Such Is My Love: A Study of Shakespeare's Sonnets*. Chicago, IL: University of Chicago Press.

Phelan, Peggy (1993) *Unmarked: The Politics of Performance*. London: Routledge.

——(1997) *Mourning Sex: Performing Public Memories*. London: Routledge.

——(2005) '*King Lear* and Theatre Architecture', in *A Companion to Shakespeare and Performance*, ed. Barbara Hodgdon and W. B. Worthen. Oxford: Blackwell, 13–35.

Plato (1974) *The Republic*, trans. Desmond Lee. Harmondsworth: Penguin.

Poel, William (1913) *Shakespeare in the Theatre*. London: Sidgwick and Jackson.

Potter, Lois and Arthur F. Kinney (eds) (1999) *Shakespeare, Text, and Theater: Essays in Honor of Jay L. Halio*. Newark, DE: University of Delaware Press.

Proudfoot, Richard, Ann Thompson and David Scott Kastan (1995) 'General Editors' Preface', The Arden Shakespeare, third series. London: Routledge.

Quiller-Couch, Sir Arthur and John Dover Wilson (eds) (1921) *The Two Gentlemen of Verona*. The New Shakespeare. Cambridge: Cambridge University Press.

——(eds) (1928) *The Taming of the Shrew*. The New Shakespeare. Cambridge: Cambridge University Press.

Rabkin, Norman (1977) 'Rabbits, Ducks, and *Henry V*', *Shakespeare Quarterly*, 28: 279–96.

Rackin, Phyllis (1987) 'Androgyny, Mimesis, and the Marriage of the Boy Heroine on the English Renaissance Stage', *PMLA*, 102: 29–41.

——(2000) 'Misogyny Is Everywhere', in *A Feminist Companion to Shakespeare*, ed. Dympna Callaghan. Oxford: Blackwell, 42–56.

Razzell, Peter (ed.) (1995) *The Journals of Two Travellers in Elizabethan and Early Stuart England*. London: Caliban.

Rees, Jasper (2006) 'The Play What I Wrote', *Daily Telegraph*, 22 June.

Reese, M. M. (1961) *The Cease of Majesty: A Study of Shakespeare's History Plays*. London: Edward Arnold.

Reynolds, Bryan (2003) *Performing Transversally: Reimagining Shakespeare and the Critical Future*. Basingstoke: Palgrave Macmillan.

Reynolds, Peter (1992) *Practical Approaches to Teaching Shakespeare*. Oxford: Oxford University Press.

Ribner, Irving (1965) *The English History Play in the Age of Shakespeare*. Princeton, NJ: Princeton University Press.

Richards, I. A. (1929) *Practical Criticism*. London: Routledge.

Richards, Jennifer and James Knowles (eds) (1999) *Shakespeare's Late Plays: New Readings*. Edinburgh: Edinburgh University Press.

Ridley, M. R. (ed.) (1958) *Othello*. The Arden Shakespeare, second series. London: Methuen.

Ridout, Nicholas (2006) *Stage Fright, Animals, and Other Theatrical Problems*. Cambridge: Cambridge University Press.

Riggio, Milla Cozart (ed.) (1999) *Teaching Shakespeare through Performance*. New York: Modern Language Association of America.

Righter, Ann (1962) *Shakespeare and the Idea of the Play*. London: Chatto and Windus.

Ripley, John (1980) *Julius Caesar on Stage in England and America, 1599–1973*. Cambridge: Cambridge University Press.

Roach, Joseph R. (1996) *Cities of the Dead: Circum-Atlantic Performance*. New York: Columbia University Press.

Roberts, Sasha (2003) *Reading Shakespeare's Poems in Early Modern England*. Basingstoke: Palgrave.

Roche, T. P. (1989) *Petrarch and the English Sonnet Sequences*. New York: AMS Press.

Rodenburg, Patsy (1993) *The Need for Words: Voice and the Text*. London: Methuen.

——(2005) *Speaking Shakespeare*. London: Methuen.

Rosenberg, Marvin (1961) *The Masks of Othello: The Search for the Identity of Othello, Iago, and Desdemona by Three Centuries of Actors and Critics*. Berkeley, CA: University of California Press.

——(1971) *The Masks of King Lear*. Berkeley, CA: University of California Press.

——(1978) *The Masks of Macbeth*. Berkeley, CA: University of California Press.

——(1993) *The Masks of Hamlet*. Berkeley, CA: University of California Press.

Rossiter, A. P. (1989 [1961]) *Angel with Horns: Fifteen Lectures on Shakespeare*, ed. Graham Storey. London: Longman.

Rothwell, Kenneth (2004) *A History of Shakespeare on Screen: A Century of Film and Television*. Second edition. Cambridge: Cambridge University Press.

Rouse, W. H. D. (ed.) (1961) *Shakespeare's Ovid: Being Arthur Golding's Translation of the Metamorphoses*. London: Centaur.

Royal Shakespeare Company (1989) *The Plantagenets*. London; Faber and Faber.

Rutter, Carol Chillington (1984) *Documents of the Rose Playhouse*. Manchester: Manchester University Press.

——(1988) *Clamorous Voices: Shakespeare's Women Today*, ed. Faith Evans. London: The Women's Press.

——(1997) 'Fiona Shaw's *Richard II*: The Girl as Player-King as Comic', *Shakespeare Quarterly*, 48: 314–24.

——(2000) 'Looking at Shakespeare's Women on Film', in *The Cambridge Companion to Shakespeare on Film*, ed. Russell Jackson. Cambridge: Cambridge University Press, 241–60.

——(2001) *Enter the Body: Women and Representation on Shakespeare's Stage*. London: Routledge.

——(2007) *Shakespeare and Child's Play: Performing Lost Boys on Stage and Screen*. London: Routledge.

Ryan, Kiernan (2002) *Shakespeare*. Third edition. Basingstoke: Palgrave Macmillan.

Ryuta, Minami, Ian Carruthers and John Gillie (eds) (2001) *Performing Shakespeare in Japan*. Cambridge: Cambridge University Press.

Sachdev, Rachana (2000) 'Sycorax in Algiers: Cultural Politics and Gynecology in Early Modern England', in *A Feminist Companion to Shakespeare*, ed. Dympna Callaghan. Oxford: Blackwell, 208–25.

Salingar, Leo (1974) *Shakespeare and the Traditions of Comedy*. Cambridge: Cambridge University Press.

Sandler, R. (ed.) (1986) *Northrop Frye on Shakespeare*. New Haven, CT: Yale University Press.

Sasayama, Takashi, J. R. Mulryne and Margaret Shewring (eds) (1998) *Shakespeare and the Japanese Stage*. Cambridge: Cambridge University Press.

Saussure, Ferdinand de (1959 [1916]) *Course in General Linguistics*, trans. Wade Baskin. London: Peter Owen.

Schafer, Elizabeth (1998) *Ms-Directing Shakespeare: Women Direct Shakespeare*. London: The Women's Press.

Schanzer, Ernest (1956) 'Thomas Platter's Observations on the Elizabethan Stage', *Notes and Queries*, 201: 465–67.

Schechner, Richard (1992) 'A New Paradigm for Theatre in the Academy', *TDR*, 36: 7–10.

——(2000) 'Theatre Alive in the New Millenium', *The Drama Review*, 44: 5–6.

——(2002) *Performance Studies: An Introduction*. London: Routledge.

Schoenbaum, S. (1977) *William Shakespeare: A Compact Documentary Life*. Oxford: Clarendon Press.

——(1991) *Shakespeare's Lives*. Revised edition. Oxford: Oxford University Press.

Schwartz, Murray M. and Coppélia Kahn (eds) (1980) *Representing Shakespeare: New Psychoanalytic Essays*. Baltimore, MD and London: Johns Hopkins University Press.

Selbourne, David (1982) *The Making of 'A Midsummer Night's Dream': An Eyewitness Account of Peter Brook's Production from First Rehearsal to First Night*. London: Methuen.

Shand, G. B. (2005) 'Guying the Girls and Girling the Shrew: (Post)Feminist Fun at Shakespeare's Globe', in *A Companion to Shakespeare and Performance*, ed. Barbara Hodgdon and W. B. Worthen. Oxford: Blackwell, 550–63.

Shapiro, James (1996) *Shakespeare and the Jews*. New York: Columbia University Press.

——(2005) *1599: A Year in the Life of William Shakespeare*. London: Faber.

——(2010) *Contested Will: Who Wrote Shakespeare?* London: Faber and Faber.

Shapiro, Michael (1994) *Gender in Play on the Shakespearean Stage: Boy Heroines and Female Pages*. Ann Arbor, MI: University of Michigan Press.

Shaughnessy, Robert (1994) *Representing Shakespeare: England, History and the RSC*. Hemel Hempstead: Harvester Wheatsheaf.

——(ed.) (1998) *Shakespeare on Film: Contemporary Critical Essays*. New Casebooks. Basingstoke: Macmillan.

——(2002) *The Shakespeare Effect: A History of Twentieth-Century Performance*. Basingstoke: Palgrave.

——(ed.) (2007) *The Cambridge Companion to Shakespeare and Popular Culture*. Cambridge: Cambridge University Press.

Shaw, George Bernard (1961) *Shaw on Shakespeare*, ed. Edwin Wilson. Harmondsworth: Penguin.

Shepherd, Simon (1986) *Marlowe and the Politics of Elizabethan Theatre*. Brighton: Harvester.

——(2006) *Theatre, Body and Pleasure*. London: Routledge.

Sher, Antony (1985) *Year of the King*. London: Methuen.

Showalter, Elaine (1985) 'Representing Ophelia: Women, Madness and the Responsibilities of Feminist Criticism', in *Shakespeare and the Question of Theory*, ed. Patricia Parker and Geoffrey Hartmann. London: Methuen, 77–94.

Shuger, Deborah K. (1996) 'Subversive Fathers and Suffering Subjects: Shakespeare and Christianity', in *Religion, Literature, and Politics in Post-Reformation England, 1540–1688*, ed. Donna B. Hamilton and Richard Strier. Cambridge: Cambridge University Press, 46–69.

Sidney, Sir Philip (1966) *A Defence of Poetry*, ed. J. A. Van Dorsten. Oxford: Oxford University Press.

Simkin, Stevie (2000) *A Preface to Marlowe*. Harlow: Longman.

——(2006) *Early Modern Tragedy and the Cinema of Violence*. Basingstoke: Palgrave.

Sinfield, Alan (1983) *Literature in Protestant England 1560–1660*. London: Croom Helm.

——(1988) 'Making Space: Appropriation and Confrontation in Recent British Plays', in *The Shakespeare Myth*, ed. Graham Holderness. Manchester: Manchester University Press, 128–44.

——(1992) *Faultlines: Cultural Materialism and the Politics of Dissident Reading*. Oxford: Clarendon Press.

——(1994) 'Royal Shakespeare: Theatre and the Making of Ideology', in *Political Shakespeare: Essays in Cultural Materialism*, ed. Jonathan Dollimore and Alan Sinfield. Manchester: Manchester University Press, 182–205.

——(2006) *Shakespeare, Authority, Sexuality: Unfinished Business in Cultural Materialism*. London: Routledge.

Slater, Ann Pasternak (1982) *Shakespeare the Director*. Brighton: Harvester.

Slights, Camille Wells (1999) 'The Politics of Conscience in *All Is True* (or *Henry VIII*)', *Shakespeare Survey*, 43: 59–68.

Smith, Emma (ed.) (2004) *Shakespeare's Histories*. Oxford: Blackwell.

——(2007) 'Shakespeare Serialized: *An Age of Kings*', in *The Cambridge Companion to Shakespeare and Popular Culture*, ed. Robert Shaughnessy. Cambridge: Cambridge University Press, 134–49.

Smith, Bruce R. (1991) *Homosexual Desire in Shakespeare's England: A Cultural Poetics*, Chicago, IL: University of Chicago Press.

——(1999) *The Acoustic World of Early Modern England: Attending to the O-Factor*. Chicago, IL: University of Chicago Press.

——(2000) *Shakespeare and Masculinity*. Oxford: Oxford University Press.

——(2004) 'E/loco/com/motion', in *From Script to Stage in Early Modern England*, ed. Peter Holland and Stephen Orgel. Basingstoke: Palgrave Macmillan, 131–50.

Smith, Peter J. (2000) 'A "Consummation Devoutly to Be Wished": The Erotics of Narration in *Venus and Adonis*', *Shakespeare Survey*, 53: 25–38.

Smith-Howard, Alycia (2006) *Studio Shakespeare: The Royal Shakespeare Company at the Other Place*. Aldershot: Ashgate.

Snyder, Susan (ed.) (1993) *Measure for Measure*. The Oxford Shakespeare. Oxford: Oxford University Press.

Sorlien, Robert (ed.) (1976) *The Diary of John Manningham of the Middle Temple, 1602–1603*. Hanover, NH: University Press of New England.

Space Doctors (2007) *Space Doctors: People: Malcolm Evans*, http://www.space-doctors.com/malcolm.htm, accessed 24 January 2007.

Spencer, Charles (2007) 'A Delirious Dream of India', *Daily Telegraph*, 30 March.

Spencer, Theodore (1966 [1942]) *Shakespeare and the Nature of Man*. Second edition. London: Collier, Macmillan.

Sprague, A. C. (1953) *Shakespearian Players and Performances*. London: Black.

——(1964) *Shakespeare's Histories: Plays for the Stage*. London: Society for Theatre Research.

Spurgeon, Caroline (1935) *Shakespeare's Imagery and What It Tells Us*. Cambridge: Cambridge University Press.

Stallybrass, Peter (1986) 'Patriarchal Territories: The Body Enclosed', in *Rewriting the Renaissance: The Discourses of Sexual Difference in Early Modern Europe*, ed. Margaret W. Ferguson, Maureen Quilligan and Nancy Vickers. Chicago, IL: University of Chicago Press, 123–42.

Stanislavski, Constantin (2008a [1937]) *An Actor Prepares*, trans. Elizabeth Reynolds Hapgood. London: Methuen.

——(2008b [1950]) *Building a Character*, trans. Elizabeth Reynolds Hapgood. London: A & C Black.

——(2008c [1961]) *Creating a Role*, trans. Hermione L. Popper. London: A & C Black.

——(2008d [1952]) *My Life in Art*, ed. and trans. Jean Benedetti. London: Routledge.

Starks, Lisa L. and Courtney Lehmann (eds) (2002) *Spectacular Shakespeare: Critical Theory and Popular Cinema*. Madison, WI: Fairleigh Dickinson University Press.

States, Bert O. (1992) *Hamlet and the Concept of Character*. Baltimore, MD: Johns Hopkins University Press.

Steggle, Matthew (2004) 'Salomon Pavy: Jonson's Avatar?', *Ben Jonson Journal*, 11: 259–64.

Stern, Tiffany (2000) *Rehearsal from Shakespeare to Sheridan*. Oxford: Clarendon Press.

——(2004) *Making Shakespeare: From Page to Stage*. London: Routledge.

——(2006) '"On Each Wall and Corner Poast": Playbills, Title-pages, and Advertising in Early Modern London', *English Literary Renaissance*, 36: 57–89.

Stern, V. F. (1979) *Gabriel Harvey: His Life, Marginalia and Library*. Oxford: Clarendon Press.

Stone, Lawrence (1965) *The Crisis of the Aristocracy, 1568–1641*. Oxford: Clarendon Press.

Strindberg, August (1982) *Plays: Two*, trans. Michael Meyer. London: Methuen.

Stubbs, Imogen (2006) 'Gertrude', in *Performing Shakespeare's Tragedies Today: The Actor's Perspective*, ed. Michael Dobson. Cambridge: Cambridge University Press, 29–40.

Styan, J. L. (1977) *The Shakespeare Revolution: Criticism and Performance in the Twentieth Century*. Cambridge: Cambridge University Press.

Taylor, Gary (1985) *Moment by Moment by Shakespeare*. London: Macmillan.

——(1990) *Reinventing Shakespeare: A Cultural History from the Restoration to the Present*. London: Hogarth Press.

——(1995) 'Shakespeare and Others: The Authorship of *Henry the Sixth, Part One*', *Medieval and Renaissance Drama in England*, 7: 145–205.

——(1999) 'Afterword: The Incredible Shrinking Bard', in *Shakespeare and Appropriation*, ed. Christy Desmet and Robert Sawyer. London: Routledge, 197–205.

——(2003) 'The Cultural Politics of Maybe', in *Theatre and Religion: Lancastrian Shakespeare*, ed. Richard Dutton, Alison Findlay and Richard Wilson. Manchester: Manchester University Press, 242–58.

Taylor, Gary and John Lavagnino (eds) (2007a) *Thomas Middleton: The Complete Works*. Oxford: Oxford University Press.

——(eds) (2007b) *Thomas Middleton and Early Modern Textual Culture: A Companion to the Collected Works*. Oxford: Oxford University Press.

Taylor, Gary and Michael Warren (eds) (1983) *The Division of the Kingdoms: Shakespeare's Two Versions of King Lear*. Oxford: Clarendon Press.

Taylor, Gary and Stanley Wells (eds) (1988) *William Shakespeare: The Complete Works*. Oxford: Clarendon Press.

Tennenhouse, Leonard (1994) 'Strategies of State and Political Plays: *A Midsummer Night's Dream, Henry IV, Henry V, Henry VIII*', in *Political Shakespeare: Essays in Cultural Materialism*, ed. Jonathan Dollimore and Alan Sinfield. Manchester: Manchester University Press, 109–28.

——(2005 [1986]) *Power on Display: The Politics of Shakespeare's Genres*. London: Routledge.

Thompson, Ann (1988) '"The Warrant of Womanhood": Shakespeare and Feminist Criticism', in *The Shakespeare Myth*, ed. Graham Holderness. Manchester: Manchester University Press, 74–89.

——(1997) 'Feminist Theory and the Editing of Shakespeare: *The Taming of the Shrew* Revisited', in *The Margins of the Text*, ed D. C. Greetham. Ann Arbor, MI: University of Michigan Press, 83–103.

Thompson, Ann and Neil Taylor (eds) (2006) *Hamlet*. The Arden Shakespeare, third series. London: Thomson.

Thompson, Ayanna (ed.) (2006) *Colorblind Shakespeare: New Perspectives on Race and Performance*. New York: Routledge.

Thompson, Marvin and Ruth Thompson (eds) (1989) *Shakespeare and the Sense of Performance: Essays in the Tradition of Performance Criticism in Honor of Bernard Beckerman*. Newark, DE: University of Delaware Press.

Thomson, Peter (1994) *Shakespeare's Professional Career*. Cambridge:

Tillyard, E. M. W. (1938) *Shakespeare's Last Plays*. London: Chatto and Windus.

——(1950) *Shakespeare's Problem Plays*. London: Chatto and Windus.

——(1954) 'Shakespeare's Historical Cycle: Organism or Compilation?', *Studies in Philology*, 51: 34–39.

——(1962 [1944]) *Shakespeare's History Plays*. Harmondsworth: Penguin.

——(1963 [1943]) *The Elizabethan World Picture*. Harmondsworth: Penguin.

Tokson, Elliot H. (1982) *The Popular Image of the Black Man in English Drama 1550–1688*. Boston, MA: G. K. Hall.

Traub, Valerie (1989) 'Prince Hal's Falstaff: Positioning Psychoanalysis and the Female Reproductive Body', *Shakespeare Quarterly*, 40: 456–74.

——(1991) *Desire and Anxiety: Circulations of Sexuality in Shakespearean Drama*. London: Routledge.

——(1994) 'The (In)Significance of "Lesbian" Desire in Early Modern England', in *Queering the Renaissance*, ed. Jonathan Goldberg. Durham, NC: Duke University Press, 62–83.

Traub, Valerie, M. Lindsay Kaplan and Dympna Callaghan (eds) (1996) *Feminist Readings of Early Modern Culture: Emerging Subjects*. Cambridge: Cambridge University Press.

Traversi, D. A. (1957) *Shakespeare from 'Richard II' to 'Henry V'*. London: Hollis and Carter.

Trewin, J. C. (1960) *Benson and the Bensonians*. London: Barrie and Rockliffe.

Trivedi, Poonam and Dennis Bartholomeusz (eds) (2005) *India's Shakespeare: Translation, Interpretation, and Performance*. Newark, DE: University of Delaware Press.

Van Lennep, William *et al.* (eds) (1960–68) *The London Stage, 1660–1800: A Calendar of Plays, Entertainments and Afterpieces*, 11 vols. Carbondale, IL: Southern Illinois University Press.

Vaughan, Alden T. and Virginia Mason Vaughan (1991) *Shakespeare's Caliban: A Cultural History*. Cambridge: Cambridge University Press.

Vaughan, Virginia Mason (1994) *Othello: A Contextual History*. Cambridge: Cambridge University Press.

——(2005) *Performing Blackness on English Stages, 1500–1800*. Cambridge: Cambridge University Press.

Veeser, H. Aram (ed.) (1989) *The New Historicism*. London: Routledge.

Vickers, Brian (ed.) (1974–81) *Shakespeare: The Critical Heritage*, 6 vols. London: Routledge and Kegan Paul.

——(1993) *Appropriating Shakespeare: Contemporary Critical Quarrels*. New Haven, CT: Yale University Press.

——(2002) *Shakespeare, Co-author: A Historical Study of Five Collaborative Plays*. Oxford: Oxford University Press.

——(2007) *Shakespeare, A Lover's Complaint, and John Davies of Hereford*. Cambridge: Cambridge University Press.

Waith, Eugene M. (ed.) (1984) *Titus Andronicus*. The Oxford Shakespeare. Oxford: Oxford University Press.

Wall, Wendy (2002) *Staging Domesticity: Household Work and English Identity in Early Modern Drama*. Cambridge: Cambridge University Press.

Wardle, Irving (1970) 'To the Heights on a Trapeze', *The Times*, 28 August.

Warren, Roger (1983) *A Midsummer Night's Dream*. Text and Performance. Basingstoke: Macmillan.

——(1987) 'Shakespeare at Stratford-upon-Avon, 1986', *Shakespeare Quarterly*, 37: 82–89.

Wayne, Valerie (ed.) (1991) *The Matter of Difference: Materialist Feminist Criticism of Shakespeare*. Brighton: Harvester.

Wearing, J. P. (ed.) (1976–93) *The London Stage, 1890–1959: A Calendar of Plays and Players*, 15 vols. Metuchen, NJ: Scarecrow Press.

Webster, Margaret (1957) *Shakespeare Today*. London: Dent.

Weimann, Robert (1969) 'Laughing with the Audience: *The Two Gentlemen of Verona* and the Popular Tradition of Comedy', *Shakespeare Survey*, 22: 35–42.

——(1978) *Shakespeare and the Popular Tradition in the Theater*, trans. Robert Schwartz. Baltimore, MD: Johns Hopkins University Press.

——(2000) *Author's Pen and Actor's Voice: Playing and Writing in Shakespeare's Theatre*. Cambridge: Cambridge University Press.

Wells, Robin Headlam (2000) *Shakespeare on Masculinity*. Cambridge: Cambridge University Press.

Wells, Robin Headlam, Glenn Burgess and Rowland Wymer (eds) (2000) *Neo-Historicism: Studies in Renaissance Literature, History and Politics*. Woodbridge: D. S. Brewer.

Wells, Stanley (1977) *Royal Shakespeare: Four Major Productions at Stratford-upon-Avon*. Manchester: Manchester University Press.

——(1989) 'Shakespeare Performances in London and Stratford-upon-Avon, 1986–87', *Shakespeare Survey*, 41: 159–81.

——(1995) *A Midsummer Night's Dream*. The New Penguin Shakespeare. Revised edition. Harmondsworth: Penguin.

——(2002) *Shakespeare for All Time*. London: Macmillan.

——(2004) *Looking for Sex in Shakespeare*. Cambridge: Cambridge University Press.

——(2006) *Shakespeare and Co*. London: Allen Lane.

Wells, Stanley and Sarah Stanton (eds) (2002) *The Cambridge Companion to Shakespeare on Stage*. Cambridge: Cambridge University Press.

Wells, Stanley and Gary Taylor (eds) (1986) *William Shakespeare: Complete Works*. The Oxford Shakespeare. Oxford: Oxford University Press.

Werner, Sarah (2001) *Shakespeare and Feminist Performance*. London: Routledge.

——(2008) 'Two Hamlets: Wooster Group and Synetic Theater', *Shakespeare Quarterly*, 59: 323–9.

West, Anthony James (2001) *The Shakespeare First Folio: The History of the Book*. Oxford: Oxford University Press.

White, Martin (1998) *Renaissance Drama in Action*. London: Routledge.

Wickham, Glynne (1980) '*The Two Noble Kinsmen* or *A Midsummer Night's Dream, Part II*?', in *The Elizabethan Theatre*, VII, ed. G. R. Hibbard. Hamden, CT: Archon Books.

Wiggins, Martin (2008) 'When did Marlowe Write *Dido, Queen of Carthage*?' *Review of English Studies*, 59: 521–41.

Willey, Basil (1968) *Cambridge and Other Memories, 1920–1933*. London: Chatto and Windus.

Williams, Gary J. (1997) *Our Moonlight Revels: A Midsummer Night's Dream in the Theatre*. Iowa City, IA: University of Iowa Press.

Williams, Raymond (1977) *Marxism and Literature*. Oxford: Oxford University Press.

Williams, Simon (1990) *Shakespeare on the German Stage, Volume 1: 1586–1914*. Cambridge: Cambridge University Press.

Willis, Deborah (1989) 'Shakespeare's *The Tempest* and the Discourse of Colonialism', *Studies in English Literature*, 29: 277–89.

Willson, Robert F., Jr (2000) *Shakespeare in Hollywood, 1929–1956*. London: Associated University Presses.

Wilson, J. Dover (1935) *What Happens in Hamlet*. Cambridge: Cambridge University Press.

——(1943) *The Fortunes of Falstaff*. Cambridge: Cambridge University Press.

——(ed.) (1947) *King Henry V*. The New Shakespeare. Cambridge: Cambridge University Press.

——(ed.) (1948) *Titus Andronicus*. The New Shakespeare. Cambridge: Cambridge University Press.

——(1956) 'Prefatory Note', in *Pericles*, ed. J. C. Maxwell. The New Shakespeare. Cambridge: Cambridge University Press, vii.

——(1957) 'Prefatory Note', in *Timon of Athens*, ed. J. C. Maxwell. The New Shakespeare. Cambridge: Cambridge University Press, vii.

——(1962) 'Prefatory Note', in *King Henry VIII*, ed. J. C. Maxwell. *The New Shakespeare*. Cambridge: Cambridge University Press, vii.

——(1969) *Milestones on the Dover Road*. London: Faber.

Wilson, John Dover and T. C. Worsley (1952) *Shakespeare's Histories at Stratford 1951*. London: Max Reinhardt.

Wilson, Richard (1993) *Will Power: Essays on Shakespearean Authority*. Brighton: Harvester Wheatsheaf.

——(1997) 'Voyage to Tunis: New History and the Old World of *The Tempest*', *ELH*, 64: 333–57.

——(2004) *Secret Shakespeare: Studies in Theatre, Religion, and Resistance*. Manchester: Manchester University Press.

Wilson, Richard and Richard Dutton (eds) (1992) *New Historicism and Renaissance Drama*. London: Longman.

Wood, Michael (2003) *In Search of Shakespeare*. London: BBC Worldwide Ltd.

Wood, Nigel (ed.) (1996) *Antony and Cleopatra*. Theory in Practice. Buckingham: Open University Press.

Woodbridge, Linda (1984) *Women and the English Renaissance: Literature and the Nature of Womankind 1540–1620*. Brighton: Harvester.

——(ed.) (2003) *Money and the Age of Shakespeare*. New York: Palgrave.

Worthen, W. B. (1997) *Shakespeare and the Authority of Performance*. Cambridge: Cambridge University Press.

——(2003) *Shakespeare and the Force of Modern Performance*. Cambridge: Cambridge University Press.

——(2008) '*Hamlet* at Ground Zero: The Wooster Group and the Archive of Performance', *Shakespeare Quarterly*, 59: 303–22.

——(2010) *Drama: Between Poetry and Performance*. Oxford: Wiley-Blackwell.

Worthen, W. B. and Peter Holland (eds) (2003) *Theorizing Practice: Redefining Theatre History*. Basingstoke: Palgrave Macmillan.

Woudhuysen, H. R. (ed.) (1998) *Love's Labour's Lost*. Arden Shakespeare, third series. Walton-on-Thames: Thomas Nelson.

Wright, George T. (1988) *Shakespeare's Metrical Art*. Berkeley, CA: University of California Press.

Yachnin, Paul and Jessica Slights (eds) (2008) *Shakespeare and Character: Theory, History, Performance and Theatrical Persons*. Basingstoke: Palgrave.

Young, David (1972) *The Heart's Forest: A Study of Shakespeare's Pastoral Plays*. New Haven, CT: Yale University Press.

Ziegler, G (1990) 'My Lady's Chamber: Female Space, Female Chastity in Shakespeare', *Textual Practice*, 4: 73–100.

Zimmerman, Susan (ed.) (1992) *Erotic Politics: Desire on the Renaissance Stage*. London: Routledge.

Index

eBooks – at www.eBookstore.tandf.co.uk

A library at your fingertips!

eBooks are electronic versions of printed books. You can store them on your PC/laptop or browse them online.

They have advantages for anyone needing rapid access to a wide variety of published, copyright information.

eBooks can help your research by enabling you to bookmark chapters, annotate text and use instant searches to find specific words or phrases. Several eBook files would fit on even a small laptop or PDA.

NEW: Save money by eSubscribing: cheap, online access to any eBook for as long as you need it.

Annual subscription packages

We now offer special low-cost bulk subscriptions to packages of eBooks in certain subject areas. These are available to libraries or to individuals.

For more information please contact webmaster.ebooks@tandf.co.uk

We're continually developing the eBook concept, so keep up to date by visiting the website.

www.eBookstore.tandf.co.uk